# SCIENTIFIC RUSSIAN

# SCIENTIFIC
# RUSSIAN

## *A TEXTBOOK*
## *for Classes and Self-Study*

### JAMES W. PERRY

*Associate Professor, Modern Language Department,*
*Massachusetts Institute of Technology.*

1950

INTERSCIENCE PUBLISHERS, INC., NEW YORK
INTERSCIENCE PUBLISHERS LTD., LONDON

INTERSCIENCE PUBLISHERS, Inc.
250 Fifth Avenue, New York 1, N. Y.

For Great Britain and Northern Ireland:
INTERSCIENCE PUBLISHERS, Ltd.
2a Southampton Row, London W. C. 1

PRINTED IN THE UNITED STATES OF AMERICA

# FOREWORD

Russian as a scientific language has been long neglected. This has been due in part to an unreasonable fear of the difficulties of the language. There has also existed a certain tendency to under-estimate Russian scientific achievements. To many it has seemed impossible that first-rate work in science could be accomplished under the Czars or within the intellectual strait jacket of Soviet terrorism. In spite of severe difficulties, the record of Russian achievements in science has continued to expand year by year.

At the present time, when the Iron Curtain makes personal contact with Russian scientists virtually impossible, it is particularly important to be able to follow their work through their publications. This would still be true even though the Soviet authorities — misguided by unrealistic fears and fanatical ambitions conjured up by a pseudoscientific materialistic philosophy — should embark on a large-scale military adventure.

The Russian nation — and Russian science — have survived many difficult times, and can be expected to outlive the Soviet era. The inalienable rights, with which all men are endowed by their Creator, cannot forever be denied the Russian people. Someday we shall be able to mingle freely with our Russian colleagues at international scientific meetings. May this book, by promoting better understanding, hasten that day.

# PREFACE

The purpose of this book is to teach a reading knowledge of scientific and technical Russian.

In order that the student may progress step by step in a systematic fashion, the book is divided into forty lessons, each of which is concerned with some important facet of the Russian language. The first few lessons are designed to impart familiarity with the Russian alphabet by directing attention to certain scientific and technical terms that are closely similar or identical in English and Russian. The next few lessons introduce the minimum of grammar required to read simple sentences. Following this introductory material, the book presents a systematic summary of those features of the Russian language essential to reading scientific and technical material. Each individual feature of the language is illustrated by carefully selected example sentences provided with interlinear translation supplemented, where necessary, by footnotes. In many of the lessons, it proved advantageous to provide an introduction to detailed treatment of the Russian by devoting the first section of the lesson to discussing points of similarity and of difference between English and Russian.

Each lesson includes a Russian reading exercise written so as to provide illustrations of those features of Russian with which the lesson is concerned. Once simple sentences have been introduced — i.e., from Lesson 7 onward — each of the reading exercises is a coherent discussion of some topic such as "The States of Matter," "Atomic Energy," "Sources of Light," "Vitamins," "Radioactivity," "Sodium," "Radar." Student interest is sustained by this selection of topics which are treated in such a fashion as to provide a series of stepping stones to reading contemporary Russian scientific literature. The scientific and technical nature of the reading exercises has proved an effective aid to acquiring understanding of Russian scientific writing. Notes appended to the reading exercises provide the student with the additional aid which experience in teaching this material has proved necessary.

The final section of each lesson consists of English material for translation into Russian. Each translation exercise is built up from words and phrases found in the accompanying Russian reading exercise.

The book has been designed for three purposes: for class room instruction, for self-study, and for reference. To facilitate reference use, an extensive table of contents and a subject index have been provided.

The Russian-English vocabulary comprises all words used in the reading exercises. Irregularly inflected forms are included as separate entries. The relationship of many Russian words to their roots is also indicated in the vocabulary.

An appendix lists abbreviations commonly encountered in reading Russian scientific and technical material.

This book could not have been written without the generous assistance of a large number of persons. Particular thanks are due to a number of Russian friends. Dr. Vladimir Nekrassoff provided most valuable assistance from the writing of the preliminary draft to the last revisions of the final manuscript. Dr. Alexander Bogrow aided in making many revisions. Thanks are also due Professors Nicolai Golub (University of Connecticut), G. A. Znamensky (Massachusetts Institute of Technology), and Dmitri Stein (New York University) and Mr. Serge Zaroodny (Aberdeen Proving Ground) for helpful suggestions.

During the course of rewriting the preliminary draft in final form, the author was greatly aided by skillful and constructive criticism generously contributed by Professor W. N. Locke and Mr. George Condoyannis (Modern Language Department, Massachusetts Institute of Technology). Their efforts were in large measure responsible for whatever merit this book may have achieved. Thanks for valuable criticism and suggestions are also due to the author's students, too numerous to be mentioned individually.

The typing of the manuscript in final form was a task of no mean proportion, for whose accomplishment the author is indebted to Mlles. Alice Perry, Ruth Volinn, Betty Park, Eunice Kazanowski and Gloria Fauci, and Mdmes. Marianne Graswich, Sophie van Bourg, Myrtle Hanke, and Elizabeth Kemp.

For assistance in final checking of the proof, the author is indebted to Capt. Victor de Guinzbourg, USA. His careful scrutiny detected a number of errors.

Miss Krista Perry helped to alphabetize the vocabularies and the index.

Finally, a word of appreciation is due the author's long-suffering wife, who for over six years has endured having our home littered with hieroglyphic notes distributed in an apparently random fashion by an absent-minded husband.

James W. Perry

Cambridge, Massachusetts
July, 1950

# CONTENTS

CONTENTS

# INTRODUCTION

## § 1. Preliminary Note.

Learning to read scientific Russian is a task consisting essentially of a multiplicity of small difficulties to be overcome one by one. Nevertheless, before plunging into details, it is helpful to consider certain fundamental characteristics of the Russian language in general and of scientific Russian in particular.

## § 2. Remarks Concerning the Russian Alphabet.

Perhaps the most striking feature of Russian is the exotic appearance of the alphabet. Fortunately, the Russian alphabet is not so difficult as it appears to be. Since there are few exceptions to the rule that each letter represents only one sound, it is surprisingly easy to learn to recognize Russian scientific terms derived from other languages. In fact, mere pronunciation of corresponding Russian and English scientific terms often suffices to disclose extremely close similarity. As we shall see, many Russian and English scientific terms are derived from the same source. The first four lessons in this book are written so as to combine practice in the Russian alphabet with acquisition of skill in recognizing well-known scientific terms in Russian disguise.

Thanks to the phonetic character of Russian spelling a rather rough approximation to correct pronunciation suffices for the purpose of learning to read scientific Russian. If, however, perfection in pronunciation is sought, the aid of a Russian-speaking person is essential. Russians tend to slur together various consonant combinations which at first might appear to defy pronunciation. There is also a tendency for unaccented vowels to lose their full value and for voiced consonants to go over to unvoiced consonants. The teaching of conversational Russian is a specialized task which will not be undertaken in this book.

## § 3. Russian Scientific Vocabulary.

As mentioned above, a surprisingly large number of Russian scientific terms correspond to well-known English terms and are

1

easily recognized once the alphabet has been learned. On the other hand, many of the words encountered in reading scientific Russian are typically Russian in character and origin. In coping with such words, it is helpful to note that the Russian language frequently derives many words from a single basic root. Although the meaning of a derived word often cannot be deduced from the meaning of the root, the memory is always aided by noting the relationship of a derived word to the root word. Attention is directed to these relationships throughout this book, and in particular in the Russian-English vocabulary.

## § 4. The Russian Grammar.

Although it is not absolutely necessary to study Russian grammar in order to read Russian, experience has shown that educated, English-speaking persons progress most rapidly in learning to read Russian if they devote a reasonable amount of effort to becoming well acquainted with the fundamentals of grammar. This is due to the fact that learning the fundamentals of grammar is the quickest and most convenient method for gaining insight into Russian methods for fitting words together to express thought.

This does not mean, however, that it is necessary to become an expert in Russian grammar before starting to read Russian scientific material. What is important is to understand the relationship of the fundamentals of grammar to Russian methods of expressing thought. In line with these considerations, the presentation of the essentials of grammar has been kept as simple as possible by using two somewhat different approaches. On the one hand, many details, relating in particular to use of endings to form various cases and tenses, are presented in tabular form for ready reference. On the other hand, the broader aspects of grammar are discussed one by one with the aid of Russian sentences selected, with very few exceptions, from the works of contemporary Russian scientific writers. The meaning of these sentences is indicated by interlinear, word for word translations, supplemented where necessary by footnotes. When studying these sentences, rephrasing the interlinear literal translation to improve the English may prove helpful. Study of these illustrative sentences provides the necessary background for understanding the Russian reading exercises given at the close of each lesson.

These methods of presentation are in harmony with the nature of the Russian language, which is characterized by extensive use

of endings to indicate how individual words fit together in phrases and sentences to express thought. As might be expected, it is easier to understand how the endings are used than it is to acquire familiarity with the endings themselves. Fortunately, the existence of phonetic similarity between certain sets of endings and related irregularities can be used to ease the task of coping with this aspect of Russian grammar.

In this connection, a word of caution appears necessary. Although it may prove helpful to memorize certain sets of important endings, it is most decidedly not advisable to attempt to memorize all of the numerous tabulations of words and inflected forms, as these tabulations are in some cases repetitious and in other cases include, for sake of completeness, many irregular forms of relatively rare occurrence.

## § 5. Notes on Study Methods.

It is important to develop the habit of associating a sound with each Russian word. The aid of a Russian speaking friend is helpful and reassuring -- but not absolutely necessary -- when acquiring an approximately correct pronunciation. The important thing is to use the voice and sense of hearing as aids in impressing Russian words and phrases on the memory. Words and idioms pronounced and heard "stick" better. This is a psychological fact and should not be forgotten. Printing Russian words out by hand is also recommended as an aid to the memory. This is particularly helpful when learning the alphabet.

The material in successive lessons is arranged so as to facilitate use of the voice and the ear as aids in learning. Thus, as already mentioned, the first group of lessons presents lists of scientific terms which, when pronounced, will be found to be very closely related to well-known English terms. Subsequent lessons are featured by Russian reading exercises made up of phrases and sentences containing many easily recognized terms having close similarity to English counterparts. Each of these reading exercises is followed by a series of ten English sentences which are built up of phrases from the reading exercise. Translation of these sentences into Russian aids the memory in retaining Russian phraseology.

In order to obtain maximum benefit from this order of presentation of Russian material, the student should cultivate the habit of reading Russian directly, i.e., without consciously translating into English. The advantages to be gained from doing this

become more apparent the further one progresses in the study of Russian. Although not evident to the beginner, it is nevertheless true that it is much more practical to retain the meaning of Russian words as such in the memory rather than to attempt to memorize an English equivalent for each Russian word. This is due to the fact that many Russian words, like many French, German, Italian, etc., words, have no exact English equivalents. That direct impression of the meaning of Russian words on the memory is by no means so difficult as might appear at first, is attested by the fact that many words of foreign origin, e.g., "blitzkrieg," "kindergarten," "samovar," "Cominform," are understood by English-speaking persons directly, i.e., without translation into English.

Use of a Russian-English dictionary is, of course, necessary when confronted with an unknown Russian word. But the meaning of a word is best impressed on the memory by observing its use in expressing thought and such impression is accomplished most efficiently by reading Russian directly without translating. In other words, reading Russian without translation is an efficient method whereby dictionary definitions of Russian words can be transformed into direct impression of their meaning on the memory.

Some students may feel tempted to insert notes on the meaning of individual Russian words into the reading exercises. This practise is to be avoided as it deflects attention from the Russian to English and thus disrupts any attempts at thinking in Russian. It is much sounder practise to avoid such interlinear notations. Any such notes needed to assist the memory in coping with Russian words should be made on separate slips of paper. Such notes should be regarded as crutches, to be discarded as quickly as the meanings of the Russian words become anchored in the memory.

Perhaps it is not out of place to point out that practicing the habit of reading without translating also lays the foundation for learning to speak Russian, if that should ever become desirable.

It should be emphasized that the advantages to be gained by reading Russian directly are not due to any peculiarity of the Russian language. The same advantages can be realized when studying other foreign languages, e.g., German.

Should difficulty be encountered in mastering the knack of reading Russian without translating, the following approach may prove helpful. After working out a reading exercise, with transla -

tion into English when necessary, lay the exercise aside for a day or so and then try to read the Russian directly, making a conscious effort to avoid the natural tendency to think in English. A certain amount of persistence may be required to master the trick. At first it may be possible to understand only the simplest phrases and sentences without translation; with practice, however, even the most complicated text can be read at sight. As the habit of reading Russian with direct understanding becomes well rooted, translating into English gradually assumes the character of a time-consuming nuisance.

Time is conserved in learning to read scientific Russian if the study periods are short and frequent. For this reason this book consists of a series of relatively short lessons which are broken up into paragraphs. It is hoped that this form of presentation will facilitate utilization of spare moments which might otherwise be lost.

## § 6. The Russian Alphabet

### RUSSIAN ALPHABET

| Russian | Transliteration (with pronunciation) | Russian | Transliteration (with pronunciation) |
|---|---|---|---|
| А - а | A - a (as in far) | Р - р | R - r (as in rose) |
| Б - б | B - b (as in bench) | С - с | S - s (as in site) |
| В - в | V - v (as in vent) | Т - т | T - t (as in tall) |
| Г - г | G - g (as in go) | У - у | U - u (as in lunar) |
| Д - д | D - d (as in deep) | Ф - ф | F - f (as in fast) |
| Е - е | E - e (Note 2) (as in chest) | Х - х | Kh - kh (Note 3) (as in Kharkov - Note 6) |
| Ж - ж | Zh - zh (Note 3) (s as in treasure) | Ц - ц | Ts - ts (Note 3) (as in pats) |
| З - з | Z - z (as in zipper) | Ч - ч | Ch - ch (Note 3) (as in check) |
| И - и | I - i (as in machine) | Ш - ш | Sh - sh (Note 3) (as in shop) |
| Й - й | Ĭ - ĭ (i as in toil - Note 5) | Щ - щ | Shch - shch (Note 3) (sh-ch as in cash-check Note 10) |
| К - к | K - k (as in kettle) | Ъ - ъ | - ' (Notes 4 and 7) |
| Л - л | L - l (as in long) | Ы - ы | Y - y (Note 4) (as in tryst - Note 8) |
| М - м | M - m (as in stem) | Ь - ь | ' - ' (Notes 4 and 9) |
| Н - н | N - n (as in net) | Э - э | E - e (as in error) |
| О - о | O - o (as in fore) | Ю - ю | Yu - yu (as in yule) |
| П - п | P - p (as in pen) | Я - я | Ya - ya (as in yard) |

## NOTES ON ALPHABET

1. The thirty-two letters of the Russian alphabet are listed above in the conventional order used in arranging words in dictionaries. The pronunciation indicated for the various letters is a good approximation of the usual Russian pronunciation, with certain exceptions noted below.

2. When the voice stress falls on Russian Е-е, it tends, to a greater or less degree, to be pronounced like "ye" in "yes." Similar pronunciation is encountered when Russian Е-е is preceded by another vowel.

In certain words, however, Е-е when stressed is pronounced like "yo" in "yokel." Such pronunciation is indicated throughout this book by the dieresis; for example, in the word идёт (pronounced idyót). Many Russian-printing establishments omit the dieresis. Thus, our example word, идёт, often is printed as идет with the result that material so printed may cause pronunciation difficulties to persons learning Russian.

3. If all the letters of a Russian word are to be transliterated into our capitals, then Ж will be transliterated as ZH, Х as KH, Ц as TS, Ч as CH, Ш as SH and Щ as SHCH.

4. The letters Ъ – ъ, Ы – ы and Ь – ь are never the first letters of a Russian word. Consequently, their capital forms are found only in words spelled out entirely in capitals as, for example, in the titles of books and papers.

5. To understand better the role of the Russian letter Й – й in pronunciation, note how the letter "i" is used in English to indicate that the pronunciation of "toil" differs from that of "told."

The letter Й – й is used as the first letter of a very few words of which Йорк, "York" is an example.

6. No sound exactly equivalent to Russian Х - х occurs in English. The Russian sound which is akin to German "ch" as in "Bach," can be approximated quite closely by strong, guttural breathing of "h" in "horse" or "hurry." The transliteration as "kh" is not to be taken too seriously.

7. This Russian letter -- the hard sign -- indicates the pronunciation of other letters (cf. § 13). It is not only represented by the apostrophe in transliteration, but is sometimes replaced by the same in printed Russian.

8. The "y" sound in "tryst" approximates rather poorly the sound represented by the letter " Ы,ы ." Some authorities state that the pronunciation of this Russian letter can be closely approximated by positioning the mouth to say "oil" and then attempting to pronounce "it" instead.

9. This Russian letter -- the soft sign -- indicates the pronunciation of other letters (cf. §§ 12, 13; pp. 17, 18). This Russian letter is transliterated by the apostrophe. Some transliteration schemes disregard the soft sign if it occurs at the end of a Russian word. In this book any transliteration of Russian words always represents the soft sign by an apostrophe.

10. The correct pronunciation of the letter Щ – щ is a palatized "sh" to which the "shch" sound is only a poor approximation.

### Discarded Letters

Shortly after its establishment, the Soviet government decreed that four letters previously used were to be eliminated by effecting the following replacements:

| Discarded Letters | | Replaced By | |
|---|---|---|---|
| I | i | И | и |
| Ѣ | ѣ | Е | е |
| V | v | И | и |
| Ѳ | ѳ | Ф | ф |

Only two of these discarded letters I-i and Ѣ-ѣ were ever used to any important extent.

# LESSON 1

## LETTERS RESEMBLING LATIN OR GREEK

§ 7.  List of Letters Resembling Latin or Greek.

Approximately half the letters of the Russian alphabet closely resemble letters of the Latin or of the Greek alphabet. These are:

| Letters Resembling Latin | | | Letters Resembling Greek | | |
|---|---|---|---|---|---|
| Capital | Small | | Capital | Small | |
| A | a | – a as in far | Б | б | – (beta) b as in bench |
| E | e | – e as in chest | Г | г | – (gamma) g as in go |
| К | к | – k as in kettle | Д | д | – (delta) d as in deep |
| M | м | – m as in stem | Л | л | – (lambda) l as in long |
| O | o | – o as in fore | П | п | – (pi) p as in pen |
| C | c | – s as in site | P | р | – (rho) r as in rose |
| T | т | – t as in tall | Ф | ф | – (phi) f as in fast |
| У | у | – u as in lunar | Х | х | – (chi) kh as in Kharkov |

### Pronunciation Unlike English

| Capital | Small | |
|---|---|---|
| H | н | – n as in net |
| B | в | – v as in vent |

§ 8.  Some Russian Technical Terms of Foreign Origin.

By using the letters listed above, it is possible to spell out a number of scientific terms adopted by the Russians from English, German or French. The degree to which the Russians are willing to use technical terms of foreign origin is surprising. At times, a foreign term may even be used in preference to an already existing, purely Russian word. Since the process of adopting foreign technical terms into Russian goes on continually, it is important to cultivate skill in recognizing well-known technical

9

terms in Russian disguise. Such recognition is facilitated by the
fact that, as a general rule, the Russians are guided by phonetic
principles when using the Russian alphabet to spell out foreign
technical terms. This important point is illustrated by lists of
examples to be presented in this and subsequent lessons. In order
to emphasize the close phonetic similarity of the Russianized terms
with their English counterparts, the Russianized terms have been
transliterated into our own alphabet, using the Chemical Abstracts
system of letter equivalents, cf. § 6, p. 6.

In this lesson two lists of nouns are presented. In accordance
with the usual convention, the nouns are listed in the nominative
singular case.

In the first of these two lists, all the nouns are masculine in
gender. This is in accord with the general rule that all nouns
whose nominative singular terminates with a consonant not followed
by the soft sign are masculine in gender.[1] (Nouns whose nominative, singular ending is -Ь, however, may be either masculine or
feminine. Thus автомобиль-- "automobile," is masculine, while
модель -- "model," is feminine).

## Masculine Nouns of Foreign Origin

| Russian | Transliteration of Russian | English |
|---------|----------------------------|---------|
| абсо́рбер | absórber | absorber |
| агар-ага́р | agar-agár | agar-agar |
| ампе́р | ampér | ampere |
| ано́д | anód | anode |
| аппара́т | apparát | apparatus |
| арго́н | argón | argon |
| арсена́л | arsenál | arsenal |
| арсена́т[2] | arsenát | arsenate |
| асбе́ст[3] | asbést | asbestos |
| а́том | átom | atom |
| аура́т[2] | aurát | aurate |

[1] See § 28, p. 43 for rules with whose aid the gender of the majority of Russian
nouns can be determined from their nominative, singular form.
[2] Russian chemical nomenclature requires special attention. See Perry, J. W.
"Chemical Russian, Self-Taught." Chemical Education Publishing Company.
Easton, Pennsylvania. 1948.
[3] An alternate spelling is азбе́ст.

| Russian | Transliteration of Russian | English |
|---------|---------------------------|---------|
| бор[1] | bor | boron |
| борáт[2] | borát | borate |
| бром[1] | brom | bromine |
| бромáт[2] | bromát | bromate |
| бутáн[2] | bután | butane |
| бутéн[2] | butén | butene |
| вáкуум | vákuum | vacuum |
| вéктор | véktor | vector |
| ветерáн | veterán | veteran |
| грамм | gramm | gram |
| декáн[2] | dekán | decane |
| дефéкт | defékt | defect |
| дефлегмáтор | deflegmátor | dephlegmator |
| додекáн[2] | dodekán | dodecane |
| дублéт | dublét | doublet |
| канáл | kanál | canal, duct |
| карбонáт[2] | karbonát | carbonate |
| карборýнд | karborúnd | carborundum |
| карбýнкул | karbúnkul | carbuncle |
| кетóн[2] | ketón | ketone |
| класс | klass | class |
| коллагéн | kollagén | collagen |
| коммутáтор | kommutátor | commutator |
| комплéкс | kompléks | complex |
| компонéнт | komponént | component |
| конденсáт | kondensát | condensate |
| конденсáтор[3] | kondensátor | condenser |
| кóнус | kónus | cone |
| куб | kub | cube |
| курс | kurs | course |
| меркаптáн[2] | merkaptán | mercaptan |
| метáлл | metáll | metal |
| момéнт | momént | moment |
| мотóр | motór | motor |
| неóн | neón | neon |
| неопрéн | neoprén | neoprene |
| нерв | nerv | nerve |
| нонáн[2] | nonán | nonane |

[1] Note the close similarity between the Russian and German names of these chemical elements.
[2] Cf. Footnote 2, p. 10.
[3] This term is used for electrical capacitors and also for devices for condensing vapors to liquids. An alternate spelling кондéнсор is also used particularly for referring to a lens system.

| Russian | Transliteration of Russian | English |
|---|---|---|
| оксалат[1] | oksalát | oxalate |
| октан[1] | oktán | octane |
| октен[1] | oktén | octene |
| ом | om | ohm |
| оператор | operátor | operator |
| параграф | parágraf | paragraph |
| параллелограм | parallelográm | parallelogram |
| параметр[2] | paramétr | parameter |
| патент[1] | patént | patent |
| пентан[1] | pentán | pentane |
| пентен[1] | pentén | pentene |
| петролатум | petrolátum | petrolatum |
| план | plan | plan |
| постулат | postulát | postulate |
| препарат | preparát | preparation (substance) |
| продукт[1] | prodúkt | product |
| пропан | propán | propane |
| пропанол[1] | propanól | propanol |
| пропен[1] | propén | propene |
| протон | protón | proton |
| профессор | proféssor | professor |
| радон | rádon | radon |
| реагент | reagént | reagent |
| регенератор | regenerátor | regenerator (Metallurgy) |
| реостат | reostát | rheostat |
| ротор | rótor | rotor |
| сатуратор | saturátor | saturator |
| секрет | sekrét | secret |
| селен[3] | selén | selenium |
| селенат[1] | selenát | selenate |
| скрап | skrap | scrap (Metallurgy) |
| скруббер | skrúbber | scrubber |
| спектр[2] | spektr | spectrum |
| спектрограф | spektrográf | spectrograph |
| спектроскоп | spektroskóp | spectroscope |
| стартер | stárter | starter |
| студент | studént | student |

[1] Cf. Footnote 2, p. 10.

[2] This use of the letter combination -тр in Russian is probably to be traced to the influence of French which in corresponding words uses "-tre" as, for example, in "mètre."

[3] Cf. Footnote 1, p. 11.

| Russian | Transliteration of Russian | English |
|---|---|---|
| суберо́н[1] | suberón | suberone |
| субстра́т | substrát | substrate |
| танта́л[3] | tantál | tantalum |
| таутоме́р[2] | tautomér | tautomer |
| теллу́р[3] | tellúr | tellurium |
| терпе́н | terpén | terpene |
| тра́ктор | tráktor | tractor |
| тра́нспорт | tránsport | transport |
| ура́н[3] | urán | uranium |
| факт | fakt | fact |
| фа́ктор | fáktor | factor |
| фено́л | fenól | phenol |
| фо́кус | fókus | focus |
| фоно́граф | fonógraf | phonograph |
| форт | fort | fort |
| фосфа́т[1] | fosfát | phosphate |
| фо́сфор[3] | fósfor | phosphorus |
| фото́граф | fotógraf | photographer |
| фо́тон | fóton | photon |
| фронт | front | front |
| хара́ктер | kharákter | character |
| хлор[3] | khlor | chlorine |
| хлора́т[1] | khlorát | chlorate |
| хлорофо́рм[1] | khlorofórm | chloroform |
| хром[3] | khrom | chromium |
| хрома́т[1] | khromát | chromate |
| хромосо́м | khromosóm | chromosome |
| хромофо́р | khromofór | chromophore |

---

[1] Cf. Footnote 2, p. 10.
[2] The dipthong -au- is more commonly transliterated as -ав- as discussed in § 25, p. 37.
[3] Cf. Footnote 1, p. 11.

Various other scientific terms of foreign origin are, in Russian, nouns whose nominative, singular case ends in " -a." This ending in the nominative, singular case usually indicates feminine gender, and the following list of nouns contains none of the rare exceptions to that general rule.

### Feminine Nouns of Foreign Origin

| Russian | Transliteration of Russian | English |
|---------|---------------------------|---------|
| анте́нна | anténna | antenna |
| атмосфе́ра | atmosféra | atmosphere |
| бала́та | baláta | balata |
| бо́мба | bómba | bomb |
| гру́ппа | grúppa | group |
| камфора́ | kamforá | camphor |
| коме́та | kométa | comet |
| конста́нта | konstánta | constant |
| ла́мпа | lámpa | lamp, radio tube |
| ле́мма | lémma | lemma |
| ма́сса | mássa | mass |
| моле́кула | molékyla | molecule |
| номенклату́ра | nomenklatúra | nomenclature |
| па́ста | pásta | paste |
| плане́та | planéta | planet |
| пробле́ма | probléma | problem |
| програ́мма | prográmma | program |
| раке́та | rakéta | rocket |
| рето́рта | retórta | retort |
| секу́нда | sekúnda | second (time period) |
| со́да | sóda | soda |
| структу́ра | struktúra | structure |
| су́мма | súmma | sum |
| сфе́ра | sféra | sphere |
| схе́ма | skhéma | scheme |
| температу́ра | temperatúra | temperature |
| фара́да | faráda | farad |
| фа́уна | fáuna | fauna |
| фло́ра | flóra | flora |
| фо́рма | fórma | form |
| фо́рмула | fórmula | formula |

## § 9. Reading Exercise.

ампе́р, ано́д, анте́нна, арсена́л, асбе́ст, атмосфе́ра, а́том, бо́мба, бром, ва́куум, ве́ктор, грамм, гру́ппа, дефе́кт, камфора́, кана́л, класс, компле́кс, компоне́нт, конденса́тор, куб, ла́мпа, ла́текс, ма́сса, мета́лл, моле́кула, моме́нт, мото́р, нерв, номенклату́ра, ом, опера́тор, пара́граф, параме́тр, па́ста, пате́нт, план, плане́та, постула́т, програ́мма, прото́н, раке́та, реоста́т, ро́тор, секу́нда, скрап, скру́ббер, со́да, спектрогра́ф, спектроско́п, структу́ра, субстра́т, су́мма, температу́ра, тра́ктор, фено́л, фо́кус, фоно́граф, фо́рма, хлорофо́рм, хромосо́м.

## § 10. Translation Exercise.

commutator, argon, comet, sphere, atom, scheme, factor, photographer, chromosome, asbestos, motor, retort, paragraph, doublet, student, atmosphere, absorber, transport, chlorine, carbonate, professor, parallelogram, dephlegmator, apparatus, photon, spectrograph, character.

# LESSON 2

## REMAINING LETTERS OF THE RUSSIAN ALPHABET

§ 11. List of Remaining Letters of the Russian Alphabet.

Fourteen letters of the Russian alphabet remain to be discussed. Six of these letters represent hissing sounds,[1] six others are vowels, while the two remaining letters are used to indicate differences in pronunciation of certain consonants.

| Hissing Sounds | | | Special Vowels | | |
|---|---|---|---|---|---|
| Ж | ж | – s as in trea<u>s</u>ure[2] | И | и | – i as in ma<u>chi</u>ne |
| З | з | – z as in <u>z</u>ipper | Й | й | – i as in to<u>i</u>l[3] |
| Ц | ц | – ts as in pa<u>ts</u> | Ы | ы | – y as in tryst |
| Ч | ч | – ch as in <u>ch</u>eck | Ю | ю | – yu as in <u>yu</u>le |
| Ш | ш | – sh as in <u>sh</u>op | Я | я | – ya as in <u>ya</u>rd |
| Щ | щ | – sh-ch as in ca<u>sh</u>-<u>ch</u>eck | Ё | ё | – yo as in <u>yo</u>kel |
| | | | Э | э | – e as in <u>e</u>rror |

### Letters Indicating Different Modes of Pronunciation

| Ъ | ъ | – hard sign |
|---|---|---|
| Ь | ь | – soft sign |

§ 12. Hard and Soft Vowels.

In learning the Russian alphabet, it is helpful to note that the pronunciation of certain vowels serves as a basis for dividing them into two groups as follows.

---

[1] Experts in phonetics prefer to describe "hissing," "hard" and "soft" sounds, respectively; as, "fricative," "unpalatized" and "palatized."

[2] The letter Ж – ж is transliterated by "zh," cf. Note 3, p. 7.

[3] The letter Й – й is used almost exclusively after vowels as in the combinations -ай, -ей, -ой, -ый, -ий.

17

| Hard Vowels | | | | Soft Vowels | | |
|---|---|---|---|---|---|---|
| А | а | - a as in f<u>a</u>r | $\longrightarrow$ | Я | Я | - ya as in <u>ya</u>rd |
| Э | э | - e as in <u>e</u>rror | | Е | е | - ye as in <u>ye</u>s |
| О | о | - o as in f<u>o</u>re | | Ё | ё | - yo as in <u>yo</u>kel |
| У | у | - u as in l<u>u</u>nar | $\longrightarrow$ | Ю | ю | - yu as in <u>yu</u>le |

Note also in this connection the following pair of vowels:

| Ы | ы | - y as in tr<u>y</u>st | | И | И | - i as in mach<u>i</u>ne |
|---|---|---|---|---|---|---|

As indicated above, the term "hard" is usually applied to one group of vowels and to " ы," while the other group and "И" are usually described as "soft." As we shall see subsequently, in certain sets of endings soft vowels may replace hard vowels and vice versa, as indicated by arrows above. Note that "О" is so replaced by "е" or "ё" depending on circumstances. Since "Э" does not occur in endings, it is not subject to such replacement.

§ 13.  Hard and Soft Consonants.

Russian also differentiates between hard and soft consonants. A few examples are given to illustrate this important point.

| Hard Consonants | | Soft Consonants | |
|---|---|---|---|
| Н | - n as in <u>n</u>et | НЬ | - ny sound in can<u>yo</u>n |
| П | - p as in <u>p</u>oor | ПЬ | - py sound in p<u>u</u>re ("pyure") |
| В | - v as in <u>v</u>ent | ВЬ | - vy sound in view ("vyoo") |
| Т | - t as in <u>t</u>ip | ТЬ | - ty sound is not common in the U.S. In England, such pronounciation as "<u>ty</u>une" for "tune" is often heard. |

This list gives examples; many other soft consonants are used in the Russian language.

Soft consonants at the end of Russian words are a matter of considerable grammatical importance, as will be pointed out in discussing various endings used with nouns and verbs. For example, the infinitives of the great majority of Russian verbs end in "-ТЬ":

| | | | |
|---|---|---|---|
| теря́ть | to be losing | жить | to be living |
| чита́ть | to be reading | крыть | to be covering |
| коло́ть | to be splitting | тере́ть | to be rubbing |
| дуть | to be blowing | фотографи́ровать | to be photographing |

The letter -ь- also forms the nominative, singular ending of certain masculine and feminine nouns.

§ 14.  More Russian Technical Terms of Foreign Origin.

The following three lists of scientific terms of foreign origin are given to provide aid in learning the Russian alphabet. These lists of nouns, as well as other lists of Russianized technical terms of foreign origin, are not intended to be exhaustive. In fact, it would be virtually impossible to make such lists complete because of the steady influx of foreign technical terms into the Russian language.. As is customary, the nouns in all three lists are in the nominative, singular case.

The nouns in the first of the three lists are all masculine in gender, in accordance with the rule that nouns whose nominative, singular case terminates in a hard consonant are masculine. It should be noted that no case ending is used in forming the nominative, singular of these masculine nouns. In other words, the nominative, singular and the stem of these nouns are identical.

| Russian | Transliteration of Russian | English |
|---|---|---|
| абце́сс | abtséss | abscess |
| ами́н | amín | amine |
| анио́н | anión | anion |
| асфа́льт | asfál't | asphalt |
| ацета́т | atsetát | acetate |
| ацето́н | atsetón | acetone |
| аэродро́м | aerodróm | aerodrome |
| аэропла́н | aeroplán | aeroplane |
| бакели́т | bakelít | bakelite |
| бактериофа́г | bacteriofág | bacteriophage |
| бензи́н | benzín | benzine, gasoline |
| бензо́л | benzól | benzene |
| бокси́т | boksít | bauxite |
| ви́рус | vírus | virus |

| Russian | Transliteration of Russian | English |
|---|---|---|
| вискóзиметр | viskózimetr | viscosimeter |
| витамúн | vitamín | vitamin |
| вóльт | vol't | volt |
| вольтмéтр | vol'tmétr | voltmeter |
| газ | gaz | gas |
| гальванóмéтр | gal'vanométr | galvanometer |
| глицерúн | glitserín | glycerol |
| градиéнт | gradiént | gradient |
| диáметр | diámetr | diameter |
| диоксáн | dioksán | dioxane |
| диск | disk | disk |
| дистиллЯ́т | distillyát | distillate |
| журнáл | zhurnál | journal, notebook |
| изопрéн | izoprén | isoprene |
| изотóп | izotóp | isotope |
| импедáнц | impedánts | impedance |
| úмпульс | ímpul's | impulse |
| индивúд | individ | individual |
| индикáтор | indikátor | indicator |
| институ́т | institút | institute |
| интегрáл | integrál | integral |
| интервáл | intervál | interval |
| иóн | ión | ion |
| каолúн | kaolín | kaolin |
| капиллЯ́р | kapillyár | capillary |
| карбúд | karbíd | carbide |
| катализáтор | katalizátor | catalyst |
| катиóн | kation | cation |
| керосúн | kerosín | kerosene |
| килогрáмм | kilográmm | kilogram |
| киломéтр | kilométr | kilometer |
| кобáльт | kobál't | cobalt |
| коллéдж | kollédzh | college |
| коллóид | kolloíd | colloid |
| колориméтр | kolorimétr | colorimeter |
| концéпт | kontsépt | concept |
| коэффициéнт | koeffitsiént | coefficient |
| крéкинг | kréking | cracking |
| крéкинг-процéсс | kréking-protsess | cracking process (petroleum chemistry) |
| криолúт | kriolít | cryolite |
| кристáлл | kristáll | crystal |

| Russian | Transliteration of Russian | English |
|---|---|---|
| лигроин | ligroin | ligroine |
| магнит | magnit | magnet |
| материал | materiál | material |
| мениск | menísk | meniscus |
| метр | metr | meter |
| механизм | mekhanism | mechanism |
| микрометр | mikrométr | micrometer |
| микроорганизм | mikroorganizm | microorganism |
| микроскоп | mikroskóp | microscope |
| миллион | millión | million |
| минерал | minerál | mineral |
| нитрид | nitríd | nitride |
| нихром | nikhróm | "Nichrome" |
| оксим | oksim | oxime |
| парафин | parafín | paraffin |
| парашют | parashyút | parachute |
| период | period | period |
| позитрон | pozitrón | positron |
| полимер | polimér | polymer |
| поташ | potásh | potash |
| потенциал | potentsiál | potential |
| процесс | protséss | process |
| радикал | radikál | radical |
| радиус | rádius | radius |
| результат | rezul'tát | result |
| рельс[1] | rel's | rail, track |
| сантиметр | sántimétr | centimeter |
| силикат | silikát | silicate |
| симптом | simptóm | symptom |
| сифилис | sifilis | syphilis |
| сульфат | sul'fát | sulfate |
| тип | tip | type |
| титан | titán | titanium |
| токсин | toksin | toxine |
| фильтр | fil'tr | filter |
| фильтрат | fil'trát | filtrate |
| характер | kharákter | character |
| хлорид | khlorid; | chloride |
| хлорофилл | khlorofill | chlorophyll |
| цемент | tsemént | cement |

[1] The Russian noun рельс is singular in spite of the fact that it is derived from the English plural noun, "rails." In Russian, the plural (nominative case) of рельс is рельсы. A similarly derived feminine noun, рельса, is also used with the same meaning.

| Russian | Transliteration of Russian | English |
|---------|----------------------------|---------|
| центр | tsentr | center |
| цикл | tsikl | cycle |
| цилиндр | tsilindr | cylinder |
| цинк | tsink | zinc |
| эбонит | ebonít | ebonite |
| эксперт | ékspert | expert |
| экстракт | ekstrákt | extract |
| электрод | elektród | electrode |
| электролизёр | elektrolizyór | electrolyzer |
| электролит | elektrolít | electrolyte |
| электрометр | elektrométr | electrometer |
| электрон | elektrón | electron |
| электроскоп | elektroskóp | electroscope |
| элемент | elemént | element |
| эндосперм | endospérm | endosperm |
| эффект | effékt | effect |

The following list of Russian scientific terms of foreign origin form their nominative, singular in some instances with the ending –а and in other instances with the ending –я. In general, use of either of these endings to form the nominative, singular of a Russian noun indicates that it is feminine in gender. None of the rare exceptions to this general rule are found in the following list.

| Russian | Transliteration of Russian | English |
|---------|----------------------------|---------|
| академия | akadémiya | academy |
| амальгама | amal'gáma | amalgam |
| амнезия | amnéziya | amnesia |
| аналогия | analógiya | analogy |
| анатомия | anatómiya | anatomy |
| анемия | anémiya | anemia |
| асимметрия | asimmetriya | asymmetry |
| бронза | brónza | bronze |
| вакцина | vaktsína | vaccine |
| геология | geológiya | geology |
| геометрия | geométriya | geometry |
| дерматология | dermatológiya | dermatology |
| дизентерия | disentériya | dysentery |
| зона | zóna | žone |
| зоология | zoológiya | zoology |

| Russian | Transliteration of Russian | English |
|---|---|---|
| изомéрия | izomériya | isomerism |
| кабина | kabína | cabin |
| коррóзия | korróziya | corrosion |
| кристаллогрáфия | kristallográfiya | crystallography |
| лаборатóрия | laboratóriya | laboratory |
| литератýра | literatúra | literature |
| малярия | malyariya | malaria |
| матрица | matritsa | matrix |
| машина | mashina | machine |
| медицина | meditsina | medicine |
| механика | mekhánika | mechanics |
| минýта | minúta | minute |
| моногрáфия | monográfiya | monograph |
| океанолóгия | okeanológiya | oceanology |
| орбита | orbíta | orbit |
| пáуза | páuza | pause |
| плáтина | plátina | platinum |
| прогрéссия | progréssiya | progression |
| психиатрия | psikhiatriya | psychiatry |
| психолóгия | psikhológiya | psychology |
| симметрия | simmetriya | symmetry |
| систéма | sistéma | system |
| токсиколóгия | toksikológiya | toxicology |
| турбина | turbína | turbine |
| фармаколóгия | farmakológiya | pharmacology |
| физика | fízika | physics |
| физиолóгия | fiziológiya | physiology |
| фотогрáфия | fotográfiya | photography |
| характеристика | kharakterístika | characteristic (noun) |
| центрифýга | tsentrifúga | centrifuge |
| шкáла | shkála | scale |
| шкóла | shkóla | school |
| экзéма | ekzéma | eczema |
| эклáмпсия | eklámpsiya | eclampsia |
| электрокардиогрáмма | electrokardiográmma | electrocardiogram |
| эмбриолóгия | embriológiya | embryology |
| эмýльсия | emúl'siya | emulsion |
| энéргия | enérgiya | energy |
| энтрóпия | entrópiya | entropy |
| эпилéпсия | epilépsiya | epilepsy |
| эпóха | epókha | epoch |

The following list of technical terms shows that English "-tion"
often corresponds to Russian "-ЦИЯ," which is also closely related
to the French "-tion." As listed here in the nominative, singular
case, these nouns bear the case ending "-Я." In accordance with
a rule given subsequently (§ 28,  p. 43), these Russian nouns are
all of feminine gender.

| Russian | Transliteration of Russian | English |
|---------|----------------------------|---------|
| аберра́ция | aberrátsiya | aberration |
| абсо́рбция | absórbtsiya | absorption |
| авиа́ция | aviátsiya | aviation |
| адсо́рбция | adsórbtsiya | adsorption |
| актива́ция | aktivátsiya | activation |
| ампута́ция | amputátsiya | amputation |
| анизотро́пия | anizotrópiya | anisotropy |
| апроксима́ция | aproksimátsiya | approximation |
| вакцина́ция | vaktsinátsiya | vaccination |
| вентиля́ция | ventilyátsiya | ventilation |
| вулканиза́ция | vulkanizátsiya | vulcanization |
| газифика́ция | gazifikátsiya | gasification |
| дезинфе́кция | dezinféktsiya | disinfection |
| деполяриза́ция | depolyarizátsiya | depolarization |
| детона́ция | detonátsiya | detonation |
| диссерта́ция | dissertátsiya | dissertation, thesis |
| диссоциа́ция | dissotsiátsiya | dissociation |
| изомериза́ция | izomerizátsya | isomerization |
| инфе́кция | inféktsiya | infection |
| иониза́ция | ionizátsiya | ionization |
| конденса́ция | kondensátsiya | condensation |
| конду́кция | kondúktsiya | conduction |
| констру́кция | konstrúktsiya | construction |
| конфигура́ция | konfigurátsiya | configuration |
| концентра́ция | kontsentrátsiya | concentration |
| кристаллиза́ция | kristallizátsiya | crystallization |
| менструа́ция | menstruátsiya | menstruation |
| модифика́ция | modifikátsiya | modification |
| навига́ция | navigátsiya | navigation |
| опера́ция | operátsiya | operation |
| полимериза́ция | polimerizátsiya | polymerization |
| по́рция | pórtsiya | portion |
| радиа́ция | radiátsiya | radiation |
| реа́кция | reáktsiya | reaction |

| Russian | Transliteration of Russian | English |
|---|---|---|
| регенера́ция | regenerátsiya | regeneration |
| фарма́ция | farmatsiya | pharmacy |
| форма́ция | formátsiya | formation |
| фра́кция | fráktsiya | fraction, portion |
| экстра́кция | ekstráktsiya | extraction |
| электриза́ция | elektrizátsiya | electrification, process of charging electrically |

## § 15. Reading Exercise.

аберра́ция, абсо́рбер, актива́ция, амальга́ма, амплиту́да, анало́гия, анато́мия, анизотро́пия, асфа́льт, аэродро́м, баке-ли́т, бо́мба, бро́нза, вакци́на, вакцина́ция, ви́рус, витами́н, вольт, вулканиза́ция, газ, газифика́ция, геоло́гия, градие́нт, дерматоло́гия, детона́ция, диа́метр, диск, диссерта́ция, дубле́т, журна́л, зо́на, изоме́р, изомериза́ция, изоме́рия, изото́п, и́мпульс, институ́т, ио́н, иониза́ция, каби́на, карби́д, кати́он, километр, коллои́д, коме́та, коммута́тор, концентра́ция, корро́зия, коэффицие́нт, криоли́т, криста́лл, кристал-лиза́ция, лаборато́рия, литерату́ра, маши́на, мени́ск, микро-ско́п, минера́л, мину́та, моногра́фия, навига́ция, орби́та, па-раллелогра́м, пери́од, позитро́н, полиме́р, полимериза́ция, постула́т, профе́ссор, радиа́ция, реаге́нт, реа́кция, реге-нера́ция, результа́т, сантиме́тр, силика́т, систе́ма, схе́ма, сфе́ра, токсиколо́гия, тра́нспорт, фи́зика, фи́льтр, фо́рма, форма́ция, фо́рмула, фотогра́фия, фра́кция, хлорофи́лл, ци-ли́ндр, цинк, шко́ла, экстра́кт, экстра́кция, электро́д, элек-тро́н, элеме́нт, эму́льсия, эне́ргия, энтро́пия, эпо́ха, эффе́кт.

§ 16.  Translation Exercise.

orbit, electrode, process, filtrate, cement, coordinate, amplitude,
asphalt, pharmacy, infection, electrification, turbine, minute,
geometry, platinum, element, potential, micrometer, period,
meniscus, aviation, modification, centrifuge, emulsion, absorption,
configuration, symmetry, physics, academy, amalgam, result,
chloride, kilometer, crystal, volt.

# LESSON 3

## USE OF RUSSIAN SUFFIXES TO FORM ADJECTIVES FROM FOREIGN TECHNICAL TERMS

§ 17.  Notes on Russian Suffixes with Foreign Technical Terms.

This lesson is devoted to consideration of Russianized technical terms formed by adding a purely Russian suffix to roots of foreign origin. In considering the derivation of words in Russian, a distinction will be made between: (1) suffixes which are affixed to roots to form the stems of derived words, and (2) endings of a purely grammatical nature, such as the case endings of nouns and adjectives.

The Russian language never uses one noun to modify another, as is done in such English expressions as "salt solution," "neutron bombardment," "power series," etc. For this reason, use of typically Russian suffixes to convert words of foreign origin, particularly nouns, into adjectives is even more extensive than might perhaps be expected.

In the following paragraphs, lists of words are given illustrating the use of a few of the more important Russian suffixes frequently used with technical terms of foreign origin. Other similar suffixes will be mentioned in subsequent lessons.

§ 18.  Adjectives Formed with Suffix, -H-.

The following list gives examples of Russian adjectives formed by adding the suffix "-H-" to foreign stems. In accordance with usual convention, the adjectives are listed here in the masculine, nominative, singular case, as is indicated by the case ending - ый.

| Russian | Transliteration of Russian[1] | English |
|---|---|---|
| абсолютный | absolyútnyĭ | absolute |
| активный | aktívnyĭ | active |
| аморфный | amórfnyĭ | amorphous |
| аналогичный | analogíchnyĭ | analogous |
| анаэробный | anaeróbnyĭ | anaerobic |
| анодный | anódnyĭ | anodic |
| аномальный | anomál'nyĭ | anomalous |
| атипичный | atipíchnyĭ | atypical |
| атомный | atómnyĭ | atomic |
| ацетатный | atsetátnyĭ | acetate (adj.) |
| ацетильный | atsetíl'nyĭ | acetyl (adj.) |
| аэробный | aeróbnyĭ | aerobic |
| валентный | valéntnyĭ | pertaining to valence (chem.) |
| вертикальный | vertikál'nyĭ | vertical |
| витаминный | vitamínnyĭ | vitamine (adj.) |
| детонационный | detonatsiónnyĭ | pertaining to detonation |
| дипольный | dipól'nyĭ | dipole (adj.) dipolar |
| диференциальный | diferentsiál'nyĭ | differential |
| идеальный | ideál'nyĭ | ideal (adj.) |
| изомерный | izomérnyĭ | isomeric |
| изотропный | izotrópnyĭ | isotropic |
| инвариантный | invariántnyĭ | invariant |
| индивидуальный | individuál'nyĭ | individual |
| интересный | interésnyĭ | interesting |
| инфекционный | infektsiónnyĭ | infectious |
| иррациональный | irratsionál'nyĭ | irrational (math) |
| капиллярный | kapillyárnyĭ | capillary (adj.) |
| катодный | katódnyĭ | cathodic |
| кетонный | ketónnyĭ | ketonic |
| коллоидальный | kolloidál'nyĭ | colloidal |
| комплексный | kompléksnyĭ | complex (adj.) |
| конвективный | konvektívnyĭ | pertaining to convection |
| кондуктивный | konduktívnyĭ | pertaining to conduction |
| координатный | koordinátnyĭ | pertaining to coordination |

[1] The use of the letter "y" to represent " ы " must not be allowed to cause confusion with respect to pronunciation. The syllable, -ный should be pronounced like the English word "knee"; pronunciation involving the sound of the English word "ye" is quite incorrect. Use of "y" to represent " ы " is in accordance with the transliteration practice of Chemical Abstracts.

| Russian | Transliteration of Russian | English |
|---|---|---|
| лаборато́рный | laborató́rnyĭ | laboratory (adj.) |
| магни́тный | magnítnyĭ | magnetic |
| макси́ма́льный | maksimál'nyĭ | maximum (adj.) |
| матри́чный | matrichnyĭ | matrix (adj.), pertaining to a matrix (math.) |
| метастаби́льный | metastabil'nyĭ | metastable |
| миллио́нный | milliónnyĭ | millionth |
| минера́льный | minerál'nyĭ | mineral (adj.) |
| минима́льный | minimál'nyĭ | minimum (adj.) |
| молекуля́рный | molekulyárnyĭ | molecular |
| моля́рный | molyárnyĭ | molar |
| мото́рный | motórnyĭ | motor (adj.) |
| навигацио́нный | navigatsiónnyĭ | navigational |
| натура́льный | naturál'nyĭ | natural |
| нейтра́льный | neĭtrál'nyĭ | neutral |
| не́рвный | nérvnyĭ | nerve (adj.) |
| норма́льный | normál'nyĭ | normal (adj.) |
| оптима́льный | optimál'nyĭ | optimum (adj.) |
| оригина́льный | originál'nyĭ | original |
| парази́тный | parazitnyĭ | parasitic |
| паралле́льный | parallél'nyĭ | parallel |
| парциа́льный | partsiál'nyĭ | partial |
| перпендикуля́рный | perpendikulyárnyĭ | perpendicular |
| поля́рный | polyárnyĭ | polar |
| прецизио́нный | pretsiziónnyĭ | precise |
| примити́вный | primitivnyĭ | primitive |
| прогресси́вный | progressivnyĭ | successive, progressive |
| пропорциона́льный | proportsionál'nyĭ | proportional |
| радиа́льный | radiál'nyĭ | radial |
| радиоакти́вный | radioaktivnyĭ | radioactive |
| рациона́льный | ratsionál'nyĭ | rational (math) |
| реакцио́нный | reaktsiónnyĭ | pertaining to a reaction |
| реа́льный | reál'nyĭ | real, actual |
| резона́нсный | rezonánsnyĭ | involving or pertaining to resonance |
| скаля́рный | skalyárnyĭ | scalar |
| спектра́льный | spektrál'nyĭ | pertaining to a spectrum |
| специа́льный | spetsiál'nyĭ | special |
| стаби́льный | stabil'nyĭ | stable |
| станда́ртный | standártnyĭ | standard |

| Russian | Transliteration of Russian | English |
|---|---|---|
| структу́рный | struktúrnyĭ | structural |
| текстильный | tekstil'nyĭ | textile (adj.) |
| тетрагона́льный | tetragonál'nyĭ | tetragonal |
| тота́льный | totál'nyĭ | total (adj.) |
| тра́нспортный | tránsportnyĭ | transport (adj.) |
| трансцendéнтный | transtsendéntnyĭ | transcendental |
| тривиа́льный | triviál'nyĭ | trivial |
| универса́льный | universál'nyĭ | universal |
| фикти́вный | fiktívnyĭ | fictitious |
| фундамента́льный | fundamentál'nyĭ | fundamental |
| функциона́льный | funktsionál'nyĭ | functional |
| характе́рный | kharaktérnyĭ | characteristic (adj.) |
| эксперимента́льный | eksperimentál'nyĭ | experimental |
| электромагни́тный | elektromagnitnyĭ | electromagnetic |
| электро́нный | elektrónnyĭ | electronic |
| элемента́рный | elementárnyĭ | elemental, pertaining to a basic unit or quantity |
| эндокри́нный | endokrínnyĭ | endocrine (adj.) |

§ 19.  Adjectives Formed with Suffix, -и́ческ-.

Another important group of adjectives are formed with the suffix "-и́ческ-." As listed below, these adjectives have the case ending "-ий," indicating the masculine, nominative, singular case.

| Russian | Transliteration of Russian | English |
|---|---|---|
| адиабати́ческий | adiabatícheskii | adiabatic |
| азеотропи́ческий | azeotropícheskiĭ | azeotropic |
| алгебраи́ческий | algebraícheskiĭ | algebraic |
| алифати́ческий | alifatícheskiĭ | aliphatic |
| аналити́ческий | analitícheskiĭ | analytical |
| аромати́ческий | aromatícheskiĭ | aromatic |
| астрономи́ческий | astronomícheskiĭ | astronomical |
| бактериостати́ческий | bakteriostatícheskiĭ | bacteriostatic |
| биологи́ческий | biologícheskiĭ | biological |
| геометри́ческий | geometrícheskiĭ | geometrical |
| графи́ческий | grafícheskiĭ | graphical |
| динами́ческий | dinamícheskiĭ | dynamic |
| диэлектри́ческий | dielektrícheskiĭ | dielectric |
| карбоцикли́ческий | karbotsiklícheskiĭ | carbocyclic |

| Russian | Transliteration of Russian | English |
| --- | --- | --- |
| каталитический | kataliticheskiĭ | catalytic |
| кинетический | kineticheskiĭ | kinetic |
| классический | klassicheskiĭ | classical |
| космический | kosmicheskiĭ | cosmic |
| кристаллический | kristallicheskiĭ | crystalline |
| критический | kriticheskiĭ | critical |
| кубический | kubicheskiĭ | cubic |
| логический | logicheskiĭ | logical |
| макроскопический | makroskopicheskiĭ | macroscopical |
| металлический | metallicheskiĭ | metallic |
| механический | mekhanicheskiĭ | mechanical |
| микроскопический | mikroskopicheskiĭ | microscopical |
| минералогический | mineralogicheskiĭ | mineral (adj.) |
| моноклинический | monoklinicheskiĭ | monoclinic (crystallography) |
| неорганический | neorganicheskiĭ | inorganic |
| несферический | nesfericheskiĭ | non-spherical |
| оптический | opticheskiĭ | optical |
| органический | organicheskiĭ | organic |
| периодический | periodicheskiĭ | periodic |
| практический | prakticheskiĭ | practical |
| призматический | prizmaticheskiĭ | prismatic |
| ромбический | rombicheskiĭ | rhombic |
| сифилитический | sifiliticheskiĭ | syphilitic (adj.) |
| спектроскопический | spektroskopicheskiĭ | spectroscopic |
| статистический | statisticheskiĭ | statistical |
| сферический | sfericheskiĭ | spherical |
| технический | tekhnicheskiĭ | technical |
| технологический | tekhnologicheskiĭ | technological |
| типический | tipicheskiĭ | typical |
| тригонометрический | trigonometricheskiĭ | trigonometrical |
| триклинический | triklinicheskiĭ | triclinic (cryst.) |
| тропический | tropicheskiĭ | tropical |
| фактический | fakticheskiĭ | factual |
| физический | fizicheskiĭ | physical |
| фотографический | fotograficheskiĭ | photographic |
| хаотический | khaoticheskiĭ | chaotic |
| характеристический | kharateristicheskiĭ | characteristic |
| химический | khimicheskiĭ | chemical |
| циклоалифатический | tsikloalifaticheskiĭ | cycloaliphatic (chem.) |
| электрический | elektricheskiĭ | electrical |
| электролитический | elektroliticheskiĭ | electrolytic |
| эллиптический | ellipticheskiĭ | elliptical |
| эмпирический | empiricheskiĭ | empirical |

## § 20.  Adjectives Formed with Suffix -CK-.

The Russian suffix -CK- is used with foreign roots or words to form adjectives, many of which designate relationship to a geographical region or a geological epoch. These latter categories of adjectives are capitalized in English, but not in Russian.

| Russian | Transliteration of Russian | English |
|---------|---------------------------|---------|
| америка́нский | amerikánskiĭ | American |
| англи́йский | angliĭskiĭ | English |
| артиллери́йский | artilleriĭskiĭ | pertaining to artillery (adj.) |
| балка́нский | balkánskiĭ | Balkan |
| брази́льский | brazíl'skiĭ | Brazilian |
| брита́нский | británskiĭ | British |
| дево́нский | devónskiĭ | Devonian |
| италья́нский | ital'yánskiĭ | Italian |
| калифорни́йский | kaliforniĭskiĭ | Californian |
| картезиа́нский | karteziánskiĭ | Cartesian |
| каспи́йский | kaspiĭskiĭ | Caspian |
| кембри́йский | kembriĭskiĭ | Cambrian |
| мезозо́йский | mezozóĭskiĭ | Mesozoic |
| мексика́нский | meksikánskiĭ | Mexican |
| палеозо́йский | paleozóĭskiĭ | Paleozoic |
| пассажи́рский | passazhirskiĭ | pertaining to passengers (transportation) |
| по́льский | pól'skiĭ | Polish |
| пру́сский | prússkiĭ | Prussian |
| ру́ский | rússkiĭ | Russian |
| силури́йский | siluriĭskiĭ | Silurian |
| текса́сский | teksásskiĭ | Texas (adj.) |
| францу́зский | frantsúzskiĭ | French |
| япо́нский | yapónskiĭ | Japanese |

## § 21.  Adjectives Formed with Suffixes -OB-, -eB, -eBCK- and -OBCK-.

A third group of adjectives is formed by using the suffix -OB- or its alternate form -eB-. Chemists should note that specific valence states are sometimes indicated by adjectives formed by adding the suffix -OB- (or -eB- ) to the names of chemical elements. Thus the Russian name for selenic acid is селе́новая кислота́ ( -ая being the nominative, feminine, singular case ending for the

adjective and КИСЛОТА́ being a feminine noun meaning acid). The suffix -ОВ- (or -ЕВ-) and the closely related suffix -ОВСК- (or -ЕВСК-) are widely used with the names of persons, as is evident from examples included in the following list. The adjectives are listed in the nominative, singular case, as indicated by the endings -ОЙ and -ЫЙ.

| Russian | Transliteration of Russian | English |
|---|---|---|
| алли́ловый | allílovyĭ | allyl (adj.) |
| алюми́ниевый | alyumínievyĭ | alluminum (adj.) |
| асбе́стовый | asbéstovyĭ | asbestos (adj.) |
| ацетиле́новый | atsetilénovyĭ | acetylenic (adj.) |
| бензи́ловый | benzílovyĭ | benzyl (adj.) |
| бу́нзеновский | búnzenovskiĭ | pertaining to Bunsen |
| вандерва́льсовский | vandervál'sovskiĭ | pertaining to van der Waals |
| вольфра́мовый | vol'frámovyĭ | made of or containing tungsten (cf. German Wolfram - tungsten) |
| га́зовый | gázovyĭ | gaseous |
| ка́льциевый | kál'tsievyĭ | calcium (adj.) |
| ко́ксовый | kóksovyĭ | pertaining to coke (cf. German Koks-coke) |
| ла́мповый | lámpovyĭ | pertaining to one or more lamps or radio tubes |
| на́триевый | nátrievyĭ | sodium (adj.) (cf. German Natrium-sodium) |
| ни́келевый | níkelevyĭ | nickel (adj.) |
| окта́новый | oktánovyĭ | octane (adj.) |
| палми́товый | palmítovyĭ | palmitic |
| парафи́новый | parafínovyĭ | paraffinic |
| пла́тиновый | plátinovyĭ | platinum (adj.) |
| рентге́новский | rentgénovskiĭ | pertaining to Roentgen and hence to X-rays. |
| спиртово́й | spirtovóĭ | pertaining to alcohol (cf. German - Spiritus) |
| терпе́новый | terpénovyĭ | terpenic |
| фронтово́й | frontovóĭ | pertaining to the front |

§ 22. Notes on Reading Exercise.

Each of the phrases in this lesson's Reading Exercise (§ 23) consists of a noun in the nominative, singular case, together with an adjective-modifier.

It is a general[1] rule that Russian adjectives bear endings which indicate agreement as to gender, number and case with the nouns that they modify. Although all nouns in the following Reading Exercise are in the nominative, singular case, some of them are masculine in gender, while others are feminine. The ending -ая is used with those adjectives which modify feminine nouns in the following Reading Exercise. The nominative, singular case forms of all adjectives mentioned in this book, up to this point, are illustrated by the following examples.

### Nominative Singular Case of Adjectives

| Adjective Stem (to which endings are attached) | Masculine | Feminine | Neuter |
|---|---|---|---|
| | Ending -ый | Ending -ая | Ending -ое |
| абсолютн- | абсолю́тный | абсолю́тная | абсолю́тное |
| максимальн- | максима́льный | максима́льная | максима́льное |
| радиоактивн- | радиоакти́вный | радиоакти́вная | радиоакти́вное |
| электронн- | электро́нный | электро́нная | электро́нное |
| | Ending -ий | Ending -ая | Ending -ое |
| алгебраическ- | алгебраи́ческий | алгебраи́ческая | алгебраи́ческое |
| критическ- | крити́ческий | крити́ческая | крити́ческое |
| синтетическ- | синтети́ческий | синтети́ческая | синтети́ческое |
| эллиптическ- | эллипти́ческий | эллипти́ческая | эллипти́ческое |
| | Ending -ий | Ending -ая | Ending -ое |
| балканск- | балка́нский | балка́нская | балка́нское |
| пассажирск- | пассажи́рский | пассажи́рская | пассижи́рское |
| русск- | ру́сский | ру́сская | ру́сское |
| японск- | япо́нский | япо́нская | япо́нское |
| | Ending -ый, -ой or -ий | Ending -ая | Ending -ое |
| алюминиев- | алюми́ниевый | алюми́ниевая | алюми́ниевое |
| газов- | га́зовый | га́зовая | га́зовое |
| рентгеновск- | рентге́новский | рентге́новская | рентге́новское |
| спиртов- | спиртово́й | спиртова́я | спиртово́е |

[1] The rule covering an adjective modifying two nouns of different gender is cited in § 68, p. 95. As noted in § 393, p. 655, it sometimes happens that a noun in the plural has modifiers, which are singular in number. After certain numerals (Cf. § 371, p. 604) a noun in the genitive singular requires an adjectival modifier to be in the genitive plural.

This summary illustrates only those adjectives already mentioned in this book. For a more complete discussion of the nominative case of adjectives, reference is made to Lesson 8, § 59, p. 80.

Usually Russian adjectives precede the nouns which they modify, as in the typical phrases given in the Reading Exercise.

In these phrases, no Russian words corresponding to "a," "an" and "the" in English are to be found, for the simple reason that no such words exist in Russian. Hence, the phrase радиоактивный элемент standing alone could be translated equally correctly as "the radioactive element" or "a radioactive element" or simply "radioactive element." In translating whole sentences or paragraphs into English, it is necessary to rely on the context of the Russian material for hints as to proper use of "a," "an," or "the" in the English translation. This turns out to be much easier than might appear possible at first, as will become evident in later lessons.

## § 23. Reading Exercise.

абсолютная температура, адиабатический процесс, алгебраическая сумма, алюминиевая амальгама, алюминиевый атом, американский патент, анаэробная бактерия, аномальный эффект, атомная бомба, атомная энергия, балканский фронт, бессемеровский процесс (met.), валентный электрон, дипольный момент, диэлектрическая константа, идеальный газ, инертная атмосфера, каталатическая реакция, классическая механика, коллоидальный компонент, космическая радиация, кристаллическая форма, критическая масса, максимальная энтропия, матричный продукт, мезозойская эпоха, металлическая платина, металлический ион, металлический анод, метастабильная система, молекуярная структура, натриевая амальгама, натуральный латекс, нециркулярная орбита, нормальный октан (chem.), оптический аппарат, оптический изомер, паразитный организм, полярная молекула, практический результат, призматический кристалл, радиоактивный элемент, радиоактивный препарат, реактивный комплекс (chem.), реальный коэффициент, синтетическая камфора, сифилитический абцесс, статистический результат, сферическая форма,

сфери́ческая аберра́ция, сфери́ческая координа́та, тригономе-
три́ческая фу́нкция, триклини́ческий криста́лл, ультравиоле́-
товая фотогра́фия, ультравиоле́товая ла́мпа, физи́ческая кон-
ста́нта, францу́зский пате́нт, характеристи́ческий параме́тр,
хими́ческая номенклату́ра, хими́ческая лаборато́рия, хими́-
ческий элеме́нт, эксперимента́льный факт, электри́ческий
импеда́нц, электри́ческий ве́ктор, электри́ческий потенциа́л,
электролити́ческая диссоциа́ция, эллипти́ческая фу́нкция,
(math.) электромагни́тная радиа́ция, электро́нный микроско́п.

## § 24. Translation Exercise.

statistical mechanics, synthetic latex, spherical orbit, critical
potential, radioactive isotop, anaerobic organism, metallic aluminum, stable molecule, normal pentane, kinetic energy, aromatic
ketone, chemical energy, critical impedance, crystalline product,
monoclinic crystal, irrational coefficient, elliptical orbit, electrical
energy, British patent, crystalline virus, potential energy, biological
problem, calcium atom, rhombic crystal, photographic emulsion,
chemical reagent, periodic function, synthetic vitamin, scalar
product, electrical apparatus, catalytic effect, radioactive platinum,
crystalline chlorophyll, sodium ion, natural camphor, amorphous
mass, aerobic bacteria, sodium atom, metallic zinc, critical
temperature, aliphatic ketone, platinum electrode, normal
temperature.

## FURTHER NOTES ON THE RECOGNITION OF RUSSIANIZED TECHNICAL TERMS

§ 25. Deviations from Phonetic Similarity in Russianizing Foreign Words.

Since Russian does not make use of certain sounds commonly used in English, e.g., the English "th" sound, the phonetic similarity between certain corresponding English and Russian terms may be imperfect. If an English word is spelled with "th," the Russian cognate is usually spelled with "T" or, rarely, with "ф." English "h," when not part of consonantal diphthong, such as "ch" or "sh," is usually rendered in Russian cognates by "Г" or, rarely, by "X" or else disregarded. The Russian "КВ," "аВ" and "еВ" (or "эВ") often correspond to English "qu," "au" and "eu," respectively. Phonetic similarity is closer in the case of less common Russian usage of "X," "аy" and "еy," respectively, for English, "qu," "au" and "eu." The Russians may use "КС" for English "x," even when the latter is pronounced like "z." These deviations from phonetic similarity might be summarized as follows:

| English | Russian | | |
|---------|---------|-----|---|
| th | T | | (rarely ф) |
| h | Г | | (rarely X sometimes omitted) |
| qu | КВ | | (occasionally X) |
| au | аВ | | (occasionaliy аy) |
| eu | еВ | эВ | (ocasionally еy) |
| x | КС | | |

The following list of nouns and adjectives illustrates these types of deviations from close phonetic similarity. The nouns are listed in the nominative, singular case. The gender of the nouns may be determined by using the rules mentioned in § 8; p. 10, 14; and § 14, pp. 19, 22. These rules are summarized in § 28, p. 43.

| Russian | Transliteration of Russian | English |
|---|---|---|
| а́втор | а́vtor | author |
| автоиониза́ция | avtoionizátsiya | autoionization |
| автомати́ческий | avtomatícheskiĭ | automatic (adj.) |
| автомоби́ль, (masc.) | avtomobil' | automobile |
| алкоголи́зм | alkogolízm | alcoholism |
| алкоголи́ческий | alkogol'ícheskiĭ | alcoholic |
| алкого́льный | alkogól'nyĭ | alcoholic, alcohol (adj.) |
| алкого́ль | alkogól' | alcohol (noun) |
| алкоголя́т | alkogolyát | alcoholate |
| альдеги́д | al'degid | aldehyde |
| анга́р | angár | hangar |
| ангидри́д | angidríd | anhydride |
| анестези́я | anezteziya | anesthesia |
| антраце́н | antratsén | anthracene |
| арифме́тика | arifmétika | arithmetic |
| арифмети́ческий | arifmeticheskiĭ | arithmetical |
| а́рфа | árfa | harp |
| арфи́ст | arfíst | harpist |
| а́стма | ástma | asthma |
| гало́ид | galóid | halide (noun) |
| гало́идный | galóidnyĭ | halogen (adj.) |
| га́фний | gáfniĭ | hafnium |
| гексагона́льный | gekzagonál'nyĭ | hexagonal |
| гекса́н | geksán | hexane |
| ге́лий | géliĭ | helium |
| гепта́н | geptán | heptane |
| гермети́ческий | germetícheskiĭ | hermetic |
| гетероцикли́ческий | geterotsiklícheskiĭ | heterocyclic |
| гигие́на | gigiéna | hygiene |
| гигроскопи́ческий | gigroskopícheskiĭ | hygroscopic |
| гидра́т | gidrát | hydrate |
| гидродина́мика | gidrodinámika | hydrodynamics |
| гидрокси́льный | gidroksil'nyĭ | hydroxyl (adj.) |
| гидростати́ческий | gidrostatícheskiĭ | hydrostatic |
| гипетрофи́я | gipertrofia | hypertrophy |
| гипо́теза | gipóteza | hypothesis |
| гистоло́гия | gistológiya | histology |
| Голла́ндия | Gollándia | Holland |
| голла́ндский | Gollándskiĭ | Dutch |
| гомо́лог | gomólog | homolog |
| горизонта́льный | gorizontál'nyĭ | horizontal |
| гормо́н | gormón | hormone |
| гу́мус | gúmus | humus |

| Russian | Transliteration of Russian | English |
|---|---|---|
| дифтерит | difterít | diphtheria |
| исторический | istorícheskiĭ | historical |
| история | istória | history |
| евклидовский | evklídovyĭ | Euclidean |
| Европа | Evrópa | Europe |
| катод | katód | cathode |
| квадрупол | kvadrúpol | quadripole |
| квази- | kvazi- | quasi- |
| квант | kvant | quantum |
| квантовый | kvántovyĭ | quantum (adj.) |
| квантомеханический | kvantomekanícheskiĭ | quantum mechanical |
| кварц | kvartz | quartz |
| квебрахо | kvebrákho | quebracho |
| ксенон | ksenón | xenon |
| ксилол | ksilól | xylene |
| ликвидация | likvidátsiya | liquidation |
| логарифм | logarífm | logarithm |
| логарифмический | logarifmícheskiĭ | logarithmic |
| максвелл | máksvell | maxwell |
| математика | matemátika | mathematics |
| математический | matematícheskiĭ | mathematical |
| метан | metán | methane |
| метил | metil | methyl (noun) |
| метилен | metilén | methylene |
| метиловый | metílovyĭ | methyl (adj.) |
| метод | métod | method |
| нафталин | naftalín | naphthalene |
| нейтрализация | neĭtralizátsiya | neutralization |
| нейтральный | neĭtrál'nyĭ | neutral (adj.) |
| нейтрон | neĭtrón | neutron |
| паталогический | patalogícheskiĭ | pathological |
| паталогия | patalógiya | pathology |
| пневматический | pnevmatícheskiĭ | pneumatic |
| псевдо- | psevdo- | pseudo- |
| ревматизм | revmatízm | rheumatism |
| ревматический | revmatícheskiĭ | rheumatic |
| синтетический | sintetícheskiĭ | synthetic |
| теорема | teoréma | theorem |
| теоретический | teoretícheskiĭ | theoretical |
| теория | teóriya | theory |
| терапевтический | terapevtícheskiĭ | therapeutic |
| терапия | terápiya | therapy |
| термический | termícheskiĭ | thermal |
| термодинамика | termodinámika | thermodynamics |

| Russian | Transliteration of Russian | English |
|---|---|---|
| термодинами́ческий | termodinamícheskiĭ | thermodynamical |
| термо́метр | termómetr | thermometer |
| тра́вма | trávma | trauma |
| физиотера́пия | fizioterápiya | physiotherapy |
| хе́нна | khénna | henna |
| хини́н | khinín | quinine |
| хиноли́н | khinolín | quinoline |
| эвте́ктика | evtéktika | eutectic |
| эквивале́нт | ekvivalént | equivalent (noun) |
| эквивале́нтный | ekvivaléntnyĭ | equivalent (adj.) |
| экзотерми́ческий | ekzotermícheskiĭ | exothermal |
| экзоте́рмный | ekzotérmnyĭ | exothermal |
| электротерми́ческий | elektrotermícheskiĭ | electrothermal |
| эндотерми́ческий | endotermícheskiĭ | endothermal |
| эндоте́рмный | endotérmnyĭ | endothermal |
| эпите́лий | epitéliĭ | epithelium |
| эта́н | etán | ethane |
| этано́л | etanól | ethanol |
| эти́л | etíl | ethyl (noun) |
| этиле́н | etilén | ethylene |
| эти́ловый | etílovyĭ | ethyl (adj.) |

The letter combination -из- (or less commonly -ез-) terminates the stems of a small but important group of Russian words which correspond to English words terminating in "-sis." The Russian termination of these words is strongly suggestive of the "-yse" termination of corresponding French words, as is evident from the following list, which includes other closely related words.

| Russian | French | English |
|---|---|---|
| автоли́з | autolyse | autolysis |
| алкоголи́з | alcoolyse | alcoholysis |
| аммо́нолиз | ammonolyse | ammonolysis |
| ана́лиз | analyse | analysis |
| гидроли́з | hydrolyse | hydrolysis |
| микроанали́з | microanalyse | microanalysis |
| некробио́з | nécrobiose | necrobiosis |
| пироли́з | pyrolyse | pyrolysis |
| протеоли́з | protéolyse | proteolysis |
| симбио́з | symbiose | symbiosis |
| си́нтез | synthèse | synthesis |
| туберкулёз | tuberculose | tuberculosis |
| электро́лиз | électrolyse | electrolysis |

## § 26. Technical Terms of French or German Origin.

| Russian | German | French | English |
| --- | --- | --- | --- |
| адвока́т | Advokat | avocat | lawyer |
| азо́т | | azote | nitrogen |
| актуа́льный | | actuel | present, existing at the time in question |
| аммиа́к | Ammoniak | | ammonia |
| амперме́тр | | ampèremètre | ammeter |
| бензи́н | Benzin | | benzine, gasoline |
| бето́н | Beton | béton | concrete (noun) |
| библиоте́ка | Bibliothek | bibliothèque | library |
| биохи́мия | Biochemie | biochimie | biochemistry |
| бор | Bor | bore | boron |
| бром | Brom | brome | bromine |
| ви́смут | Wismut | | bismuth |
| во́льтметр | | voltmètre | voltmeter |
| вольфра́м | Wolfram | wolfram | tungsten |
| вулка́н | Vulkan | volcan | volcano |
| гидри́рование | Hydrierung | | hydrogenation |
| дисциплина | Disziplin | discipline | discipline, branch of science |
| дро́ссель | Drossel | | throttle |
| изоля́тор | Isolator | isolateur | insulator, isolator |
| иммуните́т | Immunität | | immunity |
| йод | Jod | iode | iodine |
| интере́с | Interesse | intérêt | interest |
| ка́лий | Kalium | | potassium |
| ка́рта | Karte | carte | map, chart, card |
| карто́фель, (masc.) | Kartoffel | | potato |
| каучу́к | Kautschuk | caoutchouc | rubber |
| киломе́тр | Kilometer | kilomètre | kilometer |
| кле́мма | Klemme | | clamp |
| кокс | Koks | | coke |
| ко́лба | Kolben | | flask |
| куло́н | | couloumb | couloumb |
| куро́рт | Kurort | | health resort |
| курс | Kurs | | course |
| лак | Lack | laque | lacquer, varnish |
| ла́кмус | Lakmus | | litmus |
| ли́нза | Linse | | lens |
| ли́ния | Linie | ligne | line |
| луна́ | | lune | moon |
| лу́па | Lupe | loupe | magnifier, enlarging glass |
| массико́т | | massicot | litharge |
| масшта́б | Massstab | | scale |

| Russian | German | French | English |
|---|---|---|---|
| мето́дика | Methodik | | method (generalized) |
| метр | | mètre | meter |
| мра́мор | Marmor | | marble |
| на́трий | Natrium | | sodium |
| пра́ктикум | Praktikum | | laboratory course |
| при́нцип | Prinzip | principe | principle |
| про́ба | Probe | | test, experiment, sample |
| райо́н | | rayon | region |
| раффини́ровать | raffinieren | raffiner | to refine |
| реда́ктор | Redaktor | rédacteur | editor |
| результа́т | Resultat | résultat | result |
| резюме́ | | résumé | resume |
| рента́бельный | | rentable | economical, profitable |
| роль | Rolle | rôle | role |
| сантиме́тр | | centimètre | centimeter |
| скеле́т | Skelett | squelette | skeleton |
| ста́дия | Stadium | | stage, step |
| такт | Takt | | time (music), stroke (piston, etc.), tact |
| термо́метр | | thermomètre | thermometer |
| те́хника | Technik | technique | technology |
| ти́гель | Tiegel | | crucible |
| тира́ж | | tirage | edition (number of copies) |
| университе́т | Universität | université | university |
| фа́брика | Fabrik | fabrique | manufacturing plant |
| фабрика́нт | Fabrikant | fabricant | manufacturer |
| фон | | fond | background (photography) |
| фунт | Pfund | | pound |
| футеро́вка | Futter | | lining |
| хи́мия | Chemie | chimie | chemistry |
| хирурги́я | Chirurgie | chirurgie | surgery |
| хлор | Chlor | chlore | chlorine |
| хром | Chrom | chrome | chromium |
| ци́фра | Ziffer | chiffre | figure, numeral diget |
| цель | Ziel | | goal, purpose, target |
| ша́йба | Scheibe | | flat plate |
| ша́хта | Schacht | | mine shaft, pit |
| Швейца́рия | Schweiz | | Switzerland |
| швейца́рский | schweizerisch | | Swiss |
| экра́н | | écran | screen |
| эма́ль | Email | émail | enamel |
| эта́п | | étape | phase, stage |
| эфи́р | | éther | generic term including both esters and ethers |

## § 27. Caution Required with Certain Cognates.

A majority of Russian technical terms of foreign origin have substantially the same meaning in Russian as their obvious English counterparts. In some cases there exist slight differences in usage or shade of meaning which cannot be indicated conveniently in preparing lists. Occasionally, however, a Russian technical term will be encountered whose basic meaning, or scope of meaning, deviates widely from the meaning usually attached to its apparent English counterpart. The following examples illustrate this point:

| | |
|---|---|
| актуа́льный | present, existing at the time in question, actual |
| ваго́н | car, railroad car |
| дисципли́на | branch of science, teaching, military discipline |
| конта́кт | poisoning, contact, (chem.) catalyst |
| перл | pearl, bead of glass or the like |
| проце́сс | process, action, law suit |
| реакти́в | reagent |
| рези́на | rubber (noun), particularly vulcanized rubber |
| рези́новый | made of rubber, rubber (adj.) |
| ста́дия | stage, step |
| такт | time (music), stroke (piston, etc.), tact |
| торф | peat |
| фа́брика | manufacturing plant |
| фа́ктор | commission broker, agent, factor |

## § 28. Rules for Gender of Russian Nouns.

The gender of practically all Russian nouns can be determined without difficulty by examining the final letter of their nominative, singular case (as conventionally listed in dictionaries or glossaries) and applying the following simple rules:

Masculine Nouns
Nominative singular ending is
1) Absent, i.e., the nominative, singular form ends in a hard consonant. (Note that the nominative, singular form and the stem of this important group of masculine nouns are identical.)
2) -й

Feminine Nouns
   Nominative singular ending is
      1)  -а
      2)  -я

Neuter Nouns
   Nominative singular ending is
      1)  -о
      2)  -е

Some nouns ending in -ь are masculine and others are feminine. As is noted hereafter (§ 35, pp. 49-51) nouns formed with the suffixes -ОСТ- and -ест- are feminine. Those formed with the suffix -тел-, e.g., растворитель "solvent," are masculine.

## § 29.  The Genitive Singular of Russian Nouns.

The need for keeping in mind the gender of Russian nouns will become evident in considering the declension of Russian nouns. The situation in this regard may be exemplified by the genitive singular, which with regularly declined Russian nouns of feminine gender is formed by using one of the pair of endings - ы (hard) or -и (soft), whereas regularly declined nouns of both masculine and neuter gender form their genitive, singular case by using one of the pair of endings -а (hard) and -я (soft). This latter pair of endings, it will be recalled, are used to form the nominative, singular case of many feminine nouns. This and similar, as yet undiscussed, possibilities of confusion may be avoided by carefully noting the gender of Russian nouns, which usually conforms to the rules summarized in the preceding paragraph.

Perhaps the most important single use of the Russian genitive case is to indicate a dependent relationship between nouns, as for example in the phrases:

| | |
|---|---|
| синтез витамина | synthesis of (a) (the) vitamine |
| атом натрия | atom of sodium |
| фотография машины | photograph of (a) (the) machine |
| профессор физики | professor of physics |
| концентрация калия | concentration of potassium |

§ 30.  Reading Exercise.

In the following phrases, nouns in the genitive, singular case are designated by asterisks.

автоматический аппарат, активный вулкан, актуальный интерес, американский автомобиль, английский арфист, арифметическая сумма, атом азота*, биологический синтез витамина* А, Британский Гондурас, вулканизация каучука*, гексагональный кристалл, голландский патент, гомолог метана*, евклидовская геометрия  Журнал Биохимии*, изотермический процесс, изотоп висмута*, исторический факт,  история металлургии*, итальянский мрамор, квантовая механика, квантовомеханический эффект, кварцевая лампа, кварцевая линза, квазистабильная система, кинетическая теория, курс биохимии* ликвидация фашизма*, логарифмическая функция, металлический вольфрам, металлический катод, метиловый алкоголь, механическая модель атома*,  монтаж циклотрона* натуральный логарифм, нейтральная реакция, органическая химия, паталогический организм, пенсильванский антрацит, платиновый тигель, профессор математики*, псевдометаллический характер, редактор журнала*, рентабельный процесс, роль медицины* симптом туберкулёза*, синтез хинина* синтетический каучук, спектральный анализ, стандартный термометр, такт музыки* теоретический процесс, теоретический результат, терапевтический препарат, термический нейтрон, термодинамическая константа, термодинамическая функция, фотография машины* химический анализ, центр экрана* электрический изолятор, электромагнитная радиация, электротермический метод, японский лак.

§ 31.  Translation Exercise.

synthetic vitamin, rubber insulator, synthesis of rubber, sample of quinine, radioactive chlorine, British editor, crystalline hormone, mathematical analysis, metallic sodium, installation of a machine,

quartz flask, role of mathematics, anaerobic microorganism, Japanese volcano, gaseous nitrogen, course of metallurgy, photograph of (a) cyclotron, atomic theory, theoretical hydrodynamics, mathematical formula, asbestos insulator, ethyl alcohol, experimental method, Swiss chemist, biological process, chemical analysis of vitamin A, Italian fascism, hygroscopic crystal, mathematical theorem, history of music, platinum cathode, American history, molecule of methane, Dutch mathematician, natural immunity, quartz crystal, crystal of bismuth, horizontal line, colloidal litharge, natural rubber, professor of medicine, quantum mechanical problem, Brazilian author.

# LESSON 5

## INTRODUCTION TO RUSSIAN WORDS

§ 32. General Considerations.

In previous lessons, attention has been centered on various Russian scientific and technical terms of foreign origin. Due to the frequency with which they are used, such words of foreign origin are of great importance when reading scientific and technical Russian. As might be expected, however, even greater importance is attached to words of purely Russian origin.

Since Russian is a member of the Indo-European group of languages, some simple Russian words bear a family resemblance to related English words, e.g., НОС (nos) "nose," МОЛОКО́ (moloko) "milk," НО́ВЫЙ (novyĭ) "new" (c.f. Latin, "novus"), морско́й (morskoĭ) "marine" (from мо́ре "sea"), матери́нский (materınskiĭ) "maternal" (from мать "mother"). The overwhelming majority of Russian words, however, bear no resemblance whatever to English words having closely related or identical meaning. This fact constitutes one of the difficulties which must be overcome in learning to read Russian.

Fortunately, it is possible greatly to reduce the magnitude of the difficulties involved in acquiring a working knowledge of Russian words. It is particularly helpful to take careful note of relationships existing between Russian words. Building up a pattern of associations between Russian words is best accomplished by observing relationships between words when consulting a dictionary. Since it is not always easy for the beginner to detect such relationships, the Russian-English vocabulary at the end of this book points out how individual Russian words encountered in subsequent reading exercises are related to simple parent words. The introductory discussion of Russian word-building methods given in this lesson is supplemented by further notes which preface the Russian-English vocabulary. Because of space limitations, it is not possible for this book to present a thorough analysis of Russian word-building methods.[1]

---

[1] For an excellent general review of Russian word-building methods see Patrick, George Z., "Roots of the Russian Language," Pitman Publishing Corporation, New York, 1938.

This  lesson  is  devoted  to  pointing  out  certain  general
features of Russian word-building methods.


§ 33.  Relationships Between Words As an Aid to the Memory.

As  indicated  above,  it  is  possible,  by  directing  attention  to
relationships  between  Russian  words,  to  weave  a  pattern  of
associations  able  powerfully  to  assist  the  memory  in  acquiring
and  retaining  a  vocabulary  of  Russian  words.  It  should  be  kept
in  mind,  however,  that  usage  rather  than  logic  determines  the
shade  of  meaning  of  many  Russian  words.  For  this  reason,
relationships  between  Russian  words  quite  frequently  fail  as  a
logical  basis  for  deducing  their  meaning  but  do  provide  hints  as
to  the  meanings  of  words.  Such  hints  are  very  helpful  as  an  aid
to the memory.


§ 34.  General   Role   of   Prefixes   and   Suffixes   in   Forming
       Russian Words.

A  very  large  number  of  Russian  words  can  be  regarded  as
derived  from  simple  Russian  words  or  Russian  roots  by  affixing
prefixes  or  suffixes,  as  will  be  illustrated  by  citing  examples
in  subsequent  paragraphs  of  this  lesson.  Before  taking up  individual  examples,  certain  general  features  of  Russian  prefixes
and suffixes will be discussed briefly.

Prefixes   in   Russian,   with   few   exceptions,   are   either
identical  with  or  closely  related  to  prepositions.  However,
prefixes  often  impart  to  a  derived  word  a  shade  of  meaning
which  would  scarcely  be  predicted  from  the  meaning  of  the
corresponding  preposition.  Of  particular  importance  in  this
connection  is  the  fact  that  prefixes  are  widely  used with  simple
verbs  to  indicate  merely  that  the  action  designated  by  the  verb
is  being  thought  of  as  a  completed  whole.  Nouns  derived  from
such  verbs  may  also  bear  prefixes  whose  principle,  if  indeed not
only  significance  is  to  indicate completed  action.  On  the  other
hand,  the  meaning  of  a  given  preposition often  is  closely  related
to  the  change  in  meaning  caused  by  affixing  the  corresponding
prefix  to  a  simple  Russian  word.  Evidently,  Russian  words
bearing prefixes require careful attention.

In  considering  words  formed  with  suffixes,  a  possible  source
of  confusion  is  avoided  by  making  a  careful  distinction  between
roots,  stems,  suffixes  and  endings.  The  root  of  a  word  is  the

essential basic part which it has in common with other related words. When using a word in forming a sentence, some endings having particular grammatical significance are affixed to the stem of the word. The stem of a simple word may be a root. The stems of many Russian words are roots modified by affixing one or more prefixes or suffixes.

§ 35. Examples of Uses of Suffixes in Forming Russian Words.

We have already observed that the Russian suffix -Н- is used to form Russian adjectives from foreign words. (Cf. Lesson 3, § 18, pp. 27-30.) The use of this same suffix to form adjectives from simple Russian nouns is cited as typical of use of suffixes to form Russian adjectives. The similar use of other suffixes will be observed when consulting the Russian-English vocabulary.

| Adjectives | | Nouns | |
|---|---|---|---|
| ви́дный (vidnyĭ) | prominent, visible | вид (vid) | form, aspect, appearance |
| го́рный (gornyĭ) | mountainous, geological | гора́ (gora) | mountain |
| лине́йный (lineĭnyĭ) | linear | ли́ния (liniya) | line |
| приро́дный (prirodnyi) | natural | приро́да (priroda) | nature |
| ру́дный (rudnyĭ) | ore (adj.), mining (adj.) · | руда́ (ruda) | ore |
| са́харный (sakharnyĭ) | sugar (adj.) | са́хар (sakhar) | sugar |
| свобо́дный (svobodnyĭ) | free | свобо́да (cvoboda) | liberty |
| стально́й (stal'noĭ) | steel | сталь (stal )(fem.) | steel |
| холо́дный (kholodnyĭ) | cold (adj.) | хо́лод (kholod) | chill, cold (noun) |
| щелочно́й (shchelochnoĭ) | alkaline | щёлочь (shchyoloch') (fem.) | alkali |

Various suffixes also play an important role in the formation of Russian nouns. One of the most important of these suffixes is -ОСТ- (alternate form -ЕСТ-) which is used to form

feminine abstract nouns from words of foreign origin as well as from purely Russian words. The meaning of such feminine abstract nouns is most easily grasped by noting that they are closely related to adjectives.

## Words of Foreign Origin

| Nouns | | Adjectives | |
|---|---|---|---|
| акти́вность (aktivnost') | activity | акти́вный (aktivnyĭ) | active |
| вале́нтность (valentnost') | valency | вале́нтный (valentnyĭ) | pertaining to valence |
| ине́ртность (inertnost') | inertness | ине́ртный (inertnyĭ) | inert |
| кристалли́чность (kristallichnost') | crystallinity | кристалли́ческий (kristallicheskiĭ) | crystalline |
| периоди́чность (periodichnost') | periodic character | периоди́ческий (periodicheskiĭ) | periodic |
| пласти́чность (plastichnost') | plasticity | пласти́чный (plastichnyĭ) | plastic |
| радиоакти́вность (radioaktivnost') | radioactivity | радиоакти́вный (radioaktivnyĭ) | radioactive |
| реакти́вность (reaktivnost') | reactivity | реакти́вный (reaktivnyĭ) | reactive |
| стаби́льность (stabil'nost') | stability | стаби́льный (stabil'nyĭ) | stable |
| эласти́чность (elastichnost') | elasticity | эласти́ческий (elastichnost') | elastic |

## Words of Russian Origin

| Nouns | | Adjectives | |
|---|---|---|---|
| беспо́мощность (bespomoshchnost') | helplessness | беспо́мощный (bespomoshchnyĭ) | helpless |
| бли́зость (blizost') | nearness, proximity | бли́зкий (blizkiĭ) | near |
| ва́жность (vazhnost') | importance | ва́жный (vazhnost') | important |
| возмо́жность (vozmozhnost') | possibility | возмо́жный (vozmozhnyĭ) | possible |
| вя́зкость (vyazkost') | viscosity, toughness, stickiness | вя́зкий (vyazkiĭ) | viscous, tough, sticky |

| Nouns | | Adjectives | |
|---|---|---|---|
| жи́дкость (zhidkost') | liquid (noun) | жи́дкий (zhidkiĭ) | liquid (adj.) |
| лёгкость (lyogkost') | ease, lightness | лёгкий (lyogkiĭ) | light (adj.), easy, gentle |
| мо́щность (moshchnost') | power, vigor, magnitude | мо́щный (moshchnyĭ) | powerful, vigorous, strong |
| опа́сность (opasnost') | danger | опа́сный (opasnyĭ) | dangerous |
| промы́шленность (promyshlennost') | industry | промы́шленный (promyshlennyĭ) | industrial |
| ре́дкость (redkost') | rareness, rarity | ре́дкий (redkiĭ) | rare |
| све́жесть (svezhest') | freshness | све́жий (svezhiĭ) | fresh |
| ско́рость (skorost') | speed, rate | ско́рый (skoryĭ) | swift, rapid |
| твёрдость (tvyordost') | solidity, hardness, rigidity | твёрдый (tvyordyĭ) | solid, hard, rigid |
| то́чность (tochnost') | precision, exactness | то́чный (tochnyĭ) | precise, exact |

A very important group of neuter nouns are formed with the suffix -НИ-. These nouns denote an action, process or, less frequently, a concept or result associated with an action. As might be expected, such nouns are closely related to Russian verbs, which in accordance with the usual convention are listed below as infinitives. It should be noted that the infinitives of Russian verbs, with few exceptions, end with -ТЬ.

| Nouns | | Verb Infinitives | |
|---|---|---|---|
| броже́ние (brozhenie) | fermentation | броди́ть (brodit') | to be fermenting, to be wandering |
| враще́ние (vrashchenie) | rotation | враща́ть (vrashchat') | to be rotating |
| горе́ние (gorenie) | combustion | горе́ть (goret') | to be burning |
| давле́ние (davlenie) | pressure | дави́ть (davit') | to be exerting pressure |

| Nouns | | Verb Infinitives | |
|---|---|---|---|
| кипе́ние (kipenie) | act of boiling | кипе́ть (kipet') | to be boiling |
| плавле́ние (plavlenie) | fusion, act of melting | пла́вить (plavit') | to be melting, to be floating |
| расте́ние (rastenie) | plant (botanical) | расти́ (rasti) | to be growing |
| ржавле́ние (rzhavlenie) | rusting (process) | ржа́веть (rzhavet') | to be rusting |
| тече́ние (techenie) | flow, course | течь (tech') | to be flowing |
| тре́ние (trenie) | rubbing, friction | тере́ть (teret') | to be rubbing |

## § 36. An Important Relationship Between Certain Russian Adjectives and Adverbs.

Many Russian adverbs may be regarded as formed by adding -O to the stems of adjectives.

The following adverb-adjective pairs are derived from foreign words.

| Adverbs | | Adjectives | |
|---|---|---|---|
| аналоги́чно (analogichno) | analogously | аналоги́чный (analogichnyĭ) | analogous |
| вертика́льно (vertikal'no) | vertically | вертика́льный (vertikal'nyĭ) | vertical |
| горизонта́льно (gorizontal'no) | horizontally | горизонта́льный (gorizontal'nyĭ) | horizontal |
| идеа́льно (ideal'no) | ideally | идеа́льный (ideal'nyĭ) | ideal (adj.) |
| молекуля́рно (molekulyarno) | molecularly | молекуля́рный (molekulyarnyĭ) | molecular |
| официа́льно (ofitsial'no) | officially | официа́льный (ofitsial'nyĭ) | official |
| пропорциона́льно (proportsional'no) | proportionally | пропорциона́льный (proportsional'nyĭ) | proportional |
| радиа́льно (radial'no) | radially | радиа́льный (radial'nyĭ) | radial |
| центра́льно (tsentral'no) | centrally | центра́льный (tsentral'nyĭ) | central |
| эксперимента́льно (eksperimental'no) | experimentally | эксперимента́льный (eksperimental'nyĭ) | experimental |

The following adverb-adjective pairs are derived from purely Russian roots.

| | | | |
|---|---|---|---|
| беспомощно (beςpomoshchno) | helplessly | беспомощный (beςpomoshchnyĭ) | helpless |
| видно (vidno) | seemingly, apparently | видный (vidnyĭ) | visible, prominent |
| возможно (vozmozhno) | possibly | возможный (vozmozhnyĭ) | possible |
| легко (legko) | easily, lightly, gently | лёгкий (lyogkiĭ) | light (adj.), easy, gentle |
| медленно (medlenno) | slowly, sluggishly | медленный (medlennyĭ) | slow, sluggish |
| мощно (moshchno) | powerfully, vigorously | мощный (moshchnyĭ) | powerful, vigorous, strong |
| опасно (opasno) | dangerously | опасный (opasnyĭ) | dangerous |
| редко (redko) | rarely | редкий (redkiĭ) | rare |
| скоро (skoro) | swiftly, rapidly | скорый (skoryĭ) | swift, rapid |
| точно (tochno) | exactly, precisely | точный (tochnyĭ) | exact, precise |
| широко (shiroko) | widely, extensively | широкий (shirokiĭ) | wide, broad |

## § 37. Reading Exercise.

активность гормона, американская промышленность, брожение сахара, важная теорема, важность результата, важный
результат, валентный электрон, валентность алюминия, вер-
тикальная линия, видный математик, возможная важность,
возможность опасности, возможный результат, вращать медленно, вращение диска, вязкая жидкость, вязкость жидкости, горение метана, гореть скоро, давление газа, жидкий
металл, инертность гелия, Каспийское море, каталитиче-
ская активность платины, кипение жидкости, кипеть легко,
лёгкий металл, математическая точность, медленное вращение, медленная кристаллизация, молекула сахара, морское
растение, мощная машина, мощность турбины, мощный катализатор, новая машина, новый продукт, опасный эксперимент, опасная возможность, плавление металла, пластичность асфальта, пластичность натрия, природный газ, про-

мы́шленный проце́сс, радиоакти́вность ура́на, ре́дкий элеме́нт, ре́дкое расте́ние, ржа́веть ме́дленно, ржавле́ние ста́ли,   руда́ тита́на, све́жее молоко́, свобо́дное враще́ние моле́кулы, свобо́дный ио́н, ско́рость горе́ния, ско́рость реа́кции, стаби́льность систе́мы, стально́й диск, теорети́ческая возмо́жность, то́чность результа́та, то́чный результа́т,   хими́ческая промы́шленность, холо́дный мета́лл, эласти́чность рези́ны.

## § 38.  Translation Exercise.

activity   of   (the)   catalyst,   Japanese   industry,   prominent chemist,  to  be  growing  slowly,  to  be  fermenting  rapidly, rate of combustion,  combustion  of  sugar,  liquid helium, powerful turbine, important  experiment,  importance  of  (the)  experiment,  ore  of uranium, theoretical importance  of (the) result, possible result of (the)  experiment,  radioactive  aluminum,  theoretical  chemistry, horizontal  line,   importance   of   uranium,   important   element, important  plant,  chemical  product, dangerous product, product of (the)  reaction,  dangerous  rate of reaction, crystal of sugar, to be burning  slowly,  fusion  of  platinum,  biological  activity  of (the) hormone,  slow  rotation  of  (the)  disk,  hardness  of  steel, valency of  titanium,  liquid  sodium,  valence  electron of sodium, reactivity of  sodium,  tropical  plant,  to be flowing slowly, free electron, new process,  new steel, biological activity of (the) vitamin.

# LESSON 6

## BASIC FACTS CONCERNING RUSSIAN VERBS

§ 39. General Considerations.

In general, Russian verbs indicate an action or existence of a condition just as they do in English. Russian and English verbs are also similar in other respects. Endings are used in both languages in the formation of participles, past tenses, etc. Russian makes more use of endings than English, but, on the other hand, auxiliary verbs are used very much less extensively in Russian. This is shown by the following simple example sentences.

| Action Thought of As Incomplete, in Progress or Frequently Repeated | Action Thought of As a Completed Whole |
|---|---|
| (Imperfective Aspect) | (Perfective Aspect) |
| Он фотографи́ровал маши́ну. He was photographing (a) (the) machine. | Он сфотографи́ровал маши́ну. He photographed (a) (the) machine. |
| Он фотографи́рует маши́ну. He photographs (a) (the) machine. | (Perfective aspect has no present tense). |
| Он бу́дет фотографи́ровать маши́ну. He will be photographing (a) (the) machine. | Он сфотографи́рует маши́ну. He will photograph (a) (the) machine. |

As indicated by these simple sentences, nearly all Russian verbs have two parallel sets of forms, imperfective and perfective aspects, which designate different types of action. Russian has no progressive tense forms corresponding to English "was photographing," "will be photographing," etc. Nevertheless, frequent use will be made of English progressive forms to translate Russian imperfective forms in order to distinguish them from companion perfective forms.

55

## § 40. Russian Verbs Derived from Foreign Words.

In previous lessons we have reviewed various procedures whereby the Russians form nouns and adjectives from words of foreign origin. It will be recalled that such procedures were characterized by the use of suffixes such as -ИЧЕСК -, -Н-, -СК-, -ОСТ-, etc. As might be expected, a similar situation exists with regard to adoption of foreign verbs into Russian. Thus, the infinitives of Russian verbs are formed by affixing either -ИРОВАТЬ or -ОВАТЬ to foreign words or roots, as shown in the following examples.

| Russian Verb | Transliteration | Translation |
|---|---|---|
| активи́ровать | aktiví rovat' | to be activating<br>to activate |
| амальгами́ровать | amal'gamírovat' | to be amalgamating<br>to amalgamate |
| ампути́ровать | amputírovat' | to be amputating<br>to amputate |
| броми́ровать | bromírovat' | to be brominating<br>to brominate |
| денатури́ровать | denaturírovat' | to be denaturing (protein)<br>to denature (protein) |
| деформи́ровать | deformírovat' | to be deforming<br>to deform |
| диазоти́ровать | diazotírovat' | to be diazotizing<br>to diazotize |
| диссоции́ровать | dissotsiírovat' | to be dissociating<br>to dissociate |
| игнори́ровать | ignorírovat' | to be ignoring<br>to ignore |
| идентифици́ровать | identifitsírovat' | to be identifying<br>to identify |
| изомери́зовать | izomerízovat' | to be isomerizing<br>to isomerize |
| капитули́ровать | kapitulírovat' | to be capitulating<br>to capitulate |
| компенси́ровать | kompensírovat' | to be compensating<br>to compensate |
| конденси́ровать | kondensírovat' | to be condensing<br>to condense |
| куппели́ровать | kuppelírovat' | to be coupling<br>to couple |

| Russian Verb | Transliteration | Translation |
|---|---|---|
| мерсеризи́ровать | merserizírovat' | to be mercerizing<br>to mercerize |
| метили́ровать | metilírovat' | to be methylating<br>to methylate |
| нейтрализова́ть | neĭtralizovát' | to be neutralizing<br>to neutralize |
| нитрова́ть | nitrovát' | to be nitrating<br>to nitrate |
| ориенти́ровать | orientírovat' | to be orientating<br>to orient |
| постули́ровать | postulírovat' | to be postulating<br>to postulate |
| презентова́ть | prezentovát' | to be presenting<br>to present |
| реализова́ть | realizovát' | to be realizing<br>to realize |
| синтези́ровать | sintezírovat' | to be synthesizing<br>to synthesize |
| стабилизи́ровать | stabilizírovat' | to be stabilizing<br>to stabilize |
| стимули́ровать | stimulírovat' | to be stimulating<br>to stimulate |
| сульфи́ровать | sul'fírovat' | to be sulfonating<br>to sulfonate |
| хлори́ровать | khlorírovat' | to be chlorinating<br>to chlorinate |
| экстраги́ровать | ekstragírovat' | to be extracting<br>to extract |
| юсти́ровать | yustírovat' | to be adjusting<br>to adjust |

## § 41. Perfective and Imperfective Infinitives of Russian Verbs Derived from Foreign Words.

As is indicated by their translation, the Russian infinitives listed in § 40 do not distinguish between (1) action thought of as incomplete, in progress or frequently repeated and (2) action thought of as a completed whole. In general, however, each Russian verb has two distinct infinitives to distinguish between these two types of action. One infinitive -- the imperfective -- and verb forms derived therefrom designate action thought of as incomplete, in

progress or frequently repeated; while the other infinitive -- the perfective -- and verb forms derived therefrom designate action thought of as a completed whole. For these reasons, the "one-infinitive" verbs listed in § 40 may be regarded as incompletely assimilated into the Russian language.

Further assimilation of a foreign verb into Russian proceeds beyond the "one-infinitive" stage to formation of a pair of infinitives -- one perfective and the other imperfective. As might be expected, only those verbs of foreign origin which are used relatively frequently in Russian have been assimilated to the extent of having a pair of infinitives (perfective and imperfective) and parallel sets of forms derived therefrom.

| Imperfective Infinitive | Perfective Infinitive |
|---|---|
| (Indicating action thought of as incomplete, in progress or frequently repeated.) | (Indicating action thought of as a completed whole.) |
| анализи́ровать<br>to be analyzing | проанализи́ровать<br>to analyze |
| интересова́ть<br>to be arousing interest | заитересова́ть<br>to interest |
| концентри́ровать<br>to be concentrating | сконцентри́ровать<br>to concentrate |
| критикова́ть<br>to be criticizing | раскритикова́ть<br>to criticize |
| магни́тить<br>намагни́чивать<br>to be magnetizing | намагни́тить[1]<br>to magnetize |
| монти́ровать<br>to be installing, to be erecting,<br>  to be mounting | смонти́ровать<br>to install, to erect,<br>  to mount |
| патентова́ть<br>to be patenting | запатентова́ть<br>to patent |

---

[1] Note that магнетизи́ровать, "magnetizirovat'," means "to be hypnotizing, to hypnotize."

| Imperfective Infinitive | Perfective Infinitive |
|---|---|
| (Indicating action thought of as incomplete, in progress or frequently repeated.) | (Indicating action thought of as a completed whole.) |
| публикова́ть<br>to be publishing | опубликова́ть<br>to publish |
| рапортова́ть<br>to be reporting (military) | отрапортова́ть<br>to report (military) |
| фикси́ровать<br>to be fixing, to be developing (photography) | зафикси́ровать<br>to fix, to develop (photography) |
| формули́ровать<br>to be formulating | сформули́ровать<br>to formulate |
| фотографи́ровать<br>to be photographing | сфотографи́ровать<br>to photograph |
| шлакова́ть<br>to be slagging | ошлакова́ть<br>to form slag, to slag |
| экзаменова́ть<br>to be examining (school) | проэкзаменова́ть<br>to give an examination, to examine (school) |

## § 42. Prefixes Used to Alter the Meaning of Russian Verbs of Foreign Origin.

In the examples given in § 41 above, each of the various imperfective infinitives have been converted into perfective infinitives by affixing a prefix. This method of converting imperfective infinitives into perfective infinitives is very common in Russian.

The use of prefixes with Russian verbs is not limited, however, merely to forming perfective infinitives from the corresponding imperfective infinitives. In general, use of prefixes with imperfective infinitives also involves alteration of their meaning.[1]

---

[1] Prefixes are also used with Russian nouns, adjectives, verbs and adverbs to alter their meaning.

In other words, affixing a prefix to an imperfective infinitive of
a verb, in general, simultaneously (1) alters the meaning of the
verb to a greater or less degree and (2) converts the imperfective
infinitive into a perfective infinitive. Thus on affixing the prefix
пере- to the imperfective infinitive кристаллизовать[1] "to be
crystallizing," there is formed the perfective infinitive
перекристаллизовать "to recrystallize." It is perhaps
obvious that from the Russian point of view it is not enough to
form the perfective infinitive перекристаллизовать. A companion imperfective infinitive is needed, and this is formed by
inserting the letters -вы- in the stem to obtain
перекристаллизовывать "to be recrystallizing." Various
other alterations in the stems of a large number of Russian
perfective infinitives are also used to convert them into perfective
infinitives. Which alteration is used with a given perfective
infinitive is a matter of usage rather than logical consideration.

The following examples illustrate the use of Russian prefixes
with simple verbs of foreign origin to form verbs having more or
less altered meaning.

| Imperfective Infinitives | Perfective Infinitives |
|---|---|
| выкристаллизовывать | выкристаллизовать |
| to be crystallizing out | to crystallize out |
| перекристаллизовывать | перекристаллизовать |
| to be recrystallizing | to recrystallize |
| выфильтровывать | выфильтровать |
| to be filtering off | to filter off |
| отфильтровывать | отфильтровать |
| to be filtering out | to filter out |
| профильтровывать | профильтровать |
| to be filtering through | to filter through |
| переэкзаменовывать | переэкзаменовать |
| to be re-examining | to re-examine |
| размагничивать | размагнитить |
| to be demagnetizing | to demagnetize |

[1] This imperfective infinitive also exists in the alternate form кристаллизировать.

As noted above, by affixing certain prefixes to the simple verbs кристаллизовать "to be crystallizing" and фильтровать "to be filtering," various verbs having more or less altered meaning are derived. Thus, in the case of фильтровать we have verbs indicating the actions, "filtering off," "filtering out," "filtering through." From one point of view, one might be led to the conclusion that the simple verb фильтровать has no corresponding perfective infinitive. However, the action профильтровать "to filter through" is by its very nature the completed act corresponding to фильтровать "to be filtering." As will be pointed out in § 43 below, a similar situation exists with respect to verbs of purely Russian origin. It is important to note that this situation is not treated in uniform fashion by compilers of dictionaries and various authorities on Russian grammar. Thus, referring again to our example, профильтровать in view of its meaning, is sometimes cited as the perfective infinitive corresponding to the imperfective infinitive фильтровать. Others, centering attention on the technicalities of word derivation, point out that the imperfective infinitive профильтровывать "to be filtering through" forms with the perfective infinitive профильтровать the typical pair of infinitives профильтровывать (imperfective) -- профильтровать (perfective); and from this fact they draw the conclusion that фильтровать has no single, corresponding perfective infinitive. The point of view adopted in describing the existing relationships, however, is much less important than the fact that from the simple imperfective infinitive фильтровать, the Russian language derives a series of infinitives which express not only different variations of the process of filtration, but which also distinguish between (1) action thought of as incomplete, in progress or frequently repeated and (2) action thought of as complete. Derivation of a surprisingly large number of closely related verbs from one simple verb is one of the means employed by the Russian language to express fine shades of meaning with precision and subtlety.


§ 43. Prefixes Used to Alter the Meaning of Verbs of Purely Russian Origin.

The following list of verbs, derived from the simple verb лить "to be pouring," illustrates how prefixes are used with simple verbs of purely Russian origin.

| Imperfective Infinitives | Perfective Infinitives |
|---|---|
| ЛИТЬ<br>to be pouring | |
| ВЛИВА́ТЬ<br>to be pouring in, to be<br>  influencing, to be inspiring | ВЛИТЬ<br>to pour in, to inject |
| ВЫЛИВА́ТЬ<br>to be pouring out | ВЫ́ЛИТЬ<br>to pour out |
| ДОЛИВА́ТЬ<br>to be finishing filling<br>  (by pouring) | ДОЛИ́ТЬ<br>to pour full, to fill up |
| НАЛИВА́ТЬ<br>to be pouring in | НАЛИ́ТЬ<br>to pour in |
| ОБЛИВА́ТЬ<br>to be pouring over, to be<br>  drenching, to be glazing,<br>  to be varnishing | ОБЛИ́ТЬ<br>to pour over, to drench, to<br>  glaze, to varnish |
| ОТЛИВА́ТЬ<br>to be pouring off, to be<br>  decanting, to be casting<br>  (metal) | ОТЛИ́ТЬ<br>to pour off, to decant, to cast<br>  (metal) |
| ПЕРЕЛИВА́ТЬ<br>to be pouring from one vessel<br>  to another, to be recasting | ПЕРЕЛИ́ТЬ<br>to pour from one vessel to<br>  another, to recast |
| ПОЛИВА́ТЬ<br>to be pouring on, to be watering | ПОЛИ́ТЬ<br>to pour on, to water |
| РАЗЛИВА́ТЬ<br>to be pouring out (into separate<br>  containers), to be diffusing | РАЗЛИ́ТЬ<br>to pour out (into separate con-<br>  tainers), to diffuse |
| СЛИВА́ТЬ<br>to be pouring off, to be pouring<br>  together, to be mixing | СЛИТЬ<br>to pour off, to pour together,<br>  to mix |

It will be observed that prefixes are used not only to alter what might be termed the literal meaning of a verb but also to impart a figurative meaning, as e.g., ОБЛИВА́ТЬ "to be pouring

over," "to be drenching," "to be glazing or varnishing"; and its companion infinitive ОБЛИ́ТЬ "to pour over," "to drench," "to glaze or varnish." Usage, rather than logic, is the determining factor in establishing many figurative meanings.

## § 44. Citing Russian Infinitive Pairs.

In previous discussion of Russian verbs, separate translations have been given for both imperfective and perfective infinitives. This rather clumsy method of citing verbs will not be used through- out the balance of this book. Instead, when citing infinitive pairs, the imperfective infinitive will be given first, followed in order by a dash, the corresponding perfective infinitive and translation of the perfective infinitive only. Translation of the imperfective infinitives will be omitted to avoid tedious, useless repetition.

The student is urged, when learning Russian verbs, to impress both infinitive pairs on the memory. As mentioned already, a few simple Russian verbs cannot be regarded as having any one individual perfective infinitive. These will be listed in appro- priate fashion, e.g., ЛИТЬ "to be pouring." A few other verbs are unusual in that they have only one infinitive which is, in some instances, perfective. Certain other verbs, as illustrated by those cited in § 40, have only one infinitive to designate both perfective and imperfective action. The nature of such infinitives will be indicated by appropriate translation. The necessity for special care when learning such verbs is obvious.

## § 45. Notes on Some Unusual Russian Verbs.

Previous discussion has been directed to those characteristic features which the vast majority of Russian verbs have in common. Although no discussion of certain exceptional verbs will be under- taken in this lesson, it is perhaps well to mention their existence. Thus, the verbs of motion are characterized by various peculiar- ities, the most important of which is the existence of two imperfective infinitives used for distinguishing between general motion and motion toward some objective. The verbs of motion and their derivatives are discussed in  Lesson 40, pp. 626-635.

Finally, there are a small number of peculiar infinitives not mentioned as yet. One type of such infinitives is used to denote momentary or instantaneous action. Another type of infinitive emphasizes repetitive nature of an action. Yet another type of infinitive is sometimes used to indicate intermittent action.

None of these relatively uncommon types of infinitives is of much importance in scientific Russian and discussion of them is deferred to a later lesson.

## § 46. The Accusative Singular of Russian Nouns.

The accusative singular case of the majority of Russian nouns is identical as to form with the corresponding nominative case. Two large classes of feminine nouns which are readily identified from their nominative singular are exceptional and use distinctive endings to form the accusative singular. This situation might be summarized by the following tabulation.

### Accusative Case
### Singular Endings

| Masculine | Feminine | | Neuter |
|---|---|---|---|
| Accusative | Nominative | Accusative | Accusative |
| Same as | -а | -у | Same as |
| nominative | -я | -ю | nominative |
| for inanimate | -ь | -ь | |

It may be of interest to note in this connection that, aside from certain exceptions mentioned below, the accusative plural of all Russian nouns is identical as to form with their nominative plural.

The rules given above for forming the accusative case do not apply to nouns designating living entities (viz., human beings, mythological persons, animals and insects). For further discussion of this point see Lesson 9, § 67, p. 93.

## § 47. Reading Exercise.

The following phrases include some in which a noun in the accusative case is used as the direct object of an infinitive as, for example, in the phrase    сфотографировать машину[1] "to photograph (a) (the) machine." An asterisk is used to direct attention to all such nouns in the accusative case in the following phrases.

---

[1] The Russian phrase standing alone could be translated equally correctly by "to photograph a machine" or "to photograph the machine." Such ambiguity rarely becomes troublesome in reading coherent text.

активи́ровать хлорофи́лл*, амальгами́ровать алюми́ний*, анали́зи́ровать руду́* урана, вылива́ть молоко́*, вы́лить молоко́*, деформи́ровать диск*, диазоти́ровать анили́н*, идентифици́ровать органи́зм*, испари́ть ацето́н*, испаря́ть ацето́н*, калибро́ва́ть вольтме́тр*, концентри́ровать ви́рус*, критикова́ть тео́рию, лить жи́дкость*, метили́ровать ами́н*, монти́ровать турби́ну,* монти́ровать циклотро́н*, написа́ть фо́рмулу* са́хара, нейтрали́зова́ть ще́лочь*, описа́ть центрифу́гу*, описа́ть ржавле́ние* ста́ли, опи́сывать центрифу́гу*, опи́сывать ржавле́ние* ста́ли, опубликова́ть результа́т* экспериме́нта, откры́ть коме́ту*, откры́ть позитро́н*, отлива́ть мета́лл*, отли́ть мета́лл*, отфильтрова́ть проду́кт*, отфильтро́вывать проду́кт*, перекристалли́зова́ть витами́н*, перекристаллизо́вывать витами́н*, переэкзаменова́ть студе́нта*, писа́ть фо́рмулу* са́хара, перессова́ть бакели́т*, проэкзаменова́ть студе́нта*, разлива́ть во́дку*, разли́ть во́дку*, размагни́тить магни́т*, размагни́чивать магни́т*, реаги́ровать ме́дленно, смонти́ровать турби́ну*, смонти́ровать циклотро́н*, синтези́ровать гормо́н*, синтези́ровать каучу́к*, стабилизи́ровать энзи́м*, стабилизи́ровать эму́льсию*, стимули́ровать проду́кцию* витами́на, сфотографи́ровать автомоби́ль*, сфотографи́ровать плане́ту*, уско́рить ско́рость* реа́кции, ускоря́ть ско́рость* реа́кции, фильтрова́ть жи́дкость* ме́дленно, фотографи́ровать автомоби́ль*, фотографи́ровать плане́ту*, хлори́ровать кероси́н*, экзаменова́ть студе́нта*.


## § 48. Translation Exercise.

Asterisks are used to indicate English infinitives, whose corresponding Russian infinitives have both perfective and imperfective significance.

to calibrate* (a) (the) colorimeter, to chlorinate* methane, to be concentrating (the) bacteriophage, to stimulate* (the) production of vitamin, to be evaporating ether, to evaporate ether, to be casting aluminum, to cast aluminum, to amalgamate* sodium, to activate*(an) (the) enzyme, to identify*(an) (the) ore of uranium, to identify*(a) (the) comet, to criticize (a) (the) hypothesis, to be pouring milk, to methylate* aniline, to install (a) (the) centrifuge, to be installing (a) (the) centrifuge, to be describing (a) (the) voltmeter, to describe (a) (the) voltmeter, to be describing (a)

(the) planet, to describe (a) (the) planet, to be describing (a) (the) cyclotron, to describe (a) (the) cyclotron, to discover (the) electron, to be filtering out (a) (the) hormone, to filter out (a) (the) hormone, to be accelerating (the) rate of hydrolysis, to synthesize (a) (the) vitamin, to stimulate (the) production of rubber, to be filtering kerosene, to be filtering (a) (the) liquid, to be filtering vodka, to discover (the) radioactivity of uranium.

INTRODUCTION TO SIMPLE SENTENCES

## § 49. General Considerations.

In previous lessons we have discussed various simple relationships between Russian nouns, adjectives, verbs and adverbs, and their derivation from simple nouns and roots. Phrases given in reading exercises have revealed that considerable similarity exists between Russian and English methods of combining words to express thought. Perhaps the most striking difference is the much greater extent to which endings are used in Russian to convey meaning. Such use of endings must be carefully considered when reading Russian. Although in general the word order in Russian sentences deviates very little from the word order in English sentences, it is important to realize that the endings determine the meaning rather than the relative position of the words in a sentence. Thus the sentence " Челове́к куса́ет соба́ку " means "Man (Челове́к) bites (куса́ет) dog (соба́ку)." In English, transposing the words "man" and "dog" to form the sentence "Dog bites man" completely changes the meaning. Transposition of the corresponding words in the Russian sentence effects no such change in meaning.[1] Both the sentences˙ " Челове́к куса́ет соба́ку " and " Соба́ку куса́ет челове́к " indicate "dog" as being bitten and "man" as the biter. The noun, челове́к, "man" is the subject of both sentences and consequently in the nominative case; while соба́ку "dog," as the direct object of the verb куса́ет "bites," is in the accusative. In order to express in Russian the thought "Dog bites man," the word "dog" must be placed in the nominative case and the word "man" in the accusative case. When this is done, we have " Соба́ка куса́ет челове́ка " a sentence whose meaning "Dog bites man" remains unchanged on transposing челове́ка and соба́ка to form the sentence "Челове́ка куса́ет соба́ка." This simple example has been discussed at length to emphasize the important role played by noun endings in Russian methods of expressing thought.

---

[1] A difference in shade of meaning is introduced by deviation from the normal word order. Placing the direct object first directs attention to it and hence emphasizes it.

## § 50.  Role of Verbs in Russian Sentences.

As in English, the two basic components of every simple Russian sentence (and of each of the clauses into which complex sentences can be resolved) are (1) the subject of the sentence (or clause) and (2) the verb that designates what action is indicated by the sentence (or clause). In English, the form of the verb in some instances at least depends on the subject, e.g., "I am," "you are," "he goes," "they go."[1] Similarly, the form of the verb in a Russian sentence depends on the subject. Thus, in the sentences Человек кусает собаку. Собака кусает человека. and variations thereof given above, the same form кусает of the present tense is used throughout, as the subject in each case and is a singular noun requiring the present tense of the verb to be in the third person, singular form. Here -ет is the ending used to derive the required verb form.

## § 51.  Some Important Present Tense Forms.

The third person, singular and plural forms of the present tense of Russian verbs are of particular importance in reading Russian scientific material. The present tense of regular Russian verbs may be conveniently regarded as derived from the imperfective infinitives of verbs by first removing either -ТЬ or some combination of a vowel plus -ТЬ to obtain a verb stem and then affixing an ending. This ending is either -ет or -ит for the third person singular and either -ут, -ют-, -ат, or -ят for the third person plural of the present tense. Irregular formation of the present tense, almost without exception, involves some change in the stem of the verb prior to affixing the regular endings already noted. Very few Russian verbs are conjugated with irregular endings.

Both regular and irregular formation of the third person singular and plural of the present tense of various important Russian verbs are illustrated in the following table.

The present tense is formed only from imperfective infinitives. The closely related perfective future tense is formed from perfective infinitives as is discussed in §§ 185-188, pp. 280-285 and in §§ 228-229, pp. 359-360.

---

[1] However, as previously noted, § 39, p. 55, a greater number of endings are used with Russian verbs, while English makes more extensive use of auxiliary verbs.

## Present Tense

| Infinitives | 3rd Person Singular | 3rd Person Plural |
| --- | --- | --- |
| воспламеня́ть – воспламени́ть<br>to inflame, to ignite | воспламеня́ет | воспламеня́ют |
| входи́ть – войти́<br>to enter | вхо́дит | вхо́дят |
| выделя́ть – вы́делить<br>to evolve (heat, gas), to liberate, to set free | выделя́ет | выделя́ют |
| густе́ть<br>to become thick, dense or viscous | густе́ет | густе́ют |
| излуча́ть – излучи́ть<br>to emit, to radiate | излуча́ет | излуча́ют |
| испаря́ть – испари́ть<br>to evaporate | испаря́ет | испаря́ют |
| итти́<br>to be going (toward some point or place) | идёт | иду́т |
| кипе́ть<br>to be boiling | кипи́т | кипя́т |
| кристаллизова́ть<br>to be crystallizing | кристаллизу́ет | кристаллизу́ют |
| пла́вить<br>to be melting | пла́вит | пла́вят |
| поглоща́ть – поглоти́ть<br>to absorb, to suck up | поглоща́ет | поглоща́ют |
| применя́ть – примени́ть<br>to use, to adapt, to utilize | применя́ет | применя́ют |
| проводи́ть – провести́<br>to conduct, to carry through | прово́дит | прово́дят |

| Infinitives | 3rd Pers. Sing. | 3rd Pers. Plural |
|---|---|---|
| происходить – произойти<br>to proceed, to originate, to occur | происхо́дит | происхо́дят |
| разлага́ть – разложи́ть<br>to decompose, to disintegrate | разлага́ет | разлага́ют |
| размягча́ть – размягчи́ть<br>to soften | размягча́ет | размягча́ют |
| сгуща́ть – сгусти́ть<br>to thicken, to coagulate, to condense (liquid) | сгуща́ет | сгуща́ют |
| течь<br>to be flowing | течёт | теку́т |

The use of the above cited verb forms in constructing sentences is illustrated by the following examples.

Де́рево гори́т сравни́тельно бы́стро.
Wood    burns relatively    rapidly.

Мёд    течёт ме́дленно.
Honey flows    slowly.

Металли́ческий на́трий легко́ разлага́ет во́ду.
Metallic             sodium easily decomposes water.

Со́лнце    непреры́вно излуча́ет свет.
(The) sun continuously radiates light.

Серебро́ и    медь    хорошо́ прово́дят электри́чество.
Silver    and copper well    conduct    electricity.

## § 52. Reflexive Forms of Russian Verbs.

In English, reflexive pronouns, e.g., "myself," "yourself," "himself," "herself," "itself" are used with verbs to form sentences in which the action is directed back to the subject of the sentences, as, for example, in the sentence "He washes himself." Use of the reflexive form in Russian to indicate such reflexive action is comparatively unimportant in view of the much more common use of Russian reflexive verb forms to correspond to simple English intransitive verbs or to the passive voice of English transitive verbs. Such use of the Russian reflexive closely resembles corresponding use of the reflexive in German and French.

The reflexive of transitive Russian verbs may be formed with the reflexive pronoun себя. More commonly, however, the additional ending -ся (a contracted form of себя) is added to transitive verb forms to convert them into the reflexive; the ending -ся (or the pronoun себя) is used regardless of the person or number of the subject or the verb. This means, as will be pointed out in subsequent discussion, that the ending, -ся, (or the pronoun себя) when used in a true reflexive sense, will sometimes require translation by different English pronouns, e.g., "myself," "yourself," "herself," etc., depending on the subject of the sentence. For the present, however, this point is a minor concern, as the most frequent and, consequently, the most important use of the reflexive forms of Russian verbs is most conveniently translated into English by an intransitive verb (see first three sentences below) or by the passive of a transitive verb (see the last two example sentences below).

Жидкий воздух испаряется быстро.
Liquid air evaporates self (evaporates) rapidly.

Иод и камфора сравнительно быстро испаряются.
Iodine and camphor relatively rapidly evaporate self

(evaporate).

Стекло медленно кристаллизуется.
Glass slowly crystallizes self (crystallizes).

Эфир легко воспламеняется.
Ether easily ignites self (is ignited).

Сталь широко́ применя́ется.
Steel   widely   uses self (is used).


The five sentences given above illustrate the approach that has been followed in this book in attempting to use literal translation, particularly of себя́ and -ся, as a bridge to rendering the meaning of the Russian sentence into English. In those sentences in which an English reflexive pronoun is superfluous for final translation, the literal translation will nevertheless include the word "self." If the context of the sentence does not make the meaning completely obvious, an additional note in parenthesis, such as, "(is used)" -- cf. last sentence above -- will be provided. Such notes are not included as a matter of routine, but only in those sentences whose meaning might otherwise be difficult to grasp.


§ 53.  Formation of Adverbs from Adjectives with Stems Ending in - ическ-.

As already noted (§ 36, p. 52), the majority of Russian adverbs may be regarded as being formed by adding "о" (or in some instances "е") to adjective stems.

A smaller, though important, class of Russian adverbs are derived from adjectives formed with the suffix -ическ-. Thus from the adjective математи́ческий "mathematical" we obtain the adverb математи́чески "mathematically" by removing the masculine, nominative singular ending -ий to obtain the stem математическ-   and then adding the adverbial ending -и. Other examples of similarly derived adverbs are given below.


автомати́чески            автомати́ческий
automatically             automatic

алгебраи́чески            алгебраи́ческий
algebraically             algebraic

геометри́чески            геометри́ческий
geometrically             geometrical

каталити́чески            каталити́ческий
catalytically             catalytic

логи́чески                логи́ческий
logically                 logical

| | |
|---|---|
| механически | механический |
| mechanically | mechanical |
| оптически | оптический |
| optically | optical |
| физически | физический |
| physically | physical |
| химически | химический |
| chemically | chemical |
| электрически | электрический |
| electrically | electrical |

## § 54. The Russian Preposition При.

The preposition при indicates "at the time of," "in the presence of," "affiliated with." The same relationships may also be expressed by the English prepositions "in," "at," "during," "near," "on," which, consequently, may often serve as translations of при. As is often the case with Russian prepositions, it is not possible to cite any one English preposition which is the full and complete equivalent of при. The prepositional case, whose formation has not yet been discussed, is always used with при. Example sentences illustrating important uses of при are given below:

При охлаждении вода́ кристаллизу́ется.
On   cooling,      water crystallizes self.

При нагрева́нии стекло́, воск и   парафи́н размягча́ются.
On  heating,       glass,   wax  and parrafin   soften self.

При повыше́нии давле́ния   хлор   и   аммиа́к  сгуща́ются.
On  increase     of pressure, chlorine and ammonia condense self.

Жи́дкий кислоро́д кипи́т при −183°Ц.
Liquid  oxygen      boils   at    −183°C.

## § 55.  Reading Exercise.

The  following  reading  exercise  is  a  very  simple  discussion
entitled  Агрегáтные  состоя́ния  вещества́  literally "Aggregate
states of matter" or, more simply, "States of matter." In this
reading exercise, nouns in the nominative plural case are indicated
by single underlining, and their adjective modifiers (also in the
nominative plural case) are doubly underlined. All remaining
nouns are singular in number; some of them are in the genitive
case, while a few others are in the prepositional case after при.

### Агрегáтные состоя́ния вещества́

Жи́дкий кислоро́д, эфи́р, кероси́н, глицери́н, ртуть и
люба́я друга́я жи́дкость испаря́ются. Не́которые[1] жи́дкости,
как, наприме́р,[2] жи́дкий кислоро́д и́ли эфи́р, испаря́ются бы́стро,
но други́е, наприме́р глицери́н и́ли ртуть, ме́дленно.

Не́которые твёрдые вещества́[3] - наприме́р, лёд, и́од,
камфора́, нафтали́н - сравни́тельно бы́стро испаря́ются.

Испаре́ние ускоря́ется при повыше́нии температу́ры.

Жи́дкости та́кже кипя́т. Жи́дкий кислоро́д кипи́т при
-183°, вода́ при 100°, а ртуть при 357°.

Мно́гие га́зы, наприме́р, хлор, мета́н, аммиа́к, сгуща́ются
при повыше́нии давле́ния. Други́е же[4] га́зы, наприме́р, водо-
ро́д, азо́т, ге́лий, сгуща́ются при одновре́менном пониже́нии
температу́ры и повыше́нии давле́ния.

Густы́е и́ли вя́зкие жи́дкости, наприме́р, мёд, сма́зочное
ма́сло, глицери́н, теку́т ме́дленно, а подви́жные жи́дкости,
наприме́р, вода́, алкого́ль, ртуть, теку́т бы́стро.

При охлажде́нии мно́гие жи́дкости - наприме́р, вода́,
ртуть, алкого́ль - кристаллизу́ются. При э́том[5] выделя́ется
теплота́. Други́е же[4] жи́дкости, наприме́р, льняно́е ма́сло,
кероси́н, при охлажде́нии густе́ют.

Кристалли́ческие вещества́, наоборо́т,[6] пла́вятся при на-
грева́нии. При э́том поглоща́ется теплота́.

Амо́рфные тела́ - наприме́р стекло́, воск, парафи́н - при
нагрева́нии постепе́нно размягча́ются, но не[7] сра́зу[8] пла́вятся.

Не́которые твёрдые вещества́ - наприме́р, бума́га, каменный у́голь, де́рево - при нагрева́нии не пла́вятся и не
размягча́ются, но хими́чески разлага́ются.

## Notes

1. Не́которые   "certain" in the nominative plural modifies жи́дкости   the subject of the verb испаря́ются.

2. как, наприме́р   "as for example."

3. Both Не́которые   "certain" and твёрдые   "solid" are adjectives in the nominative plural case. These adjectives modify the noun вещества́   "substances," the subject of the verb испаря́ются.

4. же is used here in the usual way, to link the thought of this sentence with the preceding one. Here же might best be translated by "however."

5. При э́том literally, "at this" is more smoothly translated as "thereby."

6. наоборо́т   is an adverb meaning "on the contrary."

7. не "not" is used to negate simple sentences. (Cf. Lesson 20; §§ 180, 181; pp. 272, 274 for use of не as the so-called double negative with negative adverbs, pronouns and the like.)

8. сра́зу   is an adverb meaning "all at once."

§ 56. Translation Exercise.

The ten sentences, which make up this Translation Exercise, are built up almost entirely from words and phrases found in the preceding Reading Exercise. This same relationship exists between the Translation and Reading Exercises in all subsequent lessons.

It should be noted that most, though not all, of the verbs in the following sentences become reflexive in form on translation into Russian. Thus in the first sentence English "evaporates" is translated by Russian испаря́ется. See § 52, p. 71.

1. Liquid oxygen evaporates rapidly.
2. Mercury and glycerin evaporate slowly.
3. Water boils at 100°C.
4. Nitrogen and helium condense on simultaneous lowering of temperature and increase in (of) pressure.
5. Glycerin  and honey flow slowly, but water flows rapidly.
6. On cooling, mercury crystallizes.
7. Linseed oil thickens on cooling.
8. Ice melts on heating.
9. Glass, on heating, gradually softens.
10. Paper, on heating, chemically decomposes.

# LESSON 8

## THE NOMINATIVE CASE

§ 57. Use of the Nominative Case.

The nominative case is used in Russian:
1) To denote the grammatical subject of a sentence or clause.
2) As a predicate after the verb "to be" either expressed or implied. Note, however, that another case, the instrumental (cf. § 100, p. 145), is often used in the predicate of sentences involving such verbs as "to be," "to remain," "to become," etc.
3) In making enumerations.
4) In listing nouns and adjectives (cf. preceding lessons).

§ 58. Nominative Case Endings of Nouns.

The endings of the nominative case of the great majority of Russian nouns are as follows. Nouns which form their plural irregularly will be discussed subsequently.

### NOUNS

|  | Masculine | | Feminine | | Neuter | |
|---|---|---|---|---|---|---|
|  | Nom. Sing. | Nom. Plural | Nom. Sing. | Nom. Plural | Nom. Sing. | Nom. Plural |
| Hard | -- | -ы | -а | -ы | -о | -а |
| Soft | -й -ь | -и | -я -ь | -и | -е | -я |

The following examples illustrate the use of these endings.

77

| Noun | Key No.[1] | Stem | Nominative Singular | Nominative Plural |
|------|-----------|------|---------------------|-------------------|

### MASCULINE NOUNS

#### Hard Endings

| áтом | 1 | áтом_ | áтом<br>atom | áтомы<br>atoms |

#### Mixed Hard and Soft Endings

| луч | 2 | луч_ | луч<br>ray | лучи́<br>rays |
| проводни́к | 3 | проводник_ | проводни́к<br>conductor | проводники́<br>conductors |

#### Soft Endings

| рой | 4 | ро_ | рой<br>swarm | рои́<br>swarms |
| эпите́лий | 5 | эпители_ | эпите́лий<br>epithelium | эпите́лии<br>epithelia |
| мно́житель | 6 | мно́жител_ | мно́житель<br>multiplier | мно́жители<br>multipliers |

### FEMININE NOUNS

#### Hard Endings

| моле́кула | 7 | молекул_ | моле́кула<br>molecule | моле́кулы<br>molecules |

[1] Key numbers are used as a convenient means for designating various standard declensions of nouns and adjectives. In the vocabularies, key numbers are cited with each Russian noun and adjective to point out how they are declined.

| Noun | Key No.[1] | Stem | Nominative Singular | Nominative Plural |
|------|-----------|------|--------------------|--------------------|

### Mixed Hard and Soft Endings

| | | | | |
|------|------|------|------|------|
| единица | 8 | единиц– | единица<br>unit | единицы<br>units |
| наука | 9 | наук– | наука<br>science | науки<br>sciences |

### Soft Endings

| | | | | |
|------|------|------|------|------|
| неделя | 10 | недел– | неделя<br>week | недели<br>weeks |
| теория | 11 | теори– | теория<br>theory | теории<br>theories |
| смесь | 12 | смес– | смесь<br>mixture | смеси<br>mixtures |

## NEUTER NOUNS

### Hard Endings

| | | | | |
|------|------|------|------|------|
| вещество | 13 | веществ– | вещество<br>substance | вещества<br>substances |

### Mixed Hard and Soft Endings

| | | | | |
|------|------|------|------|------|
| училище | 14 | училищ– | училище<br>school | училища<br>schools |

### Soft Endings

| | | | | |
|------|------|------|------|------|
| поле | 15 | пол– | поле<br>field | поля<br>fields |
| явление | 16 | явлени– | явление<br>phenomenon | явления<br>phenomena |

[1] Key numbers are used as a convenient means for designating various standard declensions of nouns and adjectives. In the vocabularies, key numbers are cited with each Russian noun and adjective to point out how they are declined.

As will become evident in the next few lessons, the declension of nouns depends principally on their gender but also to a minor degree on other factors such as the final letter of their stems. The nouns mentioned above have been selected to typify the great majority of regularly declined nouns. Irregularities in noun declensions will be pointed out as the occasion requires.

§ 59.  Nominative Case Endings of Adjectives.

|  | Masc. | | Fem. | | Neuter | |
|---|---|---|---|---|---|---|
|  | Hard | Soft | Hard | Soft | Hard | Soft |
| Nom. Sing. | -ой,-ый | -ий | -ая | -яя | -ое | -ее |

| | Masc.-Fem.-Neuter | |
|---|---|---|
| | Hard | Soft |
| Nom. Plural | -ые | -ие |

The following adjectives illustrate the use of these endings.

### Hard Endings -- Adjectives

| Stems | стар- | old |
|---|---|---|
| | Key No. 17 | |
| | жив- | live, alive |
| | Key No. 18 | |

| | Masc. | Fem. | Neuter |
|---|---|---|---|
| Nom. Sing. | ста́рый живо́й | ста́рая жива́я | ста́рое живо́е |

| | Masc.-Fem.-Neuter |
|---|---|
| Nom. Plural | ста́рые живы́е |

## Soft Endings -- Adjectives

Stem         СИН-    blue
Key No. 19

| | Masc. | Fem. | Neuter |
|---|---|---|---|
| Nom. Sing. | си́ний | си́няя | си́нее |

### Masc.-Fem.-Neuter

| | |
|---|---|
| Nom. Plural | си́ние |

## Mixed Hard and Soft Endings -- Adjectives

Stems     СУХ-    dry
Key No. 20

           ЭЛЕКТРИЧЕСК-    electrical
Key No. 21

           СВЕЖ-    fresh
Key No. 22

| | Masc. | Fem. | Neuter |
|---|---|---|---|
| Nom. Sing. | сухо́й электри́ческий све́жий | суха́я электри́ческая све́жая | сухо́е электри́ческое све́жее |

### Masc.-Fem.-Neuter

| | |
|---|---|
| Nom. Plural | сухи́е электри́ческие све́жие |

    Two hard endings, namely -ый and -ой, are used in forming the masculine, nominative singular case of adjectives. The -ой ending is used only in case the ending is accented.

## § 60. Passive Past Participles of Russian Verbs.

The passive past participles of Russian verbs play an important role in scientific Russian. Although in many respects similar to corresponding English passive past participles, such as "discovered," "taken," "oxidized," etc., the Russian passive past participles (like all Russian participles) are used much more like adjectives than is the case with their English counterparts. Russian participles are used almost always as noun modifiers and are declined with regular adjective endings.

The passive past participles of most Russian verbs are formed by (1) removing −ТЬ from the infinitive, (2) adding −НН− (or less commonly −Т−) to form the stem of the participle, and (3) adding the regular adjective endings. Participles formed from infinitives ending in -ИТЬ usually change the "и" to "е" before adding the −НН− suffix to form the passive past participle.

Passive past participles are derived both from imperfective and perfective infinitives. Passive past participles derived from perfective infinitives indicate completed past action and are frequently encountered in Russian scientific literature. The following examples illustrate formation of passive past participles, including a few whose derivations involve stem changes of infinitives such as найти, поглотить, раздробить, расплавить.

| Infinitive | Passive Past Participle |
|---|---|
| активи́ровать<br>to activate | активи́рованный<br>activated |
| амальгами́ровать<br>to amalgamate | амальгами́рованный<br>amalgamated |
| взорва́ть<br>to explode, to blow up | взо́рванный<br>exploded, blown up |
| взять<br>to take | взя́тый<br>taken |
| дать<br>to give | да́нный<br>given |
| испо́льзовать<br>to utilize | испо́льзованный<br>utilized |

| Infinitive | Passive Past Participle |
|---|---|
| лиши́ть<br>to deprive, to remove | лишённый<br>removed, devoid (of) |
| назва́ть<br>to name, to call | на́званный<br>named, called |
| найти́<br>to find, to come upon | на́йденный<br>found |
| напо́лнить<br>to fill (up) | напо́лненный<br>filled (up) |
| наэлектризова́ть<br>to electrify, to charge<br>electrically | наэлектризо́ванный<br>electrified, charged<br>electrically |
| образова́ть<br>to form, to educate | образо́ванный<br>formed, educated |
| окисли́ть<br>to oxidize | окислённый<br>oxidized |
| отклони́ть<br>to deflect | отклонённый<br>deflected |
| откры́ть<br>to open, to discover,<br>to uncover | откры́тый<br>opened, discovered,<br>uncovered |
| поглоти́ть<br>to absorb, to swallow | поглощённый<br>absorbed, swallowed |
| получи́ть<br>to obtain | полученный<br>obtained |
| потере́ть<br>to rub | потёртый<br>rubbed |
| прореаги́ровать<br>to react (completely) | прореаги́рованный<br>reacted (completely) |
| раздроби́ть<br>to break up, to comminute | раздроблённый<br>broken up, comminuted |

| Infinitive | Passive Past Participle |
|---|---|
| разложи́ть<br>to decompose | разло́женный<br>decomposed,<br>    placed apart |
| распла́вить<br>to melt (down) | распла́вленный<br>melted, fused |
| рассе́ять<br>to scatter | рассе́янный<br>scattered, diffused |
| реши́ть<br>to solve (problem),<br>    to decide | решённый<br>solved, decided |
| собра́ть<br>to collect | со́бранный<br>collected |
| удали́ть<br>to remove | удалённый<br>removed |
| удовлетвори́ть<br>to satisfy | удовлетворённый<br>satisfied |

§ 61. A Note on И, а and НО.

Russian uses three words, И, а and НО to cover the range of meaning embraced by "and" and "but" in English. Overlapping relationships between these words might be indicated schematically as follows.

Russian   English

И          and (logical or similar direct relationship)

a          and (no direct relationship or very mild contrast)

           but (mild contrast)

НО         but (sharp contrast)

In addition to being used as a conjunction with the meaning "and," the Russian word И is also used adverbially to signify "as well as," "indeed," "moreover." This use of Russian И is somewhat similar to adverbial use of German "ja" to denote certainty or to impart emphasis to a statement.

§ 62. Reading Exercise.

### Химические изменения

Химические изменения веществ[1] происходят повсюду. Химические изменения наблюдаются, например, при горении[2] дерева. При этом образуются углекислый газ, вода и зола, а само дерево[3] превращается, изчезает.

Многие химические изменения происходят быстро. Каменный уголь,[4] нефтяные продукты и другие виды топлива горят сравнительно быстро. Металлический натрий бурно разлагает воду. При детонации[5] взрывчатые вещества разлагаются чрезвычайно быстро.

Другие же химические изменения происходят медленно. Железо мало-по-малу ржавеет. Нефть образуется в недрах[6] земли в течение геологических эпох.[7] Гранит, глинистый сланец, песчаник и другие горные породы разлагаются очень медленно. При этом образуется почва.

Растения, животные,[8] люди[9] растут, живут, умирают. При этом многочисленные вещества химически изменяются. Так, например, когда переваривается пища, последняя[10] химически преобразуется.

На химических заводах[11] изготовляются многие ценные продукты, например, мыло, стекло, цемент, алюминий и другие металлы, синтетический каучук, лекарства, искусственные удобрения, взрывчатые вещества, красители и т. д.[12] Как исходные материалы применяется различное природное сырьё,[13] например, растительные и животные жиры, песок, известняк, каменный уголь, природный газ, нефть, землистые и каменистые руды, и другие горные породы.[14]

При брожении получаются алкоголь и углекислый газ, а молекулы сахара расщепляются.

Горение топлива, детонация взрывчатых[15] веществ, образование почвы, пищеварение, брожение сахара – всё это[16] химические изменения.

### Notes

1. вещéств "of substances" is the genitive plural of the noun вещество́ .

2. при горéнии "during combustion." Here горéнии is the prepositional singular of горéние "combustion."

3. само́ де́рево  "the wood itself." When used, as here, to modify a noun, the pronoun adjective сам is usually best translated by "the --- itself," "the very," "even the," etc., (§ 148, p. 223). The closely related adjective са́мый is used to form one type of superlative as will be discussed in § 345, p. 544.

4. ка́менный у́голь  literally "stone coal" signifies "coal" as distinguished from древе́сный у́голь "charcoal," or бу́рый у́голь "brown coal."

5. при детона́ции "on detonation." Here детона́ции is the prepositional singular of детона́ция "detonation."

6. в не́драх земли́  "in the depths of the earth." Here не́драх is the prepositional plural of a neuter noun whose plural forms are the only ones in common use. The nominative plural of this noun is не́дра "depths," "lower regions." A few other Russian nouns are also peculiar by being used mostly in the plural and rarely, if at all, in the singular, cf. § 359, p. 579.

7. в тече́ние геологи́ческих эпо́х  "in the course of geological epochs." Both эпо́х and its modifier геологи́ческих are in the genitive plural case, while тече́ние is in the accusative case after the preposition в, cf. § 69, p. 95.

8. живо́тные "animals" is an example of an adjective used as a noun. Such use of the neuter forms of the adjective живо́тный "animal" probably arises by omission of the noun суще́ство from the phrase живо́тное суще́ство "animal being." Similarly, the feminine forms of криво́й have come to designate "curve" in place of крива́я ли́ния "curved line." Note also the use of the neuter forms of производ́ный for "derivative" (in the chemical sense) to replace производ́ное вещество́ "derived substance" and the feminine forms of производ́ный for "derivative" (in the mathematical sense) to replace производ́ная величина́ "derived magnitude." The feminine forms of постоя́нный used in place of постоя́нная величина́ "constant magnitude," have come to mean "constant" (in this instance, also a mathematical concept).

9. лю́ди "persons," "people" may be regarded as the plural of челове́к "man," "person.".

10. после́дняя "the latter" refers back to пи́ща "food." Note that the adjective после́дняя is in the feminine, nominative, singular case to bring it into agreement with the noun to which it refers. This is standard practice in Russian.

11. на хими́ческих заво́дах "in chemical plants." Both the noun заво́дах and the modifying adjective хими́ческих are in the prepositional plural case. The prepositional case is used after the preposition на when motion is not involved.

12. и т.д. is an abbreviation for и так да́лее "and so further." The Russian и т.д. corresponds to English "etc."

13. сырьё "raw material(s)" is a collective noun.

14. го́рные поро́ды "mineral substances." Russian has a number of fixed expressions of which го́рная поро́да "mineral substance" is an example.

15. детона́ция взры́вчатых веще́ств "detonation of explosive substances." Both the noun веще́ств and its adjective modifier взры́вчатых are in the genitive plural case.

16. — всё э́то literally "all this" or, in better English phrasing, "all these are" is perhaps best regarded as an idiom.


§ 63. Translation Exercise.

The student is reminded that reflexive verb forms are used much more frequently in Russian than in English (Cf. § 52, p. 71) and that the Russian language is devoid of definite and indefinite articles such as English "the," "a," "an" (Cf. § 22, p. 35).


1. Chemical changes are observed everwhere.
2. Carbon dioxide, water and ashes (ash) are formed during combustion of wood.
3. The combustion of wood proceeds rather rapidly.
4. Coal is formed in the course of geological epochs.
5. Detonation of explosives proceeds ( происхо́дит ) extremely rapidly.
6. Granite and sandstone decompose little by little.
7. Formation of petroleum ( не́фти ) proceeds slowly.

8. In chemical plants are used (use self) various mineral substances.
9. During fermentation, sugar is decomposed.
10. During rusting ( ржа́влении ), iron undergoes change (изменя́ется).

# LESSON 9

## THE ACCUSATIVE CASE

### § 64. Use of the Accusative Case.

The use of the accusative case in Russian may be summarized under the following headings:
1) As direct object of most transitive verbs.
2) After certain prepositions.
3) In expressions denoting extent of space or time or point in time. (The accusative case is used similarly in German.)
4) In a few idiomatic expressions of minor importance.

### § 65. Accusative Case Endings of Nouns (Inanimate).[1]

For the majority of regularly declined nouns, the endings[2] of the accusative case are as follows:

### NOUNS (Inanimate)

|  | Masculine | | Feminine | | Neuter | |
|---|---|---|---|---|---|---|
|  | Acc. Sing. | Acc. Plural | Acc. Sing. | Acc. Plural | Acc. Sing. | Acc. Plural |
| Hard | -- | -ы | -у | -ы | -о | -а |
| Soft | -й, -ь | -и | -ю, -ь | -и | -е | -я |

---

[1] See § 67, p. 93 for discussion of other endings for the accusative endings of nouns denoting persons or living entities.

[2] As pointed out previously, § 46, p. 64, these endings are identical with the corresponding nominative case endings except for the endings -у and -ю which are used to form the accusative singular of regularly declined feminine nouns, with exception of those whose nominative singular ends in -ь.

| Noun | Key No. | Stem | Accusative Singular | Accusative Plural |
|---|---|---|---|---|

## MASCULINE NOUNS

### Hard Endings

| а́том | 1 | атом– | а́том | а́томы |

### Mixed Hard and Soft Endings

| луч | 2 | луч– | луч | лучи́ |
| проводни́к | 3 | проводник– | проводни́к | проводники́ |

### Soft Endings

| рой | 4 | ро– | рой | рой |
| эпите́лий | 5 | эпители– | эпите́лий | эпите́лии |
| мно́житель | 6 | множител– | мно́житель | мно́жители |

## FEMININE NOUNS

### Hard Endings

| моле́кула | 7 | молекул– | моле́кулу | моле́кулы |

### Mixed Hard and Soft Endings

| едини́ца | 8 | единиц– | едини́цу | едини́цы |
| нау́ка | 9 | наук– | нау́ку | нау́ки |

### Soft Endings

| неде́ля | 10 | недел– | неде́лю | неде́ли |
| тео́рия | 11 | теори– | тео́рию | тео́рии |
| смесь | 12 | смес– | смесь | сме́си |

| Noun | Key No. | Stem | Accusative Singular | Accusative Plural |
|------|---------|------|---------------------|-------------------|

### NEUTER NOUNS

#### Hard Endings

| | | | | |
|------|------|------|------|------|
| вещество́ | 13 | веществ- | вещество́ | вещества́ |

#### Mixed Hard and Soft Endings

| | | | | |
|------|------|------|------|------|
| учи́лище | 14 | училищ- | учи́лище | учи́лища |

#### Soft Endings

| | | | | |
|------|------|------|------|------|
| по́ле | 15 | пол- | по́ле | поля́ |
| явле́ние | 16 | явлени- | явле́ние | явле́ния |

## § 66.  Accusative Case Endings of Adjectives.
### (Used to Modify Nouns Denoting Inanimate Objects)

The following case endings are used to form the accusative case of adjectives or other noun modifiers, except when they are used with nouns denoting persons or other living entities (cf. § 67, p. 93).

|  | Masc. Hard | Masc. Soft | Fem. Hard | Fem. Soft | Neuter Hard | Neuter Soft |
|--|------------|------------|-----------|-----------|-------------|-------------|
| Acc. Sing. | -ый, -ой | -ий | -ую | -юю | -ое | -ее |

|  | Masc.-Fem.-Neuter Hard | Masc.-Fem.-Neuter Soft |
|--|------------------------|------------------------|
| Acc. Plural | -ые | -ие |

Here  again  the  endings  of  corresponding  nominative  and
accusative  cases  are  identical  (cf.  § 65,  p. 89)  with  the  exception
of  the  feminine  singular.

## Hard Endings -- Adjectives

Stems    стар-,    old
         Key No. 17

         жив-,     live, alive
         Key No. 18

|  | Masc. | Fem. | Neuter |
|---|---|---|---|
| Acc. Sing. | ста́рый живо́й | ста́рую живу́ю | ста́рое живо́е |

(For animate forms,
   cf. § 67, p. 93)

## Masc.-Fem.-Neuter

| | |
|---|---|
| Acc. Plural | ста́рые живые |

(For animate forms,
   cf. § 67, p. 93)

## Soft Endings -- Adjectives

Stem     син-     blue
         Key No. 19

|  | Masc. | Fem. | Neuter |
|---|---|---|---|
| Acc. Sing. | си́ний | си́нюю | си́нее |

(For animate forms,
   cf. § 67, p. 93)

### Masc.-Fem.-Neuter

Acc.  
Plural  
(For animate forms,  
  cf. § 67, below)

си́ние

---

### Mixed Hard and Soft Endings -- Adjectives

Stems       сух-,     dry  
            Key No. 20

            электрическ-,    electrical  
            Key No. 21

            свеж-,    fresh  
            Key No. 22

|  | Masc. | Fem. | Neuter |
|---|---|---|---|
| Acc.<br>Sing.<br>(For animate<br>forms, cf. §67,<br>below) | сухо́й<br>электри́ческий<br>све́жий | суху́ю<br>электри́ческую<br>све́жую | сухо́е<br>электри́ческое<br>све́жее |

### Masc.-Fem.-Neuter

Acc.  
Plural  
(For animate forms  
  cf. § 67, below)

сухи́е  
электри́ческие  
све́жие

---

§ 67. Accusative Case Endings of Nouns Denoting Living Entities and Adjectives Modifying Such Nouns.

When nouns refer to living entities (viz., human beings, mythological persons, animals and insects), the endings of the accusative case are the same as the genitive for masculine nouns in both singular and plural and for feminine and neuter nouns in the plural only. Note, however, that the usual method of forming

the accusative (cf. § 65) is used with the names of (1) parts of the body and (2) plants. These same rules apply to the accusative endings of adjectives and other noun modifiers when used with nouns denoting persons, animals, insects and similar living entities. Endings regularly used to form the genitive case will be discussed in Lesson 14. Instances of use of the regular genitive endings to form the accusative, in accord with rules given above, will be pointed out in the notes accompanying reading exercises and in discussing example sentences.

§ 68. Nouns in Accusative Case as Direct Objects of Verbs.

In Russian sentences a noun (or pronoun)[1] which indicates the person, thing or concept subjected to the direct action of the verb is usually, though not always, in the accusative case. This general rule is illustrated by the following sample sentences in which all nouns and noun modifiers in the accusative case have been marked by an asterisk.

Аммиа́к   име́ет ни́зкую* температу́ру*кипе́ния.
Ammonia has     (a) low   temperature of boiling.

Морска́я   вода́ соде́ржит пова́ренную* соль*.
Sea        water contains   cooking       salt. (i.e., common salt.)

При расшире́нии газ      соверша́ет рабо́ту*.
On expansion   (the) gas performs  work.

Тре́ние превраща́ет механи́ческую* эне́ргию* в    теплоту́*.
Friction converts     mechanical     energy    into heat.

Твёрдые тела́ име́ют  определённую* фо́рму*и  объём*.
Solid    bodies have  (a) definite      form and volume.

---

[1] Occasionally the direct object of a verb may be an adjective or participle used in place of a noun. For further discussion of such substantive use of noun modifiers, see Note 6, p. 86; § 245, p. 389; § 283, p. 448; § 392, p. 652.

Here определённую, which modifies both фо́рму and объём, is in the feminine accusative singular to bring it into agreement with фо́рму. When the sentence is rewritten so as to interchange the position of the words фо́рму and объём then the common modifier of these two nouns takes an ending to bring it into agreement with объём. Thus we have:

Твёрдые тела́ име́ют определённый* объём* и фо́рму*
Solid bodies have (a) definite volume and form.

The general rule governing such situations is that the ending of the adjective shall indicate agreement with the noun which stands nearest to it.

§ 69. Prepositions Governing the Accusative Case.

Russian prepositions, with which the accusative case may be used, can be divided into two groups.

The first group consists of three prepositions which always govern the accusative.

| про | about, concerning |
| сквозь | through (the middle of) |
| че́рез | through, across, by way of (particularly in a figurative sense) |

Usage distinguishes between the last two prepositions to a greater extent than is apparent from their meaning as usually defined in dictionaries.

The second group of prepositions requires the accusative when used in the sense given below. These prepositions, when used with other significance, require cases other than the accusative as will be discussed subsequently. For summary, see § 127, p. 187.

| Preposition | Meaning Requiring Accusative |
|---|---|
| в ( во)[1] | "into" (when indicating motion)<br>"in" (with nouns indicating time interval) |
| за | "toward," "after," "for," "as" (range of meaning difficult to define. Cf. example sentences below.) |
| на | "onto" (when indicating motion) |
| о(об)[1] (обо)[1] | "against," "along" (when indicating contact) |
| по | "up to," "for" (in "to go for," i.e., to go to get) |
| под | "under" (when indicating motion) |

Indication of figurative motion with the aid of various prepositions listed above is usually accomplished by using them with the accusative case. This is illustrated by various sentences given below. Certain idiomatic uses of various above-mentioned prepositions with the accusative case are also illustrated.

Sentences illustrating the use of the Russian prepositions under discussion have been arranged so as to group together sentences illustrating how the accusative is used with (1) в (во) (2) за (3) на and (4) other prepositions mentioned above.

(1)  Sentences Illustrating Use of в (во) with the Accusative Case.

Воздух поступает в     компрессор.
Air     enters     into (the) compressor.

Фотография     имеет большое практическое значение.
Photography     has     great     practical     significance.

---

[1] The preposition в is pronounced as though it were the first letter of the following word, unless the latter begins with a consonant combination, e.g., вт-, or вр-, which makes such pronunciation difficult or impossible. In such instances во replaces в. A similar situation exists with regard to pronunciation of the prepositions к and с and their alternate forms, ко and со. The alternate form обо of о is used in a similar fashion.

Полное превращение теплоты в работу невозможно.
Complete conversion of heat into work (is)[1] impossible.

Термодинамика изучает в первую очередь[2] равновесные
Thermodynamic studies in (the) first instance equilibrium

состояния.
conditions.

Газ во время расширения охлаждается.
(The) gas in (the) time of expansion cools self.

Газ в течение всего процесса находится
(The) gas in (the) course of all (the) process finds self (is)

в равновесном состоянии.[3]
in equilibrium condition.

Водные растворы аммиака окрашивают лакмус в синий цвет.
Aqueous solutions of ammonia color litmus in blue color.

(2) Sentences Illustrating the Use of За with the Accusative Case.

За единицу длины принимается метр.
As (the) unit of length accepts self (the) meter.

Окисление серы происходит за счёт
Oxidation of (the) sulfur proceeds at (the) expense

кислорода воздуха.
of (the) oxygen of (the) air.

---

[1] Omission of the present tense of быть "to be" from Russian sentences is frequently encountered. Cf. Lesson 15, § 120, p. 174.
[2] The phrase в первую очередь is best regarded as an idiom equivalent to the English "in the first place."
[3] Both the adjective равновесном and the noun состоянии are in the prepositional case. Cf. Lesson 10, p. 105.

Совреме́нный     бессеме́ровский  конве́ртер перераба́тывает
(A) contemporary  Bessemer        converter  processes

за одну́ опера́цию 15-25 т. чугуна́.
in  one   operation 15-25 tons cast iron.

За  после́дние  го́ды  произво́дство  ма́гния      си́льно
In  (the) last  years (the) production of magnesium strongly

развива́ется.
develops self.

(3) Sentences Illustrating the Use of на with the Accusative Case.

Кусо́к      де́рева,  погружённый в   во́ду, всплыва́ет  на
(A) piece of wood,   immersed     into water floats up   onto

пове́рхность воды́.
(the) surface of (the) water.

Давле́ние       уменьша́ется       на  бесконе́чно   ма́лую
(The) pressure decreases self       by (an) infinitely small

величину́.
magnitude.

На  после́дний  вопро́с  даёт  отве́т  второ́й    зако́н
To  (the) latter question gives answer (the) second law

термодина́мики.
of thermodynamics.

Число́       $a$,  умно́женное  на  число́   $b$, составля́ет
(The) number $a$,  multiplied   by  number  $b$, constitutes

произведе́ние  $ab$.
(the) product  $ab$.

Зву́ки разделя́ются     на   музыка́льные   то́ны   и   шу́мы.
Sounds divide self      into musical      tones and noises.

Осо́бенно   большо́е   коли́чество   глицери́на   идёт   на
Particularly   large     quantity      of   glycerol   goes   to

произво́дство    нитроглицери́на.
(the) production of nitroglycerol.

## (4) Sentences Illustrating Use of Various Other Prepositions with the Accusative Case.

Тре́ние      части́цы      о      бума́гу уменьша́ется.
(The) friction of (the) particle along (the) paper   decreases self (is decreased).

Стальны́е     ша́рики     непреры́вно   ударя́ются   об
(The) steel    little spheres continuously   strike self    against

окру́жность      ди́ска.
(the) circumference of (the) desk.

Моле́кулы     га́за     ударя́ются о    все сте́нки
(The) molecules of (the) gas strike self   against all   (the) walls

сосу́да.
of (the) container.

Газ     выхо́дит   че́рез   специа́льные газоотво́ды.
(The) gas goes out   through special      gas outlets.

При э́том     газ    прохо́дит че́рез   ряд     состоя́ний.
Thereby,     (the) gas traverses through (a) series of conditions.

В настоя́щее вре́мя мы не мо́жем    лета́ть     сквозь
At (the) present time we not are   able to fly      through

мирово́е простра́нство.
cosmic space.

Подводная    лодка,    погрузившаяся[1]                на 100 м.
Underwater   load,     having  submerged self            to 100 m.

под воду, испытывает давление в       10 кг/см.[2]
under water, experiences pressure  of about 10 kg/cm.

Телега       стоит  по    ступицу   в   грязи.[2]
(The) cart   stands up to  hub (deep) in  mud.

Мы читали[3] про  эту реакцию в  учебнике    химии.
We read      about that reaction in (a) textbook  of chemistry.

## § 70.  Accusative Case to Indicate Time Period, Distance, etc.

Russian nouns denoting a period of time, distance, dimension
or size when not a part of a prepositional phrase may be in the
accusative case as shown by the following examples. It will be
recalled that the accusative case is used similarly in German.
When duration of time is so denoted by the accusative, it is often
conveniently rendered into English by a phrase involving the
preposition "for."

Поршень      каждый раз возвращается  в первоначальное
(The) piston each   time returns self  to (the) original

положение.
position.

Опыт        продолжается   только    минуту.
(The) experiment prolongs self  for only  (a) minute.

---

1 погрузившаяся   is a verb form characterized by three successive endings.
The ending –ся indicates the reflexive form while –ая the nominative, feminine
singular ending for adjectives and participles indicates that the word modifies лодка.
The ending -ивш- is used to form the past active participle from many verbs,
including  погружать – погрузить, "to (cause to) sink or submerge" or "to load
(e.g., goods)."
  2 в грязи "in mud." Here грязи is in the prepositional case, cf. § 76, p. 109.
  3 читали is the plural form of the past tense of читать "to be reading,"

Свече́ние    метеори́та       иногда́       продолжа́ется
Luminosity   of   (a)   meteorite    sometimes    prolongs    itself

значи́тельное     вре́мя.
(a) considerable    time.


О́чень       до́лгое вре́мя    нау́ка    рассма́тривала[1] теплоту́
For (a) very   long     time,     science   considered     heat

как невесо́мую    жи́дкость.
as   (a) weightless liquid.


Кита́йская     а́рмия   наступа́ет         приблизи́тельно
(The) Chinese   army      advances (is advancing) approximately

одну́   ми́лю   ка́ждый   день.
one    mile   each     day.


## § 71. Reading Exercise.


### На́трий

     Мно́гие со́ли - наприме́р пова́ренная соль - соде́ржат на́трий, но металли́ческий на́трий в приро́де[1] не встреча́ется. Электро́лиз разлага́ет распла́вленную пова́ренную соль на хлор и металли́ческий на́трий.

     Металли́ческий на́трий име́ет сравни́тельно ни́зкую температу́ру плавле́ния, и́менно 97. 7°Ц. На́трий кипи́т при 880. 9°Ц.

     На́трий име́ет не́которые типи́чные металли́ческие сво́йства. На́трий хорошо́ прово́дит теплоту́ и электри́ческий ток. На́трий та́кже образу́ет[2] амальга́мы и спла́вы

     Когда́ электри́ческий ток пропуска́ется че́рез на́триевые пары́, после́дние[3] излуча́ют прекра́сный жёлтый свет. На э́том при́нципе[4] стро́ятся мо́щные освети́тельные ла́мпы.

---

   [1] рассма́тривала    is the feminine singular form of the imperfective past tense of рассма́тривать – рассмотре́ть "to consider,"   "to examine,"   "to approve," cf. Lesson 24.

Áтомы нáтрия легкó отдаю́т внéшний электрóн - так
называ́емый⁵ валéнтный электрóн. При э́том áтомы нáтрия
перехóдят в катиóны.

$$Na \longrightarrow e + Na^{+}$$

Слéдовательно, нáтрий легкó вступáет в химúческие реáкции.
При э́том⁷ нáтрий произвóдит восстановлéния. Так,напримéр,
нáтрий  восстановля́ет хлорúд алюмúния.

$$3\,Na + AlCl_3 \longrightarrow Al + 3\,NaCl$$

Реáкция идёт⁸ при нагревáнии.

Металлúческий нáтрий óчень легкó разлагáет вóду.
При э́том⁷ образу́ется² éдкий натр и выделя́ется водорóд.

$$2\,Na + 2\,H_2O \longrightarrow 2\,NaOH + H_2$$

Нáтрий тáкже дéйствует⁸ на мнóгие органúческие соединéния.  Так,напримéр:

$$2\,Na + 2\,CH_3COCH_2CO_2C_2H_5 \longrightarrow H_2 + 2\,CH_3COCHCO_2C_2H_5$$
$$| $$
$$Na$$

## Notes

1. в прирóде  "in nature." Here прирóде (from прирóда
"nature") is in the prepositional case.

2. образу́ет   "(it) forms" and образу́ется   "(it) forms
(self)" i.e., " (it) is formed) " are derived from the infinitive
образовáть  "to form."

3. послéдние   "the latter" is plural because it refers to the
plural noun пáры. Note further that   послéдние is in the
nominative case because it is the subject of the verb излучáют.

4. на э́том прúнципе  "on this principle," Here both э́том
(from э́тот "this") and   прúнципе (from прúнцип "principle")
are in the prepositional case.

5. так называ́емый "so-called." Here называ́емый is the
present passive participle of the infinitive называ́ть of the verb
называ́ть - назвáть      "to call," "to name."   .

6. идёт "goes" is the third person singular of the present tense of итти "to be going (to some definite point or place)."

7. при этом "thereby" or more literally "at this." Here, again, этом is in the prepositional case.

8. действует "(it) acts" is derived from the infinitive действовать "to be acting."

## § 72. Translation Exercise.

1. Common salt contains (содержит) sodium.
2. Metallic sodium melts at 97.7°C.
3. Sodium conducts the electric current.
4. Alloys of sodium not are encountered (встречаются) in nature.
5. Sodium lamps radiate beautiful yellow light.
6. Atoms of sodium easily go over into cations.
7. Sodium decomposes aluminum chloride (chloride of aluminum) on heating.
8. Sodium very easily decomposes water.
9. Thereby, hydrogen is evolved.
10. Sodium also reacts with (acts on) alcohol (алкоголь).

# LESSON 10

## THE PREPOSITIONAL CASE

§ 73.  Use of the Prepositional Case.

The prepositional case of nouns is used only when they are in prepositional phrases, i.e., the objects of prepositions.

The following preposition always governs the prepositional case.

при,    at, near, during

The following prepositions govern the prepositional case only when they are used with certain restricted meanings as indicated below.  For a summary of the uses of these prepositions when governing other cases, see  § 127,  p. 187.

| | |
|---|---|
| в  (во)[1] | within, in (no motion) |
| на | on (no motion) |
| по | after |
| о (об, обо)[1] | about, concerning |

§ 74.  Prepositional Case Endings of Nouns.

NOUNS

| | Masculine | | Feminine | | Neuter | |
|---|---|---|---|---|---|---|
| | Prep. Sing. | Prep. Plural | Prep. Sing. | Prep. Plural | Prep. Sing. | Prep. Plural |
| Hard | -е | -ах | -е | -ах | -е | -ах |
| Soft | -е, -и | -ях | -е, -и | -ях | -е, -и | -ях |

---

[1] See Footnote 1, p. 96.

Regardless of gender, the endings –e and –и are used to form the prepositional singular of regularly declined nouns while their prepositional plural is formed with –ах and –ях, as illustrated by the following examples.

| Noun | Key No. | Stem | Prepositional Singular | Prepositional Plural |
|------|---------|------|------------------------|----------------------|

### MASCULINE NOUNS

#### Hard Endings

| Noun | Key No. | Stem | Prepositional Singular | Prepositional Plural |
|------|---------|------|------------------------|----------------------|
| а́том | 1 | а́том– | а́томе | а́томах |

#### Mixed Hard and Soft Endings

| Noun | Key No. | Stem | Prepositional Singular | Prepositional Plural |
|------|---------|------|------------------------|----------------------|
| луч | 2 | луч– | луче́ | луча́х |
| проводни́к | 3 | проводни́к– | проводнике́ | проводника́х |

#### Soft Endings

| Noun | Key No. | Stem | Prepositional Singular | Prepositional Plural |
|------|---------|------|------------------------|----------------------|
| рой | 4 | ро– | ро́е | роя́х |
| эпите́лий | 5 | эпители– | эпите́лии | эпите́лиях |
| мно́житель | 6 | мно́жител– | мно́жителе | мно́жителях |

### FEMININE NOUNS

#### Hard Endings

| Noun | Key No. | Stem | Prepositional Singular | Prepositional Plural |
|------|---------|------|------------------------|----------------------|
| моле́кула | 7 | молекул– | моле́куле | моле́кулах |

#### Mixed Hard and Soft Endings

| Noun | Key No. | Stem | Prepositional Singular | Prepositional Plural |
|------|---------|------|------------------------|----------------------|
| едини́ца | 8 | едини́ц– | едини́це | едини́цах |
| нау́ка | 9 | наук– | нау́ке | нау́ках |

| Noun | Key No. | Stem | Prepositional Singular | Prepositional Plural |
|------|---------|------|------------------------|----------------------|

### Soft Endings

| Noun | Key No. | Stem | Prepositional Singular | Prepositional Plural |
|------|---------|------|------------------------|----------------------|
| неде́ля | 10 | недел- | неде́ле | неде́лях |
| тео́рия | 11 | теори- | тео́рии | тео́риях |
| смесь | 12 | смес- | сме́си | сме́сях |

## NEUTER NOUNS

### Hard Endings

| Noun | Key No. | Stem | Prepositional Singular | Prepositional Plural |
|------|---------|------|------------------------|----------------------|
| вещество́ | 13 | вещств- | веществе́ | вещества́х |

### Mixed Hard and Soft Endings

| Noun | Key No. | Stem | Prepositional Singular | Prepositional Plural |
|------|---------|------|------------------------|----------------------|
| учи́лище | 14 | училищ- | учи́лище | учи́лищах |

### Soft Endings

| Noun | Key No. | Stem | Prepositional Singular | Prepositional Plural |
|------|---------|------|------------------------|----------------------|
| по́ле | 15 | пол- | по́ле | поля́х |
| явле́ние | 16 | явлени- | явле́нии | явле́ниях |

Note that the prepositional case ending in the singular·is "-e-" for all nouns except:

1) Nouns whose roots end in "-и-" and feminine nouns with "-ь-" as nominative singular case ending. Such nouns take "-и-" as case ending (cf. тео́рии, явле́нии and сме́си ).
2) Certain highly irregular nouns discussed in Lesson 38, p. 561.

The prepositional plural of all nouns, without exception, ends either in "-ах-" or "-ях-."

§ 75. Prepositional Case Endings of Adjectives.

| | Masc. | | Fem. | | Neuter | |
|---|---|---|---|---|---|---|
| | Hard | Soft | Hard | Soft | Hard | Soft |
| Prep. Sing. | -ом | -ем | -ой | -ей | -ом | -ем |

| | Masc.-Fem.-Neuter | |
|---|---|---|
| | Hard | Soft |
| Prep. Plural | -ых | -их |

### Hard Endings -- Adjectives

| Stems | стар-, old Key No. 17 |
|---|---|
| | жив-, live, alive Key No. 18 . |

| | Masc. | Fem. | Neuter |
|---|---|---|---|
| Prep. Sing. | ста́ром живо́м | ста́рой живо́й | ста́ром живо́м |

| | Masc.-Fem.-Neuter |
|---|---|
| Prep. Plural | ста́рых живы́х |

### Soft Endings -- Adjectives

| Stem | син-, blue Key No. 19 |
|---|---|

|  | Masc. | Fem. | Neuter |
|---|---|---|---|
| Prep.<br>Sing. | си́нем | си́ней | си́нем |

|  | Masc.-Fem.-Neuter |
|---|---|
| Prep.<br>Plural | си́них |

## Mixed Hard and Soft Endings -- Adjectives

Stems     сух-,    dry
Key No. 20

электри́ческ-,   electrical
Key No. 21

свеж-,   fresh
Key No. 22

|  | Masc. | Fem. | Neuter |
|---|---|---|---|
| Prep.<br>Sing. | сухо́м<br>электри́ческом<br>све́жем | сухо́й<br>электри́ческой<br>све́жей | сухо́м<br>электри́ческом<br>све́жем |

|  | Masc.-Fem.-Neuter |
|---|---|
| Prep.<br>Plural | сухи́х<br>электри́ческих<br>све́жих |

## § 76. Sentences Illustrating Use of the Prepositional Case.

При высо́ком давле́нии мета́н превраща́ется в жи́дкость.
At   high    pressure   methane converts self   into (a) liquid.

Одни[1] жи́дкости  при  да́нной   температу́ре   испаря́ются
Some  liquids      at   (a) given  temperature    evaporate self

бы́стро, други́е ме́дленно.
rapidly, others   slowly.


Крахма́л      соде́ржится      в    больши́х    коли́чествах   в
Starch        contains self    in   large       amounts       in

карто́феле.
(the) potato.


Пла́тина, зо́лото  серебро́ и  не́которые  други́е мета́ллы
Platinum, gold,    silver   and certain    other   metals

встреча́ются    в приро́де   в  свобо́дном  ви́де.
encounter self  in nature    in free        form.


В ма́лых  коли́чествах   и́ндий прису́тствует в ци́нковых ру́дах.
In small  quantities,    indium is present    in zinc        ores.


Водола́зы рабо́тают на дне          мо́ря.
Divers    work       at (the) bottom of the sea.


Стально́й ша́рик         пла́вает на пове́рхности   рту́ти.
(A) steel small sphere  floats   on (the) surface  of mercury.


Иссле́дования о  влия́нии       измене́ния температу́ры     на
Investigations on (the) influence of change   of temperature on

ско́рость реа́кции   продолжа́ются.
(the) rate of reaction continue self.


По       истече́нии сро́ка                    реа́кция
After    expiration of (the)   time   interval,  (the) reaction

прекраща́ется.
stops self.

---

[1] Here ОДНИ́, the plural of ОДИ́Н "one," is used with the meaning "several," "some."

§ 77. Special Form of the Prepositional Case of Certain Nouns after "на" and "в."

The endings "-у" (hard) or "-ю" (soft) may be used with various masculine and neuter nouns when they are used after the prepositions "на" and "в." There is good reason to believe that we are concerned here with the remnants of an otherwise obsolete locative case. The following sentences illustrate the use of these remnants of the locative which sometimes are referred to as a special form of the prepositional case.

Такие грибы́ ча́сто встреча́ются   в   лесу́.
Such fungi   often   encounter self   in   (the) forest.

Сле́дует      име́ть   в   виду́, что   ско́рость реа́кции
It is necessary to have in view   that   (the) rate of reaction

зави́сит от температу́ры.
depends   on (the) temperature.

На морско́м   берегу́ нахо́дится   рыба́чий   посёлок.
On (the) sea   shore   finds self   (a) fishing   village.

В расте́нии на свету́   происхо́дят поглоще́ние углеки́слого
In (a) plant   in (the) light goes on   absorption   of carbonic

га́за   и   выделе́ние кислоро́да.
acid gas and evolution   of oxygen.

Живо́тное   нахо́дится   на краю́ ги́бели.
(The) animal finds self   (is) on verge of perishing.

§ 78. Reading Exercise.

## Эне́ргия

Эне́ргия существу́ет[1] в разли́чных ви́дах. Так, например, то́пливо соде́ржит эне́ргию в хими́ческим ви́де. При горе́нии то́плива хими́ческая эне́ргия превраща́ется в теп-

лоту́. В котла́х теплота́ перево́дит во́ду в пар. В турби́-
нах и други́х паровы́х маши́нах теплова́я эне́ргия па́ра час-
ти́чно преобразу́ется[2] в механи́ческое движе́ние. Après Après Après Après Après Après Après После́днее[3]
перево́дят в электри́ческую эне́ргию динамомаши́ны. При элек-
тро́лизе,   электри́ческая эне́ргия превраща́ется вновь в
хими́ческую эне́ргию.  При таки́х проце́ссах, эне́ргия пре-
враща́ется, но не исчеза́ет и не возника́ет самопроизво́льно.

Вообще́ вале́нтные электро́ны игра́ют исключи́тельно
ва́жную роль в горе́нии и други́х хими́ческих реа́кциях. Од-
на́ко радиоакти́вные элеме́нты соде́ржат а́томные я́дра, ко-
то́рые[4] самопроизво́льно расщепля́ются. При таки́х[5] я́дерных
реа́кциях выделя́ется а́томная эне́ргия. При э́том небольши́е
коли́чества ма́ссы  превраща́ются в грома́дные коли́чества
эне́ргии.

Горе́ние то́плива и водяна́я си́ла доставля́ют эне́ргию
на совреме́нных силовы́х ста́нциях. А́томные силовы́е стан-
ции до сих пор[6] всё еще́[7] отсу́тствуют на земле́.

Одна́ко на со́лнце а́томная эне́ргия непреры́вно выдел-
я́ется в грома́дных коли́чествах. Со́лнечная а́томная эне́р-
гия испуска́ется в разли́чных ви́дах: в теплоте́, све́те и
други́х излуче́ниях. На земле́ расте́ния превраща́ют со́лнеч-
ную светову́ю эне́ргию в хими́ческую эне́ргию. Со́лнечная
а́томная эне́ргия игра́ет исключи́тельно ва́жную роль в на́-
шей  жи́зни.[8]

### Notes

1. существу́ет   "(it) exists" is derived from the infinitive
существова́ть   "to exist."

2. преобразу́ется   "(it) converts self"  "(it) is converted"
is derived from  преобразова́ть  one of the infinitives of
преобразо́вывать -- преобразова́ть   "to change, to convert."

3. после́днее   "the latter" is neuter and singular because
it refers to  движе́ние.  Note also that  после́днее is in the
accusative case because it is the direct object of the verb
перево́дят.

4. кото́рые  "which" is plural, referring to я́дра  "nuclei."
As the subject of the verb  расщепля́ются, кото́рые  is in the
nominative case.

5. таки́х  is the prepositional plural of тако́й  "such."

6. до сих пор  is a standardized phrase or idiom meaning
"up to now," "up to the present."

7. всё еще́ is another idiom meaning "still," "even yet."

8. в на́шей жи́зни "in our life." Here на́шей is the feminine
singular prepositional case of the possessive pronoun наш "our"
whose declension deviates somewhat from the regular adjective
declension,  cf.  § 138,  p. 208.


§ 79.  Translation Exercise.

1. Energy is evolved during the combustion of fuel.
2. Combustion converts the chemical energy of fuel into heat.
3. In boilers, water undergoes conversion into steam.
4. The energy of steam undergoes conversion into mechanical
   motion in turbines and other steam engines.
5. Radioactive atoms decompose spontaneously.
6. Atomic energy is evolved during nuclear reactions.
7. On earth, solar light energy is converted partially into
   chemical energy.
8. The chemical energy of fuel is converted into electrical
   energy in modern power plants.
9. The sun furnishes (доставля́ет) energy in enormous amounts.
10. Energy in various forms plays an important role in our lives
    (life).

# LESSON 11

## THE GENITIVE CASE

§ 80. Use of the Genitive Case.

The following summary of uses of the Russian genitive case shows that it is employed much more extensively than the corresponding English possessive case.

### Uses of Russian Genitive Case

1) To indicate possession (as in English).
2) To indicate relationships somewhat resembling possession. (This often corresponds to an English phrase involving the preposition "of," as illustrated in previous Reading Exercises.)
3) After a majority of Russian prepositions. (For a partial list, see § 84, p. 121.)
4) After the comparative of adjectives, cf. § 338, p. 532.
5) As the object of certain verbs, cf. § 85, p. 124.
6) After certain numerals, cf. § 371, p. 604.
7) In certain negative sentences to designate an object or person whose existence, presence or involvement is negated, cf. § 175, p. 266; § 176, p. 267; § 177, p. 269.
8) In expressions indicating quantity or amount. (Cf. § 395, p. 656, for a special form of the genitive of certain nouns occasionally used in such expressions.)
9) To express dates.
10) In various idioms to be considered individually.

§ 81. Genitive Case Endings of Nouns.

Certain peculiarities of these endings are discussed in Notes on p. 117.

# LESSON 11

## NOUNS

| | Masculine | | Feminine | | Neuter | |
|---|---|---|---|---|---|---|
| | Gen. Sing. | Gen. Plural | Gen. Sing. | Gen. Plural | Gen. Sing. | Gen. Plural |
| **Hard** | -а | -ов | -ы | —— | -а | —— |
| **Soft** | -я | -ев<br>-ей | -и | -ь<br>-ей<br>-й | -я | -ей<br>-й |

| Noun | Key No. | Stem | Genitive Singular | Genitive Plural |
|---|---|---|---|---|
| | | | | |

### MASCULINE NOUNS

#### Hard Endings

| áтом | 1 | атом- | áтома | áтомов |
|---|---|---|---|---|

#### Mixed Hard and Soft Endings

| луч | 2 | луч- | лучá | лучéй |
|---|---|---|---|---|
| проводни́к | 3 | проводник- | проводникá | проводнико́в |

#### Soft Endings

| рой | 4 | ро- | ро́я | роёв |
|---|---|---|---|---|
| эпите́лий | 5 | эпители- | эпите́лия | эпите́лиев |
| мно́житель | 6 | множител- | мно́жителя | мно́жителей |

### FEMININE NOUNS

#### Hard Endings

| моле́кула | 7 | молекул- | моле́кулы | моле́кул |
|---|---|---|---|---|

| Noun | Key No. | Stem | Genitive Singular | Genitive Plural |
|------|---------|------|-------------------|-----------------|
| **Mixed Hard and Soft Endings** | | | | |
| едини́ца | 8 | едини́ц– | едини́цы | едини́ц |
| нау́ка | 9 | нау́к– | нау́ки | нау́к |
| **Soft Endings** | | | | |
| неде́ля | 10 | неде́л– | неде́ли | неде́ль |
| тео́рия | 11 | тео́ри– | тео́рии | тео́рий |
| смесь | 12 | смес– | сме́си | сме́сей |

## NEUTER NOUNS

### Hard Endings

| | | | | |
|------|---------|------|-------------------|-----------------|
| вещество́ | 13 | вещест́в– | вещества́ | веще́ств |

### Mixed Hard and Soft Endings

| | | | | |
|------|---------|------|-------------------|-----------------|
| учи́лище | 14 | учи́лищ– | учи́лища | учи́лищ |

### Soft Endings

| | | | | |
|------|---------|------|-------------------|-----------------|
| по́ле | 15 | пол– | по́ля | поле́й |
| явле́ние | 16 | явлени– | явле́ния | явле́ний |

### Notes

1. Formation of the genitive singular of nouns is quite simple. The endings are either hard (–a and –ы) or soft (–я and –и). Feminine nouns form their genitive singular with –ы or –и, while nearly all masculine and neuter nouns take the endings –a or –я. In connection with feminine nouns it is helpful to remember that the genitive singular is formed with the ending –и, if the stem of the feminine noun ends in –Г,–Ж,–К,–Х,–Ч,–Ш,–Щ.

2.  The situation with regard to the genitive plural of nouns is
not easy to summarize, as the ending used depends not only on the
case ending of the nominative singular of the noun, but also on
other factors of which the final letter of the stem is particularly
important.  The following general rules appear worthy of mention.

(a)  The  genitive  plural  of masculine  nouns whose stems
end with Ж,Ч,Ш or Щ is formed with the ending –ей.

(b)  The  genitive  plural  of neuter  and  feminine  nouns,
whose stems end with –и–, is formed with the ending –й.
Thus we have теорий and явлéний as the genitive plural
of теóрия and явлéние, respectively.  Care must be
taken to avoid confusing the genitive plural of such
nouns  either with the masculine nominative singular of
adjectives  or with the nominative singular of certain
masculine nouns, e.g., гéний, нáтрий, алюмúний, etc.
Such confusion is readily avoided if care is taken to note
the gender of the nouns by observing the final letters of
their nominative  singular as  conventionally listed in
dictionaries, cf. § 28, p. 43.

## § 82.  Genitive Case Endings of Adjectives.

Although  the  genitive  case  endings  of nouns  are  rather
complicated, the corresponding case endings of adjectives are quite
simple as is evident from the following summary.

|  | Masculine | | Feminine | | Neuter | |
|  | Hard | Soft | Hard | Soft | Hard | Soft |
|---|---|---|---|---|---|---|
| Gen. Sing. | –ого[1] | –его[2] | –ой | –ей | –ого[1] | –его[2] |

|  | Masc.-Fem.-Neuter | |
|  | Hard | Soft |
|---|---|---|
| Gen. Plural | –ых | –их |

---

[1]  Pronounced -- ОВО.
[2]  Pronounced -- еВО.

The use of these endings is illustrated by the following examples.

### Hard Endings -- Adjectives

Stems    стар–,    old
Key No. 17

жив–,    live, alive
Key No. 18

| | Masc. | Fem. | Neuter |
|---|---|---|---|
| Gen. Sing. | ста́рого<br>живо́го | ста́рой<br>живо́й | ста́рого<br>живо́го |

**Masc.-Fem.-Neuter**

| Gen. Plural | ста́рых<br>живы́х |
|---|---|

### Soft Endings -- Adjectives

Stem    син–,    blue
Key No. 19

| | Masc. | Fem. | Neuter |
|---|---|---|---|
| Gen. Sing. | си́него | си́ней | си́него |

**Masc.-Fem.-Neuter**

| Gen. Plural | си́них |
|---|---|

## Mixed Hard and Soft Endings -- Adjectives

| Stems | сух-,  dry |
|---|---|
|  | Key No. 20 |
|  |  |
|  | электрическ-,  electrical |
|  | Key No. 21 |
|  |  |
|  | свеж-,  fresh |
|  | Key No. 22 |

|  | Masc. | Fem. | Neuter |
|---|---|---|---|
| Gen.<br>Sing. | сухо́го<br>электри́ческого<br>све́жего | сухо́й<br>электри́ческой<br>све́жей | сухо́го<br>электри́ческого<br>све́жего |

|  | Masc.-Fem.-Neuter |
|---|---|
| Gen.<br>Plural | сухи́х<br>электри́ческих<br>све́жих |

§ 83.  Use of the Genitive to Indicate Possession and Relationships Resembling Possession.

This use of the genitive to show a possession type of relationship was pointed out in § 29, p. 44 and has been exemplified by numerous phrases in example sentences and reading exercises. The following sentences further illustrate this very important use of the genitive case.

Электро́ны    игра́ют    ва́жную        роль   в    строе́нии
Electrons      play     (an) important  role   in   (the) structure

вся́кого а́тома, вся́кой  моле́кулы   и    вся́кого материа́льного
of every atom,  of every molecule  and  of every material

вещества́.
substance.

Каучу́к содержится  в   мле́чном   со́ке мно́гих  расте́ний.
Rubber  contains self in (the) milky  sap  of many  plants.

Во́дные  раство́ры  кисло́т,соле́й,  щёлочей  (электроли́тов)
Aqueous  solutions  of acids, of salts,  of alkalis  (of  electrolytes)

прово́дят  электри́ческий  ток.
conduct    (the) electrical  current.


§ 84. Some Prepositions and Prepositional Adverbs Governing
     the Genitive Case.

In this section, example sentences illustrate certain uses of
the genitive case.

Some of these sentences include prepositions and prepositional
adverbs (i.e., adverbs which may be used as prepositions), for
which translations are given below.  Unfortunately, these translations cannot be regarded as entirely precise as the vagaries of
usage make it difficult if not impossible to give exact translations
of many of the more commonly used prepositions:

| | |
|---|---|
| без  (бе́зо)[1] | without |
| вблизи́ | near, in the vicinity of |
| вме́сто | in place of |
| вне | outside |
| внутри́ | within |
| вокру́г | around |
| для | for |
| до | up to |
| из ,(и́зо)[1] | away from, of |
| кро́ме | besides, aside from |
| от | from |
| по́сле | after |
| пре́жде | before |
| про́тив | against |
| с (со)[1] | from, since (the preposition "С" has other meanings when used with other cases cf. § 127, p. 187.) |
| у | near, at by, of |

Many  other  less  common  prepositions  and  prepositional
adverbs also govern the genitive case.


[1] This form of the preposition is used for reasons of euphony, depending on the
initial letter or letters of the word which follows, cf. Footnote 1, p. 96.

Внутри со́лнца и звёзд температу́ры дохо́дят
Inside of (the) sun and of (the) stars, temperatures go as far as

до деся́тков миллио́нов гра́дусов.
to tens of millions of degrees.

Вокру́г плане́ты Сату́рна нахо́дится кольцо́.
Around (the) planet, Saturn finds self (a) ring.

Ацетиле́н употребля́ется для сва́рки мета́ллов.
Acetylene uses self for welding of metals.

Поваренная соль[1] растворя́ется в воде́ до не́которой
Cooking salt dissolves self in water up to (a) certain

определённой концентра́ции.
definite concentration.

Кокс образу́ется при нака́ливании без до́ступа во́здуха
Coke forms self on strong heating without access of air

приро́дных ка́менных у́глей.
of natural coals.

Промы́шленное произво́дство алюми́ния начало́сь[2] в 1886
Industrial production of aluminum started self in 1886

году́ в Нью-Кенсингто́не вблизи́ Питсбурга.
year in New Kensington near Pittsburgh.

Вдоль вертика́ли де́йствует си́ла тя́жести.[3]
Along (the) vertical acts (the) force of gravity.

---

[1] поваренная соль literally "cooking salt" is the Russian expression corresponding to English "common salt."

[2] начало́сь "started self" is the reflexive of the neuter singular of the past imperfective (cf. Lesson 24, p. 331) of the verb начина́ть – нача́ть "to begin," "to start."

[3] Another word, тяготе́ние is also used to refer to gravity as a mathematically defined force. Both тя́жесть and тяготе́ние are related to the simple noun тя́га whose basic meaning is "pull."

Все тела́  состоя́т  из а́томов или моле́кул.
All  bodies consist   of atoms   and  molecules.


Электропроводи́мость      га́за      зави́сит от сте́пени
(The) electrical conductivity of (a) gas depends  on (the) degree

иониза́ции.
of ionization.


Артиллери́йский снаря́д во вре́мя полёта нагрева́ется    от
(An) artillery     shell   in time  of flight heats self     from

тре́ния о      во́здух.
friction against (the) air.


Испаре́ние происхо́дит то́лько с    пове́рхности жи́дкости.
Evaporation goes on     only   from (the) surface  of (a) liquid.


Это     явле́ние      наблюда́ется     у      легкопла́вких
This   phenomenon     observes self   with    easily melted

мета́ллов уже́  при ко́мнатной температу́ре.
metals   even at   room         temperature.


## § 85.  Verbs Taking the Direct Object in the Genitive Case.

A few important Russian verbs require that their objects shall
be in the genitive case.  It will be recalled that a similar situation
exists  with  certain  German verbs, e.g., bedürfen -- "to need."

Раке́ты   достига́ют высо́ких  скоросте́й.
Rockets   attain     high     velocities.


Гео́логи  непреры́вно  и́щут[1] но́вых месторожде́ний руд.
Geologists continuously  seek   new    deposits        of ores.


---

[1]  Formation of the present tense of the verb   иска́ть - поиска́ть  involves
change of the infinitive stem иск- to иш- before affixing the usual present tense
endings, cf. § 198, p. 300.

Произво́дство    ста́ли    ежего́дно  достига́ет   грома́дных
(The)  production  of steel  yearly    attains     enormous

разме́ров.
dimensions.


Разли́чные    жи́дкости  тре́буют  разли́чного  коли́чества теплоты́
Different     liquids    require  (a) different amount      of heat

для па́рообразова́ния.
for  vaporization.


Мно́гие   герма́нские   вое́нные   престу́пники      избега́ют
Many      German       war        criminals        are evading

наказа́ния.
punishment.


## § 86. Reading Exercise.


### Пова́ренная соль

Моле́кула пова́ренной со́ли составля́ется из    а́томов
на́трия и хло́ра.  Ввиду́[1] своего́  соста́ва  пова́ренная соль
но́сит хими́ческое назва́ние хлори́да на́трия.  Хлори́д на́трия
иногда́   но́сит   по-ру́сски  друго́е хими́ческое  назва́ние, а
и́менно назва́ние хло́ристого на́трия.[2]

Хлори́д на́трия, или хло́ристый на́трий, применя́ется  в
произво́дстве со́ды, е́дкого на́тра, хло́ра, соляно́й[3] кислоты́,
стекла́, органи́ческих краси́телей, мы́ла и пр. Поэ́тому хими́-
ческая  промы́шленность ежего́дно тре́бует[4] пова́ренной со́ли
(хло́ристого на́трия) в грома́дных коли́чествах.

Пова́ренная соль та́кже име́ет обши́рное примене́ние  в
ка́честве пищево́го проду́кта. Пи́ща, лишённая[5] пова́ренной
со́ли (хлори́да на́трия), име́ет пре́сный неприя́тный вкус.

Огро́мные коли́чества поваренной со́ли, или хло́ристого на́трия, нахо́дятся в растворённом ви́де в воде́ океа́нов, море́й и не́которых озёр. Поваренная соль та́кже встреча́ется в земно́й коре́ в ви́де ка́менной со́ли. Бога́тые за́лежи ка́менной со́ли нахо́дятся в шта́тах Мичига́н, Нью-Йо́рк и Юта.

Разли́чные ме́тоды применя́ются для добы́чи поваренной со́ли. Добы́ча со́ли из земли́ произво́дится таки́м о́бразом:[е] в земле́ де́лаются ша́хты, кото́рые дохо́дят до пла́стов со́ли, и зате́м[7] пла́сты со́ли раздробля́ются при по́мощи[8] буровы́х маши́н, а иногда́ взры́вчатых веще́ств. Раздро́блённая соль поднима́ется на пове́рхность земли́.

Из воды́ соля́ных исто́чников и из морско́й воды́ поваренная соль добыва́ется при по́мощи о́чень просто́го ме́тода, и́менно выпа́ривания на огне́ или на со́лнце. При выпа́ривании воды́ поваренная соль выделя́ется в ви́де[9] куби́ческих криста́ллов. Разме́ры криста́ллов зави́сят от ско́рости выпа́ривания. При ско́ром выпа́ривании выделя́ются ме́лкие криста́ллы. При ме́дленном же[10] выпа́ривании получа́ются кру́пные криста́ллы.

Добыва́ние поваренной со́ли ежего́дно достига́ет[11] грома́дных разме́ров.

## Notes

1. Ввиду́ своего́ соста́ва  "in view of its composition." Here своего́ is in the masculine, genitive, singular case because it modifies соста́ва.    Note also that своего́ which is derived from the reflexive possessive pronoun свой refers back to соль.

2. Cf. Note 2, p. 10.

3. соляна́я кислота́  "hydrochloric acid."  Cf. the similar German term "Salzsäure."

4. трéбует  "(it) needs" is derived from the infinitive требовать  "to be requiring" which takes its direct object -- here  повáрённой сóли. (хлóристого  нáтрия) -- in the genitive case.

5. лишённая  "devoid of" is in the feminine, nominative singular case as is also the noun. пи́ща  which it modifies.

6. таки́м óбразом "thus," "in this way" may be regarded as an idiom. Grammatically, both óбразом and its modifier таки́м are in the instrumental case, cf. § 98, p. 141.

7. затéм "thereafter."

8. при пóмощи "with the aid."

9. в ви́де "in the form." Note that the scope of meaning of the Russian word ви́д is very broad. Reference is made to the previously noted phrase в виду́ "in view (of)," cf. § 77, p. 111.

10. See Note 5, p. 75.

11. The verb  достигáть -- дости́гнуть  "to attain," "to reach" requires its direct object (here громáдных размéров) to be in the genitive case.


§ 87. Translation Exercise.

1. Common salt plays an important role in our lives.
2. Hydrochloric acid is used in the production of organic dyes.
3. Food requires common salt (sodium chloride).
4. Sodium chloride is found on earth in various forms.
5. The production of rock salt is carried out with the aid of boring machines.
6. Mining of rock salt requires boring machines.
7. Sodium chloride is produced from sea water in enormous quantities.
8. Evaporation is used for the production of sodium chloride from sea water.
9. Crystals of sodium chloride are obtained on evaporation of sea water.
10. Use of sodium chloride in the production of soda annually attains enormous dimensions.

# LESSON 12

## THE INSTRUMENTAL CASE

§ 88. Use of the Instrumental Case.

To English speaking persons, the Russian instrumental case may appear at first rather strange. By affixing certain endings to nouns and noun modifiers, Russians form a case whose most important single use is to designate the agent or means by which an action is accomplished. In this lesson, we shall consider this use of the instrumental case to indicate means or agency, and also its use in certain expressions in which the implication of agency or means is more or less attenuated.

§ 89. Instrumental Case Endings of Nouns.

### NOUNS

| | Masculine | | Feminine | | Neuter | |
|------|----------------|-----------------|----------------|-----------------|----------------|-----------------|
| | Instr.<br>Sing. | Instr.<br>Plural | Instr.<br>Sing. | Instr.<br>Plural | Instr.<br>Sing. | Instr.<br>Plural |
| Hard | -ом | -ами | -ой (-ою) | -ами | -ом | -ами |
| Soft | -ем | -ями | -ей (-ею) | -ями | -ем | -ями |

Note the use of -ами and -ями (sometimes replaced by -ьми) to form the instrumental plural of all nouns regardless of gender.

| Noun | Key No. | Stem | Instrumental Singular | Instrumental Plural |
|------|---------|------|----------------------|---------------------|

### MASCULINE NOUNS

#### Hard Endings

| Noun | Key No. | Stem | Instrumental Singular | Instrumental Plural |
|------|---------|------|----------------------|---------------------|
| а́том | 1 | атом- | а́томом | а́томами |

#### Mixed Hard and Soft Endings

| Noun | Key No. | Stem | Instrumental Singular | Instrumental Plural |
|------|---------|------|----------------------|---------------------|
| луч | 2 | луч- | лучо́м | луча́ми |
| проводни́к | 3 | проводник- | проводнико́м | проводника́ми |

#### Soft Endings

| Noun | Key No. | Stem | Instrumental Singular | Instrumental Plural |
|------|---------|------|----------------------|---------------------|
| рой | 4 | ро- | ро́ем | роя́ми |
| эпите́лии | 5 | эпители- | эпите́лием | эпите́лиями |
| мно́житель | 6 | множител- | мно́жителем | мно́жителями |

### FEMININE NOUNS

#### Hard Endings

| Noun | Key No. | Stem | Instrumental Singular | Instrumental Plural |
|------|---------|------|----------------------|---------------------|
| моле́кула | 7 | молекул- | моле́кулой (моле́кулою) | моле́кулами |

#### Mixed Hard and Soft Endings

| Noun | Key No. | Stem | Instrumental Singular | Instrumental Plural |
|------|---------|------|----------------------|---------------------|
| едини́ца | 8 | единиц- | едини́цей (едини́цею) | едини́цами |
| нау́ка | 9 | наук- | нау́кой (нау́кою) | нау́ками |

| Noun | Key No. | Stem | Instrumental Singular | Instrumental Plural |
|---|---|---|---|---|
| | | | | |

### Soft Endings

| Noun | Key No. | Stem | Instrumental Singular | Instrumental Plural |
|---|---|---|---|---|
| неде́ля | 10 | недел– | неде́лей (неде́лею) | неде́лями |
| тео́рия | 11 | теори– | тео́рией (тео́риею) | тео́риями |
| смесь | 12 | смес– | сме́сью | сме́сями |

## NEUTER NOUNS

### Hard Endings

| Noun | Key No. | Stem | Instrumental Singular | Instrumental Plural |
|---|---|---|---|---|
| вещество́ | 13 | веществ– | вещество́м | вещества́ми |

### Mixed Hard and Soft Endings

| Noun | Key No. | Stem | Instrumental Singular | Instrumental Plural |
|---|---|---|---|---|
| учи́лище | 14 | училищ– | учи́лищем | учи́лищами |

### Soft Endings

| Noun | Key No. | Stem | Instrumental Singular | Instrumental Plural |
|---|---|---|---|---|
| по́ле | 15 | пол– | по́лем | поля́ми |
| явле́ние | 16 | явлени– | явле́нием | явле́ниями |

## § 90. Instrumental Endings of Adjectives.

| | Masculine | | Feminine | | Neuter | |
|---|---|---|---|---|---|---|
| | Hard | Soft | Hard | Soft | Hard | Soft |
| Instr. Sing. | –ым | –им | –ой (–ою) | –ей (–ею) | –ым | –им |

Masc.-Fem.-Neuter

| Hard | Soft |
|------|------|
| -ЫМИ | -ИМИ |

Instr.
Plural

### Hard Endings -- Adjectives

Stems

ста́р-,   old
Key No. 17

жив-,   live, alive
Key No. 18

| | Masc. | Fem. | Neuter |
|---|-------|------|--------|
| Instr. Sing. | ста́рым живы́м | ста́рой (ста́рою) живо́й (живо́ю) | ста́рым живы́м |

Masc.-Fem.-Neuter

Instr.
Plural

ста́рыми
живы́ми

### Soft Endings -- Adjectives

Stem

син-,   blue
Key No. 19

| | Masc. | Fem. | Neuter |
|---|-------|------|--------|
| Instr. Sing. | си́ним | си́ней (си́нею) | си́ним |

Masc.-Fem.-Neuter

Instr.
Plural

си́ними

## Mixed Hard and Soft Endings -- Adjectives

Stems     сух-,     dry
          Key No. 20

          электрическ-,     electrical
          Key No. 21

          свеж-,     fresh
          Key No. 22

|  | Masc. | Fem. | Neuter |
|---|---|---|---|
| Instr. Sing. | сухи́м электри́ческим свѐжим | сухо́й (сухо́ю) электри́ческой (электри́ческою) свѐжей (свѐжею) | сухи́м электри́ческим свѐжим |

Masc.-Fem.-Neuter

| Instr. Plural | сухи́ми электри́ческими свѐжими |
|---|---|

§ 91. Sentences Illustrating Use of the Instrumental Case to Indicate Means or Agency.

Perhaps the best approach to understanding the instrumental case in Russian is to consider its use to indicate means or agency whereby some action is effected. Throughout the remainder of this lesson, an asterisk is used to direct attention to the instrumental case endings of nouns and adjectives.

| Обрабо́тка | воды́ | хло́ром* | применя́ется | |
|---|---|---|---|---|
| Treatment | of water | by chlorine | uses self | (is used) |

| для | уничтоже́ния | вре́дных | бакте́рий. |
|---|---|---|---|
| for | destruction | of harmful | bacteria. |

При таких о́пытах наблюда́ется отклоне́ние
In such experiments observes self deflection of

α-части́ц электри́ческим* по́лем*.
α-particles by (an) electric field.

При захва́тывании прото́на ядро́м* Li
On capture of (a) proton by (the) nucleus Li

образу́ется Be.
forms self Be.

Струя́ кислоро́да предвари́тельно прохо́дит для
(The) stream of oxygen preliminarily passes for

осуше́ния че́рез тру́бку, напо́лненную хлори́дом*
drying through (a) tube filled with chloride

ка́льция.
of calcium.

Мо́жно извлека́ть у́ксусную кислоту́ из во́дных
(It is) possible to extract acetic acid from aqueous

раство́ров обрабо́ткой растворителями*, наприме́р, эфи́ром*.
solutions by treatment with solvents, for example, ether.

При разбавле́нии раство́ра водо́й* появля́ется
On dilution of (the) solution with water, appears self

кра́сное окра́шивание.
red coloration.

§ 92. Uses of the Instrumental Case Involving Attenuated
Instrumentality.

In the previous paragraph, example sentences were given to
illustrate the use of the instrumental case in Russian to designate
the agent or means by which an action is accomplished. Certain
other uses of this case may be regarded as more or less remotely

related or, in other words, as involving the concept of an instrumental agency in more or less attenuated form. When so used, the
instrumental case is often best translated into English by means of
an adverb or an adverbial phrase, cf. also § 98, p. 141.

The use of the instrumental case with the reflexive of verbs is
a particularly important example of attenuated instrumentality. As
seen from examples given below, combination of the instrumental
case with reflexive verb forms often results in Russian sentences
which are best translated by the passive voice of the English verb
or by an English intransitive verb.

При   ко́мнатной   температу́ре   са́хар   не   окисля́ется
At    room         temperature    sugar   not  oxidizes self

кислоро́дом*  во́здуха.
by (the) oxygen of (the) air.

Со́ли дифенилами́на   легко́  разлага́ются   водо́й.*
Salts of diphenylamine  easily  decompose self  by water.

Рентге́новские лучи́   употребля́ются   врача́ми*   для
Roentgen       rays    utilize self      by physicians  for

фотографи́рования вну́тренних   о́рганов тела.
photographing   of (the) inner   organs  of (the) body.

Вся́кое парообразова́ние   сопровожда́ется   поглоще́нием*
Every  evaporation         accompanies self  by (the) absorption

теплоты́.
of heat.

Пониже́ние     электропроводи́мости          ме́ди
(A) lowering   of (the) electrical  conductivity   of copper

на  10%  вызыва́ется   прису́тствием*        0.001%
by  10%  calls forth self  by (the) presence   (of)  0.001%

фо́сфора.
of phosphorus.

Мо́щность     маши́ны       измеря́ется     рабо́той;*
(The) power   of (a) machine    measures self    by (the) work

кото́рую производит маши́на    в едини́цу    вре́мени.
which    carries out   (the) machine in (a) unit    of time.

Хи́мия     занима́ется     изуче́нием*    веще́ств     и
Chemistry concerns   self    with the study of substances and

их    превраще́ний.
their changes.

В моме́нт     перехо́да    спла́ва     из    одного́
In (the) moment    of transition of (an)   alloy from one

состоя́ния в    друго́е теплосодержа́ние    меня́ется
state      into another, (the) heat content    changes    self

скачко́м.*
with a bound (abruptly).

На́трий легко́   ре́жется    ножо́м.*
Sodium easily   cuts self    by a knife.

В ка́чественном ана́лизе хи́мики    ча́сто по́льзуются[1]
In qualitative      analysis chemists often   avail self

       цветны́ми* реа́кциями.*
(utilize) color      reactions.

Ацетиле́н получа́ется    де́йствием* воды́    на карби́д
Acetylene obtains self    by (the) action of water on   carbide

ка́льция.
of calcium.

---

[1] This and other forms derived from the infinitive по́льзоваться "to be availing self," "to utilize" are often used in so-called impersonal sentences, i.e., in sentences whose subject is not explicitly stated, but implied by the ending. Typical translations into English would result in sentences containing such expressions as "they use," "one uses," etc., cf. § 384, p. 639.

§ 93. The Instrumental Case in Sentences Expressing Various
Types of Designation or Characterization.

Another important, closely related use of the instrumental case
is in sentences involving the idea of "being named," "being
expressed," "being characterized" and the like.

Изменéние   фóрмы       твёрдого       тéла   называ́ется
Change      of (the) form of (a) solid  body  calls  self

деформа́цией*
deformation.

Пове́рхностное   натяже́ние   обознача́ется       бу́квой*   γ.
(The) surface    tension      designates    self  by (the) letter γ.

Нéкоторые сплáвы   метáллов   окáзываются ферромагни́тными*
Certain   alloys   of metals  show self    ferromagnetic.

Состáв        водьі́     выража́ется    фóрмулой*    H₂O.
(The) composition of water  expresses  self  by the formula $H_2O$.

Проце́сс      расшире́ния     гáза        изобража́ется
(The) process of expansion   of (the) gas depicts  self

криво́й*    ABC  в диагрáмме   pv.
by (the) curve ABC in (the) diagram pv.

Графи́т   отлича́ется       мáлой* твёрдостью*
Graphite distinguishes self  by slight hardness.

Гéлий   характеризу́ется   своéй*хими́ческой*инéртностью*
Helium  characterizes self  by its chemical      inertness.

На́трий   характеризу́ется      металли́ческими* сво́йствами*,
Sodium   characterizes self      by metallic          properties,

наприме́р,  большо́й* электропроводи́мостью*, образова́нием*
for example, by big   electrical conductivity,    by formation

соле́й   и   спла́вов,   и  металли́ческим* бле́ском*.
of salts and   of alloys   and by metallic        luster.

Каучу́к   характеризу́ется           це́нными*   сво́йствами*,
Rubber   characterizes   self       by valuable  properties,

наприме́р,  высо́кой* эласти́чностью*, исключи́тельно  больши́м*
for example, high      elasticity,        extremely          big

электросопротивле́нием*   и  хими́ческой*  усто́йчивостью*.
electrical-resistance,          and chemical     stability.

Зако́н     сохране́ния            эне́ргии    счита́ется
(The) law of (the)  conservation of energy   regards    self

              · осно́вны́м*   зако́ном* приро́ды.
(is considered) (a) basic     law        of nature.


§ 94.  The Instrumental Case Used in Conjunction with the
       Reflexive of ЯВЛЯ́ТЬ – ЯВИ́ТЬ.

    Use of the reflexive forms of the verb  ЯВЛЯ́ТЬ -- ЯВИ́ТЬ
"to show" with the instrumental case of nouns is encountered very
frequently in scientific Russian.  Such sentences often may be
translated into English by some form of the verb  "to be," instead
of by more literal but clumsier expressions, such as, "shows self
as," "appears as"  or  "turns out to be."  As will be discussed
subsequently (Lesson 15), the present tense of the verb "to be" is
virtually obsolete in Russian, and this appears to be the principle
factor which has led to widespread use of the reflexive of ЯВЛЯ́ТЬ --
ЯВИ́ТЬ with the instrumental case in scientific Russian.

Во́здух явля́ется сме́сью* га́зов.
Air      shows self (is) (a) mixture of gases.


В раство́рах соле́й носи́телями* электри́чества
In solutions of salts (as) carriers of electricity

явля́ются положи́тельные и отрица́тельные ио́ны.
show self (are) positive and negative ions.


Большинство́ хими́ческих элеме́нтов явля́ется
(The) majority of chemical elements shows self

        ре́дкими* вещества́ми*.
(appears) (as) rare substances.


Калифорни́йская нефть явля́ется
Californian petroleum shows self (turns out to be)

сравни́тельно бога́той* азо́том*.
relatively rich in nitrogen.


Осо́бенно хоро́шим* раствори́телем* явля́ется вода́.
Particularly good solvent shows self (is) water.


§ 95. Reading Exercise.

### Мета́н

Мета́н явля́ется просты́м* газообра́зным* углеводоро́дом*.
Соста́в метана выража́ется фо́рмулой* $CH_4$. При обыкнове́нной
температу́ре мета́н не окисля́ется кислоро́дом* во́здуха.    При
поджига́нии мета́н гори́т бле́дным* пла́менем*.[1]
Мета́н образу́ется разли́чными* спо́собами*.  В лабора-
то́рии мета́н получа́ется сплавле́нием*ацета́та на́трия с е́дким*
на́тром*.[2]

$$CH_3COONa + NaOH \longrightarrow CH_4 + Na_2CO_3$$

Действие подкисленной воды́ на  карби́д алюми́ния явля́ется
други́м* удо́бным* спо́собом* получе́ния мета́на в лаборато́рии.

$$Al_4C_3 + 12\,H_2O \longrightarrow 3\,CH_4 + 4\,Al(OH)_3$$

При нагрева́нии вы́ше[3] 700°C  мета́н распада́ется  на
водоро́д и углеро́д.  При таки́х температу́рах мета́н та́кже
образу́ется из элеме́нтов прямы́м* присоедине́нием*

$$C + 2\,H_2 \rightarrow CH_4$$

Не то́лько[4] реа́кция образова́ния, но и реа́кция распа-
де́ния ускоря́ется катализа́тором*, наприме́р, ни́ккелем* При
ра́венстве скоросте́й обе́их[5] реа́кций устана́вливается   хи-
ми́ческое равнове́сие.

Хло́ристый мети́л и хло́ристый водоро́д образу́ются при
замеще́нии хло́ром* водоро́дного а́тома мета́на. Реа́кция идёт[6]
при рассе́янном со́лнечном све́те.

$$CH_4 + Cl_2 \longrightarrow \qquad CH_3Cl \qquad + \qquad HCl$$

Мета́н  хлор        хло́ристый   хло́ристый
                        водоро́д       мети́л

Радика́л $CH_3$  называ́ется мети́лом*

Хло́ром* замеща́ются и други́е а́томы водоро́да:

$$CH_3Cl + Cl_2 \longrightarrow CH_2Cl_2 + HCl$$
$$CH_2Cl_2 + Cl_2 \longrightarrow CHCl_3 + HCl$$
$$CHCl_3 + Cl_2 \longrightarrow CCl_4 + HCl$$

Проду́кт  $CCl_4$  называ́ется четыреххло́ристым* углеро́-
дом, а $CHCl_3$ - хлорофо́рмом* Четыреххло́ристый углеро́д и хло-
рофо́рм широко́ применя́ются как раствори́тели   для  мно́гих
веще́ств - смол, жиро́в, каучука́ и пр.[7]   Ины́ми* слова́ми* [8]
хлорофо́рм и четыреххло́ристый углеро́д явля́ются  хоро́шими*
раствори́телями*

---

## Notes

1. бле́дным* пла́менем* "with a pale flame."  As pointed out
in the next lesson, the instrumental case may be used in Russian
in such a fashion as to require translation by an adverbial phrase
in English.  Note that пла́менем* is the instrumental, singular
case of the neuter noun пла́мя "flame," which is one of a group
of neuter nouns having a special declension (cf. § 358, p. 575)
and characterized by having the nominative singular terminate in
—мя.

2. с е́дким* на́тром* "with caustic soda."  When the preposition "с" is used to mean "with" it is followed by the instrumental case, as in this instance. It is necessary to distinguish between на́трий "sodium" and е́дкий натр "caustic soda."  Note further that е́дким* на́тром* is the instrumental case of е́дкий натр.

3. вы́ше  "above," "higher"  is the irregular, undeclinable, comparative of высо́кий  "high," cf. § 334, p. 528.

4. не то́лько -- но и --, "not only  --  but also --."

5. обе́их  is the feminine prepositional plural of о́ба  "both" which is declined irregularly, cf. § 370, p. 601.

6. идёт  "goes"  is the irregularly formed third person singular of the present tense of  итти́  "to be going."

7. и пр. is an abbreviation for и про́чее "and so on."

8. ины́ми* слова́ми*  "in other words." This is another example of what is sometimes termed the "adverbial" use of the instrumental case in Russian, cf. § 98, p. 141.


§ 96. Translation Exercise.

Underlining has been used to direct attention to those nouns (and their modifiers) whose translation into Russian is to be accomplished with the aid of the Russian instrumental case.

1. The simple hydrocarbon (Просто́й   углеводоро́д), $CH_4$ is called (calls self) methane.
2. During combustion, methane reacts with oxygen.
3. Products of combustion of methane are (show self) water and carbon dioxide (углеки́слый газ).
4. The fusion (Сплавле́ние) of acetate of sodium with caustic soda is (shows self) a convenient method of obtaining (of) methane in (the) laboratory.
5. Methane is obtained (obtains self) by the action (де́йствием) of acidified water on carbide of aluminum.
6. Methane reacts with chlorine.
7. The reaction is accelerated (accelerates self) by a catalyst, for example, nickel.
8. Hydrogen chloride and methyl chloride are (show self as) gaseous (газообра́зными) products.
9. The product, $CHCl_3$, is called chloroform.
10. Chloroform is (shows self as) a good solvent (хоро́шим· раствори́телем) for fats.

# LESSON 13

## ADDITIONAL NOTES ON THE USE OF THE INSTRUMENTAL CASE

§ 97. Summary of Uses of the Instrumental Case.
  1) In general, to indicate the means or agency whereby some action is accomplished. (See preceding lesson).
  2) In expressions in which the means or agency relationship may be regarded as attenuated, cf. § 98 below.
  3) As the predicate after such verbs as "быть." (to be), "становиться," (to become), etc., cf. § 100, p. 145.
  4) As the object of certain verbs, cf. § 102, p. 148.
  5) After certain prepositions, cf. § 101, p. 146 for list.
  6) In various idiomatic expressions.

§ 98. Attenuated Instrumentality and "Adverbial" Use of the Instrumental Case.

In the previous lesson, it was pointed out that the Russian instrumental case derives its name from the fact that it may be used to indicate the agency or means whereby an action is accomplished. Certain related uses of the instrumental may be regarded as involving the concept of instrumentality in an attenuated form. When so used, it is often convenient to translate the instrumental case by an adverb or an adverbial phrase. There is, in fact, a tendency for the instrumental case of at least certain Russian nouns to assume the character of an adverb. Thus, for example, the English adverb "completely" may be rendered by ПОЛНОСТЬЮ, the instrumental of ПОЛНОСТЬ "completeness." Note also that "by night" or "during the night" may be expressed by НОЧЬЮ, the instrumental of НОЧЬ "night." Similarly, ДНЁМ the instrumental of ДЕНЬ "day" may be used to mean "during the day."

This brief discussion may suffice to indicate why this use of the instrumental is sometimes referred to as adverbial in character.

Сера горит бледным пламенем.
Sulfur burns with (a) pale flame.

Ины́ми слова́ми, окисле́ние органи́ческих веще́ств в
In other words, (the) oxidation of organic substances in

по́чве происхо́дит сравни́тельно ме́дленно.
(the) soil proceeds relatively slowly.

При кипяче́нии во́дного раство́ра избы́точная пе́рекись
On boiling of (the) aqueous solution, (the) excess peroxide

водоро́да бы́стро и по́лностью разлага́ется.
of hydrogen rapidly and completely decomposes self.

Днём пове́рхность земли́ согрева́ется со́лнцем,
By day, (the) surface of (the) earth warms self by (the) sun;

а но́чью охлажда́ется.
but at night, cools self.

Весно́й вла́жные гли́нистые по́чвы до́лго не
In (the) spring, moist clay soils long (time) not

просыха́ют и пло́хо прогрева́ются со́лнцем.
dry out and poorly warm self through by (the) sun.

Таки́м о́бразом, а́томы ура́на самопроизво́льно
In this way, atoms of uranium spontaneously

превраща́ются в а́томы ра́дия.
converts self into atoms of radium.

Пенсильва́нская нефть состои́т, гла́вным о́бразом, из
Pennsylvania petroleum consists for principal part of

углеводоро́дов алифати́ческого ря́да.
hydrocarbon of (the) aliphatic series.

Кусо́к серебра́, ве́сом в 52.5 г.,име́ет объём
(A) piece of silver with (a) weight of 52.5 g. has (a) volume

5 см$^3$.
5 cm$^3$.

Шáрик,           рáдиусом    в  0.01 см.,имéет  ёмкость,
(A) little sphere with (a) radius (in) 0.01 cm. has      (a) volume,

рáвную 0.0000042 куб. см.
equal    0.0000042 cc.

§ 99.  Use of Instrumental and Accusative Cases with Certain Verbs.

Certain Russian sentences, whose verbs take a direct object in the accusative case, also contain one or more words (usually nouns or noun modifiers), characterized by being in the instrumental case and by referring to the direct object. The following examples are typical.

Хи́мики  называ́ют[1]  коли́чественное   определе́ние кисло́т
Chemists call       (the) quantitative    determination of acids

при по́мощи   титрова́ния  ацидиме́трией.
with (the) aid  of titration  acidimetry.

Обогаще́ние            руд    име́ет   це́лью
Enrichment    (dressing) of ores  has      as  purpose  (the)

отделе́ние   поле́зных   соста́вных  часте́й  от   пусто́й
separation   of useful   component  parts   from  empty

поро́ды.
substance (gangue).

Кристаллиза́ция де́лает  стекло́[2]  полупрозра́чным.
Crystallization   makes   glass    semi-transparent.

Фо́сфор      де́лает  сталь  хру́пкой[3]  при  обыкнове́нной
Phosphorus  makes   steel   brittle    at   ordinary

температу́ре  (хладноло́мкой)[3].
temperature  (cold brittle).

[1] This verb form is often used impersonally to mean "they call," "they name," in sentences containing no explicit subject such as ХИ́МИКИ in our example.

[2] The instrumental case ending of the adjective, which refers to СТЕКЛО́ a neuter noun, is of necessity neuter in gender.

[3] The instrumental case endings of these adjectives are feminine in gender, because they refer to the feminine noun СТАЛЬ.

The verb   представля́ть -- предста́вить   "to present,"
"to offer" is often used with the instrumental case in such a way
as to be best translated into English by the verb "to constitute"
or, more simply, by "to be."  Such sentences usually involve
собо́й,  the instrumental case of the Russian reflexive pronoun,
себя́.

Применéние лёгких алюмúниевых сплáвов в авиáции
Application of light aluminum alloys in aviation

представля́ет весьмá большúе возмóжности в смы́сле
presents extremely great possibilities in (the) sense

уменьшéния мёртвого вéса и увеличéния скóрости
of decrease of dead weight and of increase of speed

движéния.
of motion.

Свет представля́ет собóй                электромагнúтные
Light presents by means of self electromagnetic

колебáния.
vibrations.

Вся́кий металлургúческий процéсс представляет собóй
Every metallurgical process presents by means

сло́жный комплéкс физúческих.
of self (constitutes) (a) complicated complex of physical

процéссов и химúческих превращéний.
processes and chemical changes.

Нáтрий и кáлий представля́ются серебристобéлыми
Sodium and potassium present self (as) silvery white

метáллами.
metals.

§ 100. Use of the Instrumental Case with Verbs Meaning "to be,"
"to remain," "to become," etc.

Closely related to the use of the instrumental case discussed
in the preceding paragraph is a similar use with verbs which
mean "to be," "to remain," "to become." This is illustrated in
the following sentences:

Цезий   и   рубидий   были   первыми   химическими
Cesium  and  rubidium  were  (the) first   chemical

элементами, открытыми при помощи спектроскопа.
elements    discovered  with (the) aid  of (the) spectroscope.

Растворимость   различных   тел   в одном   и   том   же
(The) solubility  of different  bodies in one  and the  same

растворителе может  быть весьма   различной.
solvent        may    be   extremely different.

Температура   газа   остаётся¹   постоянной.
(The) temperature of (the) gas remains   constant.

При  нагревании стеклянной   трубочки,   она начинает
On   heating     of (a) glass  little tube,  she begins

краснеть,   размягчаться,     сгибаться,    но   стекло
to  redden,  to soften self,  to bend self; but  glass

остаётся¹ стеклом.
remains     glass.

При этих  условиях  становится¹ возможным преобразование
With such conditions  becomes      possible    conversion

тепловой  энергии в   механическую.
of heat   energy   into mechanical.

¹ This reflexive verb form defies literal translation.

Следовательно,   изображение   краёв        предмета
Consequently,      (the) image    of (the) edges of (the) object

также будет плохим.
also   will   be poor.

Note that if these sentences were translated into German,
nouns and adjectives which are in the instrumental case in
Russian would be in the nominative case in German.


§ 101.  Prepositions Governing the Instrumental Case.

The  following  prepositions  always  require  the  instrumental
case:

между            -   between
над (надо)[1]     -   above

The following prepositions govern the instrumental when used
with restricted meaning[2] as indicated below.

за                behind
перед             before        with no motion implied
под (подо)[1]     under
с (со)[1]         with

The  following  sentences  illustrate  the  use  of  prepositions
governing the instrumental case of nouns and adjectives.

За       Ураном   находятся      планеты      Нептун   и
Beyond   Uranus   find self      (the) planets Neptune  and

Плутон.
Pluto.


[1] These forms of the prepositions are used for euphony, depending on the initial
letter or letters of the following word, cf. Footnote 1, p. 96.
[2] These prepositions when used with different meanings govern other cases,
cf. § 127, p. 187.

Сцепле́ние, существу́ющее   ме́жду   моле́кулами   жи́дкости,
Cohesion,      existing       between molecules    of (a) liquid,

приво́дит пове́рхностный слой   её  в   осо́бое  состоя́ние.
brings      surface       layer of  her into peculiar condition.

При   плавле́нии   твёрдых   тел   расстоя́ние   ме́жду
On   (the) melting   of solid   bodies (the) distance   between

моле́кулами   увели́чивается,   а   си́лы   сцепле́ния
molecules   increases self,   but (the) forces of cohesion

уменьша́ются.
decreases self.

В закры́том   сосу́де   испаре́ние   в   простра́нство   над
In (a) closed   vessel   evaporation   into (the) space   above

жи́дкостью   постепе́нно   замедля́ется.
(a) liquid   gradually   slows self.

Подво́дная   ло́дка   мо́жет   погружа́ться   в
(An) underwater  boat (submarine) is able  to plunge self   into

во́ду,  а  та́кже плыть   под   пове́рхностью   воды́.
water  and also  to navigate   under   (the) surface   of water.

Жи́дкости   под   де́йствием   своего́   ве́са   принима́ют
Liquids   under (the) action   of their   weight   assume

фо́рму   содержа́щего   их   сосу́да.
(the) form of (the) containing them vessels.

При   реа́кции   воды́   с   на́трием   выделя́ется
On   (the) reaction  of water  with   sodium   evolves self

водоро́д.
hydrogen.

С повышением температуры диэлектрическая
With increase of temperature, (the) dielectric

постоянная жидких веществ уменьшается.
constant of liquid substances decreases self.

С кислородом (или воздухом) метан образует
With oxygen (or air) methane forms

взрывчатую смесь.
(an) explosive mixture.

Вода, спирт, эфир, керосин и любая другая жидкость
Water, alcohol, ether, kerosene and any other liquid

с течением времени испаряются.
with (the) course of time evaporate self.

Медь легко соединяется со свободным хлором.
Copper easily combines self with free chlorine.


§ 102. Verbs Taking the Direct Object in the Instrumental Case.

A limited number of Russian verbs require that the direct
object be in the instrumental case. Most of these verbs imply
possession, control, or mastery. A particularly important
example is the verb обладать "to possess."

В сжатом виде воздух служит рабочим веществом
In compressed form, air serves as a working substance

в пневматических машинах.
in pneumatic machines.

Примером химической реакции может служить
(As an) example of chemical reaction may serve

разложение окиси ртути.
(the) decomposition of oxide mercury.

Cа́хар облада́ет   прия́тным   сла́дким   вку́сом.
Sugar   possesses   (a) pleasant sweet   taste.


В   настоя́щее   вре́мя   инжене́ры   располага́ют   са́мыми
In (the) present   time,   engineers   have available   (the) most

разнообра́зными   металли́ческими   материа́лами.
diverse   metallic   materials.


Для   простоты́   мы   пренебрега́ем[1]   измене́ниями   объёма
For   simplicity,   we   neglect   changes   of volume

воды́   при   нагрева́нии.
of water on   heating.


Заря́д   на   се́тке   трехэлектро́нной   усили́тельной
(The) charge on   (the) grid of (a) three electrode amplifier

ла́мпы   управля́ет   ано́дным   то́ком.
lamp   controls   (the) anode   current.


Так   лю́ди   проника́ют   в   глубь   земли́   и
Thus people   penetrate   into (the) depth of (the) earth   and

овладева́ют   её бога́тствами.
take control (of)   her riches.


In the preceding sentences, such actions as "possessing,"
"controlling," "taking control" and the like are expressed by
various verb forms, which take their direct object in the
instrumental case. In the following sentences, action of this type
is expressed by corresponding nouns, viz.,   управле́ние, and
овладе́ние   which, like the corresponding verbs, are followed by
the instrumental case.


[1] The   -ем   ending of the verb indicates agreement with the subject   МЫ   "we."
cf. § 188, p. 283.

| | | | | |
|---|---|---|---|---|
| В э́том | прибо́ре | управле́ние | электро́нным | пото́ком |
| In this | device | control | of (the) electron | stream |

| | | |
|---|---|---|
| осуществля́ется | | электри́ческим |
| accomplishes self | (is accomplished) by | (an) electric |

по́лем.
field.

| | | | | | |
|---|---|---|---|---|---|
| Челове́к | ведёт | непреры́вную | борьбу́ | за | овладе́ние |
| Man | conducts (a) continuous | | struggle toward mastering | | |

есте́ственными процессами.
natural          processes.


## § 103.  Reading Exercise.

### Физи́ческие сво́йства чи́стых мета́ллов

Чи́стые мета́ллы характеризу́ются[1] ма́лой твёрдостью, значи́тельным теплови́м расшире́нием, хоро́шей пласти́чностью, большо́й теплопрово́дностью и ни́зким электросопротивле́нием. Вообще́ физи́ческие сво́йства чи́стых мета́ллов ре́зко меня́ются с измене́нием температу́ры.  Так, с повыше́нием  температу́ры электропрово́дность чи́стых мета́ллов си́льно пада́ет, с пониже́нием температу́ры - растёт.

Мно́гие мета́ллы при о́чень ни́зких температу́рах облада́ют сво́йством сверхпроводи́мости.  Характе́рным[2] для сверхпроводнико́в явля́ется ре́зкое скачкообра́зное паде́ние электросопротивле́ния в о́чень у́зком интерва́ле температу́р вблизи́[3] абсолю́тного нуля́.  В настоя́щее вре́мя[4] сверхпроводи́мость наблюда́ется в мета́ллах  Ga, In, Sn, Pb, Hg, Te, Ti, Th, Ta, Mo. Nb.

Чи́стые мета́ллы облада́ют оптима́льными сво́йствам для проводо́в.  В осо́бенности высо́кая электропроводи́мость

делает чистые металлы хорошим конструкционным материалом для проводов. Чистые металлы являются фактически незаменимым материалом для электрических проводов. Кроме того[5] металлы очень высокой чистоты обладают повышенной[6] химической стойкостью против действия растворов электролитов.

Однако чистые металлы также характеризуются малой силой[7] сцепления, большим коэфициентом линейного расширения, низкой твёрдостью и недостаточной прочностью при высоких температурах. Такие свойства[8] делают чистые металлы невыгодными для многих технических употреблений. Требования техники часто удовлетворяются только сплавами с более[9] выгодными физическими свойствами.

## Notes

1. характеризуются    "(they) are characterized" is derived from the infinitive характеризовать of the verb характеризовать -- охарактеризовать, "to characterize."

2. характерным is the instrumental, neuter, singular of the adjective, характерный "characteristic." Here характерным is used with является and refers to the noun падение. The skeleton of the sentence is formed by the words падение является характерным "fall is (literally -- shows self) characteristic." This sort of inverted word order is often encountered with sentences (and clauses) in which the verb is one of the forms of являть. Cf. § 49, p. 67 for previous discussion of inverted word order.

3. вблизи "near," "in the neighborhood of" is a preposition requiring the genitive, ( абсолютного нуля ).

4. в настоящее время "at the present time." Here the irregularly declined neuter noun время is in the accusative singular case, as is also its modifier настоящее.

5. кроме того "aside from this."

6. повышенной which modifies стойкостью is the instrumental, feminine singular case of повышенный the perfective, passive, past participle of the verb повышать -- повысить "to raise," "to lift," "to increase."

7. Here сѝлой is the instrumental singular case of the noun сѝла "force," "strength." сѝла сцепле́ния which is, literally, "strength of linking (or bonding)" might best be translated by "tensile strength."

8. таки́е сво́йства "such properties." Both таки́е and сво́йства are in the nominative plural case.

9. бо́лее вы́годными "more suitable." The formation of one type of comparative with the aid of undeclinable бо́лее (literally "bigger") is discussed in § 231, p. 523.

§ 104. Translation Exercise.

Underlining has the same significance as in the preceding Translation Exercise, § 96, p. 139.

1. Sodium and potassium are characterized by high (big) plasticity.
2. The electrical resistance of pure metals changes with change of temperature.
3. Tin and lead possess the property of superconductivity.
4. The electrical resistance of pure metals in general is (shows self) low.
5. The electrical resistance of certain ( не́которых ) pure metals sharply drops in a very narrow temperature range near absolute zero.
6. High electrical conductivity makes pure metals practically irreplaceable, as material for conductors.
7. Pure metals possess good resistance to (against) the action of solutions of electrolytes.
8. The hardness of pure metals decreases with rise in (of) temperature.
9. Pure metals are (show themselves) unsuitable for many technical applications.
10. Many alloys (спла́вы ) are characterized by good (favorable) physical properties at high temperatures.

# LESSON 14

## THE DATIVE CASE

§ 105. Use of the Dative Case.

The use of the dative case in Russian might be summarized as follows:

1) As indirect object after certain verbs, such as, дава́ть-- дать "to give."
2) After certain prepositions.
3) With certain words having implied prepositional meaning.
4) To denote the object of certain verbs, § 114, p. 166.
5) In certain idiomatic expressions. (For a particularly important idiomatic use of the dative, see § 386, p. 640.)

§ 106. Dative Case Endings of Nouns.

### NOUNS

|  | Masculine | | Feminine | | Neuter | |
|---|---|---|---|---|---|---|
|  | Dat. Sing. | Dat. Plural | Dat. Sing. | Dat. Plural | Dat. Sing. | Dat. Plural |
| Hard | -у | -ам | -е | -ам | -у | -ам |
| Soft | -ю | -ям | -е -и | -ям | -ю | -ям |

Note use of the endings -ам and -ям to form the dative plural of all nouns, regardless of gender, as in the following examples.

# LESSON 14

| Noun | Key No. | Stem | Dative Singular | Dative Plural |
|------|---------|------|-----------------|---------------|

## MASCULINE NOUNS

### Hard Endings

| Noun | Key No. | Stem | Dative Singular | Dative Plural |
|------|---------|------|-----------------|---------------|
| а́том | 1 | а́том– | а́тому | а́томам |

### Mixed Hard and Soft Endings

| Noun | Key No. | Stem | Dative Singular | Dative Plural |
|------|---------|------|-----------------|---------------|
| луч | 2 | луч– | лучу́ | луча́м |
| проводни́к | 3 | проводни́к– | проводнику́ | проводника́м |

### Soft Endings

| Noun | Key No. | Stem | Dative Singular | Dative Plural |
|------|---------|------|-----------------|---------------|
| рой | 4 | ро– | ро́ю | роя́м |
| эпите́лий | 5 | эпители– | эпите́лию | эпите́лиям |
| мно́житель | 6 | мно́жител– | мно́жителю | мно́жителям |

## FEMININE NOUNS

### Hard Endings

| Noun | Key No. | Stem | Dative Singular | Dative Plural |
|------|---------|------|-----------------|---------------|
| моле́кула | 7 | моле́кул– | моле́куле | моле́кулам |

### Mixed Hard and Soft Endings

| Noun | Key No. | Stem | Dative Singular | Dative Plural |
|------|---------|------|-----------------|---------------|
| едини́ца | 8 | едини́ц– | едини́це | едини́цам |
| нау́ка | 9 | нау́к– | нау́ке | нау́кам |

### Soft Endings

| Noun | Key No. | Stem | Dative Singular | Dative Plural |
|------|---------|------|-----------------|---------------|
| неде́ля | 10 | неде́л– | неде́ле | неде́лям |
| тео́рия | 11 | тео́ри– | тео́рии | тео́риям |
| смесь | 12 | смес– | сме́си | сме́сям |

| Noun | Key No. | Stem | Dative Singular | Dative Plural |
|------|---------|------|-----------------|---------------|

## NEUTER NOUNS

### Hard Endings

| вещество́ | 13 | веществ- | веществу́ | вещества́м |

### Mixed Hard and Soft Endings

| учи́лище | 14 | учи́лищ- | учи́лищу | учи́лищам |

### Soft Endings

| по́ле | 15 | пол- | по́лю | поля́м |
| явле́ние | 16 | явлени- | явле́нию | явле́ниям |

§ 107. Dative Case Endings of Adjectives.

|  | Masculine | | Feminine | | Neuter | |
|--|-----------|--|----------|--|--------|--|
|  | Hard | Soft | Hard | Soft | Hard | Soft |
| Dative Sing. | -ому | -ему | -ой | -ей | -ому | -ему |

|  | Masc.-Fem.-Neuter | |
|--|-------------------|--|
|  | Hard | Soft |
| Dative Plural | -ым | -им |

## Hard Endings -- Adjectives

Stems      ста́р-,   old
Key No. 17

жив-,   live, alive
Key No. 18

|  | Masc. | Fem. | Neuter |
|---|---|---|---|
| Dative Sing. | ста́рому жив́ому | ста́рой жив́ой | ста́рому жив́ому |

| Masc.-Fem.-Neuter |
|---|
| Dative Plural   ста́рым жив́ым |

## Soft Endings -- Adjectives

Stem      син-,   blue
Key No. 19

|  | Masc. | Fem. | Neuter |
|---|---|---|---|
| Dative Sing. | си́нему | си́ней | си́нему |

| Masc.-Fem.-Neuter |
|---|
| Dative Plural   си́ним |

## Mixed Hard and Soft Endings -- Adjectives

Stems      сух-,   dry
Key No. 20

электрическ-,  electrical
Key No. 21

свеж-,  fresh
Key No. 22

|        | Masc. | Fem. | Neuter |
|--------|-------|------|--------|
| Dative Sing. | сухо́му, электри́ческому све́жему | сухо́й, электри́ческой све́жей | сухо́му, электри́ческому све́жему |

|        | Masc.-Fem.-Neuter |
|--------|-------------------|
| Dative Plural | сухи́м, электри́ческим све́жим |

§ 108.  Verbs Taking the Direct Object in the Accusative and the Indirect Object in the Dative Case.

This use of the dative case is not as important in scientific Russian as might, perhaps, be expected.

Спектра́льный   ана́лиз   даёт хи́микам   возмо́жность
Spectrum        analysis   gives to chemists   (the) possibility

бы́стро   анализи́ровать   спла́вы,   ру́ды,   ка́мни   и   други́е
quickly   to analyze        alloys,    ores,    rocks   and   other

го́рные   поро́ды.
mineral   substances.

Газ      отдаёт      воде́      тепло́.
(The) gas gives out   to (the) water, heat.

Нераствори́мые приме́си   придаю́т воде́   му́тность.
Insoluble       impurities impart   to water turbidity.

В   настоя́щее   вре́мя   хи́мики   припи́сывают   энзи́мам
In (the) present   time   chemists   ascribe        to enzymes

катали́тический   хара́ктер.
catalytic          character.

Отсу́тствие          заря́да          чрезвыча́йно        облегча́ет
(The) absence        of charge        extraordinarily    facilitates

нейтро́нам   проника́ние  в  а́то́мные  я́дра.
to neutrons  penetration  into atomic   nuclei.

In the above sentences, the direct object is a noun in the accusative case (or a phrase involving such a noun). Closely related to such sentences are those in which some form of the reflexive pronoun (себя́ or its contracted ending forms –СЯ or –СЬ) is, grammatically, the direct object. The Russian verbs in such sentences are usually best translated into English by the passive of the corresponding English verbs. This use of the dative is less frequent in scientific Russian than the corresponding use of the instrumental, cf. § 102, p. 148.

Мно́гие ацета́ты  легко́  подверга́ются           гидро́лизу,
Many   acetates  easily  submit self (undergo)   to hydrolysis,

т.е.легко́ разлага́ются      де́йствием   воды́.
i.e., easily decompose self  by (the) action of water.

Для  удале́ния       при́месей       цинк   подверга́ется
For  (the) removal   of impurities,  zinc   submits self

опера́ции     рафини́рования.
to (the) operation of refining.

Сре́дняя         кинети́ческая    эне́ргия   поступа́тельного
(The) average kinetic            energy   of (the) translational

движе́ния   моле́кул          га́за        не   поддаётся
movement   of (the) molecules  of (a) gas   not  submits self

непосре́дственному   и   просто́му   измере́нию.
to direct            and simple     measurement.

При э́том электри́ческий   заря́д  сообща́ется
Thereby, (an) electrical   charge imparts self   (is imparted)

ша́ру.
to (the) sphere.

## § 109. The Dative Case Used with the Preposition К (КО).[1]

The Russian preposition К(КО)[1] meaning "to" or "toward," always governs the dative case. This preposition is used in sentences indicating physical motion, as well as in other sentences indicating various relationships not involving actual motion.

При    электро́лизе    ио́ны    с    отрица́тельным    заря́дом    (анио́ны)
On     electrolysis   ions   with  negative            charge      (anions)

передвига́ются                          к      ано́ду.
displace   self   (are displaced)      to    (the) anode.


Ко[1]    второ́й         гру́ппе    паровы́х    маши́н       отно́сятся[2]
To      (the) second    group     of steam   machines    pertain

турби́ны.
turbines.


Зо́лото    облада́ет    о́чень    ма́лым    хими́ческим    сро́дством   к
Gold       possesses   very     slight    chemical       affinity     to

кислоро́ду.
oxygen.


Отноше́ние    си́лы         тре́ния    к си́ле        давле́ния
(The) ratio   of (the) force of friction to (the) force of pressure

называ́ется    коэфицие́нтом    тре́ния       и       изобража́ется
calls self     the coefficient  of friction  and     denotes self

гре́ческой    бу́квой μ.
by (the) Greek letter μ.

---

[1] The КО form of this preposition is used to facilitate pronunciation when the next word in the sentence starts with a consonant combination such as ВТ-, cf. Footnote 1, p. 96.
[2] Here, again, we have a reflexive form of a verb scarcely capable of literal translation, cf. Footnote 1, p. 145.

Вдыха́ние паро́в хлорофо́рма приво́дит к по́лной поте́ре
Inhalation of gases chloroform leads to complete loss

чувстви́тельности и созна́ния.
of feeling and consciousness.

К о́бщей гру́ппе драгоце́нных мета́ллов принадлежа́т
To (the) general group of precious metals pertain

пла́тина и пала́дий.
platinum and palladium.

В прису́тствии катализа́торов при повы́шенной
In (the) presence of catalysts at elevated

температу́ре водоро́д присоединя́ется к эти́леновым
temperature, hydrogen combines self to ethylenic

углеводоро́дам.
hydrocarbons.

Преде́льные углеводоро́ды отно́сятся[1] к числу́
Saturated hydrocarbons pertain to (the) number

веще́ств хими́чески сто́йких, ма́ло реакционноспосо́бных.
of substances chemically stable, slightly reaction-capable.

## § 110. The Dative Case Used with the Preposition ПО.

The Russian preposition ПО usually (though not always)[2]
governs the dative case. When used with the dative ПО denotes
relationships of the sort indicated by such English expressions as
"according to," "in compliance with," "in agreement with,"
"with respect to," "along."

---

[1] Cf. Footnote 2 on preceding page.
[2] The preposition ПО is occasionally used with the prepositional case to mean
"after" (cf. § 76, p. 100) and with the accusative to mean "for," "as far as"
(cf. § 69, pp. 99-100). Such use of ПО with cases other than the dative is very rare
in scientific Russian.

По        вне́шнему  ви́ду  графи́т  си́льно
With  respect  to  external  appearance,  graphite  strongly

отлича́ется  от  алма́за.
differs  self  from diamond.


По        запа́сам  кали́йных  соле́й  СССР
With  respect to  reserves  of potassium  salts,  (the) U.S.S.R.

стои́т  на  пе́рвом  ме́сте  в  ми́ре.
stands  at  (the) first  place  in (the) world.


По        содержа́нию  в земно́й  коре́ алюми́ний,  в
With respect to content  in terrestrial crust aluminum,  in

ви́де  его́  соедине́ний,  занима́ет  пе́рвое  ме́сто
(the) form  of its  compounds,  occupies  (the) first  place

среди́  мета́ллов.
among  metals.


Совреме́нная  те́хника  располага́ет  больши́м
Contemporary  technology  has  available  (a)  large

коли́чеством разнообра́зных  по        их  сво́йствам
quantity  of different  with respect to their properties

лёгких алюми́ниевых  спла́вов.
light  aluminum  alloys.


По        молекуля́рно - кинети́ческой  тео́рии  моле́кулы
According to (the) molecular  kinetic  theory,  molecules

жи́дкости  нахо́дятся  в  непреры́вном  движе́нии.
of (a) liquid  find  self  (are)  in continuous  motion.


По        свое́й  электропрово́дности  серебро́
With  respect  to  its  electrical  conductivity,  silver

превосхо́дит все  остальны́е  мета́ллы.
surpasses  all  remaining  metals.

В     атмосфе́ре            кислоро́да      аммиа́к      сгора́ет
In  (an)  atmosphere      of   oxygen,    ammonia    burns

жёлтым          пла́менем     по                      реа́кции:
with (a) yellow    flame        according to           (the) reaction:

4 NH₃   +   3 O₂   =   2 N₂   +   6 H₂O   +   366 ккал.
$4\,NH_3 + 3\,O_2 = 2\,N_2 + 6\,H_2O + 366\ \text{kcal.}$

Содержа́ние      радо́на     в атмосфе́ре          оце́нивается
(The) content   of radon   in (the) atmosphere   estimates self

                цифро́й         6 x 10⁻⁸% по  объёму.
(is estimated) by (the) figure  $6 \times 10^{-8}\%$  by   volume.

По                       ме́ре    повыше́ния     температу́ры
In accordance  with  degree  of increase    of temperature,

сте́пень       диссоциа́ции     воды́     увели́чивается.
(the) degree  of dissociation   of water   increases self.

Нефть          прохо́дит че́рез  печь,        по      тру́бам,
(The) petroleum passes    through (the) furnace, through tubes,

и   нагрева́ется                до    температу́ры   о́коло
and heats    self     (is heated) up to (a) temperature   about

400°.
400°.

§ 111.  A Partial List of Prepositions and Prepositional Adverbs
    Governing the Dative Case.

A number of important prepositions and prepositional adverbs
govern the dative case.

| | |
|---|---|
| благодаря́ | thanks to |
| вопреки́ | contrary to |
| к(ко)[1] | toward, to |
| по | according to, in conformity with, with respect to |
| подо́бно | similarly to |
| пропорциона́льно | proportional to |
| согла́сно | in agreement with |
| | according to |

Благодаря́ свои́м вы́годным физи́ческим сво́йствам спла́вы
Thanks to    their    favorable    physical       properties,    alloys

широко́ применя́ются      в те́хнике.
widely    utilize    self    in technology.

Эти́ловый спирт подо́бно воде́ явля́ется      хоро́шим
Ethyl    alcohol    like    water    shows self    (a) good

раствори́телем.
solvent.

Подо́бно други́м углеводоро́дам аромати́ческие углеводоро́ды
Like    other    hydrocarbons    aromatic    hydrocarbons

явля́ются      неполя́рными    соедине́ниями.
show self (are) non-polar    compounds.

При постоя́нной температу́ре объём      да́нной    ма́ссы
At    constant    temperature    (the) volume of (a) given    mass

идеа́льного    га́за изменя́ется    обра́тно пропорциона́льно
of (an) ideal    gas    changes self    inversely    proportionally

давле́нию,      а    при постоя́нном давле́нии – пря́мо
to (the) pressure, and at    constant    pressure — directly

пропорциона́льно абсолю́тной    температу́ре.
proportionally    to (the) absolute    temperature.

---

[1] See Footnote 1, p. 96.

Согла́сно     тео́рии     электролити́ческой     диссоциа́ции
According to (the) theory of electrolytic          dissociation

(тео́рии   иониза́ции),   кислоты́,   основа́ния   и   со́ли   при
(theory    of ionization), acids,      bases       and salts  on

растворе́нии   их    в воде́   распада́ются   на    ио́ны.
solution       of them in water decompose     into ions.

Согла́сно   при́нципу    Ле - Шателье́,   повыше́ние
According to (the) principle (of) Le Chatelier,   (an) increase of

температу́ры      благоприя́тствует          появле́нию
temperature        favors                    (the) appearance

веще́ств,    кото́рые    образу́ютсн        с    поглоще́нием
of substances which      form   self      with  absorption

тепла́.
of heat.

## § 112. Use of Dative Case with Adjectives.

In § 111, p. 162, the use of the dative case with various prepositional adverbs, e.g., пропорциона́льно was mentioned. As might be expected, the dative case is often used with corresponding adjectives, e.g., пропорциона́льный and with related adjectives, e.g., ра́вный "equal."

Сопротивле́ние     проводника́     явля́ется     пря́мо
(The)  resistance   of a  conductor  shows self     directly

пропорциона́льным    длине́,            но    обра́тно
proportional         to (the) length,   but   inversely

пропорциона́льным пло́щади     его́ попере́чного сече́ния.
proportional      to (the) area  of its cross     section.

Не́которые  кривы́е   охлажде́ния   явля́ется   аналоги́чными
Certain    curves    of cooling    show self    similar

кривы́м    нагрева́ния.
to (the) curves of heating.

Уксусная кислота содержится (2 - 3%) в уксусе,
Acetic    acid    contains  self  (2 - 3%) in vinegar,

знакомом человеку уже с древних времён.
known   to man  already from ancient  times.

Добавление          0.5% висмута  делает  скорость
(The) addition  of  0.5% bismuth  makes  (the) rate

превращения   белого   олова  в  серое  практически
of conversion  of white  tin  into gray  practically

равной нулю.
equal  to zero.

Невидимые  глазу          рентгеновские лучи  обладают
Invisible   to (the) eye  Roentgen      rays  possess

способностью  проникать  сквозь  непрозрачные
(the) ability  to penetrate through  non-transparent

обычному  свету тела.
to ordinary light bodies.


§ 113. Use of Dative Case with Nouns.

In the foregoing discussion attention was directed to use of the dative case with various verbs and adjectives. The dative case may be used similarly with certain nouns closely related to such verbs and adjectives.

Как  правило,  у  всех  металлов  с  понижением
As  (a) rule  with  all  metals  with  lowering

температуры  повышаются       твёрдость       и
of temperature  increases self  (the) hardness  and

пределы  текучести,  и  падает – сопротивление
(the) limits  of creep  and falls  (the) resistance

удару.
to impact.

Процéсс    отдáчи    теплá  гáзами    водé
Process   of giving off  of heat  by (the) gases  to (the) water

происхóдит    при    постоя́нном давлéнии.
proceeds     at    constant    pressure.


Плавлéнием    называ́ется    перехóд    тéла      из
As melting    calls self     transition  of (a) body  from

твёрдого    состоя́ния  в    жúдкое    при  сообщéнии
(the) solid   condition  into (the) liquid  on   communication

тéлу      теплоты́.
to (the) body  of heat.


Квáрцевые    лúнзы    характеризýются        высóкой
Quartz      lenses    characterize self        by high

прозрáчностью  ультрафиолéтовым      лучáм.
transparency    to ultra-violet        rays.


В противополóжность  другúм    галоидным  соля́м  серебрá,
In contrast        to other    halide    salts  of silver,

AgF  растворя́ется    в водé  óчень  легкó.
AgF  dissolves self   in water  very   easily.


§ 114.  Verbs Taking the Direct Object in the Dative Case.

A few verbs which are encountered fairly frequently in
scientific Russian require the direct object to be in the dative
case. Sentences involving some of these Russian verbs require
use of the preposition "to" for translation into English. Note, for
example, the use of COOTBÉTCTBУeт "corresponds (to)" -- from
COOTBÉTCTBOBATЬ "to correspond (to)" -- in the first sentence
of the following group.


Вéрхний      перелóм  кривóй          соотвéтствует
(The)  upper    break    of (the)  curve   corresponds

начáлу      кристаллизáции.
to (the) start of crystallization.

Такие кислотоупорные сплавы хорошо удовлетворяют
Such acid resistant alloys well satisfy

требованиям пищевой промышленности.
(the) requirements of the food industry.


При гетерогенном катализе промоторы способствуют
In heterogeneous catalysis promoters promote

созданию каталитически активных центров.
(the) creation of catalytically active centers.


Присутствие алкоголя в растворе препятствует
(The) presence of alcohol in (the) solution impairs

действию катализатора.
(the) action of (the) catalyst.


Обычно примеси различных материалов
Ordinarily admixtures (impurities) of various materials

сопутствуют самородной сере.
accompany native sulfur.


Цинк, получаемый сухим способом, по своему
Zinc, obtained by (the) dry process, as to its

качеству уступает электролитическому цинку.
quality gives way to electrolytic zinc.


Такое состояние отвечает равновесию.
Such (a) condition corresponds to equilibrium.


Такая машина противоречит второму закону
Such (a) machine contradicts (the) second law

термодинамики.
of thermodynamics.

| | | | | |
|---|---|---|---|---|
| Атмосфе́рная | вла́га | вреди́т | таки́м | катализа́торам. |
| Atmospheric | moisture | damages | such | catalysts. |

| | | | | |
|---|---|---|---|---|
| Существова́ние | а́томов | не | подлежи́т | сомне́нию. |
| (The) existence | of atoms | not | is subject | to doubt. |

§ 115.  Reading Exercise.

### Каучу́к

Каучу́к и проду́кты его́[1] перерабо́тки нахо́дят широ́кое применéние в промы́шленности благодаря́ свои́м це́нным сво́йствам - высо́кой эласти́чности, исключи́тельно большо́му электросопротивле́нию, хими́ческой усто́йчивости. При прибавлéнии к каучуку́ небольшо́го коли́чества се́ры (4-5%) получа́ется нагрева́нием[2] вулканизи́рованный каучу́к[3] - так называ́емая рези́на.[10] Проце́сс вулканиза́ции придаёт каучуку́ це́нные сво́йства. Вулканизи́рованный каучу́к противостои́т де́йствию горя́чей воды́, а та́кже мно́гих хими́ческих реаге́нтов. Одна́ко, вулканизи́рованный каучу́к ме́дленно подверга́ется де́йствию жиро́в и нефтя́ных фра́кций. По свое́й[4] молекуля́рной структу́ре каучу́к отно́сится[5] к гру́ппе высокомолекуля́рных веще́ств. Согла́сно результа́там многочи́сленных нау́чных иссле́дований,[6] каучу́к явля́ется непреде́льным[7] углеводоро́дом, и́менно полиме́ром изопре́на.

Каучу́к, подо́бно изопре́ну и други́м непреде́льным[7] углеводоро́дам, присоединя́ет бром и галоидоводоро́ды.

К приро́дному каучуку́ по свои́м[8] примене́ниям примыка́ют не́которые иску́сственные проду́кты, кото́рые обыкнове́нно но́сят о́бщее назва́ние, иску́сственные каучуки. Иску́сственные каучуки́ облада́ют мно́гими физи́ческими сво́йствами, прису́щими[9] приро́дному каучуку́.

Мно́гие так называ́емые[10] иску́сственные каучуки́ дета́лями свои́х молекуля́рных структу́р отлича́ются от приро́дного

каучука́. Так, наприме́р, в неопре́не (и́ли совпре́не)   мети́-
ловые гру́ппы приро́дного каучука́ замеща́ются а́томами хло́ра.
Тем не ме́нее[11] неопре́н явля́ется похо́жим по свои́м  физи́че-
ским сво́йствам на приро́дный каучу́к.

Фабри́чное произво́дство синтети́ческих каучуко́в при-
надлежи́т к са́мым[12] ва́жным достиже́ниям совреме́нной хими́че-
ской промы́шленности. Мно́гие ви́ды синтети́ческих  каучуко́в
по не́которым свои́м сво́йствам превосхо́дят натура́льный кау-
чу́к. Так, наприме́р, неопре́н отлича́ется высо́ким сопроти-
вле́нием де́йствию жиро́в и нефтя́ных фра́кций. Но сего́дняшние
ти́пы иску́сственного каучука́ не удовлетворя́ют всем тре́бо-
ваниям те́хники и бы́та. Хи́микам в э́той  о́бласти  всё  еще
предстоя́т нереше́нные пробле́мы.

## Notes

1. его́ "his," "its" is an undeclinable possessive pronoun
here referring to каучу́к. Thus the phrase  проду́кты его́
перерабо́тки  means "products of its processing."

2. Here  нагрева́нием, which is the instrumental, singular
case of  нагрева́ние  might well be translated ` "by means of
heating."

3. The noun каучу́к is the subject of the verb получа́ется.

4. свое́й, the dative singular feminine form of свой, the
reflexive possessive, here refers to the noun каунук  in
accordance with the general rule that this reflexive refers to the
subject of the sentence (or clause) in which it is used.

5. каучу́к  отно́сится к -- "rubber belongs to --." Some
Russian reflexives virtually defy literal translation. The verb
относи́ть -- отнести́  literally means "to carry off," "to
carry away."

6. иссле́дований is the genitive plural of иссле́дование
"investigation."

7. непреде́льный  "unsaturated" (in chemical sense) is
derived from не-+ преде́л  "limit, boundary, extent."

8., СВОИ́М here is in the dative plural case and refers to ПРОДУ́КТЫ , the subject of the sentence.

9. прису́щими the instrumental plural of прису́щий "inherent (to)" is followed by a noun and modifier in the dative case, e.g., приро́дному каучуку́.

10. так называ́емые "so called." называ́емые is the nominative plural of the present passive participle formed from называть (from называ́ть -- назва́ть) "to name," "to call."

11. тем не ме́нее "none-the-less." An excessively literal translation would be "by that not less."

12. са́мый ва́жный "the most important" is an example of one type of Russian superlative, discussed in detail in § 345, p. 544.

§ 116. Translation Exercise.

Underlining indicates nouns (and their modifiers) to be translated into Russian with the aid of the dative case.

1. Thanks to its (СВОИ́М) valuable properties, rubber plays an important role in our lives (life).
2. Vulcanization imparts to natural rubber increased (увели́ченную) elasticity (эласти́чность) at low (ни́зких) temperatures.
3. Neoprene resists the action of fats and petroleum fractions.
4. According to (По) results of scientific investigations, rubber belongs to the group of high molecular substances.
5. Isoprene belongs to the group of unsaturated hydrocarbons (непреде́льных углеводоро́дов).
6. Isoprene, like (подо́бно) other unsaturated hydrocarbons, combines with (adds on) chlorine.
7. Neoprene differs (distinguishes self) as to (по) details of its (свой) molecular structure (структу́ры) from natural rubber.
8. Neoprene surpasses (превосхо́дит) natural rubber as to certain physical properties.
9. Rubber and neoprene satisfy many (мно́гим) requirements of technology.
10. Unsolved problems confront chemists in the field of synthetic (синтети́ческого) rubber.

## LESSON 15

## IMPLIED VERBS IN SIMPLE SENTENCES

§ 117. Adjectives as Attributive and Predicative Modifiers.

Adjectives which are used to modify nouns directly are termed attributive as, for example, the adjective "red" in the following sentence.

The red book is on the table.

On rewording this sentence, the adjective "red" may be placed in the predicate and is then quite logically termed a predicative modifier, as in the following sentence.

The book on the table is red.

As seen from these two sentences, English adjectives, in general, suffer no change in form on shifting from attributive to predicate or vice versa. However, certain English possessives do undergo change as is evident from the following sentences.

My book is red.

The red book is mine.

In Russian, the majority of adjectives have predicative forms differing from their attributive forms. The predicate forms are obtained by using the endings given in the next paragraph.

The predicative form of Russian adjectives occurs only in the nominative case.

§ 118. Predicative Endings of Adjectives.

|  | Masculine | | Feminine | | Neuter | |
|---|---|---|---|---|---|---|
|  | Hard | Soft | Hard | Soft | Hard | Soft |
| Singular | -- | -ь | -а | -я | -о | -е |

Masc.-Fem.-Neuter

| | Hard | Soft |
|---|---|---|
| Plural | –ы | –и |

### Hard Endings -- Adjectives

Stems　стар–,　old
　　　　Key No. 17

　　　　жив–,　live, alive
　　　　Key No. 18

| | Masc. | Fem. | Neuter |
|---|---|---|---|
| Singular | стар | старá | старó |
| | жив | живá | живо |

Masc.-Fem.-Neuter

| | |
|---|---|
| Plural | стáры |
| | жи́вы |

### Soft Endings -- Adjectives

Stem　син–,　blue
　　　Key No. 19

| | Masc. | Fem. | Neuter |
|---|---|---|---|
| Singular | синь | си́ня | си́не |

Masc.-Fem.-Neuter

| | |
|---|---|
| Plural | си́ни |

## Mixed Hard and Soft Endings -- Adjectives

Stems       сух-,     dry
Key No. 20

электрическ-,[1] electrical
Key No. 21

свеж-, fresh
Key No. 22

|  | Masc. | Fem. | Neuter |
|---|---|---|---|
| Singular | сух | сухá | сýхо |
|  | свеж | свежá | свéже |

| | Masc.-Fem.-Neuter |
|---|---|
| Plural | сýхи |
| | свéжи |

§ 119. Nominative Case of the Personal Pronouns and the Demonstrative Pronouns ЭТОТ.

The nominative case of personal pronouns are as follows:

| Я | I | МЫ | we |
|---|---|---|---|
| ТЫ | you (singular -- familiar form) | ВЫ | you (plural -- polite form) |
| ОН | he | | |
| ОНÁ | she | ОНИ́ | they |
| ОНÓ | it | | |

The nominative case of the demonstrative pronoun ЭТОТ has the following forms:

| | Singular | | Plural |
|---|---|---|---|
| Э́ТОТ | this (masc.) | | |
| Э́ТА | this (fem.) | Э́ТИ | these |
| Э́ТО | this (neuter) | | |

[1] Adjectives whose stems end in -ИЧЕСК- have no predicative forms.

These forms of э́тот may be used either alone, as pronouns, or as noun modifiers.

§ 120.  Omission from Russian Sentences of Present Tense of быть "to be."

An English sentence is considered incomplete and ungrammatical if it does not contain a verb. It is sometimes permissible, however, in English to omit the verb "to be" from clauses, if not from sentences. Thus we have, for example:

"The stronger the acid, the more rapid is the rate of solution."

The wording of the clause "the stronger the acid" so strongly implies the verb "is," that it may be omitted. Such omission of the present tense of the verb быть "to be" occurs much more extensively in Russian than in English. In Russian not only clauses but whole sentences may contain no verb aside from the implied present tense of быть. In fact, the present tense of the verb быть "to be" is rarely used in Russian sentences and may be regarded as virtually obsolete. For this reason the presence in a simple sentence of either of the present tense forms есть "is" or суть "are" indicates rather strong emphasis that something actually exists, often coupled with the implication that the emphasized fact may be unknown to the reader or may even appear doubtful. Use may also be made at times of есть and суть to avoid ambiguity in complicated sentences. Furthermore, суть is occasionally used in connection with enumerations.

In many Russian sentences the missing present tense forms of быть are replaced by a dash, e.g., Я — хи́мик "I (am) (a) chemist." Other pronouns are used similarly. In particular, э́то standing alone in a sentence may be used to mean either "this is" or "these are" and use of всё э́то to mean "all this is" or "all these are" is particularly frequent in definitions.

Examples of such types of sentences in which the present tense of быть is omitted, but implied, are given below.

Ацетиле́н  -  деше́вое  и  досту́пное вещество́.
Acetylene  (is)  (a) cheap  and  available  substance.


Нефть  -  тёмная  маслянистая  жи́дкость.
Petroleum (is) (a) dark,  oily  liquid.

Углеро́д - гла́вная составна́я часть обыкнове́нного
Carbon (is) principal component part of ordinary

древе́сного угля́.
charcoal.

Крахма́л - бе́лый порошо́к, нераствори́мый в воде́.
Starch (is) (a) white powder insoluble in water.

Эти́ловый спирт - бесцве́тная легкоподви́жная жи́дкость.
Ethyl alcohol (is) (a) colorless mobile liquid.

Мы в состоя́нии наблюда́ть лишь сре́дний
We (are) in position to observe only (the) average

результа́т грома́дного коли́чества уда́ров
result of (the) enormous quantity of impacts

моле́кул.
of molecules.

Ири́дий - э́то ре́дкий мета́лл пла́тиновой гру́ппы.
Iridium — that (is) (a) rare metal of (the) platinum group.

Хлор, се́ра, желе́зо, ге́лий - всё э́то хими́ческие
Chlorine, sulfur, iron, helium — all these (are) chemical

элеме́нты.
elements.

Sentences from which the present tense of БЫТЬ is omitted
(except by implication) may be constructed using the word ВОТ
which like the French "voilà" means "there you see," "there
you have."

Углево́ды, белки́ и жиры́ — вот весьма́
Carbohydrates, proteins and fats — there you have extremely

ва́жные компоне́нты пи́щи.
important components of food.

Note also the frequent use of the predicative form of adjectives in constructing sentences in which the present tense of быть is implied so strongly that it is customarily omitted.

Скорость        испаре́ния        разли́чных        жи́дкостей
(The) rate      of evaporation    of different      liquids        (is)

разли́чна.
different.

Коли́чество воды́    в расте́ниях      о́чень велико́.
Quantity        of water in plants   (is) very    large.

Ато́мные      веса́    ма́рганца      и    желе́за        о́чень
Atomic        weights  of manganese  and  iron     (are)  very

бли́зки друг к дру́гу.
near       one  to (the) other.

Хими́ческие        сво́йства      бро́ма        бли́зки    к
(The)   chemical   properties    of bromine (are) near     to

сво́йствам      хло́ра.
(the) properties   of chlorine.

Формальдеги́д    да́же    в    сла́бых    раство́рах        си́льно
Formaldehyde     even    in   weak       solutions    (is)   strongly

ядови́т.
poisonous.

Кислоро́д    ма́ло    раствори́м в воде́.
Oxygen     (is) slightly soluble    in water.

Крити́ческая      температу́ра      для    азо́та        равна́
Critical          temperature       for    nitrogen (is)  equal    (to)

-147.1°, для кислоро́да   -188.8°, для водоро́да -239.9°.
-147.1°,   for   oxygen      -188.8°,   for  hydrogen -239.9°.

Эфи́р          чрезвыча́йно     лету́ч   и    о́чень   легко́
Ether    (is)    extremely        volatile  and   very    easily

воспламеня́ется.
inflames self.


Для  тел   в   амо́рфном     состоя́нии    сжима́емость,
For  bodies  in  (the) amorphous  condition      compressibility,

теплопрово́дность,  электропроводи́мость,  ско́рость све́та,
heat conductivity,     electrical conductivity,     speed      of light,

механи́ческие    сво́йства    по всем    направле́ниям
mechanical          properties  in  all     directions          (are)

одина́ковы.
identical.


Карби́ды    во́льфрама     чрезвыча́йно  тугопла́вки,  по
Carbides    of tungsten  (are)  extremely      refractory     with

                 тве́рдости бли́зки  к алма́зу   и  о́чень  ме́дленно
respect to hardness      near     to diamond  and very   slowly

понижа́ют  свою́ тве́рдость по  ме́ре    разоргева́ния.
decrease    their  hardness  with degree  of heating.


    Similar, closely related sentences involve the predicative
forms of the passive past participles of Russian verbs.  These
predicative forms are derived from passive past participles
whose stems end in –НН–, cf. § 60, p. 82, by dropping one –Н–
and then attaching the hard predicative adjective endings,
cf. p. 193.  No stem alteration is involved in deriving the
predicative forms of passive past participles whose stems end in
–Т–, cf. § 60, p. 82.

Земля́          окружена́   то́лстым    сло́ем во́здуха.
(The) earth (is) surrounded  by (a) thick  layer  of air.

На   тугоплáвкости          вóльфрама    оснóвано
On   (the) high melting    character   of tungsten    (is) based

егó применéние   для   нúтей    ламп    накаливáния.
its   use         for    filaments   of lamps of incandescence.

Рáзные    вúды    кривы́х    нагревáния    и    охлаждéния
Various    forms    of curves   of heating      and   of cooling

покáзаны       на   фигýре   48.
(are) shown     in   Figure    48.

Сравнúтельно    с   теóрией      гáзов,    кинетúческая
Comparatively    with (the) theory   of gases, (the) kinetic

теóрия жúдкостей    разрабóтана    óчень мáло.
theory   of liquids    (is) worked out     very    little.

Двойнóе лучепреломлéние    кристáллов     тéсно   свя́зано
Double    refraction         of crystals   (is) closely connected

с   их   анизотрóпией.
with their anisotropy.

Продáжный    иод    чáсто      загрязнён    разлúчными
Commercial    iodine often    (is) contaminated   by various

прúмесями.
impurities.

§ 121.   The   Partitive   and   the   Descriptive   Genitive in Simple Sentences.

     The genitive case may be used in simple sentences to indicate something of which a more or less limited amount is under consideration. Similarly, the genitive may be used to indicate a quality of which something partakes. The present tense of the verb быть may often be omitted from simple sentences involving the partitive or descriptive genitive, which is underlined in the following sentences.

Бензи́на    в не́фти        сравни́тельно    немно́го.
Of gasoline in petroleum (is) relatively        little.

В ураноно́сных      поро́дах    ра́дия        чрезвыча́йно
In uranium bearing    minerals    of radium (is) extremely

ма́ло.
little.

Изве́стно        о́чень мно́го  органи́ческих    соедине́ний.
There    are known very    many    organic        compounds.

В      во́здухе  ге́лия        ме́ньше    0.001%.
In    (the) air  of helium  (is) less than  0.001%.

Таки́х  коме́т  сейча́с        изве́стно  о́коло 170.
Of such comets  at present (are) known      about  170.

Продолжи́тельность    существова́ния    позитро́на
(The) duration    ·    of existence    of (a) positron  (is)

весьма́    мала,  поря́дка    $10^{-7}$ сек. (в  атмосфе́рном
extremely    small,  of (the) order  $10^{-7}$ sec.  (in  atmospheric

во́здухе).
air).

Газообра́зный  озо́н    голубова́того    цве́та.
Gaseous        ozone (is) of a bluish    color.

Ко́рковые про́бки  быва́ют  разнообра́зных    разме́ров  · и
Cork        stoppers exist    (of) various        dimensions  and

фо́рмы.
(of) form.

§ 122.  Sentences Involving Present Tense Forms of  Быть.

As already mentioned (§ 120,  p. 174) rather strong emphasis,
often coupled with the implication that the emphasized fact may
be unknown to the reader or even appear doubtful, is indicated by
the presence in a simple sentence of the present tense forms
есть "is" or суть "are" of Быть "to be."

Эне́ргия  есть  спосо́бность   производи́ть  рабо́ту.
Energy      is     (the) ability       to perform      work.


Давле́ние     га́за          есть   результа́т      уда́ров
Pressure      of (a)  gas    is     the  result      of  impacts

моле́кул        о   сте́нки     сосу́да,       в   кото́ром
of  molecules   on  (the) walls   of (the)  vessel   in  which

нахо́дится      газ.
finds  self     (the) gas.


Вычита́ние     есть  де́йствие,     обра́тное    сложе́нию.
Subtraction    is     (the) process   reverse     to addition.


Кро́ме        пова́ренной со́ли,  в  морско́й  воде́    есть   ещё
Besides        cooking         salt,  in  sea        water    are    also

го́рькие    со́ли.
bitter       salts.


Орби́ты       периоди́ческих       коме́т   суть   э́ллипсы    с
(The) orbits  of periodic            comets   are    ellipses   with

разли́чными    эксцентрисите́тами,  а,   сле́довательно, с
various         eccentricities           and  consequently     with

разли́чными   пери́одами враще́ний.
various        periods       of revolutions.

§ 123. Sentences Involving Russian Verbs Closely Similar in
Meaning to English "to be."

Although the present tense forms of the Russian verb быть
"to be" are little used, cf. §§ 120, 121; pp. 174, 178, several
Russian verbs having meanings closely similar to English "to be"
are widely used. Thus we have, for example, существовать
"to exist," бывать "to be in existence," "to exist," "to be,"
находиться literally "to find self," or, better, "to be located,"
"to occur," "to be." Other closely related verbs have already
been mentioned in discussing the instrumental case, (Lessons 12
and 13). Of these previously mentioned verbs, the reflexive of
являть -- явить "to show" is particularly widely used in
scientific Russian, cf. § 94, p. 136.

| Между | свойствами | звуковых | и | световых | волн |
|-------|------------|----------|---|----------|------|
| Between | properties | of sound | and | light | waves |

| существует | большое | сходство, | но | имеется | |
|------------|---------|-----------|-----|---------|-----|
| exists | great | similarity | but | has self | (there is) |

| также | и | глубокое | различие. |
|-------|---|----------|-----------|
| also | as well | (a) profound | difference. |

| Рулетки | | бывают | на 1, 2, 5, 10 и 20м. |
|---------|---|--------|----------------------|
| Tape | measures | exist | in 1, 2, 5, 10 and 20 m. |

| Громадные | количества | воды | находятся |
|-----------|------------|------|-----------|
| Enormous | quantities | of water | find self (occur) |

| на | земле. |
|----|--------|
| on | earth. |

| У | каждого | лабораторного | рабочего | стола | имеются |
|---|---------|---------------|----------|-------|---------|
| At | each | laboratory | working | desk | have |

| | | водопроводные | краны. |
|---|---|---------------|--------|
| self (there are) | | water pipe | faucets. |

| Витамины | являются | веществами, | необходимыми |
|----------|----------|-------------|--------------|
| Vitamins | show self | as substances | necessary |

для поддержания человеческой и животной жизни.
for  maintenance  of human  and animal  life.


§ 124. Reading Exercise.

### Металлы

Железо, медь, алюминий, свинец, золото, натрий –
всё это металлы, Значение металлов очень велико не
только[1] в быту и в промышленности, но также и в научном
отношении. Металлы представляют собой большинство химических элементов.

Металлы имеют всем[2] известный внешний вид, проводят
теплоту и электричество. Металлы также вытягиваются в
проволоку. Неметаллы лишены этих свойств.[3]

Металлов[4] около 70; из них[5] главные: лёгкие - щелочные, щелочноземельные, магний, алюминий; тяжёлые - цинк,
ртуть, олово, свинец, хром, марганец, железо, никкель,
кобальт, серебро, золото, платина.

Щелочные металлы - это элементы первой подгруппы I
группы периодической системы. Все[6] щелочные металлы од-
новалентны. В природе щелочные металлы встречаются почти
исключительно в виде солей. Соли щелочных металлов почти
все[5] растворимы в воде. Наиболее[7] распространённой солью
щелочных металлов является поваренная соль.

Щелочноземельные металлы - очень сходны с щелочными
металлами. Характерная особенность щелочноземельных металлов – образование нитридов $Ca_3N_2$, $Sr_3N_2$, $Ba_3N_2$ при
нагревании с азотом.

Лишь очень немногие металлы встречаются в природе
в самородным виде. Обыкновенно металлы находятся в разных рудах. Руды - это горные породы из которых добываются
металлы.

Алюминий - самый[8] распространённый металл на земле.
Алюминий - белый серебристый металл. Большие количества
электрической энергии употребляются для добывания алюминия
из руды - боксита.

Металлы - обыкновенно твёрдые вещества. Лишь ртуть
- жидкий металл при комнатной температуре.

Натрий, калий, кальций, свинец – очень мягкие металлы и легко режутся[9] ножом, в то время как хром, марганец, ванадий – очень твёрдые металлы.

Золото – драгоценный металл. В золотоносных породах золота[10] очень мало. Чистое золото прекрасного жёлтого[11] цвета. Золото применяется, главным образом,[12] в ювелирном деле.

Применение чистых металлов в производстве относительно ограничено. Сплавы соответствуют лучше[13] требованиям техники. Сплавы – это тела, которые содержат два или больше[14] химических элементов и обладают металлическими свойствами. Известно очень много сплавов.

## Notes

1. НЕ ТОЛЬКО -- НО ТАКЖЕ --, not only -- but also --.

2. ВСЕМ  "to all"  is in the dative plural case.

3. ЭТИХ СВОЙСТВ  "of these properties."  Both the noun СВОЙСТВ  and its pronoun modifier  ЭТИХ  are in the genitive plural case after  ЛИШЕНЫ  "(are) devoid."

4. Cf. § 121, sentences 3, 5.

5. ИЗ НИХ "of them."  Here НИХ one of the forms of ОН  "he," ОНО  "she," ОНА  "it" is in the genitive plural case after ИЗ.

6. ВСЕ  "all"  is the nominative plural form of the pronoun adjective ВЕСЬ  "all."

7. наиболее  "the most"  is used to form one type of superlative of adjectives as discussed in § 344, p. 541. Note that наиболее  like other adverbs has only one form.

8. самый распространённый  "the most widely distributed" exemplifies another form of superlative discussed in § 345, p. 544.

9. режутся  "cut self" is the reflexive form of the third person, plural present tense from the infinitive резать  "to be cutting," cf. § 198, p. 300.

10. Cf. § 121, sentence 2.

11.  Cf.  § 121,  sentence 7.

12.  гла́вным  о́бразом   is a phrase consisting of an adjective and noun, both in the instrumental case.  This phrase may be regarded as an idiom meaning "principally," "for the most part."

13.  лу́чше  "better" is the irregular comparative of хоро́ший "good," cf. § 334, p. 527. Here, лу́чше is used as an adverb.

14.  Various forms of бо́льшо́й  "big," "large" or бо́льший "bigger," "larger" are identical with respect to spelling, but differ as to accent.  If the first syllable is accented, then the meaning is "bigger," "larger" while placing the accent on the second syllable denotes "big," "large." The accent mark is quite often printed to avoid ambiguity.  This is one of the rare instances in which Russian printing establishments use an accent mark,  which  otherwise  is  practically  never  seen except in connection with foreign names.

§ 125.  Translation Exercise.

On translating the following sentences into Russian, the English words "is" and "are" are omitted.

1.  Zinc, chromium, manganese, silver, potassium -- all these are metals.
2.  All alkaline earth metals are divalent, (двухвале́нтны).
3.  The chlorides (хлори́ды) of metals are almost all soluble in water.
4.  The characteristic peculiarity of noble (благоро́дных) metals is resistance to the action of nitric (азо́тной) acid (кислоты́).
5.  Platinum and gold are relatively soft metals.
6.  Silver is a precious metal.
7.  In uranium bearing (ураноно́сных) ores there is of radium (ра́дия) very little.
8.  The use of silver (серебра́) in industry is relatively limited.
9.  There are known many metals.
10. Alloys are ordinarily solid substances at room temperature.

# LESSON 16

## SUMMARY OF REGULAR DECLENSION OF NOUNS AND ADJECTIVES

§ 126. Role of Noun and Adjective Endings in Expressing Thought.

The use of endings to form various cases and their role in expressing thought have been considered in previous lessons as follows:

| Case | Lesson |
|---|---|
| Nominative | 8 |
| Genitive | 11 |
| Dative | 14 |
| Accusative | 9 |
| Instrumental | 12, 13 |
| Prepositional | 10 |

§ 127. Cases Governed by Various Prepositions.

As noted in previous lessons, certain prepositions always govern the same case regardless of the shade of meaning involved. In contrast, certain other prepositions change their meaning more or less radically, depending on the case of the noun or other substantive which they govern. These two types of prepositions are separately grouped and summarized below.

Group I. Prepositions Always Governing the Same Case

Genitive[1]

| | |
|---|---|
| без (бе́зо) | without |
| вблизи́ | near, in the vicinity of |
| вме́сто | in place of |
| вне | outside |
| внутри́ | within |

---

[1] This list is incomplete.

| вокру́г | around |
| для | for |
| до | up to |
| из (изо) | away from, of |
| кро́ме | besides, aside from |
| от | from |
| по́сле | after |
| пре́жде | before |
| про́тив | against |
| у | near, at, by, of |

## Dative[1]

| благодаря́ | thanks to |
| вопреки́ | contrary to |
| к (ко) | toward, to |
| подо́бно | similarly to |
| пропорциона́льно | proportional to |
| согла́сно | in agreement with, according to |

## Accusative

| про | about, concerning |
| сквозь | through (the middle of) |
| че́рез | through, across, by way of (particularly in a figurative sense) |

## Instrumental

| ме́жду | between |
| над (на́до) | above |

## Prepositional

| при | at, near, during |

---

[1] This list is incomplete.

## Group II. Meaning of Preposition Depends on Case Governed

в (во)

with accusative<br>
into (indicating motion)<br>
in (with nouns indicating<br>
  time interval)

with prepositional<br>
within, in (no motion)

за

with accusative<br>
toward, after, for, as<br>
(range of meaning difficult<br>
  to define)

with instrumental<br>
behind (indicating position)

на

with accusative<br>
onto (indicating motion)

with prepositional<br>
on (indicating position)

о (об)(обо)

with accusative<br>
against, along (indicating<br>
  motion)

with prepositional<br>
about, concerning

перед

with accusative<br>
before (indicating motion)

with instrumental<br>
before (indicating position)

по

with dative<br>
according to, in compliance<br>
with, with respect to,<br>
along

with accusative<br>
for (indicating purpose)

with prepositional<br>
after

под (подо)

with accusative<br>
under (indicating motion)

with instrumental<br>
under (indicating position)

с (со)

| with genitive | with instrumental |
|---|---|
| from, since | with |

§ 128.  General Remarks on the Regular Declensions.

In §§ 129, 131, pp. 189, 191, the endings used to decline practically all Russian nouns and adjectives are summarized. It is much more important to understand the role of the endings in expressing thought than it is to memorize tabulations of endings. Skill in grasping the various shades of meaning expressed by endings is best developed by practice reading, using the tabulations for reference purposes as required. Becoming sufficiently familiar with these endings to be able to recognize them quickly is an important step in learning to read scientific Russian.

The burden imposed on the memory by the need to be able to recognize the various noun and adjective endings can be eased by taking note of certain similarities. Thus, in the singular, masculine and neuter nouns form most of their cases with the same endings. The corresponding adjective endings exhibit parallel similarities. In the plural, nouns, regardless of gender, take nearly the same endings, the genitive plural furnishing the majority of cases of divergence. Adjectives are declined with one set of endings in the plural regardless of gender.

Noun and adjective endings exist in two modifications, hard and soft. Certain nouns and adjectives are declined in all cases with hard endings, others exclusively with soft endings.

Another category is formed by nouns and adjectives which are declined partly with hard endings and partly with soft endings. In general, nouns and adjectives in this category are declined with hard endings except when soft endings are required for conformation with the following rules:

(1)  The letter ы may not follow any one of the letters Г, Ж, К, Х, Ч, Ш, or Щ but must be replaced by И.

(2)  The endings -е, -ее, -его, -ей, -ему, -ем, -ев, -ею are used when use of the corresponding hard endings would result in unaccented "о" following the letters Ж, Ц, Ч, Ш, Щ.

§ 129. Summary of Noun Case Endings.

## NOUNS

### Singular

| | Masc. | | Fem. | | Neuter | |
| | Hard | Soft | Hard | Soft | Hard | Soft |
|---|---|---|---|---|---|---|
| Nom. | -- | -й, -Ь | -а | -я, -Ь | -о | -е |
| Gen. | -а | -я | -ы | -и | -а | -я |
| Dat. | -у | -ю | -е | -и, -е | -у | -ю |
| Acc. | -- | -й, -Ь | -у | -ю, -Ь | -о | -е |
| Instr. | -ом | -ем | -ой (-ою) | -ей (-ею) | -ом | -ем |
| Prep. | -е | -е, -и | -е | -е, -и | -е | -е, -и |

### Plural

| | Masc. | | Fem. | | Neuter | |
| | Hard | Soft | Hard | Soft | Hard | Soft |
|---|---|---|---|---|---|---|
| Nom. | -ы | -и | -ы | -и | -а | -я |
| Gen. | -ов | -ев, -ей | -- | -Ь, -ей, -й | -- | -й |
| Dat. | -ам | -ям | -ам | -ям | -ам | -ям |
| Acc. | -ы | -и | -ы | -и | -а | -я |
| Instr. | -ами | -ями | -ами | -ями | -ами | -ями |
| Prep. | -ах | -ях | -ах | -ях | -ах | -ях |

§ 130. Tabulated Noun Declensions.

MASCULINE NOUNS

| | Hard Endings | Mixed Hard and Soft Endings | | Soft Endings | | |
|---|---|---|---|---|---|---|
| Nom. Sing. | áтом (atom) | луч (ray) | проводни́к (conductor) | рой (swarm) | эпите́лий (epithelium) | мно́житель (multiplier) |
| Key No. | 1 | 2 | 3 | 4 | 5 | 6 |
| Stem | áтом- | луч- | проводник- | ро- | эпители- | множител- |

| Hard Endings | Mixed Hard and Soft Endings | | | Soft Endings | |
|---|---|---|---|---|---|

### Singular

| | Hard | Mixed Hard and Soft | | | Soft | |
|---|---|---|---|---|---|---|
| Nom. | а́том | луч | проводни́к | рой | эпите́лий | мно́житель |
| Gen. | а́тома | луча́ | проводника́ | ро́я | эпите́лия | мно́жителя |
| Dat. | а́тому | лучу́ | проводнику́ | ро́ю | эпите́лию | мно́жителю |
| Acc. | а́том | луч | проводни́к | рой | эпите́лий | мно́житель |
| Instr. | а́томом | лучо́м | проводнико́м | ро́ем | эпите́лием | мно́жителем |
| Prep. | а́томе | луче́ | проводнике́ | ро́е | эпите́лии | мно́жителе |

### Plural

| | | | | | | |
|---|---|---|---|---|---|---|
| Nom. | а́томы | лучи́ | проводники́ | рои́ | эпите́лии | мно́жители |
| Gen. | а́томов | луче́й | проводнико́в | роёв | эпите́лиев | мно́жителей |
| Dat. | а́томам | луча́м | проводника́м | роя́м | эпите́лиям | мно́жителям |
| Acc. | а́томы | лучи́ | проводники́ | рои́ | эпите́лии | мно́жители |
| Instr. | а́томами | луча́ми | проводника́ми | роя́ми | эпите́лиями | мно́жителями |
| Prep. | а́томах | луча́х | проводника́х | роя́х | эпите́лиях | мно́жителях |

## FEMININE NOUNS

| | Hard Endings | Mixed Hard and Soft Endings | | | Soft Endings | |
|---|---|---|---|---|---|---|
| Nom. Sing. | моле́кула (molecules) | едини́ца (unit) | нау́ка (science) | неде́ля (week) | тео́рия (theory) | смесь (mixture) |
| Key No. | 7 | 8 | 9 | 10 | 11 | 12 |
| Stem | молекул- | единиц- | наук- | недел- | теори- | смес- |

### Singular

| | | | | | | |
|---|---|---|---|---|---|---|
| Nom. | моле́кула | едини́ца | нау́ка | неде́ля | тео́рия | смесь |
| Gen. | моле́кулы | едини́цы | нау́ки | неде́ли | тео́рии | сме́си |
| Dat. | моле́куле | едини́це | нау́ке | неде́ле | тео́рии | сме́си |
| Acc. | моле́кулу | едини́цу | нау́ку | неде́лю | тео́рию | смесь |
| Instr. | моле́кулой (моле́кулою) | едини́цей (едини́цею) | нау́кой (нау́кою) | неде́лей (неде́лею) | тео́рией (тео́риею) | сме́сью |
| Prep. | моле́куле | едини́це | нау́ке | неде́ле | тео́рии | сме́си |

### Plural

| | | | | | | |
|---|---|---|---|---|---|---|
| Nom. | моле́кулы | едини́цы | нау́ки | неде́ли | тео́рии | сме́си |
| Gen. | моле́кул | едини́ц | нау́к | неде́ль | тео́рий | сме́сей |
| Dat. | моле́кулам | едини́цам | нау́кам | неде́лям | тео́риям | сме́сям |
| Acc. | моле́кулы | едини́цы | нау́ки | неде́ли | тео́рии | сме́си |
| Instr. | моле́кулами | едини́цами | нау́ками | неде́лями | тео́риями | сме́сями |
| Prep. | моле́кулах | едини́цах | нау́ках | неде́лях | тео́риях | сме́сях |

NEUTER NOUNS

| | Hard Endings | Mixed Hard and Soft Endings | | Soft Endings |
|---|---|---|---|---|
| Nom. Sing. | вещество́ | учи́лище | по́ле | явле́ние |
| Key No. | 13 | 14 | 15 | 16 |
| Stem | веществ- | учи́лищ- | пол- | явлени- |

### Singular

| | | | | |
|---|---|---|---|---|
| Nom. | вещество́ | учи́лище | по́ле | явле́ние |
| Gen. | вещества́ | учи́лища | по́ля | явле́ния |
| Dat. | веществу́ | учи́лищу | по́лю | явле́нию |
| Acc. | вещество́ | учи́лище | по́ле | явле́ние |
| Instr. | вещество́м | учи́лищем | по́лем | явле́нием |
| Prep. | веществе́ | учи́лище | по́ле | явле́нии |

### Plural

| | | | | |
|---|---|---|---|---|
| Nom. | вещества́ | учи́лища | поля́ | явле́ния |
| Gen. | веще́ств | учи́лищ | поле́й | явле́ний |
| Dat. | вещества́м | учи́лищам | поля́м | явле́ниям |
| Acc. | вещества́ | учи́лища | поля́ | явле́ния |
| Instr. | вещества́ми | учи́лищами | поля́ми | явле́ниями |
| Prep. | вещества́х | учи́лищах | поля́х | явле́ниях |

## § 131. Summary of Adjective Case Endings.

## SINGULAR ADJECTIVES

| | Masc. | | Fem. | | Neuter | |
|---|---|---|---|---|---|---|
| | Hard | Soft | Hard | Soft | Hard | Soft |
| Nom. | -ый,-ой | -ий | -ая | -яя | -ое | -ее |
| Gen. | -ого | -его | -ой | -ей | -ого | -его |
| Dat. | -ому | -ему | -ой | -ей | -ому | -ему |
| Acc. | -ый,-ой | -ий | -ую | -юю | -ое | -ее |
| Instr. | -ым | -им | -ой | -ей | -ым | -им |
| Prep. | -ом | -ем | -ой | -ей | -ом | -ем |

## PLURAL  ADJECTIVES

|  | Masc.-Fem.-Neuter | |
|---|---|---|
|  | Hard | Soft |
| Nom. | -ые | -ие |
| Gen. | -ых | -их |
| Dat. | -ым | -им |
| Acc. | -ые | -ие |
| Instr. | -ыми | -ими |
| Prep. | -ых | -их |

## PREDICATIVE  FORMS  --  ADJECTIVES

|  | Masc. | | Fem. | | Neuter | |
|---|---|---|---|---|---|---|
|  | Hard | Soft | Hard | Soft | Hard | Soft |
| Sing. | — | -ь | -а | -я | -о | -е |

|  | Masc.-Fem.-Neuter | |
|---|---|---|
|  | Hard | Soft |
| Plural | -ы | -и |

§ 132.  Tabulated Adjective Declensions.

## HARD  ENDINGS  --  ADJECTIVES

Stem      стар- ,  old
            Key No. 17

### Singular

|  | Masc. | Fem. | Neuter |
|---|---|---|---|
| Nom. | ста́рый | ста́рая | ста́рое |
| Gen. | ста́рого | ста́рой | ста́рого |
| Dat. | ста́рому | ста́рой | ста́рому |

|       | Masc. | Fem. | Neuter |
|-------|-------|------|--------|
| Acc.  | ста́рый | ста́рую | ста́рое |
| Instr. | ста́рым | ста́рой | ста́рым |
|       |       | (ста́рою) |      |
| Prep. | ста́ром | ста́рой | ста́ром |

### Plural

#### Masc.-Fem.-Neuter

| | |
|--|--|
| Nom. | ста́рые |
| Gen. | ста́рых |
| Dat. | ста́рым |
| Acc. | ста́рые |
| Instr. | ста́рыми |
| Prep. | ста́рых |

### Predicative Forms

|       | Masc. | Fem. | Neuter |
|-------|-------|------|--------|
| Sing. | стар  | стара́ | ста́ро |

#### Masc.-Fem.-Neuter

| | |
|--|--|
| Plural | ста́ры |

## LESSON 16

## HARD ENDINGS -- ADJECTIVES

Stem      ЖИВ- ,    live, alive
Key No. 18

### Singular

|       | Masc.   | Fem.              | Neuter |
|-------|---------|-------------------|--------|
| Nom.  | живо́й   | жива́я             | живо́е  |
| Gen.  | живо́го  | живо́й             | живо́го |
| Dat.  | живо́му  | живо́й             | живо́му |
| Acc.  | живо́й   | живу́ю             | живо́е  |
| Instr.| живы́м   | живо́й (живо́ю)    | живы́м  |
| Prep. | живо́м   | живо́й             | живо́м  |

### Plural

**Masc.-Fem.-Neuter**

| Nom.   | живы́е  |
|--------|--------|
| Gen.   | живы́х  |
| Dat.   | живы́м  |
| Acc.   | живы́е  |
| Instr. | живы́ми |
| Prep.  | живы́х  |

### Predicative Forms

|       | Masc. | Fem.  | Neuter |
|-------|-------|-------|--------|
| Sing. | жив   | жива́ | жи́во   |

**Masc.-Fem.-Neuter**

| Plural | живы́ |
|--------|------|

## SOFT ENDINGS -- ADJECTIVES

<u>Stem</u>     син-,    blue
Key No. 19

### Singular

|       | Masc. | Fem. | Neuter |
|-------|-------|------|--------|
| <u>Nom.</u> | синий | синяя | синее |
| <u>Gen.</u> | синего | синей | синего |
| <u>Dat.</u> | синему | синей | синему |
| <u>Acc.</u> | синий | синюю | синее |
| <u>Instr.</u> | синим | синей | синим |
| <u>Prep.</u> | синем | синей | синем |

### Plural

**Masc.-Fem.-Neuter**

| | |
|---|---|
| <u>Nom.</u> | синие |
| <u>Gen.</u> | синих |
| <u>Dat.</u> | синим |
| <u>Acc.</u> | синие |
| <u>Instr.</u> | синими |
| <u>Prep.</u> | синих |

### Predicative Forms

|       | Masc. | Fem. | Neuter |
|-------|-------|------|--------|
| <u>Sing.</u> | синь | синя | сине |

**Masc.-Fem.-Neuter**

| | |
|---|---|
| <u>Plural</u> | сини |

## MIXED HARD AND SOFT ENDINGS -- ADJECTIVES

Stem        сух-,      dry
            Key No. 20

### Singular

|        | Masc. | Fem. | Neuter |
|--------|-------|------|--------|
| Nom.   | сухо́й | суха́я | сухо́е |
| Gen.   | сухо́го | сухо́й | сухо́го |
| Dat.   | сухо́му | сухо́й | сухо́му |
| Acc.   | сухо́й | суху́ю | сухо́е |
| Instr. | сухи́м | сухо́й | сухи́м |
|        |       | (сухо́ю) |      |
| Prep.  | сухо́м | сухо́й | сухо́м |

### Plural

#### Masc.-Fem.-Neuter

| Nom.   | сухи́е |
|--------|-------|
| Gen.   | сухи́х |
| Dat.   | сухи́м |
| Acc.   | сухи́е |
| Instr. | сухи́ми |
| Prep.  | сухи́х |

### Predicative Forms

|       | Masc. | Fem. | Neuter |
|-------|-------|------|--------|
| Sing. | сух   | суха́ | су́хо |

#### Masc.-Fem.-Neuter

| Plural | су́хи |
|--------|------|

## MIXED HARD AND SOFT ENDINGS -- ADJECTIVES

Stem    электрическ-,   electrical
Key No. 21

### Singular

| | Masc. | Fem. | Neuter |
|---|---|---|---|
| Nom. | электри́ческий | электри́ческая | электри́ческое |
| Gen. | электри́ческого | электри́ческой | электри́ческого |
| Dat. | электри́ческому | электри́ческой | электри́ческому |
| Acc. | электри́ческий | электри́ческую | электри́ческое |
| Instr. | электри́ческим | электри́ческой | электри́ческим |
| | | (электри́ческою) | |
| Prep. | электри́ческом | электри́ческой | электри́ческом |

### Plural

**Masc.-Fem.-Neuter**

| | |
|---|---|
| Nom. | электри́ческие |
| Gen. | электри́ческих |
| Dat. | электри́ческим |
| Acc. | электри́ческие |
| Instr. | электри́ческими |
| Prep. | электри́ческих |

### Predicative Forms

(Do Not Exist)

## MIXED HARD AND SOFT ENDINGS -- ADJECTIVES

Stem        свеж- ,      fresh
            Key No. 22

### Singular

|        | Masc.   | Fem.              | Neuter  |
|--------|---------|-------------------|---------|
| Nom.   | свéжий  | свéжая            | свéжее  |
| Gen.   | свéжего | свéжей            | свéжего |
| Dat.   | свéжему | свéжей            | свéжему |
| Acc.   | свéжий  | свéжую            | свéжее  |
| Instr. | свéжим  | свéжей            | свéжим  |
|        |         | (свéжею)          |         |
| Prep.  | свéжем  | свéжей            | свéжем  |

### Plural

#### Masc.-Fem.-Neuter

| Nom.   | свéжие  |
|--------|---------|
| Gen.   | свéжих  |
| Dat.   | свéжим  |
| Acc.   | свéжие  |
| Instr. | свéжими |
| Prep.  | свéжих  |

### Predicative Forms

|        | Masc.  | Fem.    | Neuter |
|--------|--------|---------|--------|
| Sing.  | свеж   | свежá   | свéже  |

#### Masc.-Fem.-Neuter

| Plural | свéжи  |

§ 133. Reading Exercise.

Паровы́е маши́ны[1] и турби́ны

При по́мощи паровы́х маши́н и турби́н теплова́я эне́ргия
па́ра превраща́ется в эне́ргию механи́ческого движе́ния. Пар,
кото́рый[2] применя́ется для получе́ния механи́ческого движе́ния
с по́мощью маши́н и турби́н, почти́ всегда́ есть водяно́й пар.
Преобразова́ние воды́ в пар происхо́дит в котла́х за счёт
тепла́ сгора́ния то́плива.

В паровы́х маши́нах пар из котла́ да́вит на по́ршень.
После́дний соверша́ет прямолине́йно-возвра́тное движе́ние,
кото́рое[3] при по́мощи кривоши́пного механи́зма преобразу́ется
во враща́тельное движе́ние ва́ла. В паровы́х маши́нах, два́жды[4]
во вре́мя одного́ оборо́та ва́ла ско́рость поступа́тельного дви-
же́ния по́ршня обраща́ется в нуль. Поэ́тому парово́е маши́ны
характеризу́ются сравни́тельно небольши́м число́м оборо́тов ва́-
ла в едини́цу вре́мени.[5]

Но мо́жно[6] получа́ть при по́мощи па́ра враща́тельное
движе́ние непосре́дственно без уча́стия по́ршня и кривоши́па.
Маши́ны, в кото́рых[7] эне́ргия па́ра приво́дит вал во[8] враща́-
тельное движе́ние без по́мощи по́ршня и кривоши́па, называ́ются
паровы́ми турби́нами. Сло́во ту́рбо зна́чить по-лати́ни "вихрь,
крутя́щийся".[9]

В настоя́щее[10] вре́мя име́ется о́чень мно́го паровы́х
турби́н[11] разнообра́зных констру́кций. Просты́м приме́ром па-
ровы́х турби́н мо́жет служи́ть[12] турби́на Лава́ля.

Гла́вной ча́стью турби́ны Лава́ля явля́ется стально́й
диск, о́чень утолщённый к це́нтру. По окру́жности ди́ска рас-
поло́жено большо́е число́ небольши́х лопа́точек. Тру́бки, кото́-
рые называ́ются со́плами, направля́ют струю́ па́ра на лопа́тки
турби́ны. Пар идёт[13] че́рез со́пла и при э́том постепе́нно рас-
ширя́ется. Пар, дви́жущийся[14] с большо́й ско́ростью, попада́ет
на лопа́тки и отдаёт ди́ску значи́тельную часть свое́й эне́р-
гии.

В турби́не Лава́ля ско́рости враще́ния достига́ются
о́чень больши́е. Ма́ленькая турби́на Лава́ля, мо́щностью до 10
л. с.,[15] име́ет диск диа́метром[16] 10 -15 см. Э́тот диск де́лает
3000 оборо́тов в мину́ту. Така́я больша́я ско́рость ре́дко тре́-

буется в практике.. Поэтому часто приходится соединять[17] турбину Лаваля с рабочей машиной при помощи системы зубчатых колёс, что[18] даёт возможность рабочей машине работать со значительно уменьшённой скоростью.

Современные турбины имеют сложную конструкцию с множеством дисков, которые сидят на общем валу. Скорость вращения таких турбин является сравнительно медленной – от[19] 1000 до 3000 оборотов в минуту.

## Notes

1. паровые машины    literally means  "vapor machines," but, in general, is used with the meaning  "steam engines."

2. который   "which" refers to  пар, here used in the sense of  "vapor" although quite often  пар  is used with the meaning "steam."   Use of generic terminology to designate a specific substance or property is by no means uncommon.  Thus,   алкоголь "alcohol",  is   commonly   used   to   mean   "ethyl   alcohol." растворимый   "soluble", unless  otherwise  qualified,  means "soluble in water," etc.

3. которое   "which" carries a neuter ending because it here refers to the neuter noun   движение  "movement."

4. дважды   is an adverb meaning  "twice."

5. времени   "of time" is the genitive singular of  время  a neuter noun meaning  "time."

6. можно   получать  "it is possible to obtain."  Note that the verb "to be" is implied by  можно.

7. в которых   "in which" here   которых , which refers to машины,   is in the prepositional case following  в.

8. во  is used in place of  в  to facilitate pronunciation which would otherwise be difficult due to the consonant combination  вр in  вращательное .

9. крутящийся   "whirling (self)" is one form of the present active participle (reflexive as denoted by –ся) from the infinitive  крутить  "to be turning," "to be whirling."

10. в настоя́щее вре́мя    "at the present time." Here настоя́щее is the neuter accusative form of настоя́щий which is closely related to the infinitive настоя́ть.

11. See first and fourth Russian sentences in § 123, p. 181.

12. мо́жет  служи́ть  "is able to serve."

13. For note on идёт  see  p. 139, Note 6.

14. дви́жущийся  "moving self" is one form of the present active participle (reflexive as denoted by -ся) from the infinitive дви́гать  "to move."

15. л. с. is an abbreviation for лошади́ная  си́ла "horse-power." The abbreviation is used not only for the nominative but also for other cases. The adjective лошади́ный  is derived from ло́шадь (fem.) "horse," "mare."

16. диа́метром  "with diameter." Here диа́метром is in the instrumental case, cf. § 118, sentence 7.

17. прихо́дится  соединя́ть  "it behooves self to combine." Such use of an infinitive in an impersonal sentence is quite common in Russian.

18. что даёт возмо́жность -- рабо́тать --  "which gives the possibility -- to work." Here an infinitive, namely рабо́тать,  is used as a noun.

19. от 1000 до 3000  "from 1000 to 3000."

§ 134.  Translation Exercise.

1. Steam engines and turbines are used (use self) for (для) conversion of heat energy into energy of mechanical motion.
2. Steam is produced (produces self) in boilers by evaporation (испаре́нием) of water.
3. In turbines (турби́нах)  heat energy is converted into rotatory motion without participation of piston and crank shaft.
4. The piston in steam engines carries out a linear-reciprocating movement.
5. In the Laval turbine (turbine of Laval) the steam passes through the nozzles and strikes (falls on) the blades.

x

6. The steam gradually expands in the nozzle.
7. The   Laval   turbine   (turbine   of   Laval)   is   characterized (characterizes self) by high speed of rotation.
8. In other words, the shaft of  a  Laval turbine (turbine of Laval) makes  a  large  (большóе)   number  (числó )  of rotations in a unit of time.
9. The  high  speed  of  a  Laval  turbine (turbine of Laval) often is  reduced  (уменьшáется)   with the aid of a system of gears (tooth wheels).
10. Modern steam engines have complicated construction.

## LESSON 17

## PRONOUNS AND RELATED WORDS (PART I)

§ 135. Introductory Note.

English often makes use of certain words, usually termed pronouns, e.g., "I," "we," "us," "he," "him," "it," "they," "them," for convenience in referring to persons and things. Corresponding pronouns also are used in Russian, e.g., Я "I," ОН "he," ОНИ́ "they," etc. Such pronouns are declined in Russian in a manner similar to nouns and adjectives.

Another important class of words, used like adjectives but closely related to pronouns, indicate possession. The Russian possessives МОЙ "my," НаШ "our," ТВОЙ "your" (intimate form) and ВаШ "your" (polite form) are used as noun modifiers and are declined like adjectives to indicate agreement as to gender, number and case with the noun modified. In contrast, three other Russian possessives, namely, его́ "his" or "its," её "her" and ИХ "their," are not declined but are used in one form only, in spite of the fact that these possessives are also used as direct modifiers of nouns.

The relative pronoun КОТО́РЫЙ "which" is declined with adjective endings. Special considerations governing the use of various cases of КОТО́РЫЙ are discussed in § 141, p. 210.

The Russian demonstratives э́ТОТ "this," ТОТ "that" and Тако́й "such" are used like their English counterparts, both independently as pronouns and as noun modifiers. The declension of э́ТОТ, ТОТ and Тако́й closely resembles that of adjectives.

Various other pronouns and related words are summarized in Lesson 18.

The fact that Russian pronouns and related words are declined makes it necessary to learn to recognize their various forms. The burden thereby imposed on the memory may be eased by noting numerous points of similarity to the declension of adjectives and nouns. As a further aid, the various forms of pronouns and related words are presented as tabulations in this

lesson and the one following.  These tabulations should be used
for reference purposes and not as instruments for torturing the
memory.

§ 136.  Declension of Russian Personal Pronouns.

### Singular

|        | Я - I<br>(Informal) | ТЫ - you<br>(Informal) | ОН - he, ОНА́ - she, ОНО́ - it | | |
|--------|------|------|------|------|------|
|        |      |      | ОН   | она́ | оно́ |
| Nom.   | я    | ТЫ   | ОН   | она́ | оно́ |
| Gen.   | меня́ | тебя́ | его́ | её  | его́ |
| Dat.   | мне  | тебе́ | ему́ | ей  | ему́ |
| Acc.   | меня́ | тебя́ | его́ | её  | его́ |
| Instr. | мной | тобо́й | им  | ей (е́ю) | им |
| Prep.  | мне  | тебе́ | (Footnote 1) | | |

#### Used After Prepositions

|        |      |      |      |      |      |
|--------|------|------|------|------|------|
| Nom.   |      |      | (Footnote 2) | | |
| Gen.   |      |      | него́ | неё | него́ |
| Dat.   |      |      | нему́ | ней | нему́ |
| Acc.   |      |      | него́ | неё | него́ |
| Instr. |      |      | ним  | ней (не́ю) | ним |
| Prep.  |      |      | нем  | ней | нем |

### Plural

|        | МЫ - we | ВЫ - you<br>(formal) | ОНИ́ - they | Used After Prepositions |
|--------|------|------|------|------|
| Nom.   | МЫ   | ВЫ   | они́ | (Footnote 2) |
| Gen.   | нас  | вас  | их   | них |
| Dat.   | нам  | вам  | им   | ним |
| Acc.   | нас  | вас  | их   | них |
| Instr. | на́ми | ва́ми | и́ми | ни́ми |
| Prep.  | нас  | вас  | (Footnote 1) | них |

[1] These forms are lacking since the prepositional is used only after prepositions.
[2] Since no prepositions govern the nominative, these forms are lacking.

§ 137. Sentences Illustrating Use of Russian Personal Pronouns.

As noted above, personal pronouns are declined following the same general pattern as nouns. Use of the various cases of personal pronouns follows the same rules as those which determine the use of different cases of nouns.

Various minor peculiarities in the use of Russian personal pronouns appear worthy of note.

In English, nouns referring to nearly all material objects, ideas, etc., are regarded as neuter in gender. Russian, in contrast, regards such nouns as книга "book," теория "theory," сталь "steel" as feminine; атом "atom," натрий "sodium," автомобиль "automobile" are masculine. In general, agreement as to gender exists between a Russian pronoun and the noun to which it refers. As a result, English "it" will be required to translate various forms of она "she" and он "he" when used -- as frequently occurs -- to replace nouns denoting objects, ideas, etc., regarded as neuter in English.

Another point worth noting is the fact that the Russian verb endings are such that no danger of being misunderstood arises in many sentences even if a personal pronoun -- actually, the subject of the sentence or clause -- is not explicitly stated. As a consequence of this, translation of a Russian sentence into English often requires that a verb ending be observed with care in order to determine which personal pronoun is to be used as subject of the sentence in English. We shall speak of this again when considering verb conjugations.

| Я -- американский | химик. |
|---|---|
| I (am) an American | chemist. |

| Естествознание | имеет | для | меня | очень | большое |
|---|---|---|---|---|---|
| Natural science | has | for | me | very | great |

| значение. |
|---|
| significance. |

| Соль | нам | необходима | для питания. |
|---|---|---|---|
| Salt | to us (is) essential | | for nourishment. |

Чи́стое    зо́лото    –    мя́гкий    мета́лл;    оно́    облада́ет
Pure       gold      (is)  (a) soft   metal;      it     possesses

жёлтым    цве́том    и    си́льным    бле́ском.
(a) yellow  color    and strong      luster.


Медь    –    весьма́    ва́жный    мета́лл;    она́    широко́
Copper  (is)  (a) very  important  metal;     she (it)  widely

применя́ется    в электроте́хнике.
uses (self) (is used)   in electrical technology.


Грани́т    –    твёрдый    и    пло́тный    ка́мень;    он    состои́т
Granite    (is)  (a) hard   and dense      stone;     he (it)  consists

из ква́рца, полево́го шпа́та    и    слюды́.
of quartz,  feldspar           and mica.


Стекло́    и    посу́да        из    него́    изготовля́ются
Glass      and  ware    (made)  from it       prepare self

                на стёкольных    заво́дах.
(are prepared)  at glass         factories.


Жи́дкость    выта́лкивает    погружённое    в    неё
(A) liquid    pushes out      (a) plunged    into  her (it)

те́ло    с    си́лой;    ра́вной    ве́су    вы́тесненной
body    with  (a) force  equal     to (the) weight  of (the) displaced

жи́дкости.
liquid.


Ста́рые    шра́мы на пове́рхности    земли́    говоря́т    нам
Old        scars  on (the) surface    of (the) earth  speak    to us

о    столкнове́ниях    её    с    метеори́тами    и
concerning  collisions   of her with meteorites     and

коме́тами.
comets.

§ 138.  Declension of Russian Possessives.

As already noted, cf. § 135, p. 203, the possessives МОЙ "my," НаШ "our," ТВОЙ "your" (intimate form) and ВаШ "your" (polite form) are declined like adjectives; его "his" or "its," её "her" and ИХ "their" are not declined.

МОЙ , my -- Key No. 23

### Singular

|        | Masc.           | Fem.           | Neuter     |
|--------|-----------------|----------------|------------|
| Nom.   | мой             | моя́           | моё        |
| Gen.   | моего́          | мое́й          | моего́     |
| Dat.   | моему́          | мое́й          | моему́     |
| Acc.   | мой (моего́)[1] | мою́           | моё        |
| Instr. | мои́м           | мое́й (мое́ю)  | мои́ми     |
| Prep.  | моём            | мое́й          | моём       |

### Plural

#### Masc.-Fem.-Neuter

|        |                  |
|--------|------------------|
| Nom.   | мои́             |
| Gen.   | мои́х            |
| Dat.   | мои́м            |
| Acc.   | мои́ (мои́х)[1]  |
| Instr. | мои́ми           |
| Prep.  | мои́х            |

[1] This form is used when modifying nouns referring to living entities, cf. § 158, p. 244.

наш , our -- Key No. 24

## Singular

|       | Masc.          | Fem.              | Neuter   |
|-------|----------------|-------------------|----------|
| Nom.  | наш            | на́ша             | на́ше    |
| Gen.  | на́шего        | на́шей            | на́шего  |
| Dat.  | на́шему        | на́шей            | на́шему  |
| Acc.  | наш (на́шего)[1] | на́шу           | на́ше    |
| Instr.| на́шим         | на́шей (на́шею)   | на́шим   |
| Prep. | на́шем         | на́шей            | нашем    |

## Plural

### Masc.-Fem.-Neuter

| Nom.  | на́ши          |
|-------|----------------|
| Gen.  | на́ших         |
| Dat.  | на́шим         |
| Acc.  | на́ши (на́ших)[1] |
| Instr.| на́шими        |
| Prep. | на́ших         |

§ 139. Sentences Illustrating Russian Possessives.

As pointed out before, § 137, p. 205, Russian sentences will often use the pronoun она́ "she" or a form derived therefrom in such a way as to require translation into English by the pronoun "it." For similar reasons её, literally "her," will often require translation by English "its." Note that его is used to mean both "his" and "its." Usually, in scientific writing его will require translation by "its."

По          добы́че  зо́лота  на́ша  страна́  занима́ет
With regard to production of gold    our    country   occupies

тепе́рь  тре́тье  ме́сто  в  ми́ре.
now    (the) third place  in  (the) world.

[1]  This form is used when modifying nouns referring to living entities (§ 158, p. 244).

Ткани        нашего       организма    состоят      главным
(The) tissues  of our      organism    consist      for principal

образом из   соединений   углерода.
part      of   compounds    of carbon.


Вода имеет   громадное    значение     в  нашей  жизни.
Water has    enormous     importance   in  our    life.


Массы        тел                    пропорциональны      их
(The) masses  of bodies  (are)  proportional              to their

весам.
weights.


Растворимость   газа        зависит    от  его    природы,
(The) solubility  of (a) gas  depends    on  his (its)  nature,

давления,       температуры          и     от    вида
(the) pressure,  (the) temperature    and   on    (the) type

растворителя.
of solvent.


Полярность      молекул      воды     и  её      большая
(The) polarity   of molecules  of water  and her (its)  big (high)

диэлектрическая          постоянная           обусловливают
dielectric                constant             cause

распадение      молекул      электролитов      на  ионы.
disintegration   of molecules  of electrolytes    into ions.


Электропроводимость       меди        зависит  от  её
(The) electrical conductivity  of copper  depends  from her (its)

чистоты.
purity.

§ 140. Declension of the Relative Pronoun кото́рый "which."

This is declined using the regular adjective endings.

### кото́рый which

#### Singular

| | Masc. | Fem. | Neuter |
|---|---|---|---|
| Nom. | кото́рый | кото́рая | кото́рое |
| Gen. | кото́рого | кото́рой | кото́рого |
| Dat. | кото́рому | кото́рой | кото́рому |
| Acc. | кото́рый (кото́рого) [1] | кото́рую | кото́рое |
| Instr. | кото́рым | кото́рой (кото́рою) | кото́рым |
| Prep. | кото́ром | кото́рой | кото́ром |

#### Plural

#### Masc.-Fem.-Neuter

| | |
|---|---|
| Nom. | кото́рые |
| Gen. | кото́рых |
| Dat. | кото́рым |
| Acc. | кото́рые (кото́рых) [1] |
| Instr. | кото́рыми |
| Prep. | кото́рых |

§ 141. Sentences Illustrating Use of кото́рый.

The nature of the relative pronoun кото́рый "which" is such that within its own subordinate clause it plays an independent role, from which the case to be used is determined. On the other hand, the relative pronoun, notwithstanding its independent role in its own clause, stands in a subordinate position to its antecedent noun,

[1] This form is used when referring to living entities (§ 158, p. 244).

whose gender and number determine the gender and number of the
form in which the relative pronoun is used. This point becomes
clearer on considering example sentences.

| Прекра́сный | приме́р | спа́йности | представля́ет | слюда́, |
|---|---|---|---|---|
| (A) splendid | example | of cleavage | presents | mica, |

| кото́рая | легко́ | разделя́ется | | на | то́нкие |
|---|---|---|---|---|---|
| which | easily | divides self | (is divided) | into | thin |

| пласти́нки. |
|---|
| sheets. |

| Ры́бы | непреры́вно | пропуска́ют | во́ду | че́рез |
|---|---|---|---|---|
| Fish | continuously | pass[1] | water | through |

| жа́бры, | кото́рые | заменя́ют | им | лёгкие. |
|---|---|---|---|---|
| (their) gills, | which | replace | to them | lungs. |

| Си́ла, | с | кото́рой | те́ло | притя́гивается | к |
|---|---|---|---|---|---|
| (The) force | with | which | (a) body | pulls self | to |

| земле́, | называ́ется | ве́сом | те́ла. |
|---|---|---|---|
| (the) earth | calls self | (the) weight | of (the) body. |

| Гла́вное | ква́нтовое | число́ | характеризу́ет | слой, |
|---|---|---|---|---|
| (The) principal | quantum | number | characterizes | (the) shell |

| к кото́рому | принадлежи́т | электро́н. |
|---|---|---|
| to which | pertains | (the) electron. |

| Раствори́мость | га́зов | в | воде́ | увели́чивается |
|---|---|---|---|---|
| (The) solubility | of gases | in | water | increases self (is |

| | при | увеличе́нии | давле́ния, | под | кото́рым |
|---|---|---|---|---|---|
| increased) | on | increase | of (the) pressure | under | which |

| нахо́дится | газ. |
|---|---|
| finds self (is) | (the) gas. |

---

[1] Honi soit qui mal y pense!

| Óкислы, | котóрым | соотвéтствуют | кислóты, | нóсят |
|---------|---------|--------------|---------|-------|
| Oxides, | to which | correspond | acids, | bear |

| óбщее | назвáние | – ангидрúды | кислóт. |
|-------|----------|-------------|---------|
| (the) general | name | — anhydrides | of acids. |

§ 142. Declension of Russian Demonstratives.

э́ТОТ -- this

### Singular

| | Masc. | Fem. | Neuter |
|------|-------|------|--------|
| Nom. | э́тот | э́та | э́то |
| Gen. | э́того | э́той | э́того |
| Dat. | э́тому | э́той | э́тому |
| Acc. | э́тот (э́того)[1] | э́ту | э́то |
| Instr. | э́тим | э́той (э́тою) | э́тим |
| Prep. | э́том | э́той | э́том |

### Plural

| | Masc.-Fem.-Neuter |
|------|-------------------|
| Nom. | э́ти |
| Gen. | э́тих |
| Dat. | э́тим |
| Acc. | э́ти (э́тих)[1] |
| Instr. | э́тими |
| Prep. | э́тих |

---

[1] This form is used when this demonstrative refers to living entities (§ 158, p. 244).

ТОТ -- that

### Singular

|  | Masc. | Fem. | Neuter |
|---|---|---|---|
| Nom. | тот | та | то |
| Gen. | того́ | той | того́ |
| Dat. | тому́ | той | тому́ |
| Acc. | тот (того́)[1] | ту | то |
| Instr. | тем | той(то́ю) | тем |
| Prep. | том | той | том |

### Plural

**Masc.-Fem.-Neuter**

| Nom. | те |
|---|---|
| Gen. | тех |
| Dat. | тем |
| Acc. | те (тех)[1] |
| Instr. | те́ми |
| Prep. | тех |

The declension of тако́й "such" is identical with that of the adjective сухо́й, cf. § 132, p. 196. To save space, the declension of тако́й is not presented as a separate tabulation.

---

[1] This form is used when this demonstrative refers to living entities (§ 158, p. 244).

[2] The Russian тако́й is used somewhat more frequently than English "such," and for this reason тако́й sometimes may be better translated by "this sort of," "this kind of," or simply by "this" or "that."

§ 143.  Sentences Illustrating Use of Russian Demonstratives.

Э́тот  спо́соб  измере́ния      вре́мени  употребля́ется
This   process  of measurement  of time   applies self (is applied)

ещё  и  тепе́рь.
still  even now.

Э́та          гипоте́за          подтвержда́ется
This         hypothesis         confirms self (is  confirmed)

эксперимента́льными      наблюде́ниями.
by experimental          observations.

В  све́те      э́того,     флотацио́нный      проце́сс  име́ет
In  (the) light  of this,  (the) flotation     process   has

большо́е значе́ние    для испо́льзования  бе́дных руд.
great    significance  for (the) utilization   of poor  ores.

В связи́     с    э́тим создаётся          возмо́жность
In connection with this    creates  self (arises)  (the) possibility

испо́льзования  други́х  бога́тых се́рой  ка́менных у́глей.
of utilization    of other  rich       in sulfur coals.

При     э́том           происхо́дит  превраще́ние  теплово́й
During this  (thereby)   occurs        conversion       of heat

эне́ргии в    механи́ческую    рабо́ту.
energy   into mechanical       work.

Така́я вода́  ча́сто образу́ет  на́кипь в котла́х.
Such   water  often  forms      scale   in boilers.

Приме́ром        тако́го взры́вчатого   вещества́ слу́жит
As (an) example  of such  (an) explosive   substance  serves

тринитротолуо́л.
trinitrotoluene.

Такие    явления,    при    которых    образуются
Such    phenomena    during which        form self (are formed)

новые    вещества,    относятся[1]  к    химическим    явлениям.
new    substances,    pertain    to    chemical        phenomena.

Кроме    того,    нефть    находит    широкое    применение
Aside from    that,    petroleum    finds    wide        use

в    химической    промышлености    в    качестве
in    chemical    industry        in    (the) quality

сырья.
of (a) raw material.

Эта    реакция    применима    только в    том    случае, если
This    reaction    (is) applicable    only    in that    case,    if

она        представляет    экономию.
she (the reaction) presents    economy.

Таким    образом    в тех    случаях, в которых    гидролиз
In this    manner    in those cases    in which    (the) hydrolysis

идёт    до    конца,    и    в    итоге[2]    получается
goes    to    (the) end,    and as (a) result    obtains self (is obtained)

основная    соль как осадок.
(a) basic    salt    as    (a) precipitate.

§ 144. An Important Type of Idiom    Involving    a    Demonstrative
and Же.

As shown in the two preceding paragraphs, the demonstratives
этот "this," тот "that" and такой "such" are often used to
refer to something previously mentioned. The particle Же,
cf. Note 4, p. 75, may be used to refer back to some previous
statement. In view of these facts, it is perhaps not surprising that

---

[1] See Footnote 1, p. 145.
[2] The phrase в итоге literally means "in sum."

the combination of a demonstrative with же is used idiomatically in such fashion as to be best translated into English by such expressions as "this same," "just this," "that same," "just that," "just such."

Вес　　　　　такого　же　объёма　водорода　при　тех
(The) weight of that　same volume　of hydrogen at　those

же　условиях　－　0.0449 г.
same conditions　(is) 0.0449 g.

По　　　　　весовому　составу　различные соединения
According to weight　composition various　　compounds

одних　и　тех　же　элементов　сильно　отличаются
of one　and the　same elements　strongly　differ self

одно от　другого.
one　from another.

То　же　рассуждение　годится　　　　　　　для
Just　that　reasoning　　adapts self (is suitable)　for

решения　второй　　задачи.
solution　of (the) second problem.

К　этому　　же　времени　относятся[1]　и　первые
To this　(just this) time　　pertain　　also (the) first

попытки　определить　массу　электрона.
attempts　to determine　(the) mass of (the) electron.

Звёзды　составляются　из таких　же　химических
(The) stars compose self (consist) of just　those chemical

элементов,　что　и　земля.
elements　　that (as) also (the) earth.

[1] See Footnote 1, p. 145.

§ 145. Important Type of Subordinate Clause Involving ЧТО as Conjunction.

Both Russian ЧТО and English "that" are used in more than one way in constructing sentences. One important use of ЧТО and "that" is illustrated by the following sentences.

Этот   опыт      доказывает,   что  воздух занимает место.
This   experiment proves          that air       occupies  space.

Нам  уже         известно, что амальгамы    –    сплавы
To us already (is) known,      that amalgams      (are) alloys

различных    металлов    со   ртутью.
of various    metals       with mercury.

Эта   реакция      интересна   в  том   отношении, что
This   reaction  (is) interesting  in that   respect       that

она           идёт  при очень низких температурах.
she (the reaction) goes  at    very   low    temperatures.

Оказывается,            что   различные  химические
Shows   self (It turns out),  that   different    chemical

элементы   испускают   различные спектры.
elements    emit        different  spectra.


§ 146. Reading Exercise.

## Спектральный анализ

Кусочек металлического натрия, внесённый[1] в бесцветное пламя горелки, окрашивает его в характерный ярко-
жёлтый цвет. То же явление наблюдается и при внесении
в пламя летучих натриевых солей. Последние при той температуре, которая[2] имеется в пламени, разлагаются – и
натриевые атомы обусловливают окрашивание пламени. Оказывается, что излучение жёлтого света при высоких температурах – характеристика натриевих атомов. Исследование

этого света  при  помощи спектрографа показывает,  что он
состоит[3] из   ряда   блестящих линий на тёмном фоне.Совокуп-
ность таких линий,характерных для натрия,  называется его
спектром.   Каждая линия характеризуется определённой постоянной длиной волны.  Вообще, каждый химический элемент
при  достаточном нагревании испускает спектр,  который
составляется из лучей определённых характерных для него
длин волн. Спектр этот  носит название спектра испускания.

Спектр испускания является[4] характерной физической
постоянной каждого химического элемента.  В спектре тел,
которые состоят из нескольких химических элементов,[5] ок-
азываются линии всех этих элементов.[6] Поэтому спектр дан-
ного тела, путём[7] сравнения его линий с линиями спектров
химических элементов, показывает сразу,[8] из чего состоит
данное тело.[9]

Большая  чувствительность и широкая  применяемость
характеризуют спектральный анализ. Он позволяет[10] находить
состав не только веществ.[11]доступных нам в химической ла-
бораторий,но и звёзд, солнца и других небесных светил,
которые испускают собственный свет. Эти светила (за ис-
ключением некоторых туманностей)испускают сложный спектр,
который содержит множество тёмных  так называемых фрауен-
гоферовых  линий на светловом фоне. Они происходят следующим  образом.[12] Световое излучение раскалённого тела про-
ходит через слой сравнительно холодного газа или пара,
который обволакивает светило.  При прохождении света через газообразную оболочку химические элементы, которые
составляют оболочку, поглощают лучи той длины волны, какие[13] испускаются самими химическими элементами при достаточном нагревании.  Таким образом[14] присутствие  тёмных
линий в спектре делает возможным открытие химических элементов.

Из результатов изучения спектров тысяч[15] небесных
светил мы можем[16] сделать вывод,что вся[17] вселенная содержит
те же химические элементы, которые  находятся и[18] на земле.
Наши земные химические элементы являются универсальными,
космическими.

Вид спектра раскалённого газа или пара, число и ширина его линий изменяются в зависимости[19] от температуры, до которой газ или пар нагрет, и от давления, под которым он находится. Поэтому спектр небесных светил даёт[20] не только состав их, но кроме того[21] температуру и давление их раскалённой атмосферы.

## Notes

1. внесённый в бесцветное пламя "brought into (the) colorless flame." Here внесённый is a passive past participle derived from the infinitive внести of the verb вносить - внести "to bring (in)." The ending of внесённый is in grammatical agreement with кусочек "small bit" to which внесённый refers. In this sentence пламя is the accusative singular case of the irregularly declined neuter noun пламя "flame." The accusative singular of пламя also occurs in the next two sentences of this reading exercise.

2. которая имеется literally "which has self" is better translated "which exists," cf. § 123, p. 181. Here которая is the subject of the clause and consequently in the nominative case. The feminine gender and singular number of которая are due to the fact that it refers to температуре.

3. состоит из ряда блестящих линий "consists of (a) series of shining lines." Here блестящих is the genitive plural of the active present participle of блестеть "to be shining," "to be glittering."

4. является характерной физической постоянной "shows self (is) (a) characteristic physical constant." As was previously discussed, cf. Note 8, p. 86, the feminine forms of the adjective постоянный "constant" are often used as a noun.

5. которые состоят из нескольких химических элементов "which consist of several chemical elements." As discussed in the following lesson, нескольких is the genitive form of несколькие "several."

6. всех этих элементов, "of all these elements." Here всех is the genitive plural of the collective весь "all" to be discussed in the next lesson.

7. ПУТЁМ   literally "by way of" is the instrumental singular form of the irregularly declined masculine noun ПУТЬ "way," "road." It is often possible to translate ПУТЁМ by the English preposition "by" used to indicate means or agency.

8. сразу "immediately" is an adverb.

9. из чего́ состои́т да́нное те́ло "from what consists (the) given body." Here чего́ is the genitive neuter singular of the relative-interrogative pronoun ЧТО, whose declension is given in the next lesson.

10. ПОЗВОЛЯ́ЕТ НАХОДИ́ТЬ, "enables to find." As we shall see in Lesson 19, an infinitive ( НАХОДИ́ТЬ ) of one Russian verb is often used, as here, with some other form ( ПОЗВОЛЯ́ЕТ ) of another verb.

11. веще́ств, досту́пных нам "of substances, accessible to us."

12. сле́дующим о́бразом "in the following way." Similar phrases also involving the instrumental singular case of о́браз have been noted previously, cf. Note 6, p. 126 and Note 12, p. 184. Here сле́дующим is the instrumental, masculine singular form of the present active participle from сле́довать.

13. каки́е испуска́ются сами́ми хими́ческими элеме́нтами "such (as) radiate self (are radiated) by the same chemical elements." Here каки́е, as indicated by the fact that it bears a plural ending, refers to ЛУЧИ́. The next lesson discusses сам "same," "self," whose instrumental plural here modifies элеме́нтами.

14. таки́м о́бразом "in this way," cf. Notes 7 and 12 above.

15. ТЫ́СЯЧ "of thousands" is the genitive plural of ТЫСЯ́ЧА "thousand," cf. § 369, p. 598.

16. МЫ мо́жем сде́лать вы́вод, literally, "we are able to make (the) conclusion." In English the usual phrasing is "to draw the conclusion."

17. вся вселе́нная "(the) whole universe." The word вселе́нная which is used as a noun, is declined with the feminine adjective endings, cf. § 131, p. 191. Here ВСЯ is the feminine nominative singular of ВЕСЬ "all" whose declension is given in the next lesson.

18. и "also," "in fact."  The word и is often used in this way
to impart mild emphasis to a sentence, cf. § 61, p. 84.

19. в зави́симости  от  температу́ры,  до кото́рой  "in
dependence from (the) temperature, to which."

20. даёт "gives"  is  the  irregularly  formed  third  person
singular from the infinitive дава́ть of the verb дава́ть - дать
"to give."

21. кро́ме  того́  "beside this."

§ 147.  Translation Exercise.

1. On (При) introduction of volatile salts of sodium into the
   flame of a burner, it (оно́) takes on (принима́ет) a yellow
   color.
2. With the aid of a spectroscope we (мы) observe ( наблюда́ем )
   that the spectrum of sodium consists of a series of shining
   lines on a dark background.
3. Every chemical element is characterized by its own ( свои́м )
   spectrum.
4. Spectrum analysis enables us (нам) to find the composition of
   bodies, which consist of several chemical elements.
5. The sun and the stars ( звёзды ) radiate light.
6. The light radiation of the sun passes through a relatively
   cold ( холо́дную ) gaseous envelope.
7. Rays of various ( разли́чных ) wave lengths are absorbed
   ( поглоща́ются ) by the chemical elements of the relatively
   cold gas which envelopes the sun.
8. The spectrum of the sun contains a multiplicity of dark,
   so-called Frauenhofer, lines.
9. From the results of study of the solar spectrum, we can draw
   ( сде́лать ) the conclusion that the sun consists of terrestrial
   ( земны́х) chemical elements.
10. The spectra of heavenly bodies change in dependence on
    (от) temperature and pressure.

# PRONOUNS AND RELATED WORDS (PART II)

§ 148. Declension of Reflexives and the Emphatic са́мый ( сам ).

When discussing the reflexive forms of verbs, cf. § 52, p. 71, it was pointed out that the various English reflexives, viz., "myself," "himself," "herself," "itself," "yourself," "ourselves," "themselves" are covered in Russian by a single general reflexive, себя́, whose declension is given below.

### Singular and Plural

#### Masc.-Fem.-Neuter

| | |
|---|---|
| Nom. | --- |
| Gen. | себя́ |
| Dat. | себе́ |
| Acc. | себя́ |
| Instr. | собо́й (собо́ю ) |
| Prep. | себе́ |

The absence of a nominative form is not surprising in view of the fact that this general reflexive in Russian always refers to the subject of the sentence or clause. (See example sentences in the following § 149, p. 225.)

Various nominative forms of сам "same," "self," which may be used to emphasize the subject of a sentence or clause, are most conviently considered simultaneously with себя́.

### Nominative Forms of сам

#### Singular

| Masc. | Fem. | Neuter |
|---|---|---|
| сам | сама́ | само́ |

## Plural

### Masc.-Fem.-Neuter

са́ми

As will be evident from example sentences, a close relationship exists between сам (and associated forms given above) and са́мый,[1] whose declension is identical with that of a large class of regular adjectives exemplified by ста́рый.

## Declension of the Emphatic са́мый

### Singular

|        | Masc.            | Fem.              | Neuter  |
|--------|------------------|-------------------|---------|
| Nom.   | са́мый            | са́мая             | са́мое   |
| Gen.   | са́мого           | са́мой             | са́мого  |
| Dat.   | са́мому           | са́мой             | са́мому  |
| Acc.   | са́мый (са́мого)[2] | са́мую             | са́мое   |
| Instr. | са́мым            | са́мой (са́мою)     | са́мым   |
| Prep.  | са́мом            | са́мой             | са́мом   |

## Plural

### Masc.-Fem.-Neuter

| Nom.   | са́мые           |
|--------|-----------------|
| Gen.   | са́мых           |
| Dat.   | са́мым           |
| Acc.   | са́мые (са́мых)[2] |
| Instr. | са́мыми          |
| Prep.  | са́мых           |

[1] Strictly speaking, declension of сам is not restricted to the nominative case. The other cases are not, however, encountered very often in reading scientific Russian. These other cases are closely similar to corresponding forms of са́мый. Specifically, other case forms of сам differ from corresponding forms of са́мый; (1) by replacing of -ы- by -и- in all plural endings and in certain singular endings, (2) by employing самӧ in the feminine accusative singular and само́ in the neuter accusative singular and (3) by difference in the accent. See Whitfield, p. 85 for a complete discussion. (F. J. Whitfield, "A Russian Reference Grammar," Harvard University Press, 1933, Cambridge, Mass.)

[2] This form is used when this emphatic relates to living entities (§ 158, p. 244).

The English reflexive possessives, viz., "my own," "his own," "her own," "its own," "our own," "your own" or "their own" are covered by a single Russian reflexive possessive СВОЙ, which is used like an adjective to modify nouns. The declension of СВОЙ, identical with that of МОЙ, cf. § 138, p. 207, is given below.

### Singular

|        | Masc.           | Fem.           | Neuter |
|--------|-----------------|----------------|--------|
| Nom.   | свой            | своя́          | своё   |
| Gen.   | своего́         | свое́й         | своего́ |
| Dat.   | своему́         | свое́й         | своему́ |
| Acc.   | свой (своего́)[1] | свою́         | своё   |
| Instr. | свои́м          | свое́й (свое́ю) | свои́м |
| Prep.  | свое́м          | свое́й         | своём  |

### Plural

Masc.-Fem.-Neuter

| Nom.   | свои́          |
|--------|----------------|
| Gen.   | свои́х         |
| Dat.   | свои́м         |
| Acc.   | свои́ (свои́х)[1] |
| Instr. | свои́ми        |
| Prep.  | свои́х         |

§ 149. Sentences Illustrating Use of the Russian Reflexives and the Emphatic са́мый (сам).

The reflexives себя́ and СВОЙ refer to the subject of the sentence and to no other word. The scope of meaning is such that себя́ (in its various forms) may require translation by "myself," "herself," "himself," "itself," "yourself," or "ourselves;" СВОЙ (in its various forms) may require translation by "my own," "her own," "his own," "its own," "your own," "our own" or "their own." However, Russian use of the reflexives is such that on rendering the thought of a Russian sentence into English, it sometimes may not be necessary to use

[1] This form is used when this reflexive possessive modifies a noun referring to a living entity (§ 158, p. 244).

an English word corresponding to the Russian reflexives. In other words, Russian reflexives often play a role in expressing thought which does not require use of an English reflexive pronoun or other English word. One way in which this occurs has been discussed already, § 52, p..71.

The emphatic са́мый and closely related сам may often be best translated by "very," "same" or "the very," "the same."

Мно́гие по́ристые тела́ вса́сывают в себя́ жи́дкости.
Many porous bodies suck up into self liquids.

Вся́кое материа́льное те́ло притя́гивает к себе́ друго́е
Every material body attracts to self another

с си́лой, обра́тно пропорцио́нальной
(body) with (a) force, inversely proportional

квадра́ту расстоя́ния ме́жду ни́ми.
to (the) square of (the) distance between them.

Си́ла тяготе́ния земли́ притя́гивает к
(The) force of gravity of (the) earth attracts to

себе́ луну́ и тем сообща́ет ей кругово́е
self (the) moon and by this imparts to her circular

движе́ние.
motion.

Спирт и вода́ сме́шиваются ме́жду собо́й в
Alcohol and water mix self between self in

любы́х отноше́ниях.
any proportions.

Сам а́том обладает дово́льно
Self (the) atom (The atom itself) possesses (a) rather

сло́жным строе́нием.
complex structure.

Ра́дий    сам    явля́ется              одни́м из   проду́ктов
Radium   self   shows self    (is)    one    of   (the) products

распа́да             ура́на.
of decomposition  of uranium.


Как     сама́   хлорнова́тистая      кислота́        (HOCl), так и
Both    self   hypochlorous         acid           (HOCl), and also

её      со́ли   явля́ются              о́чень    си́льными
her (its)  salts   show self  (are)    very     strong

окисли́телями.
oxidizing agents.


Хими́ческая            су́щность       са́мого              проце́сса
(The) chemical         essence        of (the) very       process

дыха́ния        состои́т     в      ме́дленном      окисле́нии
of breathing   consists    in     (the) slow      oxidation

органи́ческих        соедине́ний.
of organic          compounds.


Всле́дствие            диффу́зии        га́зы     са́ми     собо́й
As    result          of diffusion    gases    self     by    self

переме́шиваются.
mix self.


Бе́лый    фо́сфор     сам     собо́й    загора́ется.
White    phosphorus  self    by self   ignites self.


Вся́кое растворённое      вещество́     само́     по себе́     стреми́тся
Every  dissolved          substance     itself   of self     strives

к   распростране́нию      от     областе́й     раство́ра      с
to  diffusion            from    regions      of solution    with

бо́льшей   концентра́цией      к   областя́м      с      ме́ньшей
bigger    concentration      to  regions      with    lesser

концентра́цией.
concentration.

Соль      по        своему́  соста́ву     есть      проду́кт
(A) salt  with regard  to own  composition  is in fact  (a) product

замеще́ния        водоро́да        кислоты́   мета́ллом.
of replacement    of (the) hydrogen  of (an) acid  by (a) metal.



Расте́ние      для своего́  пита́ния    и    ро́ста  нужда́ется[1]
(A) plant       for  its     nourishment and growth  requires

в це́лом     ря́де     элеме́нтов,     кото́рые  в    ви́де
  (a) whole  series    of elements     which    in   (the) form

хими́ческих       соедине́ний     оно́  вса́сывает     свои́ми
of chemical       compounds       it   sucks up       by its

корня́ми    из     по́чвы.
roots       from    (the) soil.



Шерсть,    ва́та,    пух   и   мех          нетеплопрово́дны
Wool,       batting,  down and  fur   (are)   non-heat conducting

потому́,         что  ме́жду  свои́ми  воло́кнами  соде́ржат
for this reason, that between their    fibers      (they) contain

во́здух.
air.



## § 150.  Declension of Russian Collectives.

The declension of весь "all," is closely similar to that of
adjectives. For use of various forms of весь in special
expressions, see § 389, p. 647.

---

[1] Note the idiomatic use of нужда́ться в (with prepositional) "to require,"
"to need."

весь- all

### Singular

|       | Masc. | Fem. | Neuter |
|-------|-------|------|--------|
| Nom.  | весь | вся | всё |
| Gen.  | всего́ | всей | всего́ |
| Dat.  | всему́ | всей | всему́ |
| Acc.  | весь (всего́)[1] | всю | всё |
| Instr.| всем | всей (все́ю) | всем |
| Prep. | всём | всей | всём |

### Plural

#### Masc.-Fem.-Neuter

|       | |
|-------|------|
| Nom.  | все |
| Gen.  | всех |
| Dat.  | всем |
| Acc.  | все (всех)[1] |
| Instr.| все́ми |
| Prep. | всех |

Certain collectives, namely, НЕ́СКОЛЬКО "a few," "several;" СКО́ЛЬКО "how many," "how much;" СТО́ЛЬКО "so many," "so much" and МНО́ГО "many," "a multiplicity;" немно́го "a few," "a little" are declined only in the plural.[2] The declension of these collectives is exemplified by that of не́сколько given on the next page. When these collectives are used in sentences, the usual rules governing case apply. In such expressions as "several atoms," the case of the noun а́том is the same as the collective НЕ́СКОЛЬКО except when the latter is in the nominative or accusative case, in which circumstance the noun, e.g., "atom" is in the genitive plural.[3] The genitive singular of certain nouns may be used similarly, e.g., МНО́ГО ВОДЫ "much water."

---

[1] This form is used when this collective relates to living entities.

[2] The plural forms of two closely related adjectives мно́гие "many," "numerous" and немно́гие "not many," "a few," "some" are sometimes used as pronouns to signify, respectively, "many persons" or "a few persons." The neuter singular forms, e.g., мно́гое, мно́гого, мно́гому, etc., are used substantively e.g., to mean "a lot," "much" as in the sixth sentence on page 231. Declension of мно́гий and немно́гий follows that of электри́ческий (Key No. 20, § 132, p. 197).

[3] The use of the genitive plural of nouns after the nominative and accusative cases of certain numerals (Cf. § 371, p. 604) should be noted in this connection.

несколько (áтомов)
several    (atoms)

## Plural

| | | |
|---|---|---|
| Nom. | нéсколько | (áтомов) |
| Gen. | нéскольких | (áтомов) |
| Dat. | нéскольким[1] | (áтомам) |
| Acc. | нéсколько[2] | (áтомов) |
| Instr. | нéсколькими | (áтомами) |
| Prep. | нéскольких | (áтомах) |

The collectives, скóлько, стóлько, мнóго and немнóго are sometimes used in a fashion best described as adverbial. This is not surprising in view of similar use of such English words and phrases as "much," "so much," "somewhat," etc.

## § 151. Sentences Illustrating Use of Russian Collectives.

Весь      цикл процéссов    в   технúческом   масштáбе
(The) entire cycle   of processes   on   (a) technical     scale

обы́чно     производится            непрерывно.
ordinarily    conducts self (is carried out) continuously.

Все   эти    вещества́    являются      кристаллúческими,
All    these   substances   show self (are)   crystalline,

почтú все растворя́ются   в   водé.
almost all   dissolve self    in   water.

Мышья́к    и     почтú    все    егó     соединéния     —
Arsenic    and    almost    all    his (its) compounds      (are)

вещества́ ядовúтые.
substances poisonous.

---

[1] The collectives скóлько and стóлько have alternate dative forms, typified by скóльку and скóльки.

[2] When used with animate nouns, the accusative form is the same as the genitive rather than the nominative, cf. § 158, p. 244.

Всем      известно,  что жиры  совсем   не   растворяются
To all (is) known,        that fats  completely not  dissolve self

в воде.
in water.


Земля      притягивает   к  себе  все тела,  которые на
(The) earth attracts      to  self   all  bodies, which    on

ней находятся.
her find self  (are located).


На земле        много воды.
On  earth   (there is)  much  of water.


Перекись  водорода  многим    хорошо  известна.
Peroxide    of hydrogen  to many  (is) well    known.


Если в почве  содержится            много  песка,
If   in soil    contains self (is contained) much   of sand,

то  такая почва называется            песчаной.
then such  soil   calls self    (is called)  sandy.


Свойства       глинистой  почвы  во многом  зависят  от
(The) properties of clayey    soil   in much    depend   on

свойств       глины.
(the) properties  of (the) clay.


В  нижней     части трубки    этого  аппарата находится
In (the) lower  part   of (the) tube  of this  apparatus finds

            столбик  ртути,   а   над  ним  немного
self  (is)  (a) column  of mercury, but above him   a little

раствора  едкого    кали.
of solution of caustic  potash.

Элеме́нтов  совсе́м          немно́го.
Of elements altogether (are) not many.


Ура́на  в нем содержится          ро́вно сто́лько же,
Uranium in it   contains self (is contained) equally just so much,

ско́лько   и   в   пе́рвом   препара́те.
how much  also in (the) first preparation.


Ско́лько    хими́ческих     элеме́нтов     изве́стно  в
How many  (of) chemical    elements   (are) known    in

настоя́щее   вре́мя?
(the) present  time?


Сколь      вале́нтна[1]                         медь  в
How much    valent        (What is the valence of) copper in

соедине́нии     CuCl₂?
(the) compound   $CuCl_2$ ?


§ 152. Declension of Interrogatives and Relative-Interrogatives.

The pronouns КТО "who" and ЧТО "which" are declined in the singular only; ЧЕЙ "whose" is declined in both the singular and plural.


КТО – who              ЧТО – which, that


Singular

| | КТО | ЧТО |
|---|---|---|
| Nom. | КТО | ЧТО |
| Gen. | КОГО́ | ЧЕГО́ |
| Dat. | КОМУ́ | ЧЕМУ́ |
| Acc. | КОГО́ | ЧТО |
| Instr. | КЕМ | ЧЕМ |
| Prep. | КОМ | ЧЁМ |


[1] Grammatically, the word вале́нтна is the feminine singular of the predicative of the adjective вале́нтный. The close relationship between СКО́ЛЬКО and the adverb СКОЛЬ is obvious.

Plural

Lacking

чей - whose

Singular

|  | Masc. | Fem. | Neuter |
|---|---|---|---|
| Nom. | чей | чья | чьё |
| Gen. | чьего́ | чьей | чьего́ |
| Dat. | чьему́ | чьей | чьему́ |
| Acc. | чей (чьего́)[1] | чью | чьё |
| Instr. | чьим | чьей (чьéю) | чьим |
| Prep. | чьём | чьей | чьём |

Plural

Masc.-Fem.-Neuter

| Nom. | чьи |
|---|---|
| Gen. | чьих |
| Dat. | чьим |
| Acc. | чьи (чьих)[1] |
| Instr. | чьими |
| Prep. | чьих |

The declension of како́й "what kind of," "that kind of" is identical with that of the adjective сухо́й. To save space, the declension of како́й, is not presented as a separate tabulation.

---

[1] This form is used when the noun modified refers to a living entity.

§ 153.  Sentences   Illustrating   Use   of   Interrogatives   and
         Relative-Interrogatives.

Мно́гие     хими́ческие      реа́кции           сопровожда́ются
Many        chemical         reactions         accompany self

перехо́дом       электро́нов    от   одного́ элеме́нта   и́ли
by (the) transfer   of electrons   from one    element      or

ио́на к  друго́му,   всле́дствие     чего́        изменя́ются
ion  to another,   as (a) result   of which    change self

их   вале́нтности.
their valencies.


В  э́том слу́чае  всё          зави́сит  от того́, в  чьих
In that  case   all (everything) depends  on  this,   in whose

рука́х  нахо́дится   (is)   госуда́рственная   власть.
hands  finds  self  (is)   (the) government   power.


Соотноше́ние       гли́ны  и   известняка́   в мерге́ле
(The) ratio        of clay and lime         in marl      (is)

тако́е,  како́е тре́буется   для изготовле́ния  цеме́нта.
such    that  requires (self) for  preparation   of cement.


От         чего́ зави́сит  раствори́мость      га́зов   в
From (on) what  depends  (the) solubility     of gases in

воде́?
water?


Из     чего́ состоя́т  плане́ты,    звёзды  и   други́е
From  what  consist  (the) planets,  stars   and other

небе́сные  тела́?
heavenly  bodies?

На чём  основан технический  процесс превращения
On what (is) based (the) technical  process of conversion

жидких жиров  в  твёрдые?
of liquid fats  into solid (fats)?

Чем  отличается  метиловый  спирт от этилового
By what distinguishes self methyl  alcohol from ethyl

спирта?
alcohol?

Что такое  радиоактивность?
What such (What is) radioactivity?

Что такое  непредельные  углеводороды?
What such (What are) unsaturated  hydrocarbons?

Это показывает,  какие громадные  запасы  энергии
This shows  what enormous  reserves  of energy

заключаются  в  ядрах  атомов.
enclose self  in (the) nuclei  of atoms.

Какие  продукты  получаются  при
What  products  obtain self  (are obtained) on

сгорании  сероводорода?
combustion  of hydrogen sulfide?

Какое соединение  серы  при этом  прлучается?
What compound  of sulfur thereby  obtains self?

Какую часть земной  поверхности  занимает
What part of (the) terrestrial surface  occupies

вода?
water?

В како́м ви́де обы́чно  выделя́ется    из   насы́щенного
In what    form  ordinarily separates self  from (a) saturated

раство́ра   раствори́мая   соль?
solution   (a) soluble    salt?

§ 154.  Formation and Declension of Indefinites.

The formation of one group of Russian indefinites involves
hyphenating certain basic pronouns already considered in the
preceding paragraph, with one of the suffixes -ТО, -НИБУДЬ
and -ЛИБО or with the prefix КОе- (or КОЙ-). The affixes impart
somewhat different shades of meaning. Thus, -ТО, КОе- (or КОЙ-)
implies some definite person or thing that one has in mind;
-НИБУДЬ implies any person or thing at all; -ЛИБО implies any
person or thing that may be taken or chosen. The following
examples illustrate derivation of indefinite pronouns:

ко́е-кто
(ко́й-кто)              anyone at all, someone or other
кто́-нибудь

кто́-либо               anyone you like or choose

кто́-то                 someone, somebody (definite but
                          unnamed person)

ко́е-что
(ко́й-что)              anything at all, something or other
что́-нибудь

что́-либо               anything you like or choose

что́-то                 something, (definite but unnamed thing)

како́й-либо             some, any at all
како́й-нибудь           some, no matter which
како́й-то               some, some certain

In such combinations, the basic pronoun КТО or ЧТО is declined
as indicated by the tabulation given in § 152, p. 232. The suffix
or prefix КОе- (КОЙ-), -ТО, -ЛИБО or -НИБУДЬ is the same for all
cases. Thus, for example:

ЧТО́-НИБУДЬ -- anything at all, something or other

### Singular

| | |
|---|---|
| Nom. | ЧТО́-НИБУДЬ |
| Gen. | ЧЕГО́-НИБУДЬ |
| Dat. | ЧЕМУ́-НИБУДЬ |
| Acc. | ЧТО́-НИБУДЬ |
| Instr. | ЧЕ́М-НИБУДЬ |
| Prep. | ЧЁМ-НИБУДЬ |

Hyphenating СКО́ЛЬКО with -НИБУДЬ and -ЛИБО forms СКО́ЛЬКО-НИБУДЬ "somewhat" "to some degree or other" and СКО́ЛЬКО-ЛИБО "somewhat" "to any degree you like." These two indefinites, which are not encountered frequently, are used mostly in an adverbial manner.

Another group of indefinite pronouns is formed by affixing the prefix НЕ- to certain basic pronouns already discussed. The more important in this group are the following:

| | |
|---|---|
| НЕ́КОТОРЫЙ | some, certain |
| НЕ́СКОЛЬКО | several, a few |
| НЕ́ЧТО | something |
| НЕ́КТО | someone, somebody |
| НЕ́КИЙ | some, a certain |

These five indefinite pronouns are all declined in the same way as the basic pronouns from which they are derived with exception of НЕ́КИЙ. This pronoun is used so little in scientific Russian that it seems unnecessary to tabulate its declension which is quite similar to that of other pronouns. See Whitfield, p. 82.

It should be observed that this use of the prefix НЕ- is quite unusual. It will be recalled that НЕ- usually indicates negation, e.g., ВИ́ДИМЫЙ "visible," НЕВИ́ДИМЫЙ "invisible."

Cases other than the nominative of не́что and не́кто may be used with negative significance to mean "nothing" and "nobody," respectively.

§ 155. Sentences Illustrating Use of Indefinites.

При скóрости порядка 4 км./сек. свинцóвая
At velocities of (the) order of 4 km./sec. (a) lead

пýля при попадáнии в какóе-либо препя́тствие пóлностью
bullet on hit on any obstacle completely

и мгновéнно обращáется в
and instantaneously converts self (is converted) into

раскалённые пары́.
heated vapors.

С уменьшéнием давлéния скóрость испарéния
With (a) decrease of pressure (the) rate of evaporation

какóй-либо жи́дкости увели́чивается.
of any liquid increases self.

Éсли каки́м-нибудь путём давлéние
If by some way (the) pressure

увели́чивается, объём гáза уменьшáется.
increases self, (the) volume of (the) gas decreases self.

Колебáние, вы́званное в какóм-либо однóм мéсте
(A) vibration, excited in some one place

упрýгого тéла, не ограни́чивается э́тим
of (an) elastic body, not limits self (is limited) by (to) that

мéстом.
place.

Одни́м  из  ва́жных  вопро́сов  при  изуче́нии
(As) one  of  (the) important  questions  on  studying

како́го-либо  вещества́  явля́ется  вопро́с
of any  substance  shows self  (is) (the) question

об  его́ соста́ве.
concerning its  composition.

А́томы  элеме́нтов  не  явля́ются  чем-то
(The) atoms  of elements  not  show self  (are) something

сплошны́м,  недели́мым,  а  име́ют  сло́жное  строе́ние.
compact,  indivisible,  but have  (a) complex  structure.

Ско́лько-нибудь  заме́тные  результа́ты  получа́ются
To any extent  perceptible  results  obtain self

то́лько  в  прису́тствии  пла́тиновых
(are obtained)  only  in (the) presence  of platinum

катализа́торов.
catalysts.

Ка́менный у́голь  в  на́шу эпо́ху  в  ско́лько-либо
Coal  in  our  epoch  in  any

значи́тельных  коли́чествах  не  образу́ется.
considerable  quantities  not forms self.

Для  не́которых  веще́ств  раствори́мость  си́льно
For  certain  substances  (the) solubility  strongly

изменя́ется  с  температу́рой.
changes self  with temperature.

В не́которых　места́х　встреча́ются　го́рные　поро́ды,
In certain　places　encounter self　mineral　substances,

кото́рые по　соста́ву　бли́зки к той　сме́си глины
which　as to composition (are) near　to that　mixture of clay

и　известняка́,　из　кото́рой гото́вится　цеме́нт.
and limestone　from which　prepares self　cement.


Éсли　газ　и　жи́дкость нахо́дятся　в　за́мкнутом
If　(a) gas and　(a) liquid　find self　(are)　in (a) closed

простра́снство,　то　че́рез　не́которое　вре́мя
space　then　through (after)　(a) certain　time

устана́вливается　равнове́сие ме́жду　га́зом
establishes self (is established) equilibrium　between (the) gas

в раство́ре　и　га́зом над　раство́ром.
in solution　and (the) gas above　(the) solution.


Иногда́　в　ядре́　коме́ты　происхо́дит не́что
Sometimes　in (the) head　of (a) comet　occurs　something

вро́де　взры́ва,　в　результа́те　чего́
of the nature　of (an) explosion,　in　result　of which

вырыва́ется　це́лое о́блако	части́ц.
tears out self　(a) whole cloud　of particles.


Существу́ет　не́сколько	систе́м	аппара́тов
Exists　several (a number)　of systems	of apparatuses

для произво́дства	се́рной	кислоты́	конта́ктным
for　production　of sulfuric	acid	by (the) contact

спо́собом.
process.

| Éсли | металл | образует | несколько | различных | окислов, |
|---|---|---|---|---|---|
| If | (a) metal | forms | several | different | oxides |

| то | все | они | | дают | при | восстановлении |
|---|---|---|---|---|---|---|
| then | all | they | (of them) | give | on | reduction |

| водородом | металл | и | воду. |
|---|---|---|---|
| by hydrogen | metal | and water. |

<br>

| Другие | металлы, | например, | | медь, | свинец, | железо |
|---|---|---|---|---|---|---|
| Other | metals, | for example, | | copper, | lead, | iron |

| образуют | с | кислородом | по | | нескольку |
|---|---|---|---|---|---|
| form | with | oxygen | at | rate of | several |

| соединений – | окислов. |
|---|---|
| compounds — | of oxides. |

## § 156.  Formation and Declension of Negative Pronouns.

The prefix НИ- is affixed to the Relative-Interrogative pronouns (cf. § 152, p. 232) to form one group of negative pronouns. Thus we have НИКТО, "nobody;" НИКАКОЙ "no," "none;" НИЧЕЙ "no one's;" НИЧТО "nothing;" etc. These negative pronouns are declined like the relative-interrogative pronouns from which they are derived. From НИЧЕГО, the genitive of НИЧТО , is derived НЕчего a word often used in spoken Russian in expressions indicating resignation, boredom, disinterest, etc. Note that НЕчего is equivalent to НЕТ НИЧЕГО, ЧТО, translatable as "there is nothing, that."

Sentences illustrating the use of negative pronouns are presented in Lesson 21, entitled "Negative Sentences."

## § 157. Supplementary Notes on Pronouns and Related Words.

These supplementary notes are restricted to certain pronouns and related words of importance in reading scientific Russian.[1]

---

[1] For further discussion of obsolete and rarely used pronouns, the student is referred to Whitfield, pp. 77-85.

Such English expressions as "one from another," "one to another" involve in Russian a sort of double pronoun composed of друг (undeclined) together with various declined forms of друг which might be summarized as follows:

## Singular

| | |
|---|---|
| Nom. | -- -- |
| Gen. | друг дру́га |
| Dat. | друг дру́гу |
| Acc. | друг дру́га |
| Instr. | друг дру́гом |
| Prep. | друг дру́ге |

The demonstrative тако́в "that sort of," "such" has only the nominative forms.

## Singular

| Masc. | Fem. | Neuter |
|---|---|---|
| тако́в | такова́ | таково́ |

## Plural

Masc.-Fem.-Neuter

таковы́

The interrogative како́в "what sort of," "what" is similarly declined.

The demonstrative сей is obsolete except for a few fixed expressions, e.g., до сих пор "up till now," пе́ред сим "before this," при сем слу́чае "on this occasion."

Вещества́ различа́ются   друг  от   дру́га  по
Substances distinguish self   one   from another according to

приро́де  и   расположе́нию их   составны́х  а́томов.
(the) nature and (the) position  of their  component  atoms.

Величины́       хими́ческого   сродства́   к кислоро́ду
(The) magnitudes  of chemical    affinity    to oxygen

мета́ллов   А l и  Zr    сравни́тельно  бли́зки друг  к
of metals   Al and Zr (are) relatively    near    one  to

дру́гу.
the other.

Не́которые   жи́дкости,   как,   наприме́р,   вода́  и
Certain      liquids     as,    for example   water and

ами́ловый  спирт,  растворя́ются    друг в   дру́ге
amyl       alcohol, dissolve self    one in   the other

части́чно.
partially.

Таковы́     зада́чи,    кото́рые изуча́ет термодина́мика.
Such     (are) the problems, which    studies   thermodynamics.

Тако́в, наприме́р,     сплав  бабби́т.
Such,  for example,  (is)  (the) alloy babbit.

Како́в   физи́ческий   смысл   конста́нты F?
What  (is) (the) physical  significance of (the) constant F?

Каково́   значе́ние    о́лова  в те́хнике?
What   (is) (the) significance of tin   in technology?

| Вну́треннее | ядро́ | земли́ | до | сих | пор |
|---|---|---|---|---|---|
| (The) inner | core | of (the) earth | up | to these | times |

| остаётся | для нас загáдкою. |
|---|---|
| remains | for us (a) puzzle. |

## § 158.  General Remarks Concerning the Accusative Case Forms of Pronouns and Related Words.

As pointed out in § 67, p. 93, the endings of the accusative case are the same as the genitive for certain masculine nouns in both singular and plural and for certain feminine and neuter nouns in the plural only. The nouns in question refer to living entities, viz., human beings, mythological persons, animals and insects. The same changes in form of the accusative occur with adjectives and other noun modifiers when used with the above specified group of nouns. This change in form of the accusative is encountered also in various words whose declensions were cited in this lesson and in the preceding one. Such change in the accusative has not been noted in detail because it is unimportant in reading scientific Russian.

## § 159.  Reading Exercise

### Круговоро́т углеро́да в приро́де

Взро́слый челове́к ежедне́вно выдыха́ет о́коло 900 грáммов углеки́слого гáза, а всё человече́ство 438,000 миллионов килогрáммов за год. Не́которые живо́тные[1] тáкже выдыхáют значи́тельное коли́чество углеки́слого гáза.

Углеки́слый газ, кото́рый выдыхáют и живо́тные[1] и лю́ди, образу́ется всле́дствие[2] окисле́ния органи́ческих веще́ств пи́щи в живы́х ткáнях. Это окисле́ние пи́щи явля́ется исто́чником эне́ргии, необходи́мым для поддержáния жи́зни.

Все ви́ды то́плива - наприме́р, кáменный у́голь, нефть, приро́дный газ, де́рево - содéржат углеро́д как основно́й элемéнт своего́ состáва. Вся́кое то́пливо представля́ет собо́й или остáток какóго-то растéния, и́ли продýкт превраще́ния расти́тельных остáтков. При горéнии вся́кого то́плива выделя́ется эне́ргия и образу́ется углеки́слый газ - в хими́-

ческом отношéнии тот[3] же углекислый газ, котóрый выдыхáют лю́ди и живóтные.

Несмотря́ на то,[4] что таки́м óбразом ежегóдно на землé выделя́ются громáдные коли́чества углеки́слого гáза, содержáние послéднего[5] в вóздухе остаётся приблизи́тельно постоя́нным – 0.03 – 0.04% по объёму. Это[6] объясня́ется тем, что в прирóде одновремéнно протекáют процéссы, при котóрых углеки́слый газ удаля́ется из атмосфéры. Ины́ми словáми, в прирóде происхóдят нéкоторые процéссы, котóрые "исправля́ют" состáв вóздуха.

Такóе "исправлéние" явля́ется необходи́мым для поддержáния жи́зни живóтных и людéй. Однáко содержáние в вóздухе углеки́слого гáза до[7] 5% не вызывáет[8] никаки́х опáсных симптóмов ни для живóтных, ни для человéка. Таки́м óбразом углеки́слый газ сам[9] по себé не явля́ется я́дом, но мóжет[10] причини́ть смерть свои́ми удушáющими свóйствами.

Углеки́слый газ характеризу́ется своéй исключи́тельно высóкой хими́ческой прóчностью. Мы знáем[11] из закóна сохранéния энéргии, что процéссы, обрáтные окислéниям пи́щи и тóплива, трéбуют тогó[12] же коли́чества энéргии, котóрое выделя́ется при сáмом окислéнии.

Зелёные растéния питáют собóй[13] в конéчном счёте весь живóтный мир и человéка. В концé концóв всё тóпливо образу́ется из растéний. Расти́тельное происхождéние пи́щи и тóплива укáзывает на вáжность растéний в круговорóте углерóда в прирóде. Растéния поглощáют углеки́слый газ и пóльзуются им в своём рóсте.

Возникáет вопрóс, от какóго истóчника растéния черпáют энéргию, необходи́мую для превращéния углеки́слого гáза в органи́ческие продýкты. Из óпытов с растéниями мы знáем, что они́ не растýт нормáльно в отсýтствии свéта. Таки́м óбразом, лучи́ сóлнца явля́ются истóчником энéргии, необходи́мой[14] для превращéния углеки́слого гáза вновь в пи́щу и тóпливо.

Тем[15] не мéнее, растéния улáвливают тóлько мáлую дóлю солнéчной энéргии, котóрая пáдает на зéмлю. Пóлное испóль–

зование солнечной энергии представляет собой одну из самых[16] важных проблем, решение которой до[17] сих пор всё еще далеко в будущем.

## Notes

1. The use of the neuter forms of the adjective живо́тный , as a noun was discussed in  Note 8,  p. 86.

2. всле́дствие   "as a result of" is a preposition and should not be confused with other parts of speech which it may resemble.

3. тот же,  "the very same," cf. § 144, p. 215.

4. несмотря́  на то, что -- "in spite of the fact that --."

5. после́днего ,  "of the latter" referring to  углеки́слого га́за .

6. объясня́ется тем, что  -- "explains self by this, that --." Here  тем  is in the instrumental case.

7. до 5%  "up to 5%."

8. не вызыва́ет никаки́х опа́сных симпто́мов  "calls forth no dangerous symptoms." не is a so-called "double" negative and as such is omitted from translation, cf. Lesson 20, in particular § 180, p. 272; § 181, p. 274.

9. сам по себе́  "himself of self" may be regarded  as an idiom.

10. но мо́жет причини́ть смерть свои́ми удуша́ющими сво́йствами  "but is able to cause death by (means of) its suffocating properties." Here удуша́ющими  "suffocating" is the instrumental plural form of the present active participle from the infinitive удуша́ть of the verb удуша́ть -- удуши́ть "to suffocate."

11. Мы зна́ем "We know." Here зна́ем is the first person plural of the present tense of the infinitive знать "to be knowing," cf. § 187, p. 282.

12. того́ же the neuter genitive singular form of то is involved here, cf. Note 3 above.

13. собо́й is the instrumental form of the reflexive pronoun and means "by means of self."

14. необходи́мой is in the feminine genitive singular case since it refers to and modifies эне́ргии, a feminine noun in the genitive singular case.

15. тем не ме́нее "none the less" may be regarded as an idiom.

16. из са́мых ва́жных пробле́м "of the most important problems." The use of са́мый in forming one type of superlative has been noted already, cf. Note 12, p. 17·0.

17. до сих пор "up till now" and всё еще "even yet" may both be regarded as idioms.

§ 160. Translation Exercise.

1. Any adult (grown up) person daily exhales a considerable quantity of carbon dioxide.
2. The latter is formed (forms self) during (при) oxidation of food in living tissues.
3. Any kind (Вся́кая) of food contains carbon as the basic element of its (своего́) composition.
4. One (Оди́н) important (ва́жный) product of combustion of any kind of fuel is (shows self as) carbon dioxide (углски́слым га́зом).
5. In this way, enormous amounts of carbon dioxide annually enter (перехо́дят) into (в) the atmosphere.
6. Simultaneously, certain other processes remove (удаля́ют) carbon dioxide from the air.
7. Plants remove carbon dioxide from the atmosphere and in this way "regulate" its (его́) composition.

8. They[1] (Они́) obtain (получа́ют) energy from (из) the rays of the sun.
9. Carbon dioxide is converted (converts self) with the aid of plants once more into food and fuel.
10. Solar energy is (shows self as) essential for maintenance of life on earth.

## Notes

1. Here "They" (Они́) refers to "plants."

# LESSON 19

## RUSSIAN SENTENCES CONTAINING INFINITIVES OF VERBS

§ 161. Introductory Note and Summary.

Previous discussion of the infinitives of Russian verbs pointed out the existence of perfective and imperfective infinitives. It will be recalled that perfective infinitives and forms derived therefrom are used to designate action thought of as being complete. Action thought of as incomplete, continuing or frequently repeated, is expressed by using imperfective infinitives and the verb forms derived therefrom. It will also be recalled that Russian makes sparing use of auxiliary verbs. Thus, for example, имѐть "to have" is not used as an auxiliary to express past action; имѐть is used only to indicate possession or acquisition.

The fact that Russian uses a somewhat different grammar mechanism for expressing action makes it necessary to devote attention to various details relating to the use of certain Russian verb forms. In this Lesson we shall consider some of the ways in which Russian infinitives are used. These might be summarized as follows:

### Summary of Use of Russian Infinitives

1. Infinitives dependent on other verbs, cf. § 163, p. 250.
2. Infinitives dependent on nouns, cf. § 164, p. 252.
3. Infinitives dependent on adjectives, cf. § 165, p. 253.
4. Infinitives used with predicative neuter singular of adjectives, cf. § 166, p. 254.
5. Infinitives used to express purpose, cf. § 168, p. 256.
6. Infinitives used in conditional sentences, cf. § 169, p. 258.
7. Infinitives used in imperative sentences, cf. Lesson 33, § 308, p. 485.
8. Citation of verbs in dictionaries, glossaries, etc.

As we shall observe, these uses of infinitives are closely related to the fact that they express impersonal, generalized action.

249

§ 162.  Recognition of Russian Infinitives.

Infinitives are used so frequently in scientific Russian, that it is worthwhile to note that they usually end in -ТЬ. It will be recalled that the nominative and accusative singular of certain abstract, feminine nouns terminate with the letter combination -ОСТЬ or -ЕСТЬ, cf. § 35, p. 50. Aside from these feminine nouns the letter combination -ТЬ terminates very few Russian words other than the infinitives of verbs. It is also worth remembering that a few Russian verb infinitives end in  -ЧЬ, and a few others in  -ТИ.

§ 163.  Infinitives Dependent on Other Verbs.

Certain Russian verbs expressing ability, purpose, etc., are used together with dependent infinitives of other verbs as in the following sentences.  The structure of such sentences closely parallels that of their English counterparts.

Твёрдые тела́ мо́гут адсорби́ровать не то́лько га́зы, но и
Solid      bodies may   adsorb            not only      gases, but also

разли́чные растворённые вещества́ из   жи́дкостей.
various     dissolved       substances  from liquids.

В пустоте́      раке́тный    самолёт смо́жет          дости́гнуть
In (a) vacuum, (a) rocket   plane   will be able     to attain

огро́мных     ско́ростей.
enormous     velocities.

Микроско́п          помога́ет разреши́ть э́тот вопро́с.
(The) microscope helps     to solve    this question.

В   однородных        веществах    не   удаётся[1]  заме́тить
In  homogeneous      substances   not  succeeds     to detect

отде́льных   кусо́чков,   ка́пелек  и   вообще́       уча́стков
separate     fragments,  droplets and in general   component

       с   неодина́ковыми   сво́йствами.
bits with non-identical    properties.

---

[1] See Footnote 1, p. 145.

| Фотоэлементы | позволяют | преобразовать | изменения |
|---|---|---|---|
| Photo elements | permit | to transform | changes |

| интенсивности | света | в | электрические | токи. |
|---|---|---|---|---|
| of intensity | of light | into electrical | | currents. |

| Мы | не | предполагаем | здесь | следовать | историческому |
|---|---|---|---|---|---|
| We | not | propose | here | to trace | (the) historical |

| развитию | квантовой | механики. |
|---|---|---|
| development | of quantum | mechanics. |

| По | форме, | пути | движения | могут | быть |
|---|---|---|---|---|---|
| As | to form, | paths | of motion | may | be |

| прямолинейными | или | криволинейными. |
|---|---|---|
| rectilinear | or | curvilinear. |

| При | прямом | солнечном | свете | смесь | метана | с |
|---|---|---|---|---|---|---|
| In | direct | sun | light | (a) mixture | of methane | with |

| хлором | может | взорваться. |
|---|---|---|
| chlorine | is able | to explode self. |

| Под | растворами | следует | понимать | такие |
|---|---|---|---|---|
| Under | solutions | it is necessary | to understand | such |

| однородные | системы, | состав | которых | может |
|---|---|---|---|---|
| homogeneous | systems, | (the) composition | of which | may |

| меняться | в | широких | пределах, | без |
|---|---|---|---|---|
| change self (be changed) | in | wide | limits, | without |

| скачкообразного | изменения | каких-либо | свойств |
|---|---|---|---|
| abrupt | change | of any | of (the) properties |

| системы. |
|---|
| of (the) system. |

При    дальнейшем   падении   температуры,    жидкость
On     further       fall      of temperature,   (the) liquid

начинает  переходить  в   кристаллическое   состояние.
begins    to go over  into (the) crystalline  condition.


§ 164. Infinitives Dependent on Nouns.

   Nouns may also be used to express ability, purpose, etc., both
in English and also in Russian. Such nouns, like the corresponding
verbs mentioned in preceding § 163, may have infinitives dependent
on them. When infinitives are so used, they express action of an
impersonal, generalized character.

Хлорофилловые         зёрна     обладают    свойством
(The)   chlorophyll   granules  possess     (the)  property

задерживать часть света.
to retain      part   of (the) light.


Однако   имеются                 основания думать,   что
However, have self   (there exist)  reasons   to think  that

динозавры   и    теперь живут    на   земле.
dinosaurs   even  now      are living on   earth.


Этот реактив  даёт  нам  возможность   с   уверенностью
This  reagent gives to us (the) possibility with reliability

определить   количества Au    от   0.5 до 1.0 μ.
to determine quantities  (of) Au from 0.5  to  1.0 μ.


Стремление         повысить    рабочую       температуру
(The) striving     to raise    (the) working  temperature

электрических    машин    и   аппаратов, связанное с
of electrical    machines and apparatuses, connected  with

желанием    увеличить   мощность      без    изменения
the  wish   to increase (the) power   without change

их           габаритов,        в        большинстве         случаев
of  their   over-all   sizes   in       (the) majority       of cases

лимитируется                недостаточной  теплостойкостью
limits  self  (is limited by)   insufficient       heat stability

диэлектриков.
of (the) dielectrics.


## § 165.  Infinitives Dependent on Adjectives.

Adjectives  may also  be  used  to  express ability, purpose, etc.,
and   consequently   infinitives   dependent   on   adjectives   are
occasionally   encountered.   Here,   again,   infinitives   express
impersonal, generalized action.

Окись   углерода,[1]                            как   и   все газы,
Oxide    of carbon   (carbon monoxide), as      also all   gases, (is)

способна    диффузировать.
capable      to diffuse.


Ионы       неспособны     проникнуть  в   металл,         как
Ions     (are) incapable     to penetrate  into metal,    (just) as

электроны        неспособны перейти    в    раствор.
electrons        (are) incapable   to go over   into solution.


Иногда     бывает необходимо увеличить     концентрацию
Sometimes (it) is   necessary     to increase   (the) concentration

раствора.
of (a) solution.


---

[1] Carbon dioxide is   углекислый газ.  The use of the word окись  to designate
a  lower valence state of an element is  exceptional  and contrary to general practice
in Russian chemical nomenclature. Cf. Note 2, p. 10.

§ 166. Infinitives Used with Predicative Neuter Singular of
Adjectives.

As observed in preceding paragraphs of this Lesson,
Russian infinitives express action of an impersonal generalized
nature. In expressing the fact that such action is "necessary,"
"possible," "interesting," "easy," etc., the predicative neuter
singular of the adjectives in question may be used in sentences
from which the present tense of быть "to be" is omitted except
for obvious implication.

In the following example sentences, the predicative neuter
singular forms of the adjectives are designated by single asterisks
and their companion infinitives by double asterisks.

Спирты и простые эфиры можно* рассматривать**
Alcohols and　　　ethers　(it is) possible　to consider

как производные воды.
as　derivatives　of water.


Для получения кристаллического глицерина, его
For　obtaining　crystalline　glycerol,　him

надо* охладить** до 0° и внести** в него
(it is) necessary to cool　to 0° and introduce　into him

кристаллик глицерина.
(a) small crystal　of glycerol.


В этом не трудно* убедиться**
In this　not (it is) difficult　to convince self　(by means of)

весьма простым опытом.
extremely　simple　experiment.


Интересно* отметить,** что от надкрыльев жуков
(It is) interesting to note,　that from wing sheathes　of beetles

часто наблюдается "металлическое" отражение
often　observes self　"metallic"　reflection

света.
of light.

| При | за́писи | результа́тов | | измере́ния | |
|-----|---------|--------------|---|-----------|---|
| On | recording | of | results | of | (a) measurement |

| необходи́мо* | | вслед | за | число́м | писа́ть** |
|--------------|---|-------|-----|---------|-----------|
| (it is) necessary | | directly | after | (the) number | to write |

| едини́цу | ме́ры. |
|----------|--------|
| (the) unit | of measurement. |

| Легко́* | получи́ть** | эллипти́чески-поляризо́ванный | свет |
|---------|-------------|-------------------------------|------|
| (It is) | easy to obtain | elliptically | polarized | light |

| из | плоскополяризо́ванного. |
|----|-------------------------|
| from | plane polarized. |

## § 167. Use of Adjectives and Nouns Standing Alone as Clauses.

The use of the predicative, neuter singular of adjectives in impersonal sentences involving infinitives is closely related to similar use of these adjective forms standing alone as a complete clause in a complex sentence. Similar use of a noun (e.g., пра́вда in the second sentence below) is less frequently encountered in reading scientific Russian.

| Интере́сно, | что | возникнове́ние | сверхпроводи́мости |
|-------------|-----|----------------|---------------------|
| (It is) interesting, that | appearance | of superconductivity |

| в | мета́ллах | сопровожда́ется | лишь | небольши́м |
|---|-----------|------------------|------|------------|
| in | metals | accompanies self | only | by (a) small |

| измене́нием | в | теплоёмкости. |
|-------------|---|---------------|
| change | | in heat capacity. |

| Пра́вда, | производ́ство | нефтяны́х | проду́ктов | в |
|----------|---------------|-----------|------------|---|
| (It is) true (that) | (the) production | of petroleum products | in |

| настоя́щее | вре́мя | грома́дно, | но | тре́бование | на |
|------------|--------|------------|-----|-------------|-----|
| (the) present | time | (is) enormous, | but (the) demand | for |

| них | та́кже | грома́дно. |
|-----|--------|------------|
| them | also | (is) enormous. |

Понятно,       что   энергия     термоэлектрического
(It is)   understandable, that   (the) energy   of (the) thermoelectric

тока    возникает за счёт      энергии      источника
current originates   at (the) expense of (the) energy of (the) source

тепла.
of heat.

Как   известно,   сахар служит   важным       источником
As    (is) known,   sugar    serves    as (an) important source

энергии для людей   и    животных.
of energy   for    persons and animals.

Очевидно,       что при     работе   с    радиоактивными
(It is) obvious,    that during work     with   radioactive

препаратами   необходимо       охранять     себя   от
preparations    (it is) necessary   to protect    self     from

вредного действия различных    невидимых   лучей.
harmful    action       of various      invisible      rays.

Верно,       что витамины   находятся   в пище   в очень
(It is) true,   vitamins       find self      in food   in very

малых   количествах.
small    amounts.

Неясно,        почему   первая    реакция     происходит
(It is) unclear, why       (the) first reaction    proceeds

быстро, а    вторая    медленно.
rapidly,    but (the) second slowly.

## § 168. Infinitives Used to Express Purpose.

One of the more commonly used methods for expressing purpose in Russian involves the conjunction чтобы or, less commonly, чтоб followed by an infinitive. If a particular single

purpose is concerned, then the introductory phrase ДЛЯ ТОГО́
ЧТО́БЫ or, less commonly, ДЛЯ Э́ТОГО ЧТО́БЫ is often used. The
following sentences illustrate how these conjunctions (in word and
phrase form) are used with infinitives in order to indicate
purpose in Russian. Here, again, infinitives are used to express
impersonal, generalized action.

| Что́бы | поня́ть, | как | расте́ние | живёт, | на́до |
|---|---|---|---|---|---|
| In order | to understand | how | (a) plant | lives, | it is necessary |

| изучи́ть | не то́лько | вне́шнее, | но | и | вну́треннее |
|---|---|---|---|---|---|
| to study | not only | (the) external, | but | also | (the) inner |

| строе́ние | расте́ний. |
|---|---|
| structure | of plants. |

| Что́бы | осуществи́ть | ве́чный | дви́гатель, | |
|---|---|---|---|---|
| In order | to set up | perpetual | mover, | (it is) |

| ну́жно | создава́ть | эне́ргию из | ничего́. |
|---|---|---|---|
| necessary | to create | energy | from nothing. |

| Для | э́того, | что́бы | ознако́миться | со | сво́йствами |
|---|---|---|---|---|---|
| For | this | in order | to acquaint self | with | (the) properties |

| како́го-нибудь | вещества́, | необходи́мо | взять | его́ в |
|---|---|---|---|---|
| of any | substance, | (it is) necessary | to take | it    in |

| чи́стом ви́де. |
|---|
| pure    form. |

| Для | того́ | что́бы | сра́внивать | маши́ны | ра́зной |
|---|---|---|---|---|---|
| For | this | in order | to compare | machines | of different |

| производи́тельности, | необходи́мо | определи́ть, |
|---|---|---|
| productivity | (it is) necessary | to determine |

| како́е | коли́чество | рабо́ты | произво́дит | ка́ждая |
|---|---|---|---|---|
| what | quantity | of work | performs | each |

| маши́на | в едини́цу | вре́мени. |
|---|---|---|
| machine | in unit | of time. |

§ 169. Infinitives Used in Conditional Sentences.

In Russian, conditional sentences may take several forms. Impersonal conditional sentences usually involve the use of the conjunction е́сли, "if" together with the infinitive in the conditional clause. In such sentences, the conditional clause is followed by another clause usually, though not necessarily, introduced by the conjunction ТО, "then." Examples of such sentences are given below. For other types of Russian conditional sentences, see § 232, p. 364; § 313, p. 492.

Е́сли    рассма́тривать    идеа́льный    газ,    моле́кулы
If       consider          (an) ideal    gas,    molecules

кото́рого    не облада́ют    потенциа́льной    эне́ргией    от
of which    not possess     potential         energy      from

сил    сцепле́ния,    то    вну́тренняя    эне́ргия    га́за
forces of cohesion,   then  internal      energy     of (the) gas

зави́сит    то́лько    от    температу́ры.
depends     only      from (the) temperature.


Е́сли    повы́сить    температу́ру,    то    пло́тность
If       raise        (the) temperature,   then  (the) density

га́за    уме́ньшится.
of (the) gas  will decrease self.


Е́сли    кусо́чек    серебри́стой    ле́нты    ма́гния    заже́чь[1]
If       (a) piece  of silver       ribbon   of magnesium ignites

в    во́здухе, она́    загори́тся    я́рким
in   air,      she    will fire self (catch fire)    with (a) bright,

ослепи́тельным    пла́менем.
dazzling          flame.


[1] Here the meaning is "If a piece of silvery magnesium ribbon is ignited ---."

Éсли пересéчь кóнус   плóскостью,   перпендикулярной
If    cut across  (a) cone  by a plane    perpendicular

к егó        óси, то   сечéние      бýдет
to his  (the cone's) axis then (the) intersection will be

окрýжностью.
(a) circle.


§ 170. **Reading Exercise.**

### Радиоактивность
### (Часть пéрвая)

Свóйство нéкоторых вещéств самопроизвóльно испус-
кáть невидимые глáзу лучи называется   радиоактивностью.
Нетрýдно убедиться в  существовáнии этих лучéй по резуль-
тáтам их дéйствия.   Éсли положить óчень мáлое количество
радиоктивного препарáта, напримéр какóй-нибýдь сóли рáдия,
на завёрнутую[1] в чёрную бумáгу фотографическую  пластинку
и затéм проявить послéднюю,[2] то на  мéсте радиоактивного
веществá покáзывается сильное почернéние.   Éсли радиоактивный препарáт приближáется к заряжённому электроскóпу,
то послéдний быстро теряет свой[3] заряд.

Слéдует тáкже  отмéтить, что радиоактивные  препа-
рáты дáже в мáлых количествах мóгут разрушáть живые ткáни.
Нетрýдно понять, почемý[4]  при рабóте с такими препарáтами
необходимо охранять себя[5] от врéдного дéйствия их  радиáции.

Для тогó чтобы прáвильно понимáть радиоактивность,
необходимо познакóмиться с основными свóйствами радиоактивного излучéния.  Мóжно исслéдовать прирóду такóй  радиации с пóмощью óпытов над её[6] отклонéнием.

Éсли дéйствовать на радиоактивное излучéние сильным
магнитным или электрическим пóлем, мóжно наблюдáть раз-
ложéние радиáции на три вида[7] лучéй.  Один вид лучéй не
подвергáется отклонéнию и является электромагнитной ра-
диáцией с óчень корóткой длинóй волны.  Это - так называ-

емые гамма-лучи. Два других[8] вида лучей однако отклон-
яются в[9] электрическом и в магнитном полях. Из направ-
ления и размеров отклонения можно судить относительно
величин заряда, массы и скорости частиц, из которых состоят лучи. Из результатов таких опытов можно показать,
что один из[10]двух видов отклоняемых[11] лучей состоит из
двухзаряжённых[12] атомов гелия (бета-лучи), а другой из
быстро движущихся[13] электронов (альфа-лучи).

    Частицы эти, из которых составляются бета-лучи и
альфа-лучи, движутся с огромными скоростями. Поэтому
эти частицы обладают огромной кинетической энергией.
Легко понять почему радиоактивное излучение характеризуется сильным действием на различные вещества.

    В настоящее время при помощи циклотрона можно ис-
кусственно ускорять протоны и другие положительно заря-
жённые[14] частицы до высоких скоростей. Такие искусственно
ускоренные частицы, как и[15] бета-лучи, вызывают глубокие
изменения в различных веществах.

## Notes

1. завёрнутую  "wrapped" modifies пластинку "plate."
Both these Russian words are in the accusative singular case.

2. последнюю  "the latter" refers to  пластинку.

3. The reflexive, possessive pronoun свой modifies заряд
but refers back to последний "the latter" which is both the
subject of the verb теряет "loses," and also refers back to
электроскопу  which is in the dative, singular case after the
preposition по.

4. нетрудно  понять, почему -- "it is not difficult to
understand why --."

5. необходимо  охранять себя от -- "it is necessary to
protect self from --."

6. её  "its" (more literally "her") refers, as indicated by
the feminine gender of её , back to  радиации.

7. ви́да is in the genitive singular following the numeral три. The selection of the case of a noun used after a numeral is governed by an intricate set of conventions summarized in § 371, p. 604.

8. Два други́х ви́да -- "Two other forms--." Here други́х is in the genitive plural and ви́да in the genitive singular following the nominative case of the numeral два, cf. § 371, p. 604.

9. The expression в электри́ческом и в магни́тном поля́х involves two adjectives электри́ческом and магни́тном, both in the prepositional singular case and both modifying поля́х in the prepositional plural. This anomalous situation becomes more understandable if we consider that the expression under consideration is equivalent to the clumsier phrasing в электри́ческом по́ле и в магни́тном по́ле.

10. ИЗ ДВУХ ВИ́ДОВ "of two kinds." Here ВИ́ДОВ is in the genitive plural following ДВУХ which also is in the genitive case.

11. ОТКЛОНЯ́ЕМЫХ is the genitive plural of the present passive participle from the infinitive ОТКЛОНЯ́ТЬ of the verб ОТКЛОНЯ́ТЬ-- ОТКЛОНИ́ТЬ "to deflect," ОТКЛОНЯ́ЕМЫХ лучє́й literally means "of being deflected rays."

12. ДВУХЗАРЯЖЁННЫХ "doubly charged" is closely related to заряжённый the passive past participle from the infinitive заряди́ть of the verb заряжа́ть -- заряди́ть "to charge."

13. ДВИ́ЖУЩИХСЯ is the genitive plural (reflexive form as denoted by -СЯ) of the present active participle from the infinitive ДВИ́ГАТЬ of the verb ДВИ́ГАТЬ -- ДВИ́НУТЬ "to move."

14. Compare Note 12 above.

15. как и "as well as."

§ 171. Translation Exercise.

1. Radioactive preparations spontaneously emit (испуска́ют) invisible rays.
2. It is not difficult (Нетру́дно) to detect a very small amount of a radioactive preparation.

3. If there is placed (to place) a small amount ( количество ) of any radium salt on a photograph plate, then it ( Оно ) acts ( действует ) on the latter.

4. It is necessary ( Необходимо ) to protect self (себя) when working (during work) with (с) radioactive preparations.

5. It is possible ( Можно ) to deflect beta-rays by means of a strong magnetic field.

6. Beta-rays consist of doubly charged atoms of helium.

7. It is possible to show that alpha-rays consist of rapidly moving (moving self) electrons.

8. It is easy to understand why radioactive radiation is able to destroy living (live) tissue.

9. A cyclotron can    ( Может) accelerate protons to high velocities.

10. Artificially accelerated particles from (из) a cyclotron possess enormous kinetic energy.


### Notes


1. The ambiguity inherent in English "it" is removed by use of Russian Оно which being neuter in gender must refer back to the only neuter noun in the sentence, namely, количество.


2. The English "by means of" is indicated by using the instrumental case to translate "strong magnetic field."

# LESSON 20

## NEGATIVE SENTENCES

§ 172. Introductory Note and Summary.

Russian and English methods of constructing negative sentences have much in common. Both languages use negative particles не "not," нет "no," "(is) not," "(are) not"; negative pronouns (e.g., ничего "nothing"); and negative adverbs (e.g., никогда "never"). Furthermore, as already mentioned, не is used in Russian as a negative prefix to form words (e.g., невозможный "impossible;" непрерывно "uninterruptedly," "continuously;" нерастворимость "insolubility") whose use in constructing sentences offers no difficulties to English-speaking persons.

In spite of close similarity between many types of Russian negative sentences and their English counterparts, English-speaking persons must devote special attention to two characteristic features of certain types of Russian negative sentences.

One of these features is the fact that Russians prefer to use the genitive case instead of either the nominative or accusative when referring to an entity whose existence or involvement in an action is denied. It should be noted that this tendency to shift to the genitive is limited to instances where we would expect the nominative and accusative cases and does not extend to other cases (viz., the dative, instrumental or prepositional cases).

The other feature referred to above is the Russian use of не as an additional negative in sentences already containing certain negative adverbs (e.g., никогда "never") or negative pronouns (e.g., ничего "nothing"). This additional negative serves to strengthen and emphasize the negation of the simple sentence or clause rather than resulting in a positive statement as would be the case in English. For this reason, Russian sentences containing two or more negatives are discussed in detail in this Lesson.

263

§ 173.  Simple Negative Sentences.

Various examples of simple negative sentences have been presented in earlier lessons.  On reconsidering these sentences, it will be observed that they are all characterized by the negation being directed to the action expressed by the verb or to some feature of the action expressed, for example, by an adverbial phrase.  Such negation is indicated by use of the particle, не "not."  Simple negative sentences of this type are frequently encountered in scientific Russian.

Молекулы  кислорода  состоят  не  из одного, но из двух
Molecules  of oxygen  consist  not  of one  but of two

атомов.
atoms.

Однако  не все  газы и  пары  состоят из  двухатомных
However  not all  gases and vapors consist  of  diatomic

молекул.
molecules.

Свинец  -  не  магнитное  вещество.
Lead    (is) not (a) magnetic  substance.

При  очень  высоких  температурах  не  могут
At   very   high   temperatures  not  are able

существовать  живые  организмы.
to exist  living  organisms.

Вода  в  твёрдом  состоянии  также  имеет  несколько
Water  in  solid  state  also  has  several

кристаллических  форм,  существование  которых
crystalline  forms,  (the) existence  of which

относится  к  области  высоких  давлений;  эти
pertains  to  (the) field  of high  pressure;  these

формы  не  изображены  на рисунке  25.
forms  (are) not depicted  in Figure  25.

| Клетча́тка | не растворя́ется | в воде́. |
|---|---|---|
| Cellulose | not dissolves self | in water. |

## § 174. Sentences Containing Nouns, Adjectives or Adverbs Formed With the Negative Prefix не-.

Use of the negative prefix не- in forming nouns, adjectives and adverbs recalls to mind similar use of "un-," "in-" and "non-" in forming English words. The Russian nouns, adjectives and adverbs formed with не- are used in constructing sentences in the same way as any other Russian words.

| Созда́ние | ве́чного | дви́гателя | | | явля́ется |
|---|---|---|---|---|---|
| Devising | of (a) perpetual | mover (motion machine) | | | shows self |

невозмо́жным.
impossible.

| Сульфа́т | ба́рия | – | тяжёлое, | бе́лое | вещество́, |
|---|---|---|---|---|---|
| Sulfate | of barium | (is) | a heavy, | white | substance, |

| нераствори́мое | в воде́. |
|---|---|
| insoluble | in water. |

| Столкнове́ние | коме́ты | с | землёй | | весьма́ |
|---|---|---|---|---|---|
| The collision | of (a) comet | with | (the) earth | (is) | extremely |

невероя́тно.
improbable.

| Разруши́тельное | де́йствие | воды́ | | происхо́дит |
|---|---|---|---|---|
| (The) destructive | action | of | water | proceeds |

непреры́вно.
uninterruptedly.

| Рези́на | преставля́ет | собо́й | | | непроводни́к |
|---|---|---|---|---|---|
| Rubber | presents | by means of | self | (a) | non-conductor |

электри́чества.
of electricity.

It is also important to note that Russian nouns, adjectives and adverbs formed with the negative prefix не- may be used either in combination among themselves or together with не- without resulting in unusual sentence constructions of the sort to be discussed subsequently, cf. § 180, p. 272; § 181, p. 274.

После открытия витаминов причина скорбута
After (the) discovery of vitamins (the) cause of scurvy

уже не остаётся неясной.
yet not remains unclear.

Передача радиоволн при радиолокационных
Transmission of radio waves at (by) radar

приборах не происходит непрерывно.
instruments not proceeds uninterruptedly.

Искусственное превращение одного химического
Artificial conversion of one chemical

элемента в другой теперь трудное, но не
element into another now (is) (a) difficult but not

невозможное дело как раньше.
impossible thing as earlier.

Радиоактивные препараты непрерывно излучают
Radioactive preparations uninterruptedly radiate

невидимые лучи.
invisible rays.

§ 175. Use of the Genitive Case to Indicate the Direct Object in Negative Sentences.

With few exceptions, cf. § 85, p. 124; § 102, p. 148; § 114, p. 166, Russian verbs require that their direct object shall be in the accusative case. In some negative sentences the negation is directed primarily toward the direct object which, aside from this fact, would be in the accusative case. In such sentences direction of the negation toward the direct object causes it to shift from the accusative to the genitive case. The following examples are typical.

Азо́т не поддёрживае.т горе́ния.
Nitrogen not supports combustion.


Сфери́ческое зе́ркало не собира́ет отражённых
(A) spherical mirror not collects reflected

луче́й в одну́ то́чку.
rays into one point.


Алюми́ний не даёт непреры́вных твёрдых раство́ров
Aluminum not gives continuous solid solutions

с зо́лотом и с серебро́м, а образу́ет с
with gold and with silver but forms with

ни́ми хими́ческие соедине́ния.
them chemical compounds.


Раство́р спирта́ в воде́ не прово́дит
(A) solution of alcohol in water not conducts

элетри́ческсго то́ка.
electric current.


§ 176. Use of the Genitive to Indicate the Subject of Negative
      Sentences.

Direction of negation toward the subject of a Russian
sentence, which otherwise would be in the nominative case,
causes a shift from the nominative to the genitive case.

Без кислоро́да не происхо́дит дыха́ния живы́х
Without oxygen not occurs (of) breathing of living

органи́змов.
organisms.


В э́той тру́бке нахо́дятся то́лько вода́ и её
In this tube finds self only water and her (water's)

пары́, а во́здуха нет.
vapors but (of) air not.

На лунé     нет вóздуха и нет, слéдовательно,
On (the) moon (is) not (of) air and not consequently,

жи́зни.
(of) life.


В таки́х    слу́чаях    крахма́ла     в    ли́стьях    не
In such     cases      (of) starch     in    leaves     not

получáется.
obtains self.


При таки́х услóвиях реáкции окислéния не
With such conditions (of) reaction of oxidation will not

насту́пит.
set in.


Не мóжет бы́ть сомнéния в том, что молéкулы
Not is able to be (of) doubt in this, that molecules

гáзов всегдá нахóдятся в движéнии.
of gases always find self in motion.


Е́сли при дéйствии си́лы     нет перемещéния,     то
If on action of force (is) not (of) motion, then

     нет и рабóты.
(is) not also (of) work.


В молéкуле метúлового эфúра нет водорóда,
In (the) molecule of methyl ether (is) not (of) hydrogen,

спосóбного замещáться метáллом.
capable to replace self by metal.


     In translating such sentences into smooth English, it is often convenient to use such phrasing as "There occurs no," "There is no." Thus the first sentence would read "Without oxygen there occurs no breathing of living organisms."

§ 177. Negative Sentences with the Direct Object in the Dative or in the Instrumental Case.

In §§ 102, 114 attention was directed to sentences whose verbs require the direct object to be in the instrumental or dative case. When such sentences are negated, the direct object always remains in the instrumental or dative case, regardless of direction of the negation. An indirect object in the dative also undergoes no change in case.

| Крахмал | и | целлюлоза | не | образуют | видимых |
|---|---|---|---|---|---|
| Starch | and | cellulose | not | form | visible |

| кристаллов | и не обладают | сладким | вкусом. |
|---|---|---|---|
| crystals | and not possess | sweet | taste. |

| Существование | атомов | не | подлежит | сомнению. |
|---|---|---|---|---|
| (The) existence | of atoms | not | is subject | to doubt. |

| Все | реакции | не | поддаются | непосредственному |
|---|---|---|---|---|
| All | reactions | not | submit self | to direct |

| экспериментальному | изучению. |
|---|---|
| experimental | study. |

| Сильное | понижение | температуры | не делает металлы |
|---|---|---|---|
| Strong | lowering | of temperature | not makes metals |

| абсолютно | хрупкими, | неспособными | к пластической |
|---|---|---|---|
| absolutely | brittle | incapable | to plastic |

| деформации. |
|---|
| deformation. |

| Все | эти | диаграммы | настолько | просты, | что |
|---|---|---|---|---|---|
| All | these | diagrams | (are) so | simple, | that |

| не требуют[1] | отдельных | пояснений. |
|---|---|---|
| not they require | separate | explanations. |

---

[1] The various forms of требовать "to be requiring" govern the genitive even in positive sentences, cf. § 85, p. 124.

§ 178.  Negative Sentences Involving  нельзя́.

A  rather  peculiar  type  of  impersonal,  negative  sentence  is
formed  in  Russian  by  using  нельзя́  ("it is not allowed,"   "it is
impossible")  together with an infinitive of the negated verb.

| Нельзя́ | провести́ | ре́зкого | разделе́ния |
|---|---|---|---|
| It is impossible | to carry through | (a) sharp | division |

| просты́х | веще́ств | на мета́ллы | и | немета́ллы. |
|---|---|---|---|---|
| of simple | substances | into metals | | and non-metals. |

| Без | удобре́ния | по́чвы | нельзя́ | получи́ть |
|---|---|---|---|---|
| Without | fertilizer | of  soil | it is impossible | to obtain |

| высо́ких | урожа́ев. |
|---|---|
| high | harvests. |

| Нельзя́ | дава́ть | | свети́льному | га́зу |
|---|---|---|---|---|
| It  is  forbidden | to  give | (to permit) | illuminating | gas |

| вытека́ть | в | помеще́ние | лаборато́рии. |
|---|---|---|---|
| to flow out | into | (the) room | of (the) laboratory. |

§ 179.  Negative  Sentences  with  Subject  in  the  Nominative  and
Direct Object in the Accusative Case.

In  a  Russian  sentence,  negation  must  be  directed  either
toward  the  subject  or  toward  the  direct  object  if  the  subject  is
to  shift  from  the  nominative  to  the  genitive  case  or  if  the  direct
object  is  to  shift  from  the  accusative  to  the  genitive  case.  (See
§  177, p. 269  regarding  negative  sentences  having  the  direct
object in the dative or instrumental cases).

| Для | техни́ческих | целе́й, | водоро́д | получа́ется | не |
|---|---|---|---|---|---|
| For | technical | purposes, | hydrogen | obtains self | not |

| из | кисло́т. |
|---|---|
| from acids. | |

Предельные    углеводороды    не    реагируют    с
Saturated     hydrocarbons     not   react         with

металлами.
metals.


Как    правило,    неполярные    вещества    не растворяются
As     (a) rule    non-polar     substances   not dissolve self

в полярных растворителях.
in polar       solvents.


При    нагревании    клетчатка    и    крахмал    не плавятся,
On     heating       cellulose    and  starch     not melt self

но химически    разлагаются.
but chemically  decompose self.


Таким образом,    получается    практически    чистый
In  this  way     obtains self    practically    pure

газообразный    дейтерий,    в    котором    даже
gaseous         deuterium    in   which      even

спектроскопическим    путём нельзя        обнаружить
by spectroscopic        method it is impossible to detect

присутствие    атомов        $^1$H.
(the) presence  of atoms    (of) $1_H$.


Однако    этим    механизмом нельзя        объяснить те
However  by this   mechanism it is impossible to explain  those

скорости    реакции,    которые    во    многих    случаях
rates    of   reaction    which      in    many      cases

наблюдаются    при    химических    превращениях.
observe self    during chemical     changes.

§ 180.  Multiple Negatives in Russian Sentences.

An inherently negative meaning characterizes various Russian adverbs and pronouns, of which the more important are the following: НИКОГДА́, never; НИГДЕ́ nowhere (location); НИКУДА́ nowhere (motion implied); НИКТО́ no one; НИЧТО́ nothing; НИЧЕГО́ (there is) nothing; (there is) none; НИКАКО́Й, of no kind; НИ ----- НИ -------, neither ------- nor, -------.

These negative words will be termed <u>dependent negatives</u> as their presence in a sentence or clause requires simultaneous use of the independent negative НЕ (for which another independent negative, e.g., НЕЛЬЗЯ́ may sometimes be substituted). When one of the dependent negatives is used with НЕ (or other independent negative) the resulting double negative requires only a single negative for translation into correct English. In other words, a combination of one dependent and one independent negative in Russian does not correspond to a positive sentence as would be the case if each Russian negative were translated separately and interpreted by English rules. On the contrary, the simultaneous use of either НЕ or НЕЛЬЗЯ́ with one or even several dependent negatives supports and emphasizes the negation. The following sentences illustrate this important point.

Число́        1 не  причисля́ется    НИ    к просты́м,
(The) number  1 [not] reckons self    neither  to simple,

НИ   к  соста́вным   числа́м,   оно́  занима́ет  осо́бое
nor  to  composite   numbers   it    occupies   peculiar

положе́ние.
position.

Клетча́тка     не  растворя́ется   НИ   в  воде́,  НИ
Cellulose      [not] dissolves self   neither  in water,  nor

в эфи́ре, ни в спирте́.
in ether,  nor in alcohol.

В э́том слу́чае никако́го измене́ния фа́зы  не  происхо́дит.
In this case  no         change    of phase [not] occurs.

Нитроглицерин, в виду́ его́ кра́йней опа́сности,
Nitroglycerol, in view of its extreme danger,

в чи́стом ви́де никогда́ не применя́ется.
in pure form never [not] uses self.

Кре́пкие кислоты́ никогда́ нельзя́ вылива́ть в
Strong acids [never] it is forbidden to pour out into

ра́ковину.
(the) sink.

Никогда́ не сле́дует при разбавле́нии се́рной
Never [not] it ought on dilution of sulfuric

кислоты́ лить во́ду в кре́пкую кислоту́.
acid to pour water into strong acid.

Когда́ како́й-нибудь предме́т ниче́м не
When any object by nothing [not]

подде́рживается, он па́дает на зе́млю, потому́
supports self, he falls to (the) earth because

что земля́ его́ притя́гивает.
that (the) earth him attracts.

Так называ́емые "па́дающие звёзды" с настоя́щими
Thus called "falling stars" with genuine

звёздами не име́ют ничего́ о́бщего.
stars [not] have nothing common.

Звёзды – чрезвыча́йно да́лекие со́лнца – никогда́
Stars — extremely distant suns — never

никуда́ не па́дают.
nowhere [not] fall.

§ 181.  Care   Required   to Interpret   Multiple   Negatives   in
Compound Russian Sentences.

As  pointed  out  in  the  preceding  section  (§  180),  the  only
effect  of  the  presence  of  two  (and  even  three  or  four)  mutually
interdependent  negative  words  in  a  simple  Russian  sentence  (or
in  a  clause  of  a  compound  sentence)  is  to  emphasize  the  negation.
Such   interaction   to   emphasize   negation   of   combinations   of
dependent  negatives  (e.g.,  никогда  never)  and  an  independent
negative  (e.g.,  не  not)  can  occur  only  within  simple  sentences
and   individual   clauses.   When   reading   Russian   compound
sentences,  each  clause  containing  negation  must  be  considered
separately  as  is  evident  from  the  following  sentences.

Зёрна     металла       никогда   не    бывают  тождественны
Grains    of (a) metal    never    [not]  are       identical

друг с   другом,   а   потому  и   их   электрохимические
one    with (the) other, and hence    both their electrochemical

потенциалы,   а,  следовательно, и    скорости  растворения
potentials       and consequently    also rates      of solution

         не одинаковы.
(are) not identical.


Химический      анализ     метеоритов      показывает,   что
Chemical          analysis   of meteorities   shows,           that

они    состоят   из   известных    на    земле   химических
they    consist    of    known        on    earth    chemical

элементов     и    не    содержат   никаких      новых
elements       and  [not]  contain     not any       new

элементов,     которых    не существует    на земле.
elements,       (of) which   not exist          on  earth.


Известка        не    затвердевает    в    воде    и    для
Lime (mortar)   not   hardens          in   water   and   for

подводных     сооружений    совершенно       не   пригодна,
underwater     structures      completely (is)   not  suitable,

а  цемент   затвердевает   и   в воде.
but cement   hardens         even in water.

Зако́н     сохране́ния     ма́ссы     веще́ств
(The) law     of (the) conservation     of mass     of substances

подтвержда́ет     осно́вное     филосо́фское     положе́ние
confirms     (the) basic     philosophical     proposition

о     том,     что в приро́де     ничто́     не исчеза́ет
concerning this (fact), that in nature     nothing     [not] vanishes

бессле́дно     и     не появля́ется     из     ничего́.
without     trace and [not] appears     from nothing.

Нельзя́     сказа́ть,     что хими́ческие     превраще́ния
(It is) impossible to say,     that chemical     reactions

не     происхо́дят     при     радиоакти́вном     распа́де
not     occur     during     (the) radioactive     decomposition

а́томов.
of atoms.


§ 182. Reading Exercise.

### Радиоакти́вность
### (Часть втора́я)

Хими́чески реаги́рующие[1] вещества́ ча́сто испуска́ют тепло́ и свет, но они́ не испуска́ют ни га́мма-луче́й, ни заряжённых а́томов ге́лия (а́льфа-луче́й), ни бы́стро дви́жущихся электро́нов (бе́та-луче́й). Одна́ко, обыкнове́нные хими́ческие реа́кции не то́лько отлича́ются от радиоакти́вных проце́ссов таки́ми при́знаками, но та́кже ря́дом други́х характери́стик. Как[2] вообще́ изве́стно, нетру́дно в лаборато́рии уменьши́ть или увели́чить ско́рости обыкнове́нных хими́ческих реа́кций измене́ниями в температу́ре, давле́нии и концентра́циях превраща́ющихся[3] веще́ств. Таки́х[4] зави́симостей от вне́шних усло́вий нет при радиоакти́вных проце́ссах.

Очеви́дно, что радиоакти́вные проце́ссы не отно́сятся к гру́ппе обы́чных хими́ческих реа́кций. Но нельзя́ сказа́ть,

что химическое превращение не происходит при радиоактивных процессах.    Объяснить природу радиоактивных процессов невозможно без понимания современных теорий строения атомов.

Греческое слово "атом" в переводе на русский язык означает неделимую частицу.   Но атом в действительности не является неделимым. Наоборот, атомы состоят по современным теориям из положительно заряжённого ядра и электронов, которые обращаются вокруг ядра.   При обычных химических реакциях происходят изменения во внешних слоях электронов, так⁵ называемых валентных электронов. Ядро атома в таких реакциях не участвует, а остаётся неизменным. Иными словами, при обычных химических реакциях происходят образование и разложение соединений химических элементов, а сами элементы не подвергаются изменениям.   При радиоактивных процессах, наоборот, внешний слой валентных электронов не играет никакой роли. Сущность радиоактивности состоит в том, что ядро атома распадается со взрывом.   В результате взрыва ядра, атом одного элемента превращается в атом другого элемента,  Следовательно, нельзя сказать, что радиоактивное распадение не представляет собой химическую реакцию.   Радиоактивные процессы являются химическими реакциями атомных ядер.

Химические элементы сами⁶ по себе не радиоактивны в большинстве случаев.   Тем не менее,⁷ можно искусственно осуществлять радиоактивные превращения даже устойчивых атомных ядер.   Но обыкновенные химические реактивы не могут вызывать таких ядерных превращений.   Надо пользоваться такими мощными средствами, как α-частицами,  или потоками быстро движущихся положительно заряжённых частиц из циклотрона.   Можно также применять частицы другого типа - именно нейтроны - которые не обладают электрическим зарядом и поэтому не отталкиваются положительно заряжёнными атомными ядрами.

## Notes

1. реаги́рующие    "reacting"   is the nominative plural of the present, active participle from the infinitive реаги́ровать  of the verb реаги́ровать -- прореаги́ровать   "to react."

2. Как вообще́ изве́стно   "as (is) in general known."

3. превраща́ющихся        literally    "converting    self" modifies веще́ств and is the genitive plural (reflexive form as denoted by -ся) of the present active participle from the infinitive превраща́ть  of the verb.

4. таки́х зави́симостей  literally "of such dependences" is the subject of a negative sentence in which the present tense of быть "to be" is implied though omitted, cf. § 176, sentence 3.

5. так называ́емых    "so-called"  modifies электро́нов. Here называ́емых  is in the genitive, plural of the present, passive participle from the infinitive называ́ть "to be naming."

6. са́ми по себе́ "of themselves."

7. тем не ме́нее "none the less."

§ 183. Translation Exercise.

1. Chemically reacting substances   do    not    emit    neither charged atoms of helium (alpha-rays), nor gamma-rays.
2. It is not difficult to show that ordinary chemical reactions differ from radioactive processes.
3. It is obvious that   radioactive elements   do   not   belong ( ОТНО́СЯТСЯ )   to   the   group of ordinary substances.
4. It cannot be said (It is not to say) that   an   atom is (shows self) in actuality indivisible.
5. During ( При) ordinary chemical reactions,   the   nucleus of  an  atom does not undergo (submit self to) changes.
6. In other words, atomic nuclei do not participate in ordinary chemical reactions.
7. Radioactive atoms do not contain stable nuclei.
8. It cannot be said (It is not to say) that chemical elements in the majority of cases are (show self) radioactive.
9. In order to realize radioactive changes of stable atomic nuclei, it is necessary to use powerful means.
10. Positively  charged  atomic  nuclei  do  not  repulse ( ОТТА́ЛКИВАЮТ ) neutrons.

INTRODUCTION TO RUSSIAN VERB CONJUGATION
THE PRESENT TENSE AND THE PERFECTIVE FUTURE
TENSE OF REGULAR VERBS

§ 184.  General Remarks Concerning Verb Conjugations.

As a preliminary to our study of Russian verb forms, it is helpful to consider briefly English verbs which, in general, might be grouped into two main classes depending on whether their conjugation is regular or irregular. Any line drawn between these two general classes is, by its very nature, somewhat arbitrary. For purpose of definition we might regard as regular those verbs whose stems do not undergo any marked change during conjugation. On this basis, we might exemplify these two main classes of English verbs by citing some of their forms as follows:

| Infinitive | Present Tense (3rd Person Singular) | Present Participle | Past Tense | Past Participle |
|---|---|---|---|---|
| | | REGULAR | | |
| to pour | pours | pouring | poured | poured |
| to need | needs | needing | needed | needed |
| to receive | receives | receiving | received | received |
| to specify | specifies | specifying | specified | specified |

279

| Infinitive | Present Tense (3rd Person Singular) | Present Participle | Past Tense | Past Participle |
|---|---|---|---|---|

### IRREGULAR

| Infinitive | Present Tense | Present Participle | Past Tense | Past Participle |
|---|---|---|---|---|
| to throw | throws | throwing | threw | thrown |
| to go | goes | going | went | gone |
| to be | is | being | was | been |
|  |  |  | were |  |

By proceeding along these lines it is possible to effect a similar classification in Russian. The individual infinitives must be taken in Russian, however, as the basis for such classification, as quite often a Russian imperfective infinitive will be conjugated regularly and conjugation of its companion perfective infinitive will involve irregularity. This is the case, for example, with the Russian verb описывать -- описать "to describe." The conjugation of the imperfective infinitive описывать[1] is free of an important irregularity encountered in the conjugation of the perfective infinitive описать.

As discussed in detail in subsequent paragraphs of this lesson, the present tense of any given Russian verb is formed from its imperfective infinitive; from the companion perfective infinitive, a closely related tense -- the perfective future -- is formed. We shall regard as regular only those infinitives from which one or the other of these two tenses is formed by the procedures summarized in this lesson.

§ 185. Relationship Between the Russian Present and Perfective Future Tenses As to Significance.

In the introductory discussion of Russian verbs given in Lesson 6, it was noted that the majority of them have two infinitives -- one imperfective and the other perfective -- from which parallel sets of verb forms are derived. It was also pointed out that forms derived from imperfective infinitives are used when the action is thought of as being in progress, incomplete or frequently repeated. The forms derived from

---

[1] The reverse case -- an irregularly conjugated imperfective with the companion perfective infinitive regularly conjugated -- occurs relatively rarely.

perfective infinitives are used to refer to action thought of as a completed whole. This distinction is of primary importance in understanding the relationship between the Russian present and perfective future tenses.

Use of the present tense in Russian and English have much in common. First of all, the present tense is used to indicate an action characterized by unspecified time of occurrence. Thus the present tense is used both in the English sentence "Sugar dissolves in water" and in the Russian translation " Cáxap растворяется в воде́." Statements of this type are encountered very frequently in scientific writing. Other important uses of the Russian present tense are the following: (1) to indicate action actually in progress at the present time, (2) to speak of past events for the purpose of making the past more vivid (so-called historical present), and (3) to speak of future action when the context makes it clear that the action is thought of as occurring in the future. Obviously there is close relationship to similar use of the present in English.

One approach to understanding the Russian perfective future tense is to consider it as somewhat akin to the present tense, yet differing from the latter by the fact that the perfective future tense is used to indicate action regarded by the speaker or writer as completed and finished once and for all. Since such characterization, in general, does not typify action actually in progress, the perfective future is used (as its name suggests) to refer to completed action in future time. From this point of view it might be concluded that the perfective future could not be used to refer to action denoted by the English present tense. Quite often in scientific Russian, however, the perfective future tense is used to emphasize the completed character of an action with scant attention accorded to the actual time of occurrence. As will be shown by examples in §§ 206 and 207, the perfective future when so used is often best translated by the English present tense.

In reading scientific Russian, the perfective future is encountered far less frequently than the present tense.

Occasionally, the perfective future tense may be used in a fashion somewhat akin to the historical present (see preceding discussion). Thus, a speaker in considering some action may choose as reference point some moment in the past and use the perfective future to speak of some completed action which occurred between the chosen reference point and the actual present. Such use of the perfective future is not important in scientific Russian.

§ 186.  Relationship  Between  the  Russian  Present  and  Perfective
Future  Tenses  As  to  Form.

As  noted  in  previous  discussion,  a  very  close  relationship  as
to  form  exists  between  the  present  and  the  perfective  future
tenses  which  are  formed,  respectively,  from  imperfective  and
perfective  infinitives  by  following  the  same  two-step  procedure:
(1)  remove  from  the  infinitive  an  ending  to  obtain  the  infinitive
stem,  (2)  affix  various  endings  to  the  stem.

This  general  procedure  is  subject  to  minor  variations
depending  on  the  particular  infinitive  from  which  the  present
(or  perfective  future)  is  being  formed.   It  does  not  appear
profitable  to  attempt  formulation  of  rules  for  determining  which
variation  of  the  general  procedure  is  applied  to  a  given  specific
infinitive.   Due  to  the  simple  nature  of  the  variations,  such  rules
would  not  aid  materially  in  learning  to  read  scientific  Russian.

§ 187.  Regular  Formation  of  the  Present  Tense  and  the
Perfective  Future  Tense.

Only  infinitives  terminating  in  -атЬ,  -етЬ,  -итЬ,  -отЬ,
-утЬ,  -ытЬ  or  -ятЬ  (i.e.,  a  combination  of  a  vowel  and  -тЬ)
are  considered  capable  of  regular  formation  of  the  present  tense
(imperfective  infinitive)  or  the  perfective  future  tense  (perfective
infinitive).   As  already  noted  (§ 186),  regular  formation  of  these
tenses  is  subject  to  certain  variations,  which  may  be  grouped  as
follows.

Procedure  "A"
Remove  -тЬ  from  the  infinitives  to  obtain  a  stem  which,
depending  on  the  parent  infinitive,  will  terminate  in  a-,  е-,
и-.  о-,  я-  or  у-.
To  stems  so  obtained,  first  conjugation  endings  (see
below)  are  affixed.
These  infinitives  will  be  designated  as  "Regular  Class
A"  --  abbreviated,  "Reg. A."

Procedure  "B"
Remove  from  the  infinitive  the  ending  -атЬ,  -етЬ,  -итЬ,
-отЬ,  -утЬ  or  -ятЬ  to  obtain  the  infinitive  stem.
Some  of  the  stems  so  obtained  take  first  conjugation
endings  ("Regular  Class  B  --  Subclass  1"   --  abbreviated
"Reg. B-1");  other  infinitives  in  this  main  class  take
the  second  conjugation  endings  ("Regular  Class  B  --  Subclass
2"  --  abbreviated,  "Reg. B-2").

The close similarity between the first and second conjugation endings is evident from the following listing which includes the personal pronouns for reference purposes.[1]

|  | First Conjugation Endings | Second Conjugation Endings | Corresponding Pronouns (Both Conjugations) |
|---|---|---|---|

### Singular

| | | | |
|---|---|---|---|
| 1st Person | -у, -ю | -у, -ю | Я, I |
| 2nd Person | -ешь | -ишь | ТЫ,[2] you |
| 3rd Person | -ет | -ит | ОН, he; ОНа́, she; ОНо́, it |

### Plural

| | | | |
|---|---|---|---|
| 1st Person | -ем | -им | МЫ, we |
| 2nd Person | -ете | -ите | ВЫ,[3] you |
| 3rd Person | -ут, -ют | -ат, -ят | ОНи́, they |

§ 188. Examples of Regular Formation of the Present Tense and the Perfective Future Tense.

As pointed out in § 187, p. 282, regularly conjugated infinitives are grouped into classes depending on the method of formation of their present tense (imperfective infinitives) or perfective future tense (perfective infinitives). Formation of the present and perfective future tenses is given below for infinitives typifying each of the classes defined in § 187.

---

[1] Because of the distinctive nature of the present (perfective future) endings, omission of one or more pronouns from a Russian sentence often does not involve risk of ambiguity as would be the case in English. As a consequence, Russian verb endings must often be used as clues to determine which English pronoun will be required for translation.

[2] This is the familiar form.

[3] This is the formal or polite form.

In considering the examples cited below, it should not be forgotten that each of the classes of infinitives under consideration contain one or more infinitives ending in -атЬ, -етЬ, -итЬ, -утЬ, -отЬ or -ятЬ.

See also the note given at the end of the tabulations.

## TYPICAL REGULAR VERBS

| Imperfective Infinitive | де́латЬ to be doing | рватЬ to be tearing | та́ятЬ to be thawing | горе́тЬ to be burning |
|---|---|---|---|---|
| Perfective Infinitive | сде́латЬ to do | разорва́тЬ to tear apart | раста́ятЬ to thaw | сгоре́тЬ to burn |

## PRESENT TENSE

| Present Tense Stem | дела- | рв- | та- | гор- |
|---|---|---|---|---|
| Class | Reg. A | Reg. B-1 | Reg. B-1 | Reg. B-2 |

### Singular

| | | | | |
|---|---|---|---|---|
| 1st Person | де́лаю | рву | та́ю | горю́ |
| 2nd Person | де́лаешЬ | рвёшЬ | та́ешЬ | гори́шЬ |
| 3rd Person | де́лает | рвёт | та́ет | гори́т |

### Plural

| | | | | |
|---|---|---|---|---|
| 1st Person | де́лаем | рвём | та́ем | гори́м |
| 2nd Person | де́лаете | рвёте | та́ете | гори́те |
| 3rd Person | де́лают | рвут | та́ют | горя́т |

## PERFECTIVE FUTURE TENSE

| Perfective Future Tense Stem | сдела- | разорв- | раста- | сгор- |
|---|---|---|---|---|
| Class | Reg. A | Reg. B-1 | Reg. B-1 | Reg. B-2 |

### Singular

| | | | | |
|---|---|---|---|---|
| 1st Person | сде́лаю | разорву́ | раста́ю | сгорю́ |
| 2nd Person | сде́лаешь | разорвёшь | раста́ешь | сгори́шь |
| 3rd Person | сде́лает | разорвёт | раста́ет | сгори́т |

### Plural

| | | | | |
|---|---|---|---|---|
| 1st Person | сде́лаем | разорвём | раста́ем | сгори́м |
| 2nd Person | сде́лаете | разорвёте | раста́ете | сгори́те |
| 3rd Person | сде́лают | разорву́т | раста́ют | сгоря́т |

### Note

The classification of regular verbs presented here does not suffice for establishing whether a given infinitive of the "Reg. B" class uses the ending -y or -ю to form the first person singular of the present (perfective future) tense. The classification also does not permit a similar decision as to the third person plural form, which sometimes ends in -yT and sometimes in -ЮT for "Reg. B-1" while the endings -aT and -ЯT are the two possibilities for infinitives of the "Reg. B-2" subclass. For purposes of learning to read Russian, a finer, more precise classification is not necessary.

§ 189. Sentences Illustrating Use of the Perfective Future Tense.

Attention is directed to the following sentences in which the perfective future tense is used. Double asterisks are used to point out the perfective future tense, while perfective infinitives in the following sentences are marked with a single asterisk.

In order to gain further insight into the use in Russian of the perfective future tense, its use in coherent text (e.g., the Reading Exercise of § 190) should be carefully observed.


| Приливáние | раствóра | щёлочи | из | бюрéтки |
|---|---|---|---|---|
| Flowing in | of (a) solution | of caustic | from | (the) burette |

| слéдует | закóнчить* | тогдá, | когдá | цвет |
|---|---|---|---|---|
| it is necessary | to stop | then | when | (the) color |

| раствóра | сдéлается** | фиолéтовым. |
|---|---|---|
| of (the) solution | makes self | violet. |


| Éсли | внести* | в | тёплую | кóмнату | кусóк | льда, | он |
|---|---|---|---|---|---|---|---|
| If | carry | in | into (a) warm | room | piece | of ice, | he |

| растáет** |
|---|
| will melt. |


| Водá | в | чáйнике | при | нагревáнии | закипáет | и, | éсли |
|---|---|---|---|---|---|---|---|
| Water | in | teakettle | on | heating | starts to boil | and, | if |

| дóлго | кипятить | её, | то | онá | вся | превратится* |
|---|---|---|---|---|---|---|
| long | boil | her (water), | then | she | all | will convert self |

| в | пар. |
|---|---|
| into | vapor. |


| Спервá | мы | напóлним** | сосýд | водóй | и | сдéлаем** | её |
|---|---|---|---|---|---|---|---|
| First | we | will fill | (the) vessel | with water | and | will make | her |

| мýтной | прибáвкой | небольшóго | колúчества |
|---|---|---|---|
| turbid | by addition | of (a) small | amount |

| раствóра | канифóли | в | спиртý. |
|---|---|---|---|
| of (a) solution | of rosin | in | alcohol. |

| Чтобы | привести* | формулу | к | удобному | для |
|-------|-----------|---------|---|----------|-----|
| In order | to bring | (the) formula | to | (a) convenient | for |

| расчётов | виду, | умножим** | её | правую | и | левую | части |
|----------|-------|-----------|-----|--------|---|-------|-------|
| calculation | form | we will multiply | her | right | and | left | parts |

| на | длину | слоя | δ | и | разделим** | на | λ. |
|----|-------|------|---|---|------------|-----|-----|
| by | (the) length | of (the) layer | δ | and | we will divide | by | λ. |

## § 190.  Reading Exercise.

Underlining has been used to direct attention to the perfective future tense.

### Радиолокация

Основные принципы радиолокационной техники достаточно просты.  Легко уяснить их по аналогии с эхо.[1] Как общеизвестно, хлопок[3] в ущельи через несколько секунд вернётся обратно в виде слабого, отражённого от скалы звука.  Скорость звука в воздухе - 330 метров в секунду. От числа секунд, которые пройдут[4] со времени хлопка[3] до прихода эхо, нетрудно определить расстояние до скалы, от которой отражается звук хлопка.

В радиолокации также применяется явление эхо. Применяется, однако, эхо радиоволн.  Последние обладают громадной скоростью - именно 300000 километров[5] в секунду. Поэтому надо обнаружить и точно измерить весьма короткие промежутки времени.  Нетрудно понять, почему современная радиолокационная станция представляет собой сложный прибор, который составляется главным образом из передатчика и приёмника радиоволн, из вращающейся[6] антенны и из электронно-лучевой трубки.[10]

Источником радиоволн в радиолокационном приборе является ламповый передатчик,[7] который работает с перерывами и таким образом создаёт импульсы радиоволн. Пере-

да́тчик автомати́чески включа́ется на не́сколько миллио́нных до́лей секу́нды и так же автомати́чески выключа́ется. Коли́чество таки́х включе́ний и выключе́ний достига́ет 5000 в секу́нду.

По́сле ка́ждого включе́ния и выключе́ния наступа́ет па́уза, во вре́мя кото́рой на ста́нции идёт прие́м отражённых и́мпульсов. По́сланный и́мпульс достига́ет це́ли[8] - самолёта в во́здухе, корабля́ на мо́ре - и рассе́ивается е́ю[9] во все сто́роны. Очень небольша́я часть э́тих рассе́янных волн возвраща́ется обра́тно и поступа́ет в прие́мник ста́нции,а отту́да на электро́нно-лучеву́ю тру́бку.[10]

При ка́ждом выключе́нии переда́тчика, в це́нтре экра́на тако́й тру́бки возника́ет светя́щийся[11] луч, кото́рый бе́гает радиа́льно к кра́ю экра́на. Как то́лько придёт[12] и́мпульс, отражённый от самолёта и́ли корабля́, луч даст[13] бо́лее я́ркую вспы́шку. Одновреме́нно с враще́нием анте́нны радиолокацио́нной ста́нции электро́нный луч перемеша́ется по экра́ну и вновь че́ртит световы́е ли́нии. За коро́ткий промежу́ток вре́мени электро́нный луч обежи́т весь экра́н. Отражённые и́мпульсы начертя́т на нём как[14] бы "электро́нную ка́рту" ме́стности, кото́рая окружа́ет радиолокацио́нную ста́нцию. На э́той ка́рте нетру́дно определи́ть, на како́м расстоя́нии и в како́м направле́нии нахо́дятся це́ли, кото́рые отража́ют радиово́лны.

В настоя́щее вре́мя применя́ется радиолокацио́нная те́хника для навигацио́нных це́лей на не́которых комме́рческих корабля́х, в ча́стности на большо́м англи́йском пассажи́рском корабле́ "Куи́н Эли́забет."[15]

## Notes

1. ЭХО "echo." The word ЭХО is not declined but is used in one form only. Further examples of nouns of foreign origin likewise not declined include ра́дио "radio," гуа́но "guano," and КАЛИ as used in the expression е́дкое КАЛИ "caustic potash," not to be confused with ка́лий, "potassium," cf. § 363, p. 588.

2. ХЛОПОЌ when accented on the last syllable, means "clap." The corresponding plural ХЛОПКИ́ means "applause." (Note omission of second "O" in forming this plural). When accented ХЛО́ПОК the meaning is "cotton," "floc."

3. ХЛОПКА́ "of (a) clap" is the irregularly formed genitive singular of ХЛОПО́К, cf. Note 2 above.

4. ПРОЙДУ́Т "(they) pass or elapse" is the third person plural of the perfective future from the infinitive ПРОЙТИ́ of the verb ПРОХОДИ́ТЬ -- ПРОЙТИ́ "to pass, to elapse, to go through."

5. Nouns following certain numerals are in the genitive plural, provided the numerals in question are in either the nominative or the accusative case, cf. § 371, p. 604.

6. враща́ющейся is the genitive, feminine, singular (reflexive form) of the present active participle from враща́ть "to be rotating, to be turning."

7. In referring to a radio vacuum tube (or a wireless valve as such a device is sometimes called in Britain) the Russians use the word ла́мпа "lamp" usually together with an appropriate adjective as, for example, in the expression усили́тельная ла́мпа "amplifying tube." Here the adjective ла́мповый (derived from ла́мпа) is used to modify переда́тчик "transmitter," thus indicating that the transmitter uses tubes, rather than spark or other high frequency power source.

8. це́ли, самолёта and корабля́ are all in the genitive case after достига́ет, cf. § 85, p. 124.

9. е́ю (alternate form ей) literally may be translated as "by means of her." е́ю from. ОНА́ "she," is in the instrumental femine singular case and refers back to це́ли.

10. на электро́нно-лучеву́ю тру́бку "to the electron beam tube." It is perhaps obvious that reference is being made to a cathode ray tube.

11. светя́щийся "shining," "luminous" is sometimes regarded as an adjective although by origin, at least, it is the present active participle of the reflexive of свети́ть "to give light," "to shine." The reflexive ending -СЯ as used here has little, discernable reflexive meaning. A similar word is трудя́щийся used both as an adjective and a noun to mean "toiling" or "toiler."

12. придёт literally "(he) will arrive" is the irregular third person singular of the perfective future tense from the infinitive прийти of the verb приходить -- прийти "to arrive." Here the perfective future emphasizes completed action rather than future occurrence. Translation by the English present tense does not do violence to the meaning of the Russian.

13. даст literally "(he) will give" is the irregular third person singular of the perfective future tense from the infinitive дать of the verb давать -- дать "to give." Here again the Russian perfective future tense can be translated by the English present tense for the same reason as given in the preceding note.

14. как бы "as it were."

15. "Куйн Элйзабет"    -- a phonetic transliteration of "Queen Elizabeth" -- is not declined. The Russian name Елизавета, corresponding to Elizabeth in English is declined in the same way as молекула (Key No. 7, § 130, p. 190).


§ 191. Translation Exercise.

1. It is easy to explain the basic principles of radar.
2. It is not difficult to determine the speed of sound in air.
3. In radar is used the phenomena of echo or radio waves.
4. A contemporary radar station consists principally ( главным образом ) of (из) a transmitter and receiver of radio waves of (из) a rotating antenna and of (из) an electron beam tube.
5. The transmitter functions (работает ) with interruptions and thus ( таким образом ) creates pulses of radio waves.
6. The transmitted impulse is scattered  by the    target (целью) in all directions.
7. After each switching off of the transmitter proceeds the reception of the scattered waves.
8. Simultaneously with the rotation of the antenna, an electron beam flees quickly from (от) the center ( центра ) to the edge of the screen.
9. The electron beam draws bright lines on (на) the screen ( экране ) and thus ( таким образом ) sketches, as it were, an "electronic map."
10. Radar is used on the big English passenger ship "Queen Elizabeth."

# LESSON 22

## THE PRESENT TENSE AND PERFECTIVE FUTURE TENSE OF IRREGULAR INFINITIVES IN -ТЬ (BUT EXCLUDING -ЗТЬ AND -СТЬ)

§ 192. General Remarks on Irregular Formation of the Present Tense and Perfective Future Tense.

As discussed in preceding Lesson 21, regular derivation of the present tense from an imperfective infinitive (and the perfective future from a perfective infinitive) can be regarded as involving two steps: (1) removing from the infinitive a characteristic infinitive ending and (2) affixing to the stem so obtained various present (perfective future) tense endings. This general procedure and variations thereof as applied to regular infinitives were discussed in Lesson 21.

In this lesson attention is directed to infinitives, whose stems undergo change during formation of the present (or perfective future) tense. A fairly large number of such stem changes are exhibited by different infinitives, which consequently are termed irregular.

It is important clearly to understand that formation of the present (or perfective future) from the infinitives under consideration in this lesson involves three steps:

Step 1. Removal of an ending from an infinitive to obtain a stem.

Step 2. Alteration of the stem[1] in various ways preparatory to Step 3.

Step 3. Affixing regular endings previously listed, cf. § 187, p. 283. Which of the two sets of regular endings is used depends on the individual infinitive.

[1] With some infinitives a further complication is encountered by virtue of the fact that the stem alteration may not persist throughout all the forms of the present (or perfective future) tense. However, this sort of minor variation is without influence on the importance of the fact that regular endings are used to conjugate all irregular infinitives to be considered in this lesson.

291

This use of regular endings has an important consequence which becomes evident on considering an example. Once the present (perfective future) endings are known it is easy to see that verb forms, such as ПИШУТ consist of two parts, the stem ПИШ- and the known ending -УТ. This ending indicates that the verb form under consideration is the third person plural of either the present or perfective future tense. Associating the irregular, altered stem ПИШ- with the infinitive[1] ПИСАТЬ "to be writing" may prove difficult for the novice, and impede his understanding that ПИШУТ means "(they) are writing." To assist the beginner, the Russian vocabulary in this book lists as separate entries all irregular verb forms used in the Reading Exercises.

§ 193.  Importance of the Present Tense and the Perfective Future Tense with Respect to Other Verb Forms.

Stem changes encountered in formation of the present tense from irregular imperfective infinitives usually carry over to their present participles (both active and passive) their present gerunds and their imperative forms. Similarly, stem changes involved in formation of the perfective future carry over into their imperative[2] forms.  For this reason, the present and perfective future tenses are the key to the conjugation of the great majority of Russian irregular infinitives.  For a comprehensive summary, see § 324, p. 509 and accompanying table pp. 511-513.

§ 194.  Classification of Infinitive Stem Changes Discussed in This Lesson.

It is possible to group into six general classes the various stem changes encountered during irregular formation of the present (perfective future) from infinitives under discussion in this lesson.

---

[1].It should be recalled in this connection that infinitives are the verb forms conventionally listed in dictionaries.
[2] Present participles and present gerunds are not formed from perfective infinitives.

| Infinitive Class | Stem Change |
|---|---|
| Irr. A-1 | -OB- replaced by -у- |
| Irr. A-2 | -ЕВ- replaced by -Ю- |
| Irr. B | -В- removed from stem |
| Irr. C-1,2 | Addition of -Л- to stem ending in б-, в-, м-, п- or ф- |
| Irr. C-3,4,5 | Addition of -В-, -Н- or -М- |
| Irr. D | Change of final consonant |
| Irr. E | Addition of -Е-, -О- or -Ь- or removal of -Е- |
| Irr. F | Miscellaneous, more complex changes |

§ 195. Examples of Stem Changes by Replacement of -OB- or -EB- by -у- or -ю-, Respectively.

Particular attention should be directed to the irregularity encountered in the conjugation of infinitives terminating in -ировать or -овать, namely replacement of -OB- by -у-. Such infinitives typify a host of verbs, e.g., фильтровать -- профильтровать (to filter), фотографировать -- сфотографировать (to photograph), публиковать -- опубликовать (to publish). Such verbs, adopted into Russian from other languages, are of particular importance in scientific Russian.[1] There are also quite a number of purely Russian verbs with infinitives terminating in -овать. Much less importance attaches to the related class of infinitives terminating in -евать.

[1] Cf. § 40, p. 56.

| | | | |
|---|---|---|---|
| Imperfective Infinitive | фотографи́роɛать<br>to be photographing | существова́ть<br>to be existing | малева́ть<br>to be painting |
| Perfective Infinitive | сфотографи́ровать<br>to photograph | просуществова́ть<br>to exist (through to the end) | намалева́ть<br>to paint |

## PRESENT TENSE

| | | | |
|---|---|---|---|
| Present Tense Stem | фотографи́ру- | существу́- | малю́- |
| Class | Irr. A-1 | Irr. A-1 | Irr. A-2 |

### Singular

| | | | |
|---|---|---|---|
| 1st Person | фотографи́рую | существу́ю | малю́ю |
| 2nd Person | фотографи́руешь | существу́ешь | малю́ешь |
| 3rd Person | фотографи́рует | существу́ет | малю́ет |

### Plural

| | | | |
|---|---|---|---|
| 1st Person | фотографи́руем | существу́ем | малю́ем |
| 2nd Person | фотографи́руете | существу́ете | малю́ете |
| 3rd Person | фотографи́руют | существу́ют | малю́ют |

## PERFECTIVE FUTURE TENSE

| | | | |
|---|---|---|---|
| Perfective Future Tense Stem | сфотографи́ру- | просуществу́- | намалю́- |
| Class | Irr. A-1 | Irr. A-1 | Irr. A-2 |

### Singular

| | | | |
|---|---|---|---|
| 1st Person | сфотографи́рую | просуществу́ю | намалю́ю |
| 2nd Person | сфотографи́руешь | просуществу́ешь | намалю́ешь |
| 3rd Person | сфотографи́рует | просуществу́ет | намалю́ет |

### Plural

| | | | |
|---|---|---|---|
| 1st Person | сфотографи́руем | просуществу́ем | намалю́ем |
| 2nd Person | сфотографи́руете | просуществу́ете | намалю́ете |
| 3rd Person | сфотографи́руют | просуществу́ют | намалю́ют |

The following two groups of sentences illustrate the use of the present and perfective future tenses from infinitives terminating in -ИРОВАТЬ or -ОВАТЬ.

## Group A.[1]  Russianized Verbs of Foreign Origin

| Рентге́новские | лучи́ | ионизи́руют | во́здух | и | други́е |
|---|---|---|---|---|---|
| Roentgen | rays | ionize | air | and | other |

га́зы.
gases.

| Снача́ла | мы | наэлектризу́ем | | электроско́п. |
|---|---|---|---|---|
| First | we | will charge (electrically) | | (the) electroscope. |

| В | настоя́щее | вре́мя | произво́дство | лёгких | мета́ллов |
|---|---|---|---|---|---|
| At | (the) present | time | (the) production | of light | metals |

| В | большинстве́ | слу́чаев | бази́руется | | | на |
|---|---|---|---|---|---|---|
| in | (the) majority | of cases | bases | self | (is based) | on |

электроэне́ргии.
electrical energy.

| Толуо́л | нитру́ется | | сравни́тельно | легко́. |
|---|---|---|---|---|
| Toluene | nitrates self | (is nitrated) | relatively | easily. |

| Что́бы | вы́числить | pH | раство́ра, | мы | снача́ла |
|---|---|---|---|---|---|
| In order | to compute | (the) pH | of (a) solution | we | first |

| логарифми́руем | концентра́цию | Н-ио́нов, |
|---|---|---|
| take the logarithm of | (the) concentration | of H-ions, |

| вы́раженную | в грамм-эквивале́нтах. |
|---|---|
| expressed | in gram-equivalents. |

---

[1] The parent infinitives of irregular verb forms in these sentences are successively: ионизи́ровать, наэлектризова́ть, бази́ровать, нитрова́ть, логарифми́ровать, диссоции́ровать.

| Согла́сно | тео́рии | Арре́ниуса | моле́кулы | кисло́т, |
|---|---|---|---|---|
| According to | (the) theory | of Arrhenius | molecules | of acids, |

| щёлочей и | соле́й | уже́ при | само́м | растворе́нии | в воде́ |
|---|---|---|---|---|---|
| alkalies and | salts | even on | very | dissolution | in water |

| "диссоции́руют" | (т.е. распада́ются) | на |
|---|---|---|
| "dissociate" | (i.e., fall apart self ) | into |

| противополо́жно | заряжённые | части́цы, | называ́емые[1] |
|---|---|---|---|
| oppositely | charged | particles, | being called |

ио́нами.
ions.

## Group B.  Verbs of Purely Russian Character[2]

| Существу́ет | мно́го | ти́пов | желе́зных | руд. |
|---|---|---|---|---|
| (There) exist | many | types | of iron | ores. |

| В | во́здухе | всегда́ | прису́тствуют | пыль и |
|---|---|---|---|---|
| In | air | always | are present | dust and |

микроорганизмы.
microorganisms.

| Ацетиле́н | испо́льзуется | в | грома́дном |
|---|---|---|---|
| Acetylene | utilizes self (is utilized) | in | enormous |

| коли́честве | для автоге́нной | сва́рки | мета́ллов. |
|---|---|---|---|
| amount | for autogenic | welding | of metals. |

| Таки́е | явле́ния, | при | кото́рых не | образу́ется | но́вых |
|---|---|---|---|---|---|
| Such | phenomena, | during | which not | form self | new |

| веще́ств, | отно́сятся | к явле́ниям | физи́ческим. |
|---|---|---|---|
| substances, | pertain | to phenomena | physical. |

---

[1]  Here называ́емые,  is the nominative plural of the passive present participle from the infinitive называ́ть of the verb называ́ть - назва́ть "to name," cf. Lesson 30.

[2]  The parent infinitives  of irregular verb forms  in these sentences are successively: существова́ть, прису́тствовать, испо́льзовать, образова́ть.

§ 196. Examples of Stem Changes by Removal of -B- from Stem.

The imperfective infinitive давáть "to be giving" and related infinitives, e.g., издавáть "to be giving out," "to be publishing" form the present tense with alteration of the stem by removal of the letter -B-.

| Imperfective Infinitive | давáть to be giving | издавáть to be giving out |
|---|---|---|

PRESENT TENSE

| Present Tense Stem | да- | изда- |
|---|---|---|
| Class | Irr. B | Irr. B |

| | Singular | Plural | Singular | Plural |
|---|---|---|---|---|
| 1st Person | даю́ | даём | издаю́ | издаём |
| 2nd Person | даёшь | даёте | издаёшь | издаёте |
| 3rd Person | даёт | даю́т | издаёт | издаю́т |

The perfective infinitives corresponding to давáть and издавáть are, respectively, дать and издáть. Unusual irregularities are encountered in the conjugation of дать, издáть and other perfective infinitives similarly derived from дать, cf. § 207, p. 323.

§ 197. Examples of Stem Changes by Addition of a Consonant.

This type of stem change assumes one or the other of the following forms depending on the infinitive in question.

| Imperfective Infinitive | колеба́ть to be shaking | криви́ть to be twisting, bending | жить to be living | жать to be squeezing | стыть to be cooling |
|---|---|---|---|---|---|
| Perfective Infinitive | поколеба́ть to shake | покриви́ть to twist, bend | пожи́ть to live (for a while) | пожа́ть to squeeze | осты́ть to cool |

## PRESENT TENSE

| Present Tense Stem | колебл- | кривл- крив- | жив- | жм- | стын- |
|---|---|---|---|---|---|
| Class | Irr. C-1 | Irr. C-2 | Irr. C-3 | Irr. C-4 | Irr. C-5 |

### Singular

| | | | | | |
|---|---|---|---|---|---|
| 1st Person | коле́блю | кривлю́ | живу́ | жму | сты́ну |
| 2nd Person | коле́блешь | криви́шь | живёшь | жмёшь | сты́нешь |
| 3rd Person | коле́блет | криви́т | живёт | жмёт | сты́нет |

### Plural

| | | | | | |
|---|---|---|---|---|---|
| 1st Person | коле́блем | криви́м | живём | жмём | сты́нем |
| 2nd Person | коле́блете | криви́те | живёте | жмёте | сты́нете |
| 3rd Person | коле́блют | кривя́т | живу́т | жмут | сты́нут |

## PERFECTIVE FUTURE TENSE

| Future Tense Stem | поколебл- | покривл- покриб- | пожив- | пожм- | остын- |
|---|---|---|---|---|---|
| Class | Irr. C-1 | Irr. C-2 | Irr. C-3 | Irr. C-4 | Irr. C-5 |

### Singular

| | | | | | |
|---|---|---|---|---|---|
| 1st Person | поколе́блю | покривлю́ | поживу́ | пожму́ | осты́ну |
| 2nd Person | поколе́блешь | покриви́шь | поживёшь | пожмёшь | осты́нешь |
| 3rd Person | поколе́блет | покриви́т | поживёт | пожмёт | осты́нет |

### Plural

| | | | | | |
|---|---|---|---|---|---|
| 1st Person | поколе́блем | покриви́м | поживём | пожмём | осты́нем |
| 2nd Person | поколе́блете | покриви́те | поживёте | пожмёте | осты́нете |
| 3rd Person | поколе́блют | покривя́т | поживу́т | пожму́т | осты́нут |

1) Addition of -Л- to infinitive stems ending in б-, в-, м-, п- and ф-. (Note that the added -Л- persists with some infinitives throughout the present -- or the perfective future -- tense, but with others is used only in the first person singular.)
2) Addition of -В-, -Н- or -М- to an infinitive stem.

Certain infinitives in this general subclass take first conjugation endings, others take second conjugation endings.[1] Infinitives in this subclass also differ with respect to their infinitive endings. It is not practical to cite examples of all minor variations involved in the conjugation of this subclass of irregular infinitives.

The following sentences[2] illustrate use of the present and perfective future tenses of this subclass of irregular infinitives.

| На | дне | океа́на | живёт | мно́го | стра́нных |
|---|---|---|---|---|---|
| On | (the) bottom | of (the) ocean | live | many | of strange |

живо́тных.
animals.

| Хими́ческий | соста́в | бокси́тов | коле́блется | в |
|---|---|---|---|---|
| (The) chemical | composition | of bauxites | fluctuates | within |

широ́ких преде́лах.
wide    limits.

| Начну́ | с | са́мого | рожде́ния | коме́ты. |
|---|---|---|---|---|
| I will begin | from | the very | birth | of (the) comet. |

| В | настоя́щее | вре́мя[3] | жмут | съедо́бное | ма́сло | из |
|---|---|---|---|---|---|---|
| At (the) present | time | | they press | edible | fat | from |

хлопко́вого се́мени.[4]
cotton       seed.

---

[1] First and second conjugation endings are summarized in § 187, p. 283.
[2] The parent infinitives of irregular verb forms in these sentences are successively: жить, колеба́ть, нача́ть, жать.
[3] в настоя́щее вре́мя is a fixed expression or idiom discussed in Note 4, p. 151.
[4] се́мени is the genitive singular of the irregularly declined neuter noun, се́мя, cf. § 358, p. 575.

§ 198.  Examples of Changes in Final Consonant of Stem.

Certain consonant shifts are encountered rather frequently in Russian both in the conjugation of irregular infinitives but also in the derivation of words, as will be observed when using the Russian-English vocabulary. The majority of such shifts take place in verb conjugation as indicated below.

| | | | |
|---|---|---|---|
| Г → Ж | Д → Ж | Д → ЖД | З → Ж |
| К → Ч | С → Ш | Х → Ш | Ц → Ч |
| СК → Щ | СТ → Щ | Т → Ч | Т → Щ |

As shown by the following examples, with certain infinitives a stem alteration does not persist throughout all the forms of the present (or perfective future) tense. Here, again, it is not practical to cite examples of all variations involved in the conjugation of this subclass of irregular infinitives. In particular, an example has not been provided for certain of the above mentioned consonant shifts.

The following sentences[1] illustrate use of the present and of the perfective future tense formed from infinitives in this subclass.

| Металлический | натрий | легко́ | ре́жется | ножо́м. |
|---|---|---|---|---|
| Metallic | sodium | easily | cuts self | with (a) knife. |

| Е́сли | коэфицие́нт | ока́зывается | | ра́вным |
|---|---|---|---|---|
| If | (the) coefficient | proves self | (turns out to be) | equal |

| единѝце, | то | он | не | пи́шется. | |
|---|---|---|---|---|---|
| to unity, | then | he (it) | not | writes self | (is not written). |

| По | гипо́тезе | да́тского | учёного | Бо́ра |
|---|---|---|---|---|
| According to | (the) hypothesis | of (the) Danish | scientist | Bohr |

| электро́ны | дви́жутся | вокру́г | ядра́ | по |
|---|---|---|---|---|
| (the) electrons | move self | around | (the) nucleus | along |

| разли́чно | расположе́нным | орби́там. |
|---|---|---|
| differently | positioned | orbits. |

---

[1] The parent infinitives of irregular verb forms in these sentences are successively: ре́зать, писа́ть, дви́гать, рассказа́ть, хоте́ть.

| | | | | | |
|---|---|---|---|---|---|
| **Imperfective Infinitive** | писа́ть<br>to be writing | носи́ть<br>to be carrying | лгать<br>to be telling a lie | е́хать<br>to be travelling, riding | хоте́ть<br>to be wishing, desiring |
| **Perfective Infinitive** | написа́ть<br>to write | поноси́ть<br>to carry (for a time) | солга́ть<br>to tell a lie | пое́хать<br>to travel, ride | захоте́ть<br>to wish, desire |

## PRESENT TENSE

| | | | | | |
|---|---|---|---|---|---|
| **Present Tense Stem** | пиш– | нос–<br>нош– | лг–<br>лж– | ед– | хот–<br>хоч– |
| **Class** | Irr. D-1 | Irr. D-2 | Irr. D-3 | Irr. D-4 | Irr. D-5 |

### Singular

| | | | | | |
|---|---|---|---|---|---|
| **1st Person** | пишу́ | ношу́ | лгу | е́ду | хочу́ |
| **2nd Person** | пи́шешь | но́сишь | лжёшь | е́дешь | хо́чешь |
| **3rd Person** | пи́шет | но́сит | лжёт | е́дет | хо́чет |

### Plural

| | | | | | |
|---|---|---|---|---|---|
| **1st Person** | пи́шем | но́сим | лжём | е́дем | хоти́м |
| **2nd Person** | пи́шете | но́сите | лжёте | е́дете | хоти́те |
| **3rd Person** | пи́шут | но́сят | лгут | е́дут | хотя́т |

## PERFECTIVE FUTURE TENSE

| | | | | | |
|---|---|---|---|---|---|
| **Perfective Future Tense Stem** | напиш– | понос–<br>понош– | солг–<br>солж– | поед– | захот–<br>захоч– |
| **Class** | Irr. D-1 | Irr. D-2 | Irr. D-3 | Irr. D-4 | Irr. D-5 |

### Singular

| | | | | | |
|---|---|---|---|---|---|
| **1st Person** | напишу́ | поношу́ | солгу́ | пое́ду | захочу́ |
| **2nd Person** | напи́шешь | поно́сишь | солжёшь | пое́дешь | захо́чешь |
| **3rd Person** | напи́шет | поно́сит | солжёт | пое́дет | захо́чет |

### Plural

| | | | | | |
|---|---|---|---|---|---|
| **1st Person** | напи́шем | поно́сим | солжём | пое́дем | захоти́м |
| **2nd Person** | напи́шете | поно́сите | солжёте | пое́дете | захоти́те |
| **3rd Person** | напи́шут | поно́сят | солгу́т | пое́дут | захотя́т |

В на́шей   кни́жке   мы   расска́жем   об   устро́йстве
In  our       booklet   we   will tell        about (the) construction

реакти́вных   дви́гателей   и   о   том, где   и   как они́
of jet          motors          and about that, where and how they

в   настоя́щее   вре́мя   применя́ются.
at  (the) present   time     use self (are used).

В э́той главе́   я хочу́   описа́ть   о́пыт,            кото́рый
In this   chapter, I wish   to describe   (an) experiment, which

пока́зывает   влия́ние        температу́ры   на   ско́рость
shows          (the) influence   of temperature   on   (the) rate

хими́ческой   реа́кции.
of chemical   reaction.

§ 199.  Examples of Stem Changes by Addition of -е-, -о- or -ь-
or Removal of -е-.

The parent infinitives of irregular verb forms in the following
sentences are successively: брать, лить, вы́звать, бить.

Мы   берём   два   вещества́,   во́ду   и   мета́лл,   и
We   take     two   substances,   water   and   metal,      and

получа́ем   два   но́вых   вещества́:   о́кись   мета́лла   и
obtain      two   new     substances:   oxide    of metal   and

водоро́д.
hydrogen.

В   настоя́щее вре́мя   льют   колокола́   из   бро́нзи   и
At  present     time     they cast bells        from   bronze   and

из   други́х   спла́вов.
from other      alloys.

| Imperfective Infinitive | брать[1] | гнать | пить | крыть[2] | тереть |
|---|---|---|---|---|---|
| | to be taking | to be chasing | to be drinking | to be covering | to be rubbing |
| Perfective Infinitive | собрать | погнать | выпить | покрыть | потереть |
| | to collect | to chase | to drink | to cover | to rub |

## PRESENT TENSE

| Present Tense Stem | бер- | гон- | пь- | кро- | тр- |
|---|---|---|---|---|---|
| Class | Irr. E-1 | Irr. E-2 | Irr. E-3 | Irr. E-4 | Irr. E-5 |

### Singular

| | | | | | |
|---|---|---|---|---|---|
| 1st Person | беру | гоню | пью | крою | тру |
| 2nd Person | берёшь | гонишь | пьёшь | кроешь | трёшь |
| 3rd Person | берёт | гонит | пьёт | кроет | трёт |

### Plural

| | | | | | |
|---|---|---|---|---|---|
| 1st Person | берём | гоним | пьём | кроем | трём |
| 2nd Person | берёте | гоните | пьёте | кроете | трёте |
| 3rd Person | берут | гонят | пьют | кроют | трут |

## PERFECTIVE FUTURE TENSE

| Perfective Future Tense Stem | собер- | погон- | выпь- | покро- | потр- |
|---|---|---|---|---|---|
| Class | Irr. E-1 | Irr. E-2 | Irr. E-3 | Irr. E-4 | Irr. E-5 |

### Singular

| | | | | | |
|---|---|---|---|---|---|
| 1st Person | соберу | погоню | выпью | покрою | потру |
| 2nd Person | соберёшь | погонишь | выпьешь | покроешь | потрёшь |
| 3rd Person | соберёт | погонит | выпьет | покроет | потрёт |

### Plural

| | | | | | |
|---|---|---|---|---|---|
| 1st Person | соберём | погоним | выпьем | покроем | потрём |
| 2nd Person | соберёте | погоните | выпьете | покроете | потрёте |
| 3rd Person | соберут | погонят | выпьют | покроют | потрут |

[1] The perfective infinitive corresponding to брать "to be taking" is взять "to take," whose perfective future is given in § 200, p. 306 and whose full conjugation is given in § 326, p. 517. The imperfective infinitive corresponding to собрать is собирать whose conjugation is quite regular. The infinitive pairs брать – взять and собирать – собрать exemplify a rather common occurrence with Russian verbs, namely different conjugation of companion imperfective and perfective infinitives.

[2] Both infinitives of брить – побрить "to share" are declined similarly, but with addition of -е- to the stem. Thus, in the present tense we have брею, бреешь, etc. and in the perfective future побрею, побреешь, etc.

Одна́ и та же ги́ря вы́зовет разли́чное растяже́ние
One and the same weight will cause different pulling apart

пружи́ны в зави́симости от того́, где и́менно на
of (a) spring in dependence on this, where namely on

пове́рхности земли́ произво́дится о́пыт.
(the) surface of (the) earth conducts self experiment.

Пра́вда, бьёт реакти́вный снаря́д вро́де
(It is) true, (that) hits (a) reactive charge of the sort

катю́ши не так далеко́ и не так ме́тко, как
of "Katyusha" not so far and not so exactly, as

пу́шка, но в тех слу́чаях, когда́ на́до
(a) cannon, but in those cases, where (it is) necessary

забро́сать пози́ции врага́ мно́жеством
to bombard (the) position of (the) enemy with (a) multiplicity

снаря́дов, э́то не име́ет суще́ственного значе́ния.
of shells, this not has essential significance.

## § 200. Miscellaneous Irregular Formation of the Perfective Future Tense.

It will be recalled that prefixes are used in Russian to convert simple imperfective infinitives into corresponding perfective infinitives or, in the general case, to form the perfective infinitives of more or less closely related verbs. Thus we have, for example, писа́ть "to be writing," написа́ть "to write" (special case), описа́ть "to describe," переписа́ть "to transcribe," etc., (general case). Stem changes involved in the formation of the present tense of such simple imperfective infinitives carry over to the derivation of the perfective future from the closely related perfective infinitives, Thus, in our example, we have пишу́ "I am writing," напишу́ "I shall write," опишу́ "I shall describe," перепишу́ "I shall transcribe."

This type of stem changes in a perfective infinitive sometimes is accompanied by either insertion or elimination of the letter -O- from the prefix as in the following examples.[1] Occasionally, some other exceptional change in the prefix or stem may also be encountered, as in the example растере́ть given below.

| Perfective[1] Infinitive | вжа́ть to press in | обогна́ть to overtake | свить to roll or wind together | растере́ть to rub (to powder) |
|---|---|---|---|---|

## PERFECTIVE FUTURE TENSE

| Perfective Future Tense Stem | ВОЖМ- | ОБОГОН- | СОВЬ- | РАЗОТР- |
|---|---|---|---|---|
| Class | Irr. F-1 | Irr. F-2 | Irr. F-3 | Irr. F-4 |

### Singular

| | | | | |
|---|---|---|---|---|
| 1st Person | вожму́ | обогоню́ | совью́ | разотру́ |
| 2nd Person | вожмёшь | обого́нишь | совьёшь | разотрёшь |
| 3rd Person | вожмёт | обого́нит | совьёт | разотрёт |

### Plural

| | | | | |
|---|---|---|---|---|
| 1st Person | вожмём | обого́ним | совьём | разотрём |
| 2nd Person | вожмёте | обого́ните | совьёте | разотрёте |
| 3rd Person | вожму́т | обого́нят | совьют | разотру́т |

Similarly irregularities are involved in formation of the perfective future from three important perfective infinitives ending in -ЯТЬ.

---

[1] The four perfective infinitives cited in the tabulation have companion imperfective infinitives, вжима́ть - вжа́ть, обогоня́ть - обогна́ть, свива́ть - свить, растира́ть - растере́ть. The imperfective infinitives form the present tense regularly, following the example of де́лать, Class Reg. A, cf. § 188, p. 284.

| Perfective Infinitive | ПОНЯ́ТЬ to understand | ПОДНЯ́ТЬ to raise | ВЗЯТЬ to take |
|---|---|---|---|

## PERFECTIVE FUTURE TENSE

| Perfective Future Tense Stem | ПОЙМ- | ПОДНИМ- | ВОЗЬМ- |
|---|---|---|---|
| Class | Irr. F-5 | Irr. F-6 | Irr. F-7 |

### Singular

| 1st Person | пойму́ | подниму́ | возьму́ |
|---|---|---|---|
| 2nd Person | поймёшь | поднимешь | возьмёшь |
| 3rd Person | поймёт | подни́мет | возьмёт |

### Plural

| 1st Person | поймём | подни́мем | возьмём |
|---|---|---|---|
| 2nd Person | поймёте | подни́мете | возьмёте |
| 3rd Person | по йму́т | подни́мут | возьму́т |

The following sentences illustrate use of the present and of the perfective future tenses formed from infinitives in this subclass.[1]

Е́сли   маши́на       подни́мет   вес      в 1 кг. на 1 м.
If  (a)(the) machine  raises    (a) weight of 1 kg. by 1 m.

вверх,  то  она́        сде́лает  рабо́ту  в 1 кг.м.
upward,  then  she (the machine) does    work   of 1 kg.m.

[1] The parent infinitives of irregular verb forms in these sentences are successively: поня́ть, взять, растере́ть, разобра́ть.

Возьмём        тепéрь   два    состоя́ния       га́за       при
We  will take   now     two    conditions     of (a) gas   at

одно́м  и   том же    давлéнии.
one     and the   same pressure.


Снача́ла   мы   разотрём    образéц    руды́   в   порошóк.
First     we   will grind  (the) sample  of ore  into powder.


Тепéрь    разберём,       как   рабóтают   отдéльные    ча́сти
Now       we will consider  how   work       separate     parts

маши́ны.
of (the) machine.


## § 201.  Reading Exercise.

Обрати́мые реа́кции и хими́ческое равновéсие

Существýет   мнóго   обрати́мых   хими́ческих   реа́кций.
Возьмём, в[1] ка́честве примéра, реа́кцию мéжду этú́ловым спú́р-
том и у́ксусной кислотóй.  При э́том образýются два[2] нó-
вых вещества́ – этú́ловый ацета́т и вода́.  Слéдовательно, мы
напи́шем уравнéние реа́кции в тако́м ви́де:

$$C_2H_5OH \quad + \quad CH_3COOH \ --- \ CH_3COOC_2H_5 \ + \ H_2O \ (I)$$

этú́ловый         у́ксусная        этú́ловый         вода́
спирт            кислота́         ацета́т

Реа́кция эта́, одна́ко, не дойдёт[3]  до конца́,  так как
са́ми[4] продýкты реа́кции – этú́ловый ацета́т и вода́ – реа -
ги́руют мéжду собóй и, таки́м óбразом, исхóдные  вещества́
начнýт вновь образова́ться  по уравнéнию[5] обра́тному к пéр-
вому:

$$CH_3COOC_2H_5 \ + \ H_2O \ \ --- \ \ C_2H_5OH \ + \ CH_3COOH \ (II)$$

этú́ловый         вода́          этú́ловый         у́ксусная
ацета́т                         спирт            кислота́

Если мы начнём наш опыт или[e] со смесью этилового ацетата с водой, или со смесью этилового спирта с уксусной кислотой, то в обоих случаях образуется смесь всех[7] четырёх веществ. В такой смеси идут[8] одновременно обе реакции, как[9] прямая, так и обратная. Когда скорости[10] прямой и обратной реакций сделаются[11] равными, химический анализ покажет нам, что концентрации реагирующих[12] веществ не изменяются. Можно думать, что реакции прекратились.[13] В действительности же протекают всё еще обе реакции (прямая и обратная), но в каждую единицу времени образуется[14] столько же новых молекул, сколько их разлагается. Таким[15] образом устанавливается и поддерживается химическое равновесие.

Разберём сущность химического равновесия более подробно[16] при помощи математических уравнений. Лабораторные исследования показывают, что скорость и[17] прямой и обратной реакций пропорциональна концентрации каждого из реагирующих[18] веществ. Так, для прямой реакции I, мы имеем:

$$v = k[A][B]$$

где   v   =   скорость прямой реакции
      k   =   коэфициент пропорциональности прямой реакции
    [A]   =   молекулярная концентрация этилового спирта
    [B]   =   молекулярная концентрация уксусной кислоты

Для обратной реакции II мы напишем подобное уравнение:

$$v = k[C][D]$$

где   v   =   скорость обратной реакции
      k   =   коэфициент пропорциональности обратной реакции
    [C]   =   молекулярная концентрация этилового ацетата
    [D]   =   молекулярная концентрация воды

Молекулярная концентрация каждого из индивидов выражается числом молей его в единице объёма.

В состоянии равновесия скорости обеих реакций одинаковы, то-есть:[19]

$$k[A][B] = k[C][D]$$

откуда.

$$\frac{v}{v} = \frac{k}{k} = \frac{[A][B]}{[C][D]} \quad (III)$$

так как отношение двух[20] постоянных величин постоянно.

При помощи уравнения III можно предсказать влияние изменения каждого[21] реагирующего вещества на состояние равновесия. Так, например, всякое увеличение концентрации уксусной кислоты вызовет увеличение концетрации и[22] этилового ацетата и воды, но уменьшение концентрации этилового спирта.

Следует отметить,[23] что другие моменты, например, присутствие катализатора или повышение температуры, сильно влияют на скорость химических реакций.

### Notes

1. в качестве примера literally "in (the) quality of (an) example" or, more freely, as an example.

2. два новых вещества "two new substances." The fact that вещества is in the genitive singular and новых in the genitive plural is discussed subsequently, cf. § 371, p. 605, when reviewing other peculiarities of Russian numerals.

3. не дойдёт до конца, literally, "will not go to (the) end" or, more freely, "will not go to completion." Here, дойдёт is the irregular third person singular of the perfective future derived from the infinitive дойти, of the verb доходить -- дойти "to go up to," and конца is the irregular genitive singular from конец, "end."

4. сами продукты реакции, "(the) products of (the) reaction themselves," cf. § 148, p. 223.

5. по уравнению обратному к первому, "according to (the) equation inverse to (the) first."

6. или -- или, "either -- or --."

7. всех четырёх веществ   "of all four substances." The three Russian words are all in the genitive plural. The numeral четыре  has no singular declension, as might be expected.

8. идут одновременно обе реакции   "proceed simultaneously both reactions."   Here, идут is the third person plural of the present tense of итти "to go" (directed motion), cf. § 381, p. 626. Although not obvious from its form, the word  реакции is in the genitive singular after the numeral обе "both," cf. Note 2 above.

9. как прямая, так и обратная, literally, "as well (the) forward, as also (the) reverse (reaction)."

10. скорости прямой и обратной реакций   "(the) rates of (the) direct and reverse reactions," Here, прямой and обратной are in the genitive singular; реакций is in the genitive plural. The expression under consideration is equivalent to the longer and more cumbersome wording  скорости прямой реакции и обратной реакции, where реакции is in the genitive singular.

11. Cf. § 100, p. 145.

12. реагирующих      веществ,  "of (the) reacting substances." Here, реагирующих  is the genitive plural of the active present participle  реагирующий derived from the imperfective infinitive  реагировать of the verb реагировать -- прореагировать "to react," cf. Lesson 29.

13. что реакции прекратились, "that (the) reactions have stopped." Here, прекратились is the reflexive of the plural of the past tense derived from the perfective infinitive прекратить of the verb прекращать -- прекратить "to stop, to terminate, to discontinue," cf. Lesson 24, especially § 214, p. 336.

14. образуется   столько же новых молекул, сколько их разлагается, literally, "forms self just that much of new molecules, (as) how much of them decomposes self," cf. § 150, p. 228 and § 151, p. 230.

15. таким образом   "in this way" is an idiom similar to главным образом  "for the most part,"  следующим образом "in the following way," etc.

16. более подробно,   "more particularly," "more in detail."   Here, we have an example of the comparative of a Russian adverb, cf. § 336, p. 529.

17. и прямо́й и обра́тной реа́кции, "of both (the) direct and of (the) inverse reaction," cf. Note 10 on preceding page.

18. Cf. Note 12 above.

19. то-есть, "that is."

20. двух постоя́нных величи́н, "of two constant magnitudes." The three Russian words are all in the genitive plural, cf. Notes 2 and 7 above.

21. ка́ждого реаги́рующего вещества́, "of each reacting substance." Here, реаги́рующего is the neuter genitive singular of the active present participle реаги́рующий discussed above in Note 12.

22. И -- И --, "both -- and --."

23. Сле́дует отме́тить, "It is necessary to note." This impersonal expression is encountered rather frequently in scientific Russian.


§ 202. Translation Exercise.

1. The products of reversible chemical reactions react among self (собо́й).
2. The reaction between ethyl alcohol and acetic acid will not go to conclusion.
3. The products of reaction begin (will begin) to react according to the equation
$$CH_3COOC_2H_5 + H_2O = C_2H_5OH + CH_3COOH.$$
4. In a mixture of ethyl alcohol and acetic acid is formed ethyl acetate and water.
5. Both reactions proceed simultaneously and in this fashion is established chemical equilibrium.
6. In a state of equilibrium the concentrations of reacting substances do not change.
7. The rate of the first (пе́рвой) reaction is proportional to the concentration of ethyl alcohol.
8. It is possible to predict the influence of a change of temperature on the rate of chemical reactions.
9. It is necessary (Сле́дует) to mention that a change of concentration of a reacting substance strongly influences (влия́ет на) the rate of a chemical reaction.
10. The presence of a catalyst calls forth (вызыва́ет) an increase of rate of chemical reactions.

THE PRESENT TENSE AND THE PERFECTIVE FUTURE
TENSE OF REMAINING IRREGULAR INFINITIVES
(MOSTLY ENDING IN -ЧЬ, -ЗТИ, -СТИ, -ЗТЬ, -СТЬ, -ТИ)

§ 203. General Remarks.

In this lesson we consider the present tense and the perfective
future tense of the most highly irregular verbs in the Russian
language.

In coping with these verbs it is advisable to devote special
attention to their present tense (and perfective future) forms,
since these forms are usually closely related to various other
verb forms. See § 324, p. 509 and accompanying tabulation on
pp. 511-513 for a comprehensive summary. Furthermore, the
various present or perfective future tense forms of these verbs
serve as the basis in forming derived adjectives, nouns, etc.

It does not appear profitable to discuss the rather complex
relationships existing between infinitives under consideration in
this lesson on the one hand and their present (or perfective
future) tense forms, on the other hand.

§ 204. The Present Tense and the Perfective Future Tense of
Infinitives Ending in -ЧЬ.

The regular first conjugation endings are used in forming
the present and perfective future tenses from infinitives in this
subclass.

The use of present and perfective future tense forms[1] derived,
as shown above, is illustrated by the following examples.

---

[1] The parent infinitives of irregular verb forms in these sentences are
successively: мочь, казаться, мочь, влечь, растечь.

| | | | | |
|---|---|---|---|---|
| Imperfective Infinitive | берéчь<br>to be guarding, preserving | жечь<br>to be burning, roasting | влечь<br>to be dragging | мочь<br>to be able |
| Perfective Infinitive | поберéчь<br>to guard, preserve | сжечь<br>to burn, roast | повлéчь<br>to start dragging, to bring about, to induce | смочь<br>to be able (perfective) |

## PRESENT TENSE

| | | | | |
|---|---|---|---|---|
| Present Tense Stem | берег-<br>береж- | жг-<br>жж- | влек-<br>влеч- | мог-<br>мож- |
| Class | Irr. G-1 | Irr. G-2 | Irr. G-3 | Irr. G-4 |

### Singular

| | | | | |
|---|---|---|---|---|
| 1st Person | берегý | жгу | влекý | могý |
| 2nd Person | бережёшь | жжёшь | влечёшь | мóжешь |
| 3rd Person | бережёт | жжёт | влечёт | мóжет |

### Plural

| | | | | |
|---|---|---|---|---|
| 1st Person | бережём | жжём | влечём | мóжем |
| 2nd Person | бережёте | жжёте | влечёте | мóжете |
| 3rd Person | берегýт | жгут | влекýт | мóгут |

## PERFECTIVE FUTURE TENSE

| | | | | |
|---|---|---|---|---|
| Perfective Future Tense Stem | поберег-<br>побереж- | сожг-<br>сожж- | повлек-<br>повлеч- | смог-<br>смож- |
| Class | Irr. G-1 | Irr. G-2 | Irr. G-3 | Irr. G-4 |

### Singular

| | | | | |
|---|---|---|---|---|
| 1st Person | поберегý | сожгý | повлекý | смогý |
| 2nd Person | побережёшь | сожжёшь | повлечёшь | смóжешь |
| 3rd Person | побережёт | сожжёт | повлечёт | смóжет |

### Plural

| | | | | |
|---|---|---|---|---|
| 1st Person | побережём | сожжём | повлечём | смóжем |
| 2nd Person | побережёте | сожжёте | повлечёте | смóжете |
| 3rd Person | поберегýт | сожгýт | повлекýт | смóгут |

Все углеводоро́ды мо́гут го́реть.
All  hydrocarbons  are able to burn.


То, что ка́жется         нам  зако́ном, мо́жет быть
That, which shows self (seems) to us (a) law   may   be

и  случа́йным      совпаде́нием.
also (a) chance      coincidence.


Перехо́д электро́на    с   одно́й орби́ты  на  другу́ю
Transition of (an) electron from  one   orbit   to  another

влечёт за  собо́й согла́сно основны́м   постула́там Бо́ра
brings  after self according to (the) basic postulates  of Bohr

испуска́ние  лучи́стой  эне́ргии.
(the) emission  of radiant  energy.


Е́сли на  пове́рхность воды́   помести́ть  ка́пельку
If    onto (the) surface  of water  to place   (a) droplet

олеи́новой кислоты́, то  после́дняя   растечётся.
of oleic   acid,   then (the) latter  spreads self.


§ 205. The Present Tense and the Perfective Future Tense of
    Verbs Whose Imperfective Infinitives End in −ЗТИ, −СТИ,
    −ЗТЬ and −СТЬ.

    Like infinitives in the preceding subclass, infinitives grouped
together here form the present and perfective future tenses with
regular first conjugation endings.[1]

---

[1] The infinitive сади́ться (cf. second tabulation below on p. 317) does not
belong to this class of infinitives.

## INFINITIVES ENDING IN -ЗТИ AND -СТИ

| | | | | | |
|---|---|---|---|---|---|
| Imperfective Infinitive | везти́ to be travelling | нести́ to be carrying | плести́ to be weaving | грести́ to be rowing | вести́ to be leading |
| Perfective Infinitive | повезти́ to start travelling | понести́ to start carrying, to carry | заплести́ to weave | погрести́ to row (for a while) | повести́ to start, to lead |

## PRESENT TENSE

| | | | | | |
|---|---|---|---|---|---|
| Present Tense Stem | вез- | нес- | плет- | греб- | вед- |
| Class | Irr. H-1 | Irr. H-2 | Irr. H-3 | Irr. H-4 | Irr. H-5 |

### Singular

| | | | | | |
|---|---|---|---|---|---|
| 1st Person | везу́ | несу́ | плету́ | гребу́ | веду́ |
| 2nd Person | везёшь | несёшь | плетёшь | гребёшь | ведёшь |
| 3rd Person | везёт | несёт | плетёт | гребёт | ведёт |

### Plural

| | | | | | |
|---|---|---|---|---|---|
| 1st Person | везём | несём | плетём | гребём | ведём |
| 2nd Person | везёте | несёте | плетёте | гребёте | ведёте |
| 3rd Person | везу́т | несу́т | плету́т | гребу́т | веду́т |

## PERFECTIVE FUTURE TENSE

| | | | | | |
|---|---|---|---|---|---|
| Perfective Future Tense Stem | повез- | понес- | заплет- | погреб- | повед- |
| Class | Irr. H-1 | Irr. H-2 | Irr. H-3 | Irr. H-4 | Irr. H-5 |

### Singular

| | | | | | |
|---|---|---|---|---|---|
| 1st Person | повезу́ | понесу́ | заплету́ | погребу́ | поведу́ |
| 2nd Person | повезёшь | понесёшь | заплетёшь | погребёшь | псведёшь |
| 3rd Person | повезёт | пснесёт | заплетёт | погребёт | поведёт |

### Plural

| | | | | | |
|---|---|---|---|---|---|
| 1st Person | повезём | понесём | заплетём | погребём | поведём |
| 2nd Person | псвезёте | понесёте | заплетёте | погребёте | поведёте |
| 3rd Person | повезу́т | понесу́т | заплету́т | погребу́т | поведу́т |

## INFINITIVES ENDING IN -ЗТЬ OR -СТЬ

| | | | | |
|---|---|---|---|---|
| **Imperfective Infinitive** | ле́зть to climb | па́дать[a] to be falling | сади́ться[a] to be sitting | клясть to be cursing |
| **Perfective Infinitive** | влезть[1] to climb in | пасть to fall | сесть to sit | прокля́сть to curse |

### PRESENT TENSE

| | | | | |
|---|---|---|---|---|
| **Present Tense Stem** | лез- | пада- | саж-<br>сад- | клян- |
| **Class** | Irr. H-6 | Reg. A | Irr. D-2 | Irr. H-9 |

#### Singular

| | | | | |
|---|---|---|---|---|
| **1st Person** | ле́зу | па́даю | сажу́сь | кляну́ |
| **2nd Person** | ле́зешь | па́даешь | сади́шься | кляне́шь |
| **3rd Person** | ле́зет | па́дает | сади́тся | кляне́т |

[1] The perfective infinitive ВЛЕЗТЬ "to climb in" has its own imperfective infinitive ВЛЕЗА́ТЬ "to be climbing in." Note the similarity of this situation to that presented by ЛИТЬ "to be pouring" and ВЛИВА́ТЬ – ВЛИТЬ "to pour in," cf. § 43, p. 62.

[2] Formation of the present tense from ПА́ДАТЬ involves no irregularity. Note the close similarity between present tense forms from ПА́ДАТЬ and the perfective future forms from ПАСТЬ. Such close similarity is also to be found between the present and perfective future tenses of other verbs. Thus, for example, ПОЛУЧА́ТЬ – ПОЛУЧИ́ТЬ "to obtain" has the present получа́ю, получа́ешь, etc., while the perfective future forms are получу́, полу́чишь, etc.

[3] The infinitive pair САДИ́ТЬСЯ – СЕСТЬ is quite unusual in that САДИ́ТЬСЯ is reflexive in form while СЕСТЬ is not. The existence of a closely related verb САДИ́ТЬ – ПОСАДИ́ТЬ "to place," "to plant," appears worth mentioning.

Plural

| | | | | |
|---|---|---|---|---|
| 1st Person | ле́зем | па́даем | сади́мся | клянём |
| 2nd Person | ле́зете | па́даете | сади́тесь | клянёте |
| 3rd Person | ле́зут | па́дают | садя́тся | кляну́т |

## PERFECTIVE FUTURE TENSE

| Perfective Future Tense Stem | влез- | пад- | сяд- | проклян- |
|---|---|---|---|---|
| Class | Irr. H-6 | Irr. H-7 | Irr. H-8 | Irr. H-9 |

Singular

| | | | | |
|---|---|---|---|---|
| 1st Person | вле́зу | паду́ | ся́ду | прокляну́ |
| 2nd Person | вле́зешь | падёшь | ся́дешь | проклянёшь |
| 3rd Person | вле́зет | падёт | ся́дет | проклянёт |

Plural

| | | | | |
|---|---|---|---|---|
| 1st Person | вле́зем | падём | ся́дем | проклянём |
| 2nd Person | вле́зете | падёте | ся́дете | проклянёте |
| 3rd Person | вле́зут | паду́т | ся́дут | прокляну́т |

The following sentences[1] illustrate use of the present and perfective future tenses formed from infinitives in this subclass.

Вслѐдствие    но́вого    си́нтеза  хини́на   мо́жно
As a result   of (the) new synthesis of quinine (it is)  possible

ожида́ть,  что цена́  на него́    падёт.
to expect,  that price for him (it) will fall.

По́сле ѐтого мы влѐзем    в  окно́.
After   that   we will climb in (the) window.

Проце́сс      восстановле́ния ведётся              в
(The) process of reduction          conducts self  (is conducted) in

ва́кууме.
vacuum.

Электропроводи́мость        чи́стых  мета́ллов растёт    с
(The) electrical conductivity of pure  metals       increases with

пониже́нием температу́ры.
decrease      of temperature.

---

[1] The parent infinitives of irregular verb forms in these sentences are successively: пасть, влезть, вести́, расти́.

§ 206. The Present Tense and the Perfective Future Tense of Verbs Derived from ХОДИ́ТЬ and ИТТИ́.

As already noted (§ 45, p. 63,) Russian verbs of motion are characterized by various peculiarities, the most important of which is the existence of the imperfective infinitives, used for distinguishing between general motion and motion toward some objective.[1]

There are two imperfective infinitives meaning "to go (on foot)" namely ХОДИ́ТЬ (general motion) and ИТТИ́ (motion toward some objective.) The present tense of ХОДИ́ТЬ is formed with a stem change in the first person singular but is otherwise quite regular. Thus, we have ХОЖУ́, ХО́ДИШЬ, ХО́ДИТ, etc. The present tense of ИТТИ́ (sometimes also spelled ИДТИ́) is worthy of special notice.

| Imperfective Infinitive | ИТТИ́ to be going |
|---|---|

### PRESENT TENSE

| Present Tense Stem | ИД- |
|---|---|
| Class | Irr. H-10 |

|  | Singular | Plural |
|---|---|---|
| 1st Person | иду́ | идём |
| 2nd Person | идёшь | идёте |
| 3rd Person | идёт | иду́т |

From ХОДИ́ТЬ and ИТТИ́, a number of verbs are derived. The imperfective infinitives of these derived verbs are from ХОДИ́ТЬ and the perfective from ИТТИ́ as shown by the following examples.

[1] Discussion of the significance of the verbs of motion and various verbs derived from them is reserved for Lesson 40, §§ 380-382, pp. 626-635.

| Imperfective Infinitive | Perfective Infinitive | |
|---|---|---|
| входи́ть | войти́ | to enter |
| выходи́ть | вы́йти | to exit, to leave |
| находи́ть | найти́ | to find |
| обходи́ть | обойти́ | to go around, to avoid |
| переходи́ть | перейти́ | to go over |
| приходи́ть | прийти́ (приття́) | to arrive |

(The list is not complete.)

Typical of these verbs and perhaps the most important[1] in scientific writing is находи́ть -- найти́ "to find." The present and perfective future are given here for reference purposes.

| Imperfective Infinitive | находи́ть to be finding |
|---|---|
| Perfective Infinitive | найти́ to find |

## PRESENT TENSE

| Present Tense Stem | нахож- наход- |
|---|---|
| Class | Irr. D-2 |

| | Singular | Plural |
|---|---|---|
| 1st Person | нахожу́ | нахо́дим |
| 2nd Person | нахо́дишь | нахо́дите |
| 3rd Person | нахо́дят | нахо́дят |

[1] Part of the importance of находи́ть - найти́ is due to the fact that the reflexive forms derived from находи́ть are used as circumlocutions of the verb "to be," cf. § 123, p. 181, to indicate existence, usually in a certain place or condition.

## PERFECTIVE  FUTURE  TENSE

| Perfective<br>Future<br>Tense Stem | найд- |
| Class | Irr.  H-10 |

|  | Singular | Plural |
|---|---|---|
| 1st Person | найду́ | найдём |
| 2nd Person | найдёшь | найдёте |
| 3rd Person | найдёт | найду́т |

The  following  example  sentences[1]  illustrate  the  use  of  the
present  and  perfective  future  of  a  few  of  the  verbs  discussed
above.

Реа́кция      на́трия   с   мети́ловым   спи́ртом  идёт  при
(The) reaction  of sodium  with  methyl      alcohol    goes  at

обыкнове́нных   температу́рах.
ordinary         temperatures.

Таки́м   о́бразом  мы  найдём      ускоре́ние       для  любо́го
In  this way,       we will find   (the) acceleration  for  any

моме́нта    вре́мени,   т.е.   мгнове́нное     и́ли и́стинное
moment    of time,   i.e.,  (the) instantaneous   or  actual

ускоре́ние.
acceleration.

Громадные   количества   воды́   находятся      на  земле́.
Enormous    amounts    of water  find  self  (are)  on  earth.

---

[1] The  parent  infinitives  of  the  various  verb forms  in  these  sentences  are
successively:  итти́,  найти́,  находи́ть,  проходи́ть.

Гáмма-лучи́     прохо́дят      не  то́лько че́рез  бумáгу,
Gamma rays     go through (pass) not  only    through paper,

но  и   че́рез мно́гие други́е вещества́.
but also through many   other  substances.


§ 207.  Irregular Endings in Formation of the Present Tense and
the Perfective Future Tense.

As we have had occasion to observe in this and in preceding
lessons, one or another of two sets of endings is used in forming
the present and perfective future tenses from corresponding
infinitives. Irregularities encountered up to this point have been
concerned only with infinitive stem changes, not with the endings.

Discussion of formation of the present and perfective future
tenses in Russian would be incomplete, if it were not pointed out
that three simple infinitives (and certain infinitives derived
therefrom by use of prefixes) do not use the regular endings
throughout in forming the present and perfective future tenses.
These three infinitives are дать (perfective) "to give," есть
(imperfective) "to be eating" and быть (imperfective) "to be."


## THREE HIGHLY IRREGULAR INFINITIVES

| Imperfective Infinitive | Imperfective Infinitive | Perfective Infinitive |
|---|---|---|
| есть | быть | дать |
| to be eating | to be | to give |
| | | |
| Class  Irr. I-1 | Irr. I-2 | Irr. I-3 |

| | Present Tense | Present Tense | Perfective Future Tense |
|---|---|---|---|
| | Singular | Singular | Singular |
| 1st Person | ем | (есмь) | дам |
| 2nd Person | ешь | (еси́) | дашь |
| 3rd Person | ест | есть | даст |
| | Plural | Plural | Plural |
| 1st Person | еди́м | (есмы́) | дади́м |
| 2nd Person | еди́те | (есте́) | дади́те |
| 3rd Person | едя́т | суть | даду́т |

From these infinitives, various verbs are formed whose conjugation may or may not involve the irregularities cited above.

| Imperfective Infinitive | разъеда́ть[1] to be eating apart | забыва́ть to be forgetting | издава́ть to be giving out |
|---|---|---|---|
| Perfective Infinitive | разъе́сть to eat apart | забы́ть[2] to forget | изда́ть to give out |

### PRESENT TENSE

| Present Tense Stem | разъеда- | забыва- | изда- |
|---|---|---|---|
| Class | Reg. A | Reg. A | Irr. B |

[1] The reflexive forms of разъеда́ть - разъе́сть are used in scientific Russian to denote the process of undergoing corrosion. See the first Russian sentence on p. 326.

[2] Note the close relationship between the perfective future from забы́ть and the simple future of быть given in § 230, p. 360.

### Singular

| | | | |
|---|---|---|---|
| 1st Person | разъеда́ю | забыва́ю | издаю́ |
| 2nd Person | разъеда́ешь | забыва́ешь | издаёшь |
| 3rd Person | разъеда́ет | забыва́ет | издаёт |

### Plural

| | | | |
|---|---|---|---|
| 1st Person | разъеда́ем | забыва́ем | издаём |
| 2nd Person | разъеда́ете | забыва́ете | издаёте |
| 3rd Person | разъеда́ют | забыва́ют | издаю́т |

## PERFECTIVE FUTURE TENSE

| | | | |
|---|---|---|---|
| Perfective Future Tense Stem | разъед– (Plural only) | забуд– | издад– (Plural only) |
| Class | Irr. I-1 | Irr. I-4 | Irr. I-3 |

### Singular

| | | | |
|---|---|---|---|
| 1st Person | разъе́м | забу́ду | изда́м |
| 2nd Person | разъе́шь | забу́дешь | изда́шь |
| 3rd Person | разъе́ст | забу́дет | изда́ст |

### Plural

| | | | |
|---|---|---|---|
| 1st Person | разъеди́м | забу́дем | издади́м |
| 2nd Person | разъеди́те | забу́дете | издади́те |
| 3rd Person | разъедя́т | забу́дут | издаду́т |

---

[1] Note the close relationship between the perfective future from забы́ть and the simple future of бы́ть given in § 230, p. 360.

Use of the present and perfective future tenses of these verbs
is illustrated in the following sentences.[1]


Свинец      медленно    подвергается           действию
Lead        slowly      submits self (yields)  to (the) action

разбавленной   уксусной   кислоты,   но  в   конце   концов
of dilute      acetic     acid,      but in  end     of ends

            он          полностью    разъестся.
(finally)  he (the lead) completely  eats self apart (corrodes).


Только    дальнейшие    исследования дадут     возможность
Only      further       investigations will give (the) possibility

понять          природу     этих   сложных,    но   весьма
to understand   (the) nature of those complex,  but  very

интересных явлений.
interesting phenomena.


Щёлочные     металлы    суть: литий,    натрий, калий,
(The) alkali metals     are:  lithium,  sodium  potassium,

рубидий   и   цезий.
rubidium  and cesium.


Решение  проблемы       дешёвого   кислорода   создаст
Solution of (the) problem of cheap  oxygen      will create

техническую  революцию   в металлургии.
(a) technical revolution  in metallurgy.

---

[1] The parent infinitives of irregular verb forms in these sentences are
successively: расъесть, дать, быть, создать.

§ 208.  Reading Exercise.

### Влияние температуры на скорость химических реакций

Вы уже знаете, что скорость простой химической реакции растёт с увеличением концентрации реагирующих[1] веществ. В настоящей главе я опишу, что случится если я повышу температуру, при которой происходит химическая реакция между железом и водой.

Если я брошу в воду немного железных опилок, вы не увидите никаких признаков реакции. Но тем[2] не менее, реакция идёт.[3] Железо медленно ржавеет и в[4] конце концов разъестся полностью.[5] При этом железо превращается в другое вещество - в окисел железа. Процесс ржавления - вот химическая[6] реакция в этом случае. Очевидно, что реакция воды с железом не течёт так[7] бурно, как с натрием.

Теперь попробуем установить, как ведёт себя железо, когда оно соприкасается с водой при высоких температурах.

Во-первых я наполню железную трубку чистыми железными опилками. Затем я зажгу горелку и накалю железную трубку докрасна.[8] В трубку мы введём водяной пар из маленького кипятильника. При помощи крана мы пока закроем доступ пару из кипятильника в трубку. Иными словами, мы впустим в трубку пар небольшими[9] количествами.

С другой стороны печи стоит сосуд с водой, как вы видите на рисунке I. Газ, который вытекает из трубки, пропускается через воду. Таким образом я понижаю температуру этого газа. Вы помните, что водяной пар при охлаждении сгущается в воду. Но в нашем опыте газ, который выпускается из трубки, не сгущается. Таким образом[10] мы узнаем что этот газ - не пар.

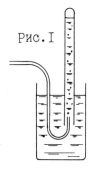

Рис. I

Чтобы определить свойства этого газа, я подвергну его другому опыту. Я буду держать[11] сосуд с газом отвер-

стием[12] вниз и поднесу к нему пламя. Вы видите, что газ зажжётся, воспламенится, даже с лёгким взрывом. Таким образом мы имеем ещё одно доказательство, что этот газ не пар. Как всем известно, пар не[13] только сам не горит, но и гасит пламя.

Другими опытами[14] я смогу доказать, что этот газ очень лёгок, что он имеет такие же свойства, как и[15] газ, выделяющийся[16] при реакции натрия с водой. Таким образом, мы найдём, что этот газ есть водород.

Когда мы получаем водород действием железных опилок на водяной пар, то в течение реакции железо изменяется; оно принимает другой, как[17] будто сожжённый вид. Вес его увеличился. Очевидно, железо при этом подвергается химической реакции, которая очень похожа на реакцию ржавления. Итак,[18] мы можем сделать вывод, что повышение температуры влечёт[19] за собой ускорение реакции воды с железом.

## Notes

1. Cf. Note 12, p. 310.

2. но тем не менее "but none the less."

3. реакция идёт "reaction goes (i.e., proceeds)."

4. в конце концов literally "at end of ends" or, more smoothly, "finally."

5. полностью -- the instrumental singular of полность "completeness" -- has virtually become an adverb meaning "completely," cf. § 98, p. 141.

6. вот химическая реакция might here be translated "that is the chemical reaction." вот is the Russian equivalent of the French "voilà."

7. так бурно, как с натрием "as vigorously as with sodium."

8. докрасна́ "to a red heat." Grammatically, докрасна́ is an adverb and should not be confused with some other part of speech.

9. небольши́ми коли́чествами "in small amounts," exemplifies the use of the instrumental case sometimes described as adverbial because of the possibility of translation by an adverbial phrase, cf. Note 5 above.

10. See Note 15, p. 310.

11. я бу́ду держа́ть "I will hold." Here we have an example of the imperfective future, discussed in Lesson 26.

12. отве́рстием вниз "with the opening downward." Here отве́рстием is in the instrumental case, cf. Note 9 above.

13. не то́лько сам не гори́т, но literally "not only self not burns, but."

14. други́ми о́пытами "by means of other experiments," cf. Note 9 above.

15. так и "as also."

16. выделя́ющийся literally "evolving self." Here выделя́ющийся is the reflexive, nominative, masculine singular form of the present active participle from the infinitive выделя́ть of the verb выделя́ть -- вы́делить.

17. как бу́дто сожжённым "as if burned."

18. ита́к "in fact."

19. влечёт за собо́й literally "drags after self" is an idiom meaning "has as consequence."

§ 209. Translation Exercise.

1. I will describe what happens (случи́тся) if sodium reacts with water.
2. Reaction of water with sodium proceeds stormily.

3. Reaction between iron and water proceeds slowly at ordinary (обычных) temperatures.
4. At the end of ends the iron completely is converted into oxide of iron.
5. When iron contacts self with water, it rusts.
6. You remember, that steam extinguishes a flame.
7. Hydrogen is not condensed (not condenses self) on cooling.
8. On reaction of sodium with water is formed hydrogen.
9. The weight of the iron filings increased in the course of reaction with water.
10. We are able to draw (to make) the conclusion that iron thereby submits self to chemical reaction.

## LESSON 24

## THE PAST TENSE -- REGULAR FORMATION
## FROM INFINITIVES ENDING IN -ТЬ

§ 210. General Remarks Concerning the Imperfective and Perfective Aspects of the Past Tense.

In speaking of past action, both Russian and English distinguish between (1) action considered as incomplete, in progress or frequently repeated and (2) action considered as a completed whole. For example, "I was buying" directs attention to an act in progress in past time, and "I bought" indicates an act completed in past time.

In Russian, past tense forms are derived from both imperfective and perfective infinitives. Past tense forms derived from imperfective infinitives are used when the action is thought of as having been incomplete, in progress or frequently repeated. When the action is thought of as a completed unit, past tense forms derived from the perfective infinitives are used.

§ 211. Regular Formation of the Past Tense of Verbs with Infinitives in -ТЬ.

In regular formation of the past tense from both imperfective and perfective infinitives, the same set of endings and the same procedure for attaching the endings to the stem are used, as is pointed out in the following paragraphs.

Practically all Russian infinitives form the past tense by a simple two step process:
1) Removal of -ТЬ from the infinitive.
2) Affixing the past tense endings listed in § 212 below.

Irregular formation of the past tense, which is observed with a remarkably small number of Russian infinitives, is discussed in the next lesson.

§ 212.  Past Tense Endings of Verbs.

The   gender  (masculine,   feminine   or   neuter)   and   number
(singular   or   plural)  of the noun or pronoun, which is the subject of
the verb,  are the factors   determining which  ending is used in the
Russian  past tense.  The  past tense  endings   do  not  depend  on
whether the subject of the verb is in the first, second or third
person.  Specifically, the past tense endings are as follows:

|          | Masc. | Fem. | Neuter |
|----------|-------|------|--------|
| Sing.    | –Л    | –Ла  | –Ло    |

|          | Masc.-Fem.-Neuter |
|----------|-------------------|
| Plural   | –Ли               |

§ 213.  Examples  of  Regular  Formation  of  the  Past  Tense.

### Examples of Verbs Regular in Past Tense and Regular in Present and Perfective Future Tenses

| Imperfective Infinitive | де́лать to be doing | рвать to be tearing | та́ять to be thawing | горе́ть to be burning |
|---|---|---|---|---|
| Perfective Infinitive | сде́лать to do | разорва́ть to tear apart | раста́ять to thaw | сгоре́ть to burn |

### PAST  TENSE -- IMPERFECTIVE

| Imperfective Past Tense Stem | дела– | рва– | тая– | горе– |
|---|---|---|---|---|
| Class | Reg. A | Reg. B-1 | Reg. B-1 | Reg. B-2 |

### Singular

|            |        |        |       |        |
|------------|--------|--------|-------|--------|
| Masc.      | де́лал  | рвал   | та́ял  | горе́л  |
| Fem.       | де́лала | рвала́  | та́яла | горе́ла |
| Neuter     | де́лало | рвало́  | та́яло | горе́ло |

### Plural

|                        |        |       |       |        |
|------------------------|--------|-------|-------|--------|
| Masc.-Fem.-Neuter      | де́лали | рва́ли | та́яли | горе́ли |

## PAST  TENSE  -- PERFECTIVE

| Perfective Past Tense Stem | сдела-  | разорва- | растая-  | сгоре-   |
|----------------------------|---------|----------|----------|----------|
| Class                      |         | Reg. B-1 | Reg. B-1 | Reg. B-2 |

### Singular

|        |         |           |          |         |
|--------|---------|-----------|----------|---------|
| Masc.  | сде́лал  | разорва́л  | раста́ял  | сгоре́л  |
| Fem.   | сде́лала | разорва́ла | раста́яла | сгоре́ла |
| Neuter | сде́лало | разорва́ло | раста́яло | сгоре́ло |

### Plural

|                   |         |           |          |         |
|-------------------|---------|-----------|----------|---------|
| Masc.-Fem.-Neuter | сде́лали | разорва́ли | раста́яли | сгоре́ли |

## Examples of Verbs Regular in Past Tense but Irregular in Present and Perfective Future Tenses

| Imperfective Infinitive | фотографи́ровать  | дава́ть | писа́ть   | брать |
|-------------------------|-------------------|---------|-----------|-------|
| Perfective Infinitive   | сфотографи́ровать | дать    | написа́ть | взять |

## PAST  TENSE -- IMPERFECTIVE

| Imperfective Past Tense Stem | фотографирова- | дава- | писа- | бра- |
|---|---|---|---|---|
| Class | Irr. A-1 | Irr. B | Irr. D-1 | Irr. E-1 |

### Singular

| | | | | |
|---|---|---|---|---|
| Masc. | фотографи́ровал | дава́л | писа́л | брал |
| Fem. | фотографи́ровала | дава́ла | писа́ла | брала́ |
| Neuter | фотографи́ровало | дава́ло | писа́ло | брало́ |

### Plural

| | | | | |
|---|---|---|---|---|
| Masc.-Fem.-Neuter | фотографи́ровали | дава́ли | писа́ли | бра́ли |

## PAST  TENSE -- PERFECTIVE

| Perfective Past Tense Stem | сфотографирова- | да- | написа- | взя- |
|---|---|---|---|---|
| Class | Irr. A-1 | Irr. I-3 | Irr. D-1 | Irr. F-7 |

### Singular

| | | | | |
|---|---|---|---|---|
| Masc. | сфотографи́ровал | дал | написа́л | взял |
| Fem. | сфотографи́ровала | дала́ | написа́ла | взяла́ |
| Neuter | сфотографи́ровало | да́ло | написа́ло | взяло́ |

### Plural

| | | | | |
|---|---|---|---|---|
| Masc.-Fem.-Neuter | сфотографи́ровали | да́ли | написа́ли | взя́ли |

As shown by the above examples, regular formation of the past tense characterizes many infinitives whose present (or perfective future) tense is formed irregularly. Specifically,

regular formation of the past tense characterizes the following
infinitives, cited in Lessons 22 and 23, in discussion of irregular
formation of the present and perfective future tenses.

| Infinitive | Class | Infinitive | Class |
|---|---|---|---|
| фотографи́ровать сфотографи́ровать | Irr. A-1 | е́хать пое́хать | Irr. D-4 |
| существова́ть просуществова́ть | Irr. A-1 | хоте́ть захоте́ть | Irr. D-5 |
| малева́ть намалева́ть | Irr. A-2 | бра́ть взя́ть | Irr. E-1 Irr. F-7 |
| дава́ть да́ть | Irr. B Irr. I-3 | собира́ть собра́ть | Reg. A Irr. E-1 |
| издава́ть изда́ть | Irr. B Irr. I-3 | гна́ть погна́ть | Irr. E-2 |
| колеба́ть поколеба́ть | Irr. C-1 | пи́ть вы́пить | Irr. E-3 |
| криви́ть покриви́ть | Irr. C-2 | кры́ть покры́ть | Irr. E-4 |
| жи́ть пожи́ть | Irr. C-3 | бри́ть побри́ть | Irr. E-4 |
| жа́ть пожа́ть | Irr. C-4 | тере́ть потере́ть | Irr. E-5 |
| сты́ть осты́ть | Irr. C-5 | вжима́ть вжа́ть | Reg. A Irr. F-1 |
| писа́ть написа́ть | Irr. D-1 | обгоня́ть обогна́ть | Reg. A Irr. F-2 |
| носи́ть поноси́ть | Irr. D-2 | свива́ть сви́ть | Reg. A Irr. F-3 |
| лга́ть солга́ть | Irr. D-3 | | |

| Infinitive | Class | Infinitive | Class |
|---|---|---|---|
| растира́ть<br>(растере́ть -- Past tense is<br>irregular, cf. § 222, p. 246.) | Reg. A | находи́ть<br>(найти́ -- Cf. § 224, p. 354<br>for past tense.) | Irr. D-2 |
| понима́ть<br>поня́ть | Reg. A<br>Irr. F-5 | бытъ | Irr. I-2 |
| поднима́ть<br>подня́ть | Reg. A<br>Irr. F-6 | дава́ть<br>датъ | Irr. B<br>Irr. I-3 |
| бра́ть<br>взятъ | Irr. E-1<br>Irr. F-7 | разъеда́ть<br>(разъе́стъ -- Cf. § 225,<br>p. 355 for past tense.) | Reg. A |
| па́дать<br>(пастъ -- Cf. § 223, p. 351,<br>for past tense.) | Reg. A | забыва́ть<br>забы́тъ | Reg. A<br>Irr. I-2 |
| сади́тъся<br>(сестъ -- Cf. § 223, p. 351,<br>Footnote 1 for past tense.) | Irr. D-2 | издава́ть<br>изда́тъ | Irr. B<br>Irr. I-3 |

## § 214. The Reflexive of the Past Tense.

A past tense form is rendered reflexive by adding -СЯ (if the form terminates with a consonant) or -СЬ (if the form terminates with a vowel).[1] This is in accord with the general rule applicable to formation of the reflexive of all verb forms excepting participles, which add -СЯ throughout.

Rendering the past tense reflexive changes the meaning in the same way as described previously for the present tense, cf. § 52, p. 71.

---

[1] Alternately, the reflexive pronoun себя́ may be used in place of -СЯ or -СЬ.

Example of Reflexive Form of Past Tense

| Imperfective Infinitive | де́лать | Perfective Infinitive | сде́лать |
|---|---|---|---|
| Class | Reg. A | | Reg. A |

|  | Reflexive of Imperfective Past | Reflexive of Perfective Past |
|---|---|---|

Singular

| Masc. | де́лался | сде́лался |
|---|---|---|
| Fem. | де́лалась | сде́лалась |
| Neuter | де́лалось | сде́лалось |

Plural

| Masc.-Fem.-Neuter | де́лались | сде́лались |
|---|---|---|

§ 215. Historical Note on the Past Tense in Russian.

The previously mentioned agreement of the past tense endings with the gender and number of the subject has an historical explanation. At one stage of the development of the Russian language, the verb forms used in modern Russian as the past tense were participial forms. In Russian, participles are declined like adjectives with respect to gender, number and case when attributive modifiers of nouns and with respect to gender and number when predicative modifiers. See § 238, p. 376; § 251, p. 398; § 263, p. 417; § 274, p. 434. From this point of view, the past tense might be regarded as a participial predicative modifier which has come to be used in one particular way.[1]

---

[1] The use of the predicative forms of adjectives was discussed in § 120, p. 176.

§ 216.   Sentences Illustrating Use of the Past Tense.

In reading the following sentences, attention should be directed to the agreement between the gender and the number of the subject of the sentence and the ending of the verb.

Óчень   дóлгое  врéмя  наýка    рассмáтривала  теплотý  как
Very    long    time   science  regarded       heat     as

   невесóмую  жúдкость.
(a) weightless  liquid.


Аррéниус считáл,    что  актúвные   молéкулы – э́то
Arrhenius reckoned,  that  activated   molecules — these (are)

бы́стрые  молéкулы  с    избы́тком   кинетúческой энéргии.
fast     molecules  with (an) excess  of kinetic      energy.


Немéцкое       комáндование  обещáло    большýю    награ́ду
(The) German   command        promised    (a) big    reward

томý,     кто раскрóет[1]    секрéт    нóвого      орýжия.
to that one, who would discover (the) secret of (the) new weapon.


Мы   вúдели  в    § 97 ,  что  двухэлектрóдная   ла́мпа
We   saw     in   § 97     that  (a) two electrode   lamp

характеризýется     её    внýтренним  сопротивлéнием
characterizes self    by its  inner        resistance

и    сúлой        тóка            насыщéния.
and  by (the) strength  of (the) current  of saturation.


Благодаря́    фотоэлемéнтам     сдéлалось    возмóжным
Thanks       to photoelements   made self     possible

изобрéтение   звуковóго    кинó.
(the) invention  of (the) sound  cinema.


---

[1] It is not unusual for the perfective future to be used to express a real condition, cf. § 232, p. 364.

В 1910, проф. Шва́рцшильд писа́л Ле́бедеву: "Я хорошо́
In 1910, Prof. Schwartzschild wrote to Lebedev: "I well

по́мню, с каки́м сомне́нием я услы́шал в 1902 г. о
remember with what doubt I heard in 1902 about

Ва́шем[1] предложе́нии изме́рить давле́ние све́та
your proposal to measure (the) pressure of light

на газ, и я преиспо́лнился тем бо́льшим
on gas, and I filled self with so much greater

удивле́нием, когда́ я прочёл, как Вы[1] устрани́ли
astonishment when I read how you eliminated

все препя́тствия."
all obstacles."

Согла́сно результа́там о́пытов Мил ликена,[2]
According to (the) results of experiments of Millikan,

заря́д электро́на оказа́лся ра́вным
(the) charge of (the) electron proved self as equal to

$4,77 \cdot 10^{-10}$ электростати́ческим едини́цам.
$4.77 \times 10^{-10}$ electrostatic units.

Мил ликен в 1910 г. эксперимента́льно определи́л
Millikan in 1910 experimentally determined

заря́д электро́на.
(the) charge of (the) electron.

Ато́мная тео́рия Дальто́на сде́лала хи́мию
(The) atomic theory of Dalton made chemistry

коли́чественной нау́кой.
(a) quantitative science.

---

[1] The pronoun Вы "you" and the possessive Ваш "your" are capitalized when used in direct address, as here. Note also the use of the plural form of the past tense with the pronoun, Вы.

[2] The names of persons are declined like other nouns. Here, Мил ликена is the genitive singular of Мил ликен, cf. § 362, p. 585.

## § 217. Special Constructions Involving Neuter Singular of Past Tense.

The subject of a Russian sentence is not necessarily a noun or pronoun, either expressed or implied. Thus, for example, an infinitive or a clause may serve as the subject of a Russian sentence with the result that the subject has no well defined grammatical gender. In such a sentence the neuter singular form of the past tense is used just as though the subject were a neuter, singular noun. Similar use of the neuter singular of the past tense is encountered in negative sentences in which, because of the negation, the normal nominative case of the subject noun (and modifiers) has been replaced by the genitive.

| Изоли́ровать | витами́н | С в чи́стом ви́де | не́ бы́ло[1] легко́. |
|---|---|---|---|
| To isolate | vitamin | C in pure form | not was easy. |

| В то вре́мя | никаки́х | общепри́нятых | а́томных весо́в |
|---|---|---|---|
| At that time | no | generally accepted | atomic weights |

| не | существова́ло. |
|---|---|
| [not] | existed. |

| Оказа́лось, | что | грома́дное | коли́чество | эне́ргии |
|---|---|---|---|---|
| Proved self, | that | (an) enormous | quantity | of energy |

| выделя́ется | при | дробле́нии | $U^{235}$. |
|---|---|---|---|
| evolves self | during | fission | (of) $U^{235}$. |

| Удало́сь | таки́м | о́бразом | осуществи́ть |
|---|---|---|---|
| Succeeded self | by this | manner | to accomplish |

| превраще́ние | $U^{238}$ | в | но́вый | элеме́нт, | плуто́ний. |
|---|---|---|---|---|---|
| (the) conversion | (of) $U^{238}$ | into | (a) new | element, | plutonium. |

| Как | уже́ | упомина́лось, | по | совреме́нным |
|---|---|---|---|---|
| As | already | mentioned self, | according to | contemporary |

| представле́ниям | я́дра | всех | а́томов | состоя́т | из |
|---|---|---|---|---|---|
| hypotheses | (the) nuclei | of all | atoms | consist | of |

| нейтро́нов | и | прото́нов. |
|---|---|---|
| neutrons | and | protons. |

---

[1] Note that не́ бы́ло is pronounced as though one word.

§ 218. **Reading Exercise.**

## Из истории металлургии алюминия
### (Часть первая)

В 1807 г.[1] английский химик Гёмфри Дэви (1778 - 1829) пропускал электрический ток через слегка[2] увлажнённую гидроокись алюминия. При этом в качестве[3] анода служила платиновая пластинка, Катодом[4] служила железная проволока. Последняя, при пропускании тока, раскалялась добела и сплавлялась. Дэви произвёл этот электролиз в атмосфере водорода. При этом, однако, Дэви получил только железо-алюминиевый сплав.

Алюминий в свободном виде впервые получил датский физик Эрстед в марте 1825 г. С этой целью Эрстед восстановил хлорид алюминия амальгамой калия. Таким образом он получил амальгаму алюминия. Затем Эрстед выдестиллировал ртуть из алюминиевой амальгамы и получил небольшие комочки[5] алюминия похожего на олово по цвету и блеску.

Позднее, в 1827 г. немецкий химик Велер улучшил метод Эрстеда. Велер заменил амальгаму калия металлическим калием. Велер помещал кусочки металлического калия, и кристаллы хлорида алюминия в фарфоровый или платиновый тигель. Затем[6] Велер закрывал тигель крышкой[7] и осторожно нагревал тигель на горелке. Таким образом, Велер получил алюминий в количествах, достаточных для определения его более важных[8] физических и химических свойств.

В 1854 г. Анри Сен-Клер-Девилль (1818 - 1881 г.) во Франции применил способ Велера для первого промышленного способа производства алюминия. При этом Сен-Клер-Девилль улучшил способ Велера. Сен-Клер-Девилль заменил металлический калий более дешёвым[9] натрием, а нестойкий и весьма гигроскопический хлорид алюминия - более прочным двойным хлоридом алюминия и натрия ($AlCl_3 \cdot NaCl$). Процесс, в отличие от бурной реакции восстановления чистого хлорида алюминия, протекал очень спокойно. Производство алю-

ми́ния   э́тим спо́собом существова́ло с 1854 до 1890 гг. Одна́ко в тече́ние 30 лет с по́мощью тако́го спо́соба произво́дство алюми́ния в о́бщей сло́жности[10] не превосходи́ло 200 т.[11] С 1884 до 1892 гг. в Áнглии и в CШA заво́ды бра́тьев[12] Ка́улес производи́ли по электротерми́ческому ме́тоду спла́вы алюми́ния с ме́дью и желе́зом — алюми́ниевую бро́нзу и ферроалюми́ний.  Для получе́ния э́тих спла́вов бра́тья[12] Ка́улес применя́ли дуговы́е пе́чи в 5000-6000 ампе́р и 60 вольт. В печь вводи́лась ши́хта из глинозёма, древе́сного у́гля и металли́ческого скра́па (желе́за или ме́ди).  Алюми́ниевая бро́нза получа́лась с содержа́нием до 17% Al и ферроалюми́ний с содержа́нием до 20% Al.

## Notes

1. 1807 г.   After numerals designating a year, the Russian places  Г.  as abbreviation for various forms of  ГОД  "year."

2. слегка́   "slightly"  is an adverb not to be confused with other parts of speech.

3. в ка́честве ано́да     literally "in (the) quality of (an) anode" or, more smoothly,  "as the anode."   Cf. Note 4 below.

4. като́дом   "as (the) cathode,"  cf. § 102, p. 148.

5. комо́чки   "lumps" is the irregular nominative plural of комо́чек  "lump."

6. затем   "thereafter" from  за  "beyond"  тем  "that."

7. кры́шкой   "by (a) cover" is the instrumental singular of кры́шка  "cover."

8. бо́лее  ва́жных  here  бо́лее  is an adverb used to form the comparative of the adjective  ва́жный  corresponding to English  "more."

9. бо́лее  дешёвым .   Cf. Note 8 above.

10. В общей сложности   is an idiom signifying "in total amount."

11. 200 т., "200 tons."

12. братьев is the irregular genitive plural of брат "brother," cf. § 359, p. 577.

13. братья is the irregular nominative plural of брат "brother," cf. § 359, p. 577.

§ 219. Translation Exercise.

1. In 1807, the English chemist, Davy, carried out the electrolysis of slightly moistened (увлажнённой) hydrated oxide (гидроскиси) of aluminum.
2. The iron (Железный) cathode on passage of electrical (электрического) current alloyed self.
3. In this way was obtained (получился) iron-aluminum alloy.
4. Davy did not (не) obtain aluminum (алюминия) in free form.
5. In March 1825, Oersted carried out (произвёл) the reduction (восстановление) of aluminum chloride by means of amalgam of potassium.
6. Wöhler reduced chloride of aluminum by means of metallic potassium.
7. Thereby the reaction of reduction of aluminum chloride proceeded quietly.
8. The process of Wöhler was used (применялся) for industrial production of aluminum.
9. Saint Clair Deville reduced the double (двойной) chloride of aluminum and sodium with (при) the aid of metallic (металлического) sodium.
10. For production of alloys of aluminum with copper and iron, the brothers Cowles used (применяли) an electrothermal process (спосоо).

# LESSON 25

## THE PAST TENSE -- IRREGULAR FORMATION

§ 220. General Remarks on Irregular Formation of the Past Tense.

It will be recalled from previous lessons that nearly all the infinitives of Russian verbs end in either -АТЬ, -ЕТЬ, -ИТЬ, -ОТЬ, -УТЬ, -ЫТЬ or -ЯТЬ, in other words in a vowel followed by -ТЬ. In Lesson 24, it was pointed out that derivation of the past tense from nearly all of these infinitives involves removing -ТЬ and then ·affixing certain endings. Only a small minority of Russian infinitives form the past tense irregularly. These will be summarized in this lesson in two groups: (1) irregular formation of the past tense from certain infinitives ending in -АТЬ, -ЕТЬ, -ОТЬ and (2) the formation of the past tense from other infinitives, namely those ending in -ЧЬ, -ЗТИ, -ЗТЬ, -СТИ, -СТЬ, -ТТИ or -ИТИ.

§ 221. Endings Used in Irregular Formation of the Past Tense.

The same endings are used both for irregular and for regular formation of the past tense, with the exception that irregular past tense formation usually, though not always, involves omission of the masculine singular ending, -Л.

### Endings Used in Irregular Formation of Past Tense

|  | Masc. | Fem. | Neuter |
|---|---|---|---|
| Sing. | (The regular ending, -Л, is usually missing.) | -ла | -ло |

|  | Masc.-Fem.-Neuter |
|---|---|
| Plural | -ли |

345

§ 222. Irregular Formation of the Past Tense from Certain Infinitives Ending in -еть, -ить or -уть

The very few verbs which constitute this class form the past tense by removing several letters from the infinitive and then adding the regular endings except in the masculine singular, cf. § 221 above.

### Irregular Past Tense of Certain Verbs with Infinitives Ending in -ить, -еть, -уть

| Imperfective Infinitive | тере́ть<br>to be rubbing | зашиба́ть<br>to be hurting | подверга́ть<br>to be subjecting |
|---|---|---|---|
| Perfective Infinitive | потере́ть<br>to rub | зашиби́ть<br>to hurt | подве́ргнуть<br>to subject |

### PAST TENSE -- IMPERFECTIVE

| Imperfective Past Tense Stem | тер- | зашиба- | подверга- |
|---|---|---|---|
| Class | Irr. E-5 | Reg. A | Reg. A |

#### Singular

| | | | |
|---|---|---|---|
| Masc. | тёр | зашиба́л[1] | подверга́л |
| Fem. | тёрла | зашиба́ла[1] | подверга́ла |
| Neuter | тёрло | зашиба́ло[1] | подверга́ло |

#### Plural

| | | | |
|---|---|---|---|
| Masc.-Fem.-Neuter | тёрли | зашиба́ли[1] | псдверга́ли |

---

[1] These forms do not involve irregularity which is encountered in the corresponding perfective past.

## PAST TENSE -- PERFECTIVE

| Perfective Past Tense Stem | потер- | зашиб- | подверг-[1] |
|---|---|---|---|
| Class | Irr. E-5 | Irr. J-1 | Irr. J-2 |

### Singular

| | | | |
|---|---|---|---|
| Masc. | потёр | зашиб | подвёрг |
| Fem. | потёрла | зашибла | подвёргла |
| Neuter | потёрло | зашибло | подвёргло |

### Plural

| | | | |
|---|---|---|---|
| Masc.-Fem.-Neuter | потёрли | зашибли | подвёргли |

The following sentences[2] illustrate use of the perfective past tense formed from infinitives in this subclass.

Анри Муассан умер 20 февраля 1907 г.
Henri Moissan died 20 February 1907.

Бах в целой серии работ подверг детальному
Bach in (a) whole series of works submitted to (a) detailed

изучению окислительные ферменты.
study oxidation enzymes.

Бор отверг применимость обычных законов
Bohr rejected (the) applicability of (the) ordinary laws

электродинамики к внутриатомным процессам.
of electrodynamics to intra-atomic processes.

---

[1] This irregularity in formation of the past tense is not encountered in all infinitives terminating in -НУТЬ. Thus, the infinitive ДВИНУТЬ of the verb двигать -- ДВИНУТЬ "to move" forms its past tense quite regularly, viz., ДВИНУЛ, ДВИНУла, etc.
[2] The parent infinitives of irregular verb forms in these sentences are successively: умереть, подвергнуть, отвергнуть, достигнуть.

Одна́ из на́ших раке́т дости́гла реко́рдной высоты́ в
One of our rockets attained (a) record height of

128 киломе́тров.
128 kilometers.

§ 223. Formation of the Past Tense from Infinitives Ending in -ЧЬ, -ЗТИ, -ЗТЬ, -СТИ or -СТЬ.

For this class of verbs, it is not possible to establish as simple and direct a relationship between the infinitives and the past tense as was the case with verbs discussed previously. In some instances, it is possible to trace a relationship between the respective stems used for conjugating the present and past tenses of these verbs.[1] Unfortunately, such relationships cannot be used as a basis for formulating useful generalities.

Past Tense of Verbs with Infinitives Ending in -ЧЬ

| Imperfective Infinitive | бере́чь | жечь | влечь | мочь |
|---|---|---|---|---|
| Perfective Infinitive | побере́чь | сжечь | повле́чь | смочь |

PAST TENSE -- IMPERFECTIVE

| Imperfective Past Tense Stem | берег- | жг- | влек- | мог- |
|---|---|---|---|---|
| Class | Irr. G-1 | Irr. G-2 | Irr. G-3 | Irr. G-4 |

Singular

| | | | | |
|---|---|---|---|---|
| Masc. | берёг | жёг | влёк | мог |
| Fem. | берегла́ | жгла | влекла́ | могла́ |
| Neuter | берегло́ | жгло | влекло́ | могло́ |

[1] See § 204, p. 314.

### Plural

| Masc.-Fem.-Neuter | берегли́ | жгли | влекли́ | могли́ |

## PAST TENSE -- PERFECTIVE

| Perfective Past Tense Stem | поберег- | сожг- | повлек- | смог- |

| Class | Irr. G-1 | Irr. G-2 | Irr. G-3 | Irr. G-4 |

### Singular

| Masc. | поберёг | сжёг | повлёк | смог |
| Fem. | поберегла́ | сожгла́ | повлекла́ | смогла́ |
| Neuter | поберегло́ | сожгло́ | повлекло́ | смогло́ |

### Plural

| Masc.-Fem.-Neuter | поберегли́ | сожгли́ | повлекли́ | смогли́ |

The following sentences[1] illustrate use of the imperfective and perfective past tenses formed from infinitives in this subclass.

| Неприя́тель | жёг | на | своём | пути́ | мно́гие | города́. |
| (The) enemy | burned | on | his | way | many | towns. |

| Для | нас | соверше́нно | очеви́дно, | что | Ле́бедев | не |
| For | us | (it is) perfectly | obvious, | that | Lebedev | not |

| мог | предви́деть | э́тих результа́тов. |
| was able | to foresee | these results. |

---

[1] The parent infinitives of irregular verb forms in these sentences are successively: жечь, мочь, извле́чь, привле́чь.

В  1807 г.   Гéмфри   Дэ́ви   впервы́е                    извлёк
In  1807,    Humphrey Davy    for the      first time   extracted

металли́ческий   на́трий   из   éдкого   на́тра.
metallic         sodium    from caustic   soda.

Одна́ко,   рабо́та      Тóмсона   не   привлекла́   к   себé
However,   (the) work   of Thomson not  attracted    to  self

осо́бого      внима́ния.
particular   attention.

### Past Tense of Verbs Ending with -ЗТИ, -ЗТЬ, -СТИ or -СТЬ

| Imperfective Infinitive | везти́[1] | нести́ | грести́ | вести́[2] | па́дать[3] |
|---|---|---|---|---|---|
| | to be travelling | to be carrying | to be rowing | to be leading | to be falling |
| Perfective Infinitive | повезти́[1] | поsnести́ | погрести́ | повести́[2] | пасть |
| | to start travelling | to start carrying, to carry | to row (for a while) | to start leading | to fall |

### PAST TENSE -- IMPERFECTIVE

| Imperfective Past Tense Stem | вез- | нес- | греб- | ве- | пада- |
|---|---|---|---|---|---|
| Class | Irr. H-1 | Irr. H-2 | Irr. H-4 | Irr. H-5 | Reg. A |

#### Singular

| | | | | | |
|---|---|---|---|---|---|
| Masc. | вёз | нёс | грёб | вёл | па́дал |
| Fem. | везла́ | несла́ | гребла́ | вела́ | па́дала |
| Neuter | везло́ | несло́ | гребло́ | вело́ | па́дало |

---

[1] The past tense is similarly formed from the infinitives лезть and полéзть (Irr. H-6). Thus we have, respectively, лез, лéзла, etc., and полéз, полéзла, etc.

[2] The past tense is formed in exactly the same way from the infinitives плести́ and заплести́ (Irr. H-3). Thus we have, respectively, плёл, плела́, etc., and заплёл, заплела́, etc.

[3] The past tense of па́дать is formed in regular fashion. It will be recalled that this was also true of formation of the present tense from the same infinitive.

### Plural

| Masc.-Fem.-Neuter | везли́ | несли́ | гребли́ | вели́ | па́дали |
|---|---|---|---|---|---|

## PAST  TENSE  --  PERFECTIVE

| Perfective Past Tense Stem | повез- | понес- | погреб- | пове-[1] | па- |
|---|---|---|---|---|---|
| Class | Irr. H-1 | Irr. H-2 | Irr. H-4 | Irr. H-5 | Irr. H-7 |

### Singular

| | | | | | |
|---|---|---|---|---|---|
| Masc. | повёз | понёс | погрёб | повёл | пал |
| Fem. | псвезла́ | понесла́ | погребла́ | повела́ | па́ла |
| Neuter | повезло́ | понесло́ | погребло́ | повело́ | па́ло |

### Plural

| Masc.-Fem.-Neuter | повезли́ | понесли́ | погребли́ | повели́ | па́ли |
|---|---|---|---|---|---|

The following sentences[2] illustrate use of the imperfective and perfective past tenses formed from infinitives in this subclass.

| В 1666 г. | Ньюто́н | произвёл | сле́дующий | просто́й, |
|---|---|---|---|---|
| In 1666, | Newton | carried out | (the) following | simple, |

| но чрезвыча́йно | ва́жный | о́пыт. |
|---|---|---|
| but extremely | important | experiment. |

---

[1] The past tense of сесть (Irr. H-8) is formed in exactly the same way. Thus, we have сел, се́ла, etc. The same is true of the infinitives, клясть and прокля́сть (Irr. H-9) whose past tense forms are, respectively, клял, кляла́, etc., and прокля́л, прокляла́, etc.

[2] The parent infinitives of irregular verb forms in these sentences are successively: произвести́, вести́, перенести́, плести́.

Реакция        велась        в   трехгорлой        литровой
(The) reaction    conducted self   in (a) three necked    liter

колбе   с   мощной   мешалкой.
flask   with powerful   stirrer.


После   заключения   мира   с   Турцией,   Пётр   Первый
After    conclusion    of peace   with   Turkey,    Peter   the First

перенёс   внимание   на   Балтийское   море.
transferred attention   to   (the) Baltic   Sea.


Прекрасные        кружева   плелись                    и     в
Beautiful           laces       wove   self   (were   woven)   also   in

Фландрии.
Flanders.


§ 224.  Irregular Past Tense of ИТТИ and Infinitives Derived
        Therefrom.

    The English verb "to go" has the highly irregular past
tense "went." Similarly, the past tense of ИТТИ is highly
irregular.


### Past Tense of ИТТИ "to be going (on foot)"

| | |
|---|---|
| Imperfective Infinitive | ИТТИ |


### PAST TENSE -- IMPERFECTIVE

| | |
|---|---|
| Imperfective Past Tense Stem | Ш- |
| Class | Irr. H-10 |

|  | Singular | | Plural |
|---|---|---|---|
| Masc. | шёл | | |
| Fem. | шла | Masc.-Fem.- | шли |
| Neuter | шло | Neuter | |

As pointed out in § 206, p. 321, the infinitives ХОДИ́ТЬ and ИТТИ́ are the parents of a number of verbs such as НАХОДИ́ТЬ -- НАЙТИ́ "to find." It will be recalled that such verbs exhibit unusual differences in form between their present and perfective future tenses. Similar large differences in form also exist between the imperfective and perfective aspects of their past tense, as is evident from the following tabulation.

| Imperfective Infinitive | НАХОДИ́ТЬ |
|---|---|
| Perfective Infinitive | НАЙТИ́ |

## PAST TENSE -- IMPERFECTIVE

| Imperfective Past Tense Stem | находи- |
|---|---|
| Class | Irr. D-2 |

|  | Singular | | Plural |
|---|---|---|---|
| Masc. | находи́л | | |
| Fem. | находи́ла | Masc.-Fem.- | находи́ли |
| Neuter | находи́ло | Neuter | |

## PAST TENSE -- PERFECTIVE

| Perfective Past Tense Stem | наш– |
| Class | Irr. H-10 |

|  | Singular |  | Plural |
| --- | --- | --- | --- |
| Masc. | нашёл |  |  |
| Fem. | нашла́ | Masc.-Fem.- | нашли́ |
| Neuter | нашло́ | Neuter |  |

The following sentences[1] illustrate use of the imperfective and perfective past tenses formed from ИТТИ́ and related infinitives.

Одновре́менно     с     о́пытным     изуче́нием     зако́нов
Simultaneously     with  experimental  investigation  of (the) laws

тепловы́х     явле́ний     шло     и     теорети́ческие
of heat       phenomena    went    also  (the) theoretical

истолкова́ние     их.
explanation       of them.

Герма́ний,     как     анало́г     кре́мния,     та́кже     нашёл
Germanium,     as      analog      of silicon,   also       found

примене́ние     при     изготовле́нии     опти́ческих стёкол.
application      during  preparation       of optical    glasses.

Бессеме́ровский     проце́сс     вошёл     в     металлурги́ю
(The) Bessemer      process      entered   into  metallurgy

в XIX     столе́тии.
in (the) 19th  century.

---

[1] The parent infinitives of irregular verb forms in these sentences are successively: ИТТИ́, найти́, войти́, найти́.

| Совершённо | ясно, что | совокупность | свойств |
|---|---|---|---|
| (It is) perfectly | clear, that | (the) aggregation | of properties |

| алюми́ния | и | потре́бность | в | нём | для | целе́й |
|---|---|---|---|---|---|---|
| of aluminum | and | (the) requirement | in | him | for | purposes |

| оборо́ны | и | ми́рного | строи́тельства | таковы́, | что |
|---|---|---|---|---|---|
| of defense | and | peaceful | construction | (are) such, | that |

| техни́ческая | мысль нашла́ | и | найдёт | но́вые | ме́тоды |
|---|---|---|---|---|---|
| technological | thought has found | and | will find | new | methods |

| увеличе́ния | произво́дства | э́того | мета́лла. |
|---|---|---|---|
| of increasing | of (the) production | of this | metal. |

§ 225. The Past Tense of есть, быть and дать and Infinitives Derived Therefrom.

The past tense of быть and дать is perfectly regular; the past tense of есть is formed by removing -сть from the infinitive and affixing regular endings. Thus we have ел, е́ла, etc.

Infinitives derived from быть and дать with prefixes also form their past tense regularly. The past from расъе́сть is formed like the past from есть, viz., разъе́л, разъе́ла, etc.

The imperfective infinitive забыва́ть, разъеда́ть, издава́ть and other similarly derived infinitives form their past tense in perfectly regular fashion.

§ 226. Reading Exercise.

### Из исто́рии металлу́ргии алюми́ния
### (Часть втора́я)

Бу́нзен (1854 г.) получи́л металли́ческий алюми́ний элек-тро́лизом распла́вленного двойно́го хлори́да алюми́ния и на́т-рия. Таки́м же о́бразом,[1] Сен-Кле́р-Деви́лль, незави́симо от Бу́нзена, в э́то же вре́мя[2] та́кже извлёк металли́ческий алю-ми́ний из двойно́го хлори́да его́ с на́трием. О́пыты Бу́нзена и Сен-Кле́р-Деви́лля не вы́шли, одна́ко, за преде́лы лаборато́-рии ввиду́ недосту́пности в то вре́мя значи́тельных коли́честв

электроэнергии.  Мощным толчком[3] для развития электроли-
тического метода получения алюминия послужило  изобретение динамомашины в 1867 г.

Чарльз Холл, будучи[4] студентом   колледжа, заинте-
ресовался вопросом получения алюминия.  В своих исследо-
ваниях Холл вначале шёл чисто эмпирическим путём.[5] Сначала, он исследовал электролиз водных растворов алюмини-
евых солей, но он не мог получить металлического алюминия.
При этом возник[6] вопрос, можно ли производить электролиз
в неводной среде.  Для того чтобы изучать этот  вопрос,
Холл искал неводные растворители для глинозёма.  С этой
целью он перепробовал различные фтористые соли.  В фев-
рале 1886 г. он внёс[7] окись алюминия  в  расплавленный
криолит и обнаружил весьма лёгкую растворимость  в  нём
глинозёма.

23 февраля 1886 г. Холл подверг[8] электролизу раствор глинозёма в расплавленном криолите и получил алюминий.

Независимо от Холла, Эру во Франции разработал современный электролитический способ производства металлического алюминия.  После неудач с электролизом алюминие-
вых солей в водных растворах Эру также перешёл к электролизу криолита и  смеси его с хлоридом алюминия.  При таких опытах Эру также пришёл к открытию растворимости глинозёма в расплавленном криолите.

Эру также разработал процесс получения  алюминие-
вых сплавов.  Для этого в электролизёр вводилось соот-
ветствующее количество металлической меди.

23 Апреля 1886 г. Эру во Франции и 9 июля того же
года  Холл в США[9]   заявили почти аналогичные патенты на
способ получения алюминия электролизом[10] глинозёма  рас-
творённого в расплавленном криолите.

Приозводство алюминия по электролитическому методу
Холла началось в 1886 г. в Нью-Кенсингтоне близ Питсбурга
(США).

Эру не смог реализовать своё изобретение во Франции и сделал это в Швейцарии на заводе в Нейгаузене,  в

конце́ 1888 г. Внача́ле заво́д э́тот[11] производи́л алюми́ниевую бро́нзу. Вско́ре (1891 г.), одна́ко, заво́д в Нейга́узене перешёл на произво́дство чи́стого алюми́ния.

## Notes

1. таки́м же о́бразом     "in the same way," cf. § 144, p. 215.

2. в э́то же вре́мя    "at the same time."

3. толчко́м  is the irregular instrumental singular of толчок "push, jolt, impetus," cf. § 357, p. 573.

4. бу́дучи студе́нтом    literally "being (a) student." Note that студе́нтом  is in the instrumental case.

5. The noun путём  and its modifier эмпири́ческим are both in the instrumental case, indicating with the verb шёл  "went," the course taken by Hall  в свои́х иссле́дованиях    "in his experiments," внача́ле  "at the start."

6. возни́к вопро́с, мо́жно ли  "arose (the) question, whether (it is) possible."   The particle ли  denotes interrogation. возни́к  is a past tense form, derived irregularly from the infinitive возни́кнуть of the verb возника́ть -- возни́кнуть "to arise," "to appear."

7. внёс  is a past tense form, derived irregularly from the infinitive внести́  of the verb вноси́ть -- внести́  "to bring in," "to put in."

8. подве́рг "submitted" is a past tense form, derived irregularly from the infinitive подве́ргнуть of the verb подверга́ть -- подве́ргнуть "to submit to," "to subject."

9. в США = в Соединённых Шта́тах Аме́рики    "in (the) United States of America."

10. электро́лизом  is in the instrumental case and for this reason may be translated as  "by means of electrolysis."

11. заво́д э́тот  "this plant." The more usual word order with э́тот preceding заво́д  is quite often reversed.

§ 227.  Translation Exercise.

1. In 1854, Bunsen passed electric current through (че́рез) fused (распла́вленный) double (ДВОЙНО́Й) chloride (хлори́д) of aluminum and sodium.

2. At that same time Saint Clair Deville interested self with the question of the preparation of aluminum.

3. Charles Hall, while a student of college, improved the method of Bunsen and Saint Clair Deville.

4. At first, Hall investigated the electrolysis of aqueous solutions of aluminum salts.

5. After many failures he went over to the electrolysis in nonaqueous medium.

6. In February 1886, Hall observed the very easy solubility of alumina in fused cryolite.

7. The 23 of February 1886, Hall obtained aluminum by electrolysis of a solution (раство́ра) of alumina in fused cryolite.

8. Independently of Hall, Héroult in France investigated the electrolysis of aqueous solutions of aluminum salts.

9. Héroult also worked out a process of production of metallic aluminum.

10. In 1886, Hall was able to accomplish his invention in a plant in New Kensington, near Pittsburgh (U.S.A.).

# LESSON 26

## THE FUTURE TENSE

§ 228. The Future Tense and Its Imperfective and Perfective Future Aspects.

In discussing infinitives, (§§ 39-43 pp. 55-63), the present and perfective future tenses (Lesson 21, § 185, pp. 280-281) and the past tense (§ 210, p. 331) it was pointed out that most Russian verbs have two parallel sets of forms derived, respectively, from the perfective and imperfective infinitives. Future tense forms are also derived from both infinitives. As might be expected from what has been said already concerning other verb forms, the imperfective future tense is used to refer to action considered as incomplete, in progress or frequently repeated. If future action is thought of as a completed whole, the perfective future tense is used.[1] A similar distinction between the two types of future action is also made in English. Thus, for example, "I will be buying" directs attention to an act in progress in future time, while "I will buy" indicates an act regarded as completed in future time.

§ 229. Formation of the Perfective Future Tense and Possible Confusion with the Present Tense.

As already discussed, cf. § 186, p. 282, the same tense endings, which are used with imperfective infinitives to form the present tense, are used with perfective infinitives to form the perfective future. Examples of the formation of the perfective future of several representative regular and irregular verbs have already been given together with companion present tense forms, cf. Lessons 21, 22, 23.

---

[1] Sometimes the Russian perfective future is best translated by the English present tense, cf. § 185, p. 280.

359

Because of the close relationship of the perfective future tense to the present tense, possibility of confusion exists. For this reason it is advisable to impress both the imperfective and perfective infinitives on the memory when learning Russian verbs.

§ 230. Formation of the Imperfective Future Tense.

The only Russian verb which forms a simple imperfective future tense is, быть "to be."

### Imperfective Future Tense of быть, (to be)

| | | | |
|---|---|---|---|
| бу́ду | I shall be | бу́дем | we shall be |
| бу́дешь | you will be | бу́дете | you will be |
| бу́дет | he will be | бу́дут | they will be |

In contrast to the simple imperfective future of быть, the imperfective future of all other verbs is compound in character. Specifically, the imperfective future is formed by using the simple future tense of быть as an auxiliary with the imperfective infinitives of Russian verbs. The formation of the imperfective future is so simple that it can be amply illustrated by a few examples.

#### Imperfective Future of Typical Verbs

| Imperfective Infinitive | де́лать | фильтрова́ть | влечь | итти́ |
|---|---|---|---|---|
| | | Singular | | |
| 1st Person | бу́ду де́лать | бу́ду фильтрова́ть | бу́ду влечь | бу́ду итти́ |
| 2nd Person | бу́дешь де́лать | бу́дешь фильтрова́ть | бу́дешь влечь | бу́дешь итти́ |
| 3rd Person | бу́дет де́лать | бу́дет фильтрова́ть | бу́дет влечь | бу́дет итти́ |
| | | Plural | | |
| 1st Person | бу́дем де́лать | бу́дем фильтрова́ть | бу́дем влечь | бу́дем итти́ |
| 2nd Person | бу́дете де́лать | бу́дете фильтрова́ть | бу́дете влечь | бу́дете итти́ |
| 3rd Person | бу́дут де́лать | бу́дут фильтрова́ть | бу́дут влечь | бу́дут итти́ |

The reflexive of the imperfective future is formed by adding to the infinitive involved either -СЯ (for infinitives ending in -ТЬ or -ЧЬ) or -СЬ (for infinitives ending in -ТИ).

### Reflexive Form of Imperfective Future

| Imperfective Infinitive | МЫТЬ |
|---|---|
| | to be washing |

| | Singular | Plural |
|---|---|---|
| 1st Person | бу́ду мы́ться | бу́дем мы́ться |
| 2nd Person | бу́дешь мы́ться | бу́дете мы́ться |
| 3rd Person | бу́дет мы́ться | бу́дут мы́ться |

| Imperfective Infinitive | ПЛЕСТИ |
|---|---|
| | to be braiding, weaving |

| | Singular | Plural |
|---|---|---|
| 1st Person | бу́ду плести́сь | бу́дем плести́сь |
| 2nd Person | бу́дешь плести́сь | бу́дете плести́сь |
| 3rd Person | бу́дет плести́сь | бу́дут плести́сь |

It is, of course, impossible to form an imperfective future tense from a perfective infinitive, as already discussed, cf. Lesson 21, § 185, p. 280.

§ 231. Sentences Illustrating Use of the Imperfective Future Tense.

In the following sentences, underlining has been used to point out the imperfective future tense, which is used to indicate an action thought of as incomplete, in progress or frequently repeated. This is to be contrasted with use of the perfective future to denote an action thought of as a completed whole.

В    случае    многоатомных    молекул    полярными
In   (the) case    of polyatomic    molecules    polar

свойствами[1]  будут  обладать  такие  молекулы,  в
properties    will   possess   such   molecules   in

которых   распределение   электрических   зарядов
which    (the) distribution   of electric   charges

в молекуле   в   целом   асимметрично.
in (the) molecule  in  whole  (is)  asymmetric.


Мы будем называть    изменения  формы  и  объёма
We  will  name (or designate) (the) changes  of form  and  volume

тел    деформациями.
of bodies   as deformations.


Диаграмма   состояния  будет выглядеть в  этом  случае,
(The) diagram  of condition  will   look   in  this  case,

как показано  на фиг. 54 и 55.
as  (is) shown  in Figs. 54 and 55.


Число    разных   линий   будет   различным   на
(The) number  of various  lines   will be  different   on

диаграммах  различных   сплавов,  но  всегда каждая
diagrams   of different   alloys,   but  always  each

линия   отвечает   какому-то изменению  в  строении
line   corresponds  to some  change   in  structure

сплава.
of (an) alloy.


The  following  passage  further  illustrates  use  of  the imperfective  future  (single  asterisks)  and  the  perfective  future (double asterisks).

---

[1] Note use of the instrumental case to designate the direct object of the infinitive обладать.

Éсли сообщи́ть те́лу не́которую нача́льную
If (to) communicate to (a) body (a) certain initial

ско́рость в вертика́льном направле́нии вверх, то
velocity in (the) vertical direction upward, then

те́ло при своём движе́нии бу́дет* находи́ться*
(the) body during its motion will find self

под де́йствием постоя́нной си́лы тя́жести,
under (the) action of (the) steady force of gravity,

напра́вленной про́тив нача́льного движе́ния. (Счита́ется,
directed against (the) initial motion. (Reckons

что сопротивле́ние во́здуха отсу́тствует.) Си́ла
self, that (the) resistance of air is absent.) (The)

тя́жести бу́дет* уменьша́ть* ско́рость те́ла,
force of gravity will decrease (the) velocity of (the) body

и те́ло бу́дет* дви́гаться* равноме́рно-заме́дленно
and (the) body will move self continually deceleratingly

с ускоре́нием -g. Сле́довательно h высота́, на
with acceleration -g. Consequently h (the) height to

кото́рую поднима́ется те́ло че́рез вре́мя t,бу́дет* равна́
which raises self (the) body after time t, will be equal

$$h = v_0 t - gt^2/2$$

где $v_0$ - нача́льная ско́рость.
where $v_0$ (is) (the) initial velocity.


Ско́рость че́рез t сек. бу́дет* равна́
(The) velocity after t sec. will be equal

$$V = v_0 - gt.$$

Когда́ ско́рость те́ла уменьши́тся** до нуля́,
When (the) velocity of (the) body will decrease to zero,

те́ло дости́гнет** са́мой высо́кой то́чки своего́
(the) body will reach (the) very high(est) point of its

подъёма; в э́той то́чке
rise;       at this   point

$$v = v_o - gt_1 = .0$$

где    $t_1$ есть вре́мя    подъёма   те́ла.      Отсю́да,
where  $t_1$ is   (the) time of rise   of (the) body.  Hence,

$$t_1 = v_o \, / \, g.$$

## § 232. Use of the Future Tense in Sentences Expressing Real Conditions.

In preceding § 231, both the imperfective future and the perfective future tenses were used to describe an imaginary experiment. Russian future tenses may also be used in conditional sentences to specify conditions which will be achieved or are capable of achievement. Russian uses another set of verb forms, cf. Lesson 34, in sentences involving conditions incapable of achievement, or contrary to fact or of a highly doubtful nature.

Е́сли   на   те́ло   не   де́йствуют   никаки́е   си́лы,
If     on   (a) body not  acts        no        forces,

ско́рость   те́ла       не  бу́дет  меня́ться,  оно́ бу́дет
(the) velocity of (the) body not will  change self, it  will

оставáться[1] в    поко́е  и́ли  бу́дет  дви́гаться   без
remain      in   rest   or   will   move self   without

измене́ния   ско́рости.
change      of velocity.

Е́сли мы каки́м-либо   спо́собом   увели́чим   ско́рости
If   we by any        process     shall increase (the) speeds

беспоря́дочного          движе́ния    моле́кул,     то
of  disorderly  (chaotic)  motion      of molecules,   then

температу́ра   те́ла       подни́мется.
(the) temperature of (the) body will raise self.

---

[1] See Footnote 1, p. 145.

Когда́ ускоре́ние стано́вится ра́вным нулю́,
When (the) acceleration will become equal to zero,

дальне́йшее движе́ние те́ла бу́дет происходи́ть
further movement of (the) body will go on

с постоя́нной ско́ростью.
with constant velocity.

Е́сли проце́сс происхо́дит в о́чень коро́ткий
If (a) process proceeds in (a) very short

промежу́ток вре́мени, он бу́дет протека́ть
interval of time, he will proceed

адиабати́чески, и́бо при э́том теплово́й обме́н не
adiabatically, since during this heat exchange not

бу́дет происходи́ть.
will proceed.

## § 233. Reading Exercise.

### Áто́мная эне́ргия

Неда́вно бы́ли изобретены́[1] но́вые ато́мные бо́мбы, в кото́рых испо́льзовано[2] получе́ние эне́ргии из а́томов ура́на и плуто́ния. Это пе́рвое примене́ние внутриато́мной эне́ргии. Оно́ показыва́ет,. что нау́ка и те́хника уже́ сде́лали в э́том направле́нии больши́е успе́хи.

Ура́н и плуто́ний - ре́дкие и дороги́е вещества́. Получе́ние их из досту́пного сырья́ тре́бует сло́жной и тру́дной обрабо́тки. Но[3] это лишь пе́рвый шаг в э́той но́вой о́бласти те́хники; нау́ка бу́дет иска́ть бо́лее[4] досту́пных спо́собов получе́ния ато́мной эне́ргии и испо́льзования бо́лее[5] распространённых материа́лов. Здесь ещё грома́дная о́бласть для изуче́ния, и мы нахо́димся лишь в са́мом нача́ле его́.

По совреме́нным тео́риям исто́чником[6] эне́ргии со́лнца явля́ется проце́сс уплотне́ния а́томов водоро́да в а́томы ге́лия. В тако́м проце́ссе уча́ствуют как "я́дерные"[7] катализа́-

торы и áтомы углеродá и áтомы азóта. Вслéдствие процéс-
са уплотнéния мáсса исхóдного материáла, именно водорóда, частúчно превращáется в энéргию, а углерóд и азóт
ввидý свой рóли катализáторов в концé концóв[8] остаáтся
неизменéнными. Возмóжно, что бýдет[9] нáйден схóдный процéсс, котóрый и[10] в земнúх услóвиях бýдет выделя́ть энéргию в громáдных колúчествах за счёт водорóдных áтомов.

Несомнéнно тáкже, что атóмная энéргия бýдет примен-
я́ться не тóлько для воéнных целéй - настýпит врéмя, когдá онá вольёт[11] нóвые мóщные потóки энéргии в промы́шлен-
ность, в трáнспорт, в сéльское хозя́йство, во все óбласти
нáшей жúзни. Онá произведёт цéлый переворóт в тéхнике.

В осóбенности измéнится вся тéхника получéния энéргии. Вмéсто совремéнных электростáнций с их котлáми,
турбúнами, динамомашúнами, когдá-нибудь вы́растут совер-
шéнно нóвые силовы́е стáнции с другúм оборýдованием. Их
прибóры и машúны бýдут создавáть необходúмые услóвия для
превращéний áтомов, при котóрых бýдет развивáться громáдная энéргия. Возмóжно, что онú бýдут горáздо[12] мéнь-
шего размéра, чем совремéнные машúны, тогдá как[13] энéргии от них бýдет получáться во мнóго раз бóльше. Во вся́-
ком слýчае "материáла"[14] для получéния э́той энéргии бýдет
трéбоваться несравнéнно мéньше,[15] чем те огрóмные колú-
чества ýгля úли нéфти, котóрые сжигáются в совремéнных
силовы́х стáнциях и в двúгателях.

Трýдно предсказáть, чéрез[16] скóлько врéмени удáст-
ся осуществúть такóе испóльзование атóмной энéргии. Мóжно тóлько сказáть, что совремéнная наýка и тéхника раз-
вивáются óчень бы́стро.

## Notes

1. были изобретены́ "were invented." This is one of the Russian equivalents, cf. § 241, p. 367, of the English passive voice.

2. испо́льзовано получе́ние эне́ргии "(is) utilized (the) production of energy."

3. Но э́то лишь--"But this (is) only -- ."

4. бу́дет иска́ть бо́лее досту́пных спо́собов "will seek more accessible methods." In general, the comparative of Russian adjectives is formed with the adverb бо́лее, cf. Lesson 36. Note that both досту́пных and спо́собов are in the genitive case after иска́ть.

5. бо́лее распространённых материа́лов "of more available materials." The word распространённый, used here like an adjective, is the passive past participle from the infinitive -- распространи́ть of the verb распространя́ть -- распространи́ть, "to extend," "to broaden," "to make available."

6. исто́чником эне́ргии -- явля́ется проце́сс -- "as (the) source of energy -- shows self (the) process --." Inverted word order with various forms, of ЯВЛЯ́ТЬСЯ is by no means rare in scientific Russian.

7. Placing this word -- namely я́дерные -- within quotation marks indicates that it is being used in a fashion which may be new or strange to the reader. Similar use of quotation marks is also encountered in English scientific writing.

8. в конце́ концо́в literally "at the end of ends," or, more smoothly, "finally." Declension of the noun коне́ц involves deletion of the "е" except in the nominative and accusative singular cases, cf. § 357, p. 573.

9. бу́дет на́йден , "will be found." Cf. Note 1 above.

10. И, "even." The use of И to impart emphasis to statements is encountered quite frequently in Russian technical writing.

11. вольёт "will pour in" is the third person singular of the irregularly formed perfective future from the infinitive ВЛИТЬ of the verb ВЛИВА́ТЬ -- ВЛИТЬ "to pour in."

12. гора́здо  ме́ньшего  разме́ра, чем -- "of much smaller dimension, than --." Here  ме́ньшего and разме́ра are in the descriptive genitive, cf. § 121, p. 178.

13. тогда́ как   "whereas."

14. материа́ла  -- бу́дет тре́боваться  -- "of material -- will require self --." Here материа́ла   is in the partitive genitive, cf. § 121, p. 178.

15. несравне́нно ме́ньше, чем  "imcomparably less, than."

16. че́рез ско́лько вре́мени уда́стся translating as literally as possible we have "through how much of time it will succeed." Note that уда́стся  is the irregular formed third person singular of the perfective future from the infinitive уда́ться of the verb  удава́ться -- уда́ться "to succeed." The parent verb дава́ть -- дать "to give" also forms the perfective future irregularly from the infinitive дать, cf. § 207, p. 323. Here вре́мени is the irregular genitive singular of the neuter noun вре́мя, "time," cf. § 358, p. 575.

§ 234. Translation Exercise.

1. The atomic bomb is (shows self) the first application ( примене́нием ) of intra -atomic energy.
2. The production of plutonium from available raw material requires difficult processing.
3. We are (find self) at the very beginning of the utilization of atomic energy.
4. Not ( Не) only (то́лько) atoms of carbon but ( но ) also ( та́кже ) atoms of nitrogen participate as (как) "nuclear" catalysts in the process of condensation of atoms of hydrogen into atoms of helium.
5. Thereby (При э́том) energy is evolved at (за) the expense ( счёт ) of the mass of the starting material.
6. The time will come when atomic energy will be used for peaceful purposes.
7. Atomic energy will bring about a complete revolution in (в) industry ( промы́шленности ),  in transportation (тра́нспорте), in agriculture (се́льском хозя́йстве ) in (во) all (всех ) fields ( областя́х ) of our life.
8. New power plants will develop atomic energy in enormous amounts.

9. Such (Такие ) power plants will be of much smaller dimension than contemporary electrostations (электростанции ).

10. The science and technology of the utilization of atomic energy is evolving (being developed) very rapidly.

# LESSON 27

## PASSIVE PAST PARTICIPLES

§ 235. Introduction to Passive Past Participles.

In previous lessons it was mentioned that Russian passive past participles usually are formed in simple fashion from infinitives. (See § 60, p. 82, Lesson 8.) Sentences involving passive past participles have also been encountered occasionally in previous lessons. We shall now review and summarize this important section of Russian grammar.

The majority of English verbs form their past participles by affixing "-d" or "-ed" to the infinitive without altering the stem of the latter. Thus we have, for example:

| Infinitive | Past Participle |
|------------|-----------------|
| to pour | poured |
| to ignite | ignited |
| to multiply | multiplied |

Another method of forming the past participle in English, namely by affixing "-n" or "-en," might also be described as regular provided the infinitive stem undergoes no change, as in the following examples.

| Infinitive | Past Participle |
|------------|-----------------|
| to beat | beaten |
| to forsake | forsaken |
| to see | seen |

371

The great majority of Russian passive[1] past participles are formed from the corresponding infinitives by equally simple procedures. Irregularities are encountered with some infinitives as is also the case in English as shown by the following examples.

| Infinitive | Past Participle |
|------------|-----------------|
| to buy     | bought          |
| to hold    | held            |
| to tell    | told            |
| to sing    | sung            |

In English, past participles are used either as modifiers of nouns either directly or in the predicate with auxiliary verbs as in the following sentences:

"The magnetized steel bar attracts iron filings."
"The steel bar, magnetized in the previous experiment, attracts iron filings."
"The steel bar is magnetized."
"The steel bar was magnetized."
"The steel bar will be magnetized."
"The steel bar can be magnetized."

As further discussion will reveal, Russian passive past participles are used in much the same fashion.

Since Russian passive past participles are used as noun modifiers, it is only natural that they should be declined exactly like adjectives using the regular adjective endings.[2] As is the case with adjectives, the gender, number and case of a given participle is determined by the noun which it modifies.

---

[1] Active past participles are also formed from Russian infinitives by affixing endings. Active past participles are discussed in Lesson 28.
[2] The adjective endings used with past participles are the so-called "hard" endings, cf. § 131, p. 191.

§ 236. Regular Formation of Stems of Passive Past Participles.

In general, either imperfective or perfective infinitives may serve as parents of passive past participles in Russian. It will be recalled that verb forms derived from imperfective infinitives usually indicate action thought of as incomplete, in progress or frequently repeated while those derived from perfective infinitives indicate action thought of as a completed whole. Since a passive past participle by its very nature indicates submission to past action, it is perhaps not surprising that the majority of passive past participles encountered in reading scientific Russian are derived from perfective infinitives.[1]

The great majority of Russian verbs form the stems of their passive past participles by a two step process:
    1) Removing -ТЬ from an infinitive.
    2) Affixing -HH- or -T- depending on the individual infinitive.

It does not appear possible to formulate a concise rule for establishing whether regular formation of the passive past participle from a given infinitive will occur by adding -HH- or -T-. It is worth noting, however, that -HH- is used almost exclusively with the very large class of infinitives ending in –аТЬ. On the other hand, -T- is used principally, though not exclusively,[2] with three small groups of infinitives ending, respectively, with –ЫТЬ, –УТЬ and –ЯТЬ. The following examples are typical:

### Passive Past Participle Formed with -HH-

|  | Infinitive | Class | Passive Past Participle |
|---|---|---|---|
| Imperfective | де́лать | Reg. A | де́ланный |
| Perfective | сде́лать |  | сде́ланный |
| Imperfective | та́ять | Reg. B-1 | та́янный |
| Perfective | раста́ять |  | раста́янный |

---

[1] Various individual infinitives, either for logical reasons or simply as a matter of usage, do not form passive past participles.

[2] Certain infinitives in –ИТЬ form their passive past participles with -T-. Thus we have вы́питый, побри́тый, прожи́тый from вы́пить, побри́ть, прожи́ть.

| | Infinitive | Class | Passive Past Participle |
|---|---|---|---|
| Imperfective | фотографи́ровать | Irr. A-1 | фотографи́рованный |
| Perfective | сфотографи́ровать | | сфотографи́рованный |
| Imperfective | писа́ть | Irr. D-1 | пи́санный |
| Perfective | написа́ть | | напи́санный |
| Imperfective | гна́ть | Irr. E-2 | по́гнанный |
| Perfective | погна́ть | | |
| Imperfective | дава́ть | Irr. B | |
| Perfective | дать | Irr. I-3 | да́нный |

### Passive Past Participles Formed with -T-

| | Infinitive | Class | Passive Past Participle |
|---|---|---|---|
| Imperfective | жа́ть | Irr. C-4 | жа́тый |
| Perfective | пожа́ть | | пожа́тый |
| Imperfective | пить | Irr. E-3 | пи́тый |
| Perfective | вы́пить | | вы́питый |
| Imperfective | кры́ть | Irr. E-4 | кры́тый |
| Perfective | покры́ть | | покры́тый |
| Imperfective | понима́ть | Reg. A | |
| Perfective | поня́ть | Irr. F-5 | по́нятый |
| Imperfective | достига́ть | Reg. A | |
| Perfective | дости́гнуть | Irr. J-3 | дости́гнутый |

**§ 237.  Irregular Formation of Stems of Passive Past Participles.**

A few infinitives ending in -ать, -еть or -ить, as the case may be, do not form their passive past participles in accordance with the procedure described above in § 236. Perhaps the most important irregularity involves a rather large group of infinitives ending in -ить, the stems of whose passive past participles usually terminate in -енн-, rather than -инн- as might be

expected. Cf. ОКИСЛЯ́ТЬ -- ОКИСЛИ́ТЬ "to oxidize" given below. Other irregularities encountered involve stem changes of the same type as described in Lesson 22 (irregular present or perfective future tense) or Lesson 25 (irregular past tense).

|  | Infinitive | Class | Passive Past Participle |
|---|---|---|---|
| Imperfective | ОКИСЛЯ́ТЬ | Reg. A | |
| Perfective | ОКИСЛИТЬ | Reg. B-2 | ОКИ́СЛЕННЫЙ |
| Imperfective | КОЛЕБА́ТЬ | | КОЛЕ́БЛЕННЫЙ |
| Perfective | ПОКОЛЕБА́ТЬ | Irr. C-1 | ПОКОЛЕ́БЛЕННЫЙ |
| Imperfective | КРИВИ́ТЬ | | КРИВЛЕ́ННЫЙ |
| Perfective | ПОКРИВИ́ТЬ | Irr. C-2 | ПОКРИВЛЕ́ННЫЙ |
| Imperfective | НОСИ́ТЬ | | НО́ШЕННЫЙ |
| Perfective | ПОНОСИ́ТЬ | Irr. D-1 | ПОНО́ШЕННЫЙ |
| Imperfective | ТЕРЕ́ТЬ | | ТЁРТЫЙ |
| Perfective | ПОТЕРЕ́ТЬ | Irr. E-5 | ПОТЁРТЫЙ |

Infinitives ending in -ЧЬ, -ЗТИ, -СТИ, -ЗТЬ, -СТЬ or -ТИ, form their passive past participle in an irregular fashion as shown by the following examples.

|  | Infinitive | Class | Passive Past Participle |
|---|---|---|---|
| Imperfective | ЖЕЧЬ | | ЖЖЁННЫЙ |
| Perfective | СЖЕЧЬ | Irr. G-2 | СОЖЖЁННЫЙ |
| Imperfective | ВЛЕЧЬ | | ВЛЕЧЁННЫЙ |
| Perfective | ПОВЛЕ́ЧЬ | Irr. G-3 | ПОВЛЕЧЁННЫЙ |
| Imperfective | ВЕЗТИ́ | | ВЕЗЁННЫЙ |
| Perfective | ПОВЕЗТИ́ | Irr. H-1 | ПОВЕЗЁННЫЙ |
| Imperfective | НЕСТИ́ | | НЕСЁННЫЙ |
| Perfective | ПОНЕСТИ́ | Irr. H-2 | ПОНЕСЁННЫЙ |
| Imperfective | ПЛЕСТИ́ | | ПЛЕТЕ́ННЫЙ |
| Perfective | ЗАПЛЕСТИ́ | Irr. H-3 | ЗАПЛЕТЕ́ННЫЙ |

| | Infinitive | Class | Passive Past Participle |
|---|---|---|---|
| Imperfective | грести́ | Irr. H-4 | погребённый |
| Perfective | погрести́ | | |
| Imperfective | вести́ | Irr. H-5 | ведённый |
| Perfective | повести́ | | поведённый |
| Imperfective | грызть | Irr. H-6 | загры́зенный |
| Perfective | загры́зть | | |
| Imperfective | клясть | Irr. H-9 | про́клятый |
| Perfective | проклясть | | |
| Imperfective | находи́ть | Irr. D-2 | на́йденный |
| Perfective | найти́ | Irr. H-10 | |
| Imperfective | разъеда́ть | Reg. A | разъе́денный |
| Perfective | разъе́сть | Irr. I-1 | |

§ 238.  Declension of Passive Past Participles.

As mentioned already, the regular hard adjective endings are used throughout in declining passive past participles. The only complication is encountered in forming the predicative forms of those passive past participles whose stems terminate in -HH-. Before adding the regular predicative adjective endings, one -H- is dropped as shown in the first of the two following examples.

## Declension of a Typical Passive Past Participle with Stem Terminating in -НН-

Stem of Passive Past Participle ДАНН-, "given"
(Perfective Infinitive ДАТЬ, "to give")

### ATTRIBUTIVE FORMS

#### Singular

|  | Masc. | Fem. | Neuter |
|---|---|---|---|
| Nom. | да́нный | да́нная | да́нное |
| Gen. | да́нного | да́нной | да́нного |
| Dat. | да́нному | да́нной | да́нному |
| Acc. | да́нный[1] | да́нную | да́нное |
| Instr. | да́нным | да́нной (да́нною) | да́нным |
| Prep. | да́нном | да́нной | да́нном |

#### All Genders

#### Plural

| Nom. | да́нные |
|---|---|
| Gen. | да́нных |
| Dat. | да́нным |
| Acc. | да́нные[1] |
| Instr. | да́нными |
| Prep. | да́нных |

### PREDICATIVE FORMS

|  | Masc. | Fem. | Neuter |
|---|---|---|---|
| Sing. | дан | дана́ | дано́ |

#### All Genders

| Plural | даны́ |
|---|---|

[1] When used to modify nouns designating living beings, as defined in § 67, p. 93, this accusative form becomes the same as the corresponding genitive.

### Declension of a Typical Passive Past Participle with Stem Terminating in -Т-

Stem of Passive Past Participle ВЗЯТ-, "taken"
(Perfective Infinitive ВЗЯТЬ, "to take")

## ATTRIBUTIVE FORMS

### Singular

|        | Masc.     | Fem.      | Neuter   |
|--------|-----------|-----------|----------|
| Nom.   | взя́тый    | взя́тая    | взя́тое   |
| Gen.   | взя́того   | взя́той    | взя́того  |
| Dat.   | взя́тому   | взя́той    | взя́тому  |
| Acc.   | взя́тый[1] | взя́тую    | взя́тое   |
| Instr. | взя́тым    | взя́той    | взя́тым   |
|        |           | (взя́тою)  |          |
| Prep.  | взя́том    | взя́той    | взя́том   |

### All Genders

### Plural

| Nom.   | взя́тые     |
|--------|------------|
| Gen.   | взя́тых     |
| Dat.   | взя́тым     |
| Acc.   | взя́тые[1]  |
| Instr. | взя́тыми    |
| Prep.  | взя́тых     |

## PREDICATIVE FORMS

|        | Masc. | Fem.   | Neuter |
|--------|-------|--------|--------|
| Sing.  | взят  | взя́та  | взя́то  |

### All Genders

| Plural | взя́ты |
|--------|-------|

[1] When used to modify nouns designating living beings, as defined in § 67, p. 93, this accusative form becomes the same as the corresponding genitive.

§ 239. Summary Note on Construction of Passive Past Participles.

As is evident from the foregoing discussion, Russian passive past participles are built up of three component parts. This fact might be represented by the following diagrammatical analysis of typical passive past participles.

| | | |
|---|---|---|
| сде́ла ———— | нн ——————— | ый from сде́лать "to do" |
| взя́ ———— | т ——————— | ый from взять "to take" |
| разъе́де ——— | нн ——————— | ый from разъе́сть "to eat |
| Infinitive stem (Sometimes in altered form) | Typical stem termination of passive past participles | Adjective apart" ending |

As already noted, the adjective endings serve to indicate which noun a given participle modifies.

§ 240. Sentences Illustrating Simple Use of Passive Past Participles as Direct Modifiers of Nouns.

In considering these sentences, particular attention should be directed to the use of the attributive adjective endings (§ 131, p. 191) to bring the participles into agreement with the modified nouns as to gender, number and case. Asterisks are used to facilitate identification of the participles. These sentences have been divided into two groups depending on whether or not the participle precedes the noun which it modifies.

Group I. Passive Past Participle Precedes Noun Modified

| Обы́чная | вода́, | во́дные | раство́ры | разли́чных | соле́й и |
|---|---|---|---|---|---|
| Ordinary | water, | aqueous | solutions | of various | salts and |

| кисло́т, | а та́кже | распла́вленные* | мета́ллы | явля́ются |
|---|---|---|---|---|
| acids, | and also | melted (fused) | metals | show self (are) |

| приме́рами | жи́дких | проводнико́в | электри́чества. |
|---|---|---|---|
| examples | of liquid | conductors | of electricity. |

| Бы́ло, | одна́ко, | тру́дно обнару́жить | предска́занный* | эффе́кт. |
|---|---|---|---|---|
| It was, | however, | difficult to detect | (the) predicted | effect. |

Си́льно сжа́тые* га́зы храня́т в про́чных стальны́х
Strongly compressed gases they store in strong steel

балло́нах.
cylinders.

Концентра́ция насы́щенного* раство́ра определя́ет
(The) concentration of (the) saturated solution determines

раствори́мость вещества́ при да́нных* усло́виях.
(the) solubility of (a) substance at given conditions.

Вода́ ка́ждой реки́ соде́ржит большо́е коли́чество
(The) water of every river contains (a) large quantity

взве́шенных* части́ц.
of suspended particles.

Число́ вы́деленных*[1] из дрожже́й стери́нов велико́.
(The) number of isolated from yeasts sterols (is) large.

### Group II. Passive Past Participle Follows Noun Modified

Число́, полу́ченное* по́сле арифмети́ческого
(The) number obtained after arithmetical

умноже́ния, называ́ется произведе́нием.
multiplication calls self (the) product.

О́пыты, произведённые* с це́лью изучи́ть
Experiments carried out with (the) purpose to study

проце́сс бомбардиро́вки металли́ческого бери́ллия
(the) process of bombardment of metallic berillium

---

[1] A smoother translation would be, "The number of sterols isolated from yeasts is large." Note carefully that вы́деленных modifies стери́нов. This sequence of words -- namely participle modifier, phrase, noun modified -- is by no means rare in scientific Russian.

α -частицами полония,      дали   повод   к   открытию
by α-particles of polonium   gave   occasion   to   discovery

нейтронов.
of neutrons.

Каждый    из этих    окислов,    взятый*    в отдельности,
Each      of these   oxides,     taken      in isolation,

обладает незначительным каталитическим действием.
possesses insignificant    catalytic      action.

Слово      "радиоактивность" происходит от     названия
(The) word  "radioactivity"   derives      from (the) name

химического    элемента радия,   открытого* в 1898 г.
of (the) chemical element  radium,  discovered in 1898.

## § 241. Use of Predicative Forms of Passive Past Participles.

The predicative forms of passive past participles are often encountered in scientific Russian. The derivation of these forms by use of regular adjective predicative endings has already been reviewed in § 238, pp. 376-378.

As might be expected, the predicative forms of participles are used in a manner analagous to the use of corresponding forms of adjectives. Thus, the predicative forms of participles may be used in sentences in which the obsolete present tense of быть "to be" is omitted but implied. (See Group I, below.) In other sentences in which the past or future tense of быть is used with the predicative forms of passive past participles, the verbal nature of the latter imparts to the sentence a shade of meaning often best translated into English by use of the passive of the corresponding English verb. (See Group II, below.) In another closely related type of sentence such expressions as может быть (literally "is able to be") or могут быть (literally "are able to be") должно быть (literally "needful to be"), etc., will be used together with the predicative form of passive past participles to indicate the possibility, necessity, etc., of accomplishing an action (See Group III, following.)

## Group I

Явле́ния        взры́ва          о́чень сло́жны  и  ещё не
(The) phenomena  of explosion  (are) very    complex  and  still not

изу́чены  во  всех  дета́лях.
studied    in   all   details.

Е́сли    дана́  си́ла      I постоя́нного[1]      электри́ческого
If    (is) given (the) strength, I, of (a) constant    (direct) electric

то́ка    в  како́м-нибудь проводнике́, и дано́ его́ сопротивле́ние,
current  in any        conductor  and given its   resistance,

то  по          зако́ну    О́ма мы  легко́ мо́жем  вы́числить
then according to (the) law of Ohm we  easily are able to  calculate

ра́зность        потенциа́лов на  конца́х    э́того проводника́.
(the) difference of potentials at  (the) ends of that  conductor.

$$V_1 - V_2 = IR$$

За  едини́цу  длины́    в  метри́ческой систе́ме      при́нят
For (the) unit  of length  in (the) metric    system    (is)  taken

метр.
(the) meter.

Для измере́ния      величины́          пове́рхностного натяже́ния
For  measurement of (the) magnitude of surface          tension

принята      та  же    едини́ца, что и    для  измере́ния
(is) taken   the  same   unit     as  also  for  measurement

други́х  небольши́х   сил, т.е.  ди́на.
of other   small       forces, i.e.,  (the) dyne.

---

[1] The two expressions постоя́нный ток  "direct current" and переме́нный ток
"alternating current" are often encountered in physics and electrical engineering.

### Group II

Химическая     природа     половых     гормонов     была выяснена
(The) chemical   nature      of sex      hormones     was elucidated

лишь за последние годы.
only in (the) last    years.

Цезий    был открыт    в 1860 г. при помощи спектрального
Cesium  was discovered in 1860      with (the) aid  of spectral

анализа.
analysis.

Другой    тип    двигателя    внутреннего сгорания    был
Another   type   of motor     of internal  combustion  was

изобретен Дизелем.[1]
invented     by Diesel.

Если    электрическая    цепь    динамомашины    будет
If     (the) electric     circuit  of (a) dynamo    will be

прервана,   т.е. разомкнута, (фиг.36),  то   по    цепи
interrupted, i.e., opened,       (Fig. 36),  then along (the) circuit

не   будет протекать   никакого тока,[2]  но   разность
not  will   flow through  no          current, but (the) difference

---

[1] Names are declined in Russian like other nouns denoting persons, animals, etc.,
cf. § 362, p. 585. Here Дизелем is the instrumental singular of Дизель "Diesel."
[2] A freer translation of this clause would be, "then no current will flow in the
circuit." For discussion of double negatives, see Lesson 20, § 180, p. 272;
§ 181, p. 274.

потенциа́лов ме́жду то́чками A и Г бу́дет существова́ть,
of potentials between points A and G will exist

и в э́том слу́чае она́ в то́чности
and in this case she (the difference) in exactness

соотве́тствует Э.Д.С.[1] динамомаши́ны.
corresponds to (the) e.m.f. of (the) dynamo.

При ско́ростях поле́та свы́ше 3000 киломе́тров в час бу́дут
At velocities of flight above 3000 kilometers per hour will be

испо́льзованы возду́шно-реакти́вные дви́гатели.
used airjet (ramjet) motors.

## Group III

Ско́рость растворе́ния твёрдого те́ла мо́жет быть увели́чена,
(The) rate of solution of (a) solid body can be increased,

е́сли раствори́тель переме́шивается и́ли нагрева́ется.
if (the) solvent stirs self or heats self.

Для изображе́ния простра́нственного строе́ния мета́на
For illustration of (the) spatial structure of methane

мо́жет быть испо́льзована моде́ль октаэ́дра.
can be utilized (the) model of octahedron.

Очеви́дно, что ско́рость испаре́ния како́го-либо
(It is) obvious, that (the) rate of evaporation of any

вещества́ должна́ быть те́сно свя́зана с величино́й
substance must be closely connected with (the) magnitude

упру́гости его́ па́ра.
of (the) tension of its vapor.

---

[1] Э.Д.С. is an abbreviation here for электродви́жущей си́ле, the dative case of электродви́жущая си́ла. The compound word электродви́жущий is derived from электро- and the active present participle derived from the imperfective infinitive дви́жущий of the verb дви́гать -- дви́нуть "to move."

Явле́ния, свя́занные с фотоэффе́ктом, не могли́
(The) phenomena, connected with (the) photoeffect, not were able

быть объяснены́ при по́мощи волново́й тео́рии све́та.
to be explained with (the) aid of (the) wave theory of light.

§ 242. The Instrumental Case of Passive Past Participles as Predicative Modifiers.

Sentences in which the instrumental case of adjectives was used predicatively with various verbs meaning "to appear," "to become," "to remain," "to be," etc., have already been discussed. See, in particular § 100, p. 145. The instrumental case of passive past participles may be similarly used as is evident from the following examples. As with adjectives, the gender and number of participles so used is determined by the noun to which the participle refers.

Легко́ объясни́ть, почему́ во вре́мя паде́ния тела́
(It is) easy to explain, why in (the) time of falling bodies

явля́ются недеформи́рованными.
show self not deformed.

Вме́сте с са́мим те́лом ока́зывается деформи́рованной
Together with the very body shows self deformed

и та подста́вка, на кото́рой те́ло лежи́т.
also that support on which (the) body lies.

Нагрева́ние га́за мо́жно осуществи́ть таки́м
Heating of gas it is possible to accomplish in such

о́бразом, что объём его́ при э́том бу́дет остава́ться[1]
a way that (the) volume of it thereby will remain

неизмене́нным.
unchanged.

[1] See Footnote 1, p. 145.

Вопрос о происхожде́нии косми́ческих
(The) question concerning (the) origin of cosmic

луче́й ещё не счита́ется решённым.
rays still not reckons self (is considered) solved.

§ 243. Passive Past Participles Used in Conjunction with the Instrumental Case of Nouns, etc.

Previous discussion has emphasized the fact that passive past participles are used to indicate submission to past action. A noun modified by a passive past participle is thereby designated as having undergone the action in question. The means (or person) whereby the action was accomplished may be designated by a noun, pronoun (or other substantive) standing in the instrumental case. This is in line with use of the instrumental case in conjunction with reflexive forms as already discussed in § 92, p. 132.

О́пыт, рассмо́тренный на́ми в § 36, пока́зывает,
(The) experiment, considered by us in § 36, shows,

что си́ла то́ка зави́сит от ско́рости
that (the) strength of (the) current depends on (the) rate

пересече́ния магни́тных ли́ний проводнико́м.
of cutting of magnetic lines by (the) conductor.

Часть излучённой со́лнцем эне́ргии па́дает на
(A) part of (the) radiated by (the) sun energy falls on

на́шу плане́ту.
our planet.

Су́щность раманэффе́кта заключа́ется
(The) essence of (the) Raman effect encloses self (consists)

в том, что в спе́ктре све́та, рассе́янного моле́кулами
in this, that in (the) spectrum of light scattered by molecules

| | | | | |
|---|---|---|---|---|
| какого-либо | вещества, | появляются | новые | линии, |
| of any | substance, | show self | new | lines, |

| | | | | |
|---|---|---|---|---|
| положение | которых | зависит | от | структуры |
| (the) position | of which | depends | on | (the) structure |

молекул.
of (the) molecules.

| | | | | |
|---|---|---|---|---|
| Явление | ассоциации | жидкостей | во многих | случаях |
| (The) phenomena | of association | of liquids | in many | cases |

| | | | | |
|---|---|---|---|---|
| обязано | своим | происхождением | описанному | выше |
| (is) connected | by its | origin | to (the) described | above |

| | | | |
|---|---|---|---|
| взаимодействию между | полярными | молекулами. |
| interaction | between polar | molecules. |

| | | |
|---|---|---|
| Часть поверхности | земли | покрыта водой. |
| Part of (the) surface | of (the earth | (is) covered by water. |

| | | | | |
|---|---|---|---|---|
| Это | объяснение фотоэлектрического | эффекта | было | впервые |
| This | explanation of (the) photoelectric | effect | was | first |

высказано Эйнштейном.[1]
stated by Einstein.

| | | | |
|---|---|---|---|
| При | нейтрализации концентрированных | растворов | кислот |
| During | neutralization of concentrated | solutions | of acids |

| | | | |
|---|---|---|---|
| и | щёлочей теплота | нейтрализации будет | замаскирована |
| and alkalis | (the) heat | of neutralization will (be) | masked |

| | | | |
|---|---|---|---|
| побочными | явлениями, | например, | появлением |
| by accessory | phenomena, | for example, | by (the) appearance |

теплот разбавления.
of heats of dilution.

---

[1] Here again, (cf. Footnote 1, p. 383), we have the instrumental case of a person's name.

Механическая    устойчивость  тела    может  быть
(The) mechanical    stability    of (a) body    can    be

улучшена увеличением площади    опоры.
improved  by increasing  of (the) area  of support.

Ещё  в  конце  XVIII    века  были  сделаны
Even  in (the) end  (of the) eighteenth  century  were  made

наблюдения,  которые не могли быть объяснены теорией
observations  which    not could be    explained  by (the) theory

теплорода.
of phlogiston.


§ 244.  Predicative  Neuter  Singular  of  Passive  Past  Participles
in Impersonal Sentences.

In § 120, p. 176, the use of the predicative neuter singular of
adjectives in constructing impersonal sentences was discussed.
Similar use of the predicative neuter singular of passive past
participles is illustrated by the following sentences.

Принято    называть  плотность  магнитного  потока
(It is) accepted  to name  (the) density  of magnetic  flux

магнитной    индукцией.
(the) magnetic  induction.

Международным  соглашением    постановлено называть эту
By international  agreement  (it is) established    to name  this

единицу  магнитной    индукции  гауссом,  в  честь
unit    of magnetic    induction  (the) Gauss,  in  honor

немецкого    учёного    Гаусса.[1]
of (the) German  scientist  Gauss.

---

[1] Here Гаусса is the genitive singular of Гаусс. Note also that гауссом. is the
instrumental singular of гаусс.

При этом        было с     абсолютной очевидностью показано,
Thereby         was   with absolute      obviousness       shown,

что при   радиоактивных процессах происходит превращение
that during radioactive      processes  occurs        conversion

малого       количества массы  в    энергию.
of (a) small amount     of mass into energy.


Как      будет       пояснено        в § 238,    имеются
As       will        be explained    in § 238,   have self

                основания считать,[1]    что  в   поглощении
(there are) grounds       to believe,    that in  (the) absorption

космических лучей образование       электрон-позитронных
of cosmic      rays  (the) formation   of electron-positron

пар играет весьма важную    роль.
pairs plays (a) very important role.


О          расчётах,    связанных  с   водяным паром в
Concerning calculations, connected  with aqueous vapor in

этих случаях, будет   сказано  в главе IV.
these cases,  will be  spoken   in Chapter IV.


§ 245.  Use of Passive Past Participles as Nouns.

    It will be recalled that adjectives are sometimes used in
Russian as nouns, cf. Note 8, p. 86. A similar use of passive
past participles is also encountered in scientific Russian.


Приведённые  данные показывают, что около половины всех
(The) cited    data   show,        that about half      of all

молекул        обладают скоростями близкими к некоторой
(the) molecules possess velocities  near      to (a) certain

определённой средней скорости.
definite      average  velocity.

---

[1] The verb считать -- счесть means also "to count," "to reckon."

Ска́занное отно́сится ко вся́кому витами́ну.
(The) said   pertains self to  every   vitamin.

Из    ска́занного   очеви́дно,    что инéртные гáзы
From  (the) said    (it is) obvious, that (the) inert gases

отлича́ются свое́й   хими́ческой инéртностью от    всех
distinguish self by their chemical  inertness   from  all

остальны́х хими́ческих элемéнтов.
other      chemical     elements.

Из    изло́женного вытека́ет, что по  мéре усилéния
From (the) expounded it flows    that with degree of strengthening

поляризацио́нного взаимоде́йствия ио́нов должно́ имéть
of polar          interaction      of ions should  take

мéсто уменьше́ние расстоя́ния  мéжду ни́ми, и   при
place (a) decrease of (the) distance between them and at

достиже́нии   после́дними    извéстной    крити́ческой
achievement   by the latter  of (a) known critical

величины́ - скачкообра́зное   изменéние  ти́па
magnitude — (an) abrupt       change     of (the) type

кристалли́ческой структу́ры.
of crystal       structure.

§ 246.  Reading Exercise.

О витами́нах

Мно́го[1] лет тому́ наза́д бы́ло обнару́жено, что мо́жно
излечи́ть заболева́ние цынго́й (иногда́ та́кже называемой скор-
бутом) при по́мощи фру́ктов и́ли их со́ков. Давно́ бы́ло та́кже
откры́то, что свéжие фру́кты и их со́ки мо́гут применя́ться как
предохрани́тельные срéдства про́тив скорбута. Мно́го[2] лет
лимо́нный сок успéшно применя́лся брита́нским фло́том для то-
го́, что́бы предохраня́ть моряко́в[3] от заболева́ния цынго́й.

Эти эмпирические наблюдения, сделанные моряками и другими не учёными людьми,[4] оставались невыясненными в научном отношении до последних лет.

Научное исследование витаминов началось в 1911 году, когда причина заболевания бери-бери была детально изучена. При этом было установлено, что появление этого заболевания у голубей связано с составом диэты. Рисовые отруби, добавленные к дефективной диэте, являлись эффективным защитным средством. К этому времени[5] был предложен термин "витамин" вследствие[6] ошибочного взгляда, что защитные вещества являлись аминами.

С того времени[7] была проделана очень большая работа в области витаминов. Исследования этого класса вещества, связанные с большими трудностями, прошли через несколько стадий.

Сначала[8] были разработаны методы отыскания витаминов в пище и природных продуктах. В основу такого исследования положены профилактические эксперименты с животными. Витамины, хотя широко распространённые в природе, всегда были найдены в ничтожно малых количествах. Тем не менее, в течение последних лет удалось[9] получить препараты витаминов, в большой степени очищенные[10] от других веществ. Выяснение состава и молекулярного строения изолированных витаминов дало возможность разработать способы синтеза, сначала в лабораториях, а затем и на заводах. Искусственно полученные (синтезированные) витамины теперь применяются для разрешения проблем, связанных с питанием как[11] людей, так и животных.

Как уже было отмечено, аминный характер был приписан витаминам в начале их научного изучения. В настоящее время[12] признано, что витамины, объединённые по той роли, которую они играют в жизненных процессах, принадлежат к различным классам химических соединений. Химия витаминов, взятая в целом, похожа на химию гормонов и ферментов.

Из вышесказанного[13] легко понять, почему до сих пор ещё не все вопросы науки о витаминах окончательно выяс-

нены.   Остаётся це́лый ряд ·нерешённых проблём.   Развитие
нау́ки витами́нов и тепе́рь продолжа́ется, и ожида́ется, что
ва́жные но́вые успе́хи бу́дут сде́ланы в э́той о́бласти.

## Notes

1. Мно́го лет тому́ наза́д--- "Many years ago ---."   The
genitive plural of ЛЕ́ТО "summer" is used after certain numerals
and after МНО́ГО "many"  to designate a number of years.

2. Мно́го лет --- "(For) many years -----."   Here МНО́ГО --
in the accusative case -- together with the genitive plural, ЛЕТ, is
used to indicate a duration of time rather than a point in time.

3. МОРЯКО́В "sailors" is in the accusative case but has the
form of the genitive, in accordance with the rule previously
given, cf. § 67, p. 93.

4. ЛЮДЬМИ́ is the irregularly formed instrumental plural of
ЛЮ́ДИ "persons," "people." Declension of ЛЮ́ДИ does not extend
to the singular, for which the various singular forms of the
noun ЧЕЛОВЕ́К are used.

5. вре́мени here is the irregularly formed dative singular
of the neuter noun ВРЕ́МЯ "time,"  cf. § 358, p. 575.

6. всле́дствие   "as a result of," is a preposition and should
not be confused with other parts of speech.

7. С того́ вре́мени--- "Since that time -----." Here ВРЕМЕНИ
is the irregularly formed genitive singular of the neuter noun
ВРЕ́МЯ "time."

8. снача́ла "at first" is an adverb.

9. удало́сь "(it) succeeded." This is the past tense of an
impersonal verb whose reflexive form defies literal translation.

10. очи́щенные   "purified." Note that the ending of this
passive past participle is such that it must refer to препара́ты
and not to ВИТАМИ́НОВ or сте́пени.

11. как люде́й, так и живо́тных "both of persons, and also of
animals."

12. Here вре́мя is the accusative singular of the neuter noun вре́мя "time."

13. Из вышеска́занного--- "From what has been said above---." Here вышеска́занного, a word derived from the passive past participle ска́занный "said," is used as a noun but is declined like its parent passive past participle with adjective endings. This calls to mind parallel use of adjectives as nouns. See Note 8, p. 86.

§ 247. Translation Exercise.

1. Many years ago it was discovered that juices of fruits may be used (мо́гут применя́ться) in order to cure scurvy.
2. The cause of scurvy was not studied in scientific respect until recent years.
3. The appearance of scurvy among sailors is connected with the composition of the diet.
4. Rice bran may be used in order to protect doves from the sickness beriberi.
5. Vitamins play an important role in the life processes both of persons and of animals.
6. Vitamins, found (на́йденные) in small quantities in food and other natural products can be isolated.
7. At first, methods of synthesis of vitamins were worked out in laboratories.
8. In the course of recent years it succeeded to synthesize (синтези́ровать) vitamins in factories.
9. Investigations of hormones are connected with great difficulties.
10. The elucidation of the molecular structure of enzymes continues (продолжа́ется).

# LESSON 28

## ACTIVE PAST PARTICIPLES

§ 248. Introduction to Active Past Participles.

As shown in the previous lesson, Russian passive past participles are verbal adjectives which, in their role of noun modifiers, are used to indicate that an object, person, etc., is thought of as having been subjected to a certain action. An object, person, etc., modified by a corresponding active past participle is thereby designated as having been performing or having performed the action denoted by the participle. When used in simple sentences, Russian active past participles usually require that some English auxiliary such as "having been" or "having," be used in translation. In complex sentences, these Russian participles are often best translated with the aid of a clause. Example sentences will be cited to make this point clearer.

As might be expected, either imperfective or perfective infinitives may serve as parents of active past participles, depending on whether the participle is used to indicate (1) action thought of as incomplete, in progress or frequently repeated or (2) action thought of as a completed whole.

As already noted, the majority of passive past participles encountered in reading scientific Russian are derived from perfective infinitives. Active past participles will be observed to be derived from imperfective infinitives rather more frequently than is the case with passive past participles.

§ 249. Time Significance of Active Past Participles.

As implied by their name, active past participles usually refer to an action thought of as having been either completed or in progress in the past. It often happens, particularly in complex sentences, that a past participle indicates action anterior in time to that of the verb to which the past participle is subordinate. As a rule, this verb to which the past active participle is

395

subordinate, is the principal verb of the sentence or of one of its component clauses. These relationships will become clearer on considering example sentences.

§ 250. Formation of Stems of Active Past Participles.

The great majority of Russian verbs form the stems of their active past participles by:
1) Removing -ТЬ from an infinitive.
2) Affixing -ВШ-, (-Ш- or -ДШ- are used with certain exceptional infinitives).

Regular formation of active past participles characterize all regular infinitives, cf. Lesson 21, as well as nearly all infinitives that form their past tense regularly as noted in § 213, p. 333. A few examples will suffice to illustrate such regular formation of active past participles.

Regular Formation of Active Past Participles
(Examples)

|  | Infinitives | Class | Active Past Participle |
|---|---|---|---|
| Imp. | де́лать | Reg. A | де́лавший |
| Perf. | сде́лать |  | сде́лавший |
| Imp. | фотографи́ровать | Irr. A-1 | фотографи́ровавший |
| Perf. | сфотографи́ровать |  | сфотографи́ровавший |
| Imp. | криви́ть | Irr. C-2 | криви́вший |
| Perf. | покриви́ть |  | покриви́вший |
| Imp. | писа́ть | Irr. D-1 | писа́вший |
| Perf. | написа́ть |  | написа́вший |
| Imp. | брать | Irr. E-1 | бра́вший |
| Perf. | взять | Irr. F-7 | взя́вший |
| Imp. | дава́ть | Irr. B | дава́вший |
| Perf. | дать | Irr. I-3 | да́вший |
| Imp. | быть | Irr. I-2 | бы́вший |

Many other infinitives whose present and perfective future tenses are formed irregularly also form their active past participles regularly as shown above.[1] These are not listed to avoid tedious repetition and to conserve space.

Irregular formation of the active past participle is exemplified by the following infinitives which, it will be recalled, also formed the present (or perfective future) tense in irregular fashion as summarized in Lessons 22 and 23.

|  | Infinitives | Class | Active Past Participle |
|---|---|---|---|
| Imp. <br> Perf. | тере́ть <br> потере́ть | Irr. E-5 | тёрший <br> потёрший |
| Imp. <br> Perf. | бере́чь <br> побере́чь | Irr. G-1 | берёгший <br> поберёгший |
| Imp. <br> Perf. | жечь <br> сжечь | Irr. G-2 | жёгший <br> сжёгший |
| Imp. <br> Perf. | влечь <br> повле́чь | Irr. G-3 | влёкший <br> повлёкший |
| Imp. <br> Perf. | мочь <br> смочь | Irr. G-4 | мо́гший <br> смо́гший |
| Imp. <br> Perf. | везти́ <br> повезти́ | Irr. H-1 | вёзший <br> повёзший |
| Imp. <br> Perf. | нести́ <br> понести́ | Irr. H-2 | нёсший <br> понёсший |
| Imp. <br> Perf. | плести́ <br> заплести́ | Irr. H-3 | плётший <br> заплётший |
| Imp. <br> Perf. | грести́ <br> погрести́ | Irr. H-4 | грёбший <br> погрёбший |
| Imp. <br> Perf. | вести́ <br> повести́ | Irr. H-5 | ве́дший <br> пове́дший |

---

[1] Various infinitives, as a matter of usage, do not form active past participles.

| | Infinitive | Class | Active Past Participle |
|---|---|---|---|
| Imp. | лезть | Irr. H-6 | лёзший |
| Perf. | влезть | | влёзший |
| Imp. | клясть[1] | Irr. H-9 | клявший |
| Perf. | проклясть | | проклявший |
| Imp. | ходить | Irr. D-2 | ходивший |
| Perf. | итти | Irr. H-10 | шёдший |
| Imp. | находить | Irr. D-2 | находивший |
| Perf. | найти | Irr. H-10 | нашёдший |
| Imp. | разъедать | Reg. A | разъедавший |
| Perf. | разъесть | Irr. I-1 | разъевший |

§ 251.  Declension of Active Past Participles.

Like  passive  past  participles,  active  past  participles  are
declined using adjective endings.[2]   These endings, however, obey
the phonetic laws governing the use of various vowels after the
letter  -Ш-,  cf. § 128, p. 188.  The same laws apply to the endings
used with adjectives with stems ending in  -Ж-.  As a consequence,
active  past  participles  are  declined  in  exactly  the  same  way  as
the adjective СВЕЖИЙ, cf. § 132, p. 198.

---

[1]  Note  similar  formation  of  the  active  past  participle  from  пасть ( павший ) and
from сесть ( севший ).

[2]  Active  past  participles  are  rarely,  if  ever,  used  as  predicative  modifiers  and
in  this  respect  differ  from  passive  past  participles.  Certain  noun  modifiers  very
closely related to active past participles do have predicative forms as pointed out in
Footnote 2, p. 456.

Stem of Active Past Participle ОКИСЛЯ́ВШ-, "having oxidized"
(Imperfective Infinitive ОКИСЛЯ́ТЬ, "to be oxidizing")

## Singular

|  | Masc. | Fem. | Neuter |
|---|---|---|---|
| Nom. | окисля́вший | окисля́вшая | окисля́вшее |
| Gen. | окисля́вшего | окисля́вшей | скисля́вшего |
| Dat. | окисля́вшему | окисля́вшей | окисля́вшему |
| Acc. | окисля́вший[1] | окисля́вшую | окисля́вшее |
| Instr. | окисля́вшим | окисля́вшей | окисля́вшим |
|  |  | (окисля́вшею) |  |
| Prep. | окисля́вшем | окисля́вшей | окисля́вшем |

## All Genders

## Plural

| Nom. | окисля́вшие |
|---|---|
| Gen. | окисля́вших |
| Dat. | окисля́вшим |
| Acc. | окисля́вшие[1] |
| Instr. | окисля́вшими |
| Prep. | окисля́вших |

§ 252. Summary Note on Construction of Active Past Participles.

Like Russian passive past participles, the active past participles are built up of three component parts as shown in the following examples.

---

[1] When used to modify nouns designating living beings as defined in § 67, p. 93, this accusative form becomes the same as the corresponding genitive.

сде́ла  —————————— вш ——— ий from сде́лать
                                       "to do"
фотографи́рова  ——— вш ——— ий from фотографи́ровать
                                       "to be photographing"
влёк  —————————————— ш ——— ий from влечь
                                       "to be dragging"
на ше́  ——————————— дш ——— ий from найти́
                                       "to find"

| Infinitive stem (Some-times in altered form) | Typical stem ter-mination of active past participle | Adjective ending, cf. § 251 before mentioned. |
|---|---|---|

In reading Russian sentences containing active past participles, it is particularly helpful to observe the adjective endings as these indicate which noun the participle modifies. This becomes particularly important as example sentences will illustrate, when one or more words are interposed between the participle and the noun it modifies.

§ 253.  The Reflexive Forms of Active Past Participles.

Conversion of active present participles to their reflexive forms is accomplished by affixing the ending -ся. Thus from окисля́вший, окисля́вшего, etc., we have окисля́вшийся, окисля́вшегося, etc.

Reflexive active past participles in general indicate an action directed back toward the noun they modify and their meaning is usually very close to that of corresponding passive past participles. Exceptions to this general rule arise because of the fact that the reflexive forms of certain verbs have acquired exceptional or idiomatic significance. Thus we have a number of verbs whose reflexive forms are generally used in a special sense, e.g., явля́ться "to be," "to turn out to be" from явля́ть "to be showing," cf. § 123, p. 181. Another group of verbs are reflexive in form only; the reflexive ending when used with these verbs is a mere grammatical formality. An example is нра́виться, "to please." Not all active present participles are capable of being converted to the reflexive form. An example is ше́дший "having gone."

§ 254. Sentences Illustrating Simple Use of Active Present Participles as Direct Modifiers of Nouns.

Active past participles may either precede or follow the modified noun, as is evident from the following example sentences, which are divided into two groups.

## Group A. Active Past Participle Precedes Noun Modified

| Мо́жно | | увели́чить | мо́щность | тако́й |
|---|---|---|---|---|
| (It is) | possible | to increase | (the) power | of such |

| парово́й | маши́ны, | е́сли | отрабо́тавший | |
|---|---|---|---|---|
| (a) steam | engine, | if | (the) having worked out | (exhaust) |

| пар | выпуска́ется | в | конденса́тор. |
|---|---|---|---|
| steam | discharges self | into | (a) condenser. |

| Эйнште́йном | был | сформули́рован | о́бщий | зако́н |
|---|---|---|---|---|
| By Einstein | was | formulated | (the) general | law |

| фотохими́ческих | реа́кций: | ка́ждой | прореаги́ровавшей | |
|---|---|---|---|---|
| of photochemical | reactions: | to each | having reacted | |

| моле́куле | соотве́тствует | оди́н | поглощённый | квант, |
|---|---|---|---|---|
| molecule | corresponds | one | absorbed | quantum, |

| т.е. | число́ | прореаги́ровавших | моле́кул | |
|---|---|---|---|---|
| i.e., | (the) number | of having reacted | molecules | (is) |

| пропорциона́льно | числу́ | поглощённых | ква́нтов. |
|---|---|---|---|
| proportional | to (the) number | of absorbed | quanta. |

| Поступи́вший | в | кровяно́е | русло́ | челове́ка |
|---|---|---|---|---|
| Having entered | into | (the) blood | circulation | of man |

| пеницилли́н[1] | уде́рживается | там | недо́лго. |
|---|---|---|---|
| penicillin | maintains self | there | not long. |

---

[1] A smoother translation is "Penicillin, after entering the human blood stream, does not remain there very-long." The key to the Russian sentence is the fact that the active past participle поступи́вший modifies the noun пеницилли́н.

Но   происше́дший[1]              с    пе́рвой      ру́сской
But  (the) having occurred     with  (the) first   Russian

подво́дной   ло́дкой  не́счастный  слу́чай   в  1838 году́
underwater   boat     unfortunate  case     in  1838

охлади́л  к  ней          интере́с  Никола́я   I   и   его́
cooled    to her (the boat) interest  of Nicholas  I  and  of his

окруже́ния.
circle.


## Group B.  Active Past Participle Follows Noun Modified

Поколе́ние,       жи́вшее      200   лет   наза́д,  ничего́ не
(The) generation, having    lived 200   years ago,   nothing (not)

слы́шало   о        микро́бах.
heard      concerning  microbes.


На    рису́нке   569    предста́влена       траекто́рия
In    figure     569   (is) presented      (the) trajectory

части́цы,       проше́дшей      сквозь   6 - миллиметро́вый
of (a) particle,  having passed    through  6 - millimeter

слой   свинца́.
layer  of lead.


Заво́д[2]      Эру́      в  Нейга́усене   был   пе́рвым   в
(The) plant  of Héroult  in Neuhausen   was   (the) first  in

Евро́пе  алюми́ниевым  предприя́тием,  рабо́тавшим   по
Europe  aluminum      enterprise,     having worked according

электролити́ческому      ме́тоду.
to (the) electrolytic      method.


---

[1]  Here the active past participle происше́дший modifies слу́чай as does also
the adjective не́счастный. The word combination не́счастный  слу́чай is an idiom
meaning "accident."

[2]  A  smoother translation  is  "Heroult's plant in  Neuhausen  was  the  first
aluminum enterprise in Europe that worked by the electrolytic method."

В то время Эванс услышал о паровых машинах,
At that time Evans heard about (the) steam engines,

существовавших[1] в Англии.
having existed in England.


§ 255. Sentences Illustrating Active Past Participles Governing a Direct Object.

Sentences considered in preceding § 254 tend to emphasize the adjectival character of active past participles. Such participles are also active verb forms and thus capable of governing a direct object as is illustrated by the following sentences.[2]


### Group I. Direct Object in Accusative Case

Атом, потерявший один или несколько электронов,
(An) atom, having lost one or several electrons,

переходит в положительно заряжённый ион —
goes over into (a) positively charged ion —

катион.
(a) cation.


По методу братьев Каулес в Англии и
According to (the) method of brothers Cowles in England and

США с 1884 до 1892 г. работали заводы,
(the) U.S.A. from 1884 to 1892 worked plants,

выпускавшие сплавы на рынок.
having placed alloys on (the) market.


---

[1] A smoother translation is "At that time Evans heard about the steam engines, that already existed in England."

[2] The ability to govern a direct object is, of course, limited to those active participles which are derived from transitive infinitives.

В нача́ле  э́того  столе́тия, проф.   П. П. Федо́тьевым[1]
At (the) start  of this  century,   by  Prof. P. P. Fedot'ev

( 1864-1934 гг.) и  други́ми   ру́сскими  учёными   был
(1864  -  1934) and  by other   Russian   scientists  was

вы́полнен   в  о́бласти   изуче́ния   совреме́нного
completed   in (the) field  of investigation  of contemporary

спо́соба произво́дства  алюми́ния   ряд    теорети́ческих
process of production  of aluminum (a) series  of theoretical

иссле́дований, получи́вших[2]   мирову́ю изве́стность.
investigations, having obtained   world    renown.

В э́том же   году́   бы́ли  опублико́ваны  о́пыты
In that  same  year  were  published   (the) experiments

Ге́ртца .    прикова́вшие   к   себе́   внима́ние
of Hertz    having attracted   to  self  (the) attention

фи́зиков   всего́   ми́ра .
of physicists  of (the) whole  world.

## Group II.  Direct Object Not in the Accusative Case

It will be recalled that the direct object in Russian sentences
is not always in the accusative case. Thus certain verbs require
the direct object to be in the genitive, cf. § 85, p. 124; other
verbs govern the instrumental, cf. § 102, p. 148; still other verbs
govern the dative, § 114, p. 166. Furthermore, in negative
sentences, direction of the negation toward a direct object
normally in the accusative case will cause a shift to the genitive,
cf. § 176, p. 267. These same factors are operative in causing
active past participles, when derived from certain verbs or when
used negatively, to govern cases other than the accusative as
illustrated by the following examples.

---

[1]  Certain Russian names are declined somewhat like adjectives, cf. § 361, p. 583.
Here, Федо́тьевым  is in the instrumental singular case.
[2]  A smoother translation of the latter part of this sentence would be "a series
of theoretical investigations, that achieved world renown."

Действительно,        формула  IV,  послужившая      выше
Actually,              formula   IV,  having served      above

основой    для всех   наших   вычислений,   правильна
as basis    for   all    our      calculations  (is) correct

лишь   при  пренебрежении   изменения   теплоёмкости
only    on   neglecting      of change    of heat capacity

с     температурой.
with  temperature.


Радиолокация,      уже     достигшая       больших успехов
Radar,             already  having achieved  great    successes

во время     войны,   будет  играть  важную        роль  в
in   time     of war   will    play   (an) important  role   in

мировой   навигации.
peaceful   navigation.


Прототипом      двигателя      внутреннего   сгорания   был
As prototype     of (the) motor  of internal     combustion  was

пороховой   цилиндр  Папена,[1]    не получивший     в
(the) powder  cylinder  of Papin,     not having obtained   in

своё               время   развития      по    тем   же
own (the cylinder's) time     development   for   the   very same

причинам,  что  и   его  паровой  цилиндр.
reason,    that  also his   steam    cylinder (did not attain

development).

---

[1] Here Папена is the genitive singular of Папен. As a rule, the pronunciation of
a name in its original language guides its transliteration into Russian, cf. § 363, p. 587.

§ 256.  Sentences  Illustrating  Use  of  Reflexive  Active  Past
Participles.

The  formation  and  significance  of  the  reflexive  forms  of
active  past  participles  was  discussed  in  § 253, p. 400.

### Group I.  Reflexive Form of Active Past Participle Precedes Noun Modified

| Во всех | ра́нее | упомина́вшихся | я́дерных | реа́кциях, |
|---|---|---|---|---|
| In  all | previously | having mentioned (self) | nuclear | reactions, |

| проце́ссы | осуществля́ются | в | масшта́бах[1] |
|---|---|---|---|
| (the) processes | realize self | on | (a) scale |

| несравне́нно | ме́ньших, | по | сравне́нию | с | обы́чными |
|---|---|---|---|---|---|
| incomparably | smaller, | in | comparison | with | ordinary |

| хими́ческими | реа́кциями. |
|---|---|
| chemical | reactions. |

| Когда́ | мы | увели́чиваем | напряже́ние, | э́то | не вы́зовет |
|---|---|---|---|---|---|
| When | we | increase | (the) voltage, | this | not causes |

| увеличе́ния | то́ка, | так как | все | вы́делившиеся[2] |
|---|---|---|---|---|
| (an) increase | of current, | since | all | having evolved  self |

| от | като́да | под | возде́йствием | све́та | электро́ны |
|---|---|---|---|---|---|
| from (the) cathode | under | (the) influence | of light | electrons |

| уже́ | испо́льзованы | в | ка́честве | переда́тчиков |
|---|---|---|---|---|
| already (are) utilized | in | (the) quality | of carriers |

| то́ка. |
|---|
| of current. |

---

[1]  Here the Russian plural  масшта́бах  is best translated, as is clear from the context, by an English singular.

[2]  The key to this sentence is the fact that the reflexive active past participle вы́делившиеся  modifies the noun  электро́ны.

Устано́вленный    Дальто́ном    зако́н кра́тных    отноше́ний
(The) established    by Dalton    law    of multiple    ratios

и   разви́вшееся      на его́ осно́ве    уче́ние о
and (the) having evolved self on its basis    doctrine concerning

хими́ческих    а́томах привели́ к поня́тию    хими́ческого
chemical    atoms    led    to (the) concept of (a) chemical

индиви́дуума    как    вещества́    стро́го    определённого
individual    as    substance    of strictly    definite

соста́ва.
composition.

Удале́ние      се́ры    в    шлак    происхо́дит    в
(The) removal   of sulfur   into   (the) slag   occurs    in

до́менной пе́чи    по      реа́кции:
blast    furnaces   according to   (the) reaction:

$$FeS + CaO + C = Fe + CaS + CO$$

образова́вшийся      сульфи́д ка́льция    растворя́ется    в
the having formed self   sulfide of calcium   dissolves self   in

шла́ке.
(the) slag.

## Group II. Reflexive Form of Active Past Participle Follows
### Noun Modified

Поэ́тому    нефть.    применя́вшаяся    до    неда́внего
Consequently   petroleum,   having used self   up to recent

вре́мени[1] то́лько как то́пливо,    в   настоя́щее    вре́мя
time    only    as    fuel    in (the) present    time

применя́ется    и    как    хими́ческое    сырьё.
uses self    also as   (a) chemical   raw material.

---

[1] вре́мени is here the irregularly formed genitive singular of the neuter noun
вре́мя, cf. § 258, p. 575.

Ток           во́здуха,  нагре́вшегося        на   пове́рхности
(The) current   of air,    having warmed self   at   (the) surface

по́чвы,        раскалённой        со́лнцем,       поднима́ется
of (the) soil,   heated             by (the) sun,   raises self

вверх  всё   вы́ше  и   вы́ше.
upward  always  higher and higher.


В результа́те      поле́мики        ме́жду      Бертолле́[1]   и
In result           of (the) polemic   between    Berthollet     and

Пру́стом,     продолжа́вшейся[2]                не́сколько   лет
Proust,        having   prolonged   self          several      years

(1801-1808 гг.),  по́ле       би́твы      оста́лось[4]       за
(1801 - 1808),     (the) field   of battle    remained          to

Пру́стом.
Proust.


Многочи́сленные       иссле́дования        я́дерных   реа́кций,
Numerous               investigations       of nuclear   reactions

проводи́вшиеся[3]          в     тече́ние     после́дних    лет,
having carried self out    in    (the) course   of (the) last   years,

приво́дят нас к  ря́ду     интере́сных    вы́водов.
lead        us   to (a) series  of interesting  conclusions.

§ 257. The Reflexive of Active Past Participles Used with the Instrumental Case of Nouns and Adjectives.

Previous discussion, cf. Lesson 12, §§ 91-94, pp. 131-137, has directed attention to the use of the reflexive of the present tense with the instrumental case of nouns and adjectives. Essentially similar use of the instrumental with the reflexive forms of active past participles is sometimes observed when reading scientific Russian. In the following sentences a double asterisk has been used to point out the reflexive past participles under consideration; the accompanying examples of the instrumental case are indicated by a single asterisk.

| Встречаются | | и | тяжёлые | отрицательные |
|---|---|---|---|---|
| Encounters self (are found) | | also | heavy | negative |

| ио́ны, | образова́вшиеся** | присоедине́нием* | | свобо́дного |
|---|---|---|---|---|
| ions, | having formed self | by combination | | of (a) free |

| электро́на | к | нейтра́льной | моле́куле | га́за. |
|---|---|---|---|---|
| electron | to | (a) neutral | molecule | of gas. |

| Образова́вшаяся** | | таки́м* | путём* | пе́рекись | мо́жет |
|---|---|---|---|---|---|
| (The) having formed self | | by this | way | peroxide | is able |

| быть | испо́льзована | для | дальне́йшего | окисле́ния. |
|---|---|---|---|---|
| be | utilized | for | further | oxidation. |

| Столе́тов, | пе́рвый | в | Росси́и, | созда́л | о́бщий | курс |
|---|---|---|---|---|---|---|
| Stoletov, | first | in | Russia, | created | (a) general | course |

| фи́зики, | сопровожда́вшийся** | | | соверше́нно |
|---|---|---|---|---|
| of physics, | having accompanied self | | (by) | completely |

| исключи́тельными* по | | тому́ вре́мени лекцио́нными* |
|---|---|---|
| exceptional | with respect to | that time lecture |

| о́пытами.* |
|---|
| experiments.[1] |

[1] A freer translation would be "Stoletov was the first in Russia to create a general physics course, which was accompanied by lecture demonstrations quite unique for that time." Note that the participle сопровожда́вшийся modifies Столе́тов.

| Все | стро́ившиеся** | | Стефенсо́ном* | до | того́ |
|-----|---------------|------|--------------|-----|------|
| All | having constructed | self | by Stevenson | up to | then |

| парово́зы | облада́ли | о́чень | суще́ственным |
|-----------|-----------|--------|---------------|
| locomotives | possessed | (a) very | essential |

| недоста́тком. |
|---------------|
| deficiency. |

§ 258.  Reading Exercise.

## О приро́де нейтро́на

По́водом[1] к откры́тию нейтро́нов послужи́л ряд иссле́до-
ваний, проводи́вшихся в тече́ние после́дних лет.  В 1930 г.
Бо́те и Бе́ккер иссле́довали проце́сс бомбарди́ровки металли́-
ческого бери́ллия α-части́цам поло́ния. Оказа́лось, что при
э́том име́ет ме́сто како́е-то излуче́ние, внача́ле  на́званное
"бери́ллиевым излуче́нием."

Бы́ло та́кже обнару́жено, что "бери́ллиевое излуче́ние",
проше́дшее сквозь то́лстые сло́и свинца́ или други́х веще́ств,
пока́зывает порази́тельно ма́лое уменьше́ние интенси́вности.
Ввиду́ результа́тов таки́х экспериме́нтов была́ предло́жена ги-
поте́за, что "бери́ллиевое излуче́ние" явля́лось электромаг-
ни́тной радиа́цией, аналоги́чной  γ-луча́м.[2]

Эта гипоте́за не[3] была́ подтверждена́ о́пытами, име́в-
шими це́лью вы́яснить приро́ду  "бери́ллиевого излуче́ния."
Кюри́ и Жолио́ (1932 г.) обнару́жили выделе́ние  прото́нов из
парафи́на при возде́йствии "бери́ллиевого излуче́ния." Про-
то́ны,[4] вы́бросившиеся под де́йствием "бери́ллиевого излуче́-
ния," пробега́ли до 25 см.  в во́здухе. Почти́ одновре́менно
Че́двиком[5] (1932 г.) бы́ло заме́чено выбива́ние прото́нов не
то́лько из водоро́да парафи́на, но и  из всех други́х изу-
ча́вшихся[6] в э́том направле́нии элеме́нтов.  Все э́ти  фа́кты
заста́вили Че́двика вы́сказать предположе́ние, в ко́рне[7] не-
согласи́мое[8] с вы́сказанной вы́ше гипоте́зой - предположе́-
ние, что[9] "бери́ллиевое излуче́ние" обя́зано свое́й приро́дой
пото́кам части́ц с ма́ссой, бли́зкой к ма́ссе прото́на, а  за-
ря́дом, ра́вным нулю́.

Частицы эти в настоящее время называются нейтронами и обозначаются символом $_0 n^1$ или просто n.

Потеря кинетической энергии нейтронов,[10] проходящих сквозь материю, имеет место вследствие столкновений с атомными ядрами, а не с электронами. Такое поведение очень сильно отличается от поведения заряжённой частицы вроде протона,[11] который растрачивает свою энергию почти исключительно вследствие столкновений[12] с электронами. При эластическом столкновении с ядром нейтрон отклоняется от своего пути, а отброшенное ядро может приобретать скорость,[13] достаточную чтобы вызывать ионизацию. Ядра, подвергнувшиеся[14] столкновениям с нейтронами, вследствие этого могут быть обнаружены измерениями ионизации в ионизационной камере, с чувствительным электрометром или электрическим счётчиком. Нейтроны были впервые обнаружены в опытах, сводившихся к наблюдению атомов, испытавших столковения с нейтронами.

При лобовых неэластических столкновениях нейтронов с атомными ядрами могли быть осуществлены такие ядерные реакции как:

$$_3 Li^6 \;+\; _0 n^1 \;=\; _1 H^2 \;+\; _2 He^4$$

$$_5 B^{10} \;+\; _0 n^1 \;=\; _3 Li^7 \;+\; _2 He^4$$

Можно с уверенностью предсказать, что использование нейтронов для осуществления ядерных превращений, уже достигшее[15] больших успехов, будет играть важную роль в дальнейшем развитии атомной энергии в большом масштабе.

## Notes

1. По́водом к откры́тию нейтро́нов послужи́л  "As a lead to the discovery of neutrons served." Note that the word, ПО́ВОДОМ is in the instrumental case.

2. аналоги́чной,  γ–луча́м  "analogous to gamma rays." Here the word луча́м is in the dative plural.

3. Э́та гипоте́за не была́ подтверждена́  "This hypothesis was not confirmed." Note the similarity of the adjective endiɴɢ used with ПОДТВЕРЖДЕНА́ to the ending of была́, cf. § 215, p. 337.

4. Прото́ны, вы́бросившиеся , literally, "Protons, having ejected self."

5. Че́двиком "by Chadwick." Note that names are declined in Russian, the instrumental case of Че́двик "Chadwick" being Че́двиком , cf. § 362, p. 585.

6. Here изуча́вшихся modifies элеме́нтов.

7. The phrase в ко́рне literally "in root" here means "fundamentally." КО́РНЕ is the irregular prepositional singular of КО́РЕНЬ (masc.) "root," cf. § 357, p. 573.

8. Here несогласи́мое refers to предположе́ние.

9. что "бери́ллиевое излуче́ние" обя́зано свое́й приро́дой пото́кам части́ц. Literally, "that beryllium radiation is connected by its nature to streams of particles."

10. нейтро́нов, проходя́щих сквозь мате́рию  "of neutrons, passing through matter." Here ПРОХОДЯ́ЩИХ is the genitive plural form of ПРОХОДЯ́ЩИЙ the active present participle of ПРОХОДИ́ТЬ "to be passing through."

11. вро́де прото́на , "of the nature of a proton." Here ВРО́ДЕ is a preposition.

12. всле́дствие столкнове́ний "as a result of collisions." Note that ВСЛЕ́ДСТВИЕ is a preposition not to be confused with other parts of speech.

13. ско́рость, доста́точную что́бы вызыва́ть иониза́цию literally, "velocity, sufficient, in order to call further ionization."

14. Ядра, подвéргнувшиеся literally, "Nuclei, having submitted self."

15. ужé достúгшее большúх успéхов "already having achieved great successes." Here большúх and успéхов are in the genitive after достúгшее, cf. § 85, p. 124. The ending of достúгшее indicates that it refers to испóльзование.

§ 259. Translation Exercise.

1. During (При) the process (процéссе) of bombardment of metallic beryllium by α–particles, takes place evolution of neutrons.

2. Neutrons, having passed (прошéдшие)through thick layers of lead cause (вызывáют) ejection of protons from paraffin.

3. These particles are characterized ( характеризýются ) by a charge equal to zero.

4. This hypothesis was confirmed by a series (рядом) of experiments carried out (having conducted self) in the course of recent years.

5. The kinetic energy of protons, passing through matter is dissipated as a result of collisions with electrons.

6. Nuclei having undergone (having submitted to) elastic ( эластúческим ) collisions with neutrons may attain a velocity sufficient in order to cause ionization.

7. Neutrons may be (мóгут быть) observed as a result of elastic collisions with atomic nuclei.

8. Nuclear reactions may be observed on inelastic collisions of neutrons with atomic nuclei.

9. It is possible to accomplish nuclear reactions with the aid (при пóмощи) of neutrons.

10. The utilization of atomic energy, already having achieved important successes, will play an important role in the technology (тéхнике ) of the future (бýдущего ).

# LESSON 29

## ACTIVE PRESENT PARTICIPLES

§ 260. Introduction to Present Participles.

English verbs add the ending "-ing" to their stems to form present participles.

| Infinitive | Present Participle |
| --- | --- |
| to pour | pouring |
| to ignite | igniting |
| to multiply | multiplying |
| to beat | beating |
| to see | seeing |
| to buy | buying |
| to sing | singing |

It should be noted that these English present participles correspond to Russian active present participles. Russian imperfective infinitives in general form both passive and active present participles, which are declined and used as noun modifiers in much the same way as the past participles discussed in the two preceding lessons. As will be discussed in the next lesson, English has no simple verb forms corresponding to Russian passive present participles. The present and the past participles in Russian have many features in common.

In English, the present participle may be used with the present tense of the verb "to be" to form the progressive present tense, examples of which are "is pouring," "are igniting," "am multiplying." In Russian, the present participles are not used in this way.

§ 261. Time Significance of Active Present Participles.

Like other verb forms, present active participles denote a process or the existence of a condition. In general, these participles modify nouns which are thereby designated as

415

performing  the  action  indicated  by  the  participle.  The  time  of
the  action  of  the  participle  is  that  of  the  main  verb  in  the  sentence
or  clause.  Consequently,  an  active  present  participle  often  is
used  to  denote  action  whose  time  of  occurrence  is  other  than  the
actual  present.

§ 262.  Stem  Formation  of  Active  Present  Participles.

The  stems  of  all  present  participles[1]  are  formed  by  the
following  two  step  process:
  1) Remove  -т  from  the  3rd  person  plural  of  the  present
     tense.
  2) Affix  the  letter  -щ-.

For  recognition  purposes,  note  that  the  stems  of  nearly  all
active  present  participles  terminate  with  the  letter  combinations
-ащ-,  -ящ-,  -ущ-  or  -ющ-.  The  terminal  letter  combination  -ющ-
will  be  encountered  most  frequently  when  reading  scientific
Russian.

The  following  examples  of  the  formation[2]  of  active  present
participles  are  typical.

### Regular Formation of Active Present Participles

| Imperfective Infinitive | Class | Present Tense Third Person Singular | Active Present Participle |
|---|---|---|---|
| де́лать | Reg. A | де́лают | де́лающий |
| фотографи́ровать | Irr. A-1 | фотографи́руют | фотографи́рующий |
| дава́ть | Irr. B | даю́т | даю́щий |
| колеба́ть | Irr. C-1 | коле́блют | коле́блющий |
| писа́ть | Irr. D-1 | пи́шут | пи́шущий |
| брать | Irr. E-1 | беру́т | беру́щий |
| бере́чь | Irr. G-1 | берегу́т | берегу́щий |
| влечь | Irr. G-3 | влеку́т | влеку́щий |

---

[1] The  only  active  present  participle  which  might  be  regarded  as  exceptional  is
су́щий  "being"  whose  stem  might  be  regarded  as  formed  from  суть  "are"  by
removing  -ть  and  affixing  -щ-.  In  use,  су́щий  more  closely  resembles  an  adjective
than  a  participle.

[2] Various  individual  imperfective  infinitives,  either  for  logical  reasons  or
simply  as  a  matter  of  usage,  do  not  form active  present  participles.

| Imperfective Infinitive | Class | Present Tense Third Person Singular | Active Present Participle |
|---|---|---|---|
| везти́ | Irr. H-1 | везу́т | везу́щий |
| нести́ | Irr. H-2 | несу́т | несу́щий |
| итти́ | Irr. H-10 | иду́т | иду́щий |
| есть | Irr. I-1 | едят | едя́щий |

§ 263. Declension of Active Present Participles.

Since active present participles, like other Russian participles are nearly always used as noun modifiers, they are declined using regular adjective endings[1] as shown by the following example.

### Declension of a Typical Active Present Participle

Stem of Active Present Participle   фотографирующ -
(Third Person Plural of Present Tense   фотографи́руют)
(Imperfective Infinitive   фотографировать, "to be photographing")

### Singular

| | Masc. | Fem. | Neuter |
|---|---|---|---|
| Nom. | фотографи́рующий | фотографи́рующая | фотографи́рующее |
| Gen. | фотографи́рующего | фотографи́рующей | фотографи́рующего |
| Dat. | фотографи́рующему | фотографи́рующей | фотографи́рующему |
| Acc. | фотографи́рующий[2] | фотографи́рующую | фотографи́рующее |
| Instr. | фотографи́рующим | фотографи́рующей (фотографи́рующею) | фотографи́рующим |
| Prep. | фотографи́рующем | фотографи́рующей | фотографи́рующем |

[1] It will be recalled that the stems of active past participles terminate with the letter -ш-, while the stems of active present participles terminate with -щ-. The fact that the stems of these participles terminate with -ш- or -щ-, as the case may be, results in their declension following that of the adjective све́жий, cf. § 132, p. 198.

[2] When used to modify nouns designating living beings as defined in § 67, p. 93, this accusative form becomes the same as the corresponding genitive.

### All Genders

### Plural

| | |
|---|---|
| Nom. | фотографи́рующие |
| Gen. | фотографи́рующих |
| Dat. | фотографи́рующим |
| Acc. | фотографи́рующие[1] |
| Instr. | фотографи́рующими |
| Prep. | фотографи́рующих |

§ 264.  Summary  Note  on  Construction  of  Active  Present
Participles.

The  three  component  parts  of  Russian  active  present
participles should be carefully noted.

| | | |
|---|---|---|
| делаю ———————— | щ | ———————— ий |
| фотографирую ———————— | щ | ———————— ий |
| влеку ———————— | щ | ————— ий |
| иду ———————— | щ | ———————— ий |
| Infinitive stem in altered form | Typical stem termination of active present participle | Adjective ending, cf. § 264 above |

As  with  other  participles,  it  is  important  when  reading
scientific Russian to observe which adjective ending is used with
any  given  active  present  participle  as  this  ending  serves  to
indicate  which  noun  the  participle  modifies.  In  complicated
sentences,  such  attention  to  the  endings  is  most  helpful  in
discerning the relationships between the various words.

§ 265.  The  Reflexive  Forms  of  Active  Present  Participles.

Active  present  participles,  like  active  past  participles,  are
rendered  reflexive[2]  by  affixing  the  ending  –ся.  Thus  from
фотографи́рующий,          фотографи́рующего,   etc.,   we   have
фотографи́рующийся,        фотографи́рующегося, etc.

---

[1]  When used to modify nouns designating living beings as defined in § 67, p. 93, this accusative form becomes the same as the corresponding genitive.

[2]  Certain active present participles have no reflexive forms. An example is иду́щий , "going." The closely related находящий, "finding," does have reflexive forms, e.g., находящийся "finding self," "being located," "existing."

Reflexive active present participles in general indicate an action directed back toward the noun they modify and, as a general rule, their meaning is close to that of the corresponding passive present participles. Exceptions to this general rule may be grouped under two headings. First, as noted in discussing reflexive active past participles, the reflexive forms of certain verbs have acquired special status of one kind or another, cf. § 253, p. 400. Secondly, the passive present participles of many infinitives, unlike their other participles, are sometimes used to indicate susceptibility to an action. Or, to state this more precisely, the passive present participle of certain verbs are sometimes used to indicate susceptibility to an action, while the corresponding reflexive active present participles always indicate actual submission to the action in question. This point will become clearer on considering specific examples, cf. in particular § 268, p. 425; § 269, p. 427.

§ 266. Sentences Illustrating Simple Use of Active Present Participles as Direct Modifiers of Nouns.

Active present participles may either precede or follow the nouns which they modify. This is illustrated by the two following groups of sentences.

Group I. Active Present Participle Precedes Noun Modified

| Простой | отве́т | на | вопро́с | о |
|---------|--------|-----|---------|---|
| A simple | answer | to | (the) question | concerning |

| существова́нии | электро́на | дал | сле́дующий |
|---------------|-----------|-----|-----------|
| the existence | of (the) electron | gave | (the) following |

| о́пыт. |
|--------|
| experiment. |

| Что́бы | привести́ | те́ло | в | движе́ние | и́ли | измени́ть |
|--------|-----------|-------|---|-----------|------|-----------|
| In order | to bring | (a) body | into | motion | or | to change |

| уже́ | существу́ющую | ско́рость | его́ | движе́ния, |
|------|---------------|-----------|------|-----------|
| (the) already | existing | velocity | of its | motion, |

необходи́мо     подействова́ть    на    него́   како́й-либо
(it is) necessary    to act          on    it    by some

вне́шней си́лой.
external force.

Со́лнце   посыла́ет   эне́ргию в    окружа́ющее простра́нство в
(The) sun   dissipates   energy   into surrounding space       in

ви́де     лучи́стой    эне́ргии.
(the) form   of radiant    energy.

Механи́ческая     рабо́та     получа́ется          в
Mechanical        work       obtains   self   (is   obtained)   in

электродви́гателях    за    счёт      притека́ющей[1]    к
electrical motors     at   (the) expense   of (the) flowing    to

да́нной    маши́не электри́ческой   эне́ргии.
(the) given machine electrical      energy.

### Group II. Active Present Participle Follows Noun Modified

Фи́зика, гла́вным    о́бразом, изуча́ет явле́ния, происходя́щие[2]
Physics, for the     most part, studies   phenomena going on

в неживо́й    приро́де.
in lifeless    nature.

Проце́ссы, протека́ющие при отсу́тствии теплообме́на    с
Processes, proceeding    with absence     of heat exchange with

окружа́ющей     средо́й, но́сят назва́ние    адиабати́ческих.
(the) surrounding   medium, bear   (the) name    of adiabatic.

---

[1] Here the participle притека́ющей modifies the noun эне́ргии. This type of participle construction, with a phrase interposed between a participle and the noun modified, is not encountered as frequently in Russian as in German.

[2] The participle окружа́ющей precedes средо́й, the noun modified.

С    термодинами́ческой    то́чки  зре́ния  вся́кий  проце́сс,
From  (the) thermodynamic     point  of view  every    process

веду́щий к уменьше́нию свобо́дной эне́ргии систе́мы,    мо́жет
leading  to (a) decrease  of free     energy  of (a) system  may

протека́ть    самопроизво́льно.
proceed      spontaneously.

Сопоставле́ние    сле́дствий,              вытека́ющих    из
Comparison       of (the) consequences,  flowing        from

рассмотре́ния моде́лей,      с    да́нными    о́пыта
consideration  of (the) models,  with  (the) data  of experiment

приво́дит   к  тому́,  что  строе́ние    мета́на    и    его́
leads      to  this,  that  (the) structure  of methane  and  its

произво́дных   нахо́дит по́лное   истолкова́ние на осно́ве
derivatives    finds    complete  explanation   on (the) basis

моде́ли    тетра э́дра.
of model  of tetrahedron.

## § 267. Sentences Illustrating Active Present Participles Governing a Direct Object.

The following two groups of sentences reveal close similarity between active present participles and active past participles with respect to their ability to govern a direct object, cf. § 255, p. 403.

### Group I.  Direct Object in Accusative Case

A double asterisk designates each of the participles under consideration and a single asterisk their direct objects (and modifiers thereof, if any).

Мно́гие вещества́,   игра́ющие**чрезвыча́йно    ва́жную*  роль*
Many    substances,  playing   (an) extremely   important  role

в   совреме́нной   хими́ческой  промы́шленности,  явля́ются
in  contemporary  chemical     industry,          show self

производными    ароматических    углеводородов, имеющих**
(are) derivatives      of aromatic      hydrocarbons,     having

в   молекуле,      подобно циклопарафинам,  замкнутую* цепь*
in (the) molecule, like    cycloparaffins,     (a) closed   chain

атомов     углерода.
of atoms    of carbon.


Запас тепловой   энергии как    газов,   так и    жидких
Supply of thermal  energy  as well of gases, as  also of liquid

и      твёрдых     тел     полностью      определяется
and    of solid    bodies   completely     determines   self

кинетической    энергией составляющих**¹ их*   частиц, т.е.
by (the) kinetic   energy   of composing      them particles, i.e.,

зависит от скоростей     движения     этих    частиц.
depends on (the) velocities  of motion   of these  particles.


В      результате    мы    получаем    закон     Ома,
As     result        we    obtain      (the) law  of Ohm,

устанавливающий**² пропорциональность*   силы
establishing         (the) proportionality   of (the) strength

тока     и     разности       потенциалов.
of current and   of (the) difference  of potentials.


Изучение      свойств       различных    веществ    при
(The) study    of (the) properties of various    substances  at

низких  температурах, составляющее**³ задачу*   целой
low     temperatures   constituting      (the) task  of (a) whole


---

¹ Here the particle составляющих  modifies the noun частиц  while the
pronoun ИХ, as the direct object of  составляющих, is in the accusative case.
² Here the  ending  -ИЙ  indicates that  the  participle   устанавливающий
modifies the noun   закон.
³ Here the ending  -ее  indicates that the participle  составляющее   modifies
the noun  изучение.

| о́бласти | фи́зики | (фи́зики | ни́зких | температу́р ), |
|---|---|---|---|---|
| field | of physics | (of physics | of low | temperatures), |

| привело́ к обнаруже́нию | сверхпроводи́мости. |
|---|---|
| led to observation | of superconductivity. |

## Group II. Direct Object Not in Accusative Case

In discussing active past participles, it was pointed out that any one of several factors may cause the direct object of such a participle to be in some case other than the accusative, cf. § 255, p. 404. The same factors are operative in causing active present participles to govern cases other than the accusative, as is shown by the following examples.

A double asterisk designates each of the participles under consideration and a single asterisk their direct objects (and modifiers thereof, if any).

| Наряду́ | с | про́волочными | сопротивле́ниями, | широко́ |
|---|---|---|---|---|
| Along | with | wire | resistors | widely |

| применя́ются | и | сопротивле́ния | из | разли́чьых |
|---|---|---|---|---|
| use self (are | used) also | resistors | from | various |

| специа́льных | веще́ств, | облада́ющих**[1] | высо́ким* | уде́льным* |
|---|---|---|---|---|
| special | substance | possessing | high | specific |

| сопротивле́нием* |
|---|
| resistance. |

| Очеви́дно, | что | большо́й | интере́с | име́ет | сопоставле́ние |
|---|---|---|---|---|---|
| (It is) obvious, | that | great | interest | has | (the) comparison |

| разли́чных | физи́ческих | свойств | и | характери́стик |
|---|---|---|---|---|
| of various | physical | properties | and | characteristics |

| сверхпроводнико́в | и | несверхпроводнико́в, | в пе́рвую |
|---|---|---|---|
| of superconductors | and | nonsuperconductors | in (the) first |

---

[1] Cf. § 102, p. 148, third Russian sentence.

о́чередь,    с        це́лью        выявле́ния      усло́вий,
place         with      (the)  purpose    of elucidating    conditions

благоприя́тствующих [1] появле́нию    сверхпроводи́мости.
favoring                   appearance    of superconductivity.

Доста́точное   освеще́ние    особенно      ва́жно       на
Sufficient        illumination   (is) particularly   important    at

том ме́сте,    где      выполня́ется    кака́я-либо    рабо́та,
that    place,    where    completes self    any              work

тре́бующая**[2] наблюде́ния:*
requiring         observation.

Явле́ние          сверхпровиди́мости    состои́т    в   том,
(The) phenomenon  of superconductivity    consists    in   this,

что  в    сверхпроводнике́ мо́жет    течь    ток,
that  in  (a) superconductor   is able  to flow  (an) electric

            не  встреча́ющий**сопротивле́ния*  и    поэ́тому
current,   not  encountering  resistance          and  consequently

не  свя́занный   с    выделе́нием    тепла́,
not  connected   with  evolution        of heat.

Для  э́того, что́бы    избежа́ть   не  име́ющих**отноше́ния*    к
For   this, in order  to avoid    not  having    relationship      to

на́шему   вопро́су   осложне́ний,[3]  бу́дем   счита́ть,    что
our          problem    complications   we will  consider,     that

образе́ц      име́ет    фо́рму    безконе́чного
(the) sample  has      (the) form   of (an) infinite

цили́ндра.
cylinder.

---

[1]  Cf. § 114, p. 166.
[2]  Cf. § 85, p. 124.
[3]  The verb избега́ть -- избежа́ть "to avoid" requires its direct object to be in
the genitive case, cf. § 85, p. 124. For this reason, in this sentence both the
noun осложе́ний and its participal modifier име́ющих are in the genitive case.

§ 268. Sentences Illustrating Use of Reflexive Active Present
       Participles.

The formation and significance of the reflexive forms of
active past participles was discussed in § 265, p. 418.

### Group I. Reflexive Form of Active Present Participle Precedes Noun Modified

| При | ни́зких | температу́рах | разма́х | колеба́ний |
|-----|---------|---------------|---------|------------|
| At | low | temperatures | (the) swing | of vibrations |

| отде́льных частиц | в криста́лле | сравни́тельно | невели́к, |
|------------------|--------------|--------------|-----------|
| of separate particles | in (a) crystal | (is) relatively | small |

| и | коле́блющийся | ио́н | не отхо́дит | ско́лько-нибу́дь |
|---|--------------|------|-------------|-----------------|
| and | (a) shaking self (vibrating) | ion | not goes | at all |

| далеко́ от | своего́ | сре́днего | симметри́чного | расположе́ния |
|-----------|---------|----------|----------------|---------------|
| far from | his | average | symmetrical | position |

| в | реше́тке. |
|---|-----------|
| in | (the) lattice. |

| При | таки́х | реа́кциях | возника́ют | слу́чаи |
|-----|--------|-----------|------------|---------|
| During | such | reactions | arise | cases |

| ка́жущегося[1] | | отклоне́ния | от | зако́на |
|---------------|---|-------------|----|---------|
| of appearing | self (seeming) | deviation | from | (the) law |

| де́йствующих | масс. |
|--------------|-------|
| of acting | masses. |

| Во всех | сообща́ющихся[2] | сосу́дах | вода́ | стои́т на одно́м |
|---------|------------------|----------|-------|------------------|
| In all | communicating | self vessels | water | stands at one |

| у́ровне. |
|----------|
| level. |

---

[1] The reflexive infinitive каза́ться and forms derived therefrom, have come
to have a special significance namely "to be appearing," "to seem" in the sense of
giving a misleading or false impression.

[2] The reflexive is sometimes used in Russian when referring to an interaction
between different individual things or persons, cf. § 394, p. 656.

За   единицу времени   может быть принята длительность
As   unit    of time    is able to be   taken    (the) duration

какого-либо    определённого повторяющегося процесса.
of any       definite      repeating self    process.

При адсорбции из   растворов можно     встретить
On   adsorption from   solutions   it is possible   to encounter

различную    степень    специфичности   взаимодействия
various      degree(s)    of specificity    of interaction

адсорбента      с   адсорбирующимися вещества́ми.
of (the) adsorbent   with   adsorbing self      substances.

---

## Group II.   Reflexive Form of Active Present Participle Follows Noun Modified

Бокситы,   встречающиеся     в   ряде     стран,
Bauxites,   encountering self   in   (a) series   of countries,

являются    важной    рудой алюминия.
show self   as important   ore    of aluminum.

Превращение      глинозёма, содержащегося   в бокси́те,
(The) conversion   of alumina,    containing self   in   bauxite,

в    алюминат натрия     может      осуществляться
into   aluminate   of sodium   is possible   to accomplish self

различными   способами.
by various     processes.

Теплотой      растворения называют    количество    теплоты,
As (the) heat   of solution    they call    (the) quantity   of heat

поглощающееся[1] или выделяющееся   при растворении одного
absorbing self    or   evolving self     on   solution      of one

---

[1] The adjective ending =ee of the participles, поглощающееся and выделяющееся     indicate that they modify the noun количество and not теплоты as might be inferred perhaps from the interlinear translation.

| мо́ля | вещества́ | в | о́чень | большо́м | коли́честве |
|-------|-----------|---|--------|----------|-------------|
| mole | of substance | in | (a) very | large | quantity |

| раствори́теля. |
|----------------|
| of solvent. |

| Двуо́кись | хло́ра | $ClO_2$ | | темножёлтый | газ |
|-----------|--------|---------|-----|-------------|-----|
| Dioxide | of chlorine | $ClO_2$ | (is) | (a) dark yellow | gas |

| отврати́тельного | запа́ха, | о́чень | легко́ | разлага́ющийся,[1] |
|------------------|----------|--------|--------|--------------------|
| of repulsive | odor, | very | easily | decomposing self, |

| иногда́ | со | взры́вом. |
|---------|-----|-----------|
| sometimes | with (an) | explosion. |

§ 269. Reflexive Active Present Participles Used with the Instrumental Case of Nouns, etc.

The role of the instrumental case of nouns and adjectives with the reflexive of active present participles is essentially the same as that already noted for other reflexive verb forms, cf. § 52, p. 71; § 214, p. 336.

In the following sentences double asterisks have been used to identify the reflexive forms of active present participles and single asterisks to identify nouns, pronouns and adjectives in the instrumental case relating to the participles under consideration.

| Добавле́ние | к | э́тому | раство́ру | концентри́рованного |
|-------------|---|--------|-----------|---------------------|
| Addition | to | this | solution | of a concentrated |

| раство́ра | броми́да | ка́лия | влечёт | за | собо́й |
|-----------|----------|--------|--------|-----|--------|
| solution | of bromide | of potassium | brings | after | self |

| выпаде́ние | амети́стово-фиоле́товых | | криста́ллов |
|------------|------------------------|---|-------------|
| precipitation | of amethyst-violet | | crystals |

---

[1] Here the participle, разлага́ющийся , as indicated by the adjective ending -ий modifies the noun, газ.

со́ли      Ni(NH₃)₆ Br₂,    характеризу́ющейся** ма́лой*
of (the) salt    $Ni(NH_3)_6 Br_2$,    characterizing self    by small

величино́й* раствори́мости.
magnitude    of solubility.

Де́ло     сво́дится   к   тому́, что не́которые приближённые
(The) thing   leads self   to this,   that certain     approximate

представле́ния о        поведе́нии    электро́нов    в
theories        concerning (the) behavior   of electrons    in

мета́ллах,    ока́зывающиеся**¹      доста́точными*    для
metal       proving self       sufficient      for

ка́чественного    описа́ния    мета́ллов   в   норма́льном
qualitative      description   of   metals    in    normal

состоя́нии, не   позволя́ют поня́ть      явле́ние
condition    not   enable    to understand (the) phenomenon

сверхпроводи́мости.
of superconductivity.

В кисло́тах, одновре́менно явля́ющихся**     окисли́телями*
In acids,      simultaneously showing self (being) oxidizing agents

(наприме́р, HNO₃),     медь и серебро́ растворя́ются легко́.
(for example, $HNO_3$), copper and silver    dissolve self    easily.

Осо́бенно    отчётливо   ещё   в   глубо́кой дре́вности   э́ти
Particularly   clearly      even in   deep     antiquity    these

сво́йства    наблюда́лись    у    янтаря́, представля́ющего**
properties   observed self   with   amber,   presenting

собо́й*       одну́ из   разнови́дностей   окамене́лой
by self (being)   one   of   (the) varieties    of petrified

смолы́.
resin.

¹ The adjective ending -ие indicates that the participle   ока́зывающиеся modifies the noun   представле́ния. The English interlinear translation fails to make this point clear.

**§ 270. Reading Exercise.**

### Фотоэлектрический эффект

Сущность фотоэффекта состоит в том , что свет определённой минимальной частоты, падающий на данную металли́ческую поверхность, вызывает испускание электронов. Металл, подвергающийся[1] действию лучей меньшей частоты, не даёт никакого эффекта. Опытами обнаружено, что электроны вылетают из металла со скоростями, возрастающими с увеличением частоты света (т.е. с уменьшением длины волны излучения). При этом оказывается, что количество вылетающих из металла электронов пропорционально количеству, падающей на поверхность металла световой энергии. Перечисленные[2] свойства фотоэффекта, являющиеся необъяснёнными с точки зрения волновой теории света, легко понять на основе квантовой теории. Эйнштейн (1905), с помощью теории квантов, дал простое уравнение, вскрывающее сущность фотоэффекта,

$$K = h\nu - (A_1 + A_2)$$

где  $K$ = кинетическая энергия электрона

$A_1$ = работа, потребная для вырывания электрона из атома (т.е. для ионизации атома)

$A_2$ = работа, необходимая для выведения электрона сквозь поверхностный слой металла

$h\nu$ = энергия кванта излучения с частотой $\nu$

$h$ = планкова постоянная действия

$$h = 6.547 \times 10^{-27} \text{ эрг сек.}$$

Мы видим, что для вылета электронов необходимо освещать поверхность металла светом,[2] характеризующимся квантами, энергия которых будет превышать сумму $A_1 + A_2$. Кинетическая энергия, а следовательно скорость вылетающих электронов увеличивается с частотой излучения. Число выброшенных электронов определяется числом падающих

на пове́рхность мета́лла ква́нтов;  поэ́тому коли́чество[4] вы-
шиба́ющихся в секу́нду электро́нов пропорциона́льно коли́честву,
поглоща́ющейся мета́ллом радиа́ции.

   Прибо́ры для наблюде́ния и испо́льзования фотоэффе́к-
та - фотоэлеме́нты - устра́иваются сле́дующим о́бразом.
Часть[5] вну́тренней пове́рхности ко́лбы покрыва́ют сло́ем ме-
та́лла, наприме́р це́сия. Э́тот слой мета́лла слу́жит като́-
дом. Часть ко́лбы оставля́ют прозра́чной[6] для освеще́ния
като́дного сло́я.

   Внутри́ ко́лбы помеща́ют[7]  второ́й электро́д (ано́д),
представля́ющий собо́й се́тку, кольцо́ или про́сто металли́че-
ский ввод в це́нтре. Ко́лба отка́чивается, и ме́жду электро́-
дами накла́дывается ра́зность потенциа́лов. Электро́ны, вы́-
брошенные под де́йствием све́та из като́дного сло́я мета́лла,
устремля́ются к ано́ду и, таки́м о́бразом, создаю́т ток.

   Си́ла[8]  то́ка, наблюда́ющегося при фотоэлектри́ческом
эффе́кте, зави́сит от освещённости и име́ет обы́чно величину́
поря́дка[9] $10^{-5}$ ампе́р. В соедине́нии с усили́тельными элек-
тро́нными ла́мпами фотоэлеме́нты[10] сде́лали возмо́жным осуще́с-
вле́ние чувстви́тельных автома́тов, реаги́рующих на измене́-
ния освещённости: открыва́ющих две́ри, включа́ющих и выклю-
ча́ющих освеще́ние, управля́ющих светофо́рмами, сорти́рующих
ме́лкие предме́ты и т. д.

## Notes

1. подверга́ющийся      де́йствию      луче́й,      literally,
"submitting self to the action of rays."

2. Перечи́сленные сво́йства фотоэффе́кта., явля́ющиеся.
"The enumerated properties of the photoeffect, which are." Note
that the reflexive form of the active present participle of ЯВЛЯ́ТЬ
may be used like other reflexive forms of ЯВЛЯ́ТЬ as a substitute
for missing parts of the verb "to be."

3. све́том, характеризу́ющимся ква́нтами literally,
"(by means of) light characterizing self by quanta."

4. коли́чество вышиба́ющихся в секу́нду электро́нов
literally, "quantity of ejecting self in (a) second electrons."

§ 208. The Influence of Temperature on the Speed of Chemical Reactions

5. Часть внутренней поверхности колбы покрывают, "Part of the inner surface of (the) bulb (they) cover." Note the impersonal verb покрывают.

6. Часть колбы оставляют прозрачной. "Part of the bulb (they) leave transparent." Here, again, оставляют is an impersonal verb while прозрачной is an adjective in the feminine, instrumental, singular case, cf. § 100, p. 145.

7. помещают второй электрод, "they place a second electrode." Here, again, the verb помещают is impersonal.

8. Сила тока, наблюдающегося literally, "(The) strength of the current observing self," or, in better English, "The strength of the current which is observed."

9. порядка 10⁻⁵ ампер "of the order of $10^{-5}$ amperes."

10. фотоэлементы сделали возможным, "photoelements made possible."

§ 271. Translation Exercise.

1. A metal, submitted (submitting self) to the action of light of a definite minimum frequency, emits electrons.
2. The speeds of the flying from the metal electrons increase ( возрастают ) with decrease in length of wave of the radiation.
3. The energy of the falling on the metal surface quanta depends on the frequency of the radiation.
4. It is easy ( легко ) to understand the simple equation describing the essence of the photoelectric effect.
5. The kinetic energy of the electrons is determined in the following manner.
6. The number of ejected electrons increases with the quantity of light falling on the surface of the metal.
7. A layer of cesium, being (presenting by means of self) the cathode, covers ( покрывает ) part of the inner surface of the bulb.
8. We see that illumination of the cathode layer with light is necessary for emission of electrons.
9. The strength of the current depends on the quantity of the ejecting self in a second electrons.

10. The strength of current, observed (observing self) during the photoelectric effect is proportional ( пропорциона́льна ) to the quantity of the light being absorbed (absorbing self) by the cathode radiation.

# LESSON 30

## PASSIVE PRESENT PARTICIPLES

§ 272. Significance of Passive Present Participles.

Passive present participles, like other Russian participles, are verb forms used as noun modifiers. As might be expected from the name, passive present participles usually indicate submission on the part of the modified noun to the action designated by the participle. English verbal expressions which correspond most nearly to Russian passive present participles are formed with the aid of an auxiliary verb form e.g., фотографируемый, "being photographed." Occasionally, a Russian passive present participle is used to designate susceptibility to an action, cf. § 278, p. 440; § 279, p. 441.

The time of the action expressed by passive present participles is that of the main verb in the sentence or clause to which the participle is subordinate. Like the corresponding active present participles, the passive present participles may be used in Russian to denote action whose time of occurrence is other than the actual present.

§ 273. Formation of Stems of Passive Present Participles.

The relationship of the stem[1] of the passive present participle to other forms of the great majority of Russian verbs is very simple. The stem of most passive present participles is identical with the first person plural of the present tense.

This relationship is illustrated by the following summary which lists the passive present participles of typical verbs together with closely related verb forms.

---

[1] Passive present participles are declined with the regular adjective hard endings as shown in § 274, p. 434.

## Regular Formation of Passive Present Participles

| Imperfective Infinitive | Class | Present Tense First Person Plural | Passive Present Participle |
|---|---|---|---|
| де́лать | Reg. A | де́лаем | де́лаемый |
| фотографи́ровать | Irr. A-1 | фотографи́руем | фотографи́руемый |
| колеба́ть | Irr. C-1 | коле́блем | коле́блемый |
| дви́гать | Irr. D-1 | дви́жим | дви́жимый |
| гнать | Irr. E-2 | го́ним | гони́мый |

This simple relationship between the first person plural of the present tense and the passive present participle is not observed with certain verbs as shown by the following examples.

## Irregular Formation of Passive Present Participles

| Imperfective Infinitive | Class | Present Tense First Person Plural | Passive Present Participle |
|---|---|---|---|
| дава́ть | Irr. B | даём | дава́емый |
| влечь | Irr. G-3 | влечём | влеко́мый |
| везти́ | Irr. H-1 | везём | везо́мый |
| нести́ | Irr. H-2 | несём | несо́мый |

As exemplified by везти́ and нести́, it is by no means unusual for the -ёМ ending of the first person plural of the present tense to go over into -ОМ in forming the stem of the passive present participle. The close phonetic relationship between -ёМ and -ОМ should be noted in this connection.

§ 274. Declension of Passive Present Participles.

Passive present participles are declined using the regular "hard" adjective endings[1] as shown by the following example.

---

[1] "Hard" adjective endings are summarized in § 131, p. 191.

Stem of Passive Present Participle ПОЛУЧАЕМ -,"being obtained"
(Second Person Plural of Present Tense получа́ем)
(Imperfective Infinitive ПОЛУЧА́ТЬ, "to be obtaining")

## Singular

|       | Masc. | Fem. | Neuter |
|-------|-------|------|--------|
| Nom.  | получа́емый | получа́емая | получа́емое |
| Gen.  | получа́емого | получа́емой | получа́емого |
| Dat.  | получа́емому | получа́емой | получа́емому |
| Acc.  | получа́емый[1] | получа́емую | получа́емое |
| Instr.| получа́емым | получа́емой (получа́емою) | получа́емым |
| Prep. | получа́емом | получа́емой | получа́емом |

## All Genders

### Plural

| Nom.  | получа́емые |
|-------|-------------|
| Gen.  | получа́емых |
| Dat.  | получа́емым |
| Acc.  | получа́емые[1] |
| Instr.| получа́емыми |
| Prep. | получа́емых |

## PREDICATIVE FORMS[2]

|       | Masc. | Fem. | Neuter |
|-------|-------|------|--------|
| Sing. | получа́ем | получа́ема | получа́емо |

### All Genders

| Plural | получа́емы |
|--------|-----------|

[1] When used to modify nouns designating living beings as defined in § 67, p. 93, this accusative form becomes the same as the corresponding genitive.

[2] The predicative forms of passive present participles are encountered only rarely, cf. § 288, p. 456.

§ 275. Summary Note on Construction of Passive Present Participles.

The three component parts of passive present participles should be noted carefully.

| | | |
|---|---|---|
| делае ——————————— | М ———————•——— | ый |
| фотографируе ————— | М ———————— | ый |
| криви ————————— | М ———————— | ый |
| влеко ——————— | М ————————— | ый |
| несо ———————— | М ——————— | ый |
| Infinitive stem in altered form | Typical stem termination of passive present participles | Adjective ending, cf. § 274 above |

As with other participles, the adjective endings serve to indicate, in the usual way, the noun modified.

§ 276. Sentences Illustrating Simple Use of Passive Present Participles as Direct Modifiers of Nouns.

The following sample sentences are divided into two groups depending on whether the passive present participles precede or follow the noun which they modify.

## Group I. Passive Present Participle Precedes Noun Modified

| Ги́ри | взве́шиваемое | те́ло | сле́дует | на |
|---|---|---|---|---|
| Weights | and (a) being weighed | body | it is necessary | on |

| ча́шки | весо́в | накла́дывать | "мя́гко" | |
|---|---|---|---|---|
| pans | of balance | to place | "softly." | |

| Отсю́да | и | произошло́ | совреме́нное | |
|---|---|---|---|---|
| From this | also | came forth | (the) contemporary | |

| наименова́ние | опи́сываемых | явле́ний, | кото́рые | |
|---|---|---|---|---|
| naming | of (the) described | phenomena | which | |

| тепе́рь | обы́чно | называ́ются | электри́ческими. | |
|---|---|---|---|---|
| now | ordinarily | call self | electrical. | |

Это    явление    испускания    электронов    освещаемой
This   phenomenon  of ejection    of electrons   by a being

          поверхностью    металла    носит    название
irradiated  surface        of (a) metal  bears    (the) name

фотоэлектрического       эффекта,      или     сокращённо
of photoelectric          effect,       or      abbreviated

фотоэффекта.
photoeffect.


Движущиеся        в      определённом      боевом   порядке,
Moving self       in     (a) definite       battle    order,

охраняемые        и      охраняющие    суда¹    носят   общее
being protected   and    protecting     vessels   bear    (the) general

название         "конвой           кораблей"       или     просто
name             of (a)  "convoy     of ships"       or      simply

"конвой".
"convoy."


### Group II.  Passive Present Participle Follows Noun Modified

Количество    теплоты,  затрачиваемое    на  нагревание
(The) quantity  of heat,  (being) expended   on  heating

одной    граммолекулы    вещества      на   $1°$, называется
one      gram-molecule    of (a) substance  by   $1°$, calls self

молекулярной       теплоёмкостью.
(the) molecular     heat capacity.


Среди    растворителей,    используемых      не   только   в
Among    solvents,          being used         not  only     in

лакокрасочной,         но    и      в    других    видах
lacquer  and  paint,    but   also   in   other     kinds


¹ суда  is  the  irregularly  formed  nominative  plural  of  the  neuter  nouns,
судно,  "ship," cf. § 359, p. 578.

**438**      LESSON 30

промышленности, на одном из первых мест стоят
*of industry, at one of (the) first places stand*

препараты ряда гликоля (получаемые[1] через
*preparations of (the) series of glycol (being obtained through*

этиленхлоргидрин).
*ethylene chlorhydrin).*

Одним из значительных неудобств, которым
*As one of (the) significant shortcomings which*

обладает вольтова дуга, применяемая в качестве
*possesses (the) Voltaic are being used in (the) quality*

источника света, является то обстоятельство,
*of (a) source of light, shows self this circumstance*

что угольные электроды непрерывно сгорают и
*that (the) carbon electrodes continuously burn away and*

расстояние между ними увеличивается.
*(the) distance between them increases self.*

На применении электрических печей (печей
*On (the) application of electrical furnaces (furnaces*

сопротивления) основано и производство
*of resistance) (is) based also (the) production*

карборунда, являющегося весьма ценным
*of carborundum, showing self (being) (a) very valuable*

материалом, употребляемым для всякого рода
*material being used for every kind*

шлифовки.
*of grinding.*

[1] The ending -ые indicates that the participle получаемые modifies the noun препараты.

§ 277.  Passive Present Participles Used with the Instrumental
        Case of Nouns, etc.

As already noted, passive present participles usually indicate
submission on the part of the modified noun to the action
designated by the participle.  The means or agency, whereby the
action of the participle is exerted, is often indicated by a noun or
pronoun in the instrumental case.

In the following example sentences, double asterisks have
been used to indicate passive present participles, while single
asterisks indicates nouns (and modifiers, if any) or pronouns
which constitute the means whereby the action of the participles
is exerted.

| Очеви́дно, | что | лёгкость | плавле́ния | криста́лла, |
|---|---|---|---|---|
| (It is) obvious | that | (the) ease | of melting | of (a) crystal, |

| ка́чественно | характеризу́емая**¹ | температу́рой* |
|---|---|---|
| qualitatively | being characterized | by (the) temperature |

| плавле́ния, | должна́ | зави́сеть | от | всех | тех | фа́кторов, |
|---|---|---|---|---|---|---|
| of melting, | must | depend | on | all | those | factors |

| кото́рые | определя́ют | си́лы | стяже́ния | ме́жду |
|---|---|---|---|---|
| which | determine | (the) forces | of coherence | between |

| ио́нами | в | криста́лле. |
|---|---|---|
| (the) ions | in | (the) crystal. |

| При | прохожде́нии | то́ка | че́рез |
|---|---|---|---|
| During | passing | of current | through |

| рассма́триваемый | электроли́т | у́гольный | като́д |
|---|---|---|---|
| (the) being considered | electrolyte | (the) carbon | cathode |

| бу́дет | покрыва́ться | сло́ем | ме́ди, | образу́емым**² |
|---|---|---|---|---|
| will | cover self | with (a) layer | of copper, | being formed |

---

¹ The ending –ая of the participle характеризу́емая  indicates that it modifies
the noun лёгкость.
² The ending –ым of the participle образу́емым  indicates that it modifies the
noun сло́ем.

отлага́ющимися*        на    като́де       положи́тельными*
by depositing self    on    (the) cathode positive

ме́дными*   ио́нами.*
copper       ions.


Вся́кое   те́ло,  ниче́м*     не    подде́рживаемое,** па́дает
Every    body,  by nothing [not]  being supported,      falls

на      зе́млю.
to     (the) earth.


Во   мно́гих    слу́чаях    для   измере́ния     механи́ческой
In    many       cases      for   measuring     of mechanical

си́лы    применя́ется       та́кже  едини́ца,    называ́емая**
force   uses self (is used) also  (the) unit,    being called

ди́ной.*
(the) dyne.


§ 278. Susceptibility to an Action Indicated by Passive Present
       Participle.

    If something is undergoing some transformation, it is by
obvious inference susceptible of such change. Since, as already
noted, the action of undergoing a transformation can be indicated
by Russian passive present participles, their use in such a
fashion as to emphasize susceptibility to the transformation is
hardly surprising.

Проница́емые       для  воды́,   но  не  для  растворённых
Permeable          for  water,  but not for  dissolved

веще́ств           перегоро́дки                    мо́жно
substances         partitions (membranes)      (it is) possible

пригото́вить       иску́сственно.
to prepare        artificially.

| Приме́р | непреры́вной, | в | смы́сле | Коши́[1] |
|---|---|---|---|---|
| (An) example | of (a) continuous, | in | (the) sense | of Cauchy, |

| нигде́ | не | дифференци́руемой | фу́нкции | был |
|---|---|---|---|---|
| nowhere | [not] | differentiable | function | was |

| опублико́ван | Ве́йерштрассом | в | 1872 г. |
|---|---|---|---|
| published | by Weierstrass | in | 1872. |

| Температу́ры, | достига́емые | в | во́льтовой | дуге́, |
|---|---|---|---|---|
| Temperatures, | attainable | in | (the) electric | arc, |

| дохо́дят | до 5000°. |
|---|---|
| go as far as | to 5000°. |

| Свежеосаждённый | сульфи́д | ме́ди, | легко́ |
|---|---|---|---|
| (The) freshly precipitated | sulfide | of copper, | easily |

| окисля́емый | кислоро́дом | во́здуха, | на́до |
|---|---|---|---|
| oxidizable | by (the) oxygen | of (the) air, | (it is) necessary |

| охраня́ть | от | соприкоснове́ния | с | во́здухом. |
|---|---|---|---|---|
| to protect | from | contact | with | air. |

## § 279. Nouns Indicating State or Condition of Susceptibility.

As noted in preceding § 278, passive present participles may be used to indicate susceptibility to some change. Thus we have, for example, проница́емый being used to express the concept "permeable." By affixing the suffix -ОСТ- to certain present active participles, Russians form feminine abstract nouns designating a state of susceptibility to some action, Thus we have проница́емость , "permeability," окисля́емость "oxidizability" from окисля́емый as well as nouns from closely related adjectives, e.g., полупроница́емый "semipermeable."

| Формальдеги́д | отлича́ется | свое́й | большо́й |
|---|---|---|---|
| Formaldehyde | distinguishes self | by his | big |

| окисля́емостью. |
|---|
| oxidizability. |

---

[1] The name Коши́ is not declined in accord with a rule already given, cf. Footnote 1, p. 408 and § 363, p. 587.

Реша́ющее влия́ние на структу́ру криста́лла
(A) deciding influence on (the) structure of (a) crystal

мо́жет ока́зывать поляризу́емость составля́ющих
is able to exert (the) polarizability of composing

его́ ио́нов.
him (the crystal) ions.

Сво́йством полупроница́емости облада́ет большинство́
(The) property of semipermeability possess (the) majority

тка́ней живы́х органи́змов, в ча́стности сте́нки
of tissues of living organisms, in particular (the) walls

расти́тельных кле́ток.
of plant cells.

Из диференци́руемости фу́нкции f(z·) в
From differentiability of (the) function f(z) at

то́чке a сле́дует и её непреры́вность в э́той
point a follows also her continuity at that

то́чке.
point.

Флотацио́нный проце́сс осно́ван на разли́чных
(The) flotation process (is) based on different

фи́зико-хими́ческих сво́йствах пове́рхности
physical-chemical properties of (the) surface

минера́лов, на разли́чной сма́чиваемости водо́й.
of minerals, on different wettability by water.

§ 280. Reading Exercise.

Источники света
(Часть первая)

Свечи, факелы, лампы накаливания, вольтовы[1] дуги, газосвечные лампы и другие приборы, применяемые[2] в качестве источников света и кажущиеся[3] разнообразными и сильно отличающимися друг от друга, тем не менее основаны[4] на одном и том же принципе. Принцип этот - превращение в световую энергию какого-нибудь другого вида затрачиваемой энергии.

Можно думать, что процессы излучения света, характеризуемые превращением различных других видов энергии в видимую радиацию, являются разнородными. В[5] конце концов, однако, свет, излучаемый каким-нибудь источником, всегда представляет собой поток квантов лучистой энергии, так называемых "фотонов". Основным механизмом излучения фотона является перескок электрона, связанного в какой-нибудь материи, с[6] состояния, характеризуемого избытком энергии, в более стабильное состояние. Энергия, необходимая для излучения фотона, соответствует разности между[7] энергиями начального и конечного состояний электрона и называется "энергией возбуждения". Необходимым условием создания светоисточника является возможность возбуждать электроны какого-либо вещества при помощи энергии, поглощаемой тем же веществом. Следует[8] отметить, что возбуждение электронов не обеспечивает излучения света, так как энергия возбуждения в зависимости от условий может превращаться не в свет, а в другие виды энергии, например в невидимую радиацию. Основным[9] требованием, предъявляемым к источникам света, является превращение в свет возможно большей части затрачиваемой энергии.

При высоких температурах молекулы и атомы, непрерывно[10] колеблющиеся, сталкиваются энергично друг с другом и, таким образом, осуществляют возбуждение электронов, необходимое для излучения света. Примером[11] объектов,

являющихся удобными для получения высоких температур, может служить проводящая нить, накаливаемая электрическим током. На этом принципе построены так называемые лампы накаливания. При температурах, достигаемых в современных лампах накаливания, сравнительно небольшая часть электрической энергии, затрачиваемой лампой, превращается в видимую радиацию.

Но высокие темпертуры, достигаемые в лампах накаливания, не является необходимыми для превращения электрической энергии в свет. Так, например, в натриевых лампах атомы натрия, возбуждаемые[12] ударами быстро[13] движущихся электронов, излучают свет без значительного повышения температуры.

## Notes

1. ВОЛЬТОВЫ ДУГИ, "voltaic arcs." Here ВОЛЬТОВЫ is the irregularly formed nominative plural of the possessive adjective whose masculine nominative singular is ВОЛЬТОВ.

2. As indicated by their endings, both применяемые and кажущиеся are nominative plural forms which here refer to the nouns свечи, факелы, лампы, дуги, лампы and приборы which form the subject of the sentence. The reflexive active present participle, кажущийся meaning "seeming to be," has no corresponding passive present participle, cf. Footnote 1, p. 425.

3. и кажущиеся разнообразными и сильно отличающимися друг от друга, "and seeming to be dissimilar and strongly differing one from another." Replacement of отличающимися, a reflexive form of an active present participle, by отличаемыми, the corresponding form of the passive present participle, would change the meaning to the following, "and appearing dissimilar and strongly distinguishable one from the other."

4. ОСНОВАНЫ is the predicative plural form of the passive past participle, ОСНОВАННЫЙ. In translating this sentence it is necessary to supply the present tense of the verb "to be." Thus, we have "Candles, torches, lamps, arcs, lamps, and other devices (are) based," cf. § 241, p. 381.

5. В конце́ концо́в , literally, "At the end of ends," or more colloquially, "When all is said and done," cf. § 357, p. 573.

6. с состоя́ния, характеризу́емого избы́тком эне́ргии, в бо́лее стаби́льное состоя́ние, literally, "from a state, being characterized by an excess of energy, into a more stable state."

7. ме́жду эне́ргиями нача́льного и коне́чного состоя́ний, "between the energies of the initial and final conditions of the electron." Note that нача́льного and коне́чного are in the genitive singular, while состоя́ний is in the genitive plural. The expression нача́льного и коне́чного состоя́ний is equivalent to the lengthier and clumsier expression нача́льного состоя́ния и коне́чного состоя́ния.

8. Сле́дует отме́тить , "It is necessary to mention." Here сле́дует is an impersonal verb, cf. § 385, p. 640.

9. Основны́м тре́бованием, предъявля́емым к исто́чникам све́та . "As the basic requirement applicable to sources of light," Note the use of the instrumental case preceding явля́ется .

10. непреры́вно коле́блющиеся, literally, "continuously shaking self," i.e., "continuously vibrating." Here replacement of the reflexive of the active present participle, коле́блющиеся, by the passive present participle, коле́блемые, would change the meaning to "continuously susceptible to vibration."

11. See Note 9 above.

12. Here the ending of возбужда́емые clearly indicates that it refers to а́томы.

13. бы́стро дви́жущихся электро́нов, literally, "of rapidly moving self electrons." Note again that дви́жущихся cannot be replaced by the corresponding passive present participle without changing the meaning.

§ 281. Translation Exercise.

1. Processes of radiating light, seeming to be (ка́жущиеся) dissimilar and strongly differing one from another none the less are based on one and the same principle.

2. Sources of light are based on the principle of conversion of some other form of (being) consumed energy into visible radiation.

3. The conversion of various other forms of energy into visible radiation is (shows self) as the basic (ОСНОВНЫМ) principle (ПРИНЦИПОМ) of creation of a light source.

4. As a necessary condition of the radiation of a photon is (shows self) the excitation of an electron.

5. The energy, (being) radiated as a photon during (ПРИ) the transition of the electron corresponds to the difference between the energies of the initial and final states of the electron.

6. A conducting thread, (being) heated by electric current, is able to radiate (ИЗЛУЧАТЬ) light.

7. So-called lamps of incandescence are used (ПРИМЕНЯЮТСЯ) for the conversion of electrical energy into light.

8. A relatively large (БОЛЬШАЯ) part of the electrical energy (being) consumed by a lamp of incandescence is converted into visible radiation.

9. Temperatures, (being) attained in sodium lamps are (show self) relatively low (НИЗКИМИ).

10. The impacts (УДАРЫ) of rapidly moving electrons accomplish the excitation of atoms of sodium.

# LESSON 31

## FURTHER NOTES ON PARTICIPLES

§ 282. The Instrumental Case of Participles as Predicative Modifiers.

In § 242, p. 385, mention was made of the fact that the instrumental case of passive past participles -- like the instrumental case of adjectives -- may be used in connection with verbs meaning "to appear," "to become," "to remain," "to be," etc. Similar use of the instrumental case of other participles will also be encountered occasionally when reading scientific Russian.

| Практически | в | любой | отрасли | развития |
|---|---|---|---|---|
| Practically | in | any | branch | of development |

| самолёта | американская | творческая | мысль |
|---|---|---|---|
| of (the) aeroplane | American | creative | thought |

| оказывалась | ведущей. |
|---|---|
| showed self | leading. |

| Непосредственно | определяемые | на | опыте | степени |
|---|---|---|---|---|
| Directly | being determined | in | experiment | degrees |

| диссоциации | сильных | электролитов | являются | лишь |
|---|---|---|---|---|
| of dissociation | of strong | electrolytes | show self | only |

| кажущимися[1] | в | том | смысле, | что | они | не | отвечают |
|---|---|---|---|---|---|---|---|
| apparent | in | this | sense, | that | they | not | correspond |

| действительным | степеням | распада |
|---|---|---|
| to actual | degrees | of falling apart |

| соответствующих | молекул | на | ионы. |
|---|---|---|---|
| of the corresponding | molecules | into | ions. |

---

[1] See Footnote 1, p. 425 for statement concerning meaning of казаться and forms derived therefrom.

В настоя́щее вре́мя иногда́, пра́вда, дово́льно
In (the) present time sometimes (it is) true, rather

ре́дко, выска́зывается мне́ние, что
rarely, expresses self (the) opinion, that

периоди́ческий зако́н Менделе́ева утра́тил своё
(the) periodic law of Mendeleev has lost his

значе́ние, явля́ется не́сколько устаре́вшим.
significance, shows self somewhat having become obsolete.

Для хара́ктера опти́ческого спе́ктра
For (the) character of (the) optical spectrum

реша́ющим представля́ется положе́ние
as being decisive presents self (is) (the) position

элеме́нта в периоди́ческой систе́ме.
of (the) element in (the) periodic system.

Ано́дные лучи́ мо́жно получи́ть не то́лько
Anode rays (it is) possible to obtain not only

состоя́щими из части́ц га́за, находя́щегося в
consisting of particles of gas finding self in

тру́бке, но и из части́ц сами́х электро́дов.
(the) tube, but also from particles of (the) very electrodes.

Э́та фу́нкция бу́дет дифференци́руемой, и
This function will be differentiable and,

поэ́тому и аналити́ческой в о́бласти G.
consequently, also analytical within (the) region G.

§ 283. Use of Participles as Nouns.

Mention has been made already (§ 245, p. 389) of the use of
passive past participles to indicate not only an action but also the
person, thing, etc., to which the action pertains. Similar use of
other Russian participles is illustrated by the following sentences.

Как      видно    из    предыдущего,    давление    и
As   (is) evident  from  (the) preceding,  (the) pressure  and

объём    данной     массы      газа     при    неизменной
volume   of (a) given  mass    of gas     at    (an) invariable

температуре     являются      обратно    пропорциональными
temperature     show self      inversely   proportional

величинами.
magnitudes.


Алюминий,    в  виде      его    соединений,    является
Aluminum,   in (the) form  of its  compounds,     shows self (is)

важной           составляющей       многих    горных пород.
(an) important    composing (part)    of many    minerals.


А    что,  если   одна из    таких    комет     налетит[1]
But  what,  if     one   of   such     comets    (should) fly

на    землю      и    уничтожит[1]    все    на ней    живущее?
to   (the) earth   and   annihilate      all    on  her    living?


Мы    отсылаем    интересующихся         этим       вопросом к
We    refer       (those) interesting self   with    this  question   to

оригинальной        литературе.
(the) original       literature.


Это    ведёт к   улучшению      культурного      уровня      всех
This   leads  to  improvement    of (the) cultural  level       of all

трудящихся.[2]
(the) toilers.

---

[1] As previously noted, cf. § 232, p. 364, the future tense (here the perfective future) is sometimes used to express a possibility.

[2] It is virtually impossible to translate literally the reflexive active present participle, трудящийся.

| Го́рные | поро́ды, | испо́льзуемые | | в | те́хнике, |
|---------|----------|---------------|---|---|----------|
| Mineral | substances, | being utilized | | in | technology, |

| называ́ются | поле́зными | ископа́емыми.[1] |
|-------------|------------|------------------|
| call self | useful | being dug. |

## § 284. Participles Used with the Dative of Nouns.

In  previous  lessons (cf.  § 255, p. 404;  § 267, p. 423) sentences have been cited in which active past and active present participles take nouns in the dative case as direct objects. The relationship between participles and the dative case is somewhat different in the following sentences, in which double and single asterisks have been used to designate, respectively, a participle and a noun (with modifiers if any) in the dative case and standing in a subordinate relationship to the participle.

| Вода́ | име́ет | соста́в, | отвеча́ющий** | просто́й* |
|-------|--------|----------|---------------|-----------|
| Water | has | (a) composition, | corresponding | to (the) simple |

| фо́рмуле* | $H_2O$, | то́лько | в | газообра́зном | состоя́нии. |
|-----------|---------|---------|---|---------------|-------------|
| formula | $H_2O$, | only | in | (the) gaseous | condition. |

| Электри́ческий | заря́д, | сообща́вшийся** | |
|----------------|---------|-----------------|---|
| (An) electrical | charge, | having imparted | self |

| металли́ческому* | те́лу, | чрезвыча́йно | бы́стро |
|------------------|--------|--------------|---------|
| to (a) metallic | body, | extremely | rapidly |

| распространя́ется | по | всей | пове́рхности |
|-------------------|----|------|--------------|
| spreads self | over | (the) whole | surface |

| те́ла. |
|--------|
| of (the) body. |

---

[1] The expression  поле́зный ископа́емый  is perhaps best regarded as an idiom meaning "exploitable mineral."

Мы    видим,  что,   как   янтарь, так   и   другие  смолы,
We    see     that   both  amber  as    also other  resins,

подвергавшиеся**           предварительному*        натиранию*,
having  submitted self     to preliminary           rubbing

обладают  свойством      притягивать   лёгкие  предметы.
possess   (the) property  to attract    light   objects.

Отдел        науки,        посвящённый** рассмотрению*
(The) branch  of science,   dedicated     to (the) consideration

превращений   веществ,       называется   химией.
of changes    of substances  calls self    chemistry.

## § 285. Participles Used with Subordinate Infinitives.

In a previous lesson (cf. § 163, p. 250) attention was directed
to the use of infinitives subordinate to various verbs meaning
"to be able," "to enable," "to wish," "to strive," "to hinder,"
"to start," etc. The participles of such verbs may also be used
with subordinate infinitives as exemplified by the following
sentences. The participles under consideration are designated by
double asterisks and their subordinate infinitives by single
asterisks.

Силу,     могущую**  привести* тело    в      движение
(A) force, being able to bring  (a) body into   motion

или  изменить* скорость      его    движения,  называют
or   to change (the) velocity of its motion     they name

механической   силой.
mechanical     force.

На   поверхности  раздела       жидкость - газ действуют
At   (the) surface of separation liquid ── gas  act

силы,   стремящиеся         уменьшить эту  поверхность.
forces  exerting self (striving) to decrease that surface.

К сожале́нию, до настоя́щего вре́мени ещё нет
To regret, till (the) present time still not

ско́лько-нибудь разрабо́танной нау́чной тео́рии,
any worked out scientific theory

позволя́ющей** объедини́ть* результа́ты отде́льных
enabling to correlate (the) results of separate

иссле́дований и вы́вести о́бщие пра́вила
investigations and to derive general rules

раствори́мости.
of solubility.

Ме́жду части́цами жи́дких и твёрдых тел
Between (the) particles of liquid and solid bodies

существу́ют си́лы взаи́много притяже́ния и́ли
exist forces of mutual attraction or

сцепле́ния, препя́тствующие**[1] части́цам свобо́дно
cohesion hindering (the) particles freely

разбега́ться* во все сто́роны.
to fly self apart to all sides.

## § 286. Compound Words Derived from Participles.

As pointed out previously, Russian participles are closely akin to adjectives both as to their use in constructing sentences and as to form. It is, therefore, not surprising that Russian participles often enter into the formation of compound words which closely resemble adjectives but nevertheless retain something of their verbal character. In the following sentences compound words formed from participles are identified by asterisks.

---

[1] The ending -ие indicates that the participle препя́тствующие modifies the noun си́лы. The noun части́цам is in the dative plural case, cf. § 114, p. 166.

Ион          магния                характеризуется
(The)   ion     of  magnesium    characterizes  self

относительной      слабостью         комплексообразующей*
by (the) relative     weakness       of complex-forming

способности.
ability.


Продукты      сочетания     солей      металлов    с
Products      of coupling   of salts    of metals    with

азотосодержащими*      компонентами      образуют
nitrogen-containing      components      form

важную      группу  комплексных    соединений.
(an) important  group    of complex     compounds.


К    аналогичны.   результатам    привели    наблюдения
To   analogous     results        led      observations

над    ураном,  который   на    основе    магнитных
on     uranium   which    on   (the) basis   of magnetic

измерений    не   является     сверхпроводящим*   до
measurements  not  shows self     superconducting    to

$T = 0.98°$ К.
$T = 0.98°$K.


По       своей способности   изменяться   на воздухе,
According to own    ability     to change self  at   air,

жидкие    растительные    масла    разделяются   на
liquid     vegetable       oils     divide self   into

высыхающие,  полувысыхающие*  и   невысыхающие.*
drying,      semi-drying      and  non-drying.

Звёзды — это громадные, чрезвычайно отдалённые,
Stars — these (are) enormous, extremely distant,

самосветящиеся* солнца.
self-luminous suns.

Образующийся осадок представляет собой
(The) forming self precipitate presents by self (is)

мелкораздроблённую* металлическую ртуть.
finely divided metallic mercury.

Эквивалентность различных видов энергии
(The) equivalence of various forms of energy

выражается вышеупомянутым* законом
expresses self by (the) above mentioned law

сохранения энергии.
of conservation of energy.

Беккерель (1896) обнаружил, что урановая смоляная
Becquerel (1896) observed, that uranium tar-like

руда действует на фотографическую пластинку,
ore acts on (a) photographic plate

защищённую обычными светонепроницаемыми*
protected by ordinary light-impenetrable

материалами.
materials.

| Такие | тела, | которые | при | быстром | движении | в | воздухе |
|---|---|---|---|---|---|---|---|
| Such | bodies, | which | on | rapid | movement | in | air |

| создают | мало | завихрений, | называются |
|---|---|---|---|
| create | little | of turbulence(s) | call self |

| удобообтекаемыми.* [1] |
|---|
| stream-lined. |

## § 287. Adverbs Formed from Present Active Participles.

It is possible to form adverbs from active present participles by affixing the ending "-е" to their stems. Adverbs so formed, e.g., "vanishingly" are encountered in Russian only rarely, in contrast to frequent occurrence of English adverbs derived by affixing "-ingly" to English verb stems.

| Трудности | эти | обусловлены | прежде | всего |
|---|---|---|---|---|
| Difficulties | these | (are) caused | before | all |

| исчезающе | малой | концентрацией | пенициллина |
|---|---|---|---|
| by (the) vanishingly | small | concentration | of penicillin |

| в | жидкости. |
|---|---|
| in | (the) liquid. |

| Упомянем | в | связи | с | этим, | что |
|---|---|---|---|---|---|
| Let us recall | in | connection | with | this, | that by |

| Н. С. Курнаковым[2] | и | его | учениками | дана |
|---|---|---|---|---|
| N. S. Kurnakov | and | his | students | (was) given |

| исчерпывающе | полная | теория | кристаллизации | солей. |
|---|---|---|---|---|
| an exhaustingly | complete | theory | of crystallization | of salts. |

---

[1] The word удобообтекаемый is composed of , удобо-, the combining form of удобный, "convenient," "favorable" and обтекаемый the passive present participle from the infinitive обтекать "to be flowing around," cf. Footnote 2, p. 536.

[2] Here Курнаковым is the instrumental singular case of the family name Курнаков, whose declensions follow that of Молотов as discussed in § 362, p. 586.

| Свои́ | воззре́ния | он | блестя́ще[1] | подтверди́л |
|-------|-----------|-----|------------|-----------|
| His | views | he | brilliantly | confirmed |

| эксперимента́льно. |
|-------------------|
| experimentally. |

| Исто́рия | наро́дов, | нау́ки, | иску́сства |
|----------|-----------|---------|-----------|
| (The) history | of nations, | of science, | of  art |

| интере́сна, | подча́с | захва́тывающе | интере́сна! |
|-------------|---------|---------------|-------------|
| (is) interesting, | sometimes | grippingly | interesting! |

§ 288.  Sentences  Involving  the  Predicative  Forms  of  Passive
Present Participles.

In  § 241, p. 381  it was  pointed  out  that  passive  past
participles  have  predicative  forms  which,  like  other  Russian
participial  forms,  resemble  adjectives  as  to  endings  but
nevertheless  indicate  action  and  consequently  are  verbal  in
character.  The  corresponding  predicative  forms  of  passive
present participles[2]  are  encountered  only  rarely  when  reading
scientific Russian.

| Су́мма | сте́пенного | ря́да | диференци́руема | в |
|--------|-----------|-------|-----------------|---|
| (The) sum | of (a) power | series | (is) differentiable | in |

| ка́ждой то́чке, | лежа́щей | внутри́ | кру́га | сходи́мости. |
|----------------|----------|---------|--------|-------------|
| each      point | lying | within | (the) circle | of convergence. |

| Да́нные | Гри́нберга | мо́гут | бы́ть | объясня́емы | с |
|---------|-----------|--------|-------|-------------|---|
| (The) data | of Grünberg | may | be | explained | from |

| то́чки | зре́ния | вышеизло́женной | | тео́рии |
|--------|---------|-----------------|---|--------|
| (the) point | of view | of (the) above | presented | theory |

| Михаэ́лиса. |
|------------|
| of Michaelis. |

[1] Translation of  блестя́ще  as "brilliantly"  fails to emphasize the relationship
of  блестя́ще  to the infinitive  блесте́ть  "to be glittering," "to be sparkling."
[2] Active  present  participles  do  not  have  predicative  forms,  but  adjectives
formed from them do, as shown by the following example.

| Бе́лое | о́лово | сверхпроводя́ще, | а | се́рое | нет. |
|--------|-------|-----------------|---|-------|------|
| White | tin | (is) superconducting, | but | gray | (is) not. |

| Для | дистиллировки | могут | быть | применяемы |
|-----|---------------|-------|------|------------|
| For | distillation | are able | to be | being applied (to be |

| | многие | различные | приборы. | | |
|---|--------|-----------|----------|---|---|
| applied) | many | different | devices. | | |


| Согласно | квантовой | теории, | энергия | может | быть |
|----------|-----------|---------|---------|-------|------|
| According to | (the) quantum | theory, | energy | is able | to be |

| отдаваема | и | принимаема | только | целыми | квантами. |
|-----------|---|------------|--------|--------|-----------|
| emitted | and | absorbed | only | in whole | quanta. |


§ 289. **Reading Exercise.**

Источники света
(Часть вторая)

Из предыдущего[1] ясно, что существует большое сходство между различными источниками света. С теоретической точки зрения, разнородность различных способов излучения видимой лучистой энергии является лишь кажущейся.[2] Практическое-же создание удобного и экономического освещения представляет собой сложную техническую проблему.

На настоящей высокоразвитой[3] стадии техники многие различные способы и приборы применяются или могут быть применяемы[4] в качестве источников света. В сегодняшней практике освещение при помощи электричества является преобладающим.[2] До изобретения электрического освещения свет, отдаваемый факелами, свечами и пламенем[5] горящих веществ вообще, играл исключительно важную роль в осветительном деле. Интенсивность света, получаемого с помощью обыкновенного пламени, не удовлетворяет многим требованиям.[6] Бывает даже так называемое несветящееся[7] пламя[5] т.е. отдающее очень малое количество света. Правда, светоотдающая способность слабосветящегося пламени[8] может быть улучшена. Такое улучшение имеет место, например, при

введении в слабосветящееся пламя некоторых летучих металлических солей в мелкораздроблённом[10] состоянии. Яркость пламени многих горящих веществ также улучшается, если горение происходит в кислороде, а не в азотосодержащем[10] воздухе. Бывают другие способы, позволяющие улучшать яркость пламени. Однако, даже при наилучших[11] условиях, пламя характеризуется сравнительно низкой степенью превращения химической энергии в свет, так как наибольшая[12] часть химической энергии горючего[13] излучается в виде теплоты.

Возникает вопрос, является ли[14] теплоотдающий процесс горения необходимым для превращения химической энергии в свет. При большинстве химических реакций, протекающих без значительного разогревания, излучение света или совсем не имеет места, или количество излучаемого света является исчезающе[15] малым.

Излучение света при обыкновенных температурах за счёт химической энергии - хемилюминесценция - имеет место при медленном окислении фосфора, а также при некоторых других химических и биохимических процессах, которыми обусловлено[16] в частности свечение светляков, гнилушек и т. д.[17] Такие процессы с химической точки зрения представляют собой медленнопротекающие реакции, при которых превращение химической энергии в свет происходит с небольшой скоростью. Следовательно, интенсивность света, соответствующая небольшой реакционной скорости, всегда мала. Из вышесказанного[1] ясно, что превращение химической энергии в свет - сложная проблема.

## Notes

1. See § 283, p. 448.

2. See § 282, p. 447.

3. высокоразвитой from высокий "high" and развитый "developed" the passive past participle derived from the infinitive развить of the verb развывать -- развить "to develop," cf. § 286, p. 452.

4. See § 288, p. 456, third Russian sentence.

5. пла́менем is the instrumental singular of the irregularly declined neuter noun пла́мя "flame." In this reading exercise, as is evident from the context, the singular of пла́мя is used several times as a generic term for flames in general.

6. мно́гим тре́бованиям are in the dative after удовлетворя́ет, cf. § 114, p. 166.

7. несветя́щееся "non-luminous" is derived from светя́щийся, the reflexive of the present active participle from свети́ть, cf. § 114, p. 166.

8. пла́мени is here the genitive singular of the irregularly declined neuter noun пла́мя "flame," cf. § 358, p. 575.

9. слабосветя́щегося from сла́бо "weakly" and светя́щийся, discussed in Note 7 above.

10. See § 286, p. 452.

11. при наилу́чших усло́виях "with the best conditions." The superlative of adjectives is discussed in Lesson 37.

12. наибо́льшая часть "the greatest part."

13. горю́чего "of the burning (substance)." For previous discussion of the use of an adjective as a noun see Note 8, p. 86.

14. явля́ется ли -- необходи́мым "whether shows self (is) -- necessary." The particle ли in Russian is used in posing questions whose wording does not involve some other word having interrogative significance, such as the interrogative pronouns of § 152, p. 232; § 387, p. 644.

15. See § 287, p. 455, first Russian sentence.

16. кото́рым обусло́влено в ча́стности свече́ние, "by which (is) caused in particular (the) glowing."

17. и т. д. is equivalent to "etc." in English. More specifically, и т.д. is the abbreviation for и так да́лее "and so further," "and so on."

§ 290.  Translation Exercise.

1. From the preceding it is clear, that many different devices
   may be used as (in the quality of) sources of light.
2. At  the  present  highly  developed  state  of technology,
   illumination with  the  aid of electricity  shows  self is
   dominating.
3. A  so-called  non-luminous ( несветящееся ) flame does not
   satisfy  the  requirements of lumination.
4. The  light-giving  ability of a  flame often ( часто ) improves
   self, if  the  combustion occurs in oxygen but not in nitrogen
   containing air.
5. The  introduction  of  certain volatile  metal  salts  into  a
   flame improves its ( его ) brightness.
6. With ( При ) the  majority of chemical reactions,  the  quantity
   of energy, (being) converted ( превращаемой ) into  light  is
   (shows self) vanishingly small.
7. The  question  arises,  whether  is  possible ( можно ли )
   the  conversion  of  chemical  energy  into  light  without
   significant heating.
8. During  the  slow  oxidation of phosphorus  conversion of
   chemical energy into light proceeds at  a  slow (not big) rate.
9. The  glowing  of  fire  flies  takes  place ( место ) without
   significant heating.
10. From  the  above said it is  clear, that  creation  of  a
    convenient and economical source  of  light  is  a  complex
    problem.

## LESSON 32

## FORMATION AND USE OF GERUNDS

§ 291. General Remarks Concerning Gerunds.

Russian gerunds[1] are sometimes described as adverbial verb forms. In particular, Russian present and past gerunds are verb forms used respectively to indicate action accompanying or preceding the action expressed by the verb to which the gerund is subordinate.

Translation of Russian phrases involving gerunds into English sometimes requires the use of a phrase or clause introduced by a word such as "while," "after," "during" or the like. These English connecting words usually have no explicit counterparts in the Russian sentence but are implied by the Russian gerund. This point will become clearer on considering various typical sentences.

Gerunds, like adverbs, are not declined.

§ 292. Time Significance of Present and Past Gerunds.

As noted above, Russian gerunds indicate an action accompanying or preceding the action of some other verb to which the gerund may be regarded as subordinate. Present gerunds are used to indicate action accompanying, i.e., occurring simultaneously, with the action of the verb to which the gerund is subordinate. Thus a present gerund, such as, фотографируя "while photographing," may be used to designate an action accompanying some other action taking place either in past, present or future time. Past gerunds, e.g., фотографировав "having photographed," are used in similar fashion to indicate an action preceding that of the verb to which

[1] This use of the term, gerund, is in accord with the usual practice among English-speaking grammarians when referring to the Russian verb forms under consideration in this lesson. Applied to English verb forms, the term gerund denotes verbal nouns, e.g., "singing," as in the sentence, "Her singing was enthusiastically applauded." Such verb forms may also be used adverbially, e.g., "She walked singing down the street." Russian gerunds are used exclusively as adverbs, never as nouns.

the gerund is subordinate. Less commonly, past gerunds are
sometimes used in place of the present gerund to designate
action which occurred in the past but which accompanied that of
the verb to which the gerund is subordinate.

It will be observed that there is a close parallelism between
the time significance of past and present gerunds on the one
hand and of past and present participles on the other.

§ 293. Formation of Present Gerunds from Imperfective
Infinitives.

Quite logically, present gerunds are derived only from
imperfective infinitives. The regular formation of gerunds is
very simple. It involves affixing one of the endings -а or -я
or, rarely, -учи to a verb stem obtained by removing -ут, -ют,
-ат or -ят from the third person plural of the present tense.
The ending -я is always used if the verb stem terminates in a
vowel. More complex rules, whose presentation does not appear
profitable, are involved in selection of the present gerund ending
to be used with verb stems not terminating with a vowel.

The following examples of the formation[1] of present gerunds
are typical.

### Regular Formation of Present Gerunds

| Imperfective Infinitives | Class | Present Tense Third Person Plural | Present Gerunds |
|---|---|---|---|
| де́лать | Reg. A | де́лают | де́лая |
| фотографи́ровать | Irr. A-1 | фотографи́руют | фотографи́руя |
| колеба́ть | Irr. C-1 | коле́блют | коле́бля |
| криви́ть | Irr. C-2 | кривя́т | кривя́ |
| дви́гать | Irr. D-1 | дви́жут | дви́жа |
| брать | Irr. E-1 | беру́т | беря́ |
| бере́чь | Irr. G-1 | берегу́т | |
| везти́ | Irr. H-1 | везу́т | везя́ |
| нести́ | Irr. H-2 | несу́т | неся́ |
| итти́ | Irr. H-10 | иду́т | идя́, и́дучи |
| есть | Irr. I-1 | едя́т | едя́ |

---

[1] Various individual imperfective infinitives, as a matter of usage, do not form
present gerunds.

Irregular formation of present gerunds, as in the following examples, is rarely encountered.

Irregular Formation of Present Gerunds

| Imperfective Infinitive | Class | Present Tense Third Person Plural | Present Gerunds |
|---|---|---|---|
| давáть | Irr. B | даю́т | давáя |
| быть | | суть | бу́дучи |

§ 294. Formation of Past Gerunds from Imperfective and Perfective Infinitives.

Past gerunds by their very nature tend to refer to completed action. For this reason past gerunds derived from imperfective infinitives are much less frequently used than those derived from perfective infinitives. Many past gerunds from imperfective infinitives are, in fact, used so rarely that they can scarcely be said to exist except in theory. For completeness the table given below contains several such imperfective past gerunds rarely, if ever, used.

The formation[1] of past gerunds for almost all verbs involves removing -Tь from the infinitive and then adding an ending, -B or -BШИ. With many infinitives, either ending may be used thus resulting in two alternative past gerund forms having identical significance.

Some of the past gerunds listed on the next two pages are used only rarely.

---

[1] Various individual infinitives, as a matter of usage, do not form past gerunds.

## Regular Formation of Past Gerunds

|        | Infinitives       | Class     | Past Gerunds                        |
|--------|-------------------|-----------|-------------------------------------|
| Imp.   | де́лать            | Reg. A    | де́лав,   де́лавши                   |
| Perf.  | сде́лать           |           | сде́лав,  сде́лавши                  |
| Imp.   | фотографи́ровать   | Irr. A-1  | фотографи́ровав                     |
|        |                   |           | фотографи́ровавши                   |
| Perf.  | сфотографи́ровать  |           | сфотографи́ровав                    |
|        |                   |           | сфотографи́ровавши                  |
| Imp.   | дава́ть            | Irr. B    | дава́в                              |
| Perf.  | дать              | Irr. I-3  | дав,   да́вши                       |
| Imp.   | криви́ть           | Irr. C-1  | криви́в,   криви́вши                 |
| Perf.  | покриви́ть         |           | покриви́в, покриви́вши               |
| Imp.   | писа́ть            | Irr. D-1  | писа́в,  писа́вши                    |
| Perf.  | написа́ть          |           | написа́в,  написа́вши                |
| Imp.   | брать             | Irr. E-1  | брав,  бра́вши                      |
| Perf.  | взять             | Irr. F-7  | взяв,  взя́вши                      |
| Imp.   | быть              | Irr. I-2  | быв,  бы́вши                        |

Infinitives  not  ending  in  a  vowel  plus  -ть  require  special
consideration.  The  past  gerund[1]  from  such  infinitives  is  usually
closely  related  to  the  past  tense,  as  is  shown  by  examples  given
below.

## Irregular Formation of Past Gerunds

|        | Infinitives | Class    | Past Tense Masculine Singular | Past Gerunds |
|--------|-------------|----------|-------------------------------|--------------|
| Imp.   | бере́чь      | Irr. G-1 | берёг                         | берёгши      |
| Perf.  | побере́чь    |          | поберёг                       | поберёгши    |

[1]  As a general rule,  the infinitives  grouped together  here  have  only  a  single past
gerund form.

|  | Infinitives | Class | Past Tense Masculine Singular | Past Gerunds |
|---|---|---|---|---|
| Imp. | влечь | Irr. G-3 | влёк | влёкши |
| Perf. | повле́чь | | повлёк | повлёкши |
| Imp. | везти́ | Irr. H-1 | вёз | вёзши |
| Perf. | повезти́ | | повёз | повёзши |
| Imp. | нести́ | Irr. H-2 | нёс | нёсши |
| Perf. | понести́ | | понёс | понёсши |
| Imp. | итти́ | Irr. H-10 | шёл | ше́дши |
| Imp. | есть | Irr. I-1 | ел | е́вши |

§ 295. Sentences Illustrating Simple Use of Present Gerunds.

As already noted, present gerunds are used to indicate action accompanying, i.e., occurring simultaneously, with the action of the verb to which the gerund is subordinate.

| Внима́тельно | наблюда́я | за | разли́чными | физи́ческими |
|---|---|---|---|---|
| Attentively | observing | after | various | physical |

| тела́ми, | мы | без | осо́бого | труда́ | замеча́ем, | что |
|---|---|---|---|---|---|---|
| bodies, | we | without | particular | difficulty | notice, | that |

| с | э́тими | тела́ми | происхо́дят | ра́зные | измене́ния. |
|---|---|---|---|---|---|
| with | these | bodies | occur | various | changes. |

| Вот, | со́бственно | говоря́, | все | необходи́мые |
|---|---|---|---|---|
| There, | strictly | speaking, (are) | all | (the) necessary |

| соотноше́ния. |
|---|
| relationships. |

| Начина́я | с | 1939 г., | ря́дом | иссле́дователей |
|---|---|---|---|---|
| Beginning | with | 1939, | by a series | of investigators |

| (Фарнсво́рстом, | Кубе́цким | Зворы́киным | и | др.)[1] | бы́ли |
|---|---|---|---|---|---|
| (Farnsworth, | Kubetskii, | Zworikin | and others) were |

[1] The abbreviation др. is used here to replace други́ми, the instrumental plural of друго́й "other," "another."

сконструи́рованы электро́нные умно́жители разли́чных
constructed electron multipliers of different

систе́м.
systems.

Если се́тка электро́нной ла́мпы заряжёна
If (the) grid of (a) electron lamp (is) charged

положи́тельно, то не́которые увлека́емые е́ю
positively, then certain being attracted by her

электро́ны, па́дая на се́тку, ча́стью[1] нейтрализу́ют
electrons, falling on (the) grid, in part neutralize

её положи́тельный заря́д.
her positive charge.

§ 296. Sentences Illustrating Simple Use of Past Gerunds.

The Russian past gerund is used in general to indicate an
action preceding that of the verb to which the gerund is
subordinate, cf. § 292, p. 462.

Попа́в на вла́жную зе́млю, спо́ры ско́ро
After falling on moist earth, spores rapidly

прораста́ют.
germinate.

Переше́дши в кристалли́ческое состоя́ние,
Having passed over into (the) crystalline condition,

каучу́к даёт рентгеногра́мму, как пока́зано на
rubber gives an X-ray diagram, as (is) shown in

рис. 23.
Fig. 23.

---

[1] ча́стью is the instrumental singular case of часть "part." For discussion of
adverbial use of the instrumental, cf. § 98, p. 141.

Разделив,        находим, что   73   в 3892   содержится   53
Having divided, we find      that   73   in 3892   contains self   53

раза,   причем   23   остаётся.[1]
times,   whereby   23   remains.

Метод           получения      алюминия     при    помощи
(The) method    of preparation   of aluminum   with   (the) aid

восстановления   металлическим   натрием, просуществовав
of reduction       by metallic        sodium,   having existed

несколько   лет,   уступил   место   электролитическому
several      years, yielded    place    to (the) electrolytic

способу.
process.


§ 297. Sentences Illustrating Gerunds Governing a Direct Object.

As discussed in preceding paragraphs, Russian gerunds designate an action accompanying or preceding some other action. As might be expected, the gerunds of transitive verbs are generally used with a direct object, as illustrated by the following example sentences.


Group I. Direct Object in Accusative Case

Double asterisks designate the gerunds under consideration and single asterisks their direct objects (and modifiers thereof, if any).

Описывая**       основной*      опыт*        индуктирования
While describing  (the) basic    experiment   of induction

электрического              тока,     мы      говорили    о
of (the) electric            current,   we      spoke        of

"пересечении"[2]            магнитных   линий.
(the) "cutting"             of magnetic  lines.


[1] See Footnote 1, p. 145.
[2] Quotation marks are sometimes used in scientific Russian to indicate that a word is being used in an exceptional or figurative way

Исследуя**     разные*    явления,*    происходящие*   в
On investigating   various    phenomena     occurring        in

природе,    физика   находит   связь    между    явленияим,
nature,      physics    finds     connection   between phenomena

объясняет,    почему   и    как   происходят    различные
explains,       why      and   how    occurs       different

явления    и    учит,    как   можно        использовать
phenomena   and   teaches   how   (it is) possible   to utilize

полученные     знания     для   различных    практических
(the) obtained   knowledge s   for   different        practical

целей.
purposes.

Приведённая    ниже    таблица[1]   показывает    какие
(The) brought     below    table       shows        what

громадные     скорости     приобретает     электрон,
enormous      velocities     attains        (an) electron

пробежав**    (без   потери энергии   на соударениях)
having traversed   (without loss   of energy   on collisions)

сравнительно    небольшие*[2]   разности*    потенциалов.
relatively       not large       differences    of potentials.

В. В. Петров,       открыв**         явление*
V. V. Petrov,       having discovered    (the) phenomenon

вольтовой    дуги,    тут   же    перешёл    к   изучению
of (the) voltaic   arc,     right   away   went over   to   (a) study

---

[1] Приведённая   ниже   таблица   might be more smoothly translated as, "The table given below."

[2] The use of the adjective небольшой, literally, "not large," to mean "small" is very common.

| | | | | | | |
|---|---|---|---|---|---|---|
| того́, | как | веду́т | себя́ | и | как "горя́т"[1] | в |
| of this, | how | conduct | self (behaves) | and | how "burn" | in |

| | | | | | |
|---|---|---|---|---|---|
| во́льтовой | дуге́ | разли́чные | вещества́ | (о́лово, | серебро́, |
| (the) voltaic | arc | various | substances | (tin, | silver, |

| | | | |
|---|---|---|---|
| зо́лото, | спирт, | масла́ | и т. д.) |
| gold, | alcohol, | oils, | etc.). |

| | | | | | |
|---|---|---|---|---|---|
| Ввиду́ | э́того, | при́нято | различа́ть | две[2] | о́бласти |
| In view | of this | (it is) accepted | to distinguish | two | fields |

| | | | | | | |
|---|---|---|---|---|---|---|
| хи́мии, | называ́я** | одну́* | из | них | органи́ческой, | а |
| of chemistry, | naming | one | of | them | organic | and |

| | |
|---|---|
| другу́ю* | неоргани́ческой. |
| (the) other | inorganic. |

| | | | | |
|---|---|---|---|---|
| Ле́бедев | доказа́л | существова́ние | давле́ния | све́та |
| Lebedev | proved | (the) existence | of pressure | of light |

| | | | | | |
|---|---|---|---|---|---|
| на | моле́кулы | га́за, | положи́в*** | тем[3] | твёрдую* |
| on | molecules | of gas, | having placed | by this | (a) solid |

| | | | | |
|---|---|---|---|---|
| осно́ву* под | тео́рию | коме́тных | хвосто́в, | разви́тую |
| basis under | (the) theory | of comet | tails, | developed |

| | |
|---|---|
| астрофи́зиком | Бреди́хиным. |
| by (the) astrophysicist | Bredikhin. |

---

[1] See Footnote 1, p. 467.

[2] In this sentence две is the feminine accusative form of the numeral два and о́бласти is in the genitive singular case after две in accord with a rule discussed in § 371, p. 605. Note that одну́ and другу́ю are in the feminine accusative singular case, while органи́ческой and неоргани́ческой are in the feminine instrumental singular case. For similar use of the accusative and instrumental cases in a simple sentence involving называ́ть, cf. § 99, p. 143. Both одну́ and другу́ю as well as органи́ческой and неоргани́ческой are feminine in gender because they refer to the feminine noun о́бласти (whose nominative singular form is о́бласть).

[3] Here тем is the neuter instrumental singular case of the demonstrative тот, cf. § 142, p. 213.

## Group II.  Direct Object Not in Accusative Case

In discussing active participles, it was pointed out that any one of several factors may cause the direct object of such participles to be in some case other than the accusative, cf. § 255, p. 404; § 267, p. 423. The same factors are operative in causing gerunds to govern cases other than the accusative, as is shown by the following examples.

Double asterisks designate the gerunds under consideration and single asterisks their direct objects (and modifiers thereof, if any).

| Пренебрегая** | изменением* | массы | движущегося |
|---|---|---|---|
| Neglecting | (the) change | of mass | of (the) moving self |

| тела | со | скоростью, | легко | интегрировать |
|---|---|---|---|---|
| body | with | velocity, | (it is) easy | to integrate |

| второе | уравнение. |
|---|---|
| (the) second | equation. |

| Пузырьки[1] | окиси[2] | углерода, | прорываясь[3] |
|---|---|---|---|
| Little bubbles | of monoxide | of carbon, | breaking out self |

| через | металл | и | шлак, | производят | их |
|---|---|---|---|---|---|
| through | (the) metal | and | slag, | effect | their |

| механическое | перемешивание, | способствуя** |
|---|---|---|
| mechanical | mixing, | promoting |

| взаимодействию* | этих | фаз. |
|---|---|---|
| interaction | of these | phases. |

[1] Пузырьки is the irregularly formed nominative plural case of пузырёк "little bubble." Note that пузырёк is the dimunitive of пузырь, (masc.) "bubble," cf. § 357, p. 573.

[2] In general окись (genitive singular окиси) refers to a higher oxidation state, while закись refers to a lower oxide. Thus we have окись железа "ferric oxide" and закись железа "ferrous oxide." The nomenclature of the oxides of carbon is exceptional with окись углерода meaning "carbon monoxide" and "carbon dioxide" being designated by углекислый газ.

[3] Reflexive gerunds, of which прорываясь is an example, are discussed in the following § 298, p. 471.

| Превращѐние | химѝческих | элемѐнтов | при |
|---|---|---|---|
| (The) conversion | of chemical | elements | during |

| радиоактѝвных | процѐссах, | ужѐ | давно́ | |
|---|---|---|---|---|
| radioactive | processes, | already | long | ago |

| достѝгнув** | большо́го* | теоретѝческого* | значѐния;* |
|---|---|---|---|
| having achieved | great | theoretical | significance, |

| бы́ло | впервы̀е | употреблено́ | в | технѝческом | масшта́бе |
|---|---|---|---|---|---|
| was | first | applied | on | (a) technical | scale |

| для | производства́ | плуто́ния. |
|---|---|---|
| for | production | of plutonium. |


| В | геометрѝческой | о́птике | рассма́тривают |
|---|---|---|---|
| In | geometric | optics | they consider |

| распространѐние | световы́х | лучѐй, | не | дѐлая** никакѝх* |
|---|---|---|---|---|
| (the) propagation | of light | rays, | [not] | making none |

| предложѐний* | об | их | приро́де. |
|---|---|---|---|
| hypotheses | concerning | their | nature. |

## § 298. Sentences Illustrating Simple Use of Reflexive Gerunds.

Gerunds, like other Russian verb forms (excepting participles), are rendered reflexive by attaching -СЯ (to gerunds terminating in a consonant) and -СЬ (to gerunds terminating in a vowel).

The use of reflexive gerunds is in line with the use of other reflexive verb forms in Russian. As shown by the following example sentences, Russian reflexive gerunds usually do not require use of English reflexive pronouns for translation.

| Тѐхника, | развива́ясь | и | совершѐнствуясь, |
|---|---|---|---|
| Technology, | developing self | and | perfecting self, |

| ока́зывает | по́мощь | развѝтию | фѝзики. |
|---|---|---|---|
| renders | aid | to (the) development | of physics. |

В    химическом    отношении    катализатор    остаётся
In    chemical        relation      (a) catalyst      remains

неизменным,    но он может    участвовать    в промежуточных
unchanged,      but he may     participate      in intermediate

процессах,    выделяясь    в    свободном    виде   из
processes,     evolving self    in    free       form   from

промежуточных    продуктов    лишь   в    конце
intermediate        products     only    at   (the)   end

реакции.
of (the) reaction.


Если исчезает    один   вид   энергии,    превращаясь
If    vanishes     one   form   of energy,    while converting self

в     другой,      то    количество    энергии    не
into    another (form),   then   (the) quantity   of energy    not

изменяется.
changes self.


Следовательно,    магниты    взаимодействуют,      даже
Consequently,      magnets     interact,           even

находясь        на    расстоянии.
finding self (being)   at   (a) distance.


Натолкнувшись       на     неодолимую       оборону
Having struck self   against   (the) unsurmountable   defense

советских     войск    под    Москвой,    немцы[1]
of (the) Soviet   troops   near   Moscow,    (the) Germans

подверглись    непрерывным      атакам    русских
submitted self   to (the) uninterrupted   attacks   of (the) Russian

партизан.
partisans.


---

[1] Here   немцы   is the irregular nominative plural of the noun   немец, "German," cf. § 357, p. 573.

§ 299.  Use  of  the  Instrumental  Case  of  Nouns,  etc.,  with
Reflexive Gerunds.

Earlier lessons have discussed the use of the instrumental
case of nouns, pronouns, and adjectives with reflexive verb forms
both  in  simple  sentences  (§§  92-94,  pp.  132-137)  and  in
more  complex  sentences  containing  participles  (§ 257, p. 409;
§ 269, p. 427).  As  the  following  example  sentences  show,
reflexive  gerunds  (double  asterisks)  are  similarly  used  in
conjunction with the instrumental case (single asterisks).

Пользуясь** приёмами,* известными* из курса геометрии,
Using        methods      known       from course of geometry,

можно,              измерив          линейные     размеры
(it is) possible,  having measured  linear       dimensions

тел        правильной    формы,   найти  их    объёмы.
of bodies  of regular     form,   to find their volumes.

Благородные¹   газы,    гелий,    неон,   аргон,   криптон,
The noble      gases,   helium,   neon,   argon,   krypton,

ксенон,  радон,  отличаясь**            своей*  химической*
xenon,   radon,  distinguishing self    by own  chemical

инертностью,* образуют  особенную  группу химических
inertness,    form      (a) special group  of chemical

элементов.
elements.

Спектральный  анализ  и   возможность   быстро  и
Spectrum        analysis and (the) possibility quickly and

точно      анализировать  металлы,  сплавы  и   другие
precisely  to analyze      metals,   alloys  and other

---

¹ The term  благородные газы  "noble gases" is formed by analogy with the
term  благородные металлы "noble metals" applied to gold and certain other metals
characterized by relatively great resistance to the attack of acids.

| вещества, | являясь** | ценным* |
|---|---|---|
| substances, | showing self (being) | (a) valuable |

| вспомогательным* | средством* | в | металлургии, |
|---|---|---|---|
| auxiliary | means | in | metallurgy, |

| базируются | на | исследованиях | Бунзена | и | Кирхгофа. |
|---|---|---|---|---|---|
| base self | on | investigations | of Bunsen | and | of Kirchhoff. |

| В | XIX | веке | железная дорога[1] | приобрела |
|---|---|---|---|---|
| In | (the) 19th | century | (the) railroad | attained |

| огромную | роль | в | народном | хозяйстве | нашей |
|---|---|---|---|---|---|
| (an) enormous | role | in | (the) national | economy | of our |

| страны, | сделавшись** | особенно | важным* |
|---|---|---|---|
| country, | having made self | (an) unusually | important |

| транспортным* | средством. |
|---|---|
| transport | means. |

## § 300. Gerunds Used with Subordinate Infinitives.

Previous discussion has pointed out that Russian infinitives may be used subordinate to other verbs. See § 163, p. 250 for relatively simple sentences and § 285, p. 451 for infinitives used subordinate to participles. As the following sentences show, infinitives (single asterisk) may also be subordinate to gerunds (double asterisk).

| Страстно | желая** | организовать* | реализацию |
|---|---|---|---|
| Passionately | wishing | to organize | (the) realization |

| электрического | освещения | в России, | П. Н. Яблочков |
|---|---|---|---|
| of electrical | illumination | in Russia, | P. N. Yablochkov |

| согласился | на | эту | чрезмерно | высокую | цену. |
|---|---|---|---|---|---|
| agreed self | to | that | extremely | high | price. |

[1] железная дорога, literally, "iron way" is the Russian term corresponding to "railroad." Note the similarity to the German "Eisenbahn."

Пар     при    вы́ходе    из     котла́    облада́ет
(The) steam   on    departure   from   (the) boiler   possesses

спосо́бностью[1]     расширя́ться,      стремя́сь**
(the) ability       to expand self,      while exerting self

заня́ть*   как   мо́жно   бо́льшее   простра́нство.
to occupy   the   largest    possible    space.


Опи́санный    о́пыт     мо́жно      повтори́ть    и
(The) described   experiment   (it is) possible   to repeat     also

в    обра́тном    направле́нии,    нача́в**      заряжа́ть*
in   (the) reverse   direction,      after starting   to charge

электроско́п     от   стекля́нной   па́лочки   и    зате́м
(the) electroscope   from   (a) glass     rod      and   then

сообща́я      ему́[2]             элетриза́цию    от
communicating   to him (the electroscope)   electrification   from

смоляно́й   па́лочки.
(a) resin     rod.


Дав**           посу́де[3]      постоя́ть*   ещё
After   having permitted   to   (the) vessel   to stand    still

2-3    мину́ты,   её       мо́ют     водо́й     как
2-3    minutes,   her (the vessel)   they wash   with water   as

обы́чно.
usually.

---

[1] Note that спосо́бностью is in the instrumental case following облада́ет.
[2] Here ему́ is in the dative case following the gerund, сообща́я.
[3] Here посу́де is in the dative case following the gerund, дав.

§ 301. **Reading Exercise.**

### Водородный показатель

Ионизируясь в весьма малой степени, вода является слабым электролитом:

$$H_2O \rightleftarrows H^{\cdot} + OH' \qquad (1)$$

Применяя закон действия масс к реакции (1), получим:

$$\frac{[H^{\cdot}][OH']}{[H_2O]} = K \qquad (2)$$

Имея в виду, что концентрация недиссоциированных молекул воды $[H_2O]$ является очень большой по сравнению с $[H^{\cdot}]$ и $[OH']$, можно считать концентрацию недиссоциированной воды постоянной величиной. Следовательно, во втором уравнении $[H_2O]$ представляет собой постоянную величину. Умножив обе[1] части уравнения (2) на[2] величину $[H_2O]$, получаем:

$$[H^{\cdot}][OH'] = K[H_2O] = K_{H_2O} \qquad (3)$$

где произведение $K[H_2O]$ также должно[3] быть постоянной величиной, которую мы обозначаем через[4] $K_{H_2O}$. Из результатов опытов мы знаем, что при 22° числовая величина $K_{H_2O}$ равна $10^{-14}$. Помня, что при средней[5] реакции вода характеризуется тождественностью величин $[H^{\cdot}]$ и $[OH']$ и имея в виду уравнение (1), найдём, что в нейтральной воде:

$$[H^{\cdot}] = 10^{-7}$$
$$[OH'] = 10^{-7}$$

Логарифмируя эти выражения, получим:

$$\log[H^{\cdot}] = -7$$
$$\log[OH'] = -7$$

Обозначая отрицательный логарифм концентрации ионов $H^{\cdot}$ через[6] символ pH, будем иметь для нейтральной воды:

$$pH = 7$$

Символ pH иногда называют[7] водородным показателем.

Зная величину водородного показателя, т.е. pH, легко вычислить концентрации и ионов $H^{\cdot}$ и ионов $OH'$ в растворе.

Рассматривая случай водного раствора с pH = 5.4, мы можем написать:

$$-\log[\text{H}^\cdot] = 6.0 - 0.6 \quad (4)$$

Изменяя[8] знаки на обратные, получим:

$$\log[\text{H}^\cdot] = -6.0 + 0.6 \quad (5)$$

Потенцируя, мы приводим уравнение (5) к виду:

$$[\text{H}^\cdot] = (10^{-6})(10^{0.6})$$

Пользуясь[9] логарифмами, найдём, что $10^{0.6} = 4$ и таким образом находим:

$$[\text{H}^\cdot] = 4 \times 10^{-6}$$

Подставив эту числовую величину в уравнение (3), получаем:

$$4 \times 10^{-6} \cdot [\text{OH}'] = 10^{-14}$$

Решив это уравнение, находим:

$$[\text{OH}'] = 2.5 \times 10^{-9}$$

Исходя из уравнения (3), мы увидим, что всякому[10] увеличению концентрации H$^\cdot$ соответствует уменьшение концентрации OH$'$ и наоборот. Соответственно, в кислых средах концентрация H — больше $10^{-7}$, а в щелочных — меньше $10^{-7}$

Желая характеризовать нейтральные, кислотные и щелочные среды, мы можем пользоваться водородным показателем. Таким образом имеем:

нейтральная среда pH = 7
кислотная среда pH < 7
щелочная среда pH > 7

### Notes

1. обе is the feminine accusative form of оба "both."   Note that части is in the genitive singular after обе. This is another instance of certain complexities involving Russian numerals.

2. на величину [H$_2$O] "by the quantity [H$_2$O]." When speaking of multiplication, "by" is usually rendered in Russian by на (followed by the accusative).

3. должно быть "must be." This is an idiomatic expression.

**4.** мы обозначаем через $K_{H_2O}$ "we designate by $K_{H_2O}$."
Use of через in this expression is worthy of careful notice.

**5.** при средней реакции "at neutral reaction." The
adjective средний has a wide scope of meaning.

**6.** Cf. Note 4 above.

**7.** Символ pH иногда называют. "(The) symbol pH
sometimes they call." Here называют is used impersonally.

**8.** Изменяя знаки на обратные, literally, "Changing signs
to reverse," or, more smoothly, "Reversing the signs."

**9.** Пользуясь логарифмами, "Using logarithms." This is
another example of the use of the instrumental (логарифмами)
with a reflexive form from the infinitive пользовать.

**10.** всякому увеличению концентрации H˙ соответствует
"to every increase of concentration of H˙ corresponds."


§ 302. Translation Exercise.

1. On applying the law of mass action to the reaction of
   dissociation (диссоциации) of water, we obtain:
   $$\frac{[\text{H}˙]\,[\text{OH}']}{[\text{H}_2\text{O}]} = K. \quad (1)$$
2. Having in view, that water is (presents self) a weak
   electrolyte, it is possible to consider the concentration of
   undissociated water as a constant quantity.
3. Consequently, it is possible to transform ( преобразовать )
   equation (1) to the form ( виду ).
   $$[\text{H}˙]\,[\text{OH}'] = K\,[\text{H}_2\text{O}].$$
4. Designating the product $K\,[\text{H}_2\text{O}]$ by the symbol $K_{H_2O}$, we
   obtain:
   $$[\text{H}˙]\,[\text{OH}'] = K_{H_2O}. \quad (2)$$
5. Remembering that at 20° the numerical value of $K_{H_2O}$
   is equal to $10^{-14}$, we find that in neutral water
   $$[\text{H}˙] = 10^{-7}$$
   $$[\text{OH}'] = 10^{-7}$$
6. Taking the logarithms of these expressions and designating
   the negative logarithm of the concentration of ions H by the
   symbol, pH, we may write for neutral water
   $$\text{pH} = 7.$$

7. Starting from (ИЗ) the value (величины) of the hydrogen ion coefficient, it is easy to calculate the concentrations both (И) of ions H° and (И) of ions OH´.

8. Proceeding from equation (3), we see (УВИДИМ) that in alkaline media the concentration of H° is less than $10^{-7}$.

9. Correspondingly, in acid media we will have pH < 7.

10. To every decrease (уменьшению) of concentration of OH´ corresponds an increase (увеличение) of concentration of H .

# LESSON 33

## THE IMPERATIVE MOOD

### § 303. The Imperative Mood in English and Russian.

The imperative mood is not used very extensively in scientific writing either in Russian or English, except in connection with instructions for carrying out experimental work, operating instruments or making calculations.

### § 304. Formation of the Imperative Mood in Russian.

Regular Formation of Imperative Mood

| | Infinitives | Class | Present Tense | Perfective Future Tense | Imperative Second Person | |
|---|---|---|---|---|---|---|
| | | | Third Person Plural | | Singular | Plural |
| Imp. | де́лать | Reg. A | де́лают | | де́лай | дела́йте |
| Perf. | сде́лать | | | сде́лают | сде́лай | сдела́йте |
| Imp. | та́ять | Reg. B-1 | та́ют | | тай | та́йте |
| Perf. | раста́ять | | | раста́ют | раста́й | раста́йте |
| Imp. | криви́ть | Irr. C-2 | кривя́т | | криви́ | криви́те |
| Perf. | покриви́ть | | | покривя́ть | покриви́ | покриви́те |
| Imp. | писа́ть | Irr. D-1 | пи́шут | | пиши́ | пиши́те |
| Perf. | написа́ть | | | напи́шут | напиши́ | напиши́те |
| Imp. | брать | Irr. E-1 | беру́т | | бери́ | бери́те |
| Perf. | взять | Irr. F-7 | | возьму́т | возьми́ | возьми́те |
| Imp. | бере́чь | Irr. G-1 | берегу́т | | береги́ | береги́те |
| Perf. | побере́чь | | | поберегу́т | побереги́ | побереги́те |
| Imp. | везти́ | Irr. H-1 | везу́т | | вези́ | вези́те |
| Perf. | повезти́ | | | повезу́т | повези́ | повези́те |
| Imp. | итти́ | Irr. H-10 | иду́т | | иди́ | иди́те |

481

Distinctive verb forms characterize the second person singular and plural of the imperative of Russian verbs. These imperative forms are derived from both imperfective and perfective infinitives. Derivation usually is accomplished by a two step process:

    1) Removal of -УТ, -ЮТ, -аТ or -ЯТ from the third person plural of the present tense (imperfective infinitives) or the perfective future tense (perfective infinitives).

    2) Addition of the following endings:

| Singular | -И, -Й, -Ь |
|---|---|
| Plural | -ИТе, -йте, -ьте. |

Rules governing the selection of these endings for use with a particular infinitive do not appear sufficiently important to warrant consideration. The great majority of Russian infinitives form the imperative mood regularly, i.e., in accord with the two step process given above.

Only a relatively few Russian infinitives form the imperative irregularly. The most important of these are (1) those listed below and (2) their derivatives and analogues.

Irregular Formation of the Imperative Mood

| | Infinitives | Class | Present Tense | Perfective Future Tense | Imperative Second Person Singular | Plural |
|---|---|---|---|---|---|---|
| | | | Third Person Plural | | | |
| Imp. | дава́ть | Irr. B | даю́т | | дава́й | дава́йте |
| Perf. | дать | Irr. I-3 | | дадут́ | дай | да́йте |
| Imp. | е́хать | Irr. D-4 | е́дут | | езжа́й | езжа́йте |
| Perf. | пое́хать | | | пое́дут | поезжа́й | поезжа́йте |
| Imp. | пить́ | Irr. E-3 | пьют | | пей | пе́йте |
| Perf. | вы́пить | | | вы́пьют | вы́пей | вы́пейте |
| Imp. | бы́ть | Irr. I-2 | (суть) | | бу́дь | бу́дьте |
| Imp. | есть | Irr. I-1 | едя́т | | ешь | е́шьте |

# THE IMPERATIVE MOOD

The derivative ИЗДА́ТЬ "to give out," "to publish" and its
parent infinitive ДАТЬ "to give" form the imperative in identical
fashion. Furthermore, the analogous verbs ПИТЬ — ВЫ́ПИТЬ
"to drink" and БИТЬ — ПОБИ́ТЬ· "to strike" form the imperative
in the same way.

## § 305. Use of Russian Imperatives.

| Перечи́слите | сво́йства | кислоро́да. |
|---|---|---|
| Recount | (the) properties | of oxygen. |

| Иссле́дуйте | жи́дкость | ла́кмусом· |
|---|---|---|
| Test | (the) liquid | with litmus. |

| Нагре́йте | раство́р, | поме́шивая, | почти́ | до кипе́ния, |
|---|---|---|---|---|
| Heat | (the) solution, | while stirring, | almost | to boiling, |

| профильтру́йте | и | фильтра́т | раздели́те | на | три |
|---|---|---|---|---|---|
| filter | and | (the) filtrate | divide | into | three |

части.
parts.

| Соста́вьте | структу́рные | фо́рмулы | всех | изоме́рных |
|---|---|---|---|---|
| Set up | (the) structural | formulas | of all | (the) isomeric |

| друг | дру́гу | амиле́нов. |
|---|---|---|
| one | to the other | amylenes. |

| Объясни́те | роль | сил | тре́ния | при |
|---|---|---|---|---|
| Explain | (the) role | of (the) forces | of friction | during |

| переда́че | движе́ния | от | одного́ | шки́ва | к | друго́му |
|---|---|---|---|---|---|---|
| transfer | of motion | from | one | pulley | to | another |

| посре́дством | приводно́го | ремня́. |
|---|---|---|
| by means | of (a) transmission | belt. |

§ 306. A Special Form of the Third Person Imperative.

The auxiliary, ПУСТЬ, corresponding to English "let" has imperative meaning when used with the third person singular and plural of the present or perfective future tense. This imperative use of ПУСТЬ extends to sentences in which the present tense of ОЫТЬ "to be" is present by implication only.

| Пусть | фиг. 53 | изображает | какой-либо | обратимый цикл. |
|---|---|---|---|---|
| Let | Fig. 53 | represent | any | reversible cycle. |

| Пусть | E | обозначает | множество | всех | точек |
|---|---|---|---|---|---|
| Let | E | signify | (the) multiplicity | of all | points |

| плоскости | за | исключением | точки | $z = 0$. |
|---|---|---|---|---|
| of (the) surface | with | exclusion | of (the) point | $z = 0$. |

| Пусть | требуется | найти | делители | числа | 420. |
|---|---|---|---|---|---|
| Let | it require self | to find | (the) divisors | of (the) figure | 420. |

| Пусть | (% FeO) | – | концентрация | FeO | в |
|---|---|---|---|---|---|
| Let | (% FeO) | (be) | (the) concentration | (of) FeO | in |

| металле, | отвечающая | равновесию | металла | со |
|---|---|---|---|---|
| (the) metal | corresponding | to equilibrium | of (the) metal | with |

| шлаком. |
|---|
| (the) slag. |

| Пусть | дроби | a/b | и | c/d | | равны. |
|---|---|---|---|---|---|---|
| Let | (the) fractions | a/b | and | c/d | (be) | equal. |

| Пусть | например | даны | два | числа: | 85 | и | 20, из |
|---|---|---|---|---|---|---|---|
| Let, | for example, | (be) given | two | numbers: | 85 | and | 20 of |

| которых | большее | не | делится | на | меньшее. |
|---|---|---|---|---|---|
| which | (the) larger | not | divides self | by | (the) smaller. |

§ 307. A Special Form of the First Person Imperative.

The first person plural of the perfective future tense is sometimes used with imperative force in scientific Russian.

Возьмём        ещё другой  пример.
Let us take    yet another  example.

Напо́мним       вкра́тце  основны́е     положе́ния    тео́рии
Let us recall  briefly  (the) basic  propositions  of (the)

          компле́ксных     чи́сел.
theory    of complex     numbers.

Обрати́мся       тепе́рь  ко второ́му     из вопро́сов,
Let us return self  now     to (the) second  of (the) questions

поста́вленных    в   нача́ле      э́той     главы́.
posed           at  (the) start  of this  chapter.

Поло́жим,         что  мы    хоти́м   то́чно      изме́рить
Let us suppose,  that  we   wish    precisely  to measure

длину́         како́й-нибудь   ли́нии.
(the) length  of any         line.

§ 308. Imperative Use of Infinitives.

The infinitives of Russian verbs are sometimes used with imperative force. This use is of little importance in the scientific literature.

Найти́ уде́льный     вес   и  уде́льный  объём    кислоро́да
Find   (the) specific  weight and specific  volume   of oxygen

при  норма́льных    усло́виях.
at   normal        conditions.

| | | | | | |
|---|---|---|---|---|---|
| Вычислить | осмотическое | давление | при | 25° С | для |
| Calculate | (the) osmotic | pressure | at | 25°C | for |

| | | | | |
|---|---|---|---|---|
| водного | раствора, | содержащего | 50 г. | сахара |
| (an) aqueous | solution | containing | 50g. | of sugar |

| | | | |
|---|---|---|---|
| $C_{12}H_{22}O_{11}$ | в 3 л. | раствора. | |
| $C_{12}H_{22}O_{11}$ | in 3 l. | of solution. | |

| | | | |
|---|---|---|---|
| Определить | значения | температур | на |
| Determine | (the) values | of (the) temperatures | at |

| | | | |
|---|---|---|---|
| граничных | поверхностях, | которые | получились |
| (the) boundary | surfaces | which | would obtain |

| | | | | |
|---|---|---|---|---|
| бы, | если бы | пробковая | изоляция | отсутствовала. |
| self | if | (the) cork | insulation | were absent. |

| | | | | |
|---|---|---|---|---|
| Показать, | что | при | горении | соблюдается |
| Show | that | during | combustion | obeys self |

| | | |
|---|---|---|
| закон | сохранения | масс. |
| (the) law | of the conservation | of mass. |

§ 309. Reading Exercise.

### Получение квасцов из каолина

В ступке смешайте 50 г.[1] каолина, 20 куб.[2] см. воды и 30 куб. см. концентрированной серной кислоты[3] (удельный вес 1.84). Эту кашицу перенесите в фарфоровую чашку под тягой[4] и нагревайте на маленьком пламени около 30 минут или более. По охлаждении[5] разбавьте 50 куб. см. воды, профильтруйте. Фильтрат до половины выпарьте и оставьте[6] кристаллизоваться.

Осевший таким образом сульфат алюминия растворите в возможно[7] малом количестве воды. В стакане с 50 куб. см. кипящей воды растворите сульфата калия в порошке до насыщения. Смешайте равные объёмы обоих растворов. Когда смесь охладится, слейте вон прозрачную жидкость с

осевшей соли. Осевшую соль растворите в кипящей воде и дайте медленно охлаждаться. Выделившиеся кристаллы представляют собой алюминиевые квасци.

### Разведение смородины отводками[8]

Сначала выберите на кусте несколько молодых (однолетних или двулетних) ветвей смородины.

Разрыхлите землю вокруг куста, наклоните выбранные ветки к земле и прикрепите их к почве деревянными вилками, слегка погрузив часть ветки в ямку. Над погружённой в землю частью ветки насыпьте небольшой холмик земли в 7-10 см.[9] вышиной и поддерживайте почву во влажном состоянии.

На таких ветвях-отводках развиваются впоследствии корни,[10] и именно в тех частях, где ветка была засыпана землёй.

Осенью или следующей весной укоренившуюся ветку можно отделить от материнского растения и использовать для посадки.

### Определение величины поверхностного натяжения воды

План работы: надо измерить высоту подъёма жидкости в капилляре и диаметр капилляра.

Ход работы. 1. Налить воды в сосуд А.

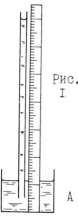

Рис. I

2. Смочить внутреннюю поверхность капиллярной трубки водой и вставить трубку в воду как показанно на рис. 1.

3. Приставить зеркальный масштаб к сосуду и измерить (в см.) высоту нижней части мениска в капилляре над уровнем жидкости в широком сосуде.

4. Для измерения диаметра капиллярной трубки вставить в её[11] нижнее отверстие иглу, заметить место, до которого игла вошла в трубку, и микрометром измерить её диаметр в отмеченном месте.

5. Сделать вычисление α по формуле:

$$\alpha = \frac{\gamma\,hg}{2}$$

где $\alpha$ – си́ла пове́рхностного натяже́ния (в дн./см. )[12]

$h$ – высота́ (в см.) столба́ воды́ в капилля́рной тру́бке

$\gamma$ – ра́диус (в см.) той же тру́бки

$g$ – 980 см./сек.$^2$ [13]

Наиме́ньшее о́бщее кра́тное[14] не́скольких чи́сел.[15]

Наиме́ньшим о́бщим кра́тным[14] не́скольких да́нных чи́сел называ́ется са́мое ме́ньшее[16]число́, кото́рое де́лится[17]на ка́ждое из э́тих чи́сел.[15]

Пусть тре́буется найти́ наиме́ньшее о́бщее кра́тное чи́сел:[15] 100, 40 и 35. Для э́того разло́жим ка́ждое из э́тих чи́сел[15] на просты́е мно́жители:

$$100 = 2{\cdot}2{\cdot}5{\cdot}5 \qquad 40 = 2{\cdot}2{\cdot}2{\cdot}5 \qquad 35 = 5{\cdot}7$$

Вы́пишем все мно́жители числа́ 100 и доба́вим к ним те мно́жители числа́ 40, кото́рых[18] недостаёт в разложе́нии 100. Тогда́ полу́чим произведе́ние $2{\cdot}2{\cdot}2{\cdot}5{\cdot}5{\cdot}2 = 200$, кото́рое де́лится и на 100 и на 40. Доба́вим тепе́рь к э́тому произведе́нию те мно́жители числа́ 35, кото́рых[18] в произведе́нии недостаёт. Тогда́ полу́чим произведе́ние:

$$2{\cdot}2{\cdot}5{\cdot}5{\cdot}2{\cdot}7 = 1400,$$

деля́щееся и на 100, и на 40 и на 35. Это и есть наиме́ньшее о́бщее кра́тное исхо́дных чи́сел.[15]

### Notes

1. Г. corresponds to our abbreviation g. for gram(s).

2. КУБ. СМ. corresponds to our abbreviation cc. for cubic centimeter(s), cf. § 405, p. 674.

3. концентрированной серной кислоты "of concentrated sulfuric acid." Russian names of oxygen containing inorganic acids require special attention, cf. Footnote 3, p. 10.

4. под тягой "Under (the) hood." Usually, тяга can be translated by "pull."

5. По охлаждении "after cooling," cf. § 76, p. 110.

6. и оставьте кристаллизоваться "and let crystallize."

7. В возможно малом количестве воды, "in the smallest possible quantity of water." This illustrates an important idiomatic use of the adverb ВОЗМОЖНО (literally, "possibly") in conjunction with the positive degree of an adjective (here МАЛОМ ), cf. § 351, p. 555.

8. ОТВОДКАМИ is the irregular instrumental plural of ОТВОДОК, cf. § 357, p. 573.

9. See Note 2 above.

10. КОРНИ is the irregular nominative plural of КОРЕНЬ, cf. § 357, p. 573.

11. В её нижнее ОТВЕРСТИЕ "into her (the capillary tube's) lower opening."

12. В ДН./СМ. "in dynes/centimeter." Note the Russian abbreviations.

13. СМ./ СЕК.$^2$ "centimeters/second/second."

14. наименьшее общее кратное, "(the) least common multiple." The neuter forms of the adjective КРАТНЫЙ "multiple" are used to replace the longer expression КРАТНОЕ ЧИСЛО "multiple number." For discussion of the form of superlative exemplified by НАИМЕНЬШИЙ, see § 344, p. 541.

15. ЧИСЕЛ is the irregular genitive plural of the noun ЧИСЛО "number," cf. § 345, p. 544.

16. самое меньшее число, "the very smallest number," exemplifies another form of superlative formed with САМЫЙ and discussed in § 355, p. 561.

17. кото́рое  де́лится  на  ка́ждое --,  "which divides by each --."

18. кото́рых is in the genitive plural because it refers to entities whose presence is being denied.

## § 310. Translation Exercise.

1. Mix equal volumes of concentrated sulfuric acid and water.
2. After cooling transfer into a porcelain evaporating dish.
3. Filter off (Отфильтру́йте) the (having) separated (self) crystals of sulfate of potassium.
4. Fasten several young branches of the bush to the ground with wooden forks.
5. On the sunk (погружённых) in the earth branches develop self roots.
6. The following autumn it is possible to separate the young (молоды́е) little stalks (ку́стики) from the mother plant.
7. Moisten the inner surface of the capillary with the above mentioned (вышеупомя́нутом) solution of caustic soda.
8. Measure the diameter of the capillary tube by a micrometer.
9. Let it be required (require self) to find all the prime factors of the number 100.
10. Let us find (Найдём) the least common multiple of the numbers 100, 40 and 35.

# LESSON 34

## THE SUBJUNCTIVE MOOD

§ 311. The Subjunctive Mood in English and Russian.

The subjunctive mood is used in both Russian and English in making statements which involve conditions contrary to fact or which express more or less doubt or uncertainty. Example sentences illustrating various uses of the subjunctive mood are given in subsequent paragraphs in this Lesson.

§ 312. Formation of the Subjunctive Mood in Russian.

Formation of the subjunctive in Russian is extremely simple. All that is involved is use of the particle бы together with the past tense forms. Consequently, each Russian infinitive has only one set of subjunctive forms. This single set of forms corresponds to the present, past and future tenses of the English subjunctive mood.[1] This failure to form different subjunctive tenses in Russian is in part compensated by the fact that Russian verbs, as a general rule, have both perfective and imperfective subjunctive forms. These two parallel sets of forms refer, as might be surmised, either to completed action or to incomplete continuing or repeated action, depending on the perfective or imperfective character of the parent infinitive.

### Examples of Formation of the Subjunctive Mood

| Imperfective Infinitive | де́лать | писа́ть | жечь | находи́ть |
|---|---|---|---|---|
| | to be doing | to be writing | to be burning | to be finding |
| Perfective Infinitive | сде́лать | написа́ть | сжечь | найти́ |
| | to do | to write | to burn | to find |

[1] Since the Russian subjunctive is derived from past tense forms, it is particularly important to take careful note of this relationship of a single set of Russian subjunctive forms to the different tenses of the English subjunctive.

### Subjunctive Mood

## IMPERFECTIVE ASPECT

### Singular

| | | | | |
|---|---|---|---|---|
| Masc. | де́лал бы | писа́л бы | жёг бы | находи́л бы |
| Fem. | де́лала бы | писа́ла бы | жгла бы | находи́ла бы |
| Neuter | де́лало бы | писа́ло бы | жгло бы | находи́ло бы |

### Plural

| | | | | |
|---|---|---|---|---|
| Masc.-Fem.-Neuter | де́лали бы | писа́ли бы | жгли бы | находи́ли бы |

## PERFECTIVE ASPECT

### Singular

| | | | | |
|---|---|---|---|---|
| Masc. | сде́лал бы | написа́л бы | сжёг бы | нашёл бы |
| Fem. | сде́лала бы | написа́ла бы | сожгла́ бы | нашла́ бы |
| Neuter | сде́лало бы | написа́ло бы | сожгло́ бы | нашло́ бы |

### Plural

| | | | | |
|---|---|---|---|---|
| Masc.-Fem.-Neuter | сде́лали бы | написа́ли бы | сожгли́ бы | нашли́ бы |

§ 313.  Use  of  the  Russian  Subjunctive  Mood  in  Sentences
Involving Conditions Contrary to Fact.[1]

A  particularly  important  use  of  the  subjunctive  mood  is  in
stating  conditions  contrary  to  fact  and  their  imaginary
consequences.  In  considering  the  following  typical  sentences,
note  that  the  particle,  бы,  quite  often  does  not  follow  immediately
after  its  companion  past  tense  form.  Thus  in  the  conditional

---

[1]  For  a  discussion  of  conditional  sentences  not  involving  impossible  or  highly
doubtful conditions, see § 232, p. 364.

clauses of the following sentences, бы follows the conjunction
е́сли , "if."

| Е́сли бы | дождевы́е | ка́пли | па́дали | в | безвозду́шном |
|---|---|---|---|---|---|
| If | rain | drops | fell | in | (an) airless |

| простра́нстве | с | высоты́ | 2 км, | то | они́ |
|---|---|---|---|---|---|
| space | from | (a) height | (of) 2 kilometers, | then | they |

| достига́ли бы | при | паде́нии | на зе́млю | ско́рости |
|---|---|---|---|---|
| would attain | during | falling | to (the) earth | (a) velocity |

200 м./сек.
(of) 200 meters/second.

| Но э́ти | чи́сла | си́льно | измени́лись бы, | е́сли бы | мы |
|---|---|---|---|---|---|
| But these | figures | strongly | would change self, | if | we |

| при́няли | во | внима́ние | де́йствие |
|---|---|---|---|
| should take | into | consideration | (the) action |

атмосфе́ры.
of (the) atmosphere.

| Е́сли бы | лю́ди, | жи́вшие | 2-3 ты́сячи | лет | наза́д, |
|---|---|---|---|---|---|
| If | persons, | having lived | 2-3 thousands | of years | ago |

| могли́ | взгляну́ть | на | не́бо, | они́ | не | нашли́ бы | в |
|---|---|---|---|---|---|---|---|
| could | look | at | (the) sky | they | not | would find | in |

| очерта́ниях | созве́здий | заме́тной | ра́зницы. |
|---|---|---|---|
| configurations | of (the) constellations | noticeable | difference. |

| Е́сли бы не́ | бы́ло | всеми́рного | тяготе́ния | и | земля́ |
|---|---|---|---|---|---|
| If | not were | universal | gravitation | and | (the) earth |

| не | уде́рживала бы | свои́м | притяже́нием | луну́, | то |
|---|---|---|---|---|---|
| not | restrained | by her | attraction | (the) moon, | then |

| луна́ | по | прямо́й | ли́нии | навсегда́ | улете́ла |
|---|---|---|---|---|---|
| (the) moon | along | (a) straight | line | forever | would fly |

| бы | прочь | от | земли́. |
|---|---|---|---|
| away | away | from | (the) earth. |

§ 314.  Use  of  the  Russian  Subjunctive  Mood  in  Statements  of
Impossible, Highly Doubtful or Hypothetical Nature.

Statements  of  this  type  are  obviously  characterized  by  a
considerable  degreee  at  least  of  doubt  or  uncertainty.  In this
general  category  are  to  be found  many  expressions  of  conjecture,
purpose,  desire,  possibility,  wonderment  and  the  like.  This
general  category  has  much  in  common  with  the  conditional
sentences  of  preceding  § 313  as  is  evident  from  the  following
examples.

Создать        машину,      которая     всё      время
To   create    (a) machine,  which       all      (the)   time

производила бы        работу    без      затраты        энергии,
would  accomplish     work      without  expenditure    of energy

оказалось     невозможным.
proved self    impossible.


Казалось бы,                                   промышленное
It might show self      (It might seem)   (that)    (the) industrial

использование      этой     реакции для синтеза     аммиака
utilization         of this  reaction for synthesis  of ammonia

невозможно.
(is) impossible.


Как    скользкая    рыба    выскальзывает     из           рук,
As     (a) slippery  fish    slips out                from    (the) hands,

так    при    отсутствии    трения       выскальзывали бы
so     during absence       of friction   would slip out

из      рук         все  предметы,  которые   мы хотели    бы
from    (the) hands  all  objects     which     we might     wish

поднять.
to pick up.

| На | Юпитере | не | видно | ничего, | никаких | деталей, |
|---|---|---|---|---|---|---|
| On | Jupiter | [not] | (is) visible | nothing, | no | details, |

| которые | принадлежали бы | твёрдой | поверхности |
|---|---|---|---|
| which | might pertain | to (the) solid | surface |

| планеты. |
|---|
| of (the) planet. |


| Но | как | отличалась бы | жизнь | разумных | существ | на |
|---|---|---|---|---|---|---|
| But | how | would differ self | (the) life | of intelligent | beings | on |

| других | планетах | от | нашей | жизни! |
|---|---|---|---|---|
| other | planets | from | our | life! |


§ 315. Clauses Involving the Russian Subjunctive Mood and the Conjunction ЧТОБЫ.

Use of the conjunction ЧТО, "that" to introduce dependent clauses was discussed in § 145, p. 217. Dependent clauses presenting a statement of an impossible, hypothetical or highly doubtful nature often involve both the conjunction ЧТО and the subjunctive mood. In such clauses the conjunction ЧТО and the particle БЫ (or Б) are printed together as one word, ЧТОБЫ (or ЧТОБ). This general type of clause is often used to express some purpose, usually hypothetical in nature.[1] It is not unusual, however, for this same type of clause to be used to more general fashion in other statements of an impossible, highly doubtful or hypothetical nature.

| Нагревание | газа | можно | производить | таким |
|---|---|---|---|---|
| (The) heating | of (a) gas | (it is) possible | to carry out | in such |

| образом, | чтобы | газ | имел | возможность |
|---|---|---|---|---|
| fashion, | that | (the) gas | might have | (the) possibility |

| изменять | свой | объём. |
|---|---|---|
| to change | its | volume. |


[1] As already noted in § 168, p. 256, the combination of ЧТОБЫ with an infinitive is used very frequently in scientific Russian to indicate purpose.

Для     того,    чтобы    реактивная    тяга         была́
For     this,    that     (the) reactive pull (thrust) may be

доста́точно   велика́,    дви́гатель    до́лжен   пропуска́ть
sufficiently great,      (the) motor   must     pass

сквозь  себя́   грома́дные   коли́чества   во́здуха.
through  self   enormous    quantities   of air.


Каза́лось      бессмы́сленным   и     невозмо́жным,   что́бы
It seemed      senseless       and   impossible      that

существова́ли       други́е   плане́ты   лишённые   жи́зни.
(there) should exist other     planets   devoid     of life.


Почти́  ни   одна́   рабо́та    в хими́ческой    лаборато́рии
Almost not  one     work      in chemical      laboratory

не производится      без   того́, что́бы не приходи́лось
not carries self out without this,  that  not should be necessary

гото́вить   какой-нибудь    раство́р.
to prepare  some            solution.


## § 316.  Other Use of the Particle  Бы.

Two idioms involving the particle бы appear worthy of special
note.  These are (1) как бы usually translatable by "as it were,"
and (2) хотя́ бы indicating concession and usually best translated
by "even though," "though only," or some similar expression.

При   превраще́нии   теплоты́ в   рабо́ту   приро́да  как  бы
On    conversion     of heat  into work    nature,   as   it were,

взима́ет    нало́г.
collects    (a) tax.


В   таки́х   слу́чаях    прохожде́ния   земли́        че́рез
In  such    cases       of passage     of (the) earth through

хвост     коме́ты     не́  было       заме́чено   каки́х-либо
(the) tail of (a) comet not was (were) noted       any

| явле́ний, | кото́рые | мо́жно | бы́ло | приписа́ть |
|---|---|---|---|---|
| phenomena | which | possible | was | to ascribe |

| де́йствию | части́ц | хвоста́ | хотя́ бы | на на́шу |
|---|---|---|---|---|
| to (the) action | of particles | of (the) tail | even | on our |

атмосфе́ру.
atmosphere.

| Пе́ред | носко́м | пу́ли | возника́ет | как бы |
|---|---|---|---|---|
| In front of | (the) nose | of (the) bullet | arises | as it were |

| упру́гая | поду́шка | уплотнённого | во́здуха, | кото́рую |
|---|---|---|---|---|
| (an) elastic | cushion | of compressed | air | which |

| пу́ля | должна́ | толка́ть | пе́ред | собо́й. |
|---|---|---|---|---|
| (the) bullet | must | push | before | self. |

| Научи́вшись | проводи́ть | в техни́ческом | масшта́бе |
|---|---|---|---|
| Having instructed self | to conduct | in (a) technical | scale |

| хотя́ бы | одну́ | лишь | реа́кцию | превраще́ния | водоро́да |
|---|---|---|---|---|---|
| even though | one | only | reaction | of conversion | of hydrogen |

| в ге́лий, | мы тем | са́мым | ста́ли бы | обладате́лями |
|---|---|---|---|---|
| into helium, | we by that | self | would be | as possessors |

| тако́го | колосса́льного | исто́чника | эне́ргии, | с кото́рым |
|---|---|---|---|---|
| of such | (a) colossal | source | of energy, | with which |

| все | испо́льзуемые | в | настоя́щее | вре́мя | потеря́ли бы |
|---|---|---|---|---|---|
| all | being used | at | (the) present | time | would lose |

| вся́кое | значе́ние. |
|---|---|
| all | significance. |

§ 317. Reading Exercise.

### Межпланетная навигация

Если бы нам[1] хотелось поехать в Нью-Йорк, Москву или какой-нибудь другой город, мы могли бы воспользоваться[2] различными транспортными средствами, так, например, железнодорожным поездом, автомобилем, пароходом, самолётом и так далее. Но без рельсов[3] поезд не двигался бы; без дороги автомобиль оказался бы беспомощным. Если бы не было океанов[4], пароходы не плавали бы. Если бы не было воздуха, самолёт не мог бы летать. Нет сомнения в том, что все вышеупомянутые транспортные средства не могут быть применимы для навигации сквозь пустоту мирового пространства.

Возникает вопрос, можно ли[5] построить какую-нибудь машину, при помощи которой было бы можно пролетать через мировое пространство? Можно дать положительный ответ на этот вопрос.

Нам уже известно из курса физики, что движение ракеты вызывается противодействием (реакцией) отбрасываемой струи какого-либо вещества. Пороховые ракеты (рис. 1) известны с древних времён. При сгорании пороха, образуется громадное количество газа, вытекающего с большой скоростью из нижнего отверстия ракеты: реакция вытекающей струи газа уносит ракету вверх.

Рис. I

Для вычисления скорости, приданной ракете при извержении некоторой массы газа, удобно применить второй закон движения Ньютона в следующей форме:

$$MV = mv$$

где M – масса ракеты, m – масса газа, V – скорость, придаваемая ракете в течение сгорания пороха, v – скорость газа, вытекающего из отверстия ракеты.

Чтобы ракета (или какой-либо другой предмет) действительно могла улететь прочь от земли, было бы нужно[6] придать ракете огромную скорость — около 700 километров в минуту. Если такая скорость не была бы придана ракете, то притяжение земли всё равно заставило бы ракету снова упасть на земную поверхность.

Однако ракета, на которой мы пролетели бы на Венеру, Марс или другую планету, являлась бы сравнительно сложным аппаратом. Было[7] бы необходимо снабдить[7] межпланетную ракету запасами пищи и питьевой воды, аппаратом для очистки воздуха в кабине, научными приборами и так далее. Межпланетная ракета немыслима без того, чтобы не было нужно сконструировать герметическую кабину.

Следовательно, наша межпланетная ракета будет иметь большой вес. Поэтому громадное количество энергии будет потребно для межпланетной навигации. Вот[8] почему до сих пор не было возможно долететь до какой-нибудь другой планеты или до луны. Сила тяжести как бы "сцепляет" нас с землёй. Может быть, атомная энергия окажется выгодной движущей силой для межпланетных ракет.

Очевидно, что полёт вне земли - хотя бы мыслимый и даже возможный, тем не менее - дело будущего.[9]

### Notes

1. Если бы нам хотелось поехать. "If we should wish to travel." Note the idiomatic use of the dative -- here нам- with an impersonal reflexive form of ХОТЕТЬ -- here ХОТЕЛОСЬ- to indicate a desire or wish.

2. восПО́льзоваться      разли́чными      тра́нспортными
сре́дствами,  "to avail self (to use) various transport means."
This construction calls to mind similar use of the reflexive forms
of по́льзовать with the instrumental, cf. Note 9, p. 478.

3. без ре́льсов ,  "without rails."  Here ре́льсов is the
genitive plural of a noun whose nominative singular is рельс
"rail" and whose nominative plural is ре́льсы  "rails."

4. океа́нов is in the genitive case because of the negative
character of the clause in which it stands. Note that во́здуха in
the next sentence is also in the genitive for the same reason.

5. мо́жно ли постро́ить,  "(is it) possible to construct." The
use of ЛИ in interrogative sentences and clauses has already been
pointed out in Note 14,  p. 459, cf. also § 387, p. 644.

6. бы́ло бы ну́жно придать раке́те,  "it would be necessary
to impart to (the) rocket."

7. снабди́ть межпланета́ную  раке́ту запа́сами.  "to furnish
(the) interplanetary rocket with supplies."

8. Вот почему́.  "That is why" might be regarded as an
idiom.

9. де́ло бу́дущего  "a thing of the future."  The word
бу́дущий,  originally the active present participle of БЫТЬ  "to
be,"  is used both as an adjective and noun with the meaning
"future."


§ 318.  Translation Exercise.

1. If we should wish to travel to New York, we could avail self
   of a railroad train.
2. If there were no road,  an automobile could not move.
3. There is no doubt (in this), that flight outside the earth is a
   matter of the future.
4. Is it (Мо́жно ЛИ) to fly through cosmic space with the aid of
   a rocket?
5. From ancient times, has been[1] known the utilization of
   powder in order (что́бы ) to impart to a rocket high (big)
   velocity.
6. Availing oneself of the second (вторы́м ) law (зако́ном) of
   Newton, it is possible to calculate (вы́числить) the velocity
   of a rocket.

7. If an enormous (громáдная) velocity not were imparted to a rocket, it (онá) would not be able to fly away from the earth.

8. Our interplanetary rocket would be (would show· self) a relatively complicated device.

9. It would be necessary to construct special scientific instruments for interplanetary navigation.

10. It is obvious (Очевúдно) also that an enormous amount of energy will be required for interplanetary rockets.

### Note

1. The English phrase "has been known" may here be translated by the single Russian word ИЗВÉСТНО, as the phrase "from ancient times" in Russian translation indicates the time existence of the fact in question.

# LESSON 35

## REVIEW OF CONJUGATION OF RUSSIAN VERBS

§ 319. Introductory Note.

This lesson is devoted to summarizing the important features of the Russian verb system as a whole. To this end attention is directed in turn to (1) perfective and imperfective infinitives and relationships between them both with respect to meaning and to form, (2) endings and their role in conjugation of Russian verbs, (3) a system of classifying infinitives based on characteristic features of their conjugation, (4) tabulation of the conjugations of some typical infinitives.

It is hoped that this summary may prove helpful in spite of the fact that it is not possible completely to embrace, within a limited number of concise rules and tables, the details of conjugation of all Russian verbs.

§ 320. Perfective and Imperfective Infinitives As Basic Verb Forms.

A majority of Russian verbs have two infinitives, the perfective and the imperfective, which it is convenient to regard as starting points for deriving other verb forms. These two classes of infinitives are distinguished as to meaning by the fact that the imperfective infinitives and forms derived therefrom are used to denote action thought of as incomplete, in progress or frequently repeated, whereas perfective infinitives and their related forms are used to indicate action thought of as a completed whole.

The relationship between the two groups of infinitives as to form was approached in Lesson 6 by considering various stages of assimilation of a verb of foreign origin into the Russian language. In this lesson we shall describe the relationship as to form between perfective and imperfective infinitives from a different point of view, shifting the emphasis to verbs of purely Russian character and origin.

503

§ 321. Derivation of Russian Verbs from Simple Imperfective Infinitives.

As might be expected, many simple infinitives in Russian refer to simple actions. Nearly all of these simple infinitives are imperfective in aspect, for example, ЛИТЬ "to be pouring," ПИСА́ТЬ "to be writing," ТЕЧЬ "to be flowing," ЧИ́СТИТЬ "to be purifying, cleaning." It will be observed that these infinitives describe actions of a general nature without designation of the direction of the action, its specific character or the like. Generally, the use of various prefixes with these simple imperfective infinitives simultaneously (1) renders them perfective and (2) changes their meaning so that the action designated is more specific in character. It is an essential feature of the Russian verb system that perfective infinitives so formed with altered meaning have, in turn, corresponding imperfective infinitives which usually are formed by inserting a syllable or letter in the stem of the perfective infinitives, as illustrated by the following examples.

| Imperfective | Perfective |
|---|---|
| течь | |
| to be flowing | |
| | |
| втека́ть | втечь |
| to be flowing in | to flow in |
| | |
| вытека́ть | вы́течь |
| to be flowing out | to flow out |
| (Both in literal and in figurative, logical sense) | |
| | |
| истека́ть | исте́чь |
| to be flowing from, | to flow from |
| to be expiring (time limit) | to expire (time limit) |
| | |
| отека́ть | оте́чь |
| to be swelling, | to swell, |
| to be flowing (light) | to flow (light) |
| | |
| перетека́ть | перете́чь |
| to be overflowing | to overflow |
| | |
| утека́ть | уте́чь |
| to be flowing away, | to flow away, |
| to be escaping | to escape |

| Imperfective | Perfective |
|---|---|
| писа́ть<br>to be writing | написа́ть<br>to write |
| впи́сывать<br>to be inscribing | вписа́ть<br>to inscribe |
| выпи́сывать<br>to be copying out,<br>to be writing out | вы́писать<br>to copy out,<br>to write out |
| испи́сывать<br>to be writing all over | исписа́ть<br>to write all over |
| опи́сывать<br>to be describing | описа́ть<br>to describe |
| перепи́сывать<br>to be transcribing | переписа́ть<br>to transcribe |
| упи́сывать<br>to be writing out (in a<br>    definite space) | уписа́ть<br>to write out (in a<br>    definite space) |

As noted above, the general effect of using a prefix with a simple imperfective infinitive is to change the meaning and to render the infinitive perfective. It is by no means unusual for some specific prefix to change a simple imperfective infinitive to perfective without appreciably changing the meaning. Thus the prefix, ПО-, is used with a large number of simple imperfective infinitives,[1] e.g., бели́ть "to be bleaching," побели́ть "to bleach"; лечи́ть "to be healing," полечи́ть "to heal"; теря́ть "to be losing," потеря́ть "to lose"; etc. Other prefixes may be similarly used, the specific prefix depending on the infinitive in question. Thus with писа́ть "to be writing," the prefix used is На-, forming написа́ть "to write," while with де́лать "to be doing" С- is used forming сде́лать "to do," etc.

With other infinitives the very nature of the action is such that no matter how it is completed, the action is more or less inevitably made specific in character. The simple imperfective

---

[1] With certain imperfective infinitives, the prefix ПО- forms perfective infinitives denoting a limited period of action, e.g., писа́ть "to be writing," попи́сать "to write for a little while," cf. § 384, p. 639.

infinitives denoting general action of this nature can scarcely be said to have a single corresponding perfective infinitive. Examples are the imperfective infinitive ТЕЧЬ "to be flowing" (cf. above) and ЛИТЬ "to be pouring," (discussed in § 43, pp. 62-64).

It should also be noted that usage sometimes creates unusual relationships requiring special care to avoid confusion. Thus, two different verbs may have an infinitive in common, as illustrated by the following example.

ТУ́ХНУТЬ -- ПРОТУ́ХНУТЬ        to spoil, to rot
ТУ́ХНУТЬ -- ПОТУ́ХНУТЬ         to go out (fire)

§ 322.  Imperfective and Perfective Infinitives Related to Nouns and Adjectives.

A rather large number of Russian verbs, which denote the attainment of some condition, are closely related to nouns or adjectives. It is possible to describe the relationships between the imperfective and perfective infinitives of these verbs in simple terms as shown below. It is convenient to consider these in two groups.

## Group I

The following relationships characterize this group.

1) The imperfective infinitives end in -ЯТЬ or, less commonly, in -АТЬ, and the corresponding perfective infinitives end in -ИТЬ.

2) The present tense is formed from the imperfective infinitives by removing -ТЬ and adding first conjugation endings (as previously described in § 187, p. 282) while the perfective future tense is formed by removing -ИТЬ from the perfective infinitives and adding the second conjugation endings (as described already in § 187, p. 282).

| Imperfective Infinitives | Perfective Infinitives | Related to Simple Noun or Adjective |
|---|---|---|
| дополня́ть<br>to be completing | допо́лнить<br>to complete | по́лный<br>complete |
| изменя́ть<br>to be changing | измени́ть<br>to change | ме́на<br>exchange |
| испаря́ть<br>to be evaporating | испари́ть<br>to evaporate | пар<br>vapor |
| окисля́ть<br>to be oxidizing | окисли́ть<br>to oxidize | о́кисел<br>oxide |
| отклоня́ть<br>to be deflecting | отклони́ть<br>to deflect | укло́н<br>slope |
| соединя́ть<br>to be uniting | соедини́ть<br>to unite | оди́н<br>one |
| облегча́ть<br>to be making easy, facilitating | облегчи́ть<br>to make easy, facilitate | лёгкий<br>light (adj.)<br>easy |
| расширя́ть<br>to be expanding | расши́рить<br>to expand | широ́кий<br>wide, broad |
| ускоря́ть<br>to be accelerating | уско́рить<br>to accelerate | ско́рый<br>fast |
| усложня́ть<br>to be making complicated | усложни́ть<br>to make complicated | сло́жный<br>complex (adj.) |

## Group II

Here the slightly more complicated characteristic relationships might be summarized as follows.

1) As in Group I, the imperfective infinitives end in -аТЬ, of -ЯТЬ. The corresponding perfective infinitives usually end in -ИТЬ.

2) As in Group I, the present tense is formed from the imperfective infinitives by removing -ТЬ and adding first conjugation endings. The perfective future is usually formed by removing -ИТЬ from the perfective infinitives and adding the second conjugation endings.

3) Due to usage, strongly influenced by phonetic factors, the basic stem word (e.g., ВОДА́) undergoes different changes in forming the imperfective and perfective infinitives (e.g., обезво́живать and обезво́дить).

| Imperfective Infinitives | Perfective Infinitives | Related to Simple Nouns and Adjectives |
|---|---|---|
| исправля́ть<br>to be correcting | испра́вить<br>to correct | пра́во<br>right |
| обезво́живать<br>to be dehydrating | обезво́дить<br>to dehydrate | вода́<br>water |
| освобожда́ть<br>to be liberating | освободи́ть<br>to liberate | свобо́да<br>freedom |
| отсыха́ть<br>to be drying out | отсо́хнуть<br>to dry out | сухо́й<br>dry |
| распи́ливать<br>to be sawing apart | распили́ть<br>to saw apart | пила́<br>saw |
| соглаша́ть<br>to be bringing into agreement | согласи́ть<br>to bring into agreement | го́лос<br>voice |
| укрепля́ть<br>to be fortifying | укрепи́ть<br>to fortify | кре́пкий<br>strong |

(Both military and figurative meaning)

| | | |
|---|---|---|
| улучша́ть<br>to be improving | улу́чшить<br>to improve | лу́чший<br>better, best |
| снижа́ть<br>to be humbling | сни́зить<br>to humble | ни́зкий  low<br>ни́же  lower |

§ 323. Miscellaneous Pairs of Imperfective and Perfective Infinitives.

In order to minimize the possibility of misleading the student with over-simplification, it seems advisable to point out that there are a number of Russian verbs[1] that do not fit into the two broad categories summarized above in §§ 321 and 322.

| Imperfective Infinitives | Perfective Infinitives | Translation of Perfective Infinitives |
|---|---|---|
| извлекать | извлечь | to extract, to pull out |
| начинать | начать | to begin, to start |
| перегонять | перегнать | to distill |
| покупать | купить | to buy |
| поднимать | поднять | to lift, to raise |
| получать | получить | to obtain |
| понимать | понять | to understand |
| растирать | растереть | to rub out |
| решать | решить | to solve, to decide |
| умирать | умереть | to die |

A few verbs[1] are exceptional in that their imperfective infinitives are not derived from the same root as their perfective infinitives, as shown by the following examples.

| Imperfective Infinitives | Perfective Infinitives | Translation of Perfective Infinitives |
|---|---|---|
| брать | взять | to take |
| говорить | сказать | to say, to speak |
| класть | положить | to place |
| находить | найти | to find |
| приходить | прийти | to arrive |

§ 324. Endings and Their Role in Conjugation of Russian Verbs.

The following table lists the endings used for the conjugation of all Russian verbs with exception of быть "to be," есть "to be eating" and дать, "to give" and certain perfective infinitives

---

[1] It is not possible to summarize concisely the differences in form between the imperfective and perfective infinitives of these verbs.

derived therefrom. Even with these exceptional infinitives,
irregular endings are used only in forming the present and
perfective future tenses as already noted in § 207, p. 323.

How the endings are used to derive verb forms is as important
as the endings themselves. It is advantageous to regard the
infinitives as the basic forms from which the other forms are
derived. In fact, for a large number of infinitives -- the
so-called regular infinitives -- the relationship of the infinitives
to the other forms is simple and direct. With other infinitives --
usually termed irregular -- a stem change is involved in
formation of the present and perfective future tenses, and with
the majority of these infinitives, such stem changes carry over
into the present participles (both active and passive), the present
gerund and the imperative forms. The relationships under
discussion are such that the following table summarizes how
endings are used to derive all the forms of regularly conjugated
infinitives and a majority of the forms of these infinitives having
one or more irregularities in their conjugation. (See pp. 511-513).

§ 325. Classification of Infinitives Based on Characteristic
       Features of Their Conjugation.

Although any definition of regular conjugation is necessarily
arbitrary and difficult to formulate precisely, we shall class as
regular those infinitives having the following characteristics:
(1) the ending of the infinitive is a vowel plus -ТЬ; (2) the present
or perfective future tense is formed by removing an infinitive
ending and affixing the regular tense endings as described in the
Table of Endings (see pp. 511-513); (3) the past tense is formed
in regular fashion by removing -ТЬ from the infinitive and affixing
the regular endings.

The conjugation of irregular infinitives involves one or more
changes in the stem prior to adding the regular endings. The
nature of these stem changes provides criteria for the
classification of irregular infinitives. (Cont'd on p. 514).

# SUMMARY OF VERB CONJUGATION

| SUMMARY OF ENDINGS | ORIGIN OF STEMS USED WITH VARIOUS ENDINGS |
|---|---|

## INDICATIVE MOOD

### Present (Perfective Future) Tense

#### 1st Conjugation

| | Singular | Plural |
|---|---|---|
| 1st Person | -у, -ю | -ем |
| 2nd Person | -ешь | -ете |
| 3rd Person | -ет | -ут, -ют |

Stem regularly derived from some infinitives by removing -ть, from other infinitives by removing -ать, -еть, -ить, -оть, -ут or -ять, i.e., a combination of a vowel and -ть.

#### 2nd Conjugation

| | Singular | Plural |
|---|---|---|
| 1st Person | -у, -ю | -им |
| 2nd Person | -ишь | -ите |
| 3rd Person | -ит | -ат, -ят |

Stem regularly derived from infinitives by removing a combination of a vowel and -ть.

*Contd. on next page.*

## SUMMARY OF ENDINGS

## ORIGIN OF STEMS USED WITH VARIOUS ENDINGS

### Past Tense

|  | Masc. | Fem. | Neuter |
|---|---|---|---|
| Singular | -Л | -ЛА | -ЛО |

Singular and Plural -- All Genders

Stem derived from infinitive. (For nearly all infinitives by removing -ТЬ).

|  | Masc., Fem., Neuter |
|---|---|
| Plural | -ЛИ |

### Future Tense

**Imperfective:** Formed by using the future tense of быть (to be) as an auxiliary with imperfective infinitives.

**Perfective:** Formed as indicated above under Present (Perfective Future) Tense.

## IMPERATIVE MOOD

| 2nd Person Singular: | -и, -й, -ь |
|---|---|
| 2nd Person Plural: | -ите, -йте, -ьте |

Stem derived from 3rd person plural of present (perfective future) tense by removing -ут, -ют, -ат, or -ят.

SUMMARY OF ENDINGS     ORIGIN OF STEMS USED WITH VARIOUS ENDINGS

## PARTICIPLES

Active Present: Russian participles are used like adjectives in constructing sentences and are declined with the regular adjective endings. See Lessons 29-33.

Stem derived by removing -Т from 3rd person plural of present tense and adding -Щ-.

Passive Present: Stem is the 1st person plural of the present tense.

Active Past: Stem is derived by removing -ТЬ from the infinitive and adding -ВШ-, -Ш- or rarely -ДШ-.

Passive Past: Stem is derived by removing -ТЬ from infinitive and adding -НН- or less commonly -Т-.

## GERUNDS

Active Present: -Я, -а rarely -ЮЧИ, -УЧИ

Stem derived by removing -УТ, ЮТ, -аТ or -ЯТ from 3rd person plural of present tense.

Active Past: -В, -ВШИ rarely -ДШИ

Stem is derived from infinitive (for majority by removing -ТЬ).

## SUBJUNCTIVE OR CONDITIONAL MOOD

The particle бы (or б), is used together with the past tense, indicative of both the imperfective and perfective aspects. The particle may be written separately or combined with a conjunction, as, for example, in чтобы (from что + бы).

## Regular Infinitives

| Infinitive Class | Refer to | Present and Perfective Future Tenses Formed by |
|---|---|---|
| Reg. A. | § 188, p. 283 | 1. Remove -ТЬ from infinitive. 2. Affix first conjugation endings. |
| Reg. B-1 Reg. B-2 | § 188, p. 283 § 188, p. 283 | 1. Remove -атЬ, -етЬ, -итЬ, -отЬ, -утЬ or -ятЬ from infinitive. 2. Affix first conjugation endings for "Reg. B-1" infinitives and second conjugation endings for "Reg. B-2" infinitives. |

## Irregular Infinitives

### Group I.  Infinitives Ending in -ТЬ (but excluding -ЗТЬ and -СТЬ)

Stem changes involved in formation of the present (or perfective future) tense characterize the following subgroups of infinitives within this class.

| Infinitive Class | Refer to | Stem Change |
|---|---|---|
| Irr. A-1 | § 195, p. 293 | -ОВ- replaced by -у-. |
| Irr. A-2 | § 195, p. 293 | -ев- replaced     -ю-. |
| Irr. B | § 196, p. 297 | -в- removed from stem. |
| Irr. C-1, 2 | § 197, p. 297 | Addition of -Л- to stem ending in б-, в-, м-, п-, or ф-. |
| Irr. C-3, 4, 5 | § 197, p. 297 | Addition of -в-, -н- or -м-. |
| Irr. D | § 198, p. 300 | Change of final consonant. |
| Irr. E | § 199, p. 302 | Addition of -е-, -о-, or -ё- or removal of -Ь-. |
| Irr. F | § 200, p. 304 | Miscellaneous more complex changes. |

## Group II. Infinitives Ending in −ЧЬ, −ЗТИ, −СТИ, −ЗТЬ, −СТЬ and −ТТИ.

Relationships between these infinitives and their present and perfective future tenses (and verb forms derived therefrom) do not lend themselves to concise summarization. In order to facilitate reference to previous discussion, these infinitives have been grouped into the following subclasses.

| Infinitive Class | Refer to | Infinitive Ending |
|---|---|---|
| Irr. G-1, 2, 3, 4 | § 204, p. 313 | −ЧЬ |
| Irr. H-1, 2, 3, 4, 5 | § 205, p. 315 | −ЗТИ and −СТИ |
| Irr. H-6, 7, 8, 9 | § 205, p. 315 | −ЗТЬ and −СТЬ |
| Irr. H-10 | § 206, p. 320 | −ТТИ (ИТТИ and related infinitives) |

## Group III. Infinitives Conjugated with Irregular Endings

This very small group is constituted by three simple infinitives and such derivatives as are formed from them with prefixes only.

| Infinitive Class | Refer to | Infinitives |
|---|---|---|
| Irr. I-1, 2, 3 | § 207, p. 323 | быть, есть, дать |

Finally, there are a few perfective infinitives (ending in a vowel plus −ТЬ), regular in the perfective future tense, but irregular in the past tense as discussed in Lesson 25. These infinitives have been divided into two subgroups and assigned the class designations "Irr. J-1" and "Irr. J-2," respectively.

§ 326.  Example Conjugations of Typical Verbs.

Previous discussion has pointed out that the great majority of Russian verbs are characterized by two parallel sets of forms derived, respectively, from two infinitives, namely the perfective and imperfective.  In §§ 321, 322, 323, attention was directed to the fact that several different means are employed in Russian to distinguish the imperfective infinitives from their perfective companions.  As a consequence of this, several different means are employed to distinguish between parallel sets of verb forms derived from different pairs of infinitives.

The following tables, giving the full conjugation of a number of typical verbs, have been drawn up so as to emphasize the different relationships as to form encountered in conjugation of various pairs of imperfective and perfective infinitives.  The more important types of these relationships are as follows.

1) Both infinitives regularly conjugated, with prefix (here с-) serving to distinguish between forms derived from the companion imperfective and perfective infinitives. Example:  де́лать -- сде́лать  "to do."

2) Both infinitives regularly conjugated but with different sets of regular endings in present and perfective future tenses serving to distinguish between parallel forms derived from companion perfective and imperfective infinitives.  Example:  ОКИСЛЯ́ТЬ -- ОКИСЛИ́ТЬ  "to oxidize."

3) Imperfective infinitive conjugated regularly but perfective infinitive conjugated irregularly.  Here, again, different sets of regular endings generally are used to form the present and perfective future tenses and this fact aids in distinguishing between parallel forms derived from companion perfective and imperfective infinitives.  Example:  ОПИ́СЫВАТЬ -- описа́ть  "to describe."

4) Both infinitives conjugated irregularly but differently. Example:  брать -- ВЗЯТЬ  "to take."

§ 327.  Concluding Remarks Regarding Irregular Conjugation.

It is important to realize that irregularities in the conjugation of infinitives cause far less difficulty in reading scientific Russian than might be anticipated.  One reason for this is the fact, already noted, that the regular endings are used almost exclusively with all infinitives regardless of whether stem changes

| | IMPERFECTIVE | PERFECTIVE | IMPERFECTIVE | PERFECTIVE |
|---|---|---|---|---|
| Inf. | де́лать | сде́лать | окисля́ть | окисли́ть |
| Class | | | | |

|  | INDICATIVE | | INDICATIVE | |
|---|---|---|---|---|
|  | Present | Perf. Future | Present | Perf. Future |
|  | Singular | | Singular | |
| 1st Per. | де́лаю | сде́лаю | окисля́ю | окислю́ |
| 2nd Per. | де́лаешь | сде́лаешь | окисля́ешь | окисли́шь |
| 3rd Per. | де́лает | сде́лает | окисля́ет | окисли́т |

|  | | Plural | | Plural |
|---|---|---|---|---|
| 1st Per. | де́лаем | сде́лаем | окисля́ем | окисли́м |
| 2nd Per. | де́лаете | сде́лаете | окисля́ете | окисли́те |
| 3rd Per. | де́лают | сде́лают | окисля́ют | окисля́т |

|  | Past Imp. | Past Perf. | Past Imp. | Past Perf. |
|---|---|---|---|---|
|  | Singular | | Singular | |
| Masc. | де́лал | сде́лал | окисля́л | окисли́л |
| Fem. | де́лала | сде́лала | окисля́ла | окисли́ла |
| Neuter | де́лало | сде́лало | окисля́ло | окисли́ло |

|  | | Plural | | Plural |
|---|---|---|---|---|
| Masc. Fem. Neuter | де́лали | сде́лали | окисля́ли | окисли́ли |

|  | Imperfective Future | | Imperfective Future | |
|---|---|---|---|---|
|  | Singular | Plural | Singular | Plural |
| 1st Per. | бу́ду де́лать | бу́дем де́лать | бу́ду окисля́ть | бу́дем окиоля́ть |
| 2nd Per. | бу́дешь де́лать | бу́дете де́лать | бу́дешь окисля́ть | бу́дете окисля́ть |
| 3rd Per. | бу́дет де́лать | бу́дут де́лать | бу́дет окисля́ть | бу́дут окисля́ть |

|  | IMPERATIVE | | IMPERATIVE | |
|---|---|---|---|---|
|  | (2nd Person) | | (2nd Person) | |
| Sing. | де́лай | сде́лай | окисля́й | окисли́ |
| Plural | де́лайте | сде́лайте | окисля́йте | окисли́те |

### CONDITIONAL        CONDITIONAL

The conditional of both the imperfective and perfective aspects is formed by using the particle бы (or б) with the forms of the corresponding indicative past tense, cf. Lesson 34.

|  | PARTICIPLES | | PARTICIPLES | |
|---|---|---|---|---|
| Present Active | де́лающий | | окисля́ющий | |
| Present Passive | де́лаемый | | окисля́емый | |
| Past Active | де́лавший | сде́лавший | окисля́вший | окисли́вший |
| Past Passive | де́ланный | сде́ланный | | окислённый |

|  | GERUNDS | | GERUNDS | |
|---|---|---|---|---|
| Present Active | де́лая | | окисля́я | |
| Past Active | де́лав | сде́лав | окисля́в | окисли́в |
|  | де́лавши | сде́лавши | окисля́вши | окисли́вши |

|  | IMPERFECTIVE | PERFECTIVE | IMPERFECTIVE | PERFECTIVE |
|---|---|---|---|---|
| Inf.<br>Class | опи́сывать | описа́ть | брать | взять |

|  | INDICATIVE | | INDICATIVE | |
|---|---|---|---|---|
|  | Present | Perf. Future | Present | Perf. Future |
|  | Singular | | Singular | |
| 1st Per. | опи́сываю | опишу́ | беру́ | возьму́ |
| 2nd Per. | опи́сываешь | опи́шешь | берёшь | возьмёшь |
| 3rd Per. | опи́сывает | опи́шет | берёт | возьмёт |
|  | Plural | | Plural | |
| 1st Per. | опи́сываем | опи́шем | берём | возьмём |
| 2nd Per. | опи́сываете | опи́шете | берёте | возьмёте |
| 3rd Per. | опи́сывают | опи́шут | беру́т | возьму́т |

|  | Past Imp. | Past Perf. | Past Imp. | Past Perf. |
|---|---|---|---|---|
|  | Singular | | Singular | |
| Masc. | опи́сывал | описа́л | брал | взял |
| Fem. | опи́сывала | описа́ла | брала́ | взяла́ |
| Neuter | опи́сывало | описа́ло | брало́ | взяло́ |
|  | Plural | | Plural | |
| Masc.<br>Fem.<br>Neuter | опи́сывали | описа́ли | бра́ли | взя́ли |

|  | Imperfective Future | | Imperfective Future | |
|---|---|---|---|---|
|  | Singular | Plural | Singular | Plural |
| 1st Per. | бу́ду опи́сывать | бу́дем опи́сывать | бу́ду брать | бу́дем брать |
| 2nd Per. | бу́дешь опи́сывать | бу́дете опи́сывать | бу́дешь брать | бу́дете брать |
| 3rd Per. | бу́дет опи́сывать | бу́дут опи́сывать | бу́дет брать | бу́дут брать |

|  | IMPERATIVE<br>(2nd Person) | | IMPERATIVE<br>(2nd Person) | |
|---|---|---|---|---|
| Sing. | опи́сывай | опиши́ | бери́ | возьми́ |
| Plural | опи́сывайте | опиши́те | бери́те | возьми́те |

| CONDITIONAL | CONDITIONAL |
|---|---|

The conditional of both the imperfective and perfective aspects is formed by using the particle бы (or б) with the forms of the corresponding indicative past tense, cf. Lesson 34.

|  | PARTICIPLES | | PARTICIPLES | |
|---|---|---|---|---|
| Present<br>Active | опи́сывающий | | | |
| Present<br>Passive | опи́сываемый | | берёмый | |
| Past<br>Active | опи́сывавший | описа́вший | бра́вший | взя́вший |
| Past<br>Passive | | опи́санный | (бра́ный) | взя́тый |

|  | GERUNDS | | GERUNDS | |
|---|---|---|---|---|
| Present<br>Active | опи́сывая | | беря́ | |
| Past<br>Active | | опи́сив<br>опи́сивши | брав<br>бра́вши | взяв<br>взя́вши |

encountered in their conjugation has caused us to classify them as irregular. Furthermore, no irregularity is involved in the derivation of certain forms from infinitives which we are classifying as irregular. Thus, for example, the past tense and the passive past participles from nearly all Russian infinitives are derived in regular fashion in accordance with the Table of Endings of pp. 511-513. The close relationship of the present and perfective future tense forms to certain other forms of irregularly conjugated infinitives also contributes to making them less troublesome than they would be otherwise.

Finally, it should also be noted that the frequency of use of irregularly derived verb forms is less than might be anticipated. This is due to a combination of circumstances. The most important of these are best explained by considering a simple example, such as ЛИТЬ "to be pouring," ВЛИТЬ "to pour in" and ВЛИВАТЬ "to be pouring in." Here the infinitive denoting general action, namely ЛИТЬ, and its closely related perfective derivative, ВЛИТЬ, exhibit certain irregularities in conjugation. It turns out, however, that the irregularly derived forms are in general encountered much less frequently in scientific writing than the regularly derived forms from ЛИТЬ, ВЛИТЬ and ВЛИВАТЬ. Note in this connection that imperfective infinitives denoting specific action as exemplified by ВЛИВАТЬ, are, in general, completely regular in their conjugation. Such imperfective infinitives as ВЛИВАТЬ and forms derived therefrom by their regular conjugation are particularly important in scientific writing.

§ 328. Reading Exercise.

## Двигатели внутреннего сгорания[1]

Двигателем внутреннего сгорания является двигатель, в котором топливо сгорает непосредственно под поршнем[2] в цилиндре. Газы, образующиеся при горении, давя на поршень, производят работу. Таким образом нет необходимости[3] предварительно превращать энергию топлива в энергию пара.

Двигатель внутреннего сгорания часто называется мотором.

В настоящее время имеется очень много моторов разнообразных конструкций, но все эти конструкции представ-

ляют собой изменения двух[4] первоначальных моторов. Один
из первоначальных моторов изобрел Отто (1861) на газообра-
зном топливе а другой - Дизель (1897) на жидком топливе.
Различные типы этих двигателей, отличаясь друг от друга
некоторыми деталями устройства, имеют[5] общую для всех
черту:  движение получается в результате давления газов,
образующихся при быстром сгорании горючей смеси в самом
цилиндре.

    В цилиндре ходит поршень, соединённый при помощи
шатуна и кривошипа с рабочим валом.  Каждый ход поршня[в]
в одну сторону называется тактом.

    В двигателе, который изобрел Отто, процесс работы
состоит из повторяющихся[7] периодически четырёх последо-
вательных движений поршня. Следовательно, такой двигатель называют четырехтактным.  Явления, происходящие в
цилиндре при каждом из четырёх тактов, резко отличаются
друг от друга.

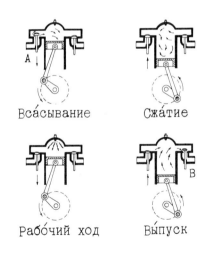

Всасывание          Сжатие

Рабочий ход          Выпуск

Первый такт (Всасывание)
    Поршень, двигаясь вниз  производит внутри цилиндра
разрежение; через клапан А засасывается горючая  смесь.

Второй такт (Сжатие)

Оба[8] клапана закрыты, поршень, поднимаясь вверх, сжимает горючую смесь. В конце этого происходит электрической искрой[9] вспышка.

Третий такт (Рабочий ход)

Образующиеся при сгорании смеси газы давят на поршень и с силой гонят его вниз.

Четвёртый такт (Выпуск)

Поднимающийся поршень через открывшийся выпускной клапан Б выталкивает из-под[10] поршня отработанные газы.

Важной частью четырехтактного двигателя является маховое колесо, укреплённое на валу мотора. Маховое колесо, получив сильный толчок во время рабочего хода, продолжает всё еще двигаться во время трёх[11] других тактов.

## Notes

1. двигатели внутреннего сгорания , literally, "movers of internal combustion" or, to use the conventional English phrasing, "internal combustion motors."

2. поршнем is the instrumental singular of поршень "piston." This noun is declined with omission of -е- from the stem in all cases except the nominative and accusative singular, cf. § 357, p. 573.

3. нет необходимости freely translated "there is no necessity." Note that необходимости is in the genitive singular case.

4. двух первоначальных моторов "of two basic motors." Both the numeral двух and the two following Russian words are in the genitive plural case, cf. § 371, p. 604.

5. имеют общую для всех черту, literally, "(they) have a common for all trait" or, more freely, "(they) all have a trait in common."

6. по́ршня  is the genitive singular of  по́ршень, cf. Note 2 above.

7., из   повторя́ющихся   периоди́чески   четырёх последова́тельных   движе́ний, literally, "of repeating self periodically   four   successive   movements."   Here   the повторя́ющихся   modifies the numeral четырёх.   Both these words and also the two words following четырёх are in the genitive plural case, cf. Note 4 above.

8. О́ба кла́пана  "Both valves."   Here кла́пана as required by the numeral о́ба is the genitive singular of  кла́пан valve.

9. электри́ческой  и́скрой.   These  words  are  in  the instrumental singular case.

10. из-под    "from   under."   Double   prepositions   are encountered occasionally in Russian.

11. трёх други́х та́ктов  "of (the) three other strokes."   All three Russian words are in the genitive plural case.

§ 329.  Translation Exercise.

1. In  a  prime  mover  of internal combustion,  the  fuel burns rapidly in a cylinder.
2. Gases, forming self during (при) combustion of fuel, exert pressure (да́вят) on  a  piston.
3. Otto (1861) invented one of these two original motors.
4. Availing  self  (По́льзуясь)  of  a  prime  mover,  it  is possible, to  convert  energy  of  fuel  into  mechanical ( меха́ническую )  energy.
5. Various, types  of  motors  differ  (distinguish  self), (отлича́ются)  by certain details of construction.
6. The motor which Otto invented, they call four-stroke.
7. During the first stroke, the combustible mixture is sucked into the cylinder.
8.  The  combustible mixture ignites self (загора́ется) by  an electric spark.
9. The  gases,  formed  during  rapid  combustion  of  the combustible mixture, drive the piston downward with force.
10. Each piston, united with the aid of a connecting rod and the crankshaft to the shaft, continues none the less to move during the time of the four strokes.

LESSON 36

THE COMPARATIVE DEGREE OF ADJECTIVES
AND ADVERBS

§ 330. The Comparative Degree of English Adjectives and Adverbs.

In English, regular formation of the comparative degree of adjectives and adverbs may occur by two distinctly different methods, (1) by using the auxiliary adverb "more" with the positive degree of an adjective or adverb and (2) by adding the ending "-er" to the positive degree of adjectives.

The first method is exemplified by such adjectives as "successful" -- "more successful," "irregular" -- "more irregular" and by corresponding adverbs "successfully" -- "more successfully," "irregularly" -- "more irregularly." In the second method, the ending "-er" is usually added directly to the positive degree of the adjective, e.g., "fast" -- "faster." However, with some adjectives, formation of the comparative may be regarded as consisting of a minor alteration in the stem of the positive degree followed by addition of the ending "-er," e.g., "pretty" -- "prettier"; "red" -- "redder," etc. Similar stem alterations occur in Russian in forming the comparative degree.

It should also be noted that irregular formation of the comparative degree, as exemplified by English "good" -- "better," "bad" -- "worse," is also encountered in Russian.

§ 331. General Method of Forming the Comparative Degree of Russian Adjectives (Attributive Forms).

When Russian adjectives are used as direct modifiers of nouns (i.e., attributively) (cf. § 117, p. 171), the general method of forming the comparative degree consists of using the adverb, бóлее, together with the positive degree of the adjective which is declined in the usual way as shown by the following example phrases.

| | |
|---|---|
| бо́лее бы́страя реа́кция | faster reaction |
| бо́лее ре́дкий мета́лл | rarer metal |
| бо́лее чи́стая кислота́ | purer acid |
| бо́лее то́чные да́нные | more exact data |
| бо́лее го́рький вкус | more bitter taste |

This use of the Russian adverb, бо́лее, to form the comparative degree of Russian adjectives is quite comparable to the above mentioned, similar use of the English adverb, "more."

Closely related to the use of бо́лее, as illustrated above, is the use of ме́нее "less" as in the phrases ме́нее бы́страя реа́кция "less rapid reaction," ме́нее ре́дкий мета́лл "less rare metal," etc.

| Почти́ | одновре́менно | появи́лись | и | бо́лее |
|---|---|---|---|---|
| Almost | simultaneously | showed self (appeared) | also | more |

| мо́щные | звездообра́зные | мото́ры | возду́шного |
|---|---|---|---|
| powerful | star-shaped (radial) | motors | of air |

охлажде́ния.[1]
cooling.

| О́чень | мо́жет | быть,[2] | что | за | Плуто́ном | есть[3] | и |
|---|---|---|---|---|---|---|---|
| Very | (it) is able | to be, | that | beyond Pluto | | are | even |

| ещё | бо́лее | далёкие | плане́ты. |
|---|---|---|---|
| farther | more | distant | planets. |

| Бо́лее | ни́зкие | температу́ры | достига́ются | лишь | в |
|---|---|---|---|---|---|
| More | low | temperatures | attain self | only | in |

| результа́те | примене́ния | ме́тода | адиабати́ческого |
|---|---|---|---|
| result | of use | of (the) method | of adiabatic |

| размагни́чивания | парамагни́тных | соле́й. |
|---|---|---|
| demagnetization | of paramagnetic | salts. |

---

[1] возду́шного охлажде́ния is an example of the descriptive genitive. A smoother translation of this sentence would be: "Almost simultaneously, more powerful, air cooled, radial engines also made their appearance."

[2] О́чень мо́жет быть is more smoothly translated: "It is very likely."

[3] For significance of есть as adding emphasis to the affirmation see § 122, p. 180.

Реа́кции   с   ма́лой  эне́ргией  актива́ции   приобрета́ют
Reactions  with  small   energy    of activation  attain

больши́е   ско́рости   уже́ при бо́лее   и́ли  ме́нее  ни́зких
big        velocities  even at  more    or   less    low

температу́рах;  реа́кции  с   большо́й эне́ргией актива́ции
temperatures;   reactions with big     energy   of activation

достига́ют  таки́х   ско́ростей   лишь   при  высо́ких
attain     such    velocities   only   at   high

температу́рах.
temperatures.


§ 332.  Unusual  Forms  Encountered  in  Comparison  of  Certain
        Adjectives.

A few Russian adjectives are exceptional in that they have
forms whose translation sometimes requires the comparative
forms and sometimes the superlative forms of English adjectives.
An example is ЛУ́ЧШИЙ "better," "best" corresponding to ХОРО́ШИЙ
"good." Note that ЛУ́ЧШИЙ, and similar comparative-superlative
forms listed below are declined with regular adjective endings
and used as direct modifiers of nouns.[1] Thus ЛУ́ЧШИЙ is declined
like СВЕ́ЖИЙ (Key No. 22, § 132, p. 198). Formation of
exceptional comparative-superlative forms from the positive
degree usually involves a stem change.

The following list though incomplete, includes all such
exceptional forms of importance in scientific Russian.

| Positive Degree | | Special Comparative - Superlative Forms |
|---|---|---|
| большо́й | big | бо́льший |
| вели́кий | great | бо́льший |
| высо́кий | high | вы́сший |
| ма́лый | small | ме́ньший |
| молодо́й | young | мла́дший |
| ни́зкий | low | ни́зший |
| плохо́й | poor, bad | ху́дший |

---

[1] Predicative comparative forms of Russian adjectives are discussed in the
following § § 333 and 334.

|  | Positive Degree | | Special Comparative - Superlative Forms |
|---|---|---|---|
| ста́рый | old | | ста́рший |
| хоро́ший | good | | лу́чший |
| худо́й | bad, evil, slender | | ху́дший |

The special forms under discussion are used with comparative force in the following sentences. Regular formation of the comparative using the adverb бо́лее is illustrated by the last sentence given below.

| Е́сли | освеща́ть | це́зий | луча́ми | бо́льшей | и́ли |
|---|---|---|---|---|---|
| If | (to) illuminate | cesium | with rays | of greater | or |

| ме́ньшей | частоты́, | то | выбра́сывается | ме́ньшее | число́ |
|---|---|---|---|---|---|
| lesser | frequency, | then | eject self | lesser | number |

| электро́нов. |
|---|
| of electrons. |


| По | зако́ну | всеми́рного | тяготе́ния, | ме́ньшие |
|---|---|---|---|---|
| According to | (the) law | of universal | gravitation | (the) smaller |

| плане́ты | притя́гивают | га́зы | с | ме́ньшей си́лой. |
|---|---|---|---|---|
| planets | attract | gases | with less | force. |


| Лу́чшие | электро́нные | умножи́тели | даю́т | усиле́ние |
|---|---|---|---|---|
| (The) better | electron | multipliers | give | amplification |

| первонача́льного | электро́нного | то́ка | в не́сколько |
|---|---|---|---|
| of (the) original | electron | current | of several |

| миллио́нов | раз. |
|---|---|
| million | times. |


| Поэ́тому | не | исключено́, | что | при бо́лее ни́зких |
|---|---|---|---|---|
| Hence | (it is) not | excluded, | that | at more low |

| температу́рах | не́которые | мета́ллы, | кото́рые | мы сейча́с |
|---|---|---|---|---|
| temperatures | certain | metals, | which | we at present |

| не | счита́ем | сверхпроводя́щими, | ока́жутся | таковы́ми. |
|---|---|---|---|---|
| not | consider | superconducting | will prove self | such. |

§ 333. Regular Formation of the Predicative Form of the Comparative Degree of Adjectives.

It will be recalled that the predicative forms of the positive degree are formed by adding a certain set of endings to the stems of Russian adjectives, cf. § 118, p. 171. In the comparative degree, only a single predicative form exists which usually[1] is formed by adding ‑ee to the stem of adjectives, i.e., to the stem of the positive degree.

| Adjective (Positive Degree) | Stem | Comparative Degree Predicative Form (Regularly Formed) |
|---|---|---|
| быстрый<br>fast | быстр‑ | быстрее |
| медленный<br>slow | медленн‑ | медленнее |
| свежий<br>fresh | свеж‑ | свежее |
| симметричный<br>symmetrical | симметричн‑ | симметричнее |
| тяжёлый<br>heavy | тяжел‑ | тяжелее |
| холодный<br>cold | холодн‑ | холоднее |

§ 334. Irregular Formation of the Predicative Form of the Comparative Degree.

Instead of merely affixing ‑ee to their stems, to form the predicative of the comparative degree, a number of Russian adjectives first undergo a stem change and then affix ‑e (or occasionally ‑ee). These phonetic changes are closely related to those noted in the conjugation of certain infinitives, namely, Class Irr. D, § 198, p. 300. Some of the comparatives listed on the next page are rarely used.

---

[1] Exceptions to this rule are noted in the following § 334.

| Adjective (Positive Degree) | | Comparative Degree (Predicative) Form (Irregularly Formed) | Adjective (Positive Degree) | | Comparative Degree (Predicative) Form (Irregularly Formed) |
|---|---|---|---|---|---|
| бли́зкий | near | бли́же | ме́лкий | small, fine | ме́льче |
| бога́тый | rich | бога́че | | | |
| большо́й | big | бо́льше | молодо́й | young | моло́же |
| вели́кий | great | бо́льше | мя́гкий | soft | мя́гче |
| высо́кий | high | вы́ше | ни́зкий | low | ни́же |
| вя́зкий | viscous, sticky | вя́зче | пло́ский | flat | пло́ше |
| | | | плохо́й | poor, bad | ху́же |
| га́дкий | nasty, repulsive | га́же | | | |
| | | | просто́й | simple | про́ше |
| гла́дкий | smooth | гла́же | ра́нний | early | ра́ньше |
| глубо́кий | deep | глу́бже | | | ра́нее |
| го́рький | bitter | го́рче | ре́дкий | rare | ре́же |
| гро́мкий | loud, strong | гро́мче | сла́дкий | sweet | сла́ще |
| | | | сто́йкий | stable, firm | сто́йче |
| густо́й | viscous, thick | гу́ще | | | |
| | | | стро́гий | strict | стро́же |
| дешёвый | cheap | деше́вле | сухо́й | dry | су́ше |
| дорого́й | dear, expensive | доро́же | твёрдый | solid, hard | твёрже |
| е́дкий | corrosive, sharp | е́дче | ти́хий | quiet | ти́ше |
| | | | то́лстый | thick | то́лще |
| жа́ркий | hot | жа́рче | то́нкий | thin, fine | то́ньше |
| жи́дкий | liquid, fluid | жи́же | у́зкий | narrow | у́же |
| | | | хоро́ший | good | лу́чше |
| коро́ткий | short | коро́че | худо́й | bad, evil, slender | ху́дее ху́же |
| кра́ткий | | кра́тче | | | |
| кре́пкий | strong | кре́пче | ча́стый | often | ча́ще |
| лёгкий | light, easy | ле́гче | чи́стый | clean, pure | чи́ще |
| ма́ленький | tiny, slight, small | ме́ньше | широ́кий | wide | ши́ре |
| | | | я́ркий | bright | я́рче |

## § 335. Sentences Illustrating Use of the Predicative Form of the Comparative Degree.

Use of the predicative form of the comparative degree of adjectives as modifiers of the subject of sentences is illustrated by the following examples.[1]

Note that the single predicative form of the comparative degree is used regardless of varying gender or number of the subject of the sentence.

---

[1] See also sentences given in subsequent § § 336-339, of this lesson.

| Скорость | света | во | второй | среде́ | в | n | раз |
|----------|-------|-----|--------|--------|-----|-----|------|
| (The) speed | of light | in | (the) second | medium | (is) by | n | times |

| ме́ньше | и, | сле́довательно, | соотве́тственно | ме́ньше | |
|---------|-----|------------------|------------------|---------|-----|
| less | and, | consequently, | correspondingly | less | (is) |

| длина́ | светово́й | волны́. |
|--------|-----------|---------|
| (the) length | of (the) light | wave. |

| Но | про́ще | и | то́чнее | в | э́том | слу́чае |
|-----|--------|-----|---------|-----|-------|---------|
| But | (it is) simpler | and | more precise | in | this | case |

| провести́ | микроскопи́ческий | ана́лиз. |
|-----------|--------------------|----------|
| to carry out | microscopic | analysis. |

| "Коэфици́ент | поле́зного | де́йствия" | у[1] |
|--------------|-------------|-------------|------|
| The coefficient | of useful | activity | near (of) |

| совреме́нного | парово́за | не́сколько | вы́ше. |
|----------------|-----------|-------------|--------|
| (a) contemporary | locomotive | (is) somewhat | higher. |

§ 336.  The Comparative Degree of Russian Adverbs.

The comparative degree of English adverbs is formed by using "more" together with the positive degree of the adverb. Thus we have "more rapidly," "more rarely," "more precisely," etc. In Russian, бо́лее corresponding to English "more" may be used to form the comparative of adverbs. Alternatively, the comparative of Russian adverbs may be, quite simply, identical in form with the predicative form of the comparative degree of the corresponding adjective. This need not lead to confusion, if the context of sentences is taken into account as is illustrated by the following sentences.

| Освое́ние | морски́х | нефтяны́х | месторожде́ний | тепе́рь |
|-----------|----------|-----------|------------------|---------|
| Exploitation | of sea | petroleum | deposits | now |

| пойдёт[a] | быстре́е | и | ле́гче. |
|-----------|----------|-----|---------|
| goes on | quicker | and | easier. |

---

[1] The preposition у "near" is also used to indicate possession as discussed in § 388, p. 646.

[a] This is another case of a perfective future which denotes completed action but which is best translated by the present tense, cf. § 185, pp. 280.

Ещё   значи́тельно   ра́ньше   Ано́сов   в   Росси́и  (1841 г.)
Even  considerably   earlier   Anosov   in  Russia   (1841)

применя́л   для   иссле́дования   ста́ли   обы́чный
used        for   investigation    of steel  (the) ordinary

микроско́п.
microscope.

Ещё   лу́чше   зерни́стое   строе́ние   тако́го   спла́ва
Even  better  (the) granular  structure  of such  (an) alloy

    ви́дно   под   микроско́пом   при   увеличе́нии   в
(is) visible  under  (a) microscope   at  (a) magnification  of

1000  раз.
1000  times.

Гора́здо   быстре́е   происхо́дит   разделе́ние   жи́дкой
Enormously  faster    occurs       separation   of (the) liquid

сме́си,   е́сли   при   перего́нке   по́льзоваться[1]
mixture,  if    during  distillation  avail self (is used)

ректификацио́нными   коло́нками.
rectifying           columns.

§ 337. Use of ЧЕМ with Comparative Degree of Adjectives and Adverbs.

In English the word "than" is often used in making a comparison. In Russian a similar role is played by the word ЧЕМ.

Вообще́   мета́ллы   облада́ют   бо́лее   высо́кими
In general  metals   possess    more    high

коэфицие́нтами   отраже́ния   све́та,   чем диэле́ктрики.
coefficients     of reflection  of light  than dielectrics.

---

[1] The use of по́льзоваться, and forms derived therefrom, with the instrumental here ректификацио́нными коло́нками, has been pointed out previously in Note 9, p. 478.

| Не́которые | образцы́ | руды́, | из | кото́рой | добыва́ется |
|---|---|---|---|---|---|
| Certain | samples | of ore, | from | which | extracts self |

| ура́н, | дава́ли | излуче́ние | гора́здо | бо́льшее | чем | сам |
|---|---|---|---|---|---|---|
| uranium, | gave | radiation | much | greater | than | self |

| ура́н | в | чи́стом | ви́де. |
|---|---|---|---|
| uranium | in | pure | form. |

| На | Ма́рсе | | холодне́е, | чем | на | земле́. |
|---|---|---|---|---|---|---|
| On | Mars | (it is) | colder | than | on | earth. |

| Осмоти́ческое | давле́ние | коллои́дных | раство́ров |
|---|---|---|---|
| (The) osmotic | pressure | of colloidal | solutions |

| гора́здо | ме́ньше, | чем | осмоти́ческое | давле́ние |
|---|---|---|---|---|
| (is) enormously | less, | than | (the) osmotic | pressure |

| исти́нных | раство́ров. |
|---|---|
| of true | solutions. |

| Реа́кции | большинства́ | органи́ческих | веще́ств |
|---|---|---|---|
| Reactions | of (the) majority | of organic | substances |

| протека́ют | значи́тельно | ме́дленнее, | чем | реа́кции | ме́жду |
|---|---|---|---|---|---|
| proceed | considerably | slower, | than | reactions | between |

| ио́нами | неоргани́ческих | веще́ств. |
|---|---|---|
| ions | of inorganic | substances. |

| Алифати́ческие | углеводоро́ды | нитру́ются | и |
|---|---|---|---|
| Aliphatic | hydrocarbons | nitrate self | and |

| сульфиру́ются | значи́тельно | трудне́е, | чем |
|---|---|---|---|
| sulfonate self | considerably | more difficultly, | than |

| аромати́ческие |
|---|
| aromatic. |

Выделе́ние           нио́бия      и   танта́ла    э́тим     реакти́вом
(The) separation   of niobium  and tantalum   by this  reagent

происхо́дит   бо́лее   бы́стро   и   по́лно,   чем   ме́тодом
occurs       more    rapidly  and completely, than by the method

"виннокислого      гидро́лиза."
"of tartrate       hydrolysis."

Гидрокси́льный        водоро́д      у    фено́ла     замеща́ется
Hydroxyl             hydrogen      in   phenol      replaces self

мета́ллом      ле́гче,   чем   у   спи́ртов.
by metal      easier,   than  in  alcohols.

Приро́дный     газ  значи́тельно      бо́льше    применя́ется     для
Natural       gas  considerably     greater   uses self        for

нагрева́ния,      чем   для   освеще́ния.
heating,         than  for   illumination.

При    турбуле́нтном     движе́нии    жи́дкости    теплообме́н
During  turbulent       movement     of (a) liquid  heat exchange

ме́жду      жи́дкостью      и     сте́нкой     тру́бы
between    (the) liquid   and   (the) wall   of (the) tube

происхо́дит    бо́лее    интенси́вно    чем   в    слу́чае
goes on       more     intensely,    than  in   (the) case

ламина́рного     движе́ния.
of laminar      movement.

§ 338.  Use of the Genitive Case with the Comparative Degree of
        Adjectives and Adverbs.

As pointed out in the preceding § 337, Russian often uses чем,
corresponding to English "than," in connection with the comparative
of adjectives and adverbs. It is by no means unusual for чем
to be omitted and the comparative degree of an adjective or

adverb to be followed by the genitive case of the noun to which
the comparison is directed.  The following example sentences
are typical.

| Коллоида́льные | части́цы | | гора́здо | кру́пнее |
|---|---|---|---|---|
| Colloidal | particles | (are) | enormously | larger |

моле́кул.
(than) molecules.

| Для | движе́ния | вверх | на́до, | чтобы | тя́га[1] |
|---|---|---|---|---|---|
| For | movement | upward | (it is) necessary, | that | (the) pull |

| была́ | бо́льше | ве́са | раке́ты. |
|---|---|---|---|
| be | greater than | (the) weight | of (the) rocket. |

| Второ́й | о́пыт | оказа́лся | уда́чнее |
|---|---|---|---|
| (The) second | experiment | proved self | more successful |

пе́рвого.
than (the) first.

| Така́я | пу́шка | ве́сит | бо́лее | одно́й | то́нны. |
|---|---|---|---|---|---|
| Such | (a) cannon | weighs | more than | one | ton. |

| Оди́н | а́том | одновале́нтного | элеме́нта | не | мо́жет |
|---|---|---|---|---|---|
| One | atom | of monovalent | element | not | is able |

| уде́рживать | в | соедине́нии | бо́лее | одного́ | а́тома |
|---|---|---|---|---|---|
| to retain | in | combination | more | (than) one | atom |

друго́го элеме́нта.
of another element.

| Эфи́р | испаря́ется | быстре́е | спи́рта, | воды́ | и |
|---|---|---|---|---|---|
| Ether | evaporates | more rapidly | (than) alcohol | water | and |

| мно́гих | други́х | жи́дкостей. |
|---|---|---|
| many | other | liquids. |

---

[1] Russian speaks of the тя́га "pull" of a rocket, but English speaks of its "thrust."

| Изучéние | химúческой | | прирóды | витамúна | B₁ |
|---|---|---|---|---|---|
| Study | of (the) chemical | | nature | of vitamin | B₁ |

| начáлось | рáньше | изучéния | | всех | другúх |
|---|---|---|---|---|---|
| started self | earlier | (than) (the) study | | of all | other |

| витамúнов. |
|---|
| vitamins. |

| Éсли | óколо | твёрдой | стéнки | протекáет | жúдкость, |
|---|---|---|---|---|---|
| If | near (along) | (a) solid | wall | flows | liquid, |

| температýра | котóрой | | вúше | úли | нúже |
|---|---|---|---|---|---|
| (the) temperature | of which | (is) | higher | or | lower |

| температýры | стéнки, | то | мéжду | жúдкостью |
|---|---|---|---|---|
| (than the) temperature | of (the) wall, | than | between | (the) liquid |

| и | стéнкой | происхóдит | теплообмéн. |
|---|---|---|---|
| and | (the) wall | occurs | heat exchange. |

§ 339. Use of ЧЕМ and ТЕМ in Making Comparisons.

A change in the degree of magnitude or intensity of some attribute may be coupled with a similar change in another attribute by using ЧЕМ in combination with ТЕМ as in the following sentences. Note that in English this type of relationship is usually denoted by "the ---, the ---."

| Чем | бóльше | инéрция | тéла, | | тем бóльше | |
|---|---|---|---|---|---|---|
| The | greater | (the) inertia | of (a) body, | | the greater | (is) |

| егó | мáсса. |
|---|---|
| its | mass. |

| Чем | мéньше | длинá | световóй | волнú, | тем | бóльше |
|---|---|---|---|---|---|---|
| The | less | (the) length | of (the) light | wave, | the | bigger |

| | частотá | колебáний | и | тем | бóльше | |
|---|---|---|---|---|---|---|
| (is) | (the) frequency | of vibration | and | the | bigger | (is) |

| величинá | квáнта. |
|---|---|
| (the) magnitude | of (the) quantum. |

Чем        бо́льшей    анизотро́пией    облада́ют
By  so  much    bigger        anisotropy        possess

моле́кулы,        тем              сильне́е    эффе́кт.
(the) molecules,    by  so  much (is)    stronger    (the) effect.


Светово́й    пото́к    па́дает    на      като́дный        слой
(The) light    flux    falls      on    (the) cathode      layer,

фотоэлеме́нта,          освобожда́я      с        пове́рхности
of (the) photoelement,    liberating      from    (the) surface

сло́я        тем          бо́льшее число́    электро́нов,
of (the) layer    by so much    greater    number    of electrons,

чем          я́рче          па́дающий      на    фотоэлеме́нт    луч.
by so much    brighter (is)    the falling    on    (the) photoelement ray.


Чем    бо́льше    мы    изуча́ем    витами́ны,        тем    ясне́е
The      more      we    study        vitamins,        the    clearer

стано́вится    их    роль  в  пита́нии      люде́й        и
becomes        their  role  in  nourishment    of persons    and

живо́тных.
animals.


Чем          бо́льше    у́гол        при́змы          и
By  so  much    bigger    (the) angle    of (the) prism    anɑ

показа́тель    преломле́ния    вещества́,          тем
index          of refraction    of (the) substance,    by so much

сильне́е        отклоня́ется          луч            от
stronger        deflects      self    (the) ray        from

первонача́льного    направле́ния.
(the) original          direction.

## § 340. Formation of the Comparative Degree of Participles.

Since Russian participles are used as noun modifiers, they have many features in common with adjectives. Consequently, it is scarcely surprising that participles occasionally form a comparative degree in the same way as adjectives.

| Мо́жно | достигнуть | бо́лее | исче́рпыва́ющего |
|---|---|---|---|
| (It is) possible | to achieve | more | exhausting |

| извлече́ния | при | по́мощи | аппара́та | Сохле́та, |
|---|---|---|---|---|
| extraction | with | (the) aid | of (an) apparatus | of Soxhlet. |

| Увели́чить | ско́рость | самолёта[1] | | мо́жно |
|---|---|---|---|---|
| To increase | (the) velocity | of (the) plane | (is) | possible |

| други́м | спо́собом | прида́нием | самолёту |
|---|---|---|---|
| by another | process | by imparting | to (the) plane |

| бо́лее | обтека́емой[2] | фо́рмы. |
|---|---|---|
| of (a) more | around flowable | form. |

| Атмосфе́ра | Ма́рса | гора́здо | разрежённее |
|---|---|---|---|
| (The) atmosphere | of Mars | (is) enormously | more rarified |

| и | су́ше | на́шей | и | для | челове́ка | недоста́точна, |
|---|---|---|---|---|---|---|
| and | drier | than ours | and for | | (a) human being | insufficient. |

| В | коне́чном | счёте | тела́ | бо́лее | нагре́тые |
|---|---|---|---|---|---|
| In | (the) final | reckoning | (the) bodies | more | heated |

| отдаю́т | часть | свое́й | теплоты́ | тела́м | ме́нее |
|---|---|---|---|---|---|
| give out | part | of own | heat | to (the) bodies | less |

| нагре́тым. |
|---|
| heated. |

---

[1] The word самолёт is derived from сам "self" and лёт "flight."
[2] The Russian phrase бо́лее обтека́емой фо́рмы is more understandably translated by "of a better streamlined form," cf. Footnote 1, p. 455.

§ 341. Reading Exercise.

In works on astronomy, it is not unusual to capitalize the English words "Sun," "Moon" and "Earth," when referring to specific heavenly bodies. Corresponding capitalization of the Russian words Со́лнце, Луна́ and Земля́ also occurs.

## О вселе́нной[1]

В дре́вние времена́[2] лю́ди ду́мали, что земна́я пове́рхность в о́бщем пло́ска, что Со́лнце и звёзды гора́здо ме́ньше Земли́. До́лгое вре́мя Зе́млю счита́ли[3] гла́вной ча́стью вселе́нной.[4]

Мы зна́ем тепе́рь, что Земля́ представля́ет собо́й шар, что диа́метр Со́лнца в 109.5 раз[5] бо́льше диа́метра Земли́. Земля́ всё вре́мя обраща́ется вокру́г Со́лнца. При э́том Земля́ дви́жется со ско́ростью гора́здо бо́льшей, чем ско́рость артиллери́йского снаря́да.

Земля́ не одино́ка в свое́м ве́чном круже́нии о́коло Со́лнца. Существу́ет мно́жество други́х плане́т, одни́ бли́же к Земле́, други́е - да́льше. Хотя́ плане́ты име́ют вид звёзд, они́ в действи́тельности бо́лее похо́жи на Зе́млю, чем на звёзды. Все плане́ты гора́здо бли́же звёзд, но гора́здо да́льше Лу́ны.

Сло́во "плане́та" по-гре́чески означа́ет "бродя́чая звезда́". В дре́вности звёзды бы́ли на́званы неподви́жными звёздами а плане́ты - подви́жными звёздами. Мы зна́ем тепе́рь, что са́ми звёзды,[6] кото́рые пре́жде счита́лись неподви́жными, о́чень бы́стро дви́жутся.

Все звёзды нахо́дятся от нас о́чень далеко́. Наприме́р звезда́, Альфа Цента́вра, отстои́т от нас в 270000 раз[7] да́льше, чем Со́льнце. Други́е же звёзды расположёны от нас ещё гора́здо да́льше. Поэ́тому кака́я-нибудь звезда́ должна́ пролете́ть о́чень мно́го миллио́нов киломе́тров, пока́ мы не заме́тим,[8] что она́ чуть-чуть сдви́нулась со своего́ ме́ста. Чем да́льше звезда́, тем трудне́е определи́ть её расстоя́ние от нас и тем трудне́е заме́тить её движе́ние сравни́тельно[9] с на́шей со́лнечной систе́мой.

Из звёзд, ви́димых у нас невооружённым гла́зом,[10] сравни́тельно бы́стро дви́жется я́ркая желтова́тая звезда́, Арктур

в созве́здии Волопа́са. Есть звёзды, кото́рые изменя́ют своё положе́ние ещё скоре́е, но просты́м гла́зом они́ не ви́дны.

Со́лнце, как и[11] Земля́, враща́ется вокру́г свое́й оси́, но с ме́ньшей ско́ростью. При э́том наблюда́ется, что ча́сти Со́лнца, находя́щиеся на его́ эква́торе, де́лают оди́н оборо́т за 25 су́ток[12] ча́сти Со́лнца, располо́женные бли́же к по́люсам Со́лнца, враща́ются ме́дленнее. И Со́лнце и звёзды состоя́т из раскалённых га́зов, нагре́тых на пове́рности до не́скольких ты́сяч гра́дусов.[13] Существу́ют звёзды ме́нее горя́чие, чем Со́лнце; они́ кра́сного цве́та[14] и име́ют температу́ру всего́ лишь о́коло 3000°. Други́е, бо́лее горя́чие, име́ют температу́ру доходя́щую до 30,000°[15] на пове́рхности. Внутри́ же Со́лнца и звёзд существу́ют гора́здо вы́сшие температу́ры, кото́рые дохо́дят[16] до деся́тков миллио́нов гра́дусов.

## Notes

1. вселе́нной  is here  the  prepositional  singular  of вселе́нная  a word which is declined with feminine adjective endings and which means  "universe."

2. времена́  is here the accusative singular of the irregular neuter noun  вре́мя  "time,"  cf. § 358, p. 575.

3. счита́ли  "(they) considered."  This is an impersonal sentence, cf. § 385, p. 640.

4. вселе́нной  is here in the genitive singular case, see Note 1.

5. что диа́метр Со́лнца в 109.5 раз бо́льше "that the diameter of (the) sun (is) 109.5 times bigger."  Note the idiomatic expression в 109.5  раз, cf. § 374, p. 610.

6. са́ми звёзды "the very stars" or "the stars themselves," cf. § 148,  p. 223.

7. в  270000  раз да́льше.  See Note 5 above.

8. пока́ мы не заме́тим, "until we note,"  cf. § 391, p. 651.

9. сравни́тельно    с, literally, "relatively with" is more smoothly rendered by "relatively to."

10. ви́димых у нас невооружённым гла́зом, literally, "visible with us by means of (the) unaided eye." Here невооружённый is analogous as to its origin to the German "unbewaffnet." In a smoother translation one might say "visible to the naked eye."

11. как и, "as also."

12. су́ток is the genitive plural corresponding to the nominative plural су́тки "24 hour period," "day and night." The noun су́тки exists only in plural forms, cf. § 359, p. 579. The genitive plural is used here after the numeral 25, cf. § 371, p. 604.

13. до не́скольких ты́сяч гра́дусов    "to several thousands of degrees," cf. § 369, p. 598.

14. кра́сного цве́та    presents an example of the descriptive genitive, cf. § 121, p. 178.

15. име́ют температу́ру всего́ лишь о́коло 3000°, literally, "have (a) temperature of all only about 3000°," or more freely "have a temperature at most of about 3000°," cf. § 389, p. 647.

16. дохо́дят до деся́тков миллио́нов гра́дусов, "go up to tens of millions of degrees." The Russian prefers to speak of "tens," where we would speak of "dozens."

§ 342. Translation Exercise.

1. The Earth is enormously smaller than the Sun.
2. The velocity of the Earth is (shows self) enormously larger (бо́льшей) than the velocity of an artillery shell.
3. The Moon is enormously closer to the Earth than the Sun. sun.
4. The planets are (show self) (явля́ются) more similar (похо́жими) to (на) the Earth than to the stars.
5. All the planets are enormously nearer to the Earth than the stars.
6. Certain (Не́которые) planets to the unaided (simple) eye are not visible.
7. The planets move relatively rapidly.

8. The stars previously were considered (считались) immobile.
9. Certain stars change their position more rapidly than others.
10. There exist stars, which have temperatures going up to 30,000° on the surface.

### Note

1. Here "there exist" is translated by существуют. A Russian word corresponding to English "there" is not required for translating this sentence, as is often the case.

# LESSON 37

## THE SUPERLATIVE DEGREE OF ADJECTIVES AND ADVERBS

§ 343. The Superlative Degree of English Adjectives and Adverbs.

The superlative degree of English adjectives and adverbs is formed from the positive degree (1) by using the auxiliary adverb "most" or (2) by adding the ending "-est." The first method of forming the superlative is exemplified by the adjectives "successful" -- "most successful," "irregular" -- "most irregular" and by the corresponding adverbs "successfully" -- "most successfully," "irregularly" -- "most irregularly." Formation of the superlative degree of many English adjectives and adverbs is accomplished by adding the ending "-est" directly to the positive degree of the adjective, e.g., "fast" -- "fastest." With some adjectives, however, a minor alteration in the stem occurs before adding the ending, e.g., "pretty" -- "prettiest," "red" -- "reddest." Similar irregularities are encountered in Russian.

A few English adjectives have irregular superlatives, e.g., "good" -- "best," "bad" -- "worst." Irregular Russian superlatives are usually closely related to the irregular comparatives discussed in the preceding lesson. See § 332, p. 525; § 334, p. 527.

§ 344. Formation of the Superlative Degree of Adjectives by Using the Prefix наи-.

There are two general methods of forming the superlative of Russian adjectives. One of these is to add the prefix наи- to the comparative degree. Thus, in the general case of comparatives formed with the adverb, более, "more," the prefix is added to the adverb to form наиболее "most," as in the following examples.

541

| наибо́лее | бы́страя | реа́кция | the fastest reaction |
| наибо́лее | ре́дкий | мета́лл | the rarest metal |
| наибо́лее | чи́стая | кислота́ | the purest acid |
| наибо́лее | то́чные | да́нные | the most precise data |
| наибо́лее | го́рький | вкус | the bitterest taste |

Closely related to this formation of the superlative is the use of the adverb наиме́нее "least" (from ме́нее "less") to form a sort of negative superlative as in the phrases, наиме́нее бы́страя реа́кция "the least fast reaction," наиме́нее ре́дкий мета́лл "the least rare metal," etc.

As noted in § 332, p. 525 a few Russian adjectives are exceptional in that they have special forms sometimes requiring translation by the comparative degree and sometimes by the superlative degree of English. Examples are ме́ньший "smaller," "smallest" (from ма́лый "small") and лу́чший "better," "best" (from хоро́ший "good"). Adding to prefix наи- to these special forms renders them exclusively superlative,[1] e.g., наиме́ньший "smallest," "least," "lowest" and наилу́чший "best," "the best."

The following sentences illustrate the use of Russian superlatives formed as described above.

| Наибо́лее | ва́жное | сво́йство | бутадие́на | – | э́то | |
| The most | important | property | of butadiene | | that | (is) |

| больша́я | скло́нность | его́ | к | полимериза́ции. |
| (the) great | tendency | of him | to | polymerization. |

| Наибо́лее | высо́ким | коэфицие́нтом | отраже́ния | облада́ет |
| The most | high | coefficient | of reflection | possesses |

| серебро́ | – | о́коло | 95%. |
| silver | | about | 95%. |

---

[1] Sometimes the superlative of these adjectives is formed by using наибо́лее with the positive degree, e.g., наибо́лее хоро́ший "best."

| С | помощью | бетатро́нов | возмо́жно | получа́ть |
|---|---|---|---|---|
| With | (the) aid | of betatrons | (it is) possible | to obtain |

| γ-лучи́ | разли́чной | длины́ | волны́, | включа́я | наибо́лее |
|---|---|---|---|---|---|
| γ-waves | of various | length | of wave | including | the most |

| коротковолно́вые.[1] |
|---|
| short-wave. |

| Произво́дство | нитроглицери́на | отно́сится[2] | к числу́ |
|---|---|---|---|
| Production | of nitroglycerol | pertains | to (the) number |

| наибо́лее | опа́сных. |
|---|---|
| of the most | dangerous. |

| Наиме́нее | раствори́мым | сульфа́том | щелочно-земе́льных |
|---|---|---|---|
| (As) the least | soluble | sulfate | of alkaline earth |

| мета́ллов | явля́ется | сульфа́т | ба́рия. |
|---|---|---|---|
| metals | shows self | sulfate | of barium. |

| Абсолю́тный | нуль | температры, | т.е. | наиме́ньшая |
|---|---|---|---|---|
| (The) absolute | zero | of temperature, | i.e., | the lowest |

| возмо́жная | температу́ра, при | кото́рой | теплово́е |
|---|---|---|---|
| possible | temperature   at | which | thermal |

| движе́ние | в  тела́х | отсу́тствует, | соотве́тствует |
|---|---|---|---|
| movement | in  bodies | is absent, | corresponds |

| -273.16°С. |
|---|
| to  -273.16°C. |

---

[1] The expression включа́я наибо́лее коротковолно́вые is more smoothly translated as "including those of shortest wavelength." There is no English adjective equivalent to the Russian adjective коротковоло́новый which modifies γ-лучи́ and indicates that the γ-rays are characterized by short wave length.

[2] See Footnote 1, p. 145.

| В | га́зах | си́лы | сцепле́ния | име́ют | наиме́ньшее |
|---|---|---|---|---|---|
| In | gases | (the) forces | of cohesion | have | the |

| значе́ние, | сравни́тельно | с | други́ми | агрега́тными |
|---|---|---|---|---|
| value | comparatively | with | other | aggregate |

| состоя́ниями. |
|---|
| states. |

| Други́е | мета́ллы, | как | пра́вило, | наибо́лее | хоро́шие |
|---|---|---|---|---|---|
| Other | metals, | as | (a) rule, | the very | best |

| проводники́, | не | стано́вятся[2] | сверхпроводя́щими | при |
|---|---|---|---|---|
| conductors, | not | become | superconducting | at |

| таки́х | температу́рах. |
|---|---|
| such | temperatures. |

## § 345.  Formation of the Superlative Degree of Adjectives by Using the Auxiliary Adjective  са́мый.

Another general method of forming the superlative is to use the auxiliary adjective  са́мый  with the positive degree of an adjective. (For another type see the next paragraph.) Thus, to illustrate the general case, we have the following example phrases.  Note that  са́мый  when so used is declined like the regular adjective  ста́рый (Key No. 17 § 132, p. 192).

| са́мая | бы́страя | реа́кция | the fastest reaction |
|---|---|---|---|
| са́мый | ре́дкий | мета́лл, | the rarest metal |
| са́мая | чи́стая | кислота́ | the purest acid |
| са́мые | то́чные | да́нные | the most precise data |
| са́мый | го́рький | вкус | the bitterest taste |

The procedure of using  са́мый  to form the superlative is usually somewhat different with those exceptional adjectives having comparative-superlative forms used as direct modifiers of nouns, but which are not formed with the adverb  бо́лее, cf. § 332, p. 525.  With such adjectives  са́мый  is generally used in conjunction with the comparative-superlative forms.[1]

---

[1] Occasionally, however,  са́мый  is used with the positive degree, e.g.,  са́мый большо́й, "the biggest." See the last of the example sentences.

[2] See Footnote 1, p. 145.

Thus we have, for example, са́мый ни́зший "the lowest," са́мый лу́чший "the best," са́мый бо́льший "the biggest," etc.

The following sentences illustrate the use of Russian superlatives formed with the auxiliary adjective са́мый.

| Са́мый | ва́жный | из | э́тих | зако́нов | – | зако́н |
|--------|---------|-----|-------|----------|-----|--------|
| The most | important | of | these | laws | (is) | (the) law |

| сохране́ния | эне́ргии. |
|-------------|-----------|
| of (the) conservation | of energy. |

| Са́мым | просты́м | амфоте́рным | соедине́нием | явля́ется |
|--------|----------|-------------|--------------|-----------|
| As the most | simple | amphoteric | compounds | shows self |

| сама́ вода́. |
|-------------|
| self   water. |

| То́пливо | явля́ется | одни́м | из | са́мых | основны́х |
|----------|-----------|--------|-----|--------|-----------|
| Fuel | shows self | as one | of | the most | basic |

| материа́лов, | употребля́ющихся | в | промы́шленности. |
|--------------|------------------|-----|------------------|
| materials | using self | | in industry. |

| Одни́м | из | са́мых | лу́чших | проводнико́в | явля́ется |
|--------|-----|--------|---------|--------------|-----------|
| As one | of | the very | best | conductors | shows self |

| медь. |
|-------|
| copper. |

| Са́мый | большо́й | из спу́тников | Юпи́тера | немно́го |
|--------|----------|---------------|----------|----------|
| The most | big | of (the) satellites | of Jupiter (is) | (a) little |

| бо́льше | Мерку́рия | и | Плуто́на | – | са́мых |
|---------|-----------|-----|----------|-----|--------|
| bigger | (than) Mercury | and | Pluto | — | the   most |

| ма́леньких | плане́т | со́лнечной | систе́мы. |
|------------|---------|------------|-----------|
| small | planets | of (the) solar | systems. |

| Са́мым[1] | просты́м | и | удо́бным | движе́нием | явля́ется |
|---|---|---|---|---|---|
| As the most | simple | and convenient | motion | | shows self |

| не | прямолине́йно-возвра́тное, | | а |
|---|---|---|---|
| not | straight line—reversible | (reciprocatory) | but |

| враща́тельное, | вокру́г | неподви́жной | оси́. |
|---|---|---|---|
| rotatory | around | (a) motionless | axis. |

§ 346.  Formation of Another Type of Superlative Adjective with the Suffix -ейш- or Variation Thereof.

Another type of Russian superlative is used principally[2] to indicate a high degree of a quality often best translated by such English expressions as "very rare," "extremely fast," etc.  This type of Russian superlative, which for purposes of description might perhaps be termed the attenuated superlative, is formed regularly by attaching the suffix -ейш- to the stem of the positive degree thus generating a new adjective stem which is declined like the regular adjective све́жий, (Key No. 22, § 132, p. 198).  This type of superlative is used attributively, i.e., to modify nouns directly, as shown by sample sentences given in § 347, p. 548.

### Regular Formation[3] of the Superlative with the Suffix -ейш-

| бога́тый | rich | богате́йший |
|---|---|---|
| бы́стрый | fast, rapid | быстре́йший |
| густо́й | viscous, thick | густе́йший |
| ме́дленный | slow | ме́дленнейший |
| просто́й | simple | просте́йший |
| све́жий | fresh | свеже́йший |
| твёрдый | solid, hard | тверде́йший |
| то́лстый | thick | толсте́йший |
| то́чный | precise | точне́йший |
| ча́стый | often | часте́йший |
| чи́стый | clean | чисте́йший |

[1] As with English "most," са́мым applies here to both the following adjectives namely просты́м and удо́бным.  In such constructions са́мый (or one of its forms) may be repeated for emphasis.

[2] Occasionally, however, such superlatives are used to indicate the supreme degrees of an attribute.  See the first sentence in § 347, p. 548.

[3] Not all adjectives form this type of superlative.  Usage, rather than logical considerations, determine which adjectives fail to form this superlative.

With some adjectives formation of this type of superlative involves a consonant shift in the stem before attaching the suffix -айш- or variation thereof. This stem shift is often, though not always, similar to that previously observed during irregular formation of the predicative of the comparative degree of the same adjective, cf. § 334, p. 527. Some of the superlatives included in the following table, though listed in dictionaries, are rarely used.

### Irregular[1] Formation of the Superlative with Suffix -айш- or Variation Thereof

| | | |
|---|---|---|
| бли́зкий | near | ближа́йший |
| вели́кий | large | велича́йший |
| высо́кий | high | вы́сший |
| | | (also высоча́йший ) |
| гла́дкий | smooth | гладча́йший |
| глубо́кий | deep | глубоча́йший |
| дорого́й | dear, expensive | дража́йший |
| жа́ркий | hot | жарча́йший |
| жи́дкий | liquid | жидча́йший |
| коро́ткий | short | |
| кра́ткий | | кратча́йший |
| кре́пкий | strong | крепча́йший |
| лёгкий | light, easy | легча́йший |
| ма́ленький | tiny, slight, small | мале́йший |
| ме́лкий | small, fine | мельча́йший |
| мя́гкий | soft | мягча́йший |
| ни́зкий | low | нижа́йший |
| плохо́й | poor, bad | ху́дший |
| ре́дкий | rare | редча́йший |
| сла́дкий | sweet | сладча́йший |
| стро́гий | strict, severe | строжа́йший |
| ти́хий | quiet | тиша́йший |
| то́нкий | thin | тонча́йший |
| тя́жкий | heavy, oppressive | тягча́йший |

[1] Drawing a line between regular and irregular is particularly difficult with respect to formation of the superlative under consideration from adjectives whose stems end in - к - (e.g., ре́дкий). Many of these adjectives change -к- to -ч-, and then add -айш- to form the superlative stem. Since other changes in stem are encountered with some adjectives with stem ending in -к-, placing them all under the irregular heading seems best.

| | | |
|---|---|---|
| хоро́ший | good | лу́чший |
| широ́кий | wide | широча́йший |
| я́ркий | bright | ярча́йший |

§ 347. Sentences Illustrating Use of the Superlative Formed
with Suffix -ейш- or Variation Thereof.

Ближа́йший    из спу́тников    Ма́рса      раз    в
(The) nearest  of (the) satellites  of Mars (is)  times  about

60 бли́же   к Ма́рсу,  чем    Луна́      к Земле́.
60  nearer  to Mars   than  (the) moon  to (the) earth.

Вероя́тно,      что уже́   в  ближа́йшие[1]  го́ды  примене́ние
(It is) probable, that even in (the) nearest   years the use

электро́нных          мультиплика́торов          значи́тельно
of   electron          multipliers              considerably

расши́рится.
will expand self.

По          совреме́нным    нау́чным  да́нным  тела́  состоя́т
According to contemporary   scientific data   bodies consists

из мельча́йших        части́ц,   называ́емых    моле́кулами.
of  extremely   small particles,  being called   molecules.

Те́хника     снабжа́ет    фи́зику     точне́йшими
Technology   supplies    physics     with extremely precise

прибо́рами,   маши́нами,    с      по́мощью   кото́рых фи́зика
devices,    with machines  with  (the) aid   of which physics

открыва́ет  все но́вые   и  но́вые  явле́ния.
discovers  ever new   and new    phenomena.

---

[1] The Russian phrase в ближа́йшие го́ды is more freely, and also more
accurately, translated as "within the next few years."

| Дальне́йшие[1] | иссле́дования | показа́ли, | что | перехо́д |
|---|---|---|---|---|
| Further | investigations | showed | that | transition |

| в | сверхпроводя́щее | состоя́ние | | свя́зан | с |
|---|---|---|---|---|---|
| into | (the) superconducting | state | (is) | connected | with |

| це́лым | ря́дом | други́х | измене́ний | сво́йств |
|---|---|---|---|---|
| (a) whole | series | of other | changes | of properties |

металла.
of (the) metal.

§ 348. Predicative Superlative Forms of Russian Adjectives.[2]

Predicative superlative forms of adjectives are obtained by using the adverb наибо́лее with the predicative forms of the ⌐ositive degree as in the following example.

### Superlative Predicative Forms

ста́рый, "old" Key No. 17

| | Masc. | Fem. | Neuter |
|---|---|---|---|
| Singular | наибо́лее стар | наибо́лее ста́ра | наибо́лее ста́ро |

| | Masc., Fem., Neuter |
|---|---|
| Plural | наибо́лее стары́ |

Occasionally, when reading scientific Russian, another type of predicative superlative form will be encountered. This is formed by using the predicative comparative forms (see §§ 333, 334, p. 527) followed by всего́ or всех (genitive forms of весь "all").

---

[1] As ordinarily used, дальне́йший is virtually without superlative significance and, as here, is best translated by "further." There is a general tendency, by no means restricted to Russian, for superlative forms gradually to lose some of their full force.

[2] The predicative superlative forms of adjectives are used relatively little in contemporary Russian scientific writing.

В твёрдых  телах  атомы           наиболее близки друг
In solid       bodies  (the) atoms  (are) most       near     one

к другу, а   силы       сцепления имеют  самое большое
to another and (the) forces  of cohesion  have   the greatest

значение.
value.


Наиболее       характерны     для  аммиака          реакции
The  most      characteristic  for  ammonia  (are)  reactions

присоединения.
of combination.


Мы  уже  знаем,   что  сульфат   бария         наименее
We  already know      that (the) sulfate  of barium (is) the least

растворим   из  всех  сульфатов   щелочно-земельных
soluble         of   all    (the) sulfates   of alkaline — earth

металлов.
metals.


Жидкое топливо  -  удобнее  всех      для таких целей.
Liquid    fuel      (is)  the most  convenient for  such    purposes.


Легче    всего        превратить электрическую    энергию
Easiest  of all   (is)  to convert   electrical         energy

в  тепловую энергию.
into heat       energy.


§ 349.  The Superlative of Russian Adverbs.

The superlative of Russian adverbs is formed in general in
two different ways.  The superlative adverb more frequently used
in scientific writing is identical in form with such predicative
superlatives of adjectives as  быстрее всех,    лучше всего,
etc., cf. § 348, p. 549.

The superlative of Russian adverbs may also be formed by using наибо́лее with the positive degree of the adverb, e.g., ча́сто "often," практи́чески "practically" to form their superlative degree, i.e., наибо́лее ча́сто "most often," наибо́лее практи́чески "most practically." This use of наибо́лее is very closely related to its use in forming the superlative degree of adjectives.

Медь  и  серебро́  встреча́ются  в приро́де  гла́вным
Copper and silver      encounter self   in nature    for the most

о́бразом в  ви́де  се́рнистых[1]  соедине́ний
part      in  (the) form  of sulfurous (i.e., sulfide) compounds

и  ча́ще  всего́[2]  совме́стно  с  се́рнистыми
and most often of all  together    with sulfurous   (i.e.,

ру́дами други́х  мета́ллов.
sulfide) ores   of other  metals.


Ле́гче  всего́  мо́жно  познако́миться  с
Most easily of all  it is possible  to acquaint self   with

бакте́риями  при  по́мощи  микроско́па.
bacteria     with  (the) aid  of (a) microscope.


В лаборато́рных  усло́виях  $CO_2$  удо́бнее  всего́
In laboratory   conditions  $CO_2$  most conveniently  of all

получа́ют  де́йствием  кисло́т  на $CaCO_3$ (известня́к,
they obtain  by (the) action  of acids  on $CaCO_3$ (lime,

мра́мор,  мел)  наприме́р  по  реа́кции –
marble,  chalk)  for example  according to  (the) reaction

$$CaCO_3 + 2\ HCl \longrightarrow CaCl_2 + CO_2 + H_2O.$$

---

[1] See Footnote 2, p. 10.
[2] The expression ча́ше всего́, literally, "oftenest," is used frequently as an idiom translatable as "in particular."

В лаборато́риях     наибо́лее     ча́сто     применя́ются     во́дные
In laboratories     the most     often     use self     aqueous

раство́ры.
solutions.


Из     свойств     карбору́нда     наибо́лее
Of     (the) properties     of carborundum     (as) the most

практи́чески     ва́жным     явля́ется     его́     исключи́тельная
practically     important     shows self     his     exceptional

твёрдость.
hardness.


§ 350.  Superlative Forms of Participles.

The use of  наибо́лее  to form the superlative of participles
parallels the previously noted use of бо́лее to form the
corresponding comparatives, cf. § 331, p. 523.

В     настоя́щее     вре́мя     наибо́лее     распространённым
In     (the) present     time     (as) the most     widely distributed

электри́ческим     исто́чником     све́та     явля́ется
electrical     source     of light     shows self     (is)

ла́мпа     нака́ливания
(the) lamp     of incandescence.


Среди́     алюмосилика́тов     наибо́лее     распространены́[1]
Among     aluminosilicates     the most     widely distributed

          полевы́е шпа́ты,     наприме́р,     ортокла́з,
(are)     (the) feldspars     (for     example     orthoclase

---

[1] Here  наибо́лее распространены́  might be regarded as the plural predicative superlative form of the participle распространённый.

$(K_2O \cdot Al_2O_3 \cdot 6SiO_2)$ являющиеся главнейшей
$(K_2O \cdot Al_2O_3 \cdot 6SiO_2)$ showing self the most important

составляющей вулканических пород.
composing (part) of vulcanic minerals.

Одним из наименее диссоциированных веществ,
As one of the least dissociated substances

могущих образоваться при ионных реакциях,
being able to form self during ionic reactions

является вода.
shows self water.

Главная заслуга Томаса заключается в
(The) main service of Thomas contains self (consists) in

том, что он нашёл наиболее подходящий[1] огнеупорный
this, that he found the most suitable refractory

материал для основной футеровки конвертера.
material for basic lining of (the) convertor.

§ 351.  Other  Expressions  for  Unusual  Degree  of  a  Quality.

Before concluding discussion of the superlative, it should be noted that Russian, like English may use certain adverbs to indicate an unusual degree of a quality. The more important of these adverbs are the following:

весьма
very

особенно
particularly

гораздо
very much,
    enormously

очень
very

исключительно
exceptionally

сильно
strongly

---

[1] the word подходящий originated as the present active participle of the verb подходить – подойти "to come under," "to approach."

кра́йне                              сравни́тельно
extremely                           comparatively

ма́ло                                чрезвыча́йно
slightly                            unusually,
                                    excessively


These adverbs are used quite generally with the positive
degree either of adjectives or adverbs, e.g., чрезвыча́йно
ре́дкий мета́лл "unusually rare metal," e.g., окисля́ть о́чень
ме́дленно "to be oxidizing very slowly."

О́бласть        о́чень    ни́зких температу́р    (ни́же 1°К)
(The) region   of very   low      temperatures  (below 1°K)

представля́ет   основно́й  интере́с  с   то́чки    зре́ния
presents       basic      interest  from (the) point of view

дальне́йшего    прогре́сса всей          фи́зики   ни́зких
of further     progress   of (the) whole physics  of low

температу́р.
temperatures.


Температу́ры        плавле́ния   и   кипе́ния   водоро́да
(The) temperatures of melting  and boiling   of hydrogen

      чрезвыча́йно  ни́зки́.
(are) unusually    low.


Теплопереда́ча    в ге́лии II происхо́дит   чрезвыча́йно
Heat transfer    in helium II occurs       unusually

бы́стро, гора́здо  быстре́е,  чем в  мета́ллах.
fast,   enormously faster,  than in metals.


С    хими́ческой   стороны́, ли́тий   и   други́е ще́лочны́е
From (the) chemical side,   lithium and other   alkali

мета́ллы        явля́ются                   исключи́тельно
metals         show     self     (are)     exceptionally

реакцио́нноспосо́бными.
reaction capable.

| Большие | толщины | воды | сравнительно | легко |
|---|---|---|---|---|
| Big (thick) | layers | of water | relatively | easily |

| прогреваются | солнечными | лучами | лишь | до |
|---|---|---|---|---|
| heat self through | by (the) sun's | rays | only | up to |

| температуры | наибольшей | плотности | воды; |
|---|---|---|---|
| (the) temperature | of the greatest | density | of water; |

| дальнейшее | прогревание | идёт | крайне | медленно. |
|---|---|---|---|---|
| further | heating through | goes | extremely | slowly. |

An important type of idiom involves the use of ВОЗМОЖНО   or
КАК МОЖНО   together with the comparative degree of an adjective
or adverb to express the upper limit of possibility as  exemplified
by the following sentences.

| Большой | интерес | представляет | изучение |
|---|---|---|---|
| Great | interest | presents | (the) study |

| сверхпроводимости, | сверхтекучести, | обычной |
|---|---|---|
| of superconductivity, | of superfluidity, | of ordinary |

| проводимости | и | других | явлений | при |
|---|---|---|---|---|
| conductivity | and | of other | phenomena | at |

| возможно более | низких | температурах. |
|---|---|---|
| the lowest  possible | | temperatures. |

| Мы | заставляем | наши | машины | работать | как |
|---|---|---|---|---|---|
| We | compel | our | machines | to work | as fast |

| можно быстрее, | производить | как | можно | больше |
|---|---|---|---|---|
| as possible, | to produce | as | much as | possible |

| нужных | нам | вещей. |
|---|---|---|
| of necessary | to us | things. |

§ 352. Reading Exercise.

## О планетах

Са́мая бли́зкая к со́лнцу плане́та называ́ется Мерку́-рием.[1] Уви́деть Мерку́рий о́чень тру́дно, так как он всегда́ стои́т на не́бе бли́зко к Со́лнцу. Мерку́рий лишь немно́го бо́льше Луны́.

За Мерку́рием,[2] е́сли итти́ да́льше от Со́лнца, сле́дует плане́та Вене́ра, всем[3] изве́стная вече́рняя и у́тренняя звезда́. Э́то са́мая я́ркая звезда́ на всём не́бе. Вене́ра све́тит так я́рко, что её нетру́дно уви́деть да́же днём,[4] то́лько на́до зара́нее знать ме́сто на не́бе, где она́ нахо́-дится. В зри́тельную трубу́ пове́рхность Вене́ры представ-ля́ется о́чень све́тлой, соверше́нно ро́вной, бе́лой без вся́-ких пя́тен.[5] Очеви́дно, э́то не твёрдая пове́рхность само́й плане́ты, а её га́зовая оболо́чка, атмосфе́ра.

Тре́тье[6] ме́сто по поря́дку от Со́лнца занима́ет на́ша Земля́ с её[7] спу́тником Луно́й. Да́льше, сле́дует четвёртая плане́та - Марс. Ка́ждые два го́да[8] Марс подхо́дит к Земле́ на са́мое бли́зкое расстоя́ние, в сре́днем вдво́е бли́же Со́лнца. Во вре́мя тако́го приближе́ния к нам, Марс на не́сколько не-де́ль де́лается одно́й из ярча́йших звёзд.

Вокру́г Ма́рса обраща́ются два ма́леньких спу́тника.[9] Они́ о́чень бли́зки к свое́й плане́те, ближа́йший из них в 60 раз[10] бли́же к Ма́рсу, чем Луна́ к Земле́.

В простра́нстве ме́жду орби́той Ма́рса и орби́той сле́-дующей плане́ты Юпи́тера, мно́жество ма́лых плане́т дви́жется вокру́г Со́лнца.

За о́бластью ма́лых плане́т дви́жется са́мая бо́льшая плане́та со́лнечной систе́мы - Юпи́тер. По́сле Вене́ры Юпи́тер са́мая я́ркая из всех звёзд и плане́т. При наблюде́нии Юпи́тера в зри́тельную трубу́ са́мое интере́сное[11] - э́то его́ спу́тники. Уже́ в са́мую ма́лую зри́тельную трубу́ ви́дны че-ты́ре спу́тника[12] во́зле Юпи́тера, кото́рые постоя́нно меня́ют свое́ положе́ние.

Сле́дующая плане́та Сату́рн - она́ одна́ из са́мых ин-тере́сных. Вокру́г Сату́рна нахо́дится кольцо́, кото́рое яв-ля́ется грома́дным скопле́нием мельча́йших спу́тников.

За Ура́ном нахо́дятся плане́ты Непту́н и Плуто́н.[13] Всле́дствие большо́го расстоя́ния от Со́лнца, на э́тих плане́тах до́лжно быть чрезвыча́йно хо́лодно, гора́здо холодне́е, чем в на́ших поля́рных стра́нах.

По общеизве́стному зако́ну интенси́вность со́лнечной радиа́ции обра́тно пропорциона́льна квадра́ту расстоя́ния от Со́лнца. Благодаря́ своему́[14] положе́нию относи́тельно к Со́лнцу, Мерку́рий явля́ется са́мой "нагре́той" из всех плане́т.

Все плане́ты обраща́ются о́коло Со́лнца. Вре́мя соверше́ния одного́ враще́ния - т.е. "год" плане́ты - увели́чивается в ря́де от Мерку́рия до Плуто́на. Таки́м о́бразом, "год" Мерку́рия - коро́че всех, а "год" Плуто́на - длинне́е всех.

## Notes

1. Мерку́рием is the instrumental singular of Мерку́рий "Mercury," a masculine noun which, like the names of the other planets, is declined regularly. For a fuller discussion of the declension of names see § 362, p. 585.

2. за Мерку́рием, "beyond Mercury." It should be recalled that за means "beyond" when followed by the instrumental, cf. § 101, p. 146 and § 127, p. 187.

3. всем изве́стная, literally, "to all known" or, more smoothly, "known to all." Here изве́стная modifies звезда́.

4. днём which here is to be translated "by day" (cf. § 98, p. 141) is the irregular instrumental singular день, which is declined like по́ршень in § 357, p. 573.

5. пя́тен  is the irregular genitive plural of  ПЯТНО́  spot.
This type of irregular genitive is discussed in  § 355,  p. 561.

6. Тре́тье   ме́сто,  "(the) third place," As discussed in
§ 360,  p. 581,  the  ordinal  numeral,  тре́тий,  "third," is not
declined with the same endings as used with  си́ний  (Key No. 19,
§ 132,  p. 195).

7. с её спу́тником,  "with her satellite." When её is used
as a possessive adjective, it does not change in form when
following a preposition (here с). As pointed out in  § 136,  p. 204,
if её is used as a pronoun then it assumes the form неё after
prepositions as, for example, in the phrase с неё "from her."

8. After the nominative and accusative cases of the numeral
два,  the genitive of the noun (here   го́да) is required, cf.  § 371,
p. 604.

9. Here, again, the genitive singular (спу́тника) follows
the nominative of the numeral два.  In accordance with a rule
given in § 371, p. 604, the adjective ( ма́леньких ) modifying
спу́тника   is in the genitive plural.

10. в 60 раз бли́же  "(about) 60 times closer." For further
sentences illustrating use of раз to mean "times" in an
arithmetical sense, see  § 374,  p. 610.

11. са́мое   интере́сное -- э́то его́ спу́тники,   literally,
"the most interesting (thing) -- that (is) his satellites."

12. The genitive singular (here   спу́тника) is also required
after the  nominative  and  accusative  of  четы́ре  "four,"
cf.  § 371,  p. 604.

13. Плуто́н  "Pluto" not to be confused with the chemical
element   плуто́ний,  "plutonium."

14. In accord with the rule given in § 149, p. 225,  своему́
refers to the subject of the sentence  Мерку́рий .


§ 353.  Translation Exercise.

1. It is difficult to see Mercury, the very nearest (са́мую
   бли́зкую) to the Sun planet.
2. Mercury always stands in the sky very near to the Sun.

3. The Moon is only slightly smaller than Mercury ( Меркурия ).
4. The planet Venus is the most bright star of all the sky.
5. Beyond Venus (Венерой), if we go farther from the Sun, follows our Earth.
6. Around the Earth ( Земли ) revolves its (его) satellite -- the Moon.
7. Jupiter -- the very largest planet of our solar system -- is (shows self) one (ОДНОЙ ) of the brightest stars.
8. On (При) observation of Saturn in a observing tube the most interesting -- that is its ring.
9. The ring of Saturn is (shows self) an enormous accumulation of very small satellites.
10. The planets Pluto and Neptune are (find self) more distant from the sun than Uranus.

## LESSON 38

## SUPPLEMENTARY NOTES ON DECLENSION OF
## NOUNS AND ADJECTIVES

§ 354.  Introduction and Summary.

The overwhelming majority of nouns and adjectives encountered in reading scientific Russian are declined regularly as summarized in Lesson 16.  Occasionally, however, it is necessary to take cognizance of various peculiarities in the declension of certain nouns and adjectives.  Stem changes are of major importance in this connection.  Thus, a fairly large number of nouns form the genitive plural with insertion of -е-, -ё- or -о- in the stem (§ 355, p. 561). Similar insertion of -е- or -о- characterizes the predicative masculine singular of certain adjectives (§ 356 (a), p. 565).  Certain nouns are declined with removal of -е- or -о- from the stem (§ 357, p. 573).  Unusual endings are encountered in the declension of certain nouns (§ 358, p. 575; § 359, p. 576), a few adjectives (§ 360, p. 581) and a special class of possessives and related names (§ 361, p. 583).  A general summary of the declension of names is given in § 362, p. 585.  The failure to decline certain names and nouns is discussed in § 363, p. 588.

§ 355.  Nouns Forming the Genitive Plural with Insertion of -е-, -ё- or -о- in Stem.

Certain classes of feminine and neuter nouns are declined in such a way that their genitive plural forms are identical with their stems.  Thus, the stem of the feminine noun наýка (Key No. 9) is наýк- and its genitive plural is наýк.  Similarly, the stem of the neuter noun вещество́ (Key No. 13) is вещество- and its genitive plural вещéств.  Certain nouns declined with the same endings as наýка and вещество́ have stems terminating with consonant combinations which are either difficult to pronounce or un-euphonious.  Examples are the feminine noun ошибка "error" whose stem is ошибк- and the neuter noun стекло́ "glass" whose stem is стекл-.  If strict regularity were preserved in declension of these nouns, their genitive plurals would be ошибк and стекл, respectively.  In

order to render these forms more easily pronounceable (or more
euphonious) an -o- is inserted in the stem with the result that
the genitive plural of ошибка is ошибок while стёкол becomes
the genitive plural of стекло.

The vowel insert in the genitive plural is the only feature
distinguishing the declension of ошибка from that of наука
(Key No. 9, § 130, p. 190) and the declension of стекло from
that of вещество (Key No. 13, § 130, p. 191).

|                | FEMININE |         | NEUTER  |         |
|----------------|----------|---------|---------|---------|
| Nom. Sing.     | ошибка   | (error) | стекло  | (glass) |
| Key No.        | 9a       |         | 13a     |         |
| Stem           | ошиб -   |         | стекл - |         |

|        | Singular            | Plural    | Singular | Plural   |
|--------|---------------------|-----------|----------|----------|
| Nom.   | ошибка              | ошибки    | стекло   | стёкла   |
| Gen.   | ошибки              | ошибок    | стекла   | стёкол   |
| Dat.   | ошибке              | ошибкам   | стеклу   | стёклам  |
| Acc.   | ошибку              | ошибки    | стекло   | стёкла   |
| Instr. | ошибкой<br>( ошибкою ) | ошибками  | стеклом  | стёклами |
| Prep.  | ошибке              | ошибках   | стекле   | стёклах  |

An important variation of this mode of formation of the
genitive plural is insertion of an -e- or -ё- rather than an -o-.
Replacement of -ь- or -й- in the stem by -e- may also occur.
Note further that some nouns declined entirely with soft endings,
e.g., капля "drop," insert -e- in the stem when forming the
genitive plural. These variations might be summarized as
follows.

## FEMININE NOUNS

| Noun | Key No. | Genitive Plural | Otherwise Declined Like Noun | Key No. |
|---|---|---|---|---|
| ка́пля<br>drop | 10a | ка́пель | неде́ля | 10 |
| ка́пелька<br>little drop | 9b | ка́пелек | нау́ка | 9 |
| сестра́<br>sister | 7a | сестёр | моле́кула | 7 |
| копе́йка<br>kopek | 9b | копе́ек | нау́ка | 9 |

## NEUTER NOUNS

| Noun | Key No. | Genitive Plural | Otherwise Declined Like Noun | Key No. |
|---|---|---|---|---|
| зерно́<br>grain | 13b | зёрен | вещество́ | 13 |
| письмо́<br>letter | 13c | пи́сем | вещество́ | 13 |
| кольцо́<br>ring | 13d | ко́лец | вещество́ | 13 |
| се́рдце<br>heart | 14a | серде́ц | учи́лище | 14 |

The use in sentences of the genitive forms under discussion requires no special comment.

| Изготовле́ние | си́льно | окра́шенных | сте́кол, |
|---|---|---|---|
| (The) preparation | of strongly | colored | glasses, |

| поглоща́ющих | ультрафиоле́товые | лучи́, не | представля́ет |
|---|---|---|---|
| absorbing | ultraviolet | rays, not | presents |

затрудне́ний.
difficulties.


| По | э́той | тео́рии | ма́сса | ато́много | ядра́ |
|---|---|---|---|---|---|
| According to | this | theory | (the) mass | of (an) atomic nucleus | |

| определя́ется | су́ммой | чи́сел | прото́нов | и |
|---|---|---|---|---|
| determines self | by (the) sum | of (the) numbers | of protons | and |

нейтро́нов.
neutrons.


| Проце́сс | дробле́ния | я́дер | ура́на | с |
|---|---|---|---|---|
| (The) process | of splitting | of nuclei | of uranium | with |

| образова́нием | бо́лее усто́йчивых | ато́мных | я́дер |
|---|---|---|---|
| formation | of stabler | atomic | nucleı |

| сре́дних | элеме́нтов | сопровожда́ется |
|---|---|---|
| of intermediate[1] | elements | accompanies self |

| выделе́нием | о́чень | больши́х | коли́честв | эне́ргии. |
|---|---|---|---|---|
| by evolution | of very | great | quantities | of energy. |


| Охлажде́нные | водяны́е | пары́ | осажда́ются | на |
|---|---|---|---|---|
| Cooled | water | vapors | precipitate self | on |

| пове́рхности | предме́тов | в ви́де | ка́пелек | росы́. |
|---|---|---|---|---|
| (the) surface | of objects | in (the) form | of droplets | of dew. |


[1] "Intermediate elements" here refers to elements of intermediate atomic weight.

§ 356. Adjectives Distinctive with Regard to One or More Predicative Forms.

(a) Adjectives Forming the Predicative Masculine Singular with Insertion of -e- or -o- in the Stem.

As already noted in § 131, p. 192, the predicative masculine singular form of nearly all regularly declined[1] adjectives is the same as their stems. Thus, for example, the stems стар- and жив- of the adjectives ста́рый and живо́й are identical with their predicative masculine singular forms стар and жив. The stems of certain adjectives end in consonant combinations, which are unpronounceable or at least non-euphonious, e.g., the stem важн- from ва́жный or редк- from ре́дкий. With some of these adjectives -e- is introduced into the stem when forming the predicative masculine singular. Thus the predicative nominative singular of ва́жный is ва́жен. Other adjectives of this group introduce -o- into the stem as is illustrated by ре́док the predicative masculine singular of ре́дкий. Replacement of -й- or -ь- of the stem by -e- is a closely related irregularity encountered in formation of the predicative masculine nominative singular of a few other adjectives.

It should be noted that the masculine singular of the predicative presents the sole instance of deviation from the usual pattern of adjective declension. In particular, the attributive or direct modifier forms follow one or another of the familiar patterns summarized in Lesson 16. Specifically, ва́жный follows the same pattern as ста́рый (Key No. 17, § 132, p. 192) with больно́й and смешно́й following живо́й (Key No. 18, § 132, p. 194) and ре́дкий, го́рький and сто́йкий following электри́ческий (Key No. 21, § 132, p. 197). It should also be noted that no insertion of a vowel into the stem occurs in those predicative forms which themselves end with a vowel.

---

[1] A very few adjectives, e.g., си́ний (Key No. 19, § 132, p. 195) employ -ь as and ending for the predicative masculine singular.

## PREDICATIVE FORMS

| Adjective | Key No.[1] | Root | Singular | | Plural (Masc., Fem., Neuter) |
|---|---|---|---|---|---|
| ва́жный important | 17a | важн- | Masc. Fem. Neuter | ва́жен важна́ ва́жно | ва́жны́ |
| си́льный strong | 17b | | Masc. Fem. Neuter | силён, сильна́ си́льно | си́льны |
| злой evil | 18a | зл - | Masc. Fem. Neuter | зол зла зло | злы |
| больно́й sick | 18b | больн- | Masc. Fem. Neuter | бо́лен больна́ бо́льно | больны́ |
| ре́дкий rare | 21a | редк- | Masc. Fem. Neuter | ре́док ре́дка ре́дко | ре́дки |
| го́рький bitter | 21b | горьк- | Masc. Fem. Neuter | го́рек го́рька го́рько | го́рьки |
| сто́йкий stable, firm | 21c | стойк- | Masc. Fem. Neuter | сто́ек сто́йка сто́йко | сто́йки |

In coping with this type of irregularity it may prove helpful to note that insertion of the vowel in the stem of the adjective usually takes place in accordance with the following rules:

    1) Insertion of -O- usually occurs if the final letter of the stem is -K preceded by another consonant.

---

[1] The numeral parts of Key Nos. given in this column points out which adjective summarized in Lesson 16 (§ 132, p. 192) exemplifies derivation of the regular forms, while the lower case letter identifies the various individual variations in formation of the predicative masculine singular.

2) Insertion of -е- usually occurs if the final letter of the stem is -н preceded by another consonant.[1]
3) The letter -е- replaces penultimate -й- or -ь- followed by a consonant.

Predicative, Masculine, Singular Formed with Insertion of -О-
in Adjective Stems Ending in -К-
(See Rule 1, p. 566)

(All adjectives listed in this table are declined in the same way as ре́дкий , Key No. 21-a, p. 566)

| Adjective | Root | Predicative Masculine Singular |
|---|---|---|
| бли́зкий near | близк- | бли́зок |
| гла́дкий smooth | гладк- | гла́док |
| гро́мкий loud | громк- | гро́мок |
| кре́пкий strong | крепк- | кре́пок |
| лёгкий easy, light | легк- | лёгок |
| ме́лкий small, fine | мелк- | ме́лок |
| мя́гкий soft | мягк- | мя́гок |
| ни́зкий low | низк- | ни́зок |
| ре́дкий rare | редк- | ре́док |

[1] In connection with this rule it is well to note that certain adjective stems terminating in -нн- drop one -н- while others insert an -е- to convert terminal -нн- of the stem to -нен in forming the predicative, masculine, singular.

| Adjective | Root | Predicative Masculine Singular |
|-----------|------|-------------------------------|
| ре́зкий<br>sharp | резк- | ре́зок |
| сла́дкий<br>sweet | сладк- | сла́док |
| то́нкий<br>thin | тонк- | то́нок |
| хру́пкий<br>brittle | хрупк- | хру́пок |
| я́ркий<br>bright | ярк- | я́рок |

## Predicative, Masculine, Singular Formed with Insertion of -e- in Adjective Stems Ending in -H-
### (See Rule 2, p. 567)

(All adjectives listed in this table are declined in the same way as ВА́ЖНЫЙ  , Key No. 17-a, p. 566)

| Adjective | Root | Predicative Masculine Singular |
|-----------|------|-------------------------------|
| возмо́жный<br>possible | возможн- | возмо́жен |
| вы́годный<br>suitable | выгодн- | вы́годен |
| непреры́вный<br>uninterrupted,<br>continuous | непрерывн- | непреры́вен |
| одновале́нтный<br>monovalent | одновалентн- | одновале́нтен[1] |
| однородный<br>homogeneous | однородн- | однородeн |

[1] Similarly двухвале́нтен  (or двувале́нтен) from двухвале́нтный (or двувале́нтный ), "divalent," трехвале́нтен from трехвале́нтный, "trivalent," etc.

| Adjective | Root | Predicative Masculine Singular |
|---|---|---|
| сло́жный complicated, complex | сложн- | сло́жен |
| схо́дный similar | сходн- | схо́ден |
| то́чный precise | точн- | то́чен |
| тру́дный difficult | трудн- | тру́ден |
| у́мный intelligent, wise | умн- | умён |
| чёрный black | черн- | чёрен |
| я́сный clear | ясн- | я́сен |

## Predicative, Masculine, Singular Formed with -е- Replacing -ь- or -й- in Adjective Stem
### (See Rule 3, p. 567)

| Adjective | Attributive Forms Follow Key No. | Stem | Predicative Masculine Singular[1] |
|---|---|---|---|
| бо́йкий clever | 21 | бойк- | бо́ек |
| больно́й sick | 18 | больн- | бо́лен |
| го́рький bitter | 21 | горьк- | го́рек |

[1] Other predicative forms are obtained in the usual way from the stem, namely by adding -а for the feminine singular -о for the neuter singular and -ы for the plural (all genders). This is also true of the adjectives listed in other tables in this section.

| Adjective | Attributive Forms Follow Key No. | Root | Predicative Masculine Singular |
|---|---|---|---|
| поко́йный quiet, dead | 17 | поко́йн- | поко́ен |
| нейтра́льный neutral | 17 | нейтра́льн- | нейтра́лен[1] |
| сто́йкий stable, firm | 21 | сто́йк- | сто́ек |

### Other Adjectives Forming Predicative, Masculine, Singular in Various Irregular Ways

| Adjective | Attributive Forms Follow Key No. | Stem | Predicative Masculine Singular |
|---|---|---|---|
| до́лгий long | 21 | долг- | до́лог |
| есте́ственный natural | 21 | естественн- | есте́ствен |
| злой evil | 18 | зл- | зол |
| по́лный complete | 17 | полн- | по́лон |
| прозра́чный transparent | 17 | прозрачн- | прозра́чен |
| све́тлый bright, clear | 17 | светл- | све́тел |

---

[1] Similarly пропорциона́лен from пропорциона́льный "proportional," норма́лен from норма́льный "normal," etc.

| Adjective | Attributive Forms Follow Key No. | Stem | Predicative Masculine Singular |
|---|---|---|---|
| смешно́й funny | 18 | смешн- | смешо́н |
| тёплый warm | 17 | тепл- | тёпел |

(b)  Adjectives Having Predicative Forms Only.

Before concluding this discussion of unusual features encountered in formation of the predicative forms of adjectives, it should be pointed out that a very few adjectives are used only as predicative modifiers.  Examples are рад "glad" and гора́зд "capable, skillful."

The adjective forms under discussion are employed in the usual way in constructing sentences.

| Соста́в | пове́рхностных | вод | о́чень |
|---|---|---|---|
| (The) composition | of surface | waters   (is) | very |

разнообра́зен
variable.

| Графи́т | в | противополо́жность | алма́зу | |
|---|---|---|---|---|
| Graphite | in | contrast | to  diamond | (is) |

чрезвыча́йно   мя́гок.
extremely       soft.

| Витами́н | А в отсу́тствии | окисли́телей | дово́льно |
|---|---|---|---|
| Vitamin | A in (the) absence | of oxidizing agents   (is) | rather |

сто́ек   к нагрева́нию.
stable   to heating.

| Кору́нд | практи́чески | не | гигроскопи́чен. |
|---|---|---|---|
| C·borundum   (is) | practically | not | hygroscopic. |

Так как в    це́лом    а́том    электри́чески
Because in (i.e., as) (a) whole (an) atom (is) electrically

нейтра́лен,    то    положи́тельный    заря́д    ра́вен,
neutral,      so     (the) positive      charge    is equal

очеви́дно, о́бщему   заря́ду внутриато́мных   электро́нов.
obviously to (the) total charge of the intra-atomic electrons.

Что́бы    разви́ть   необходи́мую     для   приведе́ния   в
In order to develop (the) necessary    for   bringing      into

движе́ние   по́езда    тя́гу,    парово́з     до́лжен   быть
motion     of train    pull,    (a) locomotive must     be

доста́точно    тяжёл.
sufficiently     heavy.

А́том       в          це́лом      нейтра́лен,    и   все
(An) atom in (i.e., as) (a) whole (is) neutral,      and all

его́    положи́тельные     заря́ды    сосредото́чены    в
its    positive           charges    (are) concentrated    in

ядре́.
(the) nucleus.

В свои́х    статья́х     В. Н. Чи́колев    всегда́ горя́ч и
In his     publications, V. N. Chikolev (is) always firey and

полеми́чен.
polemical.

Я     всегда́ рад[1]    рабо́тать   в    лаборато́рии.
I (am) always glad      to work    in   (the) laboratory.

---

[1] If the speaker were of the feminine sex, the form of the adjective would be ра́да.

§ 357. Nouns Declined with Elimination of Vowel from Stem.

Nouns of this group deviate from regularity only by virtue of elimination of a vowel from the stem during declension. The vowel eliminated may be either -е-, -ё- or -О-. With a few nouns of this class, the vowel -е- or -ё- is replaced by -Ь-. The regular endings -- either hard, soft or mixed -- are used in declining these nouns as shown by the following examples.

MASCULINE NOUNS

| Noun | у́гол angle | пёс dog | лёд ice | бело́к protein | по́ршень piston |
|---|---|---|---|---|---|
| Key No. | 1a | 1b | 1c | 3a | 6a |
| Stem Unaltered | угол- | пёс- | лед- | белок- | поршен- |
| Stem Altered | угл- | пс- | льд- | белк- | поршн- |

Singular

| Nom. | у́гол | пёс | лёд | бело́к | по́ршень |
|---|---|---|---|---|---|
| Gen. | угла́ | пса | льда́ | белка́ | по́ршня |
| Dat. | углу́ | псу | льду́ | белку́ | по́ршню |
| Acc. | у́гол | пса | лёд | бело́к | по́ршень |
| Instr. | угло́м | псом | льдо́м | белко́м | по́ршнем |
| Prep. | угле́ | псе | льде́ | белке́ | по́ршне |

Plural

| Nom. | углы́ | псы | льды́ | белки́ | по́ршни |
|---|---|---|---|---|---|
| Gen. | угло́в | псов | льдо́в | белко́в | по́ршней |
| Dat. | угла́м | псам | льда́м | белка́м | по́ршням |
| Acc. | углы́ | псов | льды́ | белки́ | по́ршни |
| Instr. | угла́ми | пса́ми | льда́ми | белка́ми | по́ршнями |
| Prep. | угла́х | пса́х | льда́х | белка́х | по́ршнях |

Nearly all feminine nouns having the nominative singular ending -ь are declined regularly as illustrated by смесь (Key No. 12, § 130, p. 190). A very few feminine nouns with nominative singular ending in -ь are declined with elimination of -O- from the stem, as exemplified by the feminine noun рожь, "rye."

## FEMININE NOUNS

| Noun | рожь | Stem Unaltered | рож- |
|------|------|----------------|------|
| Key No. |  | Stem Altered | рж- |

|  | Singular | Plural[1] |
|------|----------|--------|
| Nom. | рожь | ржи |
| Gen. | ржи | ржей |
| Dat. | ржи | ржам |
| Acc. | рожь | ржи |
| Instr. | рожью | ржами |
| Prep. | ржи | ржах |

Белки́ вхо́дят в соста́в протоплазмы
Proteins enter into (the) composition of (the) protoplasm

всех живы́х кле́ток.
of all living cells.

Ледники́ – э́то грома́дные, ме́дленно дви́жущиеся
Glaciers — these are enormous slowly moving self

ре́ки льда́.
rivers of ice.

---

[1] The plural is used only in the sense of "growing rye," "rye field."

| Из | ка́менноу́гольного | де́гтя, | полу́ченного | при |
|---|---|---|---|---|
| From | coal | tar, | obtained | during |

| сухо́й | перего́нке | ка́менного у́гля, | выде́лывают |
|---|---|---|---|
| dry | distillation | of coal, | they separate |

| це́лый | ряд | це́нных | проду́ктов. |
|---|---|---|---|
| (a) whole | series | of valuable | products. |

| Рассмо́трим | повнима́тельнее | строе́ние |
|---|---|---|
| Let us examine | more attentively | (the) structure |

| цветка́ | ржи, | что́бы | на | э́том | приме́ре |
|---|---|---|---|---|---|
| of (the) flower | of rye, | in order | on | this | example |

| познако́миться | с | осо́бенностями | строе́ния |
|---|---|---|---|
| to acquaint self | with | (the) peculiarities | of (the) structure |

| своеобра́зных | цветко́в | зла́ков. |
|---|---|---|
| characteristic | flowers | of cereals. |

## § 358.  Irregular Neuter Nouns in -МЯ.

This small group includes several nouns of considerable importance in scientific Russian, viz., вре́мя, "time"; се́мя,[1] "seed"; и́мя, "name"; пла́мя "flame." Their declension is quite irregular as seen from the following example.

вре́мя        time          Key No. 25

|  | Singular | Plural |
|---|---|---|
| Nom. | вре́мя | времена́ |
| Gen. | вре́мени | време́н |
| Dat. | вре́мени | времена́м |
| Acc. | вре́мя | времена́ |
| Instr. | вре́менем | времена́ми |
| Prep. | вре́мени | времена́х |

[1] Note that семя́н, the genitive plural of се́мя "seed" differs slightly in form from the genitive plural of вре́мя.

| Так как | это ускоре́ние | о́чень | мало́, | то |
|---|---|---|---|---|
| Because | this acceleration | (is) very | small, | hence |

| ну́жно | мно́го | вре́мени, | что́бы | получи́ть |
|---|---|---|---|---|
| (is) necessary | much | of time, | in order | to obtain |

| заме́тную | ско́рость. |
|---|---|
| (a) noticeable | velocity. |

| Когда́ прораста́ет | се́мя, | заро́дыш | его́ | пита́ется |
|---|---|---|---|---|
| When germinates | (a) seed, | (the) | of it | nourishes self |

| те́ми | пита́тельными | вещества́ми, | кото́рые |
|---|---|---|---|
| with those | nutritive | substances, | which |

| нахо́дятся | в се́мени. |
|---|---|
| find self | in (the) seed. |

| Для | прораста́ния | семя́н | пре́жде всего́ | |
|---|---|---|---|---|
| For | germination | of seeds | first of all | (is) |

| необходи́ма | вода́. |
|---|---|
| necessary | water. |

§ 359. Miscellaneous Irregular Noun Declensions.

## MASCULINE NOUNS

| Noun | глаз | клин | англича́нин | ребёнок |
|---|---|---|---|---|
| | eye | wedge | Englishman | child |
| Key No. | 26 | 27 | 28 | 29 |

### Singular

| | | | | |
|---|---|---|---|---|
| Nom. | глаз | клин | англича́нин | ребёнок |
| Gen. | гла́за | кли́на | англича́нина | ребёнка |
| Dat. | гла́зу | кли́ну | англича́нину | ребёнку |
| Acc. | глаз | клин | англича́нина | ребёнка |
| Instr. | гла́зом | кли́ном | англича́нином | ребёнком |
| Prep. | гла́зе | кли́не | англича́нине | ребёнке |

### Plural

| Nom. | глаза́ | кли́нья | англича́не | ребя́та |
|------|--------|---------|------------|---------|
| Gen. | глаз | кли́ньев | англича́н | ребя́т |
| Dat. | глаза́м | кли́ньям | англича́нам | ребя́там |
| Acc. | глаза́ | кли́нья | англича́н | ребя́т |
| Instr. | глаза́ми | кли́ньями | англича́нами | ребя́тами |
| Prep. | глаза́х | кли́ньях | англича́нах | ребя́тах |

## OTHER IRREGULAR NOUN DECLENSIONS

| | Masculine | | | Feminine | |
|------|------|------|------|------|------|
| Noun | судья́[1] | путь | брат | мать | ку́рица |
| | judge | way, road | brother | mother | hen |

### Singular

| Nom. | судья́ | путь | брат | мать | ку́рица |
|------|--------|------|------|------|---------|
| Gen. | судьи́ | пути́ | бра́та | ма́тери | ку́рицы |
| Dat. | судье́ | пути́ | бра́ту | ма́тери | ку́рице |
| Acc. | судью́ | путь | бра́та | мать | ку́рицу |
| Instr. | судьёй (судьёю) | путём | бра́том | ма́терью | ку́рицей (ку́рицею) |
| Prep. | судье́ | пути́ | бра́те | ма́тери | ку́рице |

### Plural

| Nom. | су́дьи | пути́ | бра́тья | ма́тери | ку́ры |
|------|--------|-------|---------|---------|-------|
| Gen. | суде́й | путе́й | бра́тьев | матере́й | кур |
| Dat. | су́дьям | путя́м | бра́тьям | матеря́м | ку́рам |
| Acc. | суде́й | пути́ | бра́тьев | матере́й | кур |
| Instr. | су́дьями | путя́ми | бра́тьями | матеря́ми | ку́рами |
| Prep. | су́дьях | путя́х | бра́тьях | матеря́х | ку́рах |

[1] This noun is one of the relatively few exceptions to the rule that nouns with nominative singular ending in -а or -я are feminine. Further exceptions are дя́дя "uncle," and " ба́тюшка " "little (dear) father," "priest." Names ending in -а, e.g., Капи́ца "Kapitsa" or Дюма́, "Dumas" are regarded as masculine in gender when used to refer to persons of the male sex.

## OTHER IRREGULAR NOUN DECLENSIONS

### Neuter

| Noun | крыло́ | чу́до | су́дно | у́хо |
|------|-------|-------|--------|------|
|      | wing  | wonder, miracle | ship | ear |

### Singular

| | | | | |
|------|--------|--------|---------|-------|
| Nom. | крыло́ | чу́до | су́дно | у́хо |
| Gen. | крыла́ | чу́да | су́дна | у́ха |
| Dat. | крылу́ | чу́ду | су́дну | у́ху |
| Acc. | крыло́ | чу́до | су́дно | у́хо |
| Instr. | крыло́м | чу́дом | су́дном | у́хом |
| Prep. | крыле́ | чу́де | су́дне | у́хе |

### Plural

| | | | | |
|------|----------|---------|--------|--------|
| Nom. | кры́лья | чудеса́ | суда́ | у́ши |
| Gen. | кры́льев | чуде́с | судо́в | уше́й |
| Dat. | кры́льям | чудеса́м | суда́м | уша́м |
| Acc. | кры́лья | чудеса́ | суда́ | у́ши |
| Instr. | кры́льями | чудеса́ми | суда́ми | уша́ми |
| Prep. | кры́льях | чудеса́х | суда́х | уша́х |

| Noun | лист[1] |
|------|---------|
|      | leaf, sheet |

### Singular

| | |
|------|--------|
| Nom. | лист |
| Gen. | листа́ |
| Dat. | листу́ |
| Acc. | лист |
| Instr. | листо́м |
| Prep. | листе́ |

---

[1] The declension of зуб "tooth" is identical with that of лист. In the plural, when declined зу́бы, зубо́в, зуба́м, etc., the meaning is "teeth (of animal or person)" but when declined зу́бья, зу́бьев, зу́бьям, etc., the meaning is "teeth (of saw, gear or the like)."

| Noun | листы́ | ли́стья |
|------|--------|---------|
|      | sheets | leaves |
|      |        | (plant) |

### Plural

| | | |
|------|--------|---------|
| Nom. | листы́ | ли́стья |
| Gen. | листо́в | ли́стьев |
| Dat. | листа́м | ли́стьям |
| Acc. | листы́ | ли́стья |
| Instr. | листа́ми | ли́стьями |
| Prep. | листа́х | ли́стьях |

A few other nouns are peculiar in that they have plural forms[1] only, even though, in some instances at least, the only discernible reason appears to be usage. The following list is incomplete.

### Plural Declined Like

| Noun (Plural Only) | Noun | Key No. | Remarks |
|--------------------|------|---------|---------|
| воро́та <br> gate, portal | вещество́ | 13 | |
| квасцы́ <br> alum | а́том | 1 | |
| но́жны <br> sheath, especially of sword | моле́кула | 7 | |
| сли́вки <br> cream | оши́бка | 9 a | Cf. § 355, p. 562. |
| су́тки <br> 24-hour period | оши́бка | 9 a | Cf. § 355, p. 562. |
| щи <br> cabbage soup | mostly like нау́ка | 9 | Gen. plural щей |
| щипцы́ <br> tongs, shears | а́том | 1 | |

---

[1] Depending on the context, these plural forms may have either singular or plural significance.

Certain nouns existing in the plural only have forms identical with or closely similar to other nouns. An example is весы́ "balance," "scale (for weighing)" a noun which exists only in the plural and which is closely related to вес "weight." These two nouns are declined as follows.

| | вес | weight | весы́ | balance, scale (for weighing) |
|---|---|---|---|---|
| | Singular | Plural | Plural (No singular exists) | |
| Nom. | вес | веса́ | весы́ | |
| Gen. | ве́са | весо́в | весо́в | |
| Dat. | ве́су | веса́м | веса́м | |
| Acc. | вес | веса́ | весы́ | |
| Instr. | ве́сом | веса́ми | веса́ми | |
| Prep. | ве́се | веса́х | веса́х | |

The noun час "hour," regularly declined throughout like а́том (Key No. 1, § 130, p. 190), has plural forms meaning either "hours" or "timepiece," (such as a watch or clock). The meaning of the plural forms of час must be decided from the context.

The plural forms of очко́ "little eye," "eyelet," "pip (on playing card)" also perform double duty, having the additional meaning of "eyeglasses," "spectacles."

| Там | где | тепе́рь | нахо́дятся | за́лежи | ка́менного у́гля, |
|---|---|---|---|---|---|
| There | where | now | finds self | deposits | of coal |

| когда́-то, | миллио́ны | лет | наза́д, | бы́ли |
|---|---|---|---|---|
| at some time, | millions | of years | ago | were |

| грома́дные | леса́.[1] |
|---|---|
| enormous | forests. |

| Заво́д | бра́тьев | Ка́улес | производи́л | спла́вы |
|---|---|---|---|---|
| (The) plant | of (the) brothers | Cowles | produced | alloys |

| алюми́ния | путём | термоэлектри́ческого | спо́соба. |
|---|---|---|---|
| of aluminum | by way | of (the) thermoelectric | process. |

[1] The declension of лес, "forest," "lumber" is the same as that of глаз (Key No. 26, p. 576) except that the genitive plural of лес is лесо́в.

| Углекислый | газ | растение | добывает | из | воздуха |
|---|---|---|---|---|---|
| Carbonic acid | gas | (a) plant | acquires | from | (the) air |

листьями.
by means of leaves.

| Различные | виды | точнейших | весов | были |
|---|---|---|---|---|
| Various | forms | of very precise | balances | were |

| употреблены | в то | время | для | определения | атомных |
|---|---|---|---|---|---|
| utilized | in that | time | for | determination | of atomic |

весов.
weights.

| Технически | квасцы | обычно | изготовляются | из |
|---|---|---|---|---|
| Technically | alum | ordinarily | prepares self | from |

чистой глины.
pure    clay.

§ 360.  Declension of Третий and Related Adjectives.

The summary of adjective declensions given in Lesson 16 covered all but a very few exceptional adjectives.  One of these is the ordinal numeral, Третий "third" whose declension is given below:

третий ,    third
Key No. 30

### Singular

| | Masc. | Fem. | Neuter |
|---|---|---|---|
| Nom. | третий | третья | третье |
| Gen. | третьего | третьей | третьего |
| Dat. | третьему | третьей | третьему |

|        | Masc. | Fem. | Neuter |
|--------|-------|------|--------|
| Acc.   | тре́тий[1] | тре́тью | тре́тье |
| Instr. | тре́тьим | тре́тьей | тре́тьим |
|        |        | (тре́тьею) |       |
| Prep.  | тре́тьем | тре́тьей | тре́тьем |

## Plural

### Masc.-Fem.-Neuter

|        | |
|--------|---|
| Nom.   | тре́тьи |
| Gen.   | тре́тьих |
| Dat.   | тре́тьим |
| Acc.   | тре́тьи[1] |
| Instr. | тре́тьими |
| Prep.  | тре́тьих |

A small group of relative-possessive adjectives are declined in the same way as тре́тий. These include: бо́жий "God's"; во́лчий "wolf's"; коро́вий "cow's"; коша́чий "cat's"; ли́сий "fox's"; пти́чий "bird's"; ры́бий "fish's"; соба́чий "dog's" etc.

The use in sentences of the adjectives under discussion requires no special comment.

| В     | коро́вьем | ма́сле | содержатся | сравни́тельно |
|-------|-----------|--------|------------|---------------|
| In    | cow       | fat (butter) | contain self | relatively |

| больши́е | коли́чества | ма́сляной | кислоты́. |
|----------|-------------|-----------|-----------|
| large    | quantities  | of butyric | acid.    |

| По   |          |    | произво́дству | | суперфосфа́та |
|------|----------|----|---------------|---|---------------|
| With | respect  | to | production    | of | super phosphate |

| Сове́тский | Сою́з | занима́ет | тепе́рь | тре́тье | ме́сто | в |
|-----------|-------|-----------|---------|---------|--------|---|
| (the) Soviet | Union | occupies | at present | (the) third | place | in |

| ми́ре. |
|--------|
| (the) world. |

---

[1] This form becomes identical with the corresponding genitive when used to modify a noun denoting a human being, animal or mythological person, cf. § 67, p. 93.

§ 361.  Declension of Certain Possessives and Related Names.

Previous discussion has covered the declension of possessives closely related to pronouns (§ 138, p. 207). Attention is now directed to another group of possessive adjectives, to which are closely related certain names some of which may be used as possessive adjectives.

The following examples illustrate derivation of this type of possessives and related names.

| Suffix | Derived from Noun Type | Examples |
|---|---|---|
| -ОВ- | Masculine declined with hard endings | СЫНО́В "son's" from СЫН "son"<br>ОТЦО́В "father's" from ОТЕ́Ц "father"<br>ВО́ЛЬТОВ "voltaic" from Volta<br>МО́ЛОТОВ "Molotov" from МО́ЛОТ "hammer"<br>Па́ВЛОВ "Pavlov" from Па́вел "Paul" |
| -ЕВ- or -ЁВ- | Masculine declined with soft endings | царе́в "Tsars'" from царь "Tsar"<br>Андре́ев "Andreev" from Андре́й "Andrew"<br>Соловьёв "Solov'yov"[1] from соловей "nightingale" |
| -ИН- or -ЫН- | Feminine | се́стрин "sister's" from сестра́ "sister"<br>се́стрицын "little sister's" from сестри́ца "little sister"<br>Ста́лин "Stalin" from сталь "steel" |

The declension of these possessives and also of the names closely related thereto is illustrated by the following example.

[1] A common, though less phonetic, transliteration would be "Solov'ev," cf. § 12, p. 17.

[2] The Christian name Па́вел, "Paul" is declined with regular endings but with elimination of the -е-, thus: Nom. Па́вел, Gen. Па́вла, Dat. Па́влу, Acc. Па́вла, etc.

ВО́ЛЬТОВ     voltaic
Key No. 31

## Singular

| | Masc. | Fem. | Neuter |
|---|---|---|---|
| Nom. | ВО́ЛЬТОВ | ВО́ЛЬТОВА | ВО́ЛЬТ·ОВО |
| Gen. | ВО́ЛЬТОВА | ВО́ЛЬТОВОЙ | ВО́ЛЬТОВА |
| Dat. | ВО́ЛЬТОВУ | ВО́ЛЬТОВОЙ | ВО́ЛЬТОВУ |
| Acc. | ВО́ЛЬТОВ | ВО́ЛЬТ·ОВУ | ВО́ЛЬТОВО |
| Instr. | ВО́ЛЬТОВЫМ | ВО́ЛЬТОВОЙ | ВО́ЛЬТОВЫМ |
| | | ( ВО́ЛЬТОВОЮ ) | |
| Prep. | ВО́ЛЬТОВОМ | ВО́ЛЬТОВОЙ | ВО́ЛЬТОВОМ |

## Plural

### Masc.-Fem.-Neuter

| | |
|---|---|
| Nom. | ВО́ЛЬТОВЫ |
| Gen. | ВО́ЛЬТОВЫХ |
| Dat. | ВО́ЛЬТОВЫМ |
| Acc. | ВО́ЛЬТОВЫ |
| Instr. | ВО́ЛЬТОВЫМИ |
| Prep. | ВО́ЛЬТОВЫХ |

Во́льтовы ду́ги обы́чно применя́ются в тех слу́чаях,
Voltaic   arcs   ordinarily   apply self    in   those   cases,

когда́    необходи́м исто́чник све́та о́чень большо́й
when   (is) necessary   (a) source   of light   of very   great

я́ркости.
brightness.

Пла́нкова конста́нта явля́ется одно́й из основны́х
Planck's    constant    shows self   (is) one    of   (the) basic

величи́н приро́ды.
magnitudes   of nature.

Старуха      глянула прямо  в   сыново   лицо.
(The) old woman  looked    straight into  (her) son's  face.


Внезапное     цыганкино        появление    испугало
(The) sudden    gypsy's (female)   appearance   startled

его[1]
him.


§ 362. Declension of Names.

The declension of names, particularly surnames,[2] is not without importance in reading scientific Russian. In general, names are declined either like nouns or like adjectives and, consequently, may be grouped under two general headings.

I.  Names Declined Like Nouns.
  a.  Names terminating with a hard consonant, e.g., Эйнштейн "Einstein" or Бостон[3] "Boston," are declined like the noun атом (Key No. 1, § 130, p. 190).
  b.  Surnames terminating with a soft sign, e.g., Фридель, "Friedel" are declined with the regular masculine soft endings. Following the example of множитель (Key No. 6, § 130, p. 190).
  c.  Names terminating with a vowel followed by -й, e.g., Фарадей "Faraday," are declined like эпителий (Key No. 5, § 130, p. 190).
  d.  Names of Russian origin ending in -a are declined like feminine nouns, even though they may refer to persons of the male sex. An example of such a name is Капица "Kapitsa," declined like единица (Key No. 8, § 130, p. 190).


[1] The use of the suffix -ин- to form possessives is not as general as might be suggested by this example in which from цыганка "gypsy (female)" is derived цыганкин "(female) gypsy's." A more common wording would be внезапное появление цыганки, "(the) sudden appearance of (the) gypsy (female)."
[2] The declension of the names of persons involves the rule given in § 67, p. 93 concerning the identity of certain accusative forms with corresponding genitive forms.
[3] A card game and a dance -- as well as the New England city -- are known by the name Бостон in Russian. Usually, a name is accented in Russian in the same way as in the original language.

II. Names Declined Like Adjectives.

(This group includes a very large number of Russian surnames.)

a. Names with masculine nominative singular terminating in -СКИЙ (case ending -ИЙ, stem, terminating in -СК-). These are declined like электрический (Key No. 21, § 132, p. 197). The feminine adjectival forms are used if the surname refers to a person of the feminine sex.

b. Names with stem terminating in -ОВ, -ЕВ, -ЁВ, or -ИН, e.g., Мо́лотов, "Molotov"; Менделе́ев, "Mendeleev"; Соловьёв, "Solov'yov";[1] Ста́лин, "Stalin." These are declined[2] like the possessive adjectives having the same stem termination, except for the masculine prepositional singular which for names has the ending -е rather than -ОМ. (See preceding § 361.) Here, again, the feminine adjectival forms are used if the surname refers to a person of the feminine sex.

The declension of place names exhibits a number of peculiarities whose detailed discussion does not appear profitable. It may be said in general, however, that the declension of place names is quite similar to that of the surnames of persons.

| Тео́рия | бро́уновского | движе́ния | была́ разрабо́тана |
|---|---|---|---|
| (The) theory | of Brownian | movement | was worked out |

| Эйнште́йном и | Смолухо́вским[3] | и | эксперимента́льно |
|---|---|---|---|
| by Einstein and | Smoluchowski | | and experimentally |

| подтверждена́ | рабо́тами | Перре́на | и | Сведбе́рга. |
|---|---|---|---|---|
| confirmed | by works | of Perrin | and | of Svedberg. |

| Прибо́р | Роги́нского | и | Ша́льникова | явля́ется |
|---|---|---|---|---|
| (The) device | of Roginskii | and | Shal'nikov | shows self |

| осо́бенно | удо́бным | для | получе́ния | золе́й | щелочны́х |
|---|---|---|---|---|---|
| particularly | convenient | for | obtaining | sols | of alkali |

---

[1] Cf. Footnote 1, p. 583.

[2] Ordinarily such names are not used adjectivally and consequently they do not have the neuter forms as tabulated for ВО́ЛЬТОВ on p. 584.

[3] Polish names ending in "-ski" are well suited for declension which transliterated into Russian.

металлов   в   бензоле,   толуоле,   гексане   и   других
metals      in  benzene,   toluene,    hexane   and other

угдеводородах.
hydrocarbons.


К    явлениям,    не    наблюдаемым                   при
To   phenomena,   not   being observed (observable)   at

обычных   температурах, относятся[1]   сверхпроводимость,
ordinary  temperatures, pertain        superconductivity,

открытая    в   1911 г.   Камерлинг-Оннесом        и
discovered  in  1911      by Kamerlingh-Onnes      and

сверхтекучесть    гелия     II,   открытая    в   1938 г.
superfluidity     of helium II,   discovered   in  1938

Капицей.
by Kapitza.


С   другой    стороны,   какая-то   часть научных
On  (the) other side,    some       part  of (the) scientific

знаний    древнего    Египта    проникла    в   Европу
knowledge s  of ancient  Egypt    penetrated  into  Europe

ещё    раньше   через   Грецию.
even   earlier   through  Greece.


§ 363. Nouns and Names of Foreign Origin Not Declined in
       Russian.

   To provide background for discussing undeclined nouns of
foreign origin, it should be recalled to mind that many nouns of
foreign origin have been fitted without apparent difficulty into the
Russian declension system.

[1] See Footnote 2, p. 159.

Many  foreign  nouns  ending  in  a  consonant  are  assimilated
into  Russian  as  masculine  nouns,  regularly[1]  declined  with  hard
endings  as  exemplified  by  áтом  "atom,"  нафтóл  "naphthol"
(Key No. 1, § 130, p. 190).

A  smaller  number  of  nouns  of  foreign  origin  are  spelled  with
terminal  -а  or  -я  (nominative  singular  case),  and  these  as  a
rule[2]  are  declined  like  feminine  nouns.  Examples  are  молéкула
"molecule"  (Key No. 7, § 130, p. 190) and  мелóдия  "melody"
(Key No. 11, § 130, p. 190).  Another  group  of  nouns  of  foreign
origin,  particularly  nouns  with  terminal  "-l,"  are  spelled  with
the  ending  -ь  in  the  nominative  singular  case.  Such  nouns  are
regularly  declined,  some,  e.g.,  автомобúль  "automobile"
(Key No. 6, § 130, p. 190)  with  soft  masculine  endings,  others,
e.g.,  модéль  "model,"  (Key No. 12, § 130, p. 190) with  soft
feminine  endings.  Latin  neuter  nouns  terminating  in  "-ium"  often
become  masculine  nouns  in  Russian,  e.g.,  Latin  "natrium"
becomes  Russian  нáтрий  (Key No. 5, § 130, p. 190).

Many  nouns  --  and  especially  names  --  of  foreign  origin
cannot  be  incorporated  easily  into  the  Russian  language.  There
are  two  basic  reasons  for  this.  In  the  first  place,  certain  sounds
occurring  in  other  languages,  e.g.,  English  "h,"  "w,"  "th,"  and
the  French  nasal  sounds,  do  not  occur  in  Russian.  As  a  result
the  Russian  spelling,  Эйзенгоуэр,  fails  to  indicate  in  full
detail  the  pronunciation  of  English  "Eisenhower."  Similarly,
Ле  Блан  is  only  an  approximation  of  French  "Le Blanc."  In  the
second  place,  certain  words,  in  particular  certain  English  and
French  names,  contain  so  many  unpronounced  letters  that  a
phonetic  rendition  in  Russian  can  scarcely  be  relied  on  to  suggest
the  original  spelling.  Examples  are  Юз  for  "Hughes"  and  Эрý
for  "Héroult."

Another  factor  in  the  situation  is  the  fact  that  the  nominative
case  of  Russian  nouns  never  ends  with  -й  or  -ы,  while  only  neuter
nouns  have  terminal  -о  or  -е  in  the  nominative  singular  case.

In  the  face  of  these  difficulties,  the  Russians  usually  proceed
along  the  following  lines.

---

[1]  Irregularities  are  occasionally  encountered  in  the  declension  of  such  nouns.
Thus  профéссор,  though  otherwise  regularly  declined,  has  the  nominative  plural
form  профессорá.

[2]  Nouns  of  foreign  origin  with  terminal  accented  -á  are  not  declined,  e.g.,
антрашá  "entrechat."

Foreign names, and in general nouns of foreign origin, are spelled out in Russian letters as nearly phonetically as possible. Nouns or names ending in -e, -и, -o or -y are usually not declined, e.g., Ле Шателье́ "Le Chatelier," Кюри́ "Curie," Па́ули "Pauli," Карно́ "Carnot," ра́дио "radio," гуа́но "guano," э́хо "echo," Эру́ "Héroult." Nouns and names which end in unaccented -a or -я usually are declined, e.g., Филаде́льфия "Philadelphia," (Key No. 11, § 130, p. 190). On the other hand, names which end in accented -a are not declined, e.g., Дюма́ "Dumas."

In the following sentences asterisks have been used to direct attention to names and nouns not declined in Russian.

| Пра́вило | Дюло́нга[1] | и | Пти* | 1819 г. | формули́руется |
|---|---|---|---|---|---|
| (The) rule | of Dulong | and | Petit | (1819) | formulates self |

| сле́дующим | о́бразом: | произведе́ние | из а́томного |
|---|---|---|---|
| by (the) following | form: | (the) product | of (the) atomic |

| ве́са | элеме́нта | на его́ | уде́льную | теплоёмкость |
|---|---|---|---|---|
| weight | of (an) element | by his | specific | heat conductivity |

| в | твёрдом | состоя́нии | есть | приблизи́тельно |
|---|---|---|---|---|
| in | (the) solid | state, | is | approximately |

| постоя́нная | величина́. |
|---|---|
| (a) constant | magnitude. |

| Отсю́да, | в | соотве́тствии | с | при́нципом |
|---|---|---|---|---|
| From this | in | correspondence | with | (the) principle |

| Ле Шателье́,* | мо́жно | заключи́ть, | что | адсо́рбция |
|---|---|---|---|---|
| of Le Chatelier | it is possible | to conclude, | that | adsorption |

| сопровожда́ется | выделе́нием | тепла́. |
|---|---|---|
| accompanies self | by evolution | of heat. |

[1] This name, as indicated by its ending, is declined in accordance with general rules summarized in § 362, p. 585.

Количества      кислорода    и   азота         воздуха    были
(The) quantities   of oxygen    and of nitrogen            were

особенно        точно       определены      Дюма*         и
particularly    accurately   determined      by Dumas     and

Буссэнго*       в 1841 г.
Boussingault    in 1841.

Англичанином       Максвеллом,[1]    немцем      Герцем,[1]
By (the) Englishman,   Maxwell,        (the) German, Hertz,
(
русским        Поповым[1]    и   итальянцем    Маркони*    были
(the) Russian,   Popov,      and (the) Italian,    Marconi,    were

сделаны  теоретические    и   экспериментальные      работы,
done      theoretical      and experimental            works,

являющиеся              основными    для   развития
showing self (being)     basic        for   (the) development

радио.
of radio.


§ 364.  Reading Exercise.

In the following Reading Exercise, asterisks have been used
to direct attention to those noun and adjective forms with which
this lesson is concerned.


### О значении растений для человека

Наступает весна.  Воздух переполняется мелодиями
птичьих*песен*. На голых ветвях деревьев* появляются[1] первые нежные листья*. Трава покрывает землю зелёным покро-
вом. Радуга цветов украшает поля и леса*. Как отрадны
чудеса* природы!  Как рады*мы видеть опять весеннее воскресение растительного мира!

---

[1]  See Footnote 1, p. 589.

Практи́ческое значе́ние расте́ний та́кже громадно. Они́ даю́т нам основну́ю ма́ссу пищевы́х веще́ств, материа́л для вы́работки на́шей оде́жды, строи́тельные материа́лы и то́пливо. Пра́вда, мы та́кже пита́емся мя́сом, молоко́м, коро́вьим* ма́слом, сы́ром, я́йцами и други́ми вещества́ми живо́тного[2] происхожде́ния. Из ше́рсти выраба́тываем оде́жду. В конце́* концо́в,[3] одна́ко, весь живо́тный мир пита́ется расте́ниями. Без расте́ний не[4] бы́ло бы ни коро́в, ни ове́ц* ни кур* ни други́х окружа́ющих нас живо́тных. Проду́кты живо́тного[2] ми́ра представля́ют собо́й как бы перерабо́танные живо́тными расте́ния.

Мы по́льзуемся разли́чными частя́ми ра́зных расте́ний. Хлеб изготовля́ем из семя́н* (зёрен*) пшени́цы, ржи* и други́х зла́ков. Мы еди́м ли́стья* шпина́та, а коро́вы, ло́шади, о́вцы и мно́гие други́е живо́тные едя́т траву́. Из сте́бля льна́* получа́ют[6] це́нные тексти́льные воло́кна. Из льняно́го се́мени* выжима́ют[7] одно́ из наилу́чших высыха́ющих ма́сел* - а и́менно льняно́е ма́сло, широко́ применя́емое для изготовле́ния ма́сляных кра́сок* и ла́ков. Мо́рфий и други́е алкало́иды содержа́тся в со́ке незре́лых семенны́х голо́вок* ма́ка. Бо́лее или ме́нее си́льно видоизменённые ко́рни* не́которых расте́ний - наприме́р морко́ви, ре́пы - нахо́дят примене́ние в ка́честве пи́щи.

Хими́ческий хара́ктер расти́тельных проду́ктов сравни́тельно сло́жен* Расте́ния же пита́ются просте́йшими вещества́ми, и́менно углеки́слым га́зом, водо́й и неоргани́ческими соля́ми. Углеки́слый газ извлека́ется из во́здуха ли́стьями* - а вода́[8] и растворённые в ней неоргани́ческие со́ли вса́сываются из по́чвы корня́ми* Исто́чником пита́тельных веще́ств для расте́ний та́кже слу́жат отбро́сы живо́тного происхожде́ния в ви́де коро́вьего* навоза, гуа́но* и т.д. Расти́тельный мир, в свое́й ро́ли как "хими́ческий заво́д"[9] для синте́за углево́дов, жиро́в, белко́в* и пр., о́чень ва́жен* для челове́ка.

Расте́ния та́кже весьма́ важны́ в энергети́ческом отноше́нии. В су́тки* на́ша плане́та получа́ет от со́лнца громадное коли́чество лучи́стой эне́ргии - в сре́днем о́коло 367 000 000 000 000 000 000 больши́х кало́рий. А лучи́стая эне́ргия

со́лнца распространя́ется на весь земно́й шар; она́ сли́шком
разрежена́ для удо́бного испо́льзования  челове́ком, да́же в
на́ши дни высокоразви́той те́хники.  Расте́ния же, непосре́д-
ственно по́льзуясь со́лнечной эне́ргией, сосредото́чивают её
в проду́ктах своего́[11] ро́ста.  Така́я эне́ргия сохраня́ется и
при глубоча́йших измене́ниях расти́тельных и живо́тных оста́т-
ков* - наприме́р при образова́нии ка́менного у́гля* и́ли не́фти.
Запа́сы горю́чего, необходи́мые для поддержа́ния на́шей про-
мы́шленности, име́ют расти́тельное происхожде́ние.

И в тре́тьем* отноше́нии расте́ния чрезвыча́йно  важны́
для нас.  Ли́стья* расте́ний, извлека́я из во́здуха углеки́с-
лый газ, освобожда́ют из после́днего кислоро́д, без  кото́-
рого мы задо́хлись бы.

Больша́я кало́рия - коли́чество тепла́, необходи́мое для того́,
что́бы нагре́ть 1 килогра́мм воды́ на 1°.

## Notes

1. ПОЯВЛЯ́ЮТСЯ   and companion forms from      ПОЯВЛЯ́ТЬСЯ--
ПОЯВИ́ТЬСЯ    emphasize an  actual  physical  appearance  or
beginning and thus differ by a definite  shade  of  meaning  from
ЯВЛЯ́ТЬСЯ - ЯВИ́ТЬСЯ  and forms derived therefrom.

2. Here   ЖИВО́ТНОГО, a genitive form of   ЖИВО́ТНЫЙ, is used
as an adjective, cf. last Russian sentence in § 392, p. 655.

3. В КОНЦЕ́   КОНЦО́В, cf. Note 5, p. 445.

4. не бы́ло бы ни---ни---ни---ни---        "there would be neither --- nor --- nor --- nor ---." This sentence combines the double negative of § 180, p. 272, with the subjunctive mode discussed in Lesson 34.

5. Here ЖИВО́ТНЫХ , the genitive plural of ЖИВО́ТНЫЙ, is used as a noun, cf. Note 2 above.

6. Из сте́бля льна получа́ют -, "From (the) stalk of flax they obtain --." This type of impersonal sentence is discussed in § 385, p. 640.

7. Из льняно́го се́мени выжима́ют , "From linseed they press out--." This is another impersonal sentence, cf. preceding Note 6.

8. вода́ и растворённые в ней неоргани́ческие со́ли, "water and dissolved in her (water) inorganic salts."

9. "хими́ческий заво́д"        Here the quotation marks indicate that an unusual comparison is being made, cf. Note 7, p. 367.

10. и пр. is an abbreviation for и про́чее equivalent to English "and the like."

11. Here своего́, in accordance with the previously discussed rule (§ 149, p. 225), refers to the subject of the sentence, расте́ния.


§ 365. Translation Exercise.

1. How happy we are to see the wonders of nature!
2. We utilize ( по́льзуемся ) various substances of plant origin for manufacture of own clothing.
3. Enormous quantities ( Грома́дные коли́чества ) of seeds -- grains -- of wheat, rye and other cereals find application in quality of food.
4. We do not eat the stalk of flax.
5. The oil, obtained (being obtained, получа́емое) from linseed is (shows self) one ( ОДНИ́М ) of the best drying oils.
6. The chemical character of foodstuffs is relatively complex.

7. Plants utilize ( по́льзуются ) carbonic acid gas, water and inorganic salts for the synthesis of carbohydrates, fats, proteins and the like.

8. In our days, industry is distributed (distributes self) over (на) the whole terrestrial sphere.

9. Supplies of coal and petroleum are very important for our industry.

10. Plants, while utilizing solar energy, liberate oxygen from carbonic acid gas.

# LESSON 39

## RUSSIAN NUMERALS

§ 366.  Introductory Note.

Grammatical peculiarities of Russian numerals are summarized in this lesson for reference purposes.  Relationships between different numerals and types of numerals are also pointed out.

§ 367.  Lists of Cardinal and Ordinal Numerals.

The following list includes the basic cardinal and ordinal numerals and illustrates the derivation of compound numerals up to five million from their basic components.

| | Cardinal Numerals | | Ordinal Numerals | |
|---|---|---|---|---|
| 1 | оди́н | one | пе́рвый | first |
| 2 | два | two | второ́й | second |
| 3 | три | three | тре́тий | third |
| 4 | четы́ре | four | четвёртый | fourth |
| 5 | пять | five | пя́тый | fifth |
| 6 | шесть | six | шесто́й | sixth |
| 7 | семь | seven | седьмо́й | seventh |
| 8 | во́семь | eight | восьмо́й | eighth |
| 9 | де́вять | nine | девя́тый | ninth |
| 10 | де́сять | ten | деся́тый | tenth |

| | Cardinal Numerals | Ordinal Numerals |
|---|---|---|
| 11 | одиннадцать | одиннадцатый |
| 12 | двенадцать | двенадцатый |
| 13 | тринадцать | тринадцатый |
| 14 | четырнадцать | четырнадцатый |
| 15 | пятнадцать | пятнадцатый |
| 16 | шестнадцать | шестнадцатый |
| 17 | семнадцать | семнадцатый |
| 18 | восемнадцать | восемнадцатый |
| 19 | девятнадцать | девятнадцатый |
| 20 | двадцать | двадцатый |
| 21 | двадцать один | двадцать первый |
| 22 | двадцать два | двадцать второй |
| 23 | двадцать три | двадцать третий |
| 24 | двадцать четыре | двадцать четвёртый |
| 25 | двадцать пять | двадцать пятый |
| 26 | двадцать шесть | двадцать шестой |
| 27 | двадцать семь | двадцать седьмой |
| 28 | двадцать восемь | двадцать восьмой |
| 29 | двадцать девять | двадцать девятый |
| 30 | тридцать | тридцатый |
| 40 | сорок | сороковой |
| 50 | пятьдесят | пятидесятый |
| 60 | шестьдесят | шестидесятый |
| 70 | семьдесят | семидесятый |
| 80 | восемьдесят | восьмидесятый |
| 90 | девяносто | девяностый |
| 100 | сто | сотый |
| 101 | сто один | сто первый |
| 110 | сто десять | сто десятый |
| 111 | сто одиннадцать | сто одиннадцатый |
| 120 | сто двадцать | сто двадцатый |
| 121 | сто двадцать один | сто двадцать первый |
| 200 | двести | двухсотый |
| 300 | триста | трёхсотый |
| 400 | четыреста | четырёхсотый |
| 500 | пятьсот | пятисотый |
| 600 | шестьсот | шестисотый |
| 700 | семьсот | семисотый |
| 800 | восемьсот | восьмисотый |
| 900 | девятьсот | девятисотый |
| 1000 | тысяча | тысячный |
| 1001 | тысяча один | тысяча первый |
| 1010 | тысяча десять | тысяча десятый |
| 1011 | тысяча одиннадцать | тысяча одиннадцатый |
| 1020 | тысяча двадцать | тысяча двадцатый |
| 1021 | тысяча двадцать один | тысяча двадцать первый |

| | Cardinal Numerals | Ordinal Numerals |
|---|---|---|
| 2000 | две тысячи | двухтысячный |
| 3000 | три тысячи | трёхтысячный |
| 4000 | четыре тысячи | четырёхтысячный |
| 5000 | пять тысяч | пятитысячный |
| 6000 | шесть тысяч | шеститысячный |
| 7000 | семь тысяч | семитысячный |
| 8000 | восемь тысяч | восьмитысячный |
| 9000 | девять тысяч | девятитысячный |
| 10000 | десять тысяч | десятитысячный |
| 100000 | сто тысяч | стотысячный |
| 200000 | двести тысяч | двухсоттысячный |
| 1000000 | миллион[1] | миллионный |
| 2000000 | два миллиона | двухмиллионный |
| 5000000 | пять миллионов | пятимиллионный |

§ 368. Declension of Ordinal Numerals.

The ordinal numerals which are used as noun modifiers are all declined like regular hard adjectives. More specifically, all numerals whose nominative singular end in -ый, e.g., пе́рвый "first" are declined like ста́рый (Key No. 17, § 132, p. 192), while those with nominative singular in -ой, e.g., второ́й "second," are declined like живо́й (Key No. 18, § 132, p. 194). As discussed in § 360, p. 581, the declension of тре́тий and related ordinal numerals, e.g., два́дцать тре́тий "twenty-third," is exceptional.

With all composite ordinal numerals, e.g., два́дцать пе́рвый "twenty-first," два́дцать второ́й "twenty-second," два́дцать тре́тий "twenty-third," the non-adjectival portion of the numeral, e.g., два́дцать "twenty," remains undeclined.

The following sentences illustrate the use of Russian ordinal numerals.

Второ́й    член    четвёртой    гру́ппы периоди́ческой
(The) second member of (the) fourth group of (the) periodic

систе́мы    элеме́нтов ———— кре́мний,    находя́щийся    в
system    of (the) elements — silicon,    finding self    in

---

[1] Sometimes also spelled мильо́н.

тре́тьем    ма́лом      пери́оде,    по         фо́рмулам
(the) third  small (short)  period,     with regard to  formulas

свои́х  соедине́ний   явля́ется   ана́логом   углеро́да.,   но
of own  compounds    shows self  (an) analog  of carbon,    but

по              сво́йствам   значи́тельно   отлича́ется
with regard to   properties   considerably   distinguishes self

от       после́днего.
from     (the) latter.


Вот              план     металлурги́ческого        заво́да
There  you have   (a) plan  of (a) metallurgical        plant

конца́       семна́дцатого    ве́ка.
of (the) end  of (the) seventeenth  century.


## § 369.  Nouns Used as Numerals.

Authorities on Russian grammar usually regard Russian
cardinal numerals as forming a word class separate and distinct
from nouns.  Before discussing the general class of Russian
cardinal numerals, attention is directed to certain typical cardinal
numerals which resemble nouns in all respects, particularly with
regard to declension and use in constructing phrases and sentences.
These typical numerals are па́ра (Key No. 3a, § 130, p. 190)
"pair," ПЯТО́К (Key No. 3a, § 357, p. 573) "five," ДЕСЯ́ТОК[1]
(Key No. 3a, § 357, p. 573) "ten," СО́ТНЯ (Key No. 10-a,
§ 355, p. 563) "hundred," ТЫ́СЯЧА (Key No. 9, § 130, p. 190)
"thousand," МИЛЛИО́Н (Key No. 1, § 130, p. 190) "million,"
МИЛЛИАРД (Key No. 1, § 130, p. 190) "billion," ТРИЛЛИО́Н
(Key No. 1, § 130, p. 190) "trillion," etc. It should be noted
that the numerals па́ра, ПЯТО́К, ДЕСЯ́ТОК and СО́ТНЯ, like
"dozen," or "score" in English, have collective significance
and as a consequence cannot be used to replace ПЯТЬ "five,"
ДЕ́СЯТЬ "ten" and СТО "hundred" in forming cardinal numerals.

The following sentences illustrate the use of the numerals
having the character of nouns.

_____

[1] The word ДЕСЯ́ТОК is used in Russian much like "dozen" in English. For
example, eggs are sold in units of ten, ( ДЕСЯ́ТОК ), rather than by the dozen.
The word ДЮ́ЖИНА "dozen" means 12.

| | | | | | |
|---|---|---|---|---|---|
| Температу́ры | внутри́ | звёзд | дохо́дят | до | |
| Temperatures | within | (the) stars | go up to | as far as | |

| | | |
|---|---|---|
| деся́тков | миллио́нов | гра́дусов. |
| tens | of millions | of degrees. |

| | | | | | |
|---|---|---|---|---|---|
| Среди́ | звёзд | на | не́бе | рассы́пано | мно́го |
| Among | (the) stars | in | (the) sky | (are) scattered | many |

| | |
|---|---|
| ты́сяч | тума́нностей. |
| thousands | of nebulae. |

| | | | | |
|---|---|---|---|---|
| В | тече́ние | со́тен | миллио́нов | лет | оста́тки |
| In | (the) course | of hundreds | of millions | of years | residues |

| | | | | |
|---|---|---|---|---|
| дре́вних расте́ний | преврати́лись | в | ка́менный у́голь. |
| of ancient plants | converted self | into coal. |

| | | | | |
|---|---|---|---|---|
| В | ка́ждой | ка́пле | воды́ | соде́ржатся | милли́арды |
| In | each | drop | of water | contains self | billions |

| | |
|---|---|
| милли́ардов | моле́кул. |
| of billions | of molecules. |

## § 370. Declension of Cardinal Numerals.

An understanding of this class of numerals is best approached by first noting the many features which they have in common with nouns. Most important, perhaps, is the fact that cardinal numerals are used, as a general rule, substantially, i.e., like nouns or pronouns rather than like adjectives. Furthermore, the case of a Russian cardinal numeral in a sentence, clause or phrase is determined by the same rules that apply to nouns. The declension of Russian cardinal numerals in general recalls to mind the declension of nouns, particularly the declension of irregular nouns. This is evident from the following tabulations provided for reference purposes.

ОДИН      one[1]

|        | Singular |        |        | Plural[2] |
|--------|----------|--------|--------|-----------|
|        | Masc. | Fem. | Neuter | Masc.-Fem.-Neuter |
| Nom. | одúн | однá | однó | однú |
| Gen. | сдногó | однóй | одногó | однúх |
| Dat. | одномý | однóй | одномý | однúм |
| Acc. | одúн[3] | однý | однó | однú[3] |
| Instr. | однúм | однóй (однóю) | однúм | однúми |
| Prep. | однóм | однóй | однóм | однúх |

The declension of два "two," три "three" and четы́ре "four" calls to mind irregularly declined nouns.

|        | два  two | | три  three | четы́ре  four |
|--------|----------|-----|------------|---------------|
|        | Masc. and Neuter | Fem. | Masc.-Fem.-Neuter | Masc.-Fem.-Neuter |
| Nom. | два | две | три | четы́ре |
| Gen. | двух | двух | трёх | четырёх |
| Dat. | двум | двум | трём | четырём |
| Acc. | два[3] | две[3] | три[3] | четы́ре[3] |
| Instr. | двумя́ | двумя́ | тремя́ | четы́рьмя́ |
| Prep. | двух | двух | трёх | четырёх |

The declension of полторá[4] "one and a half" and óба "both" is best considered at this point.

---

[1] The declension of одúн is exceptional in that it resembles that of a possessive adjective.

[2] The plural forms of одúн are used in the meaning "some," "several."

[3] When referring to persons, animals, etc., (cf. § 67, p. 93) this form of the numeral becomes the same as the corresponding genitive.

[4] The fact that полторá was originally a compound is attested by the vestigial declension of пол-, "semi," cf. also § 375, p. 614.

полтора́ one and a half

| | Masc. and Neuter | Fem. |
|---|---|---|
| Nom. | полтора́ | полторы́ |
| Gen. | полу́тора | полу́тора |
| Dat. | полу́тора | полу́тора |
| Acc. | полтора́ | полторы́ |
| Instr. | полу́тора | полу́тора |
| Prep. | полу́тора | полу́тора |

The prefix пол- (полу-), "semi-," "half a," is used in a rather general fashion as discussed in § 375, p. 612 and exemplified by such words as полго́да "half a year," полукру́г "semicircle," полупрозра́чный "semitransparent," "translucent."

A close relationship exists between the ordinal numeral второ́й "second" and полтора́ meaning "one and a half." The dropping of an initial в from a root in forming a derivative occurs only rarely in Russian. Another example is о́бласть "realm," "territory," "region," "field," from об- and вла́сть "power," "authority."

о́ба both

| | Masc.-Neuter | Fem. |
|---|---|---|
| Nom. | о́ба | о́бе |
| Gen. | обо́их | обе́их |
| Dat. | обо́им | обе́им |
| Acc. | о́ба[1] | о́бе[1] |
| Instr. | обо́ими | обе́ими |
| Prep. | обо́их | обе́их |

[1] When referring to persons, animals, etc., (cf. § 67, p. 93) this form of the numeral becomes the same as the corresponding genitive.

The  numerals  ПЯТЬ  "five,"  ШЕСТЬ  "six,"  СЕМЬ  "seven,"
ДЕ́ВЯТЬ  "nine"  and  ДЕ́СЯТЬ  "ten"  are  declined  like  regular
feminine  nouns,  (Key No. 12,  § 130, p. 190).  The  declension  of
ВО́СЕМЬ  "eight"  is  slightly  irregular  but  closely  related.

|        | ПЯТЬ<br>five | ДЕ́СЯТЬ<br>ten | ВО́СЕМЬ<br>eight |
|--------|--------|--------|--------|
| Nom.   | ПЯТЬ   | ДЕ́СЯТЬ | ВО́СЕМЬ |
| Gen.   | ПЯТИ́  | ДЕСЯТИ́ | ВОСЬМИ́ |
| Dat.   | ПЯТИ́  | ДЕСЯТИ́ | ВОСЬМИ́ |
| Acc.   | ПЯТЬ   | ДЕ́СЯТЬ | ВО́СЕМЬ |
| Instr. | ПЯТЬЮ  | ДЕСЯТЬЮ | ВОСЕМЬЮ |
| Prep.  | ПЯТИ́  | ДЕСЯТИ́ | ВОСЬМИ́ |

The  cardinal  numerals  ending  in  -НАДЦАТЬ  (11-19)  are
declined  in  the  same  way,  as  ПЯТЬ  "five."  The  same  is  true  of
ДВА́ДЦАТЬ  "twenty"  and  ТРИ́ДЦАТЬ  "thirty,"  while  the  declension
of  СО́РОК  "forty"  is  highly  irregular.

|        | оди́ннадцать<br>eleven | два́дцать<br>twenty | со́рок<br>forty |
|--------|--------|--------|--------|
| Nom.   | оди́ннадцать   | два́дцать  | со́рок  |
| Gen.   | оди́ннадцати  | двадцати́ | сорока́ |
| Dat.   | оди́ннадцати  | двадцати́ | сорока́ |
| Acc.   | оди́ннадцать  | двадцать  | со́рок  |
| Instr. | оди́ннадцатью | двадцатью́| сорока́ |
| Prep.  | оди́ннадцати  | двадцати́ | сорока́ |

Those  numerals  which  end  in  - ДЕСЯТ ,  namely  ПЯТЬДЕСЯ́Т
"fifty,"  ШЕСТЬДЕСЯ́Т  "sixty,"  СЕ́МЬДЕСЯТ  "seventy,"
ВО́СЕМЬДЕСЯТ  "eighty,"  decline  both  the  component  parts,  as
shown  by  the  following  examples.

|  | пятьдеся́т<br>fifty | во́семьдесят<br>eighty |
|---|---|---|
| Nom. | пятьдеся́т | во́семьдесят |
| Gen. | пятиде́сяти | восьми́десяти |
| Dat. | пятиде́сяти | восьми́десяти |
| Acc. | пятьдеся́т | во́семьдесят |
| Instr. | пятью́десятью | восемью́десятью |
| Prep. | пятиде́сяти | восьми́десяти |

The numerals СТО "100" and девяно́сто "90" are declined irregularly.

|  | СТО<br>100 | девяно́сто<br>90 |
|---|---|---|
| Nom. | сто | девяно́сто |
| Gen. | ста | девяно́ста |
| Dat. | ста | девяно́ста |
| Acc. | сто | девяно́сто |
| Instr. | ста | девяно́ста |
| Prep. | ста | девяно́ста |

Numerals denoting multiples of СТО "100" decline both component parts as shown in the following examples.

|  | две́сти<br>200 | три́ста<br>300 | пятьсо́т<br>500 | восемьсо́т<br>800 |
|---|---|---|---|---|
| Nom. | две́сти | три́ста | пятьсо́т | восемьсо́т |
| Gen. | двухсо́т[1] | трёхсо́т[1] | пятисо́т[1] | восьмисо́т[1] |
| Dat. | двумста́м[1] | трёмста́м[1] | пятиста́м[1] | восьмиста́м[1] |
| Acc. | две́сти | три́ста | пятьсо́т | восе́мьсо́т |
| Instr. | двумяста́ми[1] |  | пятьюста́ми[1] |  |
|  |  | тремяста́ми[1] |  | восемьюста́ми[1] |
| Prep. | двухста́х[1] | трёхста́х[1] | пятиста́х[1] | восьмиста́х[1] |

[1] Sometimes written as two words, thus, for example ДВУХ СОТ.

The declension of a compound number requires declension of each of its component parts as in the following example.

|        | две "two | тысячи thousand | триста three hundred | пятьдесят fifty | один[1] one" |
|--------|----------|-----------------|----------------------|-----------------|--------------|
| Nom.   | две      | тысячи          | триста               | пятьдесят       | один         |
| Gen.   | двух     | тысяч           | трёхсот              | пятидесяти      | одного       |
| Dat.   | двум     | тысячам         | трёмстам             | пятидесяти      | одному       |
| Acc.   | две      | тысячи          | триста               | пятьдесят       | один[2]      |
| Instr. | двумя    | тысячами        | тремястами           | пятьюдесятью    | одним        |
| Prep.  | двух     | тысячах         | трёхстах             | пятидесяти      | одном        |

§ 371.  Cases Used with Numerals.

As already noted, the same rules apply to the use of the cases of cardinal numerals as govern the use of the cases of nouns.

Complications are encountered when one of the overwhelming majority of[3] Russian cardinal numerals is used with a noun, as for example, in phrases corresponding to the English "two metals," "five atoms," "twenty compounds," "one hundred one molecules."

If the cardinal numeral is ОДИН "one" or a compound thereof, e.g., ДВАДЦАТЬ ОДИН, "twenty-one," МИЛЛИОН ОДИН "one million one," then the following noun is in the singular number and in the same case as the numeral.

With the remaining cardinal numerals the following special rules apply. If the cardinal numeral is used in such a way as to require it to be in the genitive, dative, instrumental or prepositional case, then the noun following the numeral is used

[1] The forms of ОДИН listed here are those that would be used if the following nouns were masculine in gender. (With regard to the accusative case with animate masculine noun, see Note 2 below). If the noun following the numeral were feminine or neuter then the appropriate forms of ОДИН listed in p. 600 would be used.

[2] With masculine animate nouns (as defined in § 67, p. 93) this accusative form of ОДИН becomes ОДНОГО, i.e., identical with its genitive form.

[3] In a preceding paragraph (§ 369, p. 598) the use of the genitive plural following the numerals МИЛЛИОН "million," МИЛЛИАРД "billion," ТРИЛЛИОН "trillion," СОТНЯ "hundred," ТЫСЯЧА "thousand," has been discussed. There is a tendency for the case of nouns used after ТЫСЯЧА to be the same as is used after СТО. When ТЫСЯЧА is so used, the instrumental singular form becomes ТЫСЯЧЕЙ.

in the plural of the same case. If, on the other hand, the cardinal numeral is used in the nominative or accusative case, then the case of the noun accompanying the numeral is determined according to the following rules:

1) After два[1] (or две) "two," три "three," четы́ре "four," and after compound cardinal numerals ending with these simple numerals, e.g., со́рок два "forty-two," сто три "one hundred three," два́дцать четы́ре "twenty-four," the noun is in the genitive singular.

2) After all other numerals, e.g., пять "five," де́сять "ten," оди́ннадцать "eleven," четы́рнадцать "fourteen," сто "one hundred," etc., the genitive plural of nouns is used.

3) When a noun, which follows a numeral, has an adjective or participle as modifier, the modifier is in the same case and number as the noun which it modifies except that nouns in the genitive singular in accord with Rule (1) above require their adjective modifiers to be in the genitive plural.

§ 372. Sentences Illustrating Use of Cardinal Numerals.

Неме́цкие генера́лы счита́ли, что они́ в тече́ние
(The) German generals estimated, that they in (the) course

полу́тора-двух ме́сяцев суме́ют дойти́
of one and a half to two months will be able to proceed up

до Ура́ла.
as far as (the) Ural(s).

Изве́стны два основны́х ти́па хими́ческих
(Are) known two basic types of chemical

реа́кций: реа́кция разложе́ния и реа́кция
reactions: reaction of decomposition and reaction

соедине́ния.
of combination.

[1] The rules cited with regard to два (две) "two," also apply to о́ба (о́бе) "both" and полтора́ (полторы́) "one and a half."

При реа́кции разложе́ния из одного́ вещества́
During reaction of decomposition from one substance

получа́ются два или бо́лее но́вых веще́ств.
obtain self two or more new substances.

Распа́д ядра́ ура́на на два лёгких
Decomposition of (the) nucleus of uranium into two light

ядра́ сопровожда́ется выделе́нием весьма́
nuclei accompanies self by (the) evolution of extremely

большо́го коли́чества эне́ргии.
large amount of energy.

Вода́ — хими́ческое соедине́ние двух га́зов —
Water (is) (a) chemical compound of two gases —

водоро́да и кислоро́да.
hydrogen and oxygen.

Э́та реа́кция прохо́дит в двух ста́диях.
This reaction proceeds in two steps.

Мальта́за разлага́ет мелеци́тозу сра́зу на три
Maltase decomposes melezitose all at once into three

моле́кулы — две моле́кулы глюко́зы и одну́
molecules — two molecules of glucose and one

моле́кулу фрукто́зы.
molecule fructose.

Из трёх возмо́жных по тео́рии
Of (the) three possible according to (the) theory

строе́ния аминобензо́йных кисло́т наибо́льшее
of structure aminobenzoic acids the greatest

значе́ние    име́ет    ортоаминобензо́йная    и́ли
importance    has    orthoaminobenzoic    or

антрани́ловая    кислота́.
anthranilic    acid.

В криста́ллах    просты́х    веще́ств    а́томы    облада́ют
In crystals    of simple    substances atoms    possess

тремя́    степеня́ми    свобо́ды    движе́ния
three    degrees    of freedom    of motion

(кинети́ческой    эне́ргии).
(of kinetic    energy).

Ближа́йший    гомо́лог    анили́на,    аминопроизво́дное
(The) nearest homolog    of aniline    (the) aminoderivative

толуо́ла,    изве́стен    в    ви́де    четырёх    изоме́ров.
of toluene (is)    known    in    (the) form    of four    isomers.

Изве́стны    шесть    диаминобензо́йных    кисло́т
(There are) known    six    diaminobenzoic    acids

соста́ва    $C_6H_4(NH_2)COOH$.
of composition    $C_6H_4(NH_2)COOH$.

На́ша    Земля́    —    одна́    из девяти́    изве́стных    нам
Our    earth    (is)    one    of nine    known    to us

плане́т,    входя́щих    в    со́лнечную    систе́му.
planets,    entering    into (the) solar    system.

Хи́мики    мо́гут,    взяв    два    гра́мма    неви́димого
Chemists are able, having taken two    grams    of (an) invisible

бесцве́тного    га́за – водоро́да и    16 гра́ммов    друго́го,
colorless    gas — hydrogen and 16 grams    of another

то́же    неви́димого    га́за    —    кислоро́да, заста́вить    их
also    colorless    gas    —    oxygen,    to make    them

| химически | соединиться | и | образовать | 18 | граммов |
|---|---|---|---|---|---|
| chemically | to combine self | and | to form | 18 | grams |

| воды́. |
|---|
| of water. |

| Уже́ | при | пяти́ | атмосфе́рах | первонача́льного |
|---|---|---|---|---|
| Even | at | five | atmospheres | of initial |

| давле́ния | пар | вырыва́ется | из | сосу́да, |
|---|---|---|---|---|
| pressure | steam | pulls self out (escapes) | from | (the vessel, |

| в | кото́ром | он | заключён, | со | ско́ростью |
|---|---|---|---|---|---|
| in | which | it | (is) enclosed, | with | (a) speed |

| пятисо́т | ме́тров | в | секу́нду, | тогда́ как |
|---|---|---|---|---|
| of five hundred | meters | in | (a) second, | whereas |

| быстрота́ | ве́тра, | да́же | при | урага́не, | не |
|---|---|---|---|---|---|
| (the) swiftness | of wind, | even | during | (a) hurricane, | not |

| превыша́ет | сорока́ | ме́тров | в | секу́нду. |
|---|---|---|---|---|
| exceeds | forty | meters | in | (a) second. |

§ 373.  Fractions.

The word дробь  "fraction" denotes the general mathematical concept.

Certain fractions are designated by special nouns, viz., 1/2, полови́на (Key No. 7, § 130, p. 190) 1/3, треть and 1/4, че́тверь (Key No. 12, § 130, p. 190). Other fractions are expressed by using the appropriate ordinal numeral to modify one of the feminine nouns, часть, "part" or до́ля "share," "portion," "fraction," e.g., со́тая часть "hundredth part," две седьмы́х ча́сти "two seventh parts," шесть пятна́дцатых доле́й "six fifteenth portions." Fractions are often expressed without using either часть or до́ля. Thus, we have, for example, со́тая "hundredth," две седьмы́х, "two sevenths," шесть пятина́дцатых,  "six fifteenths."

Since one of two nouns (часть or до́ля), either expressed or implied, forms the basis of Russian fractions, nouns subordinate to fractions are in the genitive singular, e.g., две седьмы́х ча́сти миллиме́тра "two seventh parts of a millimeter," Шесть пятна́дцатых ли́тра "six fifteenths of a liter." The same rule extends to decimal fractions and numerals terminating with a decimal fraction, e.g., 1.05 гра́мма, "1.05 of a gram."

| | | | | | |
|---|---|---|---|---|---|
| Затра́ты | на | земляны́е | рабо́ты | соста́вили | о́коло |
| Expenditures | for | earth | works | constituted | about |

| | | | |
|---|---|---|---|
| пя́той | ча́сти | сто́имости | всей |
| (a) fifth | part | of (the) cost | of (the) whole |

| | |
|---|---|
| желе́зной | доро́ги. |
| railroad. | |

| | | | | | |
|---|---|---|---|---|---|
| В после́дние | де́сять —— | пятна́дцать | лет | не | то́лько |
| In (the) last | ten | to fifteen | years | not only | |

| | | | | | |
|---|---|---|---|---|---|
| микро́н, | но его́ деся́тые | и | со́тые | до́ли | получи́ли |
| (a) micron, | but his tenth | and hundredth | parts | acquired | |

| | | | | |
|---|---|---|---|---|
| огро́мное | значе́ние | не | то́лько | в | исследова́тельских |
| enormous | importance | not | only | in | research |

| | | | | |
|---|---|---|---|---|
| лаборато́риях, | но и | в | це́хах | заво́дов. |
| laboratories | but also | in | shops | of factories. |

| | | | | | |
|---|---|---|---|---|---|
| Кислоро́д | составля́ет | по объёму | 21% | (о́коло | одно́й |
| Oxygen | constitutes | by volume | 21% | (about | one |

| | | | | | |
|---|---|---|---|---|---|
| пя́той) | во́здуха, | а азо́т | – 78% | (приблизи́тельно |
| fifth) | of (the) air | and nitrogen -- 78% | (about | |

| | |
|---|---|
| четы́ре | пя́тых). |
| four | fifths). |

| | | | | | |
|---|---|---|---|---|---|
| Вода́ | составля́ет | почти́ | три | че́тверти | всего́ |
| Water | constitutes | almost | three | fourths | of all |

| | | |
|---|---|---|
| ве́са | челове́ческого | те́ла. |
| (the) weight | of (the) human | body. |

В одно́м  объёме    воды́     растворя́ется    при 0°  о́коло
In one     volume    of water  dissolves self    at 0°   about

0.05   объёма    кислоро́да.
0.05   volume     of oxygen.

§ 374.  Prepositional Phrases Involving Numerals.

Certain prepositions are used with numerals in special
expressions, as follows:

до        "up to," "as far as"
на        "by" (with regard to both multiplication and division)
на        "per"
в         "of"
в - -     раз ( бо́льше ) ( ме́ньше )
- - -     "times (more) (less)"

Example sentences follow.

Пирофосфо́рная      кислота́       образу́ется        при
Pyrophosphoric      acid          forms self          on

продолжи́тельном  нагрева́нии   до   200 - 300°.
prolonged          heating       to   200  - 300°.

При       благоприя́тных     усло́виях       азотоба́ктерии
With      favorable          circumstances   nitrobacteria

спосо́бны   за   год      накопи́ть      в   по́чве    до
(are) capable in   (a) year  to accumulate  in  (the) soil  up to

50  кг. свя́занного     азо́та       на   ге́ктар.
50  kg. of fixed        nitrogen    per  hectare.

Оди́н    объём    сероуглеро́да      поглоща́ет          до
One      volume   of carbon disulfide  absorbs (dissolves)  up to

250  объёмов   SbH₃ .
250  volumes    (of) SbH$_3$.

Реа́кция    $P_2O_5$    с    водо́й    сопровожда́ется
(The) reaction   (of) $P_2O_5$ with   water    accompanies self

выделе́нием      значи́тельного     коли́чества
with (the) evolution    of (a) considerable    quantity

тепла́ (47 ккал.    на   г.- мол.   $P_2O_5$).
of heat (47 kcal.    per. g.   mol.   $P_2O_5$).


Когда́   85   умножа́ется    на   6,   то   85   есть
When    85   multiplies self   by   6,   then   85   is

мно́жимое,[1]      6    -    мно́житель,[1]     а
(the) multiplicand,   6   (is)   (the) multiplier,    and

получи́вшееся      по́сле   умноже́ния   число́   510
(the) having obtained self   after    multiplication   number   510

- произведе́ние.
(is) (the) product.


Для   реше́ния   пе́рвой     зада́чи      на́до    75
For    solution   of (the) first   problem   (it is) necessary 75

раздели́ть     на 3;   здесь    дели́мое[1]      75,
to divide     by   3;   here    (the) dividend   (is)   75,

дели́тель   3,   ча́стное[1]   25.
(the) divisor   3,   (the) quotient   25.


Мы зна́ем,   что диа́метр    Со́лнца      в 109.5 раз
We know,    that (the) diameter of (the) Sun   (is) 109.5 times

бо́льше    диа́метра    Земли́.
larger than   (the) diameter   of (the) Earth.


[1] The neuter forms of adjectives are often used to replace more cumbersome expressions involving the noun число́ such as мно́жимое число́, дели́мое число́, ча́стное число́, cf. also Note 14, p. 489.

На рис. 66 даны́              увели́ченные в    50 миллио́нов раз
In  Fig.  66 (are) given    magnified        50 million      times

разме́ры                      нейтра́льного     а́тома    се́ры
(the) dimensions             of (a) neutral    atom     of sulfur

и    двух    её    ио́нов.
and of two  of her  ions.

Электро́н                     приблизи́тельно  в  1840    раз
(The) electron               (is) approximately   1840    times

ле́гче   са́мого    лёгкого    а́тома,   и́менно –   а́тома
lighter than the   lightest   atom,    namely     (the) atom

водоро́да.
of hydrogen.


§ 375. Numerals Used as Prefixes.

Prefixes derived from numerals are important in scientific nomenclature.

| Derived from Russian roots | Derived from Greek or Latin | English Translation |
|---|---|---|
| пол-(полу-)[1] | семи-[4] | semi- |
| одно- | моно- | mono- |
| полутора- | сескви- | sesqui- |
| дву-[2] | ди- | di- |
| тре-[3] | три- | tri- |

---

[1] See page 614, for sample declension of nouns formed with the prefix пол- (полу-).
[2] Also sometimes двух-.
[3] Also sometimes трех-.
[4] The use of семи- for "semi-" is restricted to words such as семиполя́рный "semipolar" in which translation of семи- as "hepta-" would be meaningless. Russian prefers пол- (полу-) as the prefix meaning "semi-."

| Derived from Russian roots | Derived from Greek or Latin | English Translation |
|---|---|---|
| четырех- | тетра- | tetra- |
| пяти- | пента- | penta- |
| шести- | гекса- | hexa- |
| семи-[1] | гепта- | hepta- |
| восьми- | окта- | octa- |
| девяти- | нона- | nona- |
| десяти- | дека- | deca- |
| одиннадцати- | ундека- | undeca- |
| двенадцати- | додека- | dodeca- |
| двадцати- | эйкоза- | eicosa- |
| сто- | центи- | centi- |
| тысяче- | кило- | kilo- |
|  | мега- | mega- |
| много- | поли-[2] | poly- |

Decimal fractional parts may also be indicated by prefixes as follows:

|  | Prefixes Used In Russian | Prefixes Used In English |
|---|---|---|
| 1/10 | деци- | deci- |
| 1/100 | центи-[3] | centi- |
|  | санти-[3] |  |
| 1/1000 | милли- | milli- |
| 1/1,000,000 | микро- | micro- |

It is obvious that the decimal prefixes used in English and in Russian have a common origin.

---

[1] See Footnote 4, p. 612.

[2] Different use of the prefix "centi-" in English, as in "centimeter" and "centipede" also characterizes Russian use of центи-. The prefix санти- taken from French, always mean a hundredth part as in сантиметр "centimeter."

[3] The prefix поли- meaning "poly-" as in полимер "polymer" must not be confused with полу- meaning "semi-."

The declension of nouns bearing the prefix пол– (полу-) requires special attention and recalls to mind the declension of полтора́ as given in § 370, p. 601.

полчаса́     half (an) hour

|          | Singular    | Plural       |
|----------|-------------|--------------|
| Nom.     | полчаса́     | получасы́     |
| Gen.     | получа́са    | получасо́в    |
| Dat.     | получа́су    | получаса́м    |
| Acc.     | полчаса́     | получасы́     |
| Instr.   | получа́сом   | получаса́ми   |
| Prep.    | получа́се    | получаса́х    |

Note that the noun, here час, "hour," to which the prefix пол– (полу-) is applied takes its regular endings, except for use of the genitive singular ending in the nominative and accusative singular. The same situation occurs with feminine nouns, e.g. полмину́ты "half (a) minute," полмоле́кулы "half (a) molecule."

Nouns whose nominative singular case is formed with the prefix полу-, as for example полукру́г "semi-circle," semi-circular area," do not exhibit the above illustrated peculiarities in declension. Regular declension also characterizes adjectives formed with the prefix полу- as for example полумёртвый "half-dead."

Example sentences follow.

| Компле́ксные | соедине́ния | гексамми́нового | ти́па |
|---|---|---|---|
| Complex | compounds | of (the) hexamine | type |

| (т.е. соедине́ния, | заключа́ющие | шесть | нейтра́льных |
|---|---|---|---|
| (i.e., compounds, | containing | six | neutral |

| моле́кул | аммиака́) | произво́дятся | не | то́лько | из |
|---|---|---|---|---|---|
| molecules | of ammonia) | derive self | not | only | from |

| трехвале́нтного | коба́льта, | но | та́кже | из |
|---|---|---|---|---|
| trivalent | cobalt, | but | also | from |

четырехвале́нтной пла́тины, двухвале́нтных[1] ме́ди,
quadrivalent · platinum divalent copper,

желе́за и пр.
iron and the like.


Изуче́ние многочи́сле́нных соедине́ний азо́та
(The) study of numerous compounds of nitrogen

с други́ми хими́ческими элеме́нтами пока́зывает,
with other chemical elements shows,

что полмоле́кулы азо́та есть а́том азо́та.
that (a) half molecule of nitrogen is (an) atom of nitrogen.


За́мкнутый многоуго́льник с десятью́ сторона́ми
(A) closed polygon with ten sides

называ́ется десятиуго́льником.
calls self (a) decagon.


Раство́ры, в ли́тре кото́рых соде́ржатся 2, 0,5,
Solutions in (a) liter of which contain self 2, 0.5,

0,1, 0,01 грамм-эквивале́нта, называ́ются
0.1, 0.01 gram - equivalent(s) call self

соотве́тственно: двунорма́льным, полунорма́льным,
correspondingly; two normal half normal,

децинорма́льным, центинорма́льным.
tenth normal, hundredth normal.


[1] Here двухвале́нтных is in the plural of the genitive case since it modifies ·
two nouns, viz., ме́ди and желе́за both of which are in the genitive singular. Further
examples of such a relationship between modifiers and nouns are given in § 393, p. 655.

| Одна́ | ты́сячная | до́ля | ампе́ра | называ́ется |
|---|---|---|---|---|
| One | thousandth | part | of (an) ampere | calls self |

| миллиампе́ром, | а одна́ миллио́нная | ампе́ра — |
|---|---|---|
| (a) milliampere, | and one millionth | of (an) ampere -- |

микроампе́ром.
(a) microampere.

## § 376. Collective Numerals.

I. Introductory Note.

Along with adjectives and adverbs closely similar to English "twice," "double," etc., Russian has a group of collective numerals differing with regard to several features from English collectives. To this group we shall next direct attention.

II. Collective Numerals Resembling Nouns.

The following list includes all numerals of this group that are at all important. Note the close relationship to Russian cardinal numerals.

| | Collective Numeral | Cardinal Numeral |
|---|---|---|
| 2 | дво́е | два(две) |
| 3 | тро́е | три |
| 4 | че́тверо | четы́ре |
| 5 | пя́теро | пять |
| 6 | ше́стеро | шесть |
| 7 | се́меро | семь |
| 8 | во́сьмеро | во́семь |
| 9 | де́вятеро | де́вять |
| 10 | де́сятеро | де́сять |

The collectives дво́е and тро́е are declined alike while the others listed above are declined like че́тверо.

## Declension of Collective Numerals

| | | |
|---|---|---|
| **Nom.** | двóе | чéтверо |
| **Gen.** | двоúх | четверы́х |
| **Dat.** | двоúм | четверы́м |
| **Acc.** | двóе[1] | чéтверо[1] |
| | (двоúх) | (четверы́х) |
| **Instr.** | двоúми | четверы́ми |
| **Prep.** | двоúх | четверы́х |

The use of the collective numerals may be summarized as follows:

    a. With masculine nouns denoting persons as alternates for the cardinal numerals. Thus we have the alternative expressions for "two brothers."

| | | | | |
|---|---|---|---|---|
| **Nom.** | двóе | брáтьев | два | брáта |
| **Gen.** | двоúх | брáтьев | двух | брáтьев |
| **Dat.** | двоúм | брáтьям | двум | брáтьям |
| **Acc.** | двоúх | брáтьев | двух | брáта |
| **Instr.** | двоúми | брáтьями | двумя́ | брáтьями |
| **Prep.** | двоúх | брáтьях | двух | брáтьях |

    b. The collective numerals are also used to denote some number of pairs of various objects usually occurring in pairs, e.g. трóе сапóг "three pairs of boots."

    c. The collective numerals двóе, трóе and чéтверо are used exclusively (and the other collective numerals alternately with the cardinal numerals) to designate the plural of those nouns having plural forms only, cf. § 359, p. 579. Thus we have for example двóе ворóт "two gates," чéтверо нóжниц "four shears," пя́теро or пять сýток "five periods of twenty-four hours," etc.

    III. Adjectives and Adverbs as Collective Numerals.

    These can be divided -- at least roughly -- into two groups (1) those expressing a composite or collective multiplicity as exemplified by English "double" and (2) those expressing a repetitive multiplicity such as English "twice."

---

[1] When referring to persons, this form of the numeral becomes the same as the corresponding genitive.

The precise shades of meaning are best learned by observing how these collectives are used in sentences.

Though the lists given below are not intended to be complete, they contain a number of words which are rarely if ever used.

## Group I

### Composite or Collective Multiplicity

| Parent Numeral | Adjectives | | | Adverbs | |
|---|---|---|---|---|---|
| оди́н 1 | одино́кий | еди́ный | еди́нственный[1] | | |
| два 2 | двоя́кий | двойно́й | дво́йственный | вдвойне́ | вдво́е |
| три 3 | троя́кий | тройно́й | тро́йственный | втройне́ | втро́е |
| четы́ре 4 | | четверно́й | | | вче́тверо |
| пять 5 | | пятерно́й | | | впя́теро |
| шесть 6 | | шестерно́й | | | вше́стеро |
| семь 7 | | семерно́й | | | все́меро |
| во́семь 8 | | восьмерно́й | | | вво́сьмеро |
| де́вять 9 | | девятерно́й | | | вде́вятеро |
| де́сять 10 | | десятерно́й | | | вде́сятеро |

## Group II

### Repetitive Multiplicity

| Parent Numeral | Adjectives | Adverbs | Adverbs | |
|---|---|---|---|---|
| оди́н 1 | однокра́тный | однокра́тно | одна́жды | оди́н раз |
| два 2 | двукра́тный | двукра́тно | два́жды | два ра́за |
| три 3 | троекра́тный | троекра́тно | три́жды | три ра́за |
| четы́ре 4 | четырехкра́тный | четырехкра́тно | четы́режды | четы́ре ра́за |
| пять 5 | пятикра́тный | пятикра́тно | | пять раз |
| шесть 6 | шестикра́тный | шестикра́тно | | шесть раз |

[1] The corresponding adverb еди́нственно "solely," "only" is often used.

| Parent Numeral | Adjective | Adverbs | |
|---|---|---|---|
| семь 7 | семикра́тный | семикра́тно | семь раз |
| во́семь 8 | восьмикра́тный | восьмикра́тно | во́семь раз |
| де́вять 9 | девятикра́тный | девятикра́тно | де́вять раз |
| де́сять 10 | десятикра́тный | десятикра́тно | де́сять раз |
| двадца́ть 20 | двацатикра́тный | двацатикра́тно | двадца́ть раз |
| сто 100 | стокра́тный | стокра́тно | сто раз |
| ты́сяча 1000 | тысячекра́тный[1] | тысячекра́тно | ты́сячу раз |
| миллио́н 1000000 | миллионнокра́тный | миллионнокра́тно | миллио́н раз |

## IV. Sentences Illustrating Collective Numerals.

В то вре́мя бы́ли в Моско́вских стена́х пя́теро
At that time were in Moscow's walls five

воро́т.
gates.

Двойно́е лучепреломле́ние криста́ллов те́сно
Double refraction of crystals (is) closely

свя́зано с их анизотро́пией.
connected with their anisotropy.

Англи́йское сло́во "kid," име́ет троя́кое
(The) English word "kid," has (a) triple

значе́ние.
meaning.

До пе́рвой мирово́й войны́ существова́л
Up to (the) first world war existed

тро́йственный сою́з Герма́нии, А́встрии и Ита́лии.
(the) triple alliance of Germany, Austria and Italy.

---

[1] In conversation тысячекра́тный and the corresponding adverb is often used in speaking of an action repeated an indefinite number of times.

| В | паровы́х | маши́нах, | два́жды | во | вре́мя | одного́ |
|---|---|---|---|---|---|---|
| In | steam | engines, | twice | in | (the) time | of one |

| оборо́та | ва́ла, | ско́рость | движе́ния |
|---|---|---|---|
| rotation | of (the) shaft, | (the) rate | of motion |

| по́ршня | обраща́ется | в нуль. |
|---|---|---|
| of (the) piston | changes self | to zero. |

§ 377. **Reading Exercise.**

## Криста́ллы

Всё многообра́зие кристалли́ческих форм разли́чных веще́ств мо́жет быть сведено́ к шести́ кристалли́ческим систе́мам. Э́ти шесть кристалли́ческих систе́м характеризу́ются шестью́ ти́пами координа́тных осе́й, кото́рые различа́ются ме́жду собо́ю и[1] свое́ю относи́тельною длино́ю и угла́ми, под кото́рыми пересека́ются о́си.

1. Пра́вильная (куби́ческая) систе́ма.
Все три о́си взаи́мно перпендикуля́рны и ра́вны[2] по величине́. По куби́ческой систе́ме кристаллизу́ется о́коло 8% всех иссле́дованных веще́ств, наприме́р, NaCl, ZnS, алма́з.

2. Квадра́тная (тетрагона́льная) систе́ма.
Все три о́си взаи́мно перпендикуля́рны. Две из них равны́, тре́тья - гла́вная - ось мо́жет быть коро́че и́ли длинне́е двух остальны́х. Из о́бщего числа́ изу́ченных криста́ллов на до́лю квадра́тной систе́мы прихо́дится о́коло 5% - т.е. одна́ двадца́тая всех изве́стных криста́ллов.

3. Ромби́ческая систе́ма.
Все три о́си взаи́мно перпендикуля́рны, но неодина́ковой[3] величины́. В ромби́ческой систе́ме кристаллизу́ется о́коло 28% - приме́рно че́тверть - всех изве́стных криста́ллов.

4. Гексагональная система.

В отличие от других систем гексагональная характеризуется четырьмя осями, из которых одна - главная - перпендикулярна к остальным трём осям, которые составляют между собой равные 60° углы. Эти три оси имеют одинаковую длину. Однако четвёртая - главная - ось может быть длиннее или короче трёх остальных. Около 7% всех известных кристаллов относится к гексагональной системе.

5. Моноклиническая система.

Все три оси имеют различную величину. Две оси взаимно перепендикулярны, третья наклонна по отношению к их[4] плоскости, а перпендикулярна к одной из двух остальных осей. Около 42% - приблизительно четыре десятых - всех изученных кристаллов кристаллизуется в моноклинической системе.

6. Триклиническая система.

Все три оси расположены под различными углами друг к другу и имеют различную величину. По триклинической системе кристаллизуется около 10% - т.е. одна десятая - всех исследованных кристаллов.

Важную роль в кристаллографии играет понятие оси симметрии. Если через кристалл может быть проведена ось симметрии, то это значит, что при определённом повороте около неё[5] получается полное совпадение нового положения с прежним. Порядок оси симметрии определяется углом, необходимым для такого совмещения поворота, выраженным[6] в долях от 360°. Так, например, если кристалл совмещается со своим исходным положением при повороте около данной оси на 120°, то она является осью третьего[7] порядка (так как 120° - треть 360°). Вообще в кристаллах могут фигурировать оси симметрии второго, третьего, четвёртого и шестого порядка. Когда около оси второго (третьего, четвёртого, шестого) порядка совершается одно полное вращение кристалла, его положение совпадает с исходным - дважды (трижды, четырежды, шесть раз).

Рис. I
Кристалл, обладающий
осью третьего порядка

В частности куб - как показано в рис. 2 - имеет три
оси четвёртого порядка (проходящие через середины  гра-
ней), четыре оси третьего порядка (через противоположные
углы) и шесть осей второго порядка(через середины рёбер).

Рис. II
оси симметрии у куба

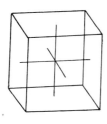 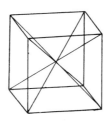 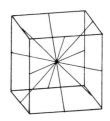

Три оси           Четыре оси        Шесть  осей
четвёртого        третьего          второго
порядка           порядка           порядка

Резюмируя, мы видим,что признаки, являющиеся особенно важными характеристиками кристаллов, трояки[8] по
категории: во-первых: число и относительная длина коорди-
натных осей, во-вторых: углы под которыми  пересекаются
координатные оси,во-третьих:число и порядок осей симметрии.

## Notes

1. И--- И---,  "both --- and ---."

2. Все три о́си взаи́мно перпендикуля́рны и равны́, "all three axes (are) mutually perpendicular and equal." Note the use of the plural predicate form of the two adjectives.

3. неодина́ковой величины́ "of unequal magnitude." This is an example of the descriptive genitive.

4. Here ИХ is a possessive adjective meaning "their," cf. Note 7, p. 558.

5. о́коло неё "about her" (referring to the axis of symmetry). Here нее is a pronoun, cf. preceding Note 4.

6. вы́раженным в доля́х от 360°, "expressed in fractions of 360°." The -ым ending of вы́раженным indicates that it refers back to угло́м.

7. ось симметри́и тре́тьего поря́дка, literally, "axis of symmetry of third order" is known in English as a "three-fold axis" or a "triad." Similarly, a "two-fold axis" or "dyad" in Russian is ось симметри́и второ́го поря́дка.

8. троя́ки is the predicative plural form of троя́кий "triple," cf. p. 618, Group I.


§ 378.  Translation Exercise.

1. All crystals (криста́ллы) pertain (отно́сятся) to six crystal systems.
2. These six crystal systems are (суть): cubic, tetragonal, rhombic, hexagonal, monoclinic and triclinic.
3. The cubic and tetragonal systems are characterized by three (тремя́) mutually perpendicular axes.
4. Of the total number of investigated crystals about 8% pertain to the cubic system.
5. One twentieth of all investigated substances crystallize (self) according to (по) the tetragonal (тетрагона́льной) system.

6. The third axis is perpendicular to the plane of the two remaining.

7. On (При) rotation about an axis of symmetry a crystal coincides (self) with own starting position.

8. A cube has axes of symmetry of second, fourth and sixth order.

9. These crystals have three axes of the third order.

10. Axes passing through centers of edges of a cube (куба) are (show self) axes of second order.

# LESSON 40

## SUPPLEMENTARY NOTES
## ON VERBS, IDIOMS AND PHRASING

§ 379. Introduction and Summary.

The basic facts concerning nearly all Russian verbs have been summarized in Lesson 35. In this lesson attention is directed to certain unusual categories, namely, simple verbs of motion (§ 381, p. 626) and their derivatives (§ 382, p. 630). Certain special infinitives denoting action characterized as either instantaneous, repetitive or intermittent are noted in § 383, p. 636.

Sentences having an infinitive or clause as the subject are discussed in § 384, p. 639. Impersonal sentences are reviewed in § 385, p. 640. A special type of use of the dative case in such sentences is reviewed in § 386, p. 642.

The use of the interrogative particle ЛИ forms the subject matter of § 387, p. 644.

Idioms reviewed involve the preposition у (§ 388, p. 646), various forms of весь (§ 389, p. 647), various forms of пора (§ 390, p. 650) and пока alone or with не (§ 391, p. 651). Adjectives used as nouns are discussed in § 392, p. 652, and an unusual type of agreement between adjectives and nouns is noted in § 393, p. 655.

Other subjects covered are the use of reflexive verb forms to denote interaction (§ 394, p. 656), an occasionally used, special form of the genitive having partitive significance (§ 395, p. 657) and the italic form of the Russian alphabet (§ 396, p. 658).

625

§ 380.  Verbs of Motion -- Two Important Groups.

For  purposes  of  subsequent  discussion,  a  large  number  of
verbs  of  motion  are  classified  into  two  groups.[1]   The  first  of
these consists of the simple verbs of motion which, as discussed
below,    have    two    imperfective    infinitives,    e.g.,    ХОДЍТЬ
"to    be    going"    (indefinite    action)    and    ИТТЍ    "to    be    going"
(definite    action).    The    other    group    consists    of    verbs    whose
infinitives  are  formed  by  using  prefixes  with  the  imperfective
infinitives  of  the  simple  verbs  as,  for  example,  ВХОДЍТЬ-
ВОЙТЍ[2]  "to enter,"  "to go in."

§ 381.  The  Imperfective  Infinitives  of  Simple  Verbs  of  Motion.

As  already  noted,  many  simple  verbs  of  motion  are  peculiar
in  that  each  of  them  has  two  imperfective  infinitives  as  listed
below.[3]  Difference  in  shade  of  meaning  between  the  indefinite  and
definite  infinitives  is  discussed  below  (p. 627).

| Imperfective INDEFINITE Infinitives | Imperfective DEFINITE Infinitives | Basic Meaning |
|---|---|---|
| бе́гать | бежа́ть | to be running, to be fleeing |
| броди́ть | брести́ | to be wandering, to be roaming |
| води́ть | вести́ | to be leading, to be driving or operating (a vehicle, machine, animal) |
| вози́ть | везти́ | to be transporting, to be conveying |
| гоня́ть | гнать | to be chasing |
| е́здить | е́хать | to be traveling, to be riding (intransitive) |
| ката́ть | кати́ть | to be rolling (transitive) |

[1]  To avoid misunderstanding, it is necessary to state that the two groups of
verbs to be discussed do not embrace all verbs indicating motion. Specifically,
we shall be concerned with those verbs listed on pp. 626-627 and their derivatives.
The verb  ДВИГАТЬ - ДВИ́НУТЬ  "to move" may be cited as an example of verbs
indicating motion yet falling outside the scope of the present discussion.
[2]  Note that the verb under consideration here has  ВХОДЍТЬ  as the imperfective
infinitive while  ВОЙТЍ  is its perfective infinitive.
[3]  This list is complete as given here.

| Imperfective INDEFINITE Infinitives | Imperfective DEFINITE Infinitives | Basic Meaning |
|---|---|---|
| ла́зить (ла́зать) | лезть | to be climbing |
| лета́ть | лете́ть | to be flying |
| носи́ть | нести́ | to be carrying |
| пла́вать | плыть | to be floating, swimming, to be traveling (by water) |
| по́лзать | ползти́ | to be crawling |
| таска́ть | тащи́ть | to be dragging |
| ходи́ть | итти́ | to be walking, going, proceeding |

The indefinite and definite infinitives listed above differ as to meaning in a fashion difficult to define with precision. In general, it may be said that the indefinite infinitives indicate motion characterized as being repetitive or aimless or of a general character. The definite infinitives on the other hand, indicate motion characterized as being directed toward some goal or proceeding in some one direction or partaking of a specific nature. It is perhaps hardly necessary to point out that these shades of meaning, which characterize the infinitives, also characterize the other verb forms (e.g., tenses, gerunds, participles) derived from the parent infinitives by conjugation in the usual way.

The three following pairs of sentences provide an introduction to the different shades of meaning characterizing these two groups of infinitives.

Indefinite    Соба́ка    хо́дит    по двору́.
(The) dog   is walking around in   the yard.

Definite    Де́душка    идёт    по у́лице.
Grandfather is walking down the street.

Indefinite   Дéдушка      вóдит                      корóву
             Grandfather  leads (usually or often leads)  (the) cow

             на   водопóй.
             to  (the) water-trough.


Definite     Дéдушка        ведёт              корóву      на
             Grandfather    is (now) leading   (the) cow   to

             водопóй.
             (the) water-trough.


Indefinite   Двóрник      катáет  бóчки   в   подвáл .
             (The) yard-man rolls   barrels into (the) cellar.


Definite     Двóрник      кáтит          бóчку       в
             (The) yard-man is (now) rolling  (the) barrel   into

             подвáл.
             (the) cellar.


The two following groups of sentences further illustrate the
use of the indefinite and definite infinitives of the simple verbs
of motion. These sentences also illustrate the fact that usage, as
well as more logical considerations, must be considered an
important factor in connection with these two groups of infinitives.


Group I.  Sentences Illustrating Indefinite Infinitives of Motion


Пóршень   хóдит  бы́стро  в  цили́ндре.
(The) piston moves   rapidly   in (the) cylinder.


Над   гóродом  летáют           аэроплáны.
Above (the) city   are flying (about) aeroplanes.

Хлор, бром, иод и фтор носят общее
Chlorine, bromine, iodine and fluorine bear (the) general

назвáние галогéнов.
name of halides.


Он хорошó éздит на велосипéде.
He well rides (knows how to ride) on (a) bicycle.


Éсли тéло плáвает, то егó вес рáвен
If (a) body floats, then its weight (is) equal

вéсу вытесняемой им жúдкости.
to (the) weight of (the) being displaced by it liquid.


Он мнóго лет водúл кораблú.
He (for) many years sailed (commanded) ships.


## Group II. Sentences Illustrating Definite Infinitives of Motion

Реáкция идёт быстро при нагревáнии.
(The) reaction proceeds rapidly on heating.


Воздýшные шары летят по вóздуху тудá,
Air globes (i.e., balloons) fly by air there,

кудá несёт их вéтер.
where carries them (the) wind.


Когдá мы éдем úли летúм, то нам кáжется, что
When we ride or fly, then to us shows self (seems), that

все предмéты двúжутся нам навстрéчу.
all objects move self to us toward.

При прекраще́нии движе́ния    летя́щего снаря́да та́кже
On   cessation        of (the) motion  of (a) flying  projectile also

возника́ет   тепло́.
arises       heat.

Ка́ждый  ио́н несёт   коли́чество   электри́чества,   ра́вное
Each    ion  bears  (a) quantity  of electricity,   equal

его́    заря́ду.
to his  charge.

Я плыл  из   Га́мбурга  в Ло́ндон  на небольшо́м  парохо́де.
I  sailed from Hamburg   to London  on (a) small   steamer.

В  то же    вре́мя маши́нист            ведёт  по́езд,
At the same time   (the) machinist (engineer)  runs  (the) train,

управля́я  им          при  по́мощи  электри́ческих   и
controlling  him (the train) with  (the) aid  of electrical     and

пневмати́ческих    аппара́тов.
pneumatic          devices.

Сравни́тельно   ре́дко  повыше́ние  температу́ры  ведёт к
Relatively      rarely  (an) increase  of temperature  leads  to

уменьше́нию  раствори́мости  со́ли   в воде́.
decrease     of (the) solubility  of (a) salt  in water.


§ 382.  Verbs Derived from the Imperfective Infinitives of Simple
       Verbs of Motion.

As previously discussed in  § 43, p. 61;  § 321, p. 504, the
Russian language uses a number of prefixes to alter the meaning
of simple verbs.  In this way a host of derived verbs are formed.
The same prefixes are also used to alter the meaning of the verbs
of motion.  The change in meaning is often well in line with what
might be expected in view of the general meaning of the prefixes

(cf. § 404, p. 674) and the meaning of the simple verbs of motion.
The following list[1] includes, however, a number of verbs whose
meaning scarcely could be deduced from the usual significance of
their component parts. In considering this list, it should be noted
that the perfective infinitives are nearly all derived from the
definite action infinitives of preceding § 381, while the imperfective infinitives with few exceptions have as parent an indefinite
action infinitive. This situation prevails with all infinitives
derived from the simple verbs of motion with exception of those
derivatives formed with the prefix ПО-, whose use with the simple
verbs of motion is discussed on p. 632.

| Imperfective Infinitives | Perfective Infinitives | Basic Meaning[2] |
|---|---|---|
| влета́ть | влете́ть | to fly in |
| возгоня́ть | взогна́ть | to sublime (e.g., iodine) |
| входи́ть | войти́ | to enter, to come in |
| выводи́ть | вы́вести | to lead out, to remove, to derive (a conclusion) |
| вылеза́ть | вы́лезть | to crawl out, to get out of or off (a vehicle) |
| вылета́ть | вы́лететь | to fly out |
| выходи́ть | вы́йти | to go out, to emerge |
| долета́ть | долете́ть | to fly up to, to penetrate to (sound) |
| доходи́ть | дойти́ | to come up to |
| заводи́ть | завести́ | to initiate, to begin |
| заходи́ть | зайти́ | to come upon, to go down (sun, etc.) |
| исходи́ть | изойти́ | to go out, to come to an end |
| находи́ть | найти́ | to find |
| наплыва́ть | наплы́ть | to float or swim toward or against |
| обходи́ть | обойти́ | to go around, to wander, to evade |
| относи́ть | отнести́ | to carry away, to relate to |

[1] The verbs under consideration are so numerous that the list given below must
be regarded as citing only certain typical examples.

[2] Verbs listed in this table are used in many special or idiomatic expressions.
This fact makes it virtually impossible to define their meaning with precision and
conciseness. It is helpful to note in this connection that English verbs of motion are
also involved in expressions having special meanings, e.g., "to go out" may be
used to indicate both the exit of a person from a room and the extinguishing of a
flame or light. The situation is further complicated in Russian by the fact that the
reflexives of certain of the verbs under discussion have come to have special
significance. Thus, for example, НАХОДИ́ТЬСЯ – НАЙТИ́СЬ, as discussed in
§ 123, p. 181, is used with the meaning "to be located," "to be."

| Imperfective Infinitives | Perfective Infinitives | Basic Meaning |
|---|---|---|
| переводи́ть | перевести́ | to take across, to use up |
| перевози́ть | перевезти́ | to transport across |
| перегоня́ть | перегна́ть | to drive away, to overtake, to distill |
| переходи́ть | перейти́ | to go over, to move (dwelling) |
| подходи́ть | подойти́ | to approach |
| приводи́ть | привести́ | to bring close, to bring about |
| приходи́ть | прийти́ | to arrive, to come to |
| проводи́ть | провести́ | to lead through, to conduct (heat, etc.) |
| производи́ть | произвести́ | to carry out, to bring forth |
| произноси́ть | произнести́ произне́сть | to utter, to pronounce |
| разгоня́ть | разогна́ть | to chase apart, to distill (into fractions) |
| сходи́ть | сойти́ | to go down, to go away |
| убега́ть | убежа́ть | to run away, to escape |
| угоня́ть | угна́ть | to chase away |
| уезжа́ть | уе́хать | to travel away |
| улета́ть | улете́ть | to fly away |
| уходи́ть | уйти́ | to pass away, to elapse, to resign (position) |

As already mentioned, the prefix ПО- when used with the imperfective infinitives of the simple verbs of motion of § 381, p. 626, requires special attention. General statements concerning such use of ПО- inevitably involve a certain amount of over-simplification. With this reservation, it may be said that in general ПО-, with the simple indefinite infinitives, forms perfective infinitives meaning: "to perform for a time the action in question." Thus, for example, we have полета́ть "to fly for a time" from лета́ть "to be flying (indefinite)." With the definite infinitives of motion ПО- forms, in general, perfective infinitives meaning "to start or to finish the action in question." An example is полете́ть "to start flying." Dictionaries often list these perfective infinitives formed with ПО- as the perfective companions of the simple imperfective infinitives. There is at least some justification for doing this as is evident from the general meaning of these perfective infinitives.

In conclusion, it should be noted that certain infinitives and verbs of the general group under discussion may be used in more than one way. Thus, the infinitive ПОХОДИ́ТЬ may be used either

as a perfective infinitive meaning  "to walk for a time,"  or as an imperfective infinitive meaning "to resemble." This latter use of ПОХОДИ́ТЬ usually involves a phrase introduced by на followed by the accusative case of a noun denoting the person or thing resembled. A similar example is the verb ДОНОСИ́ТЬ – ДОНЕСТИ́ when used with a phrase involving the preposition ДО means "to carry as far as."  Otherwise, this verb means "to report on," "to spy on," and is then used with a phrase involving the preposition на. Evidently, careful attention is necessary if pitfalls are to be avoided in interpreting various verbs included in this important group.

| В | соста́в | воды́ | вхо́дит | элеме́нт | водоро́д. |
|---|---|---|---|---|---|
| Into | (the) composition | of water | enters | (the) element | hydrogen. |

| Из | при́нципа | Ферма́ | | легко́ | вы́вести |
|---|---|---|---|---|---|
| From | (the) principle | of Fermat | (it is) | easy | to derive |

| зако́ны | отраже́ния | и | преломле́ния. |
|---|---|---|---|
| (the) laws | of reflection | and | of refraction. |

| Вы́летевший | из | ору́дия | снаря́д | облада́ет |
|---|---|---|---|---|
| (A) having flown | from | (a) gun | projectile | possesses |

| кинети́ческой | эне́ргией. |
|---|---|
| kinetic | energy. |

| Пло́тносъ | земно́й | коры́ не превосхо́дить 3 г./см$^3$. |
|---|---|---|
| (The) density | of (the) terrestrial | crust not exceeds      3 g./cm$^3$. |

| Нельзя́ | заводи́ть | мото́р | автомоби́ля | в |
|---|---|---|---|---|
| It is forbidden | to start | (the) motor | of (an) automobile | in |

| закры́том | гараже́, так как | вы́хлопные | га́зы | соде́ржат |
|---|---|---|---|---|
| (a) closed | garage, because | (the) exhaust | gases | contain |

| о́кись | углеро́да. |
|---|---|
| oxide | of carbon (carbon monoxide). |

| Мно́гие | вещества́, | не | перегоня́ющиеся | без |
|---|---|---|---|---|
| Many | substances, | not | distilling self | without |

разложе́ния    под    атмосфе́рным    давле́нием,    мо́жно
decomposition   under atmospheric    pressure,    (it is) possible

перегна́ть    в    ва́кууме.
to distill    in   (a) vacuum.

При    перехо́де    кинети́ческой    эне́ргии    в    теплоту́
On    transition    of kinetic    energy    into    heat

пра́вильное    движе́ние    те́ла    перехо́дит    в
regular    motion    of (a) body    goes over    into

неорганизо́ванные    беспоря́дочные    движе́ния
disorganized    disorderly    motions

моле́кул.
of molecules.

В    табли́це 1    приведены́    уде́льные    веса́    разли́чных
In    Table 1    (are) cited    (the) specific   weights   of various

мета́ллов    в    твёрдом    состоя́нии.
metals    in   solid    condition.

Ско́рость    исчеза́ния    пеницилли́на    из    органи́зма
(The) rate    of vanishing    of penicillin    from   (the) organism

     челове́ка    приво́дит   к необходи́мости    вводи́ть
(body)   of man    leads    to (the) necessity    to introduce

больно́му    непреры́вно    значи́тельные
to (a) sick (person)    uninterruptedly    considerable

коли́чества    препара́та.
quantities    of (the) preparation.

Разви́тие    нау́ки    о    строе́нии
(The) development    of science   concerning   (the) structure

мате́рии    дало́    возмо́жность    подойти́    к
of matter    gives    (the) possibility    to arrive    to (at)

определе́нию      значе́ний теплоёмкостей   и     чи́сто
(the) determination of values   heat capacities      also by (a) purely

теорети́ческим    путём.
theoretical       way.


Вся́кий степенно́й   ряд    схо́дится      в   определённом
Every    power      series  converges self  in  (a) definite

интерва́ле    $(a - x, a + x)$,   называ́емом      интерва́лом
interval      $(a - x, a + x)$,   being called    an interval

схо́димости     степенно́го    ря́да,   и    расхо́дится
of convergence  of (the) power  series,  but  diverges self

вне    э́того интерва́ла.
outside that   interval.


Самолёт      улете́л    на    се́вер.
(The) plane  flew away   to   (the) north.


В   э́том отноше́нии    совреме́нная    тео́рия  ещё   бо́льше
In  this  respect       contemporary    theory   even  more

похо́дит    на   тео́рию   Ломоно́сова.
resembles   to   (the) theory  of Lomonosov.


Пе́рвая       ста́дия   иониза́ции    фо́сфорной      кислоты́
(The) first   stage    of ionization  of phosphoric   acid

пойдёт[1]   по     схе́ме:
proceeds    according  to (the) scheme:

$$H_3PO_4 = H^{\bullet} + H_2PO_4'$$
$$H_3PO_4 = H^+ + H_2PO_4^-$$

[1] This is another example of translation of the Russian perfective future by the English present tense.

§ 383.  Further Notes on Special Types of Infinitives.

The use of prefixes to form derived verbs has already been discussed at some length in § 43, p. 61; § 321, p. 504; § 382, p. 630, cf. also § 404, p. 624. Furthermore, the Russian-English vocabulary presents numerous examples of the use of prefixes in deriving verbs.

In general, it may be said that each prefix changes the meaning of various simple imperfective infinitives in an approximately similar fashion. Thus the prefix ВЫ-- denotes "out of," either literally or figuratively. The situation is complicated somewhat by certain prefixes which do not always shift the meaning in the same way. Thus the prefix с-(со-) is used (1) to mean "down," "off," "away" as in    сдава́ть-сдать[1] "to give up," "to yield," "to surrender"; (2) to mean "together," "with" as in   собира́ть-собра́ть[2] "to collect," "to reap." Like other prefixes, с-(со-) is also used to form the perfective infinitive without shift of meaning as, for example, with the verbs де́лать-сде́лать         "to do"      or        фотографи́ровать-сфотографи́ровать  "to photograph." Usage rather than logic is the factor determining the influence of a prefix on the meaning of a verb.

The prefix ПО- is very often used to form a perfective infinitive. As already noted in § 382, p. 630, ПО- is used with the simple definite infinitives of the verbs of motion to form a perfective infinitive denoting performance of the action for a limited period of time. With certain other verbs, ПО- is similarly used to form special perfective infinitives, such as ПОЧИТА́ТЬ[3] "to read for a time" (from ЧИТА́ТЬ "to be reading"), ПОПИСА́ТЬ "to write for a time" (from ПИСА́ТЬ "to be writing"), ПОДЫША́ТЬ "to breathe (blow) for a time" (from ДЫША́ТЬ "to be breathing (blowing)" etc. Use of ЗА- to indicate the start of an action is also perhaps worthy of special mention. Thus we have ЗАКИПА́ТЬ-ЗАКИПЕ́ТЬ "to start boiling" (from КИПЕ́ТЬ "to be boiling"), ЗАЖИГА́ТЬ-ЗАЖЕ́ЧЬ "to start (something) burning," "to ignite" (from ЖЕЧЬ "to be burning"), etc.

Similar characterization of an action with regard to duration, repetition, etc., is sometimes also indicated by the final letters in an infinitive stem. Thus certain perfective infinitives terminating

[1]  Derived from дава́ть – дать "to give."
[2]  Derived from бра́ть "to be taking."
[3]  Note that ПОЧИТА́ТЬ may also be used as the imperfective infinitive of the verb ПОЧИТА́ТЬ – ПОЧЕ́СТЬ "to honor," "to revere," "to esteem."

in -НУТЬ[1] are used to express: (1) a single occurrence of an action ordinarily involving a multiplicity of strokes or movements or (2) action of very short duration.

| | | |
|---|---|---|
| стучать - | постучать | to knock |
| | стукнуть | to knock once |
| дышать - | подышать | to breathe, to blow |
| | дохнуть[2] | to exhale, to blow once or briefly |
| плевать - | наплевать | to spit, to despise |
| | плюнуть | to spit once |
| свистать - | посвистать | to whistle |
| | свистеть | to whistle once or briefly |
| | свистнуть | to whistle once or briefly |

A few verbs have a special imperfective infinitive used to emphasize recurrent, habitual or continuing character of the action.

| Usual Imperfective | Repetitive Imperfective | Action Expressed |
|---|---|---|
| быть | бывать | to be, to exist |
| знать | знавать | to be knowing |
| ездить | езживать | |
| | езжать | to be traveling |
| ходить | хаживать | to be going on foot |
| читать | читывать | to be reading |

The only member of this class encountered at all frequently in scientific Russian is бывать.

At an earlier stage in the development of the Russian language, repetitive imperfectives were much more important as a class than at present. During the course of evolution of the language the trend has been for repetitive imperfectives to lose their special character and merge into the general class of imperfectives. Repetitive imperfective forms other than the infinitive and the past tense are rarely, if ever, used today. The present tense of бывать is exceptional in this respect.

---

[1] Instantaneous action is not denoted of all infinitives ending in -НУТЬ as is evident from consideration of the verb ТУХНУТЬ - ПОТУХНУТЬ "to go out." "to be extinguished."

[2] Note that ДОХНУТЬ is also used as an imperfective infinitive meaning "to perish (animals)."

A few verbs have special imperfective infinitives to denote intermittent action. These special infinitives, which are of little importance in scientific Russian, stand in close relationship to the repetitive imperfective infinitives discussed above.

| | |
|---|---|
| ломáть – сломáть | to tear (down) (apart) |
| полáмывать | to be tearing (down) (apart) intermittently |
| писáть – написáть | to write |
| попи́сывать | to be writing intermittently |
| свистáть}<br>свисте́ть} –посвистáть | to whistle |
| посви́стывать | to be whistling intermittently |
| стучáть – постучáть | to knock |
| посту́кивать | to be knocking intermittently |
| читáть – прочитáть | to read |
| почи́тывать | to be reading intermittently |

Больнóй[1]                   подышáл                   кислорóдом.[2]
(The) sick (person)   breathed (for a while)   oxygen.

Я почитáл[3]   полчасá           пéред   снóм.[4]
I read           for (a) half hour   before   sleep (sleeping).

Жи́дкость     закипáет,           когдá   упру́гость   её       парóв
(A) liquid     starts boiling, when   (the) tension   of her   vapors

достигáет   величины́         атмосфéрного   давлéния.
attains       (a) magnitude   of atmospheric   pressure.

Бу́дучи   зажжён   на вóздухе,   ацетилéн   гори́т   бéлым,
Once       ignited   in   air       acetylene   burns   with (a) white,

си́льно   коптя́щим   (вслéдствие   непóлного   сгорáния
strongly   smoking     (as a result   of incomplete   combustion

углерóда)   плáменем.
of carbon)   flame.

---

[1] Here the adjective больнóй, "sick" is used in place of больнóй человéк "sick person," cf. § 392, p. 652.

[2] Note that кислорóдом is the instrumental singular of кислорóд "oxygen."

[3] The perfective infinitive прочитáть means "to read (e.g., a book) to an end."

[4] СНОМ is the instrumental singular of СОН, "sleep," declined with omission of the vowel -о- from the stem, cf. § 357, p. 573.

Как вихорь,[1]   свистнул  острый   меч.
Like (a) whirlwind, whistled  (the) sharp  sword.


Стукнем   чашу  с  чашей  дружно!
Let us strike  cup  with  cup  friendly (in friendship)!


Он знавал   много  огорчений.
He had known  much  afflictions (affliction).


Бывают   шесть  основных  классов  кристаллов.
(There) are  six  basic  classes  of crystals.


Он задумчиво  посвистывал,   сидя  на скамеечке.
He thoughtfully  whistled now and then, sitting on (a) little bench.


§ 384. Sentences Having an Infinitive or Clause As Subject.

To encounter a sentence having an infinitive or a clause as its subject is by no means uncommon either in English or in Russian.

The use, in such sentences, of the neuter, singular form of the Russian past tense has already been noted in § 217, p. 340. For similar sentences in which infinitives are used with the neuter, singular predicative form of adjectives, see § 166, p. 254.


Отсюда   следует, что $a$ = $b$ = $c$.
Therefrom  it follows, that a = b = c.


Следует        отметить, что пыль     вредна для
It is necessary  to mention, that dust (is) harmful for

лёгких.
(the) lungs.

---

[1] In this quotation from a poem, the word вихрь has been made bisyllabic to fit the meter.

Пе́ред    употребле́нием    прода́жного    ио́да   в  ка́честве
Before    utilization        of commercial   iodine  in (the) quality

хими́ческого    реаге́нта   рекоменду́ется     подве́ргнуть[1]
of (a) chemical    reagent    (it) recommends self  to submit

его́  возго́нке.
him  to sublimation.

В  техни́ческой  термодина́мике    никогда́  не   прихо́дится[1]
In technical      thermodynamics     never    [not] is necessary

интересова́ться      абсолю́тным значе́нием[2] вну́тренней
to interest self     (in)  absolute     value     of inner

эне́ргии,  а  лишь    её  измене́ниями.
energy,    but only  (in)  her  changes.

Таки́м  о́бразом   удало́сь   изоли́ровать  ра́дий.
In this  way      it succeeded  to isolate    radium.

## § 385. Impersonal Sentences.

In English such expressions as "they say," "they use," etc.,
are often used without referring to any specific group of individuals. In similar Russian sentences the pronoun "they" is not
explicitly stated but is implied by the ending of the verb, e.g.,
говоря́т   "they say."

Тако́е  измере́ние    веду́т      сле́дующим     о́бразом.
Such a  measurement  they conduct  in (the) following fashion.

До́лгое  вре́мя пу́шки  ли́ли    то́лько из  бро́нзы.
(For a) long  time   cannons they cast  only    from bronze.

---

[1] Note the close relationship between   приходи́ться – прийти́сь   "to happen,"
"to be necessary," "to fit" and the verb   приходи́ть – прийти́   "to arrive," "to
come to."

[2] An excessively literal translation of   интересова́ться абсолю́тным
значе́нием   would be "to interest self by means of (the) absolute value." The only
advantage of such a translation would be the fact that it might aid in understanding
how значе́нием and its modifier абсолю́тным come to be in the instrumental case.

В этом случае говорят, что истиная теплоёмкость C
In this case    they say,    that (the) true    specific heat    C

есть предел, к которому стремится
is    (the) limit, to which    directs self to    (rushes toward)

$C_m$ при приближением Δt к нулю.
$C_m$ at    approach    of Δt to zero.

Электроэнергией    пользуются    также для
By means of electric energy    they avail self    also    for

искусственного освещения помещений.
artificial    illumination    of rooms.

Обычно,    характеристики    усилительных    ламп
Ordinarily,    (the) characteristics    of amplifier    lamps[1]

представляют в виде графиков зависимости
they present    in    (the) form    of graphs    of dependence

силы    анодного    тока    от    напряжения    на
of strength    of (the) anode    current    from    (the) charge    on

сетке    или от    напряжения    на    аноде.
(the) gride    or    from    (the) charge    on    (the) anode.

В древние времена словом    "физика" называли    все
In ancient    times    by (the) word    "physics"    they named    all

сведения, которые были известны о    природе.
informations, which    were known    concerning    nature.

---

[1] "Amplifier tubes" would be preferred to "amplifier lamps" in this country.

## § 386.  An Important Use of the Dative Case.

The dative case in Russian may be used to indicate participation or involvement in some action or situation. As a result the structure of certain Russian sentences may appear somewhat unusual to persons speaking English as a mother tongue.[1]

To aid in studying this type of sentence structure in Russian, the key words in the dative are underlined in the following example sentences.

| Это явление | свойственно, как | истинным, так и |
|---|---|---|
| This phenomenon (is) peculiar | both | to true, as also |

| коллоидным | растворам . |
|---|---|
| to colloidal | solutions. |

<br>

| Осмий | в | этих | соединениях | | шестивалентен, | и |
|---|---|---|---|---|---|---|
| Osmium | in | this | compound | (is) | hexavalent, | and |

| ему | присуще | координационное | число 6. |
|---|---|---|---|
| to him (is) | present | (the) coordination | number 6. |

<br>

| В | одежде | нам | тепло | не | потому, | что | она | нас |
|---|---|---|---|---|---|---|---|---|
| In | clothing | to us (is) | warm | not | for this, | that | she | us |

| греет, | а | потому, | что | одежда | сохраняет | тепло |
|---|---|---|---|---|---|---|
| heats, | by | for this, | that | clothing | conserves | (the) heat |

| нашего | тела. |
|---|---|
| of our | body. |

<br>

| Вот | почему | каждому | необходимо | познакомиться |
|---|---|---|---|---|
| That is | why | to everyone | (it is) necessary | to acquaint self |

---

[1]  In approaching this type of sentence, it may be helpful to note that a similar construction occurs quite frequently in German, e.g., "mir gelingt es" (with infinitive), literally: "to me succeeds (to)" or, somewhat more freely, "to me it is possible," "I am succeeding (to)." Another example from German -- "Es ist mir nötig," literally: "It is to me necessary."

с      растительным   миром,   узнать   строение      и
with    (the) plant      world,   to learn  (the) structure  and

жизнь   растения.
life      of plant.

Если телу      мешают         падать, подставив    под
If    to (a) body  (they) hinder   to fall,   having placed  under

него         подставку,    оно         на неё
it (the body)  (a) support,  it (the body)  on her (the support)

давит.
exerts pressure.

В     конце    1920 г.    Майкельсону       удалось
At   (the) end   of  1920    to Michelson      it succeeded

измерить     диаметр      звезды    Бетельгейзе.
to measure   (the) diameter  of (the) star  Betelgeuse.

В    этом    случае    наблюдателю      кажется,      что
In   this     case      to (an) observer   (it) appears,     that

световые    лучи исходят  от    перевёрнутого  предмета.
(the) light   rays go out   from   (an) inverted     object.

Работа,  с   которой нам    приходится обычно    иметь
Work,     with which   to us   is necessary ordinarily  to have

дело    на практике,  выражается    очень     большим
business  in  practice    expresses self  by (a) very   large

числом  эргов.
number   of ergs.

Отсюда         ясно, что Ломоносов   тогда,      т.е.
From this   (it is) clear, that Lomonosov  at that time,  i.e.,

почти  200  лет  назад,  правильно  представлял  себе
almost  200  years ago,    correctly   represented   to self

заря́д       о́блака      распределённым    по    всему́
(the) charge  of (a) cloud  as distributed    over  (the) whole

о́блаку.
cloud.


§ 387.  Interrogative Sentences and Clauses Involving the Particle
ЛИ.[1]

We have already discussed interrogative sentences and
clauses formed using such pronouns and related possessive
adjectives as: ЧТО "what"; КТО "who," "which"; ЧЕЙ "whose";
СКО́ЛЬКО "how many", cf. § 150, p. 229; and adverbs such as ГДЕ
"where," КОГДА́ "when," КУДА́ "whither," etc. In the absence of
such interrogative pronouns, adjectives and adverbs, sentences
and clauses are rendered interrogative by use of the particle ЛИ.

It should also be noted that ЛИ is sometimes used in idiomatic
expressions of which the most important are, perhaps, едва́ ли
and вряд ли both of which mean "scarcely," "hardly."

The use of ЛИ in sentences is illustrated by the following
examples.

Име́ет ли  вес   во́здух?
Has        weight  air?


Далеко́ ли  от   нас   Со́лнце?
Far         from  us (is)  (the) sun?


Зна́ете ли  вы, с   како́й ско́ростью   распространя́ется
Know        you, with what  velocity      propagation

звук?
sound?


Приходи́лось[1]  ли  вам   стреля́ть  из   ружья́?
(Has it) happened   to you  to shoot   from  a gun?


<hr>

[1]  An alternate spelling, ЛЬ, will also be encountered occasionally.
[2]  See Footnote 1, p. 640.

| Как | убедиться, | | | растворимо | ли |
|---|---|---|---|---|---|
| How | to convince self, | (whether) | | soluble | (is) |

| данное | вещество | в воде | или | нет? | |
|---|---|---|---|---|---|
| (a) given | substance | in water | or | not? | |

| Существует | ли | между | превращениями | различных |
|---|---|---|---|---|
| Exists | | between | transformations | of various |

| форм | энергии | одной | в | другую | закономерная |
|---|---|---|---|---|---|
| forms | of energy | of one | into | (the) other | (a) rule type |

| связь[1] | или | нет? |
|---|---|---|
| connection | or | not? |

| Необходимо | было | выяснить, | | существует | ли |
|---|---|---|---|---|---|
| Necessary | was | to explain | (whether) | exists | |

| числовое | количественное | соотношение | между |
|---|---|---|---|
| (a) numerical | quantitative | ratio | between |

| затрачиваемым | количеством | работы | и | возникающим |
|---|---|---|---|---|
| expended | amount | of work | and | arising |

| количеством | теплоты, | и | обратно. |
|---|---|---|---|
| quantity | of heat | and | vice versa. |

| Перед | началом | взвешивания | надо |
|---|---|---|---|
| Before | (the) beginning | of weighing | (it is) necessary |

| проверить, | | правильны | ли | весы. |
|---|---|---|---|---|
| to confirm, | (whether) | correct | | (is) (the) balance. |

| После | окончания | рабочего | дня, следует |
|---|---|---|---|
| After | conclusion | of (the) working | day, it is necessary |

| проверить, | | закрыты | ли | все | шкафы, |
|---|---|---|---|---|---|
| to confirm, | (whether) | closed | (are) | all | cupboards, |

---

[1] The phrase закономерная связь might be translated as "relationship involving a law or rule," "correlation."

óкна,   выключены   ли моторы,      закрыт ли общий
windows, switched off     (the) motors, closed      (the) general

газовый   кран.
(main) gas      cock.

Едва́   ли   уда́стся     пе́рвым     ме́тодом   удали́ть
Hardly   will succeed   by (the) first   method   to remove

все   следы́   воды́.
all   traces   of water.

## § 388. Idioms Involving the Preposition У.

The simplest use of the preposition у is to denote nearness or
proximity. The preposition is also used to denote involvement
and -- particularly with pronouns -- to indicate possession. This
range of meaning of у makes it worthy of special attention.

У    всех   а́томов   одного́   и   того́   же    элеме́нта
With   all   atoms   of one   and   the   same   element

свойства           одина́ковы   и   отлича́ются     от
(the) properties   (are)   identical.   and distinguish self   from

свойств           а́томов   други́х   элеме́нтов.
(the) properties   of atoms   of other   elements.

Объём            перегре́того    па́ра    при    ра́вном
(The) volume    of superheated   steam   at    (the) same

давле́нии         бо́льше,   чем у   тако́го же   коли́чества
pressure    (is)   greater,   than with   the same   quantity

насы́щенного.
of saturated (steam).

Корне́й      у      расте́ний            мно́го.
Of roots      with plants      (are)   many.[1]


Необходи́мо,            одна́ко,      име́ть      в      виду́      сле́дующее:
(It is) necessary,      however,      to have      in      view      (the) following:


(1) не      вся́кие   два      элеме́нта      мо́гут            дава́ть      ме́жду
(1) not   every      two      elements      are able      to give      between


собо́ю      соедине́ние      и   (2) у      не́которых   элементов      в
self      (a) compound      and (2) with   certain      elements      in


одни́х      соедине́ниях            одна́   вале́нтность,      в други́х —
some      compounds      (is)   one      valency            in others


друга́я.
another.[2]


§ 389.  Idiomatic Use of Various Forms of весь "whole," "all."

As is evident from the following sentences, various forms   of
the   adjective-pronoun   весь[3]   may   be   used   idiomatically   in
expressions   denoting   totality,   continuation,   prolongation,
inclusiveness, etc.

Бу́рное            разви́тие      те́хники            тре́бует      всё   бо́льшей
(The) rapid   development   of technology   requires   ever   greater


специализа́ции      ламп.
specialization      of lamps.


Всего́      таки́х   групп   в   систе́ме      име́ется   де́вять.
In all      of such   groups   in (the) system   has self   nine.


<hr>

[1] A smoother translation would be: "Plants have many roots." Note that
корне́й   is a partitive genitive, cf. § 121, p. 178. It should also be recalled that
ко́рень   (masc.) "root" is declined with elimination of -е- from the stem,
cf. § 357, p. 573.

[2] The latter part of this sentence might be translated more smoothly as
follows:   "(2) certain elements have one valency in some compounds and another
valency in others."

[3] The declension of весь "whole," "all" resembles that of an adjective,
cf. § 150, p. 229.

Паровоз      "Ракета"   Стефенсона   превращал   в
(The) locomotive   "Rocket"   of Stephenson   converted   into

механическую   работу   всего   около   четырёх   процентов
mechanical      work    in all   about   four      per cent

тепловой   энергии   топлива .
of (the) heat   energy   of (the) fuel.


"Коэфициент      полезного   действия"   у   современного
"(The) coefficient   of useful   action"   with (a) contemporary

паровоза         несколько   выше,      но   всё-таки      не
locomotive   (is)   somewhat   higher,   but   all the same   not

превышает   семи-восьми   процентов.
exceeds    seven to eight   per cent.


Постепенно,      но   очень   медленно,      человек   всё
Gradually,        but   very   slowly,          man      ever

больше         и   больше         для   нужд   мирной,      а
more greatly   and   more greatly   for   needs   of peaceful,   and

также   военной   промышленности   прибегал   к процессам
also    war       industry          resorted   to processes

химическим,      то   разрабатывая      глубже
chemical,         now   working out       more deeply

металлургические   процессы,      то   изобретая
metallurgical      processes,       now   inventing

зажигательные   (греческий   огонь)   и   взрывчатые
incendiary      (Greek      fire)   and   explosive

смеси   (порох),      то   добывая      для   разных   нужд
mixtures   (gun powder),   now   producing   for   various   needs

кислóты органи́ческие    (у́ксусная)    и    неоргани́ческие
acids    organic          (acetic)       and  inorganic

(азóтная,[1]  сéрная  и т. д. )
(nitric,      sulfuric and so on).

В    послéднее    врéмя    бýстер    всё    чáще        и
In   last (recent) time    (a) booster ever  more often and

чáще        применяется    не    тóлько в    грузовы́х,    но
more often  applied self    not   only   in   freight,     but

и     в    скóростных  паровóзах,    для    тогó,    чтóбы
also  in   express     locomotives    for    this     in order

умéньшить    врéмя,     нýжное      для    достижéния
to decrease  (the) time, necessary   for    attainment

наибóльшей    скóрости    движéния.
of greatest   velocity     of movement.

Всегó    шестьдесят    лет    назáд    учёный,      произнóся
Only     sixty         years  ago      (a) scientist, pronouncing

слóво      "áтом",    ассоции́ровал    это     слóво    с
(the) word "atom"     associated       this    word     with

представлéнием    об           изчезáюще       мáлом
(the) notion       concerning (of)  (a) vanishingly  small

упрýгом шáрике.
elastic little sphere.

---

[1] азóтная кислотá    "nitric acid,"    азóтистая кислотá    "nitrous acid,"
сéрная кислотá   "sulfuric acid,"   сернистая кислотá   "sulfurous acid."   For
Russian nomenclature pertaining to other acids, bases and salts both organic and
inorganic, reference is made to: Perry, J. W. "Chemical Russian, Self-Taught."
Chemical Education Publishing Company. Easton, Pennsylvania. 1948.

§ 390. Use of пора́ to Indicate Start or End of Time Period.

The following sentences illustrate use of prepositional phrases, involving either a singular or plural form of пора́, to indicate the start or end of a time period. The otherwise virtually obsolete[1] demonstrative сей "this," "those" is often used with пора́ in such expressions.

| До | сих | пор | | мы | ограни́чивались |
|---|---|---|---|---|---|
| Until | those | times (Up to now) | | we | have limited self |

| сообще́нием | о́пытных | фа́ктов. |
|---|---|---|
| to communication | of experimental | facts. |

| Уже́ | с | тех | пор, | как | бы́ли | откры́ты | электро́ны, |
|---|---|---|---|---|---|---|---|
| Already | from | those | times, | when were | | discovered | electrons |

| не | вызыва́л | сомне́ния | тот | факт, | что | и́менно | они́ |
|---|---|---|---|---|---|---|---|
| not | called forth | doubt | this | fact, | that | namely | they |

| явля́ются | | носи́телями | электри́ческого | то́ка | в |
|---|---|---|---|---|---|
| show self | (are) | (the) carriers | of electric | current | in |

| мета́ллах. |
|---|
| metals. |

| Основны́е | сво́йства | па́ра | бы́ло | изве́стны | лю́дям |
|---|---|---|---|---|---|
| (The) basic | properties | of steam | were | known | to people |

| о́чень | давно́, | с | той | поры́ | как | впервы́е | котёл | с |
|---|---|---|---|---|---|---|---|---|
| very | long ago, | from | this | time | when | first | (a) kettle with |

| водо́й | был | поста́влен | на | ого́нь.[2] |
|---|---|---|---|---|
| water | was | placed | on | (a) fire. |

---

[1] Various forms of сей also occur as component parts of such words as сейча́с "at once," "right away" (from сей + час "hour"), сего́дня "to-day" (from сего + дня, the genitive singular of день "day").

[2] The masculine noun ого́нь "fire" drops the -о- from the stem during declension.

§ 391.  Sentences Involving ПОКА́ Alone and with НЕ.

If used as an adverb, ПОКА́ has the meaning "now," "as long as," "at present."  As a conjunction, ПОКА́ alone usually means "while," but together with НЕ means "until". Rather rarely ПОКА́ is used alone to mean "until."

| Подо́бная | коли́чественная | характери́стика | поля́рности |
|---|---|---|---|
| Similar | quantitative | characterization | of (the) polarity |

| хими́ческой | свя́зи | мо́жет | бы́ть | пока́ | дана́ | лишь | в |
|---|---|---|---|---|---|---|---|
| of (a) chemical | bond | may | be | at present | given | only | in |

| немно́гих | просте́йших | слу́чаях. |
|---|---|---|
| (a) few | very simple | cases. |

| Бо́лее | подро́бные | све́дения | об | э́тих |
|---|---|---|---|---|
| More | detailed | knowledge(s) | concerning | these |

| соедине́ниях, | облада́ющих | больши́м | гистере́зизом, |
|---|---|---|---|
| compounds, | possessing | great | hysteresis, |

| пока́ | отсу́тствуют. |
|---|---|
| at present | are absent. |

| Пока́ | я | спал, | шёл | дождь. |
|---|---|---|---|---|
| While | I | slept, | proceeded | (the) rain.[1] |

| Находя́сь | | в | норма́льном | состоя́нии, | а́том | не |
|---|---|---|---|---|---|---|
| Finding self | (being) | in | normal | state, | atom | not |

| мо́жет | излуча́ть | до | тех | пор, | пока́ | он | не | бу́дет |
|---|---|---|---|---|---|---|---|---|
| is able | to radiate | until | those | times | until | he | [not] | will be |

| возбуждён | вне́шними | причи́нами. |
|---|---|---|
| excited | by external | causes. |

---

[1] A somewhat less literal, but smoother, translation of  ШЁЛ ДОЖДЬ  would be "it was raining." Note the companion expression ДОЖДЬ ИДЁТ "it is raining."

В      ко́нтуре        электромагни́тные        колеба́ния
In     (the) circuit    electromagnetic          oscillations

подде́рживаются    до    тех    пор ,    пока́    весь    запа́с
maintain self      until  those  times,   until   all     (the) store

эне́ргии,       первонача́льно      сообщё́нный    конденса́тору ,
of energy,      originally          imparted      to (the) condensor,

израсхо́дуется    на    джо́улево     тепло́[1]    (и      на
dissipates self   to    Joule's       heat        (and    to

излуче́ние).
radiation).


Суде́бный       проце́сс      заста́вил      Тревити́ка      впредь
(The) court     action        compelled      Trevitik       henceforth

вести́    свои́    рабо́ты    та́йно    в     ожида́нии,      пока́[2]
to conduct  his    works      secretly  in    expectation,    until

око́нчится      срок          де́йствия        пате́нтов
would end self  (the) period  of action (validity)  of (the) patents

Уа́тта.
of Watt.


§ 392.  Adjectives Frequently Used As Nouns.

As already pointed out, it is by no means unusual in Russian
for an adjective (cf. Note 8, p. 86) or participle (cf. § 245,
p. 389; § 283, p. 448) to be used independently of a noun to
designate some entity. Some adjectives are used so frequently
in this way that special mention appears advisable. The following
table lists certain adjectives that are often used in scientific

---

[1] The expression джо́улево тепло́ refers to the electrical energy converted
into heat by virtue of the presence of resistance in the circuit.
[2] The final clause might be more smoothly translated as: "until Watt's
patents had expired."

Russian to replace an adjective-noun combination. When so used the adjectives retain the gender of the omitted noun as noted below.[1]

| Adjective Forms Used As Noun | Adjective Forms Used to Replace | | Meaning of Adjective So Used As Noun |
|---|---|---|---|
| Feminine forms of кривой | кривая curved | линия line | curve |
| Feminine forms of прямой | прямая straight | линия line | straight line |
| Feminine forms of постоянный | постоянная constant | величина magnitude | constant (in mathematical sense) |
| Feminine forms of производный | производная derivative | величина magnitude | derivative (in mathematical sense) |
| Neuter forms of производный | производное derivative | вещество substance | derivative (in chemical sense) |
| Neuter forms of кратный | кратное multiple | число number | multiple (in arithmetical sense) |
| Neuter forms of животный | животное animal | существо being | animal |
| Masculine and Feminine forms of больной | больной sick | человек man, person | sick man, person |
| | больная sick | женщина woman | sick woman |

The following sentences illustrate such use of adjectives as nouns.

[1] It is of interest to note in this connection that certain full-fledged Russian nouns are declined with adjective endings. An example is вселённая, "universe" (cf. § 341, p. 537) which, though declined with feminine adjective endings, is never used as an adjective.

В общем     случае    зависимость    теплоёмкости
In (the) general case    (the) dependence   of (the) heat capacity

от      температуры     графически    выражается
from    (the) temperature    graphically    expresses self

кривой.
by (a) curve.


Кривая   эта    для    большинства    теплотехнических
Curve    this    for    (the) majority    of thermotechnical

расчётов    обычно    замещается    близкой    к   ней
calculations   ordinarily   replaces self   by (a) near   to her

прямой.
straight (line).


В   уравнении    pv = RT    коэффициент    R   называется
In   (the) equation   pv = RT   (the) coefficient   R   calls self

универсальной    газовой постоянной.
(the) universal     gas     constant.


Производная     производной    называется    второй
(The) derivative   of (the) derivative   calls self     (the) second

производной   начальной     функции.
derivative     of (the) original   function.


Нафтолы    являются     гидроксильными    производными
Naphthols   show self    (are)   hydroxyl     derivatives

нафталина.
of naphthalene.


Общее    наименьшее   кратное[1]   нескольких   чисел   есть
General   least     multiple    of several    numbers   is


[1] The more common English expression is "least common multiple."

наиме́ньшее   из   це́лых      чи́сел,   деля́щихся   на   любо́е
(the) least      of  (the) whole   numbers  dividing self   by  any

из     да́нных    чи́сел.
of   (the) given   numbers.

Лю́ди   выдыха́ют  тот же   углеки́слыи    газ,
People  exhale    that same  carbonic acid   gas  (carbon dioxide)

что  и    живо́тные.
as  also animals (exhale).

Кисло́ты   быстре́е     разъеда́ют          воло́кна
Acids      more rapidly  eat apart (disintegrate)   fibers

расти́тельного       происхожде́ния,      чем
of vegetable          origin             than      (those)

живо́тного. [1]
of animal        (origin).

## § 393.  Nouns in Plural Modified by Adjectives or Participles in Singular.

In view of the usual rules for agreement between nouns and their modifiers it may cause surprise to find a plural noun having one or more modifiers in the singular. This occurs when the adjective refers to one of several individuals which are denoted collectively by the plural noun. Thus, in the first of the following sentences, the adjectives  пальмити́новой , стеари́новой and олеи́новой are all in the genitive singular and refer to individual acids, while the word КИСЛО́Т is in the genitive plural since it denotes all three acids. A similar situation exists in the other two example sentences cited below.

[1] Here ЖИВО́ТНОГО (the neuter genitive singular of ЖИВО́ТНЫЙ) stands alone but none the less is used as an adjective rather than as a noun as is clear from the context. This sentence illustrates the point that the principles of Russian grammar should be regarded as stepping stones toward understanding the language rather than as a set of tools for undertaking to translate in a mechanical fashion.

Смеси   натриевых   солей   пальмитиновой,   стеариновой
Mixtures of sodium    salts   of palmitic,       stearic

и   олейновой   кислот   составляют,    главным
and   oleic      acids     compose,       for (the) most

образом,   обыкновенные   мыла.
part,      ordinarily      soaps.


Между   верхним   и   нижним   электродами   накладывается
Between (the) upper and lower   electrodes     applies self

разность    потенциалов   в   500 в.
(a) difference   of potentials   of   500 V.


Это   влияние    наглядно   показано    на рис. 66, где
This   influence   (is) clearly    shown      in Fig. 66, where

     даны   увеличенные   в   50   миллионов   раз
(are)   given   magnified      in   50   million      times

размеры    нейтрального   атома   серы   (заряд = 0)
(the) dimensions   of (a) neutral    atom   of sulfur (charge = 0)

и   двух   её   ионов — присоединившего      два
and   two   of her   ions   — (one) having acquired   two

электрона   (заряд 2-)   и   отдавшего      шесть
electrons    (charge 2-)   and   (one) having given off   six

собственных       (заряд 6+).
of its own (electrons)   (charge 6+).


§ 394.   Use of the Reflexive to Denote Interaction.


As ordinarily used, the reflexive in Russian denotes action
directed back to the person or thing exerting such action.
Occasionally, however, the reflexive is used in Russian to denote
interaction taking place between a plurality of persons or things.

Разноимённые                           электри́ческие                заря́ды
Differently named       (unlike)       electrical                    charges

притя́гиваются,           одноиме́нные     —    отта́лкиваются.
attract each other       one named (like)     repel each other.


Во  всех   сообща́ющихся                           сосу́дах,     вода́
In   all    communicating with each other    vessels     (the) water

стои́т  на  одина́ково́м    у́ровне.[1]
stands at  (the) same       level.


Температу́ра,          при   кото́рой    о́бе   жи́дкости    начина́ют
(The) temperature,    at    which      both  liquids      begin

сме́шиваться                  во  всех   отноше́ниях,    называ́ется
to mix one with another   in   all    proportions,    names self

крити́ческой    температу́рой    растворе́ния.
(the) critical    temperature    of solutions.


Отноше́ние               концентра́ций             вещества́,
(The) ratio             of concentrations         of a substance,

распределя́ющегося       ме́жду  двумя́  несмешива́ющимися
distributing self       between two    not mixing self

жи́дкостями   при  да́нной   температу́ре,  есть  величина́
liquids      at   (a) given  temperature,  is    (a) magnitude

постоя́нная,
constant.


§ 395.  A Special Form of Partitive Genitive.

    In discussing various uses of the genitive case, mention was
made in § 121, p. 178, of the fact that the genitive may be used
to refer to a part or portion of a whole. Use of the genitive case
in connection with expressions involving weights and measures

_____

[1] The masculine noun у́ровень "level" drops the -е- from the stem during
declension, cf. § 357, p. 573.

will be frequently encountered when reading scientific Russian. Phrases such as the following are typical: литр кислорода "(a) liter of oxygen," миллиграмм радия "(a) milligram of radium," грамм-молекула серной кислоты "(a) gram-molecule of sulfuric acid," кулон электричества, "(a) coulomb of electricity." The usual genitive forms are ordinarily used as is shown by the examples cited.

Certain masculine nouns referring to objects of everyday household use have a special form of genitive used exclusively with various words denoting amount or measure such as "pound" or "spoonful." This special partitive genitive is formed with the ending -у (strong) or -ю weak. Thus, we have, for example, ложка сахару "spoonful of sugar," фунт чаю, "pound of tea." This special form of the genitive is used only in expressions of amount. In other expressions, such as those referring to various attributes, the usual form of genitive is used, e.g., вкус сахара "taste of sugar," цена чая "price of tea," etc.

§ 396. The Russian Italic Alphabet and an Alternate Method of Denoting Emphasis.

The Russian italic alphabet is given herewith for reference purposes. When italicized, Russian т becomes *m* whose rounded shape distinguishes it from the *и* which is the italic form of м. Other letters which may appear rather strange at first are *n* (italic for п), *б* (italic б), *д* (italic д) and *г* (italic г). In general, however, the italic alphabet presents no real difficulties.

As in English the italic alphabet is used in Russian to lend emphasis to a word, phrase, clause or sentence.

Italicizing and the speical form of printing discussed on page 660 must not be regarded as the only means for achieving emphasis in Russian. Choice of words end phrasing also serve the same general purpose. In particular, departure from normal word order may be used to impart emphasis in Russian. Deviation from normal word order may be much more drastic than in English. As noted in § 49, p. 67, the endings in Russian are effective, within wide limits, in forestalling the ambiguity and loss in meaning which might result if the same deviations from normal word order were made in English sentences.

| Capital Italic | Capital Usual | Small Italic | Small Usual | Capital Italic | Capital Usual | Small Italic | Small Usual |
|---|---|---|---|---|---|---|---|
| *А* | А | *а* | а | *Р* | Р | *р* | р |
| *Б* | Б | *б* | б | *С* | С | *с* | с |
| *В* | В | *в* | в | *Т* | Т | *т* | т |
| *Г* | Г | *г* | г | *У* | У | *у* | у |
| *Д* | Д | *д* | д | *Ф* | Ф | *ф* | ф |
| *Е* | Е | *е* | е | *Х* | Х | *х* | х |
| *Ж* | Ж | *ж* | ж | *Ц* | Ц | *ц* | ц |
| *З* | З | *з* | з | *Ч* | Ч | *ч* | ч |
| *И* | И | *и* | и | *Ш* | Ш | *ш* | ш |
| *Й* | Й | *й* | й | *Щ* | Щ | *щ* | щ |
| *К* | К | *к* | к | *Ъ* | Ъ | *ъ* | ъ |
| *Л* | Л | *л* | л | *Ы* | Ы | *ы* | ы |
| *М* | М | *м* | м | *Ь* | Ь | *ь* | ь |
| *Н* | Н | *н* | н | *Э* | Э | *э* | э |
| *О* | О | *о* | о | *Ю* | Ю | *ю* | ю |
| *П* | П | *п* | п | *Я* | Я | *я* | я |

The following sentences provide further opportunity for observing the characteristic features of the Russian italic alphabet.

*Механи́ческий*       *эквивале́нт*       *теплоты́,*   *есть*   *величина́,*
Механи́ческий       эквивале́нт       теплоты́   есть   величина́,
(The) mechanical   equivalent       of heat    is     (the) magnitude,

*измеря́емая*   *тем*   *коли́чеством*   *рабо́ты,*   *кото́рое*
измеря́емая   тем   коли́чеством   рабо́ты,   кото́рое
measured     by that  quantity       of work,    which

*на́до*                *затра́тить,*   *что́бы*   *получи́ть*   *едини́цу*
на́до                затра́тить,   что́бы   получи́ть   едини́цу
(it is) necessary    to expend,   in order  to obtain   (a) unit

*коли́чества*   *тепло́ты́.*
коли́чества   тепло́ты́.
of quantity    of heat.

| | | | |
|---|---|---|---|
| *Коэфициент* | *объёмного* | *расширения* | *всех* |
| Коэфициент | объёмного | расширения | всех |
| (The) coefficient | of volume | expansion | of all |

| | | | | |
|---|---|---|---|---|
| *идеальных* | *газов* | *при* | *постоянном* | *давлении* |
| идеальных | газов | при | постоянном | давлении |
| ideal | gases | at | constant | pressure |

| | | | |
|---|---|---|---|
| *одинаков* | *и* | *равен* | *1/273.* |
| одинаков | и | равен | 1/273. |
| (is) identical | and | equal | 1/273. |

| | | | | |
|---|---|---|---|---|
| *Высота,* | *подъёма* | *смачивающей* | *жидкости* | *в* |
| Высота | подъёма | смачивающей | жидкости | в |
| (The) height | of rise | of (a) wetting | liquid | in |

| | | | |
|---|---|---|---|
| *капиллярной* | *трубке* | *обратно* | *пропорциональна* |
| капиллярной | трубке | обратно | пропорциональна |
| (a) capillary | tube | (is) inversely | proportional |

| | | | |
|---|---|---|---|
| *диаметру* | *трубки* | *и* | *плотности* |
| диаметру | трубки | и | плотности |
| to (the) diameter | of (the) tube | and | to (the) density |

| |
|---|
| *жидкости.* |
| жидкости. |
| of (the) liquid. |

As noted above, emphasis in Russian may be indicated by italicizing. Alternately, emphasis may be indicated by printing with more than usual spacing between letters as in certain words in the second of the following two sentences.

| | | | | | | |
|---|---|---|---|---|---|---|
| При | трении | и | при | всяком | другом | способе |
| During | friction | and | during | every | other | process |

| | | | |
|---|---|---|---|
| электризации, | одно | тело | электризуется |
| of electrification, | one | body | electrifies self |

| | | | |
|---|---|---|---|
| положительно, | другое | — отрицательно, | но |
| positively, | (the) other | — negatively, | but |

| так, | что | алгебраическая | сумма | зарядов |
|------|-----|----------------|-------|---------|
| so | that | (the) algebraic | sum | of (the) charges |

| остаётся[1] | неизменной. |
|-------------|-------------|
| remains | unchanged. |

| С | химической | стороны | фтор | может | быть |
|---|------------|---------|------|-------|------|
| From | (the) chemical | side | fluorine | may | be |

| охарактеризован | как | одновалентный | металлоид, |
|-----------------|-----|---------------|------------|
| characterized | as | (a) monovalent | metalloid, |

| притом | самый | реактивный | из | всех | металлоидов. |
|--------|-------|------------|-----|------|--------------|
| furthermore | the most | reactive | of | all | metalloids. |

## § 397. Reading Exercise.

### О строении атомов
### Исторический очерк

Первоначальное представление об атомах зародилось у философов древней Греции. Они думали,[1] что вся матёрия состоит из невидимых, физически неделимых, неразрушимых, вечных и непроницаемых частиц, которые они называли атомами. Следует рассматривать греческую атомную теорию древних времён как чисто философское учение, лишённое всякого экспериментального подтверждения.

Учёным нашей эпохи впервые удалось экспериментально доказать существование атомов. Особенно важное место среди этих учёных принадлежит английскому химику Дальтону. Определяя состав окиси углерода (CO) и углекислого газа ($CO_2$), он нашёл, что количества кислорода в них относятся как 1:2, если принять, что в этих соединениях содержится одно и то же[2] количество углерода. Такие же соотношения были установлены для множества других соединений, и ни в одном случае не было найдено такого соотношения[3] между

---

[1] See Footnote, p. 145.

соединяющимися элементами, которое не могло бы быть выражено простыми целыми числами. Это привело Дальтона[4] к открытию им закона кратных отношений: если два элемента образуют между собой несколько соединений, то весовые количества одного из них, соединяющиеся с одним и тем же весовым количеством другого, относятся между собой, как простые целые числа.

В последующие годы XIX века, результаты обширных лабораторных изысканий целого ряда химиков и физиков подтвердили гипотезу, что атом есть наименьшая частица химического элемента, образующая соединения или получаемая из соединений, и что каждый химический элемент состоит из присущих только ему[5] простых атомов, отличных от атомов другого элемента.

Ко времени Дальтона и его современников атом обычно представляли себе маленьким упругим шариком. Явления известные химикам и физикам этого времени, они могли легко объяснить себе соударениями и сцеплениями этих шариков. Задумываться над вопросом, имеет ли структуру сам атом, учёным этого времени не было необходимости.[6]

С тех пор сделались - и делаются - известными многие новые явления, при помощи которых оказалось возможным проникнуть всё глубже и глубже в тайны внутреннего строения атомов. В течение XVIII века внимательное изучение статического электричества - уже известного древним грекам - показало, что свойство притягивать лёгкие предметы присуще телам, если на поверхности последних существует или избыток, или недостаток "чего-то,"[6] движение которого по проводникам, например, по металлическим проволокам, представляет собой электрический ток. Физикам удалось к концу XIX века изолировать это "что-то" в виде так называемых катодных лучей, представляющих собой поток электронов, самых маленьких частиц отрицательного электричества. К тому же времени были открыты Гольдштейном анодные лучи (иногда называемые также положительными, закатодными или каналовыми лучами). Эти лучи в результате исследований Вина и Дж. Томсона оказались потоками положительно заряжённых ионов. Таким образом было доказано, что

всякое материальное вещество, т.е. всякая молекула и всякий атом, содержит в себе и отрицательный и положительный виды электричества.

К началу хх века оставалось неясным, какую роль играет во внутреннем строении атома положительное электричество. Известные в то время опыты не давали также ответа на вопрос, является ли равновесие двух видов электричества внутри атома статическим или динамическим. Следовательно физики этого времени (Кельвин, Дж. Томсон и др.) предположили, что положительный заряд атома распределен с равномерной плотностью по объёму шара, радиус которого совпадает с радиусом атома.

Решающее влияние на дальнейшее развитие теорий, относящихся к строению атомов, оказали опыты по изучению рассеяния а-лучей радия, проведённые Резерфордом, Гейгером и Марсденом. Было обнаружено, что большинство а-частиц, пронизывающих металлическую пластинку толщиной[7] в сотые доли миллиметра, отклоняется от прямолинейного пути на незначительный угол, обычно не превышающий 2-4°.

Другому исследователю, Вильсону, удалось фотографировать траектории а-частиц, пролетающих через слой газа толщиной в несколько сантиметров. Было найдено, что а-частицы, неизбежно встречающие на своём пути десятки тысяч атомов, обычно пролетают через них насквозь. Тем не менее - правда очень редко - наблюдается отброс а-частицы, иногда в обратном направлении.

Эти факты заставили Резерфорда[8] предложить теорию, согласно которой весь положительный заряд атома и почти вся его масса сосредоточены в ядре атома, которое занимает ничтожный объём в сравнении с общим объёмом атома. Гипотеза эта находится в прекрасном согласии с выводом экспериментальных исследований. Гипотеза Резерфорда однако не могла быть приведена в согласие с законами классической электродинамики.

Следующий шаг был сделан датским физиком Бором. Он отверг применимость обычных законов электродинамики к внутриатомным процессам и совместил гипотезу Резерфорда с теорией квантов, выдвинутой Планком ещё в 1900 г. Та-

ким образом была основана современная квантовая механика, дальнейшие развитие которой при помощи изучения преимущественно спектральных явлений является основным для наших новейших теорий, объясняющих участие электронов в строении атомов.

Первое указание на то, что сами ядра атомов имеют сложное строение, дало открытие радиоактивности. Типы частиц, принимающих участие в строении атомных ядер, и природа сил, действующих между такими частицами, полностью не изучены и до сих пор. Исследованиями в этом направлении занимается в наши дни большое число институтов и учёных.

## Notes

1. Some 200 or more years ago, a Russian author might have written Они думывали instead of Они думали. Such use of думывали (the plural of the past tense of the obsolete infinitive думывать) would have emphasized the repetitive nature of the action in remote past time as discussed in § 383, p. 636.

2. одно и то же количество, "one and the same amount." Note the idiomatic expression одно и то же.

3. The genitive is used because of the negation, cf. § 176, p. 267.

4. Это привело Дальтона "This led Dalton." Note that Дальтона, the accusative singular case of Дальтон, has the same form as the corresponding genitive in accordance with a rule stated in § 67, p. 93 and further discussed in § 362, p. 585.

5. состоит из присущих только ему простых атомов, literally, "consists of pertaining only to him simple atoms." Here, ему refers to элемент.

6. Cf. Note 3 above.

7. The instrumental is used here in indicating a dimension. For a previous instance of similar use of the instrumental, see § 98, p. 141 and last sentence on p. 142.

8. Here Резерфо́рда is in the accusative singular case having the same form as the corresponding genitive in accord with the rule referred to in Note 4 above.

§ 398.  Translation Exercise.

1. The philosophers (фило́софы) of ancient Greece thought that all matter consists of atoms, invisible, indestructible and impenetrable particles.
2. To Dalton succeeded to establish ( установи́ть ) the law ( зако́н ) of multiple proportions.
3. For a multiplicity of compounds it was found that the weight ( весовы́е ) ratios between combining (self) elements express self ( выража́ются ) by simple whole numbers.
4. Facts known to Dalton confirmed the hypothesis that every chemical element consists of atoms, different from the atoms of another element.
5. Since that time (to) scientists succeeded to become acquainted ( познако́миться ) with (со) the properties ( сво́йствами) of negative electricity.
6. At the start of the 20th century, to physicists was known that positive electricity plays an important role in the inner structure of the atom.
7. It showed self, that deflection of an α-particle observes self very rarely.
8. According to the hypothesis ( гипо́тезе) of Rutherford, the nucleus of the atom carries ( несёт) all the his positive charge.
9. Contemporary quantum mechanics is based (осно́вывается) on (на) the theory ( тео́рии) of quanta, developed (вы́двинутой) by Planck.
10. Even (да́же) up to this time, the complex structure of nuclei of atoms is not completely investigated.

# RUSSIAN ABBREVIATIONS

§ 399. Introductory Notes.

Scientific and technical abbreviations are much the same in Russian as in English. In fact, many abbreviations, e.g., atomic symbols, such as C for carbon or Fe for iron, are identically the same in both languages. The use of Greek letters in abbreviations follows familiar usage, e.g., μ, micron; mμ, millimicron. The Russian abbreviations for many other scientific terms are closely similar to their English counterparts, e.g., Г. for грамм "gram," ММ. for миллиметр "millimeter" or сек. for секунда "second." Many scientific terms derived from Russian roots are similarly abbreviated, e.g., л.с. for лошадиная сила "horse power." Case endings are not used with such abbreviations.

A certain amount of care may be necessary at times when interpreting Russian abbreviations. More than one abbreviation may be used for the same term. Thus, температура "temperature" may be abbreviated as Т. or темп. or even as т-ра. This latter abbreviation, formed by dropping letters from the middle of the word, differs from other types of abbreviations discussed above by taking regular case endings, e.g.; Nom. т-ра ( температура ); Gen. т-ры (температуы); Dat. т-ре (температуре), etc.

Certain abbreviations are used with more than one meaning. Thus, Г. is used both for грамм "gram" and год "year." The meaning of such abbreviations is determined by the context.

Some abbreviations form pronounceable combinations of letters. There is a tendency for such abbreviations to become nouns which, if the final letter is a consonant, may be declined. Thus, the abbreviation ВТУЗ — высшее техническое учёбное заведение "higher technical educational establishment" — is used like a noun and declined with the regular masculine endings.

667

§ 400. List of Abbreviations.

No attempt has been made to prepare an exhaustively complete list. The more common abbreviations are given together with a few less frequently encountered. Abbreviations used by Russian writers in citing certain of their more important scientific periodicals are also included.

а. ампе́р ampere; арши́н arshin
абс. абсолю́тный absolute
ам. америка́нский American
АН Акаде́мия Нау́к Academy of Sciences
ат. атмосфе́ра atmosphere
Арх. биол. наук. Архи́в биологи́ческих нау́к Archives des sciences biologiques.
ат. в. ато́мный вес tomic weight
а-ч ампе́р-час ampere-hour
б. бар bar (unit of pressure)
булл. бюллете́нь bulletin
в. век century; вес weight; вольт volt; восто́к east; враще́ние rotation
ВА. Вое́нная акаде́мия Military Academy
вт. ватт watt
выч. вы́численный calculated
г. год year; го́род city; грамм gram
га. гекта́р bectare
гл. глава́ chapter
гс. гаусс gauss
ДАН Докла́ды акаде́мии нау́к Comptes rendus de l'Académie des Sciences
дб. дециба́л decibel
дж. джо́уль joule
диам. диа́метр diameter
др. друго́й other, others
ед. едини́ца unit
ж.; жур. журна́л journal (Cf. examples below)
ж. д. желе́зная доро́га railroad (*noun*)
ж.-д. железнодоро́жный railroad (*adj.*)
ЖОХ Журна́л о́бщей хи́мии Journal of General Chemistry
ЖРФХО Журна́л ру́сского физико-хими́ческого о́бщества Journal of the Russian Physical-Chemical Society
ЖТФ Журна́л техни́ческой фи́зики Journal of Technical Physics
ЖЭТФ Журна́л эксперимента́льной и теорети́ческой фи́зики Journal of Experimental and Theoretical Physics
з. за́пад west
и т д. и так да́лее and so forth, etc.

и т. п.  и так прóчее and so forth, etc.

Изв. АН ОХН Извéстия акадéмии наýк. отдéл химúческих наýк. Bulletin de l'acadéмie des sciences. Classes des sciences chimiques.

к.  копéйка kopek

к.  кулóн çoulomb

кал.  калóрия calorie

кв.  киловóльт kilovolt

квт.  киловáтт kilowatt

квтч. or квт-ч киловáттчас киловáтт-час Kilowatt-hour

кг. килогрáмм kilogram

кдж. килоджóуль, kilojoule

ккал.  килокалóрия kilocalorie

км. километр kilometer

коэф.  коэфициéнт coefficient

КП. коммунистúческая пáртия communist party

кпд. коэфициéнт полéзного дéйствия coefficient of useful action, efficiency factor

л. лéт year; лúтр liter; ЛОТ half an ounce

л. с. лошадúная сúла horse power

м.  мéсяц month; мéтр meter

молекулярный molecular

мг. миллигрáмм milligram

мгом. мегóм megohm

мин. минýта minute

мка. микроампéр microampere

мкв. микровóльт microvolt

мкмкф.  микромикрофарáда micromicrofarad

мкс. мáксвелл maxwell

мкф. микрофарáда microfarad

млн. миллиóн million

мм. миллимéтр millimeter

мсек. миллисекýнда millisecond

н.  нóвый new

найд. нáйденный found

напр. напримéр for example

непопр. непопрáвленный uncorrected

о.  óстров island; óзеро lake

об./мин. обóроты в минýту revolutions per minute

ов. отравляющее веществó poisonous substance, poison gas, chemical warfare agent

отв. отвéт answer

п. пýд pood

пат. патéнт patent

попр. попрáвленный corrected

прик. приклáдный applied

р. рекá river; рýбль ruble

разл. разложе́ние decomposition
размягч. размягче́ние softening
рис. рису́нок drawing, illustration
рт.ст. рту́тный столб mercury column
с. се́вер north; село́ village
сек. секу́нда second
след.обр. сле́дующим о́бразом in the following way
см. сантиме́тр centimeter; смотри́ see
соотв. соотве́тствующий corresponding
ср. сравни́ compare
СССР Сою́з Сове́тских Социалисти́ческих Респу́блик Union
of Soviet Socialist Republics.
стр. страни́ца page
США Соединённые Шта́ты Аме́рики United States of America,
USA
т. температу́ра temperature; том volume (book); тон ton; то́чка
point; ты́сяча thousand
табл. табли́ца table
так.обр. таки́м о́бразом in this way
т.е. то есть that is
темп. температу́ра temperature
т. кип. температу́ра кипе́ния boiling point
т.н. так называ́емый so-called
т. пл. температу́ра плавле́ния melting point
т-ра температу́ра temperature
Тр. геол. ин-та АН Труды́ геологи́ческого институ́та
акаде́мии нау́к. Transactions of the Geological Institute of
the Academy of Sciences.
тыс. ты́сяча thousand
уд. в. уде́льный вес specific gravity
Усп. хим. Успе́хи хи́мии Progress of Chemistry
ф. фара́да farad; фот phot
ч. час hour; часть part
черт. чертёж sketch
э. эрг erg; эрсте́д oersted
э.д.с. электродви́жущая си́ла electromotive force, emf.
экз. экземпля́р copy, specimen
эл.–магн. электромагни́тный electromagnetic
эл.–ст. электростати́ческий electrostatic
ю. юг south

## NOTES ON RUSSIAN-ENGLISH VOCABULARY

§ 401. Scope of Vocabulary.

All Russian words found in the Reading Exercises are listed. In accordance with the usual conventions, nouns are given in the nominative singular case, adjectives in the masculine nominative singular and verbs as infinitives. All irregular forms found in the reading exercises, together with a few regular forms, sometimes troublesome, appear as separate entries, which are provided, as occasion may require, with cross references to other vocabulary entries and with various supplementary notes.

Various idioms and fixed expressions are also separately entered after either the first word or the principle word involved.

§ 402. Notes Relating to Grammar.

Immediately following each Russian word, an abbreviation in italics indicates the part of speech; e.g., *n.* for noun, *adj.*, for adjective, etc. With nouns, the gender is next noted. Listing of verbs is in harmony with various factors already discussed in § 44, p. 63. Thus, a pair of infinitives with the imperfective infinitive preceding the perfective is usually given for each Russian verb and the transitive, intransitive or reflexive nature of the verb is noted. With those few verbs having only a single infinitive, the latter is also designated as being imperfective, perfective or -- with some verbs mostly of foreign origin as noted in § 40, p. 56 -- as both imperfective and perfective.

Key numbers refer to sample declensions of nouns and adjectives and class designations indicate the conjugation type of infinitives. For details regarding declensions and conjugations various sections noted below should be consulted.

NOUNS     Regular Declension. Lesson 16. §§ 129-130, pp. 189-191.

                       Irregular Declension. Lesson 38, §§ 355, p. 561. (Key numbers with lower case letter, for example, 9a or 13b)

PRONOUNS — In listing each pronoun, reference is made to its declension by citing the appropriate section and page in Lessons 17 and 18.

ADJECTIVES — <u>Regular Declension.</u> Lesson 16. §§ 131-132, pp. 191-198

<u>Irregular Declension.</u> Lesson 38. § 356, p. 565
(Key numbers with a lower case letter, for example, 17a or 18b)

VERBS — <u>Regular and Irregular Conjugation.</u> Lesson 35 (§§ 325-326, pp. 510-515) summarizes various types of conjugation with reference to more detailed discussion in other lessons.

The cases governed by the various prepositions are noted and any shift in meaning with change in case governed is also given.

In similar fashion, an appropriate note points out verbs which govern the instrumental, dative or genitive cases as discussed in § 99, p. 143; § 114, p. 166; § 85, p. 123. The reflexive forms of verbs are often used in a transitive sense and, in some instances, with a special meaning. Such uses of reflexive forms are indicated as shown in the following examples.

ДОСТИГА́ТЬ (Reg. A) - ДОСТИ́ГНУТЬ (Irr. J-3)  *v.tr.* (*with gen.*)  to attain, to achieve, to reach
   -СЯ  to be attained, achieved, arrived at
ЯВЛЯ́ТЬ (Reg. A) - ЯВИ́ТЬ (Irr. C-2)*v.tr.*  to show
   -СЯ  to show self, to appear, to be (Cf. § 94, p. 136; § 123, p. 181)

In the last example, § 94, p. 136 and § 123, p. 181 present a discussion of the idiomatic use of the reflexive forms as a circumlocution of little used or obsolete forms of БЫТЬ "to be."

§ 403.  Notes on Relationships Between Words.

As discussed in Lesson 5 (Cf. §§ 32-33, pp. 47-48), by directing attention to relationships between words, it is possible to weave a pattern of associations which is able powerfully to assist the memory in acquiring and retaining a vocabulary of Russian words.

Asterisks have been used to indicate one frequently encountered and usually obvious type of relationship, namely, that existing between a Russian word and an English cognate or closely related English word. Typical examples are:

*а́том *n.masc.* (1) atom
*мета́н *n.masc.* (1) methane
*хими́ческий *adj.* (21) chemical (*adj.*)
*фотографи́ровать - *сфотографи́ровать (Irr. A) *v.tr.*
*электри́чество *n.neuter* (13) electricity          to photograph

The relationship of words of purely Russian origin to their roots is indicated as shown in the following examples.

бесцве́тный *adj.* (17a) colorless
  бес- + цвет   color
заса́сывать (Reg. A)- засоса́ть (Reg. B-1) *v.tr.* to suck into
  -СЯ to be sucked into
  за- + соса́ть - пососа́ть   to suck
золотоно́сный *adj.* (17a) gold bearing
  зо́лото  gold; носи́ть  to be carrying
электросопротивле́ние *n.neuter* (16) electrical resistance
  *электро- electro-;  со- + про́тив against

In the last of these examples, the asterisk points out that электро- is cognate with "electro-." It will also be noted that Russian root words are individually translated but that prefixes are merely cited. A list of common prefixes is provided for reference purposes in the next section.

§ 404. Russian Prefixes.

The following list of the more important prefixes indicates in a general way the usual effect of prefixes on the meaning of roots. It is impossible to do more than this because of vagaries in usage. Most of these prefixes, when used with imperfective infinitives, convert them to perfective infinitives, as well as causing a shift in meaning as discussed in §§ 41-43, pp. 57-63.

| без-, бес- | without, -less, un- |
|---|---|
| в-, во- | into, in |
| воз-, вз-, вос-, вс- | (1) up, off, away, <br> (2) return |
| вы- | from within, out of |
| до- | (1) up to, <br> (2) sufficiency |
| за- | (1) beyond, behind, <br> (2) initiation of action |
| из-, изо-, ис- | away from, out |
| между-, меж- | between, inter- |
| на- | toward, onto, to |
| над- | above, super-, per- |
| не- | un-, non- |
| о-, об-, обо- | (1) about, around, <br> (2) establishment of condition |
| от-, ото- | out, from, away |
| пере- | (1) across, back and forth, <br> (2) above, super- |
| по- | (1) to form perfective infinitives, <br> (2) short duration of action <br> (3) in fashion of, <br> (4) initiation of action (especially with motion) |
| под-, подо- | (1) under, <br> (2) establishment of condition |
| полу- | semi-, half |
| пред- | before, in front of |
| при- | near, in vicinity of |
| про- | through, past |
| противо- | against, in opposition to |
| раз-, разо-, рас- | (1) separate, apart, to pieces, <br> (2) intensification of action |
| с-, со- | (1) with, together, <br> (2) down, off |
| у- | (1) establishment of condition or intensification of action, <br> (2) away from (with words implying motion) |

## § 405. Russian Suffixes.

Only those Russian suffixes which are most important in forming scientific and technical terms are listed here. In general, any given Russian suffix is used to form some one certain word type as is evident from the following summary.

| Adjectives | Notes |
|---|---|
| -ИЧЕСК- | Used with words of foreign origin. |
| -Н-<br>-ОВ-, -ЕВ-<br>-СК-, -ОВСК-, -ЕВСК-<br>-ИЧН- | Used both with words of foreign origin and with Russian words and roots. |
| -ИСТ-, -ОВАТ, -ЕВАТ-<br>-ОВАТИСТ-, -ЕВАТИСТ- | Used to form adjectives indicating limited intensity or relationship. |

| Adverbs | Notes |
|---|---|
| -ИЧЕСКИ | Used with words of foreign origin. |
| -О, -Е | Suffixes generally used to form adverbs. |

| Nouns<br>*Suffix* | *Nom. Sing. Ending* | Notes |
|---|---|---|
| -ТЕЛ-<br>-ИК | -Ь<br>None | Masculine nouns denoting person or thing performing some action. |
| -аК<br>-ОК, -ЯК | None | Persons, concepts or things closely related to parent word. |
| -ОСТ-, -ЕСТ- | -Ь | Feminine nouns denoting abstract class of things. |
| -К- | -а | Persons, concepts or things closely related to parent words. Also diminutives. |
| -ЕНИ-<br>-АНИ- | -Е<br>-Е | Neuter nouns denoting an action or -- rarely -- the result of an action. |
| -СТВ- | -О | Abstract concepts. |

| Verbs<br>*Infinitive Endings* | Notes |
|---|---|
| -ИРОВАТЬ | Used with foreign words. |
| -ОВАТЬ | Used with both Russian and foreign words. |
| -АТЬ,-ЕТЬ,-ИТЬ<br>-ОТЬ,-УТЬ,-ЫТЬ<br>-ЯТЬ | Endings typifying the majority of infinitives. |

§ 406. Russian Alphabet and Abbreviations Used in Vocabularies.

## Alphabet

| а | б | в | г | д | е | ж | з | и | й | к | л | м | н | о | п |
|---|---|---|---|---|---|---|---|---|---|---|---|---|---|---|---|
| А | Б | В | Г | Д | Е | Ж | З | И | Й | К | Л | М | Н | О | П |

| р | с | т | у | ф | х | ц | ч | ш | щ | ъ | ы | ь | э | ю | я |
|---|---|---|---|---|---|---|---|---|---|---|---|---|---|---|---|
| Р | С | Т | У | Ф | Х | Ц | Ч | Ш | Щ | Ъ | Ы | Ь | Э | Ю | Я |

## Abbreviations Used in Vocabularies

*abbr.*, *abbrev.* abbreviation
*acc.* accusative (case)
*act.* active
*adj.* adjective
*adv.* adverb
*chem.* chemistry
*comp.* comparative (degree)
*conj.* conjunction
*dat.* dative (case)
*decl.* declension
*def.* definite
*expr.* expression
*fem.* feminine
*fut.* future
*gen.* genitive (case)
*ger.* gerund
*imp.* imperative
*imperf.* imperfective
*impers.* impersonal
*instr.* instrumental (case)
*interj.* interjection

*interr.* interrogative
*intr.* intransitive
*irr.* irregular
*n.* noun
*nom.* nominative (case)
*part.* participle
*pas.* passive
*perf.* perfective
*pers.* person
*plu.* plural
*poss.* possessive
*pred.* predicative
*prep.* preposition,
*prep.*, *prepl.* prepositional
*pres.* present
*refl.* reflexive
*sing.* singular
*superl.* superlative (degree)
*tr.* transitive
*undecl.* undeclined
*v.* verb

# A

а *conj.* and, but (Cf. § 61, p. 84)
*аберра́ция *n.fem.* (11) aberration
*абсолю́тный *adj.* (17) absolute
*абсо́рбер *n.masc.* (1) absorber
*абцéсс *n.masc.* (1) abscess
*автома́т *n.masc.* (1) automatic device
*автомати́чески *adv.* automatically
*автомати́ческий *adj.* (21) automatic
*автомоби́ль *n.masc.* (6) automobile
*агрега́тный *adj.* (17) aggregate, pertaining to an aggregation
*адиабати́ческий *adj.* (21) adiabatic
азо́т *n.masc.* (1) nitrogen
азотосодержа́щий *adj.* (22) nitrogen containing (Cf. § 286, p. 452)
   азо́т nitrogen; содержа́ть to be containing
*актива́ция *n.fem.* (11) activation
*активи́ровать *v.tr.* (Irr. A-1) to be activating, to activate
*акти́вность *n.fem.* (12) activity
*акти́вный *adj.* (17a) active
*актуа́льный *adj.* (17b) present, existing at the time in question,
*алгебраи́ческий *adj.* (21) algebraic                            actual
*алкало́ид *n.masc.* (1) alkaloid
*алкого́ль *n.masc.* (6) alcohol
алма́з *n.masc.* (1) diamond
*а́льфа-, *А́льфа-*prefix* alpha-, Alpha-
*а́льфа-лу́ч *n.masc.* (3) alpha-ray
*алюми́ниевый *adj.* (17) aluminum (*adj.*)
*алюми́ний *n.masc.* (5) aluminum
*амальга́ма *n.fem.* (7) amalgam
*амальгами́ровать *v.tr.* (Irr. A-1) to be amalgamating,
*америка́нский *adj.* (21) American                  to amalgamate
*ами́н *n.masc.* (1) amine
*ами́нный *adj.* (17) amine (*adj.*)
*аммиа́к *n.masc.* (3) ammonia
*амо́рфный *adj.* (17a) amorphous
*ампе́р *n.masc.* (1) ampere
*амплиту́да *n.fem.* (7) amplitude
*ана́лиз *n.masc.* (1) analysis
*анализи́ровать *v.tr.* (Irr. A-1) to be analyzing, to analyze

*аналоги́чный *adj.*(17a) analogous, identical
*анало́гия *n.fem.*(11) analogy
*анато́мия *n.fem.*(11) anatomy
*анаэро́бный *adj.*(17) anaerobic
*англи́йский *adj.*(21) English
*А́нглия *n.fem.*(11) England
*анизотро́пия *n.fem.*(11) anisotropy
*анили́н *n.masc.*(1) aniline
*ано́д *n.masc.*(1) anode
*ано́дный (*adj.*) (17) anodic, anode, (*adj.*)
*анома́льный *adj.*(17b) anomalous
*Анри́ *n.masc.*(undecl.* § 363, p. 587) Henri
*анте́нна *n.fem.* (7) antenna
*антраци́т *n.masc.* (1) anthracite
*аппара́т *n.masc.* (1) apparatus, machine
*апре́ль *n.masc.* (6) April
*арифмети́ческий *adj.*(21) arithmetical
*Аркту́р *n.masc.* (1) Arcturus
*арсена́л *n.masc.*(1) arsenal
*артиллери́йский *adj.*(21) artillery
*арфи́ст *n.masc.* (1) harpist
*асбе́ст *n.masc.* (1) asbestos
*асфа́льт *n.masc.* (1) asphalt
*атмосфе́ра *n.fem.* (1) atmosphere
*а́том *n.masc.* (1) atom
*ато́мный *adj.* (17a) atomic
*ацета́т *n.masc.*(1) acetate
*ацето́н *n.masc.*(1) acetone
*аэродро́м *n.masc.* (1) aerodrome

Б

*бакели́т *n.masc.* (1) "Bakelite"
*бакте́рия *n.fem.* (11) bacteria
*балка́нский *adj.* (21) Balkan
бе́гать - побе́гать *v.intr.* (Reg. A) to run, to move rapidly (back and
                              forth) (Cf. §§ 380-382, p. 626-635)
*Бе́ккер *n.masc.*(1) Becker
белко́в *gen.plural of* бело́к
бело́к *n.masc.*(3a) white (of egg or eye), protein
бе́лый *adj.* (17) white
*бе́ри-бе́ри *n.neuter (undecl.* § 363, p. 587) beri-beri
*бери́ллиевый *adj.*(17) made of or containing beryllium
*бери́ллий *n.masc.*(5) beryllium
беспо́мощный *adj.*(17a) helpless
    бес- + по́мощь, aid, help

\*бессеме́ровский *adj.*(21) pertaining to Bessemer

бесцве́тный *adj.*(17a) colorless
   бес- + цвет color

\*бе́та-лу́ч *n.masc.*(3) beta-ray

\*биологи́ческий *adj.*(21) biological

\*биохими́ческий *adj.*(21) biochemical

\*биохи́мия *n.fem.*(11) biochemistry

благодаря́ *conj. and prep.* (*with dat.*) thanks (to)

благоро́дный *adj.* (17a) noble

бле́дный *adj.* (17a) pale

блеск *n.masc.*(3) luster

блесте́ть – заблесте́ть *v.intr.* (Irr. D-2, СТ → Щ ) to shine,
бл́ижа́йший *adj.superl.*(22) nearest        to glitter

бли́же *adj.comp.* (*undecl.* ) nearer

близ *prep.* (*with gen.*) near

бли́зкий *adj.*(21a) near

бога́тый *adj.*(17) rich

\*бокси́т *n.masc.*(1) bauxite

бо́лее *adj. and adv.comp.*(*undecl.*) bigger, more (Cf. § 331, p. 523)

бо́льше *adj.comp.* (*undecl.*) bigger, greater, larger, higher

бо́льший *adj.comp.*(22) bigger, greater, larger, higher

большинство́ *n.neuter* (13) majority

большо́й *adj.* (20) big, great, large, high

\*бо́мба *n.fem.* (7) bomb

\*бомбардиро́вка *n.fem.* (9) bombardment

\*Бор *n.masc.* (1) Bohr

\*Бо́те *n.masc.* (*undecl.* § 363, p. 587) Bothe

брат *n.masc.* (Irr. § 359, p. 577) brother

брать (Irr. E-1) – взять (Irr. F-7) *v.tr.* to take

бра́тьев *gen. and acc. plural of* брат

бра́тья *nom.plural of* брат

\*брита́нский *adj.* (21) British

бродя́чий *adj.* (22) wandering

броже́ние *n.neuter* (16) fermentation

\*бром *n.masc.* (1) bromine

\*бро́нза *n.fem.* (7) bronze

броса́ть (Reg. A) – бро́сить (Irr. D-2) *v.tr.* to throw

бро́шу *perf. future tense, first pers. sing of* бро́сить
                                 (Cf. броса́ть )

бу́дто *conj.* as if, as though

бу́дем, бу́дет, бу́ду, бу́дут *imperf. future tense*
                      *forms of* БЫТЬ to be (Cf. § 230, p. 360)

бу́дучи *conj.* when, while,
   быть to be

бу́дущий *adj.*(22) future

бума́га *n.fem.*(9) paper

\*Бу́нзен *n.masc.*(1) Bunsen

бу́рно *adv*. violently, stormily, vigorously
бу́рный *adj*.(17a) stormy, violent
*буровóй *adj*. (18) pertaining to boring
быва́ть *v.,intr*. (Reg. A) to be usually (Cf. § 383, p. 637)
был, была́, бы́ло, бы́ли, *imperf. past tense forms of* БЫТЬ
бы́стро *adv*. quickly, rapidly, swiftly                          to be
быт *n.masc*. (1) daily life
БЫТЬ *v.intr*. (Irr. I-2) to be


# В

В, ВО (*prep*.(*with acc*. *and prep*.) into (*with acc*.) in (*with prep*.)
В ВИДУ *fixed expr*. in view (of)                    (Cf. § 127, p. 185)
В ка́честве *fixed expr*. in the quality of, as,
В настоя́щее вре́мя *fixed expr*. at the present time (Cf. Note 10, § 133,
В ТО вре́мя *fixed expr*. at that time                          p. 200)
В э́то же вре́мя *fixed expr*. at the same time (Cf. § 144, p. 215)
ва́жен *pred.masc.sing*. of ва́жный
ва́жность *n.fem*.(12) importance
ва́жный *adj*. (17a) important
*ва́куум *n.masc*. (1) vacuum
*вакци́на *n.fem*. (7) vaccine
*вакцина́ция *n.fem*. (11) vaccination
*вал *n.masc*. (1) shaft (in a machine), wall
*вале́нтность *n.fem*.(12) valency
*вале́нтный *adj*.(17a) pertaining to valence, valence (*adj*.)
*вана́дий *n.masc*.(5) vanadium
вблизи́ *adv*. *and prep*. (*with gen*.) near, in the neighborhood
   В- + бли́зкий near                                of
введём *fut. tense,first pers. plural of* ВВЕСТИ́
                                   (Cf. ВВОДИ́ТЬ)
введе́ние *n.neuter* (16) introduction
вверх *adv*. upward
   В- + верх upper part, peak
ввиду́ *prep*. (*with gen*.) in view of
   В- + ВИД view, aspect, form
ввод *n.masc*.(1) something brought in
вводи́ть (Irr. D-2, Д → Ж) - ВВЕСТИ́(Irr. H-5) *v.tr*.to lead in,
                              to introduce (Cf. § 382, p. 626)
   В- + води́ть; вести́ to be leading (Cf. § 381, p. 626)
вдво́е *adv*. twice
   В- + два two
веде́т себя́ behaves, conducts self *pres. tense, third pers.
                              sing. refl. of* вести́
веду́щий leading (*pres. act. part. of* вести́) to be leading
век *n.masc*. (26 *gen. plu*. веко́в) century, lifetime

*ве́ктор *n.masc.* (1) vector
*Ве́лер *n.masc.* (1) Wöhler
вели́кий *adj.* (21) great
величина́ *n.fem.* (7) magnitude, value, quantity
*Вене́ра *n.fem.* (7) Venus (planet)
вернётся *perf.future tense third person sing.refl.*
                                    *of* верну́ть
верну́ть *v.tr.perf.* (Reg. B-1) to bring back, to call back
   -ся, to return, to come back
*вертика́льный *adj.* (17a) vertical
вес *n.masc.* (§ 359, p. 580) weight, (*plural only*) balance
весе́нний *adj.* (19) spring-time (adj.)
весна́ *n.fem.* (7a) spring (season of year)
весово́й *adj.* (18) (pertaining to) weight
весы́ *n.plural* (§ 359, p. 580) weights, balance
весь *adj.,pronoun* (Cf. § 150, p. 229) whole, all
весьма́ *adv.* very, extremely
ветвь *n.fem.* (12) branch, twig
ве́тка *n.fem.* (9) little branch
вече́рний *adj.* (19) evening
ве́чный *adj.* (17a) eternal, everlasting
   век    century
вещество́ *n.neuter* (13) substance, matter
взаи́мно *adv.* mutually
взгляд *n.masc.* (1) view, opinion
взро́слый *adj.* (17) adult
   вз- + расти́ to be growing
взрыв *n.masc.* (1) explosion
взры́вчатый *adj.* (17) pertaining to an explosion, explosive
взя́тый (17) taken *pas. past part. of* взять
взять *see* брать
вид *n.masc.* (1) view, aspect, form, shape, kind, condition, type
ви́деть – уви́деть *v.tr.* (Irr. D-2, д→ж) to see, to catch sight of
ви́димый *adj.* (17) visible
ви́дный *adj.* (17a) visible, prominent
видоизменённый *adj.* (17) changed (as to form, type, etc.)
   вид view, aspect form; из- + ме́на exchange
ви́лка *n.fem.* (9a) fork
*Ви́льсон *n.masc.* (1) Wilson
*Вин *n.masc.* (1) Wien
*ви́рус *n.masc.* (1) virus
*ви́смут *n.masc.* (1) bismuth
*витами́н *n.masc.* (1) vitamin
вихрь *n.masc.* (6) whirlwind
включа́ть (Reg. A) – включи́ть (Reg. B-2) *v.tr.* to switch on
   -ся to switch self on, to be switched on
   в- + ключ key

ВКЛЮЧЕ́НИЕ *n. neuter* (16) (act of) switching on
ВКУС *n. masc.* (1) taste
  В- + КУСА́ТЬ to be biting
ВЛА́ЖНЫЙ *adj.* (17a) moist
ВЛЕЧЁТ *pres. tense third pers. s ing. of* ВЛЕЧЬ
ВЛЕЧЬ *v. tr. imp.* (Irr. G-3 ) to be dragging, to be pulling
ВЛИВА́ТЬ (Reg. A) – ВЛИТЬ ( Irr. F-3) *v. tr.* to pour in
  В- + ЛИТЬ to be pouring
ВЛИЯ́НИЕ *n. neuter* (16) influence
ВЛИЯ́ТЬ – ПОВЛИЯ́ТЬ (на) *v. intr.* (Reg. A) to exert influence (on)
ВМЕ́СТО *prep.* (with gen. ) in place of
  В- + МЕ́СТО place
ВНАЧА́ЛЕ *adv.* at the beginning
  В- + НАЧА́ЛО beginning
ВНЕ *prep.* (with gen. ) outside
ВНЁС *past tense masc. s ing. of* ВНЕСТИ́ (Cf. ВНОСИ́ТЬ)
ВНЕСЕ́НИЕ *n. neuter* (16) introduction, bringing into
ВНЕСЁННЫЙ (17) brought in, introduced (*pas. past part. of*
ВНЕ́ШНИЙ *adj.* (19) outer, external    ВНЕСТИ́; cf. ВНОСИ́ТЬ)
ВНИЗ *adv.* down, downward
ВНИМА́ТЕЛЬНЫЙ *adj.* (17b) attentive
ВНОВЬ *adv.* anew, again
  В- + НО́ВЫЙ new
ВНОСИ́ТЬ (Irr. D-2) – ВНЕСТИ́ (Irr. H-2) *v. tr.* to carry in, to bring in
                                  (Cf. § 382, p. 630)
  В- + НОСИ́ТЬ, НЕСТИ́ to be carrying, to be bringing (Cf. § 381,
ВНУ́ТРЕННИЙ *adj.* (19) inner, internal, interior      p. 626)
ВНУТРИ́ *prep.* (with gen. ) within, inside
*ВНУТРИАТО́МНЫЙ *adj.* (17a) intra-atomic, subatomic
  ВНУТРИ́ within;  *АТО́МНЫЙ atomic
ВО *see* В
ВО-ВТОРЫ́Х *adv.* secondly, in the second place
  ВО- + ВТОРО́Й second
ВОДА́ *n. fem.* (7) water
ВО́ДКА *n. fem.* (9a) vodka
ВО́ДНЫЙ *adj.* (17) aqueous
ВОДОРО́Д *n. masc.* (1) hydrogen
  ВОДА́ water; РОД birth, tribe, genus
ВОДОРО́ДНЫЙ *adj.* (17) hydrogen (*adj.*)
ВОДЯНО́Й *adj.* (18) aqueous, containing or made from water
ВОЕ́ННЫЙ *adj.* (17) warlike, military
  ВОЙНА́ war
ВОЗБУЖДА́ТЬ (Reg. A) – ВОЗБУДИ́ТЬ (Irr. D-2, Д → Ж) to excite
  ВОЗ- + БУДИ́ТЬ to be awakening
ВОЗБУЖДЕ́НИЕ *n. neuter* (16) excitation
ВОЗВРА́ТНЫЙ *adj.* (17) returning (Cf. *next entry*)

возвращать (Reg. A) - возвратить (Irr. D-2, т — щ) to bring back,
  -ся to return                      to give back
  воз- + вращать to be turning
воздействие n. neuter (16) action (on)
  воз- + действовать to be acting
воздух n. masc. (3) air
возле prep. (with gen.) near, around
возможно adv. and pred. adj. possibly, (it is) possible (Cf. § 167,
                      p. 525). (For idiomatic use with the comp.
                      degree of adjs. and advs., Cf. § 351, p. 555)
  воз- + можно (it is) possible
возможно больший fixed expr. the greatest (or most) possible
возможность n. fem. (12) possibility
возможный adj. (17a) possible
возник past tense masc. sing of ВОЗНИКНУТЬ
возникать (Reg. A ) - возникнуть (Irr. J-3 ) v. intr. to arise,
                               to appear
возрастать (Reg. A) - возрасти ( Irr. H-2 ) v. intr. to grow up,
                              to increase
  воз- + расти to be growing
возьмём perf. future tense, first pers. sing of ВЗЯТЬ
вокруг prep. (with gen. ) around
волна n. fem. (7) wave, (shorn) wool
волновой adj. (18) (pertaining to a) wave
волокно n. neuter (13a) fiber
Волопас n. masc. (1) Boötes ("The Herdsman")
вольёт perf. future tense, third pers. sing. of ВЛИВАТЬ -
*вольт n. masc. (1) volt                            ВЛИТЬ
*вольтметр n. masc. (1) voltmeter
*вольтов poss. adj. (§ 361, p. 584) voltaic
*вольфрам n. masc. (1) tungsten
вон adv. away, off
вообще adv. in general, generally
во-первых adv. in the first place, first of all
  во- + первый first
вопрос n. masc. (1) question
воск n. masc. (3) wax
воскресение n. neuter (16) resurrection
воспламенять (Reg. A) - воспламенить (Reg. B-2 ) to ignite, to
                              to enflame
  -ся to become ignited, to burst into flame
  вос- + пламя flame
воспользоваться see пользоваться
восстановлять (Reg. A) - восстановить (Irr. C-2) v. tr. to restore,
  вос- + становиться to become            to reduce (chem.)
восстановление n. neuter (16) (chemical) reduction, restoration
вот interj. here is, there you see or have

во-тре́тьих *adv.* thirdly, in the third place
  в- + тре́тий third
вошла́ *perf.past tense,fem.sing. of* ВХОДИ́ТЬ-ВОЙТИ́
впервы́е *adv.* for the first time, first
  в- + пе́рвый first
впосле́дствии *adv.* subsequently
  в- + по- + след trace, track
впуска́ть (Reg. A) - впусти́ть (Irr. D-2, СТ → Щ) *v.tr.* to let in,
  в- + пуска́ть - пусти́ть to allow, to cause  to cause to enter
впу́стим *see* ВПУСКА́ТЬ - ВПУСТИ́ТЬ
враща́тельный *adj.* (17b) rotatory
враща́ть *v.tr.imperf.* (Reg. A) to be turning, rotating *(tr.)*
  -СЯ to be turning, rotating *(intr.)*
враща́ющийся *act.pres.part.refl. of* враща́ть (Cf. Note 6,
враще́ние *n.neuter* (16) rotation    § 190, p. 289)
вре́дный *adj.* (17a) harmful
вре́мена, вре́мени *see decl. of* вре́мя
вре́мя *n.neuter* (§ 358, p. 575) time
вро́де *prep. (with gen.)* of the nature of, like
  в- + род birth, tribe, genus
вса́сывать ( Reg. A) - всоса́ть ( Reg. B-1) *v.tr.* to suck up
  -СЯ to be sucked up
  в- + соса́ть - пососа́ть to suck
вса́сывание *n.neuter* (16) sucking in (process)
все, всё *cf.* весь
всё вре́мя *fixed expr.* all the time
всё еще́ *fixed expr.* still, even yet
всё равно́ *fixed expr.* all the same
всё э́то *fixed expr.* all this (or these) is (or are)
всегда́ *adv.* always
всего́, всей, всем, всех, вся *cf.* весь
вселе́нная *n.fem.* (17) (Note 17, p. 220) universe
вско́ре *adv.* soon
  в- + ско́рый fast
вскрыва́ть (Reg. A) - вскрыть (Irr. E-4) *v.tr.* to open up, to
  вс- + крыть to be covering                    uncover
всле́дствие *adv. and prep. (with gen.)* as a result of,
  в- + след trace, track              consequently
вспы́шка *n.fem.* (9a) flash, (mild) explosion
  вс- + пы́хать - пыхну́ть to breath deeply, to flare up
вставля́ть (Reg. A) - вста́вить (Irr. C-2) *v.intr.* to place (inside),
  в- + ста́вить - поста́вить to put          to fit in,
встреча́ть (Reg. A) - встре́тить (Irr. D-2) *v.tr.* to encounter,
  -СЯ to be encountered, (*impers.*) to happen    to receive
вступа́ть (Reg. A ) - вступи́ть (Irr. C-2) *v.intr.* to enter into
  в- + ступа́ть - ступи́ть to walk, to stride

всякий *adj.* (21) any, any kind (of), every

  вся *from* весь   whole, all

второй *adj.* (18) second

*вулкан *n.masc.* (1) volcano

*вулканизация *n.fem.* vulcanization

*вулканизировать *v.tr.* (Irr. B-1) to be vulcanizing, to vulcanize

*вулканизированный *pas. past part. of* вулканизировать

входить (Irr. D-2, Д → Ж) - войти (Irr. H-10) *v.intr.* to enter

                                      (Cf. § 382, p. 630)

  в- + ходить, итти to be going (Cf. § 381, p. 626)

вы *pronoun* (§ 136, p. 204) you

выберите *perf. imp. second pers. plu. of* выбирать - выбрать

выбивание *n. neuter* (16) emission, ejection

  вы- + бить - побить to strike

выбирать (Reg. A) - выбрать (Irr. E-1) *v.tr.*   to select,

  вы- + брать   to be taking           to choose, to take

выбранный (17) chosen, selected (*perf. pas. past part. of*

                                       выбирать - выбрать)

выбрасывать (Reg. A) - выбросить (Irr. D-2,   С → Ш) to throw

  вы- + бросать - бросит to throw             out, to eject

выброшенный (17) ejected, thrown out (*perf. pas. past part.*

                      *of* выбрасывать - выбросить)

выведение *n. neuter* (16) leading out (process)

  вы- + водить   to be leading

вывод *n. masc.* (1) (logical) conclusion

выгодный *adj.* (17a) advantageous, useable

  вы- + годный   suitable

выдвигать (Reg. A) - выдвинуть (Irr. J-3) *v.tr.* to move ahead or

  вы- + двигать - двинуть   to move            forward

выдвинутый (17) moved ahead, advanced

выделение *n. neuter* (16) ejection, excretion, evolution

  вы- + делить - разделить   to divide

выделять (Reg. A) - выделить (Reg. B-2) *v.tr.*   to isolate, to

                        remove, to evolve (heat or gas)

  -ся   to be evolved, to separate out

выделяющийся (22) being evolved (*act. pres. part. refl. of*

                      выделять - выделить)

выдестиллировывать - выдестиллировать (Irr. A-1 ) *v.tr.*

  вы- + дестиллировать   to be distilling       to distill off

выдыхать Reg. A) - выдохнуть (Reg B-1) *v.tr.* to exhale

  вы- + дышать - подышать   to breathe

выжимать (Reg. A) - выжать ( Irr. C-4 ) *v.tr.*   to press out,

                          to squeeze out

  вы- + жать - сжать   to press, to squeeze

вызовет *perf. fut. tense third pers. sing. of* вызывать -

                                  вызвать

вызыва́ть (Reg. A) - вы́звать (Irr. E-2) *v.tr.* to call forth
  -ся    to be called forth, to be caused
  вы- + звать - позва́ть    to call
выключа́ть (Reg. A) - вы́ключить (Reg. B-2) *v.tr.* to switch off
  -ся    to switch self off, to be switched off
  вы- + ключ    key
выключе́ние *n.neuter* (16) (act of) switching off
вы́лет *n.masc.* (1) flight from, (act of) flying from
вылета́ть (Reg. A) - вы́лететь (Irr. D-2, Т → Ч) *v.intr.* to
                                    fly out (Cf. (Cf.§ 382, p. 630)
  вы + лета́ть, лете́ть to be flying (Cf. § 381, p. 626)
вылива́ть (Reg. A) - вы́лить (Irr. E-3) *v.tr.* to pour out
  вы- + лить    to be pouring
выпа́ривание *n.neuter* (16) (process of) evaporation
  вы- + пар    vapor
выпа́ривать (Reg. A) - вы́парить (Reg. B-2) *v.tr.* to evaporate off
выпи́сывать (Reg. A) - вы́писать (Irr. D-1, с → ш) *v.tr.*
  вы- + писа́ть - написа́ть    to write        to write out
вы́пишем *perf.fut. tense first pers. plu. of* выпи́сывать -
вы́пуск *n.masc.* (3) exhaust                        вы́писать
выпуска́ть (Reg. A) - вы́пустить (Irr. D-2, ст → щ) *v.tr.* to let
                                    out, to cause to emerge
  -ся    to emerge, to come out
  вы- + пуска́ть - пусти́ть    to start, to cause
выпускно́й *adj.* (18) exhaust
выраба́тывать - вы́работать (Reg. A) *v.tr.* to work out
  вы- + рабо́та    work
вы́работка *n.fem.* (9) processing, working out
выража́ть (Reg. A) - вы́разить (Irr. D-2, з → ж) *v.tr.* to ex-
  -ся    to be expressed, stated                    press, to state
выраже́ние *n.neuter* (16) expression
вы́раженный (17) expressed (*perf. pas. past part. of*
                                    выража́ть - вы́разить)
вы́растут *perf.fut. tense third pers. plu. of* расти́ -
вырыва́ние *n.neuter* (16) tearing out          вы́расти
  рыть - поры́ть to dig
вы́сказанный (17) expressed, stated (*perf. pas. past part.
                          of* выска́зывать - вы́сказать)
выска́зывать (Reg. A) - вы́сказать (Irr. D-1, з → ж) to speak out,
  вы- + сказа́ть to speak                    to state, to express
высо́кий *adj.* (21) high
высокомолекуля́рный *adj.* (17a) high molecular
  высо́кий high; *молекуля́рный molecular
высокоразвитый *adj.* (17) highly developed (Cf. § 286, p. 452)
  высо́кий high; развива́ть-разви́ть to develop
высота́ *n.fem.* (7) height
вы́сший *adj. comp. and superl.* (22) higher, highest (Cf. § 332,
                                    p. 525)

ВЫСЫХА́ТЬ (Reg. A) - ВЫ́СОХНУТЬ (Irr. J-3 ) v.tr. and intr.
  ВЫ- + СУХО́Й dry                      to dry out
ВЫТА́ЛКИВАТЬ - ВЫ́ТОЛКАТЬ (Reg. A) v.tr. to force out
  ВЫ- + ТОЛКА́ТЬ - ТОЛКНУ́ТЬ to push, to shove
ВЫТЕКА́ТЬ (Reg. A) - ВЫ́ТЕЧЬ (Irr. G-3 ) v.intr. to flow out
  ВЫ- + ТЕЧЬ to be flowing                or from
ВЫТЯ́ГИВАТЬ (Reg. A ) - ВЫ́ТЯНУТЬ (Reg. B-1) to pull out, to stretch
  -СЯ to be pulled out, stretched
  ВЫ- + ТЯ́ГА pull
ВЫХОДИ́ТЬ (Irr. D-2, Д→ Ж) ВЫ́ЙТИ (Irr. H-10) v.intr. to go out,
                        to exit (Cf. § 382, p. 630)
  ВЫ- + ХОДИ́ТЬ, ИТТИ́ to be going (Cf. § 381, p. 626)
ВЫЧИСЛЕ́НИЕ n.neuter (16) calculation
  ВЫ- + ЧИСЛО́ number
ВЫЧИСЛЯ́ТЬ (Reg. A) - ВЫ́ЧИСЛИТЬ (Reg. B-2) v.tr. to calculate
ВЫ́ШЕ adv. and adj. undecl. higher, above
ВЫ́ШЕСКА́ЗАННЫЙ adj. (17) above stated, foregoing (Cf. § 286, p. 452)
  ВЫ́ШЕ higher; СКАЗА́ТЬ to speak
ВЫ́ШЕУПОМЯ́НУТЫЙ adj. (17) above mentioned (Cf. § 286, p. 452)
  ВЫ́ШЕ higher; У- + ПОМНИТЬ to be remembering
ВЫШИБА́ТЬ (Reg. A) - ВЫ́ШИБИТЬ (Irr. J-3) v.tr. to break or knock
  -СЯ to be broken or knocked out, ejected    out, to eject
ВЫШИНА́ n.fem. (17) height
ВЫ́ШЕЛ, ВЫ́ШЛИ perf. past tense forms of ВЫХОДИ́ТЬ - ВЫ́ЙТИ
ВЫЯСНЕ́НИЕ, n.neuter (16) elucidation
  ВЫ- + Я́СНЫЙ clear
ВЫЯСНЕННЫЙ (17) indicated, explained (perf. pas. past part. of
                  ВЫЯСНЯ́ТЬ - ВЫ́ЯСНИТЬ)
ВЫЯСНЯ́ТЬ (Reg. A) - ВЫ́ЯСНИТЬ (Reg. B-2) v.tr. to explain
ВЯ́ЗКИЙ adj. (21a) tough, viscous
ВЯ́ЗКОСТЬ n.fem. (12) viscosity


# Г

Г abbr. for ГОД year
Г abbr. for *ГРАММ gram
*ГАЗ n.masc. (1) gas
*ГАЗИФИКА́ЦИЯ n.fem. (11) gasification
*ГА́ЗОВЫЙ adj. (17) gaseous
*ГАЗООБРА́ЗНЫЙ adj. (17a) gaseous
  *ГАЗ gas; О́БРАЗ form, shape
ГАЗОСВЕ́ЧНЫЙ adj. (17) gas-luminous
  *ГАЗ gas; СВЕТ light
ГАЛОИДОВОДОРО́Д n.masc. (1) hydrogen halide
  *ГАЛО́ИД halide; ВОДОРО́Д hydrogen
*ГА́ММА-ЛУЧ n.masc. (3) gamma-ray

гасить - погасить (Irr. D-2) *v.tr.* to extinguish
гг. *abbr. for plural forms of* ГОД year
где *adverb* where
*Гейгер *n.masc.* (1) Geiger
*гексагональный *adj.* (17b) hexagonal
*гелий *n.masc.* (5) helium
*Гемфри *n.masc.* (*undecl.* § 363, p. 587) Humphrey
*геологический *adj.* (20) geological
*геология *n.fem.* (11) geology
*геометрия *n.fem.* (11) geometry
*герметический *adj.* (20) hermetic
*гигроскопический *adj.* (21) hygroscopic
*гидроокись *n.fem.* (12) hydroxide, hydrated oxide
*гипотеза *n.fem.* (7) hypothesis
глава *n.fem.* (7) chapter
главный *adj.* (17) principal, main, important
главным образом *fixed expr.* for the most part, principally
глаз *n.masc.* ( § 359, p. 576 ) eye　　　(Cf. § 98, p. 141)
глинистый *adj.* (17) clayey
глинозём *n.masc.* (1) alumina, aluminum oxide
　　глина clay;　земля earth
*глицерин *n.masc.* (1) glycerol
глубже *pred. comp. adj. and adv.* (*undecl.* § 334, p. 527)
глубокий *adj.* (21) deep, far reaching　　　　　　　deeper
глубочайший *adj.superl.* (22) deepest (Cf. § 346, p. 547)
гнать - погнать ( Irr. E-2 ) *v.tr.* to chase, to drive
гнилушек *gen.plu. of* ГНИЛУШКА (Cf. §§ 380-382, pp. 626-635)
гнилушка *n.fem.* (9) rotten wood
　　гнилой rotten
говорить (Reg. B-2)- сказать (Irr. D-1,　з → Ж) *v.intr.*
год *n.masc.* (1) year　　　　　　　　　　to speak, to say
*голландский *adj.* (21) Dutch
головка *n.fem.* (9a) little head
головок *gen.plural of* ГОЛОВКА
голубь *n.fem.* (12) pigeon, dove
голый *adj.* (17) bare, barren
*Гольдштейн *n.masc.* (1) Goldstein
*гомолог *n.masc.* (1) homolog
*Гондурас *n.masc.* (1) Honduras
гонят *pres. tense third pers.plu. of* ГНАТЬ-ПОГНАТЬ
гораздо *adv.* much, enormously
горелка *n.fem.* (9a) burner
　　гореть - сгореть to burn
горение *n.neuter* (16) combustion
гореть - сгореть (Reg. B-2) *v.intr.* to burn
*гормон *n.masc.* (1) hormone
горная порода *fixed expr.* mineral

го́рный *adj.* (17) mountainous, pertaining to mining
    гора́ mountain
го́род *n.masc.* (26 *gen. plu.* городо́в) city
горю́чий *adj.* (21), combustible, fuel
    горе́ть - сгоре́ть to burn
горя́чий *adj.* (21) hot, heated
*гради́ент *n.masc.* (1) gradient
гра́дус *n.masc.* (1) degree
*грамм *n.masc.* (1) gram
*грани́т *n.masc.* (1) granite
грань *n.fem.* (12) face (of crystal)
*грек, *n.masc.* (3) Greek
*Гре́ция *n.fem.* (11) Greece
*гре́ческий *adj.* (21) Greek
грома́дный *adj.* (17a) enormous
*гру́ппа *n.fem.* (7) group
*гуано́ *n.neuter* (*undecl.* § 363, p. 587) guano
густе́ть - загусте́ть (Reg. A) *v.intr.* to become thick or viscous
густо́й *adj.* (18) thick, viscous


# Д

дава́ть (Irr. B) - дать (Irr. I-3) *v.tr.* to give, to permit
дави́ть (на) (Irr. C-1) *v.intr.* to be exerting pressure (on)
давле́ние *n.neuter* (16) pressure
давно́ *adv.* long ago
даёт *pres. tense third pers.sing* of дава́ть - дать
да́же *adv.* even, in fact
да́йте *perf.imp. second pers.plu.* of дава́ть - дать
да́лее *pred. adj. comp. and adv.* (*undecl.* § 333, p. 527)
                                                              further
далёкий *adj.* (21) distant
далеко́ *adv.* distantly
дальне́йший *adj.* (22) further (Cf. Footnote 1, p. 549)
*Да́льтон *n.masc.* (1) Dalton
да́льше *adv.comp.* further, more distant
да́нные *perf. pas. past part.* used as *noun* (§ 245, p. 389) data
да́нный (17) given (*perf. pas. past part.* of дава́ть - дать)
даст *perf. future tense third pers.sing.* of дава́ть-
да́тский *adj.* (21) Danish                                    дать
дать *see* дава́ть
даю́т *pres. tense third pers. plu.* of дава́ть - дать
два *numeral* (§ 370, p. 600) two
двадца́тый *numeral adj.* (17) twentieth
два́жды *adv.* twice
две *see* два
дверь *n.fem.* (12) door

дви́гатель *n.masc.* (6) prime mover, motor

дви́гать (Irr. D-1, г → ж) - дви́нуть (Reg. B-1) *v.tr.* to move
  -ся to be moved, to move (*intr.*)

движе́ние *n.neuter* (16) motion

дви́жется *pres. tense third pers.plu.refl. of* дви́гать
                                                дви́нуть

дви́жется, дви́жутся *pres. tense third pers.sing·andplu.*
                    *refl. of* дви́гать - дви́нуть

дви́жущий (22) moving, motive (*adj.*) (*act. pres. part., of*
                                        дви́гать - дви́нуть)

  -ся / undergoing motion, moving (Cf. Note 13, p. 261)

двойно́й *adj.* (18) double

двух *see* два

двухзаряжённый *adj.* (17) doubly charged (Cf. § 286, p. 452)
  два two; заря́д charge (elec.)

двухле́тний *adj.* (19) two year (old), biannual
  два two; ле́то summer

де́йствие *n.neuter* (16) action

действи́тельно *adv.* actually

действи́тельность *n.fem.* (12) actuality

де́йствовать - поде́йствовать (на ) (Irr. A-1)*v.intr.*
                                        to act (on)

де́йствует *pres. tense third pers.sing. of* де́йствовать -
                                        поде́йствовать

де́йствующий (22) acting (*act. pres. part. of* де́йствовать -
                                        поде́йствовать)

де́лать - сде́лать (Reg. A) *v.tr.* to make, to do
  -ся to be made, to become

де́лать вы́вод *fixed expr.* to draw (a) (the) conclusion

дели́ть - раздели́ть (Reg. B-2)*v.tr.* to divide
  -ся  to be divided

де́ло *n.neuter* (13) thing, affair, business

день *n.masc.* (6a) day

де́рево *n.neuter* (*declined like* крыло́, §359,p.578) wood,tree

дере́вьев *gen.plu. of* де́рево

деревя́нный *adj.* (17) wooden

держа́ть - подержа́ть *v.tr.* (Reg. B-2) to hold

*дерматоло́гия *n.fem.* (11) dermatology

деся́тки *nom. and acc. plural of* деся́ток

деся́тков *gen. plural of* деся́ток

деся́ток *n.masc.* (3a) ten, group of ten (Cf. § 369, p. 598, Foot-
деся́тый *adj.* (17) tenth                              note 1)

*дета́ль *n.fem.* (12) detail

*дета́льно *adv.* in detail

*детона́ция *n.fem.* (11) detonation

*дефе́кт *n.masc.* (1) defect

*дефекти́вный *adj.* (17a) defective, inadequate

*деформи́ровать *v.tr. perf. and imperf.* (Irr. A-1) to be deforming, to deform

деше́вый *adj.* (17) cheap

*Дж. *used to represent initial J or G in French or English names*

*диазоти́ровать *v.tr. perf. and imperf.* (Irr. A-1) to be diazotizing, to diazotize

*диа́метр *n.masc.* (1) diameter

*Ди́зель *n.masc.* (6) Diesel

*динами́ческий *adj.* (21) dynamic

*динамома́шина (7) dynamo (machine)

*дипо́льный *adj.* (17b) dipole

*диск *n.masc.* (1) disk

*диссерта́ция *n.fem.* (11) dissertation

*диссоциа́ция *n.fem.* (11) dissociation

*диэлектри́ческий *adj.* (21) dielectric

*диэта *n.fem.* (7) diet

длина́ *n.fem.* (7) length

для *prep.* (with gen.) for

для того́ чтобы *fixed expr.* in order to (Cf. § 315, p. 495)

днём *instr.sing* of день

дни *nom. and acc. plural of* день

до *prep.* (with gen.) up to, to, until

до сих пор *fixed expr.* up till now (Cf. § 390, p. 650)

доба́вленный (17) added (*perf. pas. past part. of* добавля́ть – доба́вить)

добавля́ть (Reg. A) – доба́вить (Irr. C-2) to add

добела́ *adv.* to white (heat)

до- + бе́лый white

добыва́ние *n.neuter* (16) obtaining, production extraction

добыва́ть (Reg. A) – добы́ть (Irr. I-4) *v.tr.* to achieve, to acquire

-ся to be achieved, acquired, produced

до- + быть to be

добы́ча *n.fem.* (9 -instr.sing. добы́чей) yield, production

дойдёт *perf. future tense third pers. sing. of* доходи́ть – дойти́

доказа́тельство *n.neuter* (13) indication

дока́зывать (Reg. A) – доказа́ть (Irr. D-1,3 → Ж) *v.tr.* to prove

до- + казать to show

докрасна́ *adv.* to red heat

до- + кра́сный red

до́лгий *adj.* (21a) long

долета́ть (Reg. A) – долете́ть (Irr. D-2,Т → Ч) *v.tr.* to fly up to (Cf. § 382, p. 630)

до- + лета́ть, лете́ть to be flying (Cf. § 381, p. 626)

до́лжно *pred.adj.* (it is) necessary (Cf. § 167, p. 255)

до́лжно быть *fixed expr.* ought to be

до́лжный *adj.* (17a) needed, required, owed

до́ля, *n.fem.* (10 *gen.plu.* доле́й) share, fraction

доро́га, *n.fem.* (9) road

дорого́й *adj.* (20) expensive, dear

доставля́ть (Reg. A) - доста́вить (Irr. C-1) *v.tr.* to supply, to furnish

доста́точно *adv.* rather, quite

доста́точный *adj.* (17a) sufficient

достига́ть (Reg. A) - дости́гнуть (Irr. J-3) *v.tr.* (*with gen.*) to attain, to achieve, to reach

-ся, to be attained, achieved, arrived at

дости́гшее (22) having achieved (*perf. act. past part. of* достига́ть - дости́гнуть)

достиже́ние *n.neuter* (16) achievement

до́ступ *n.masc.* (1) entrance, acess

досту́пный *adj.* (17a) available, accessible

доходи́ть (Irr. D-2, д → ж) - дойти́ (Irr. H-10) *v.tr.* to go up to (Cf. § 382, p. 630)

до- + ходи́ть, итти́ to be going (Cf. § 381, p. 626)

драгоце́нный *adj.* (17a) precious

древе́сный *adj.* (17) pertaining to or made from wood, wood (*adj.*)

древе́сный у́голь *fixed expr.* charcoal

дре́вний *adj.* (19 _*pred. forms* дре́вен, дре́вня, -е, -и) ancient

дре́вность *n.fem.* (12) antiquity

друго́й *adj.* (20) other

друг к дру́гу *fixed expr.* one to another

друг от дру́га *fixed expr.* one from another

друг с дру́гом *fixed expr.* one with another

*дубле́т *n.masc.* (1) doublet

дуга́ *n.fem.* (9) arc

дугово́й *adj.* (18) (pertaining to an) arc

ду́мать - поду́мать (O) (Reg. A-1) *v.intr.* to think (about)

*Дэ́ви *n.masc.* (*undecl.* § 363, p. 587) Davy

## Е

евкли́довый *adj.* (17) Euclidean

его́ *pronoun and poss.* him, his (Cf. ОН, § 136, p. 204, also § 138, p. 207)

еди́м *pres.tense first pers.plu.* of есть to be eating

едини́ца (8) unit

е́дкий *adj.* (21a) caustic, sharp, biting

е́дкий на́тр *fixed expr.* caustic soda

е́дкое ка́ли *fixed expr.* caustic potash

её *pronoun and poss.* her (Cf. ОН § 136, p. 204, also § 138, p. 207)

ежего́дно *adv.* annually

еже- + год year

ежедне́вно *adv.* daily, every day

еже- + день day

ему́ *dat.sing.masc. and neuter of* OH
е́сли *conj.* if
есть (Irr. I-1 ) *imperf. v.tr.* to be eating
есть *third pers. pres. tense form of* БЫТЬ is or are (in
                                                fact) (Cf. § 122, p. 180)
е́хать – пое́хать (Irr. е́ду, е́дешь, etc.)  *v.intr.* to travel
ещё *adv.,* even, still, also, furthermore
ещё одно́ *fixed expr.* yet another
ею *instr.sing.fem. of* OH

# Ж

же, ж *conj. adv.* however, but (Cf. Note 4, § 55, p. 75; § 144,
жела́ть – пожела́ть (Reg. A) *v.tr.* to wish, to desire       p. 215)
желе́зный *adj.* (17) (made of or containing) iron, iron (*adj.*) ferric
желе́зо *n.neuter* (13) iron
железоалюми́ниевый *adj.* (17) iron-aluminum
железнодоро́жный *adj.* (17) pertaining to a railroad or
    желе́зо iron; доро́га road                       railroading
желтова́тый *adj.* (17) yellowish
жёлтый *adj.* (17) yellow
жи́дкий *adj.* (21a) liquid (adj.)
жи́дкость *n.fem.* (12) liquid
жи́зненный *adj.* (17 – *pred. masc. sing.* жи́знен, § 356,
жизнь *n.fem.* (12) life                    p. 507) pertaining to life
жир *n.masc.,* (1) fat
жить – пожи́ть (Irr. C-3) *v.intr.* to live
*Жолио́ *n.masc.* (*undecl.* § 363, p. 587) Joliot
живо́й *adj.* (18) alive, living
живо́тный *adj.* (17) animal (*For use of neuter forms as noun
    meaning* animal, *see* Note 8, § 62, p. 86 and § 392, p. 652)
живу́т *pres. tense third pers. plu. of* ЖИТЬ
*журна́л *n.masc.* (1) journal

# З

за *prep.* (*with acc.*) toward, for, during, as (*with instr.*)
за счёт *fixed expr.* at the expense                    beyond
заболева́ние *n.neuter* (16) sickness
завёрнутый (17) wrapped, (*perf. past part. of* завёртывать –
                                    заверну́ть, to wrap)
зави́сеть (от) (Reg. B-2) *imp.v.intr.* to be dependent (on)
зави́симость *n.fem.* (12) dependence
заво́д *n.masc.* (1) factory, plant (manufacturing establishment)

загора́ть (Reg. A) - загоре́ть (Reg. B-2) *v. intr.* to become
  -ся to catch fire, become ignited                sunburned
задо́хлись *perf. past tense plu.* of задыха́ться -
                                      задохну́ться
заду́мывать - заду́мать (Reg. A) *v. tr.* to conceive, to plan,
  -ся to think over, to ponder                to imagine
  за- + ду́мать - поду́мать, to think
заду́ть *v. intr. perf.* (Reg. A) to start blowing
зажéчь *see* зажига́ть

зажгу́ *perf. future tense first pers. sing.* of заживать -
                                      зажéчь
зажжётся *perf. future tense third pers. sing. refl.* of
                                      зажига́ть - зажéчь
зажига́ть (Reg. A) - зажéчь (Irr. G-2) *v. tr.* to set on fire,
  -ся to be ignited, set on fire                to ignite
  за- + жечь to be burning     (*tr.*)
*заинтересова́ть *see* *интересова́ть
*закато́дный *adj.* (17) anticathodic (ray)
за́кись *n. fem.* (12) oxide, especially lower oxide (Cf. о́кисел)
зако́н *n. masc.* (1) law
зако́н де́йствия масс *fixed expr.* law of mass action
закро́ем *perf. future tense first pers. plu.* of закрыва́ть -
                                      закры́ть
закрыва́ть (Reg. A) - закры́ть (Irr. E-4) *v. tr.* to cover up,
  за- + крыть - покры́ть to cover          to close, to shut
закры́тый (17) covered, closed, shut (*perf. pas., past part.*
                                      of закрыва́ть - закры́ть)
за́лежь *n. fem.* (12) (mineral) deposit
заменя́ть (Reg. A) - замени́ть (Reg. B-2) *v. tr.* to replace
  за- + меня́ть - поменя́ть to exchange
замеча́ть (Reg. A) - заме́тить (Irr. D-2, Т → Ч) *v. tr.*
                          to observe, to mark, to note
заме́ченный (17) noted, observed (*perf. pas. past part.,* of
                                      замеча́ть - заме́тить)
замеща́ть (Reg. A) - замести́ть (Irr. D-2, СТ → Щ) *v. tr.*
  -ся to be replaced                to replace, to occupy
  за- + ме́сто place
замеще́ние *n. neuter* (16) replacement
занима́ть (Reg. A) - заня́ть (Irr. F-5) *v. tr.* to occupy, to take,
  -ся to occupy self, to be engaged (in)          to assume
запа́с *n. masc.* (1) store, supply, reserve
зара́нее *adv.* before hand
  за- + ра́нее earlier, previously
зарожда́ть (Reg. A) - зароди́ть (Irr. D-2, Д → Ж) *v. tr.*
                          to bring forth, to bear, to produce
  -ся to be born, to originate
  за- + род birth, tribe genus

заря́д *n.masc.* (1) charge (electrical or explosive)
заряжа́ть (Reg. A) - заряди́ть (Irr. D-2, Д → Ж ) *v.tr.*
         to charge (electricity), to load (ammunition, gun)
заряжённый (17) charged (electricity) loaded (ammunition, gun)
         (*perf. pas. past part. of* заряжа́ть - заряди́ть)
заса́сывать (Reg. A) - засоса́ть (Reg. B-1) *v.tr.* to suck into
  -ся   to be sucked into
    за- + соса́ть - пососа́ть  to suck
заставля́ть (Reg. A) - заста́вить (Irr. C-2) *v.tr.*  to compel,
    за- + ста́вить - поста́вить  to put          to force
засыпа́ть (Reg. A) - засы́пать (Irr. C-1) *v.tr.* to cover, to
    за- + сы́пать - посы́пать  to strew         bury
зате́м *adv.* thereafter
    за- + тем *instr.sing. of* ТОТ
затра́чивать (Reg. A) - затра́тить (Irr. D-2, Т → Ч ) *v.tr.*
            to use up, to dissipate
    за- + тра́та  utilization, wasting
защи́тный *adj.* (17) protective
    за- + ЩИТ shield
заявля́ть (Reg. A) - заяви́ть (Irr. C-2) to announce, to apply
    за- + явля́ть - яви́ть  to show         (for patent)
звезда́ *n.fem.* (7) star
звук *n.masc.* (3) sound
здесь *adv.* here
зелёный *adj.* (17) green
земли́стый *adj.* (17) earthy
земля́ *n.fem.* (10) earth
земно́й *adj.* (18) terrestrial
зёрен *gen. plu. of* зёрно
зерка́льный *adj.* (17) mirror
зёрно *n.neuter* (13b) grain
злак *n.masc.* (3) grass, (*plu.*) cereals
знак *n.masc.* (3) sign
знако́мить - познако́мить (Irr.C-2) *v.tr.* to make acquainted
  -ся   to become acquainted
знать (Reg. A) *v.tr.* to be knowing
значе́ние *n.neuter* (16) significance, meaning, importance
зна́чить (Reg. B-2) *v.intr. imperf.* to be signifying, meaning
значи́тельно *adv.* considerably
значи́тельный *adj.* (17b) considerable
зола́ *n.fem.* (7) ash
зо́лото *n.neuter* (13) gold
золотоно́сный *adj.* (17a) gold bearing
    зо́лото gold;  носи́ть to be carrying
*зо́на *n.fem.* (7) zone
зре́ние *n.neuter* (16) view

зри́тельный *adj.* (17) viewing
зубно́й *adj.* (18) pertaining to tooth or teeth (persons or
    зуб, tooth                                     animals)
зубча́тый *adj.* (17) pertaining to tooth or teeth (gear or other
    зубча́тое колесо́ *fixed expr.* gear            machine part)

## И

И *conj. and adv.* and, also, even (Cf. § 61, p. 84)
И--- и--- *fixed expr.* both--- and---
и пр., и про́чее *fixed expr.* and so on
и т.д.; и так да́лее *fixed expr.* and so forth
игла́ *n.fem.* (7) needle
игра́ть – сыгра́ть (Reg. A) *v.tr. and intr.* to play
*идеа́льный *adj.* (17b) ideal
*идентифици́ровать (Irr. A-1)*v.tr. perf. and imperf.* to be
                                              identifying
идёт, иду́т *pres. tense third pers. sing. and plu. of*
                        итти́ – пойти́ (Cf. § 320, p. 206)
из *prep.* (*with gen.*) from, of, away from
избы́тке *prep.sing. of* избы́ток
избы́тком *instr. sing. of* избы́ток
избы́ток *n.masc.* (3a) excess
изверже́ние *n.neuter* (3a) ejection
изве́стно *pred. adj.* known, (is) (are) known (Cf. § 167, p. 255)
изве́стный *adj.* (17a) known
известня́к *n.masc.* (3) limestone
извлёк *perf.past tense masc. sing. of* извлека́ть –
                                                извле́чь
извлека́ть (Reg. A) – извле́чь (Irr. G-3)*v.tr.* to extract,
                                              to pull out
    из- + влечь to be pulling, dragging
изготовле́ние *n.neuter* (16) preparation
    из- + гото́вый ready
изготовля́ть (Reg. A) – изгото́вить (Irr. C-2)*v.tr.* to prepare,
    -ся to be prepared, made                    to manufacture
излечивать (Reg. A) – излечи́ть (Reg. B-2) *v.tr.* to cure
    из- + лечи́ть – полечи́ть to treat, to cure      (completely)
излуча́ть (Reg. A) – излучи́ть (Reg. B-2) *v.tr.* to radiate
    -ся to be radiated
    из- + луч ray
излуче́ние *n.neuter* (16) radiation
измене́ние *n.neuter* (16) change, variation
    из- + ме́на exchange

изменять (Reg. A) – изменить (Reg. B-2) *v.tr.* to change (*tr.*)

  –ся to undergo change, to be changed, to change (*intr.*)

измерение *n.neuter* (16) measurement

  из- + мера measure

измерять (Reg. A) – измерить (Reg. B-2) *v.tr.* to measure

изо *see* из

изобрёл *perf.past tense masc.sing. of* изобретать – изобрести

изобретать (Reg. A) – изобрести (Irr. H-3) *v.tr.* to invent

  изо- + брести – побрести to wander

изобретение *n.neuter* (16) invention

изобретённый (17) invented (*perf. pas. past part. of* изобретать – изобрести)

*изолировать (Irr. B-1) *v.tr. perf. and imperf.* to be isolating, to isolate

*изолятор *n.masc.* (1) insulator

*изомер *n.masc.* (1) isomer

*изомеризация *n.fem.* (11) isomerization

*изомерия *n.fem.* (11) isomerism

*изопрен *n.masc.* (1) isoprene

*изотермический *adj.* (21) isothermal

*изотоп *n.masc.* (1) isotop

изучать (Reg. A) – изучить (Reg. B-2) *v.tr.* to study out, to learn

  –ся to be studied out, learned

  из- + учение learning

изучение *n.neuter* (16) study, investigation

изученный (17) studied, investigated (*perf. pas. past part of* изучать – изучить)

изыскание *n.neuter* (16) investigation

  из- + искать – поискать to seek

или *conj.* or

или--- или--- *fixed expr.* either--- or---

им *instr.sing.masc. and neuter and dat. plu. of* он

именно *adv.* namely

  имя name

иметь (Reg. A) *v.tr. imperf.* to have

  –ся to exist, to be on hand

*импеданц *n.masc.* (3) impedance

*импульс *n.masc.* (3) impulse

*индивид *n.masc.* (1) individual

*инертность *n.fem.* (12) inertness

*инертный *adj.* (17a) inert

иногда *adv.* sometimes

иной *adj.* (18) other, different

*институт *n.masc.* (1) institute

*интенсивность *n.fem.* (12) intensity

*интервал *n.masc.* (1) interval

*интерес *n.masc.* (1) interest

*интере́сный *adj.* (17a) interesting
*интересова́ть - *заитересова́ть (Irr. A-1)*v. tr.* to interest
 -СЯ  to become interested
*йо́д *n. masc.* (1)  iodine
*ио́н *n. masc.* (1)  ion
*иониза́ция *n. fem.* (11) ionization
*иониза́ционный *adj.* (17) ionization (adj.)
*иониэи́ровать (Irr. A-1)*v. tr.* *perf. and imperf.* to be ioniz-
*иониэи́руясь *pres. ger. refl.* of *иониэи́ровать   ing, to ionize
иска́ть - поиска́ть (Irr. D-1, СК → Ш) *v. tr.* to seek
исключе́ние *n. neuter* (16) exclusion
 из- + ключ key
исключи́тельно *adv.* extremely, exclusively
и́скра *n. fem.* (9) spark
иску́ственно *adv.* artificially
иску́сственный *adj.* (17 - *pred. masc. sing.* иску́ствен § 356,
испаре́ние *n. neuter* (16) evaporation          p. 570) artificial
 ис- + пар vapor
испаря́ть (Reg. A) - испари́ть (Reg. B-2) *v. tr.* to evaporate (*tr.*)
 -СЯ to undergo evaporation, to evaporate (*intr.*)
ис-под *prep. with gen.* from, out of
испо́льзование *n. neuter* (16) utilization
 из- + поле́зный useful
испо́льзованный (17) utilized, used (*pas. past part.* of
                                  ИСПОЛЬЗОВАТЬ)
испо́льзовать (Irr. A-1) *v. tr.* *perf. and imperf.* to utilize
исправле́ние *n. neuter* (16) correction
 из- + пра́во right
исправля́ть (Reg. A) - испра́вить (Irr. C-2) *v. tr.* to correct,
испуска́ние *n. neuter* (16) emission, radiation        to control
испуска́ть (Reg. A) - испусти́ть (Irr. D-2, СТ → Щ) *v. tr.*
 -СЯ to be emitted, radiated              to emit, to radiate
 ис- + пуска́ть - пусти́ть to start, to cause
испы́тывать - испыта́ть (Reg. A) *v. tr.* to experience, to test
иссле́дование *n. neuter* (16) investigation, research
 ис- + след trace, track
иссле́дованный (17) investigated (*pas. past part. of*
                                  of иссле́довать)
иссле́дователь *n. masc.* (6) investigator
иссле́довать (Irr. A-1)*v. tr.* *perf. and imperf.* to investigate
*истори́ческий *adj.* (21) historical
*исто́рия *n. fem.* (11) history
исто́чник *n. masc.* (3) source, spring (of water)
 ис- + ТОК current
исхо́дный *adj.* (17) starting, initial
 ис- + ходи́ть to be going

ИСХОДИ́ТЬ (Irr. D-2, д → ж) - ИЗОЙТИ́ (Irr. H-10) *v. intr.*
to depart, (Cf. § 381, p. 626)
ИС- + ХОДИ́ТЬ, ИТТИ́ to be going (Cf. § 381, p. 626)
ИСЧЕЗА́ТЬ (Reg. A) - ИСЧЕ́ЗНУТЬ (Irr. I-3) (ИЗ or С) *v. intr.*
ИСЧЕЗА́ЮЩЕ *adv.* vanishingly (Cf. § 287, p. 455)   to vanish (from)
ИТА́К *adv.* in fact
*ИТАЛЬЯ́НСКИЙ *adj.* (21) Italian
ИТТИ́ - ПОЙТИ́ (Irr. H-10) *v. intr. def.* to go (Cf. §§ 380-382,
pp. 626-635)
ИХ *pronoun and poss.* them, their (Cf. § 136, p. 204, also § 138,
*ИЮ́ЛЬ *n. masc.* (6) July                                 p. 207)


# К


К (КО) *prep.* (*with dat.*) to
*КАБИ́НА *n. fem.* (7) cabin
КА́ЖДЫЙ *adj.* (17) each, every
КА́ЖУЩИЙСЯ (22) appearing, seeming (*act. pres. part. refl.* of
КАЗА́ТЬ; Cf. Footnote 1, p. 425)
КАЗА́ТЬ (Irr. D-1, з → ш) *v. tr. imperf.* to show
-СЯ to appear, to seem
КАК *adv., conj.* how, as
КАК БЫ *fixed expr.* as it were (Cf. § 316, p. 496)
КАК И *fixed expr.* as also, as well as
КАК---, ТАК И--- *fixed expr.* both--- and also---
КАК ТО́ЛЬКО *fixed expr.* as soon as
КАКО́Й *adj. pronoun* (19) what, what kind of
КАКО́Й-ЛИБО *pronoun, indefinite* any, any you please (Cf.
§ 154, p. 236)
КАКО́Й-НИБУДЬ *pronoun, indefinite* any, any you please
(Cf. § 154, p. 236)
КАКО́Й-ТО *pronoun, indefinite* some sort of (Cf. § 154, p. 236)
КАЛИ *see* Е́ДКОЕ КА́ЛИ
*КАЛИБРОВА́ТЬ (Irr. A-1) *v. tr. perf. and imperf.* to be
calibrating, to calibrate
*КА́ЛИЙ *n. masc.* (5) potassium
*КАЛО́РИЯ *n. fem.* (11) calory
*КА́ЛЬЦИЙ *n. masc.* (5) calcium
КАМЕНИ́СТЫЙ *adj.* (17) stony, rocky
КА́МЕННЫЙ *adj.* (17) rocky, pertaining to stones or rocks,
resembling stones or rocks
КА́МЕННЫЙ У́ГОЛЬ *fixed expr.* coal (Cf. Note 4, p. 86)
КА́МЕНЬ *n. masc.* (6a) stone
*КА́МЕРА *n. fem.* (7) chamber

*камфора́ *n.fem.* (7) camphor
*кана́л *n.masc.* (1) canal
*кана́ловый *adj.* (17) canal　(*adj. in the expr.* кана́ловый
*каоли́н *n.masc.* (1) kaolin　　　　　　　　　　лу́ч canal ray)
*капилля́р *n.masc.* (1) capillary
*капилля́рный *adj.* (17a) capillary (*adj.*)
*карби́д *n.masc.* (1) carbide
*ка́рта *n.fem.* (7) map, chart
*Каспи́йский *adj.* (21) Caspian
*катализа́тор *n.masc.* (1) catalyst
*каталити́ческий *adj.* (21) catalytic
*катего́рия *n.fem.* (11) category
*катио́н *n.masc.* (1) cation
*като́д *n.masc.* (1) cathode
*като́дный *adj.* (17) cathode (*adj.*)
*Ка́улес *n.masc.* (1) Cowles
*каучу́к *n.masc.* (3) rubber (unvulcanized)
ка́чественный *adj.* (17) qualitative
ка́чество *n.neuter* (13) quality
в ка́честве *fixed expr.* (*with gen.*) in quality (of), as
ка́шица *n.fem.* (8) slurry
*квадра́т *n.masc.* (1) second power, square
*квадра́тный *adj.* (17) quadratic
*квант *n.masc.* (1) quantum
*квантовомехани́ческий *adj.* (21) quantum mechanical
*ква́нтовый *adj.* (17) quantum
*ква́рцевый *adj.* (17) quartz (adj.)
*квазистаби́льный *adj.* (17a) quasistable
квасцы́ *n.* (*plu. forms only* § 359, p. 579) alum
*Ке́львин *n.masc.* (1) Kelvin
*Ке́нсингтон *n.masc.* (1) Kensington
*кероси́н *n.masc.* (1) kerosene
*килогра́мм *n.masc.* (1) kilogram
*киломе́тр *n.masc.* (1) kilometer
*кинети́ческий *adj.* (21) kinetic
кипе́ние *n.neuter* (16) (process of) boiling
кипе́ть (Irr. C-2) *v.intr. imperf.* to be boiling
кипяти́льник *n.masc.* (3) (little) boiler
кислоро́д *n.masc.* (1) oxygen
　ки́слый sour, acidic;　род birth, tribe, genus
кислота́ *n.fem.* (7) acid
кисло́тный *adj.* (17) acidic
ки́слый *adj.* (17a) sour, acidic
кла́пан *n.masc.* (1) valve
*класс *n.masc.* (1) class
*класси́ческий *adj.* (21) classical

\*кобальт *n.masc.* (1) cobalt

когда *conj.* when

когда-нибудь *adv.* somewhere, anywhere

колба *n.fem.* (7) flask, glass envelope

колебать - поколебать (Irr. C-1) *v.tr.* to shake

  -ся to vibrate, to swing, to fluctuate

колеблющийся (22) vibrating (*act. pres. part. refl. of* колебать - поколебать)

колесо *n.neuter* (13) wheel

количество *n.neuter* (13) quantity, number

\*колледж *n.masc.* (3) (*instr. sing.* \*колледжем, *gen. plu.* \*колледжей) college

\*коллоид *n.masc.* (1) colloid

\*коллоидальный *adj.* (17b) colloidal

кольцо *n.neuter* (13b) ring

\*комета *n.fem.* (7) comet

\*коммерческий *adj.* (21) commercial

\*коммутатор *n.masc.* (1) commutator

комнатный *adj.* (17) room (*adj.*)

  комната room (*noun*)

комочек *n.masc.* (3a) (small) lump, bit

  комок lump

комочки *nom. and acc.plu. of* комочек

\*комплекс *n.masc.* (1) complex

\*компонент *n.masc.* (1) component

\*конденсатор *n.masc.* (1) condenser

конец *n.masc.* (1a) end

конечный *adj.* (17) end, final

\*константа *n.fem.* (7) constant

\*конструировать - \*сконструировать (Irr. A-1) *v.tr.* to construct

\*конструкционный (17) pertaining to construction

\*конструкция *n.fem.* (11) construction, design

конца *gen.sing. of* конец

конце *prep.sing. of* конец

\*концентрация *n.fem.* (11) concentration

\*концентрированный (17) concentrated (*imperf. pas. past part of following verb*)

\*концентрировать - \*сконцентрировать (Irr. A-1) *v.tr.* to concentrate

концов *gen. plu. of* конец

концу *dat.sing. of* конец

\*координата *n.fem.* (7) coordinate

\*координатный pertaining to coordinates

\*кора *n.fem.* (7) crust, rind

корабль *n.fem.* (6) ship

корень *n.masc.* (6a) root

корне *prep.sing. of* корень

ко́рни *nom. and acc. plu. of* ко́рень
ко́рнями *instr. plu. of* ко́рень
коро́ва *n.fem.* (7) cow
коро́вий *poss.adj.* (§ 360, p. 581) cow's
коро́вье ма́сло butter
коро́ткий *adj.* (21) short
коро́че *pred. comp. adj. (undecl.) and adv.* shorter
*корро́зия (11) corrosion
*косми́ческий *adj.* (21) cosmic
коте́л *n.masc.* (1a) kettle, boiler
котла́ *gen.sing of* коте́л
котла́ми *instr. plu. of* коте́л
котла́х *prep. plu. of* коте́л
кото́рый *pronoun* (17) which
*коэффицие́нт *n.masc.* (1) coefficient
край *n.masc.* (4) edge, border, locality
кран *n.masc.* (1) cock (gas or water)
краси́тель *n.masc.* (6) dyestuff
кра́ска *n.fem.* (9a) color, dye, paint
кра́сный *adj.* (17a) red
кра́сок *gen.plu. of* кра́ска
кра́тный *adj.* (17a) multiple
кра́тче *pred. comp. adj. (undecl.) and adv.* shorter
кра́тче всех *pred. supl. adj. (undecl.) and adv.* shortest
кривоши́п *n.masc.* (1) crankshaft
кривоши́пный *adj.* (17) (pertaining to) crank or crankshaft
*криста́лл *n.masc.* (1) crystal
*кристаллиза́ция (11) crystallization
*кристаллизова́ть (Irr. A-1) *v.tr. imperf.* to be crystallizing
   -ся to be crystallizing (*intr.*)        (*tr.*)
*кристаллизу́ет, *кристаллизу́ют *pres. tense third person*
                   *sing. and plu. of* *кристаллизова́ть
*кристалли́ческий *adj.* (21) crystalline
*кристаллогра́фия *n.fem.* (11) crystallography
*критикова́ть - *раскритикова́ть (Irr. A-1) *v.tr.* to criticize
*крити́ческий *adj.* (21) critical
кро́ме *prep. (with gen.)* aside from
кро́ме того́ *fixed expr.* aside from this
круговоро́т *n.masc.* (1) cycle
   круг circular area;    во́рот turn
круже́ние *n.neuter* (1) rotation
кру́пный *adj.* (17a) large
крутя́щийся (22) whirling, turning (*act. pres. part. refl. of*
кры́шка *n.fem.* (7a) cover, lid    крути́ть to whirl, to turn)
   крыть - покры́ть to cover
*куб *n.masc.* (1) cube
*куб. см. *abbrev. of* *куби́ческий *сантиме́тр cubic centimeter

\*кубический *adj.* (21) cubic
\*Куин \*Элизабет *undecl.* *name of the ship* Queen Elizabeth
кур *gen. and acc. plu. of* курица (Cf. Note 15, p. 290)
курица *n.fem.* (§ 359, p. 577) hen, chicken
\*курс *n.masc.* (1) course (in school, college, or university)
кусок *n.masc.* (3a) piece
кусочек *n.masc.* (3a) small piece
кусочки *nom. and acc. plu. of* кусочек
куст *n.masc.* (1) bush
\*Кюри *n.masc.* ( *undecl.* § 363, p. 587) Curie

# Л

\*лаборатория *n.fem.* (11) laboratory
\*лабораторный *adj.* (17) (relating to or accomplished in the)
\*Лаваль *n.masc.* (6) Laval                 laboratory, laboratory (*adj.*)
\*лак *n.masc.* (3) lacquer, lac.
\*лампа *n.fem.* (7) lamp, (radio or electronic) tube
\*ламповый *adj.* (17) (pertaining to or containing) lamp (s)
\*латекс *n.masc.* (1) latex                 or vacuum tubes
латунь *n.fem.* (12) brass
лёгкий *adj.* (21a) easy, light, mild, slight
легко *adv.* easily, readily
легко *pred. adj.* (it is) easy (Cf. § 167, p. 255)
лёгок *pred.masc.sing. of* лёгкий
лёд *n.masc.* (1c) ice
лекарство *n.neuter* (13) medicine
лён *n.masc.* (1c) flax, linen
лес *n.masc.* (Footnote 1, p. 580) forest, lumber
летать – полетать (Reg. A) *v.intr.* to fly (Cf. §§ 380-382,
лето *n.neuter* (13) summer, year              pp. 626-630)
летучий *adj.* (22) volatile
    лёт flight
ли *particle used to indicate interrogation* (Cf. § 387,
\*ликвидация *n.fem.* (11) liquidation              p. 644)
\*лимонный *adj.* (17) lemon, lime
    \*лимон lemon
\*линейный *adj.* (17) linear
    \*линия line
\*линза *n.fem.* (7) lens
\*линия *n.fem.* (11) line
лист *n.masc.* (§ 359, p. 578) leaf, sheet (of paper)
листья *nom. and acc.plu.,* листьями *instr.plu. of*
                лист *when meaning* leaf (Cf. § 359, p. 578)
\*литература *n.fem.* (7) literature

ЛИТЬ (Irr. E-3) *v.tr. imperf.* to be pouring
ЛИШАТЬ (Reg. A) – ЛИШИТЬ (Reg. B-2) *v.tr.* to remove, to take away
ЛИШЁННЫЙ (17) devoid, freed of (*perf. pas. past part. of* ЛИШАТЬ – ЛИШИТЬ)
ЛИШЬ *adv.* only
ЛОБОВОЙ *adj.* (18) head on, direct
*ЛОГАРИФМ *n.masc.*(1) logarithm
*ЛОГАРИФМИРОВАТЬ (Irr. A-1)*v.tr. perf. and imperf.* to be taking (or to take) the logarithm of
*ЛОГАРИФМИРУЯ *pres. ger. of* ЛОГАРИФМИРОВАТЬ
*ЛОГАРИФМИЧЕСКИЙ *adj.* (21) logarithmic
ЛОПАТКА *n.fem.*(7a) (little) shovel,
ЛОПАТОЧКА *n.fem.* (7a) (Cf. next entry) (little) shovel,
ЛОПАТОЧЕК *irr.gen.plu. of* ЛОПАТОЧКА
Л.С. *abbrev. for* ЛОШАДИНАЯ СИЛА horse power
ЛОШАДЬ *n.fem.* (12) horse
*ЛУНА *n.fem.* (7) moon
ЛУЧ *n.masc.* (2) beam, ray
ЛУЧИСТЫЙ *adj.* (17) radiant, light (adj.)
ЛУЧШЕ *pred. comp. adj. (undecl.) and adv.* better
ЛЬНА *gen.sing. of* ЛЁН     (Cf. § 334, p. 527)
ЛЬНЯНОЙ *adj.* (17) (pertaining to) flax, linseed or linen
ЛЮБОЙ *adj.* (18) any
ЛЮБИТЬ – ПОЛЮБИТЬ to love
ЛЮДИ *n.plu. only* (§ 359, p. 579) persons, people

# M

МАГНИЙ *n.masc.* (5) magnesium
*МАГНИТ *n.masc.* (1) magnet
*МАГНИТНЫЙ *adj.* (17) magnetic
МАК *n.masc.* (3) poppy
*МАКСИМАЛЬНЫЙ *adj.* (17b) maximum (adj.)
МАЛЕНЬКИЙ *adj.* (21) small, tiny, little
МАЛО-ПО-МАЛУ *adv.* little by little
МАЛЫЙ *adj.* (17) slight, small
МАРГАНЕЦ *n.masc.*(3a) (*instr. sing.* МАРГАНЦЕМ) manganese
*МАРС *n.masc.*(1) Mars
*МАРСДЕН *n.masc.*(1) Marsden
*МАРТ *n.masc.*(1) March
МАСЕЛ *gen.plu. of* МАСЛО
МАСЛО *n.neuter* (13b) oil, fat
МАСЛЯНАЯ КРАСКА *fixed expr.* paint
МАСЛЯНЫЙ *adj.* (17) fatty
*МАССА *n.fem.* (7) mass
МАСШТАБ *n.masc.* (1) scale

\*матема́тик *n.masc.* (3) mathematician
\*матема́тика *n.fem.* (9) mathematics
\*материа́л *n.masc.* (1) material, substance
\*материа́льный *adj.* (17b) material  (*adj.*)
\*матери́нский *adj.* (21) maternal, mother (adj.) .
\*мате́рия *n.fem.* (11) matter
\*матри́чный *adj.* (17) matrix
маховое колесо́ *fixed expr.*  flywheel
маховой *adj.* (18) pertaining to momentum
\*маши́на *n.fem.* (7) machine, engine
мёд *n.masc.* (1) honey
\*медици́на *n.fem.* (7) medicine
ме́дленно *adv.* slowly
медленнопротека́ющий *adj.* (22) slowly proceeding (Cf. § 286,
    ме́дленный slow;    теку́т (they) flow            p. 452)
ме́дленный *adj.* (17) slow
медь *n.fem.* (12) copper
ме́жду *prep.* (*with instr.*) among, between
\*межплане́тный *adj.* (17) interplanetary
    ме́жду between;    \*плане́та planet
\*мезозо́йский *adj.* (21) Mesozoic
ме́лкий *adj.* (21a) small
мелкораздро́блённый *adj.* (22) finely divided (Cf. § 286, p. 452)
    ме́лкий small;  раз- + дробь fraction
\*мело́дия *n.fem.* (11) melody
мельча́йший *superl.adj.* (22) smallest (Cf. § 346, p. 546)
ме́нее *pred. comp. adj.* (*undecl.*) *and adv.* less
\*мени́ск *n.masc.* (1) meniscus
ме́ньше *pred. comp. adj.* (*undecl.*) *and adv.* less (than)
                                (Cf. § 334, p. 527)
ме́ньший *comp. adj.* lesser, smaller (Cf. § 332, p. 525)
меня́ть – поменя́ть (Reg. A) *v.tr.* to exchange
    -ся  to undergo change, to change (*intr.*)
\*Мерку́рий *n.masc.* (5) Mercury
ме́стность *n.fem.* (12) locality
ме́сто *n.neuter* (13) place
\*мета́лл *n.masc.* (1) metal
\*металли́ческий *adj.* (21) metallic
\*металлу́ргия *n.fem.* (11) metallurgy
\*мета́н *n.masc.* (1) methane
\*метаста́бильный *adj.* (17a) metastable
\*матема́тический *adj.* (21) mathematical
\*мети́л *n.masc.* (1) methyl
\*метили́ровать (Irr. A-1) *v.tr.  perf. and imperf.*
\*мети́ловый *adj.* (17) methyl        to be methylating, to methylate
\*ме́тод *n.masc.* (1) method
\*метр *n.masc.* (1) meter

\*механизм  *n.masc.* (1) mechanism
\*механика  *n.fem.* (9) mechanics
\*механический  *adj.* (21) mechanical
\*микрометр  *n.masc.* (1) micrometer
\*микроскоп  *n.masc.* (1) microscope
\*миллиметр  *n.masc.* (1) millimeter
\*миллион  *n.masc.* (1) million
\*миллионный  *adj.* (17) millionth
\*минерал  *n.masc.* (1) mineral
\*минимальный  *adj.* (17b) minimum
\*минута  *n.fem.* (7) minute
 мир  *n.masc.* (1) world, peace
 мировой  *adj.* (18) peaceful, cosmic, universal
\*Мичиган  *n.masc.* (1) Michigan
 многие  *adj.* (20) many
 много  *pronoun* (§ 150, p. 230) many, multiplicity
 много раз  *fixed expr.* many times
 многообразие  *n.neuter* (16) multiplicity, multiformity
    много, many; образ form, shape
 многочисленный  *adj.* (17) numerous
    много many; число number
 множество  *n.neuter* (13) plurality, multiplicity
 множитель  *n.masc.* (6) multiplier, coefficient, factor
 простой множитель  *fixed expr.* prime factor
 мог, могла, могло, могли,  *imperf. past tense forms*
                                    *of* МОЧЬ - СМОЧЬ
 могут  *pres. tense third pers. plu. of* МОЧЬ - СМОЧЬ
\*модель  *n.fem.* (12) model
 можем  *pres. tense first pers. plu. of* МОЧЬ - СМОЧЬ
 может  *pres. tense third pers. sing. of* МОЧЬ - СМОЧЬ
 можно  *pred.adj.* (it is) possible (Cf. §§ 166-7, pp. 254-5)
 можно ли  *fixed expr.* is it possible?  (Cf. § 387, p. 644)
\*молекула  *n.fem.* (7) molecule
\*молекулярный  *adj.* (17a) molecular
 молодой  *adj.* (18) young
✱молоко  *n.neuter* (13) milk
\*моль  *n.fem.* (12) molecular amount, mol
\*момент  *n.masc.* (1) moment, factor
\*монель  *n.fem.* (12) "Monel"
\*монография  *n.fem.* (11) monograph
\*моноклинический  *adj.* (21) monoclinic
\*монтаж  *n.masc.* (3 instr. sing. МОНТАЖЕМ)  installation
\*монтировать - ✱смонтировать (Irr. A-1)  *v.tr.* to install,
\*море, *n.neuter* (15) sea                    to erect, to mount
 морковь  *n.fem.* (12) carrot
✱морской  *adj.* (20) sea (adj.)
\*морфий  *n.masc.* (5) morphine

моря́к *n.masc.* (3) sailor
*мо́ре sea
*Москва́ *n.fem.* (7) Moscow
*мото́р *n.masc.* (1) motor
мочь – смочь (Irr. G-4) *v.intr.* to be able
мо́щность *n.fem.* (12) powerfulness, power
мо́щный *adj.* (17a) powerful
мра́мор *n.masc.* (1) marble
*му́зыка *n.fem.* (9) music
мы *pronoun* (§ 136, p. 204) we
мы́ло *n.neuter* (13) soap
мыть – помы́ть to wash
мы́слимый *adj.* (17) thinkable
мысль thought
мя́гкий *adj.* (21a) soft
мя́со *n.neuter* (13) meat

<h1 style="text-align:center">Н</h1>

на *pred.* (*with acc. implying motion; with prep implying
repose*) on, at, to, into, after, in (Cf. § 127, p. 185)
на by (*referring to multiplication division and the like,
Cf.* § 374, p. 610)
наблюда́ть (Reg. A) – наблюсти́ (Irr. H-5) *v.tr.* to observe
–ся to be observed
наблюде́ние *n.neuter* (16) observation
наблюдённый (17) observed (*perf. pas. past part. of
наблюда́ть – наблюсти́*)
*навигацио́нный *adj.* (17) navigational
*навига́ция *n.fem.* (11) navigation
наво́з *n.masc.* (1) manure
нагрева́ть – нагре́ть (Reg. A) *v.tr.* to heat
на- + горе́ть – сгоре́ть to burn
нагрева́ние *n.neuter* (16) heating (process)
нагрева́нии *prep. sing. of* нагрева́ние
нагре́ть *see* нагрева́ть
нагре́тый (17) heated (*perf. pas. past part. of
нагрева́ть – нагре́ть*)
над *prep.* (*with instr.*) on, above
на́до *pred. adj.* (it is) necessary (Cf. § 165, p. 253)
наза́д *adv.* back, backward
назва́ние *n.neuter* (16) designation, name
на́званный (17) named, called (*perf. pas. past part. of
называ́ть – назва́ть*)
называ́емый (17) (being) called (Cf. Note 10, p. 170) (*pas. pres.
part. of* называ́ть – назва́ть)

называть (Reg. A) - назвать (Irr. E-1,   O insert)  *v.tr.*
to name, to call
  -ся  to be named, called
называнный (17) called, named (*imperf. pas. past part. of*
назыать - назвать)
наиболее *adv.* most, greatest (Cf. § 344, p. 541)
наибольший *superl. adj.* (22) largest
наилучший *superl. adj.* (22) best
наименьший *superl. adj.* (22) least, smallest
найдём *perf. future tense first pers. plu. of*
находить - найти
найденный (17) found, discovered (*perf. pas. past part of*
найти *see* находить          находить - найти)
накаливание *n.neuter* (16) incandescence
  на- + калить to be glowing
накаливать (Reg. A) - накалить (Reg. B-2) *v.tr.* to heat (to
incandescence)
накладывать (Reg. A)  - накласть (Irr. H-7) *v.tr.* to lay on,
  -ся  to be attached                    to place on
  на- + класть to be placing
накласть *see* накладывать
наклон *n.masc.* (1) incline
наклонять (Reg. A) - наклонить (Reg. B-2) *v.tr.* to bend down
  на- + КЛОН incline
наливать (Reg. A)  - налить (Irr. E-3)  *v.tr.* to pour in
  на- + лить to be pouring
нам *dat. of.* МЫ
наоборот *adv.* on the contrary, vice versa
написать *see* писать
напишем *perf. future tense first pers. plu. of* писать -
написать
наполнять (Reg. A) - наполнить (Reg. B-2) *v.tr.* to fill
  на- + полный  full
направление *n.neuter* (16) direction
направлять (Reg. A) - направить (Irr. C-2) *v.tr.* to direct
  на- + право right
например *adv.* for example
  на- + пример example
нас *gen. and acc. of* МЫ
насквозь *adv.* straight through
настоящий *adj.* (22) present, actual
  на- + стоять to be standing
настоящее время *fixed expr.* present time
наступать (Reg. A) - наступить (Irr.C-2) *v.intr.* to approach
  на- + ступать - ступить to walk, to stride
насыпать (Reg. A) *v.tr. imperf.* to strew upon, to fill
  на- + сыпать - посыпать to strew

насыще́ние *n. neuter* (16) saturation, (process of) saturating
\*на́тр *see* е́дкий \*на́тр
\*на́триевый *adj.* (17) sodium
\*на́трий *n. masc.* (5) sodium
\*натура́льный (17b) natural
натяже́ние *n. neuter* (16) tension
    на- + тя́га  pull
нау́ка *n. fem.* (9) science
нау́чный *adj.* (17a) scientific
\*нафтали́н *n. masc.* (1) naphthalene
нахо́дятся find self, are located (Cf. § 123, p. 181 *and follow-*
находи́ть (Irr. D-2, д → ж) – найти́(Irr. H-10) *v. tr.* to find,
                                   (Cf. § 382, p. 630)
    -ся to be found, to be located, (Cf. § 123, p. 181)
    на- + ходи́ть, итти́  to be going (Cf. § 381, p. 626)
нача́ло *n. neuter* (13) start, beginning
нача́ть *see* начина́ть
нача́льный *adj.* (17) initial, beginning
начерти́ть *see* черти́ть
начина́ть (Reg. A) – нача́ть (Irr. C-3, H added) *v. tr.* to start,
                                            to begin
начнём, начну́т *perf. future tense forms of* начина́ть –
наш *poss. adj.* (§ 136, p. 208) our                     нача́ть
на́ша, на́шего, на́шей, на́шем, на́ши, на́ших *forms of* наш
нашёл *perf. past tense masc. sing. of* находи́ть –
                                 найти́ (Cf. § 224, p. 354)
не not, no (*for use in sentences* Cf. Lesson 20, p. 263)
не то́лько *fixed expr.* not only
не то́лько --- но и ---; не то́лько --- но та́кже *fixed*
                           *expr.* not only --- but also ---
небе́сный *adj.* (17) heavenly, pertaining to the sky
не́бо *n. neuter* (§ 359, p. 578) sky
небольшо́й *adj.* (20) not big, small
    не- + большо́й  big
неви́димый *adj.* (17) invisible
    не- + вид  sight, form
нево́дный *adj.* (17) non-aqueous
    не- + вода́  water
невозмо́жный *adj.* (17a) impossible
    не- + воз- + мо́жно  (it is) possible
невооружённый *adj.* (17) unaided
    не- + во- + ору́жие  weapon
невы́годный *adj.* (17a) unsuitable, unusable
    не- + вы- + го́дный  suitable
невы́ясненный *adj.* (17) unexplained (Cf. § 286, p. 452)
    не- + вы- + я́сный  clear

него́ *see declension of* ОН *given in* § 136, p. 452
неда́вно *adv.* not long ago, recently
   не- + да́вно long ago
недели́мый *adj.* (17) indivisible
   не- + дели́ть - раздели́ть to divide
неде́ля *n.fem.* (10) week
недиссоции́рованный *adj.* (17) undissociated (Cf. § 286, p. 452)
   не- + *диссоции́ровать to dissociate, to be dissociating
недостава́ть (Irr. B) - недоста́ть (Irr. C-5) *v.tr.* to be
                          insufficient or lacking
   не- + до- + стать to stand, to become
недоста́ток *n.masc.* (3a) insufficiency, lack, inadequacy
недоста́точный *adj.* (17a) insufficient
недосту́пность *n.fem.* (12) non-availability
не́дра *n. plu. only* (Cf. § 359, p. 579) depths
неё *see* ОН
не́жный *adj.* (17a) tender
незави́симо *adv.* independently
   не- + зави́сеть to be dependent
незамени́мый *adj.* (17) irreplaceable
   не- + за- + меня́ть - поменя́ть to exchange
незначи́тельный *adj.* (17b) insignificant
   не- + знать to be knowing
незре́лый *adv.* (17) unripe, immature
   не- + зре́лый ripe
неизбе́жно *adv.* unavoidably
   не- + из- + бе́гать - побе́гать to flee
неизмене́нный *adj.* (17) unchanged
   не- + из- + меня́т - поменя́ть to exchange
ней *see* ОН
*Не́йгаузен *n.masc.* (1) Neuhausen
*нейтрализова́ть (Irr. A-1) to be neutralizing, to neutralize
*нейтра́льный *adj.* (17b) neutral
*нейтро́н *n.masc.* (1) neutron
не́который *adj. and pronoun* (17) certain, some
нельзя́ *adv.* it is impossible, it is forbidden (Cf. § 178, p. 270)
нем *see* ОН
*неметалл *n.masc.* (1) non-metal
   не- + *металл metal
неме́цкий *adj.* (21) German
немно́гие *adj.* (21) few
   не- + мно́гие many
немно́го *pronoun* a little, small amount
   не- + мно́го much
нему́ *see* ОН
немы́слимый *adj.* (17) unthinkable
   не- + мысль thought

необходи́мо *pred. adj.* (it is) necessary (§§ 166-7, pp. 254-5)
   не- + об- + ходи́ть to be going
необходи́мость *n.fem.* (12) necessity, unavoidability
необходи́мый *adj.* (17) necessary, required
необъяснённый *adj.* (17) unexplained (Cf. § 286, p. 452)
   не- + об- + я́сный clear
неодина́ковый *adj.* (17) non-identical
   не- + оди́н one
*неопре́н *n.masc.* (1) Neoprene
*неоргани́ческий *adj.* (21) inorganic
непосре́дственно *adv.* directly
   не- + по- + сре́дство means, agency
неподви́жный *adj.* (17a) immovable
   не- + по- + дви́гать - дви́нуть to move
непреде́льный *adj.* (17) unsaturated (chemical compounds not
   не- + преде́л limit                                    solutions)
непреры́вно *adv.* uninterruptedly, continuously
не- + пре- + рвать to be tearing apart
неприя́тный *adj.* (17a) unpleasant
   не- + приятный pleasant
непроница́емый *adj.* (17) impenetrable, inscrutible (Cf. § 286, p. 452)
   не- + проника́ть - прони́кнуть to penetrate
*Непту́н *n.masc.* (1) Neptune (planet)
неразруши́мый *adj.* (17) indestructible (Cf. § 286, p. 452)
   не- + разруша́ть - разруши́ть to destroy
*нерв *n.masc.* (1) nerve
нерешённый *adj.* (17) undecided, unsolved (Cf. § 286, p. 452)
   не- + реша́ть - реши́ть to decide, to solve
несветя́щийся *adj.* (22) non-luminous (Cf. § 286, p. 452)
   не- + свети́ться to be shining
не́сколько *pronoun, adv.* (§ 150, p. 230) several, somewhat
   не- + ско́лько how many
несмотря́ на *prep. expr.* (*with acc.*) in spite of
   не- + смотре́ть - посмотре́ть to view
несогласи́мый *adj.* (17) disagreeing
несомне́нно *pred. adj. and adv.* certain, certainly, doubtless,
                       (it is) certain (Cf. §§ 166-7, pp. 254-5)
   не- + сомне́ние doubt
несравне́нно *adv.* incomparably
   не- + с- + ра́вный equal
несто́йкий *adj.* (21c) unstable
   не- + стоя́ть to be standing
*несфери́ческий *adj.* (21) non-spherical
   не- + *сфери́ческий spherical
нет *adv.* not, (is) not (Cf. Lesson 20, p. 263)
нетру́дно *pred. adj.* (it is) not difficult (Cf. §§ 166-7, pp. 254-5)
   не- + тру́дный difficult

неуда́ча *n.fem.* (7 *instr. sing.* неуда́чей) non-success, failure
   не- + удава́ться - уда́ться   to succeed
неучёный *adj.* (17) uneducated (Cf. § 286, p. 452)
   не- + учи́ть   to be teaching, learning
нефть *n.fem.* (12) petroleum
нефтяно́й *adj.* (18) (pertaining to) petroleum
*нециркуля́рный *adj.* (17) non-circular
не́что *pronoun* something (Cf. § 154, p. 237)
*неэласти́ческий *adj.* (21) inelastic
   не- + *эласти́ческий   elastic
*неэлектризо́ванный *adj.* (17) unelectrified (Cf. § 286, p. 452)
   не- + *электризова́ть - *наэлектризова́ть  to electricity
нея́сный *adj.* (17a) unclear, uncertain
   не- + я́сный   clear
НИ --- НИ --- *fixed expr,* neither--- nor---
ни́же *adv. and comp. adj.* (*undecl.* § 334, p. 527) lower, less
ни́жний *comp. adj.* (19) lower, lesser (Cf. § 332, p. 525)
ни́зкий *adj.* (21a) low, slight
никако́й *neg. adj.* none (Cf. § 156, p. 241 and § 172, p. 263)
*ни́келлевый *adj.* (17) nickel (*adj.*)
*ни́ккель *n.masc.* (6) nickel
*нитри́д *n.masc.* (1) nitride
нить *n.fem.* (12) thread, filament
НИХ *see* ОН
*нихро́м *n.masc.* (1) nichrome
ничто́жно *adv.* insignificantly, negligibly
   не- + что   that, which
ничто́жный *adj.* (17a)   insignificant, vanishingly small
НО *conj.* but (Cf. § 61, p. 84)
нове́йший *superl. adj.* (22)   newest
*но́вый *adj.* (17) new
НОЖ *n.masc.* (2) knife
*номенклату́ра *n.fem.* (7) nomenclature
*норма́льно *adv.* normally
*норма́льный *adj.* (17b) normal
носи́ть - поноси́ть (Irr. D-2) *v.tr.* to carry, to hear (Cf. § 282, p. 632)
ну́жно *pred. adj.* (it is) necessary (Cf. §§ 166-7, pp. 254-5)
*нуль *n.masc.* (6) null, zero
*Нью-Йо́рк *n.masc.* (5) New York
*Нью-Ке́нсингтон *n.masc.* (1) New Kensington
*Нью́тон *n.masc.* (1) Newton

# O

О (об, обо) *prep.* (*with acc.*) against, along (*with prep.*)
об *see* О                    about, concerning (Cf. § 127, p. 187)

о́ба *numeral* (§ 370, p. 601) both

обволáкивать (Reg. A) - обволóчь (Irr. G-3) *v. tr.* to enclose, to envelop

о́бе *see* о́ба

обéгать (Reg. A) - обежáть (Reg. B-2)
  о- + бéгать - побéгать to flee (Cf. § 382, p. 632)

обежáть *see* обéгать

обéих *see* о́ба

обеспéчивать (Reg. A) - обеспéчить (Reg. B-2) *v. tr.* to guarantee, to insure
  о- + бес- + печáть seal, press

облада́ть (Reg. A) *v. tr. imperf.* (*with instr.*) to possess

о́бласть *n. fem.* (12) realm, territory, region, field
  об- + влáсть power, authority

обóих *see* о́ба

обнарýженный (17) observed, detected (*perf. pas. past part. of* обнарýживать - обнарýжить)

обнарýживать (Reg. A) - обнарýжить (Reg. B-2) *v. tr.* to observe
  об- + нарýжий outside

обозначáть (Reg. A) - обозна́чить (Reg. B-2) *v. tr.* to designate
  обо- + знáть to be knowing

оболóчка *n. fem.* (9a) envelop, sheath

оборóт *n. masc.* (1) revolution, rotation
  об- + вóрот turn

оборýдование *n. neuter* (16) equipment
  об- + орýжие weapon

обрабóтка *n. fem.* (9) processing
  об- + рабóта work

о́браз *n. masc.* (1) form, shape, fashion, manner
  глáвным о́бразом *fixed expr.* for the most part

образовáние *n. neuter* (16) formation

образóвывать - образовáть (Irr. A-1) *v. tr.* to form
  -ся to be formed

образýет, образýется, образýют, образýются *perf. tense forms of* образóвывать - образовáть (*These forms usually are best translated by the English present tense as discussed in* Cf. § 185, p. 280)

образýющий *act. pres. part. of* образовáть

образýющийся *act. pres. part. refl. of* образовáть

обрати́мый *adj.* (17) revisible
  об- + вращáть to be turning

обрáтно *adv.* backward, inversely, back

обрáтный *adj.* (17) reverse, inverse

обращáть (Reg. A) - обрати́ть (Irr. D-2) *v. tr.* to turn, to rotate (*tr.*)
  -ся to rotate (*intr.*)
  об- + вращáть to be turning

обращéние *n. neuter* (16) rotation

обуслóвленный (17) caused, brought about (*perf. pas. past part of* обуслóвливать - обуслóвить)

обусло́вливать (*Reg. A*) – обусло́вить (*Irr. C-2*) *v.tr.*
to cause, to bring. about, to stipulate
  об- + усло́вие condition
общеизве́стный *adj.* (17a) generally, known
  о́бщий general, common; изве́стный known
о́бщий *adj.* (22) common, general, total
  в о́бщем *fixed expr.* in general
обши́рный *adj.* (17a) wide, extensive
объединённый (17) united (*perf. pas. past part. of*
объединя́ть – объедини́ть)
объединя́ть (*Reg. A*) – объедини́ть (*Reg. B-2*) *v.tr.* to unite
*объе́кт *n.masc.* (1) object
объём *n.masc.* (1) volume
объяснённый (17) explained (*perf. pas. past part of*
объясня́ть – объясни́ть)
объясня́ть (*Reg. A*) – объясни́ть (*Reg. B-2*) *v.tr.* to explain,
  -ся to be explained, clarified         to elucidate
  себе́ to explain to self, to understand
  об- + я́сный clear
обыкнове́нно *adv.* ordinarily, usually
обыкнове́нный *adj.* (17a) ordinary, usually
обы́чно *adv.* ordinarily
обы́чный *adj.* (17a) ordinary
обя́занный (17) bound, obliged (*perf. pas. past part. of*
обя́зывать – обяза́ть to bind, to oblige)
ове́ц *gen. plu. of* овца́
овца́ *n.fem.* (8 *gen.plur.* ове́ц Cf. § 355, p. 561) sheep
огне́ *prep. sing. of* ого́нь
ого́нь *n.masc.* (6a) fire
ограни́ченный (17) limited, restricted (*perf. pas. past*
  *part. of* ограни́чивать – ограни́чить to limit, to restrict)
  о- + грани́ца border, boundary
огро́мный *adj.* (17a) enormous
оде́жда *n.fem.* (7) clothing
оди́н *numeral, adj., pronoun* (§ 370, p. 600) one, single, (*plu.*)
several, some
оди́н и тот же *fixed expr.* one and the same (Cf. § 144, p. 215)
одина́ковый *adj.* (17) identical, same
одино́кий *adj.* (20) alone, lonely
одна́ *see* оди́н
одна́ко *adv.* however
одно́ *see* оди́н
одновале́нтный *adj.* (17a) monovalent
  оди́н one; *валє́нтный pertaining to valence
одновре́менно *adv.* simultaneously
  оди́н one; вре́мя time
одновре́менный *adj.* (17) simultaneous

одного́ *see* оди́н
одноле́тний *adj.* (19) one-year (old)
   оди́н one;  ле́то summer
одну́ *see* оди́н
ожида́ть (Reg. A) *v.tr.* to be awaiting, expecting
  -ся to be awaited, expected
о́зеро *n.neuter* (13) lake
означа́ть (Reg. A) - озна́чить (Reg. B-2) *v.tr.* to designate,
  о- + знать to be knowing              to signify
ока́жется *perf. fut. third pers. sing. refl. of*
                        ока́зывать - оказа́ть
ока́зывать (Reg. A) - оказа́ть (Irr. D-1,  з → ж) *v.tr.*
                     to prove, to show, to exert
  -ся to be proved, to turn out to be
  о- + каза́ть to show
*океа́н *n.masc.* (1) ocean
о́кисел *n.masc.* (1a) oxide (general term -- Cf. о́кись and
  о- +, ки́слый sour, acid                      за́кись)
окисле́ние *n.neuter* (16) oxidation
окисля́ть (Reg. A) - окисли́ть (Reg. B-2) *v.tr.* to oxidize
  -ся to become oxidized
о́кись *n.fem.* (12) oxide, especially higher oxide (Cf. о́кисел)
о́кись углерода́ *fixed expr.* carbon monoxide (Cf. Note 2, p. 470)
о́коло *prep.* (*with gen.*) about, approximately
оконча́тельно *adv.* conclusively, finally
  о- + коне́ц end
окра́шивать (Reg. A) - окра́сить(Irr. D-2) *v.tr.* to paint,
  о- + кра́сный red                      to color
окра́шивание *n.neuter* (16) coloration
окружа́ть (Reg. A) - окружи́ть (Reg. B-2) *v.tr.* to surround
  о- + круг circular area
окру́жность *n.fem.* (12) circumference
*окта́н *n.masc.* (1) octane
о́лово *n.neuter* (13) tin
*ом *n.masc.* (1) ohm
он, она́, оно́, они́ *pronoun third pers.* (Cf. §136, p. 204) he,
опа́сность *n.fem.* (12) danger             she, it they
опа́сный *adj.* (17a) dangerous
*опера́тор *n.masc.* (1) operator
опи́лки *n.plu. only* (9a Cf. § 359, p. 579) filings
опи́лок *gen. plu. of* ОПИ́ЛКИ
опи́сывать (Reg. A) - описа́ть (Irr. D-1) *v.tr.* to describe
  о- + писа́ть - написа́ть to write
опишу́ *perf. fut. first pers. sing. of* опи́сывать -
                            описа́ть
определе́ние *n.neuter* (16) determination, regulation, order
  о- + преде́л limit

определённый (17) established, (*perf. pas. past part. of* определять - определить)

определять (Reg. A) - определить (Reg. B-2) *v.tr.* to determine, to establish, to set up

  -ся to be determined, to be established, to be set up

*оптимальный *adj.* (17a) optimum

*оптический *adj.* (21) optical

опыт *n.masc.* (1) experiment

опять *adv.* again

*орбита *n.fem.* (7) orbit

*организм *n.masc.* (1) organism

*органический *adj.* (21) organic

осветительный *adj.* (17) illuminating

  о- + свет light

освещать (Reg. A) - осветить (Irr. D-2, Т → Ч) *v.tr.*      to illuminate

освещение *n.neuter* (16) illumination

освещённость *n.fem.* (12) illumination

освобождать (Reg. A) - освободить (Irr. D-2, Д → Ж) *v.tr.*

  -ся to be liberated, set free    *v.tr.* to liberate, to set free

  о- + свобода freedom

осевший (22) precipitated, settled out, sunk (*perf. act. past part. of* оседать - осесть)

  о- + садиться - сесть to sit (down)

  осадок precipitate

осей *see* ось

осень *n.fem.* (12) autumn, fall

оси *see* ось

основа *n.fem.* (7) basis

основанный (17) based (*perf. pas. past part. of* основывать - основать to establish, to base)

основной *adj.* (18) basic, fundamental

основный *adj.* (17) basic (in chemical sense)

особенно *adv.* particularly, especially

особенность *n.fem.* (12) peculiarity

  в особенности *fixed expr.* in particular

оставаться (Irr. B) - остаться (Irr. C-5) *v.refl.* to remain

  о- + стать to become, to remain      (Cf. Footnote 1, p. 145)

оставлять (Reg. A) - оставить (Irr. C-2) *v.tr.* to leave, to give up, to allow

остаётся, остаются *pres.tense third pers. sing. and plural*

остальной *adj.* (18) remaining      *of* оставаться - остаться

остатков *gen. plu. of* остаток

остаток *n.masc.* (3a) residue, radical (chem.)

  о- + стать to become, to remain

осторожно *adv.* cautiously, carefully

осуществле́ние *n. neuter* (16) realization, accomplishment
 О- + СУТЬ are
осуществлённый (17) achieved, realized, accomplished (*perf.*
      *pas. past part. of* ОСУЩЕСТВЛЯ́ТЬ - ОСУЩЕСТВИ́ТЬ)
осуществля́ть (Reg. A) - осуществи́ть (Irr. C-2) *v. tr.*
 О- + СУТЬ are          to accomplish, to achieve, to realize
ОСЬ *n. fem.* (12) axis
ОТ *prep.* (*with gen.*) from, away
отбра́сывать (Reg. A) - отбро́сить (Irr. D-2) *v. tr.* to eject,
 ОТ- + броса́ть - броси́ть to throw          to throw away
отбро́с *n. masc.* (1) something thrown away, (*plu.*) rubbish,
                               waste products
отбро́шенный (17) ejected, thrown away (*perf. pas. past*
                *part. of* ОТБРА́СЫВАТЬ - ОТБРО́СИТЬ)
отве́рг *perf. past tense masc. sing. of* ОТВЕРГА́ТЬ -
                               ОТВЕ́РГНУТЬ
отверга́ть (Reg. A) - отве́ргнуть (Irr. J-3) *v. tr.* to reject
отве́рстие *n. neuter* (16) opening, hole
отве́т *n. masc.* (1) answer
отво́дками *instr. plu. of* ОТВО́ДОК
отво́дках *prep. plu. of* ОТВО́ДОК
ОТВО́ДОК *n. masc.* (3a) shoot (of plant)
отдава́емый (17) (*pas. pres. part. of* ОТДАВА́ТЬ - ОТДА́ТЬ)
отдава́ть (Irr. B-2) - отда́ть (Irr. I-3) *v. tr.* to give off,
                               to release
отдаёт, отдаю́т *pres. tense third pers. sing. and plu.*
                *of* ОТДАВА́ТЬ - ОТДА́ТЬ
отда́ющий (21) *act. pres. part. of* ОТДАВА́ТЬ - ОТДА́ТЬ
отделя́ть (Reg. A) - отдели́ть (Reg. B-2) *v. tr.* to separate,
 ОТ- + дели́ть - раздели́ть to divide          to isolate
отка́чивать - откача́ть (Reg. A) *v. tr.* to pump out, to evacuate
 -СЯ to be pumped out, evacuated
отклоне́ние *n. neuter* (16) deflection
 ОТ- + КЛОН incline
отклоня́емый (17) *pas. pres. part. of* ОТКЛОНЯ́ТЬ -
                               ОТКЛОНИ́ТЬ
отклоня́ть (Reg. A) - отклони́ть (Reg. B-2) *v. tr.* to deflect
 -СЯ to be deflected
открыва́ть (Reg. A) - откры́ть (Irr. E-4) *v. tr.* to discover, to open up
 -СЯ to be discovered, to open up
 ОТ- + крыть - покры́ть to cover
откры́тие *n. neuter* (16) discovery
откры́тый (17) discovered, opened up (*perf. pas. past part.*
отку́дка *adv.* from this, hence          *of* ОТКРЫВА́ТЬ - ОТКРЫ́ТЬ)
отлива́ть (Reg. A) - отли́ть (Irr. E-3) *v. tr.* to pour off,
 ОТ- + ЛИТЬ to be pouring          to decant, to cast (metal)

ОТЛИЧА́ТЬ (Reg. A) - ОТЛИЧИ́ТЬ (Reg. B-2) *v. tr.* to distinguish
  -СЯ (ОТ) to be distinguished (from), to differ (from)
  ОТ- + ЛИЦО́ face, person

ОТЛИ́ЧИЕ *n. neuter* (16) distinction, difference

ОТЛИ́ЧНЫЙ *adv.* (17a) distinct, different

ОТМЕЧА́ТЬ (Reg. A) - ОТМЕ́ТИТЬ (Irr. D-2. Т → Ч) *v. tr.*
  ОТ- + МЕ́ТИТЬ to be marking         to note, to mention

ОТМЕ́ЧЕННЫЙ (17) noted, mentioned (*perf. pas., past part., of*

ОТНОСИ́ТЕЛЬНО *adv.* relatively         ОТМЕЧА́ТЬ - ОТМЕ́ТИТЬ)

ОТНОСИ́ТЕЛЬНЫЙ *adj.* (17) (*pred. masc. sing.* ОТНОСИ́ТЕЛЕН
                          Cf. § 356, p. 569) relative

ОТНОСИ́ТЬ (Irr. D-2) - ОТНЕСТИ́ (Irr. H-2) *v. tr.* to carry away, to
  -СЯ to pertain, to behave (toward), to belong (to)         attribute
  ОТ- + НОСИ́ТЬ, НЕСТИ́ to be carrying (Cf. § 381, p. 626)

ОТНОШЕ́НИЕ *n. neuter* (16) regard, ratio, respect

ОТРАБА́ТЫВАТЬ - ОТРАБО́ТАТЬ (Reg. A) *v. tr.* to work out
  ОТ- + РАБО́ТА work

ОТРА́ДНЫЙ *adj.* (17a) pleasant, exhilarating
  ОТ- + РАД happy

ОТРАЖА́ТЬ (Reg. A) - ОТРАЗИ́ТЬ (Irr. D-2, З → Ж) *v. tr.* to reflect
  ОТ- + РАЗИ́ТЬ to be hitting         (light, etc.), to throw back

ОТРАЖЁННЫЙ (17) reflected         (*perf. pas. past part. of*
                          ОТРАЖА́ТЬ - ОТРАЗИ́ТЬ)

ОТРИЦА́ТЕЛЬНО *adv.* negatively

ОТРИЦА́ТЕЛЬНЫЙ *adj.* (17) negative

О́ТРУБИ, *n. plu. forms only* (Cf. ШИ § 359, p. 579) bran

ОТСТОЯ́ТЬ (Reg. B-2) *v. intr.* to be distant, far away
  ОТ- + СТОЯ́ТЬ - ПОСТОЯ́ТЬ to stand, to remain

ОТСУ́ТСТВИЕ *n. neuter* (16) absence
  ОТ- + СУТЬ are

ОТСУ́ТСТВУЮТ *pres. tense third pers. plu. of* ОТСУ́ТСТВОВАТЬ
                          (Irr. A-1) *v. intr.* to be absent

*О́ТТО, *n. masc.* (*undecl.* § 363, p. 589) Otto

ОТТА́ЛКИВАТЬ (Reg. A) - ОТТОЛКНУ́ТЬ (Reg. B-1) *v. tr.* to thrust
  -СЯ to be thrust aside, repelled         aside, to repel
  ОТ- + ТОЛКА́ТЬ to be

ОТТУ́ДА *adv.* from here
  ОТ- + ТУДА́ (to) there

*ОТФИЛЬТРУ́ЙТЕ *perf. imp. second pers. plu. of*
                          *ОТФИЛЬТРО́ВЫВАТЬ - *ОТФИЛЬТРОВА́ТЬ

*ОТФИЛЬТРО́ВЫВАТЬ (Reg. A) - *ОТФИЛЬТРОВА́ТЬ (Irr. A-1) *v. tr.*
  ОТ- + *ФИЛЬТРОВА́ТЬ to be filtering         to filter out

ОХЛАЖДА́ТЬ (Reg. A) - ОХЛАДИ́ТЬ (Irr. D-2, Д → ДЖ) *v. tr.* to cool
  -СЯ to cool off, to become cold
  О- + ХОЛО́ДНЫЙ cold

охлаждение *n. neuter* (16) cooling (process)
охранять (Reg. A) - охранить (Reg. B-2) *v. tr.* to protect
очевидно *adv.* obviously, (it is) obvious
  очи eyes; вид view, aspect, form
очень *adv.* very
очерк *n. masc.* (3) sketch, outline
  о- + чёрный black
очистка *n. fem.* (9) purifying, purification
  о- + чистый clean, pure
очищать (Reg. A) - очистить (Irr. D-2, СТ → Щ) *v. tr.* to clean,
                                 to purify
очищенный (17) purified (*perf. pas. past part. of*
ошибочный *adj.* (17a) erroneous         очищать - очистить)
  ошибка error

## П

падать (Reg. A) - пасть (Irr. H-7) *v. intr.* to fall
падение *n. neuter* (16) drop, fall, decrease
пар *n. masc.* (1) vapor, steam
*пара *n. fem.* (7) pair
*параграф *n. masc.* (1) paragraph
*параллелограмм *n. masc.* (1) parallelogram
*параметр *n. masc.* (1) parameter
*паразитический *adj.* (21) parasitic
*паразитный *adj.* (17) parasitic
*парафин *n. masc.* (1) paraffin
паровая *машина *fixed expr.* steam engine
паровой *adj.* (18) (pertaining to) steam or vapor
пароход *n. masc.* (1) steamer (type of ship)
*пассажирский *adj.* (21) (pertaining to) passenger
*паста *n. fem.* (7) paste
*паталогический *adj.* (21) pathological
*патент *n. masc.* (1) patent
*пауза *n. fem.* (7) pause
*пенсильванский *adj.* (21) Pennsylvanian
первоначальный *adj.* (17) basic, fundamental
  первый first; начало beginning
первый *adj.* (17) first
переваривать (Reg. A) - переварить (Reg. B-2) *v. tr.* to digest
  -ся to be digested
  пере- + варить to cook
перевод *n. masc.* (1) transference, translation
  пере- + водить, вести to be leading (Cf. § 381, p. 626)
переводить (Irr. D-2, д → ж) - перевести (Irr. H-5) *v. tr.*
                           to transfer, to convert

переворо́т *n.masc.* (1) revolution, (radical) change

пе́ред, (пе́редо) *prep. with instr.* before, in front of

переда́тчик *n.masc.* (3) transmitter

    пере- + дава́ть - да́ть to give

*перекристаллизо́вывать - *перекристаллизова́ть (Irr. A-1)

                                               *v.tr.* to recrystallize

    пере- + *кристаллизова́ть to be crystallizing

перемеща́ть (Reg. A) - перемести́ть (Irr.D-2, СТ → Щ) *v.tr.*

    -ся to be displaced                         to displace

    пере- + ме́сто place

перенеси́те *perf. imp. second pers. plu. of* переноси́ть -

                                           перенести́

переноси́ть (Irr. D-2) - перенести́ (Irr. H-2) *v.tr.* to carry

                          over, to transfer (Cf. § 381, p. 626)

    пере- + носи́ть, нести́ to be carrying (Cf. § 382, p. 630)

переполня́ть (Reg.A)- перепо́лнить (Reg.B-2) *v.tr.* to fill (to

    пере- + по́лный complete                   overflowing)

перепро́бовать (Irr. A-1) *v.tr.* to test exhaustively, to test

    пере- + про́бовать to be testing         one after another

перераба́тывать - перерабо́тать (Reg. A)     *v.tr.* to process,

    пере - + рабо́та work                      to rework

перерабо́тка *n.fem.* (9) processive

переры́в *n.masc.* (1) interruption

    пере- + рыть to be digging

пересека́ть (Reg. A) - пересе́чь (Irr.G-3) *v.tr.* to cut across,

    -ся to be cut across, to intersect            to cut off

    пере- + сечь to hack, to whip

переско́к *n.masc.* (3) leap, jump, transition

    пере- + скака́ть to be jumping, galloping

переходи́ть (Irr. D-2, д → ж) - перейти́ (Irr. H-10) *v.intr.*

                     to go over (Cf. § 382, p. 630)

    пере- + ходи́ть, итти́ to be going (Cf. § 381, p. 626)

перечи́сленный (17) enumerated (*perf. pas, past part, of*

                    перечисля́ть - перечи́слить)

перечисля́ть (Reg. A) - перечи́слить (Reg. B-2) to enumerate

    пере- + число́ number

перешёл *perf. past tense masc. sing. of* переходи́ть -

                                     перейти́

*переэкзамено́вывать - *переэкзаменова́ть (Irr.A-1) *v.tr.* to re-

                          examine (student)

    пере- + *экзаменова́ть - *проэкзаменова́ть to examine

*перио́д *n.masc.* (1) period                    (student)

*периоди́чески *adv.* periodically

*периоди́ческий *adj.* (21) periodic

*перпендикуля́рный *adj.* (17a) perpendicular

пе́сен *gen. plu. of* пе́сня

пе́сня *n. fem.* (10 *gen. plu.* пе́сен) song
песо́к *n. masc.* (3a) sand
песча́ник *n. masc.* (3) sandstone
печь *n. fem.* (12) furnace, heater
писа́ть – написа́ть (Irr.D-1) *v. tr.*  to write
пита́ние *n. neuter* (16) nutrition
пита́тельный *adj.* (17 *pred. masc. sing.* пита́телен § 356,
пита́ть (Reg. A) *v. tr. imperf.* to nourish       p. 569) nutritive
   –ся   to be nourished
*Пи́тсбург *n. masc.* (3) Pittsburgh
питьево́й *adj.* (18) drinkable, potable
   пить – вы́пить  to drink
пи́ща *n. fem.* (8) food
пищеваре́ние *n. neuter* (16) (food) digestion
   пи́ща, food;  вари́ть to cook
пищево́й *adj.* (18) pertaining to food, food  (*adj.*)
пла́вать – попла́вать (Reg. A) *v. tr.* to swim, to float, to sail
                                 (Cf. § 282, p. 632)
пла́вить – распла́вить (Irr. C-2) *v. tr.*  to melt
плавле́ние *n. neuter* (16) fusion, melting
пла́мени, пла́менем *see* пла́мя
пла́мя *n. neuter* (§ 358, p. 575) flame
*план *n. masc.* (1) plan
*плане́та *n. fem.* (7) planet
*Планк *n. masc.* (3) Planck
*пла́нков *poss. adj.* (§ 361, p. 584) Planck's
пласт *n. masc.* (1) layer, stratum
пласти́нка *n. fem.* (9a) (photographic) plate, foil
*пласти́чность *n. fem.* (12) plasticity
*пла́тина *n. fem.* (7) platinum
*пла́тиновый *adj.* (17) pertaining to or made of platinum
пло́ский *adj.* (21a) flat
пло́скость *n. fem.* (12) plane
пло́тность *n. fem.* (12) density
   пло́тный dense, thick
*Плуто́н *n. masc.* (1) Pluto
*плуто́ний *n. masc.* (5) plutonium
по *prep.* (*with dat.*) according to, with respect to, along, by
way of  (*with acc.*)for (purpose), about (*with prepl.*) after,
                            following (Cf. § 127, p. 187)
по сравне́нию *fixed expr.* by comparison
пова́ренный *adj.* (17) (*pred. masc. sing.* пова́рен Cf. § 356,
                            p. 570) pertaining to cooking
   по- + вари́ть  to be cooking
пова́ренная *соль *fixed expr.* common salt
поведе́ние *n. neuter* (16) behavior
   по- + води́ть, вести́ to be leading (Cf. § 381, p. 626)

поверхностное натяжение *fixed expr.* surface tension
поверхностный *adj.* (17a) surface (*adj.*)
поверхность *n.fem.* (12) surface
 по- + верх upper part, peak
повод *n.masc.* (1) lead, clue
 по- + водить, вести to be leading (Cf. § 381, p. 626)
поворот *n.masc.* turn, rotation
 по- + ворот winch, windless
повсюду *adv.* everywhere
повторять (Reg. A) - повторить (Reg. B-2) *v.tr.* to repeat
 по- + второй second
повышать (Reg. A) - повысить (Irr. D-2) *v.tr.* to raise,
 по- + выше higher                                    to increase
повышение *n.neuter* (16) increase, rise
повышенный (17) raised, increased (*perf. pas. past part. of*
                                    ПОВЫШАТЬ - ПОВЫСИТЬ)
повышу *perf. future first pers. sing. of* ПОВЫШАТЬ -
                                    ПОВЫСИТЬ
поглощать (Reg. A)-поглотиь (Irr. D-2, Т → Щ) *v.tr.* to
 по- + глотка throat                          absorb, to swallow
по-*гречески *adv.* in Greek
погружать (Reg. A) - погрузить (Irr. D-2) *v.tr.* to submerge,
 по- + груз load, freight                               to bury
под, (подо) *prep.* (*with acc. implying motion*) under,
toward (*with prep. implying no motion*) under, near (Cf. § 127, p. 187)
подверг *perf. past tense masc. sing. of* ПОДВЕРГАТЬ -
                                    ПОДВЕРГНУТЬ
подвергать (Reg. A) - подвергнуть (Irr. J-3) *v.tr.* to subject
 -ся (*with dat.*) to submit to, to undergo, to yield to        (to)
подвижной *adj.* (18) (*pred. masc. sing.* ПОДВИЖЕН Cf. § 356,
                          p. 568) mobile, movable
 по- + двигать - двинуть to move
*подгруппа *n.fem.* (7) subgroup
 под- + *группа group
поддержание *n.neuter* (16) maintenance, support
 под- + держать - подержать to hold
поддерживать (Reg. A) - поддержать (Reg. B-2) *v.tr.* to
 -ся to be maintained, sustained              maintain, to sustain
поджигание *n.neuter* (16) ignition
 под- + жечь to be burning (*tr.*)
подкисленный (17) acidified (*perf. pas. past part. of*
                          ПОДКИСЛЯТЬ - ПОДКИСЛИТЬ)
подкислять (Reg. A) - подкислить (Reg. B-2) *v.tr.* acidified
 под- + кислый sour, acid
поднесу *perf. future tense first pers. plu. of* ПОДНОСИТЬ -
                                    поднести

поднимать (Reg. A) - поднять (Irr. F-6) *v.tr.* to lift, to raise
   -ся to be lifted or raised, to move upward
подносить (Irr. D-2) - поднести (Irr. H-2) to bring close, to
                              offer, to present (Cf. § 382, p. 630)
   под- + носить, нести to be carrying (Cf. § 381, p. 626)
подобно *prep.* (*with dat.*) similar to, like (to)
подробно *adv.* in detail, more particularly
подставлять (Reg. A) - подставить (Irr. C-2)*v.tr.* to place under,
   под- + ставить - поставить to place     to substitute (math.)
подтверждать (Reg. A) - подтвердить (Irr. D-2, д → ж)
   -ся to be confirmed                     *v.tr.* to confirm
   под- + твёрдый hard, solid
подтверждение *n.neuter* (16) confirmation
подтверждённый (17) confirmed (*perf. pas. past part.* of
                         подтверждать - подтвердить)
подходить (Irr. D-2, д → ж) - подойти (Irr. H-10) *v.intr.*
                  to come near, to approach (Cf. § 382, p. 630)
   под- + ходить, итти to be going (Cf. § 381, p. 626)
подъём *n.masc.* (1) rise
поезд *n.masc.* (1) (railroad) train
поехать (Irr. D-4) *v.intr. perf.* to travel (for a time)
                              (Cf. § 382, p. 632)
позволять (Reg. A) - позволить (Reg. B-2) *v.tr.* to permit,
                                             to enable
позднее *adj. pred. comp.* (*undecl.*) later on, thereafter
поздний *adj.* (19) later, subsequent
*позитрон *n.masc.* (1) positron
познакомиться *see* знакомить
пока *adv. and conj.* almost, until
пока ни *fixed expr.* until (§ 391, p. 651)
покажет *perf. future tense third pers. plu.* of
                         показывать - показать
показанный (17) shown, set forth (*perf. pas. past part.* of
                         показывать - показать)
показатель *n.masc.* (6) indicator, exponent
показывать (Reg. A) - показать (Irr. D-1, з → ж) *v.tr.*
   по- + казать to show     to exhibit, to make evident, to show
покров *n.masc.* (1) veil, cover
покрывать (Reg. A) - покрыть (Irr. E-4) *v.tr.* to cover over,
   по- + крыть - покрыть to cover          to meet (expense)
полагать (Reg. A) - положить (Reg. B-2)*v.tr.* to place, to pro-
   по- + ложиться to be lying down          pose, to assume
по-латини *adv.* in Latin
поле *n.neuter* (15) field

ПОЛЁТ *n. masc.* (1) flight

по- + летать, лететь to be flying (Cf. § 381, p. 626)

*ПОЛИМЕ́Р *n. masc.* (1) polymer

*ПОЛИМЕРИЗА́ЦИЯ *n. fem.* (11) polymerization

ПО́ЛНОСТЬ *n. fem.* (12) completeness

ПО́ЛНОСТЬЮ (§ 98, p. 141) completely

ПО́ЛНЫЙ *adj.* (17) (*pred. masc. sing.* ПО́ЛОН Cf. § 356, p. 570)

ПОЛОВИ́НА *n. fem.* (7) half                          whole, complete, entire

ПОЛОЖЕ́НИЕ *n. neuter* (16) position

по- + ложи́ться to be lying down

ПОЛО́ЖЕННЫЙ (17) placed (*perf. pas. past part. of*
                                    полага́ть – положи́ть)

ПОЛОЖИ́ТЕЛЬНО *adv.* positively

ПОЛОЖИ́ТЕЛЬНЫЙ *adj.* (17b) positive

*ПОЛО́НИЙ *n. masc.* (5) polonium

ПОЛУЧА́ТЬ (Reg. A) – ПОЛУЧИ́ТЬ (Reg. B-2) *v. tr.* to obtain,

-ся to be obtained, produced, prepared                to acquire

ПОЛУЧЕ́НИЕ *n. neuter* (16) production, acquisition

ПОЛУ́ЧЕННЫЙ (17) obtained, acquired, produced (*perf. pas. past
                               part. of* ПОЛУЧА́ТЬ – ПОЛУЧИ́ТЬ)

ПО́ЛЬЗОВАТЬСЯ – ВОСПО́ЛЬЗОВАТЬСЯ (Irr. B-1) *v. refl.* (*with instr.*)

ПОЛЕ́ЗНЫЙ useful                   to utilize, to avail self (of), to use

ПО́ЛЬЗУЕМСЯ, ПО́ЛЬЗУЮТСЯ *pres. tense forms of* ПО́ЛЬЗОВАТЬСЯ –
                                                    ВОСПО́ЛЬЗОВАТЬСЯ

ПО́ЛЬЗУЯСЬ *pres. ger. of* ПО́ЛЬЗОВАТЬСЯ – ВОСПО́ЛЬЗОВАТЬСЯ

ПО́ЛЮС *n. masc.* (1) pole

*ПОЛЯ́РНЫЙ *adj.* (17a) polar

ПОМЕЩА́ТЬ (Reg. A) – ПОМЕСТИ́ТЬ (Irr. D-2, СТ → Щ) *v. tr.*

по- + ме́сто place                              to place, to arrange

ПО́МНИТЬ – ВСПО́МНИТЬ (Reg. B-2) *v. tr.* to remember

ПО́МОЩЬ *n. fem.* (12) aid, help

при по́мощи; с по́мощью *fixed expr.* with the aid (of)

ПОНИЖА́ТЬ (Reg. A) – ПОНИ́ЗИТЬ (Irr. D-2, З → Ж) *v. tr.*

по- + ни́же lower                              to lower, to decrease

ПОНИЖЕ́НИЕ, *n. neuter* (16) decrease, lowering

ПОНИЖЕ́НИЙ *prep. sing. of* ПОНИЖЕ́НИЕ

ПОНИМА́НИЕ *n. neuter* (16) understanding

ПОНИМА́ТЬ (Reg. A) – ПОНЯ́ТЬ (Irr. F-5) *v. tr. and intr.*

ПОНЯ́ТИЕ *n. neuter* (16) concept                     to understand

ПОНЯ́ТЬ *see* ПОНИМА́ТЬ

ПОПАДА́ТЬ (Reg. A) – ПОПА́СТЬ (Irr. H-7) *v. intr.* to fall into,
                               to strike against, to impinge on

ПОПРО́БУЕМ *perf. future tense first pers. plu. of*
                               про́бовать – попро́бовать

пор, пора́ *n.* (Cf. § 390, p. 650) *used in certain fixed exprs.*

порази́тельно *adv.* surprisingly
  по- + рази́ть to hit, to strike
поро́да *n.fem.* (7) type, genus, geological formation
  по- + род birth, tribe, genus
по́рох *n.masc.* (3) gun powder
порохово́й *adj.* (18) (pertaining to) gun powder
порошке́ *prep. sing. of* порошо́к
порошо́к *n.masc.* (3a) powder
по-*русски *adv.* in Russian
по́ршень *n.masc.* (6a) piston
по́ршнем *instr. sing. of* по́ршень
по́ршня *gen. sing. of* по́ршень
поря́дку *dat. sing. of* поря́док
поря́дка *gen. sing. of* поря́док
поря́док *n.masc.* (3a) order
  по- + ряд series
поса́дка *n.fem.* (9a) planting
  по- + сади́ть - посади́ть to plant
по́сланный (17) dispatched, sent, transmitted  (*pas. past part.*
  по- + слать - посла́ть to send   *of* посыла́ть - посла́ть)
по́сле *prep.* (*with gen.*) after
после́дний *adj.* (19) latter, recent
  по- + след track, trace
после́довательный *adj.* (17b) successive
после́дующий (22) following (*act. pres. part. from*
                после́довать Cf. сле́довать)
постепе́нно *adv.* gradually, stepwise, little by little
  по- + сте́пень degree, rank
постоя́нно *adv.* constantly, continuously
  по- + стоя́ть - постоя́ть to stand, to remain
постоя́нный *adj.* (17a) constant, continuous, invariable
     (*For use of fem. forms as noun* Cf. § 392, p. 652)
постро́енный (17) constructed (*perf. pas. past part. of*
постро́ить *see* стро́ить         стро́ить - постро́ить)
*постула́т *n.masc.* (1) postulate
поступа́ть (Reg. A) - поступи́ть (Irr. C-2) *v.intr.* to enter, to
                         occur, to proceed
  по- + ступа́ть - ступи́ть to stride, to walk
поступа́тельный *adj.* (17) progressive
посыла́ть (Reg. A) - посла́ть (Irr. пошлю́, пошлёшь *etc.*)
          to dispatch, to send, to transmit
*потенциа́л *n.masc.* (1) potential
*потенци́руя *pres. ger. of* *потенци́ровать (Irr. A-1) *v.tr.*
  *imperf. and perf.* to be converting (to convert) to exponential
поте́ря *n.fem.* (10) loss         or power expression (math.)

ПОТОК *n.masc.* (3) stream, current
   ПО- + ТОК  current
потребный *adj.* (17a) necessary, required
похожий *adj.* (22) similar
   ПО- + ХОДИТЬ, ИТТИ to be going (Cf. § 381, p. 626)
почва *n.fem.* (7) soil
почему *interr. adv.* why
   ПО- + ЧТО  who, that
почернение *n.neuter* (16) blackening
   ПО- + чёрный  black
почти *adv.* almost
поэтому *adv., conj.* hence
   ПО- + ЭТОМУ *dat. sing. of* ЭТОТ this
появление *n.neuter* (16) appearance
   ПО- + ЯВЛЯТЬ - ЯВИТЬ to show
появляться (Reg. A) - появиться (Irr. C-2) *v.refl.* to put
                              in an appearance, to show up
   ПО- + ЯВЛЯТЬ - ЯВИТЬ to show
пр. *abbrev. for* ПРОЧЬ away, off
правда *n.fem.* (7) truth, (it is) true (that)
правильно *adv.* correctly
правильный *adj.* (17b) correct, regular (crystals)
*практика *n.fem.* (9) practice, practical work
*практический *adj.* (21) practical
превосходить (Irr. D-2, д → ж)  - превозойти (Irr. H-10)
               *v.tr.* to exceed, to surpass (Cf. § 382, p. 630)
   пре- + вос- (воз-) + ХОДИТЬ, ИТТИ to be going (Cf. § 381, p. 626)
превращать (Reg. A)- превратить (Irr. D-2,  Т → Щ)  *v.tr*
                              to convert, to change
   -ся to be changed, converted, to undergo change or conversion
   пре- + вращать  to be turning
превращающийся (22)  being changed, changing, reacting (chem.)
      (*act. pres. part. refl. of* превращать - превратить)
превышать (Reg. A) - превысить (Irr. D-2,  с → ш )  *v.tr.*
   пре- + выше  higher                        to exceed
пред *see* перед
предварительно *adv.* preliminarily
предел *n.masc.* (1) limit, border
предлагать (Reg. A) - предложить (Reg. B-2) to offer, to
   пред- + ложиться  to be lying down                   propose
предложенный (17) proposed, offered (*perf. pas. past part.*
                        *of* предлагать - предложить)
предмет *n.masc.* (1) object
предохранительный *adj.* (17) protective, prophylactic
предохранять (Reg. A) - предохранить (Reg. B-2)*v.tr.*
                              to protect, to forestall
   пред- + охранять - охранить  to guard

предполага́ть (Reg. A) - предположи́ть (Reg. B-2) *v.tr.*
         to presume, to hypothesize, to plan
  пред- + по- + ложи́ться  to be lying down
предположе́ние *n.neuter* (16) proposition, idea, hypothesis
предположенный (17) proposed, hypothesized (*perf. pas.*
     *past part.* of предполага́ть - предположи́ть)
предска́зывать (Reg. A) - предсказа́ть (Irr. D-1, 3 → Ж)
           *v.tr.* to predict
  пред- + сказа́ть  to speak
представле́ние *n.neuter* (16) notion, idea, hypothesis
  пред- + ста́вить - поста́вить  to place
представля́ть (Reg. A) - предста́вить (Irr. C-2) *v.tr.* to present,
          present, to show, to display
  себе́  to represent to self, to imagine, to conceive
  собо́й  to constitute, to be (Cf. § 99, p. 144)
  -ся  to present self, to be (Cf. § 99, p. 144)
предстоя́ть (Reg. A) *v.tr. imperf.* (*with dat.*) to confront
  пред- + стоя́ть - постоя́ть  to stand, to remain
предыду́щий *adj.* (22) foregoing, preceding
  пред- + ходи́ть, итти́  to be going (Cf. § 381, p. 626)
предъявля́ть (Reg. A) - предъяви́ть (Irr. C-2) *v.tr.* to present,
         to impose (demands)
  пред- + явля́ть - яви́ть  to show
пре́жде *adv.* formerly
пре́жний *adj.* (19) former
преиму́щественно *adv.* predominantly
прекра́сный *adj.* (17a) splendid, beautiful
  пре- + кра́сный  red, beautiful
прекраща́ть (Reg. A) - прекрати́ть (Irr. D-2, Т → Щ) to quit,
  -ся  to be concluded, to come to a stop     to stop
  пре- + кра́ткий  short
преоблада́ть (Reg. A) *v.intr. imperf.* to be predominating, to
          be dominating
преобразова́ние *n.neuter* (16) conversion, (complete) change
  пре- + о́браз  form, shape
преобразо́вывать (Reg. A) - преобразова́ть (Irr. A-1) to
  -ся  to undergo change or conversion   convert, to transform
преобразу́ется *perf. fut. tense third pers. sing. refl.*
       of преобразо́вывать - преобразова́ть
*препара́т *n.masc.* (1) preparation
пре́сный *adj.* (17a) flat (taste), insipid
*прессова́ть - *спрессова́ть (Irr. A-1) *v.tr.* to press
при *prep.* (*with prep.*) at, during, by
при э́том *fixed expr.* thereby
прибавле́ние *n.neuter* (16) addition
приближа́ть (Reg. A) - прибли́зить (Irr. D-2, 3 → Ж) *v.tr.*
  -ся  to be brought near, to come near, to approach   to bring
  при + бли́зкий  near

приближе́ние *n.neuter* (16) approach, approximation

приблизи́тельно *adv.* approximately

прибо́р *n.masc.*(1) device, apparatus, instrument

приведённый (17) brought (about, forward) (*perf. pas. past part. of* приводи́ть - привести́)

приводи́ть (Irr. D-2, д → ж) - привести́ (Irr. H-5) *v.tr.*
to bring (about, forward) to lead, to cause (Cf. § 382, p. 630)

при- + води́ть, вести́ to be leading (Cf. § 381, p. 626)

привело́ *perf. past tense neuter sing. of* приводи́ть - привести́

придава́емый (17) being imparted (*pas. pres. part. of* придава́ть - прида́ть)

придава́ть (Irr. B) - прида́ть (Irr. I-3) *v.tr.* to impart

при- + дава́ть - дать to give

придаёт (*pres. tense third pers. sing. of* придава́ть - прида́ть)

прида́нный (17) imparted (*pas. past part of* придава́ть - прида́ть)

придёт (*perf. fut. third pers. sing. of* приходи́ть - прийти)

прие́м *n.masc.* (1) reception

при- + име́ть to be having

прие́мник *n.masc.* (3) receiver

*призмати́ческий *adj.* (21) prismatic

при́знак *n.masc.* (3) indication

при- + знать to be knowing

прикрепля́ть (Reg. A) - прикрепи́ть (Irr. C-2) *v.tr.* to fasten

при- + кре́пкий strong

примене́ние *n.neuter* (16) use, application

при- + ме́на exchange

примени́мость *n.fem.*(12) applicability

примени́мый *adj.* (17) usable, applicable

применя́емость *n.fem.* (12) usability, application

применя́ть (Reg. A) - примени́ть (Reg. B-2) *v.tr.*to apply, to use
-ся to be applied, used

приме́р *n.masc.* (1) example

при- + ме́ра measure

приме́рно *adv.* approximately, about

примыка́ть (Reg. A) - примкну́ть (Reg. B-1) (К) *v.intr.*
to attach to, to pertain to

принадлежа́ть (Reg. B-2)(К) *v.intr. imperf.* to belong (to)

при- + над- + лежа́ть to be lying

принима́ть (Reg. A) - приня́ть *v.tr.* to assume, to take on, to achieve

*при́нцип *n.masc.*(1) principle

приобрета́ть (Reg. A) - приобрести́ (Irr.H-3) *v.tr.* to acquire, to attain

при- + о- + брести́ - побрести́ to wander

приписывать (Reg. A)- приписа́ть (Irr. D-1) *v.tr.* to ascribe

при- + писа́ть to write

приро́да *n.fem.* (7) nature
приро́дный *adj.* (17) natural
присоедине́ние *n.neuter* (16) combination
    при- + со- + оди́н one
присоединя́ть (Reg. A) - присоедини́ть(Reg.B-2)*v.tr.*to combine
                               with, to add on, to take up
приставля́ть (Reg. A) - приста́вить (Irr.C-1) *v.tr.*to place
    при- + ста́вить- поста́вить to put       near, to put near
прису́тствие *n.neuter* (16) presence
    при- + суть are
прису́щий (22) *adj.* (*with dat.*) peculiar (to), inherent (to)
притя́гивать (Reg. A) - притяну́ть (Reg. B-1) *v.tr.* to attract
    при- + тя́га pull
притяже́ние *n.neuter* (16) attraction
прихо́д *n.masc.* (1) arrival
    при- + ходи́ть, итти́    to be going (Cf. § 381, p. 626)
приходи́ть (Irr. D-2, Д → Ж) - прийти́ (Irr. H-10) *v.intr.*
                      to arrive (Cf. § 382, p. 630)
  -ся *v.refl.* to be necessary, to be suitable
причи́на *n.fem.* (7) cause
причиня́ть (Reg. A) - причини́ть(Reg. B-2)*v.tr.* to cause
прише́л *perf. past masc. sing.* of приходи́ть - прийти́
                            (Cf. § 224, p. 352)
пробега́ть (Reg. A) - пробежа́ть (Reg. B-2) *v.tr. and intr.*
               to run across, to traverse (Cf. § 382, p. 630)
    про- + бе́гать, бежа́ть to be fleeing (Cf. § 381, p. 626)
*пробле́ма *n.fem.* (7) problem
про́бовать - попро́бовать (Irr. A-1) *v.tr.* to test
    про́ба sample, test
проведённый (17) performed, carried out (*perf. pas. past*
                      *part. of* проводи́ть - провести́)
про́вод (1) conductor, conduit, leading
проводи́ть (Irr. D-2, Д → Ж) - провести́ (Irr. H-5) *v.tr.*
  to lead through, to conduct, to carry out, to perform (Cf. § 382, p. 630)
    про- + води́ть, вести́ to be leading (Cf. § 381, p. 626)
проводни́к *n.masc.* (3) conductor
про́волока *n.fem.* (7) wire
*програ́мма *n.fem.* (7) program
проде́лывать - проде́лать (Reg. A) *v.tr.* to perform (a lengthy
    про- + де́ло thing       task), to do, to knock (a hole through)
продолжа́ть (Reg. A) - продо́лжить (Reg.B-2)*v.tr.* to prolong
  -ся to be prolonged, to continue
    про- + до́лгий long
*проду́кт *n.masc.* (1) product
*проду́кция *n.fem.* (11) production
прозра́чный *adj.* (17a) transparent
    про- + зреть to be seeing

пройду́т *perf. fut. tense third person plu. of*
$\qquad$ проходи́ть - пройти́
произведе́ние *n. neuter* (16) product (multiplication)
про- + из- + води́ть to be leading (Cf. § 381, p. 626)
произведё,т *perf. fut. third pers. sing. of*
$\qquad$ производи́ть - произвести́
произвё́л *perf. past masc. sing. of* производи́ть -
$\qquad$ произвести́
производи́ть (Irr. D-2) - произвести́ (Irr. H-5) *v. tr.* to effect,
$\qquad$ to cause, to bring about (Cf. § 382, p. 630)
-ся to be caused, to come about, to be carried out
про- + из- + води́ть, вести́ to be leading (Cf. § 381, p. 626)
произво́дный *adj. and noun* (17) derived, derivative (math. and chem.)
производ́ство *n. neuter* (13) production (Cf. § 392, p. 652)
произноси́ть (Irr. D-2) - произнести́ (Irr. H-2) *v. tr.*
$\qquad$ to pronounce (Cf. § 382, p. 630)
про- + из- + носи́ть, нести́ to be carrying (Cf § 381, p. 626)
происходи́ть (Irr. D-2, Д → Ж) произойти́ (Irr. H-10) to proceed,
$\qquad$ to occur (Cf. § 382, p. 630)
про- + из- + ходи́ть, итти́ to be going (Cf. § 381, p. 626)
происхожде́ние *n. neuter* (16) origin, source
пролета́ть (Reg. A) - пролете́ть (Irr. D-2, Т → Ч) *v. tr.*
$\qquad$ to fly across, to fly through (Cf. § 382, p. 630)
про- + лета́ть, лете́ть to be flying (Cf. § 381, p. 626)
промежу́тки *n. and acc. plu. of* ПРОМЕЖУ́ТОК
промежу́ток *n. masc.* (3a) interval
про- + ме́жду between
промы́шленность *n. fem.* (12) industry
про- + мысль thought
промы́шленный *adj.* (17) industrial
прони́зывать, (Reg. A) - прониза́ть (Irr. D-1. З → Ж) *v. tr.*
про-, + ни́зкий low $\qquad$ to penetrate
проника́ть (Reg. A) - прони́кнуть (Irr. J-3) to penetrate, to
проникнове́ние *n. neuter* (16) penetration $\qquad$ work into
*пропорциона́льность *n. fem.* (12) proportionality
*пропорциона́льный *adj.* (17b) proportional
пропуска́ть (Reg. A) - пропусти́ть (Irr. D-2, СТ → Щ)
$\qquad$ *v. tr.* to pass through, to cause to pass or elapse
-ся to be passed through
про- +, пуска́ть - пусти́ть to start, to cause
пропуска́ние *n. neuter* (16) passage (through)
просте́йший *adj. superl.* (22) simplest (Cf. § 346, p. 546)
про́сто *adv.* simply
просто́й *adj.* (18) simple
простра́нство *n. neuter* (13) space
про- + страна́ country, neighborhood

протекáть (Reg. A) - протéчь (Irr. G-3) *v.tr.* to flow through,
   про- + течь to be flowing          to flow along, to proceed
прóтив *prep.* (*with gen.*) against, opposite
противодéйствие *n.neuter* (16) counter action, reaction
   прóтив against;   дéйствовать to be acting
противополóжный *adj.* (17) (diagonally) opposite
   прóтив against;   по- + пожúться to be lying down
противостоять (Reg. B-2)- противостáть (Irr. C-5) *v.tr.*
                         to resist, to oppose
   прóтив against;  стоять - постоять to stand, to remain
*протóн *n.masc.* (1) proton
*профéссор *n.masc.* (1 Footnote 1, p. 588) professor
*профилактúческий *adj.* (21) prophylactic
*профильтрóвывать - *профильтровáть (Irr. A-1) *v.tr.* to filter
   про- + *фильтровáть to be filtering            through
*профильтрýйте *perf. imp. second pers. plu. of*
                  *профильтрóвывать - *профильтровáть
проходúть (Irr. D-2, д → ж) - пройтú (Irr. H-10) *v.intr.*
             to pass through (Cf. § 382, p. 630)
   про- + ходúть, иттú to be going (Cf. § 381, p. 626)
проходящий (22) passing through (*act. pres. part. of*
                 проходúть - пройтú)
прохождéние *n.neuter* (16) passage (through)
*процéсс *n.masc.* (1) process, lawsuit
прóчность *n.fem.* (12) stability, strength, resistance
прóчный *adj.* (17a) stable
прочь *adv.* away, off
прошéдший (22) having passed through (*act. past part. of*
                 проходúть - пройтú)
прошлú *perf. past plu. of* проходúть - пройтú (Cf. § 224, p. 352)
проявлять (Reg. A) - проявúть (Irr. C-2) *v.tr.* to develop
   про- + являть - явúть to show          (photography)
прямóй *adj.* (18) direct, straight
прямолинéйно-возврáтный *adj.* (17) reciprocating
   прямóй straight; *лúния line;   возвращáть - возвратúть
прямолинéйный *adj.* (17) linear, straight line        to return
*псевдометаллúческий *adj.* (21) pseudometallic
птúчий *poss. adj.* (§ 360, p. 581) birds
   птúца bird
*публиковáть - *опубликовáть (Irr.A-1) *v.tr.* to publish
пустотá *n.fem.* (7) emptiness
пусть *verbal auxiliary* let (Cf. § 306, p. 484)
путём *instr. sing. of* путь
путú *see decl. of* путь (Cf. § 359, p. 577)
путь *n.masc.* (§ 359, p. 577) way, path

пшени́ца *n.fem.* (8) wheat
пя́тен *gen. plu.* of ПЯТНО́
ПЯТНО́ *n.neuter* (13b) spot


## Р


рабо́та *n.fem.* (7) work
рабо́тать – порабо́тать (Reg. A) *v.intr.* to work
рабо́чий *adj.* (22) working, pertaining to work or workers
ра́венство *n.neuter* (13) equality
равнове́сие *n.neuter* (16) equilibrium
   ра́вный equal; вес weight
равноме́рный *adj.* (17a) uniform
   ра́вный equal;   ме́ра measure
ра́вный *adj.* (17a) equal
рад *adj.* (Cf. § 357, p. 571) happy
*радиа́льно *adv.* radially
*радиа́ция *n.fem.* (11) radiation
*ра́дий *n.masc.* (5) radium
*радика́л *n.masc.* (1) radical
*радиоакти́вность *n.fem.* (12) radioactivity
*радиоакти́вный *adj.* (17a) radioactive
радиоволна́ *n.fem.* (7) radio wave
   *ра́дио radio;   волна́ wave
*радиолокацио́нный *adj.* (17) radar (*adj.*)
*радиолока́ция *n.fem.* (11) radio location, radar
*ра́диус *n.masc.* (1) radius
ра́дуга *n.fem.* (9) rainbow
раз *n.masc.* time, times (in arithmetical sense) (Cf. § 374, p. 610;
                                     § 376, p. 616)
разбавля́ть (Reg. A) – разба́вить (Irr. C-2) *v.tr.* to dilute
разберём *perf. future tense   first pers. plu.* of
                         разбира́ть – разобра́ть
разбира́ть (Reg. A) – разобра́ть (Irr. F-4) *v.tr.* to take apart,
   раз- + брать to be taking          to analyze, to investigate
разведе́ние *n.neuter* (16) propagation (of plant)
   раз- + води́ть, вести́ to be leading (Cf. § 381, p. 626)
развива́ть (Reg. A) – разви́ть (Irr.E-3) *v.tr.* to develop,
   -ся to be developed, worked out       to evolve, to work out
   рас- + вить   to wind
разви́тие *n.neuter* (16) evolution, development
раздроблённый (17) broken to bits, crushed to pieces (*perf.*
              *pas. past part.* of раздробля́ть – раздроби́ть)
раздробля́ть (Reg. A) – раздроби́ть (Irr. C-2) *v.tr.* to break
   -ся to be broken to bits, broken up              to bits
   раз- + дробь fraction

разлага́ть (Reg. A) - разложи́ть (Reg. B-2) *v.tr.* to disintegrate,
  -ся to undergo decomposition             to decompose
  раз- + ложи́ться   to be lying down

разлива́ть (Reg. A) - разли́ть (Irr. E-3) *v.tr.* to pour out (into
  раз- + лить to be pouring           separate containers)

различа́ть (Reg. A) - различи́ть (Reg. B-2) *v.tr.* to distinguish
  -ся to be distinguished (ОТ, from), to differ     (ОТ, from)
  раз- + лицо́ face, person

разли́чный *adj.* (17a) different, various

разложе́ние *n.neuter* (16) decomposition, disintegration, separation,
  раз- + ложи́ться to be lying down           factoring (math.)

разло́жим *perf. future tense second person plu. of*
                         разлага́ть - разложи́ть

*размагни́чивать (Reg. A) - *размагни́тить (Irr. D-2, Т → Ч)
  раз- + *магни́т magnet          *v.tr.* to demagnetize

разме́р *n.masc.* (1) dimension, magnitude
  раз- + ме́ра measure

размягча́ть (Reg. A) - размягчи́ть (Reg. B-2) *v.tr.* to make
  -ся to become soft, to soften          soft, soften
  раз- + мя́гкий soft

разнообра́зный *adj.* (17a) different, dissimilar, diverse (as to
  ра́зный different; о́браз form, shape        form or type)

разноро́дность *n.fem.* (12) diversity, inhomogeniety
  ра́зный different; род birth, tribe, genus

разноро́дный *adj.* (17a) different (as to type)

ра́зность *n.fem.* (12) difference

ра́зный *adj.* (17) different, various

разогрева́ние *n.neuter* (16) heating up (process)
  раз- + горе́ть to be burning

разраба́тывать - разрабо́тать (Reg. A) *v.tr.* to work out,
  раз- + рабо́та work            to develop

разрабо́тать *see* разраба́тывать

разрежа́ть (Reg. A) - разреди́ть (Irr. D-2, Д → Ж) *v.tr.*
  раз- + ре́же rarer         to rarefy, to render diffuse

разреже́ние *n.neuter* (16) rarefaction

разрежённый (17) rarefied, diffused (*perf. pas. past part.* of
                разрежа́ть - разреди́ть)

разреше́ние *n.neuter* (16) solution (of problem), decision
  раз- + реши́ть to decide, to solve

разруша́ть (Reg. A) - разру́шить (Reg. B-2) *v.tr.* to destroy

разрыхли́ть *see* рыхли́ть

разъеда́ть (Reg. A) - разъе́сть (Irr. I-1) *v.tr.* to eat apart,
  -ся to be eaten apart, to undergo corrosion      to corrode
  раз- + есть to be eating

разъе́стся *refl. perf. future tense third pers. sing. of* разъеда́ть – разъе́сть

\*раке́та *n.fem.* (7) rocket

раскалённый (17) heated (to glowing) (*perf. pas. part. of* раскаливать – раскали́ть)

раска́ливать (Reg. A) – раскали́ть (Reg. B-2) *v. tr.* to heat
  –СЯ to be heated (to glowing) (to glowing)
  рас- + кали́ть to be glowing

распада́ться (Reg. A) – распа́сться (Irr. H-7) *v.refl.* to decom-
  рас- + па́дать to be falling    pose, undergo decomposition
распаде́ние *n.neuter* (16) decomposition

расплавленный (17) fused, melted (*perf. pas. past part. of* расплавля́ть – распла́вить)

расплавля́ть (Reg. A) – распла́вить (Irr. C-2) *v. tr.* to fuse, to
  –СЯ to be melted, fused    melt
  рас- + пла́вить to melt, to float

располага́ть (Reg. A) – расположи́ть (Reg. B-2) to distribute,
    to arrange, to place, to control
  –СЯ to be distributed, placed, arrayed
  рас- + ложи́тся to be lying down
располо́женный (17) distributed, placed (*perf. pas. past part. of* располага́ть – расположи́ть)

распределённый (17) distributed, divided (*perf. pas. past part. of* распределя́ть – распредли́ть)

распределя́ть (Reg. A) – распредели́ть (Reg. B-2) *v. tr.* to dis-
  рас- + предел limit    tribute, to divide (e.g., into classes)
распространённый (17) diffused, extended, spread (*perf. pas. past part. of* распространя́ть – распространи́ть)

распространя́ть (Reg. A) – распространи́ть (Reg. B-2) *v.tr.* to ex-
    tend, to diffuse, to spread
  –СЯ to be extended, diffused, spread
  рас- + про- + страна́ country, locality
рассева́ть – рассе́ять (Reg. A) *v. tr.* to sow (widely), to scatter,
  –СЯ to be sowed (widely), scattered, diffused  to diffuse
  рас- + се́ять to be sowing
рассе́яние *n.neuter* (16) scattering, diffusion
рассе́ять *see* рассева́ть – рассе́ять
рассма́тривать (Reg. A) – рассмотре́ть (Reg.B-2) *v.tr.* to con-
  рас- + смотр observation    sider, to examine
расстоя́ние *n.neuter* (16) distance
  рас- + стоя́ть to be standing
раство́р *n.masc.* (1) solution
  рас- + твори́ть to be creating

раствóренный (17) dissolved (*perf. pas. past part. of* растворя́ть – раствори́ть)

раствори́мость *n.fem.*(12) solubility

раствори́мый *adj.* (17) soluble

раствори́тель *n.masc.* (6) solvent

растворя́ть (Reg. A) – раствори́ть (Reg. B-2) *v.tr.* to dissolve
 –ся to be dissolved

растéние *n.neuter* (16) plant (vegetable organism)
 расти́ to be growing

растёт *pres. tense third person s.ing. of* расти́ – вы́расти

расти́тельный *adj.*(17) vegetable, plant

расти́ – вы́расти (*Irr.* расту́, –ёшь, –ёт etc.) *v.intr.* to grow, to increase

растра́чивать (Reg. A) – растра́тить (*Irr.* D-2, Т → Ч) *v.tr.* to dissipate, to expend
 рас- + тра́та expenditure, waste

расту́т *pres. tense third person sing. of* расти́ – вы́расти

расширéние *n.neuter* (16) expansion
 рас- + широ́кий wide

расширя́ть (Reg. A) – расши́рить (Reg.B-2) *v.tr.* to expand, to extend
 –ся to be expanded, extended

расщепля́ть (Reg. A) – расщепи́ть (*Irr.* C-2) *v.tr.* to disintegrate, to decompose, to breakdown
 –ся to undergo disintegration, decomposition, breakdown
 рас- + щепа́ (wood) shaving

*реагéнт *n.masc.* (1) reagent

*реаги́ровать – *прореаги́ровать (*Irr.*A-1)*v.intr.* to react

*реаги́руют *pres. tense third person plu. of* *реаги́ровать – *прореаги́ровать

*реаги́рующий (22) reacting (*pas. pres. part. of* *реаги́ровать – *прореаги́ровать)

*реакти́в *n.masc.* (1) reagent

*реакти́вный *adj.* (17) reactive

*реакцио́нный *adj.* (17) (pertaining to) reaction

*реа́кция *n.fem.*(11) reaction

*реализова́ть(*Irr.* A-1) *v.tr. imperf. and perf.* to realize, to accomplish

*реа́льный *adj.*(17b) real

рёбер *gen. plu. of* ребро́

ребро́ *n.neuter* (13b) rib, edge (e.g. of cube)

*ревмати́зм *n.masc.* (1) rheumatism

*регенера́ция *n.fem.* (11) regeneration

*реда́ктор *n.masc.* (1) editor

ре́дкий *adj.* (21a) rare

ре́дко *adv.* rarely

ре́жутся *refl. pres. tense third person plu. of* ре́зать – нареза́ть

ре́зать – нареза́ть (Irr. D-1, з → ж ) to cut
  –ся to be cut, to fight (one another)
*Резерфо́рд n. masc. (1) Rutherford
*рези́на n. fem. (7) rubber (vulcanized)
ре́зкий adj. (21) sharp, keen
ре́зко adv. sharply, abruptly
*результа́т n. masc. (1) result
*резюми́ровать (Irr. A-1) v. tr. imperf. and perf. to summarize, to
*резюми́руя pres. gerund of *резюми́ровать      prepare a resume
*рельс n. masc. (1) rail
рента́бельный adj. (17b) economical, profitable
*реоста́т n. masc. (1) rheostat
ре́па n. fem. (7) beet
реша́ть (Reg. A) – реши́ть (Reg. B-2) v. tr. to solve, to decide
реше́ние n. neuter (16) solution (of problem)
ржа́веть – заржа́веть (Reg. A) v. intr. to rust
ржа́вление n. neuter (16) (process of) rusting
ржи see decl. of рожь in § 357, p. 574
рис. abbr. for рису́нок
ри́совый adj. (17) rice (adj.)
рису́нке prep. sing. of рису́нок
рису́нок n. masc. (3a) illustration, figure
ро́вный adj. (17a) even, equal, smooth, level
рожь n. fem. (§ 357, p. 574) rye
*роль n. fem. (12) role
*ромби́ческий adj. (21) rhombic
рост n. masc. (1) growth
*ро́тор n. masc. (1) rotor
ртуть n. fem. (12) mercury
руда́ n. fem. (7) ore
*ру́сский adj. (21) Russian
рыхле́ть – разрыхле́ть (Reg. B-1) v. tr. to loosen
ряд n. masc. (1) series, order

## С

с (со) prep. (with gen.) from, away from (with instr.)
с тех пор fixed expr. from those times    with
с того́ вре́мени fixed expr. from that time
сам pronoun same, self (Cf. § 148, p. 223)
са́ми see сам
са́ми по себе́ fixed expr. of themselves (Cf. сам)
само́ по себе́ fixed expr. of itself (Cf. сам)
самолёт n. masc. (1) aeroplane
  сам self; лёт flight

самопроизвольно *adv.* spontaneously

  сам self;  про- + из- + воля will, freedom

самородный *adj.* (17) virgin, native (form of metals)

  сам self;  род birth, tribe, genus

самый (17) same, self same, the very same (Cf. § 148, p. 223)

*сантиметр *n.masc.* (1) centimeter      most (Cf. § 354, p. 544)

*Сатурн *n.masc.* (1) Saturn

*сахар *n.masc.* (1) sugar

сведённый (17) lead down or away, correlated (*perf. pas.*

свежий *adj.* (21) fresh    *past part.* of сводить – свести)

сверхпроводимость *n.fem.* (12) superconductivity

  сверх- super- + про- + водить to be leading

сверхпроводник *n.masc.* (3) superconductor

свет *n.masc.* (1) light

светило *n.neuter* (13) shining body, star

светить (Irr.D-2)*v.intr.imp.* светиться (Irr. D-2) *v.refl. imp.*

светлый *adj.* (17a) bright          to be shining

светляк *n.masc.* (3) firefly

световой *adj.* (18) (pertaining to) light

светоисточник *n.masc.* (3) light source

  свет light;  ис- + ток current

светоотдающий *adj.* (22) light giving (Cf. § 286, p. 452)

  свет light;  от- + дать to give

светофор *n.masc.* (1) semaphore

светящийся (22) shining, luminous ( *act. pres. part refl.* of

свеча *n.fem.* (8 *gen. plu.* свечей) candle     светить)

свечение *n.neuter* (16) glowing (process)

свинец *n.masc.* (3a) lead (the metal)

свинца *gen. sing.* of свинец

свободный *adj.* (17a) free

сводить (Irr. D-2, д → ж) – свести (Irr.H-5)*v.tr.* to lead

                down, to bring together (Cf. § 382, p. 626)

  -ся to be brought, to consist (in)

  с- + водить, вести to be leading (Cf. § 381, p. 626)

своею *fem. inst. sing.* of свой

свой *possessive* (18) own (Cf. § 148, p. 225)

свойство *n.neuter* (13) property

связанный (17) connected, bound (*perf. pas. past part.* of

                  связывать – связать)

связывать (Reg. A) – связать (Irr. D-1, з → ж) *v.tr.*

  с- + взять to take          to bind, to connect

связь *n.fem.* (12) bond, link

сгорание *n.neuter* (16) combustion

сгорать (Reg. A) – сгореть (Reg. B-2)*v.intr.* to burn (down),

  с- + гореть to be burning          to rot

сгущать (Reg. A) - сгустить (Irr. D-2, СТ → Щ) *v.tr.*
  -ся to become thick, to condense    to thicken, to condense
  с- + густой thick, viscous
сдвигать (Reg. A) - сдвинуть (Reg. B-1) to shove or push away,
                                               to shove or push together
  -ся to be moved (away or together)
  с- + двигать to be moving
сдвинуть *see* сдвигать
сделать *see* делать
себе, *dat. of* себя
себя, *refl. pronoun* self (Cf. § 148, p. 223)
сегодняшний *adj.* (19) present day
  сей this; день day
сек., *abbrev. for* *секунда
*секунда *n.fem.* (7) second (time unit)
сельский *adj.* (21) country (*adj.*), village (*adj.*)
сельское хозяйство *fixed expr.* agriculture
семени *see decl. of* семя *in* § 358, p. 575
семенной *adj.* (18) (pertaining to) seed
семя, *n.neuter* (§ 358, p. 575) seed
семян *gen. plural of* семя
*Сен-Клер-Девилль *n.masc.* (6) Saint-Claire-Deville
сера *n.fem.* (7) sulfur
серебристый *adj.* (17) silvery
серебро *n.neuter* (13) silver
середина *n.fem.* (7) center
серная кислота *fixed expr.* sulfuric acid (*used in chem.*
                                          *nomenclature*)
серный *adj.* (17) pertaining to or containing сера, sulfur
сетка *n.fem.* (9a) net, grid
сжатие *n.neuter* (16) compression
  с- + жать to be pressing
сжигать (Reg. A) - сжечь (Irr. G-2; сожгу, сожжёшь etc.)
                    *v.tr.* to burn (up), to reduce to ashes
  -ся to undergo combustion
  с- + жечь to be burning
сжимать (Reg. A) - сжать (Irr.F-1)*v.tr.* to squeeze together,
  с- + жать to be pressing            to compress
сидеть - посидеть (Irr.D-2, Д → Ж) *v.intr.* to sit, to be
сила *n.fem.* (7) power, strength, force      located
сила сцепления *fixed expr.* tensile strength
*силикат (1) silicate
силовой *adj.* (18) (pertaining to) power
  сила power
сильно *adv.* strongly, greatly

си́льный *adj.* (17b) strong, intense, powerful

*си́мвол *n.masc.* (1) symbol

*симметри́чный *adj.* (17a) symmetrical

*симме́три́я *n.fem.* (11) symmetry

*симпто́м *n.masc.* (1) symptom

*си́нтез *n.masc.* (1) synthesis

*синтези́рованный (17) synthesized (*pas. past part. of* *синтези́ровать)

*синтези́ровать (Irr. A-1) *v.tr. imp. and perf.* to be synthesizing, to synthesize

*синтети́ческий *adj.* (21) synthetic

*систе́ма *n.fem.* (7) system

*сифилити́ческий *adj.* (21) syphilitic

сказа́ть *see* ГОВОРИ́ТЬ

скала́ *n.fem.* (7) rock (cliff)

скачкообра́зный *adj.* (17a) abrupt

скака́ть to be galloping; о́браз form, shape

сквозь *prep.* through, across

ско́лько *pronoun, adv.* how many, how much (Cf. § 150, p. 230)

сконструи́ровать *see* КОНСТРУИ́РОВАТЬ

скопле́ние *n.neuter* (16) accumulation

с- + КОПИ́ТЬ to collect

скорбу́т *n.masc.* (1) scurvy

ско́ро *adv.* rapidly

ско́рость *n.fem.* (12) velocity, speed, rate

ско́рый *adj.* (17) rapid, fast

*скрап *n.masc.* (1) scrap (metal)

*скру́ббер *n.masc.* (1) scrubber

слабосветя́щийся *adj.* (22) weakly, shining (Cf. § 286, p. 452)

сла́бый weak; свет light

сла́бый *adj.* (17) weak

сла́нец *n.masc.* (7a *instr. sing.* СЛА́НЦЕМ) slate

слегка́ *adv.* lightly, slightly

с- + ЛЁГКИЙ light

сле́довательно *adv.* consequently, accordingly

след track, trace

сле́довать - после́довать (Irr. A-1) *v.tr. and intr.* to follow, to be necessary

сле́дует *pres. tense third person sing.* of СЛЕ́ДОВАТЬ - после́довать

сле́дующий (22) following (*act. pres. part.* of сле́довать - после́довать)

сле́дующим о́бразом *fixed expr.* in the following way

слива́ть (Reg. A) - слить (Irr. E-3) *v.tr.* to pour off, to pour together

с- + ЛИТЬ to be pouring

сли́шком *adv.* too, too much, excessively

сло́во *n.neuter* (13) word

сло́жен *pred., nom., masc. sing* of СЛО́ЖНЫЙ

СЛОЖНОСТЬ *n.fem.* (12) sum, accumulation, complexity, amount
  C- + ЛОЖИТЬСЯ to be lying down
СЛОЖНЫЙ *adj.* (17a) complex, complicated
СЛОЙ *n.masc.* (4) layer, shell (of electrons)
СЛУЖИТЬ - ПОСЛУЖИТЬ (Reg. B-2) *v.intr.* (*with instr.*) to serve (as)
СЛУЧАЙ *n.masc.* (4) case
СЛУЧАТЬСЯ (Reg. A) - СЛУЧИТЬСЯ (Reg. B-2) *v.refl.* to happen, to occur
СМ. *abbrev. for* \*САНТИМЕТР centimeter
СМАЗОЧНЫЙ *adj.* (17) lubricating
СМАЧИВАТЬ (Reg. A) - СМОЧИТЬ (Reg. B-2) *v.tr.* to moisten
СМЕРТЬ *n.fem.* (12) death
СМЕСЬ *n.fem.* (12) mixture
СМЕШИВАТЬ - СМЕШАТЬ (Reg. A) *v.tr.* to mix
СМОГ *perf. past tense masc. sing of* МОЧЬ - СМОЧЬ
СМОГУ *perf. future tense first person sing. of* МОЧЬ - СМОЧЬ
СМОЛА *n.fem.* (7) resin
СМОРОДИНА *n.fem.* (7) currant plant
СМОЧИТЬ *see* СМАЧИВАТЬ
СНАБЖАТЬ (Reg. A) - СНАБДИТЬ (Irr. D-2, Д → Ж) *v.tr.* to supply
СНАРЯД *n.masc.* (1) shell (artillery)
СНАЧАЛА *adv.* at first, in the beginning
  C- + НАЧАЛО start
СНОВА *adv.* anew
  C- + НОВЫЙ new
СО *see* С
СОБОЙ *instr. sing. of* СЕБЯ
СОБСТВЕННЫЙ *adj.* (17) own, personal
СОВЕРШАТЬ (Reg. A) - СОВЕРШИТЬ (Reg. B-2) *v.tr.* to complete, to perform
  -СЯ to be performed, completed
СОВЕРШЕНИЕ *n.neuter* (16) completion
СОВЕРШЕННО *adv.* completely
СОВМЕЩАТЬ (Reg. A) - СОВМЕСТИТЬ (Irr. D-2, СТ → Щ) *v.tr.* to unite, to bring into agreement, to combine, to coordinate
  -СЯ to coincide, to agree
  СОВ- + МЕСТО place
СОВМЕЩЕНИЕ *n.neuter* (16) agreement, congruence
СОВОКУПНОСТЬ *n.fem.* (12) collection, totality
СОВПАДАТЬ (Reg. A) - СОВПАСТЬ (Irr. H-7) *v.intr.* to coincide
  СОВ- + ПАДАТЬ to be falling
СОВПАДЕНИЕ *n.neuter* (16) congruence, coincidence
\*СОВПРЕН *n.masc.* Sovprene
  \*СОВЕТ Soviet; \*ИЗОПРЕН isoprene
СОВРЕМЕННИК *n.masc.* (3) contemporary
СОВРЕМЕННЫЙ *adj.* (17a) contemporary
СОВСЕМ *adv.* completely, totally
  СО- + ВЕСЬ all

согла́сие *n. neuter* (16) agreement
  со- + го́лос voice
согла́сно *prep.* (*with dat.*) according to
*со́да (7) soda
содержа́ние *n. neuter* (13) content
содержа́ть (Reg. B-2) *v. tr. imperf.* to be containing
  -ся to be contained (in)
соедине́ние *n. neuter* (16) (chemical) compound, combination
  со- + оди́н one
соединённый (17) united, combined (*perf. pas. past part.*
                                   *of* соединя́ть – соедини́ть)
соединя́ть (Reg. A) – соедини́ть (Reg. B-2) *v. tr.* to unite,
  -ся to undergo combination, to unite        to combine
сожжённый (17) burnt (*perf. pas. past part. of* сжига́ть –
                                                    сжечь)
созве́здие *n. neuter* (16) constellation
  со- + звезда́ star
создава́ть (Irr. B) – созда́ть (Irr. I-3) *v. tr.* to create,
                                            to establish
создаёт, создаю́т *pres. tense third person sing. and plu.*
                                *of* создава́ть – созда́ть
созда́ние *n. neuter* (16) creation, establishment
сок *n. masc.* (3) juice
со́лнечный *adj.* (17a) solar
со́лнце *n. neuter* (16) sun
*соль *n. fem.* (12) salt
*соляна́я кислота́ *fixed expr.* hydrochloric acid
*соляно́й *adj.* (18) pertaining to salt
сомне́ние *n. neuter* (16) doubt
соотве́тственно *adv.* correspondingly
соотве́тствовать (Irr. A-1) *v. intr. imperf.* (*with dat.*) to
  со- + отве́т answer                        correspond (to)
соотве́тствует, соотве́тствуют *pres. tense third person*
                      *sing. and plu. of* соотве́тствовать
соотве́тствующий (22) corresponding (*act. pres. part. of*
                                         соотве́тствовать)
соотноше́ние *n. neuter* (16) relationship, ratio
  со- + от- + носи́ть to be carrying
со́пло *n. neuter* (13b) nozzle
соприкаса́ться (Reg. A) – соприкосну́ться (Reg. B-1) *v. refl.*
  со- + при- + каса́ться to touch            to be in contact
сопротивле́ние *n. neuter* (16) resistance
  со- + про́тив against
*сорти́рующий (22) sorting (*pres. act. part. of*
                                          *сорти́ровать)
*сорти́ровать (Irr. A-1) *v. tr. imp. and perf.* to be sorting, to sort

сосредото́ченный (17) concentrated (*perf. pas. past.* part. *of* сосредото́чивать – сосредото́чить)

сосредото́чивать (Reg. A) – сосредото́чить (Reg. B-2) *v.tr.* to concentrate, to direct (attention)

соста́в *n.masc.* (1) composition

со- + ста́вить to be putting, placing

составля́ть (Reg. A) – соста́вить (Irr. C-2) to constitute, to compose, to form

-ся to be constituted, composed, formed

состоя́ние *n.neuter* (16) condition, state

со- + стоя́ть to be standing

состоя́ть (Reg. B-2) *v.intr. imperf.* to be consisting

сосу́д *n.masc.* (1) vessel

со́тый *adj.* (17) hundreth

соударе́ние *n.neuter* (16) collision

со- + уда́р blow

сохране́ние *n.neuter* (16) conservation

со- + храни́ть to be protecting

сохраня́ть (Reg. A) – сохрани́ть (Reg. B-2) *v.tr.* to preserve, to conserve

-ся to be preserved, conserved

*спектр *n.masc.* (1) spectrum

*спектра́льный *adj.* (17) spectrum (*adj.*) (pertaining to)

*спектрогра́ф *n.masc.* (1) spectrograph spectra

*спектроско́п *n.masc.* (1) spectroscope

*спирт *n.masc.* (1) alcohol

сплав *n.masc.* (1) alloy

сплавле́ние *n.neuter* (16) fusion (together)

с- + пла́вить to be melting, to be floating

сплавля́ть (Reg: A) – спла́вить (Irr. C-2) *v.tr.* to alloy

-ся to become alloyed

с- + пла́вить – распла́вить to smelt

споко́йно *adv.* quietly, smoothly

спо́соб *n.masc.* (1) process, method

спосо́бность *n.fem.* (12) ability, capability

спу́тник *n.masc.* (3) satellite

с- + путь way, path

сравне́ние *n.neuter* (16) comparison

с- + ра́вный equal

сравни́тельно *adv.* relatively

сра́зу *adv.* all at once, immediately

с- + раз time (multiplicity)

среда́ *n.fem.* (7) medium

среди́ *prep.* (*with gen.*) among

сре́дний *adj.* (19) middle, neutral, average, neuter

сре́дство *n.neuter* (13) means, agency

*стабилизи́ровать (Irr. A-1) *v.tr.* to be stabilizing, to stabilize

*стаби́льность *n.fem.* (12) stability

*стаби́льный *adj.* (17b) stable

ста́дия *n. fem.* (11) status, condition

стака́н *n. masc.* (1) glass

ста́лкивать – столка́ть (Reg. A) *v. tr.* to shove away, to thrust,
  –ся  to collide                                       to strike
  с- + толка́ть to be pushing, thrusting

*сталь *n. fem.* (12) steel

*стально́й *adj.* (18)  steel (*adj.*)

*станда́ртный (*adj.*) (17a) standard

стано́вится (Irr. C-1) *v. refl.* to become

ста́нция *n. fem.* (11) station, installation

*статисти́ческий *adj.* (21) statistical

*стати́ческий *adj.* (21) static

сте́бель *n. masc.* (6a) stalk

сте́бля *gen. sing. of* сте́бель

стекло́ *n. neuter* (13a) glass

сте́пень *n. fem.* (12) degree

*стимули́ровать *v. tr.*    *v. tr.* (Irr. A-1) to be stimulating,

сто́йкость *n. fem.* (12) stability                     to stimulate

столб́ *n. masc.* (1) column

столкнове́ние *n. neuter* (16) collision
  с- + толкну́ть  to strike

сто́лько *pronoun, adv.* so many (Cf. § 150, p. 230)

сто́лько же *fixed expr.* just so many

сторона́ *n. fem.* (7) side, land, direction

стоя́ть – постоя́ть (Reg. B-2) *v. intr.* to stand, to halt

страна́ *n. fem.* (7) country, region

строе́ние *n. neuter* (16) structure

строи́тельный *adj.* (17) (pertaining to) construction, building
  стро́ить to be constructing                           (*adj.*)

стро́ить – постро́ить (Reg. B-2) *v. tr.* to construct, to build
  –ся  to be constructed, built

*структу́ра *n. fem.* structure

струя́ *n. fem.* (11) jet, stream

*студе́нт *n. masc.* (1) student

сту́пка *n. fem.* (9a) (little) mortar

*субстра́т *n. masc.* (1) substrate

суди́ть – посуди́ть (Irr. D-2, Д → Ж)  *v. tr.* to judge, to

*сульфа́т *n. masc.* (1) sulfate                  estimate, to decide

*су́мма *n. fem.* (7) sum

су́тки *n. plural* (§ 359, p. 579) twenty-four hour period

су́ток *gen. plural of* су́тки

существова́ние *n. neuter* (16) existence
  суть are
существова́ть – просуществова́ть (Irr. A-1) *v. intr.* to exist

существу́ет, существу́ют *pres. tense third person sing.*
                              *and plu. of* существова́ть

сущность *n.fem.* (12) essence
*схема *n.fem.* (7) scheme
сходный *adj.* (17) similar
   с- + ХОДИТЬ, ИТТИ to be going (Cf. § 381, p. 626)
сходство *n.neuter* (13) similarity
*сфера *n.fem.* (7) sphere
*сферический *adj.* (20) spherical
сцепление *n.neuter* (16) cohesion, linking together
   с- +, цепь chain
сцеплять (Reg. A) – сцепить (Irr. C-2) *v.tr.* to link together,
                                    to couple, to fasten
счёт *n.masc.* (1) reckoning, expense
счётчик *n.masc.* (3) counter
считать (Reg. A) – счесть (Irr. сочту, -ёшь -ёт etc.) *v.tr.*
                                 to reckon, to consider, to regard
   -ся to be considered, to be considered, to be paid
США *abbr. for* Соединённые *Штаты* Америки *fixed expr.*
                              United States of America
сыр *n.masc.* (1) cheese
сырьё *n.neuter* (16) raw material

# Т

Т. *abbr. for* ТОМ, volume, *тонна, ton, тысяча, thousand
Т.Д. *abbrev. for* так далее in и так далее *fixed expr.*
                            and so forth, etc.
Т.е. *abbr. for* то есть *fixed expr.* that is
тайна *n.fem.* (7) secret
так *adv.* so, thus
так как *fixed expr.* since, because
так --- как и --- *fixed expr.* both --- as well as ---
так называемый *fixed expr.* so called
также *adv.* also
таким же образом *fixed expr.* in that same way
таким образом *fixed expr.* in this way
такой *adj. and pronoun* (18) such, that (Cf. § 142, p. 213)
такт *n.masc.* (1) stroke, time (music)
твёрдость *n.fem.* (12) hardness
твёрдый *adj.* (17) solid, hard
те *pronoun* those (Cf. ТОТ § 142, p. 213)
те же *fixed expr.* those same (Cf. § 144, p. 215)
*текстильный *adj.* (17) textile
текут *pres. tense third person plu. of* течь
тело *n.neuter* (13) body, object
тем *see* ТОТ
тем не менее *fixed expr.* none the less
тёмный *adj.* (17a) dark

\*температу́ра *n. fem.* (7) temperature
\*теоре́ма *n. fem.* (7) theorem
\*теорети́ческий *adj.* (21) theoretical
\*тео́рия *n. fem.* (11) theory
тепе́рь *adv.* now, at present
тепло́ *n. neuter* (13) heat
теплово́й *adj.* (18) (pertaining to) heat, thermal
теплоотда́ющий *adj.* (22) heat supplying, exothermal (Cf. § 286,
   тепло́ heat; от- + дать to give           p. 452)
теплопрово́дность *n. fem.* (12) heat conductivity
   тепло́ heat; про- + води́ть to be leading
теплота́ *n. fem.* (7) heat
\*терапевти́ческий *adj.* (21) therapeutic
\*те́рмин *n. masc.* (1) term
\*терми́ческий *adj.* (21) thermal
\*термодинами́ческий *adj.* (21) thermodynamical
\*термо́метр *n. masc.* (1) thermometer
теря́ть - потеря́ть (Reg. A) *v. tr.* to lose
\*тетрагона́льный *adj.* (17) tetragonal
тех *gen. and prep. plu. of* ТОТ (Cf. § 142, p. 213)
\*те́хника *n. fem.* (9) technology, technique
\*техни́ческий *adj.* (21) technical
тече́ние *n. neuter* (16) flow, course (of time)
тече́т *pres. tense third person sing. of* течь
течь (Irr. G-3) *v. intr. imperf.* to be flowing
ти́гель *n. masc.* (6) crucible
\*тип *n. masc.* (1) type
\*типи́чный *adj.* (17a) typical
\*тита́н *n. masc.* (1) titanium
ткань *n. fem.* (12) tissue, fabric
ТО *pronoun, demonstrative* that    (Cf. ТОТ § 142, p. 213)
ТО *conj.* then (*For use to introduce clause following a
                  conditional clause beginning with
                  е́сли see* § 169, p. 258, §§ 313-4; pp. 492-5)
ТО ЖЕ  (ТОТ ЖЕ) (ТА ЖЕ) that same (Cf. § 144, p. 215)
тогда́ *adv., conj.* then
тогда́ как *fixed expr.* whereas
тожде́ственность *n. fem.* (12) equality, identity
   ТОТ ЖЕ  just the same (Cf. § 144, p. 215)
ТОЙ *see* ТОТ
ТОК *n. masc.* (3) stream, current
\*токсиколо́гия *n. fem.* (11) toxicology
то́лстый *adj.* (17) thick
толчко́м *instr. sing. of* ТОЛЧО́К
толчо́к *n. masc.* (3a) push, shove, impulse
толщина́ *n. fem.* (7) thickness
   то́лстый  thick

ТО́ЛЬКО *adv.* only
ТОМ *see* ТОТ
*ТО́МСОН *n. masc.* (1) Thompson
ТОМУ́ *see* ТОТ
ТОМУ́ наза́д *fixed expr.* ago
ТО́ПЛИВО *n. neuter* (13) fuel
ТОТ *pronoun, demonstrative* (Cf. § 142, p. 213) that
ТОТ же *fixed expr.* that same (Cf. § 144, p. 215)
ТО́ЧКА *n. fem.* (9) point
ТО́ЧНО *adv.* precisely
ТО́ЧНОСТЬ *n. fem.* (12) precision, exactness
ТО́ЧНЫЙ *adj.* (17a) precise, exact
ТРАВА́ *n. fem.* (7) grass
*ТРАЕКТО́РИЯ *n. fem.* (11) trajectory
*ТРА́КТОР *n. masc.* (1) tractor
*ТРА́НСПО́РТ *n. masc.* (1) transport
*ТРА́НСПО́РТНЫЙ *adj.* (17) (pertaining to) transport
ТРЕ́БОВАНИЕ *n. neuter* (16) demand, need, requirement
ТРЕ́БОВАТЬ (Irr. A-1) *v. tr. imperf.* to be needing, to require
   –СЯ to be needed, required
ТРЕ́БУЕТ, ТРЕ́БУЮТ *pres. tense third person sing. and plu.*
ТРЁМ *see* ТРИ                          *of* ТРЕ́БОВАТЬ
ТРЕ́ТИЙ *adj. numeral* (§ 360, p. 581) third
ТРЕТЬ *n. fem.* (12) third (part)
ТРЕУГО́ЛЬНИК *n. masc.* (3) triangle
   ТРИ three; У́ГОЛ angle
ТРЕХ *see* ТРИ
ТРЕХФА́ЗНЫЙ *adj.* (17) three phase
   ТРИ three; *ФА́ЗА phase
ТРИ *numeral* (§ 370, p. 600) three
*ТРИГОНОМЕТРИ́ЧЕСКИЙ *adj.* (21) trigonometrical
*ТРИ́ЖДЫ *adv.* thrice
*ТРИКЛИНИ́ЧЕСКИЙ *adj.* (21) triclinic
ТРОЯ́КИЙ *adj.* (21) triple
ТРУ́БКА *n. fem.* (9a) tube
ТРУ́ДНЕЕ *comp. adj.* more difficult
ТРУ́ДНО *adv. and pred. adj.* difficulty, (it is) difficult
ТРУ́ДНОСТЬ *n. fem.* (12) difficulty
ТРУ́ДНЫЙ *adj.* (17a) difficult
*ТУБЕРКУЛЁЗ *n. masc.* (1) tuberculosis
ТУМА́ННОСТЬ *n. fem.* (12) nebula
*ТУРБИ́НА *n. fem.* (7) turbine
*ТУРБО– *part of compound words* turbo-
ТЫ́СЯЧА *n. fem.* (8) thousand
ТЯ́ГА *n. fem.* (9) pull, thrust (of rocket), hood (laboratory)
ТЯЖЁЛЫЙ *adj.* (17) heavy
ТЯ́ЖЕСТЬ *n. fem.* (12) gravity, weightiness

## У

У *prep.* (*with gen.*) with, near, at (*For idiom indicating possession* Cf. § 388, p. 646)

убедиться *see* убеждать

убеждать (Reg. A) – убедить (Irr. D-2,д → жд) *v. tr.* to persuade, to convince

-ся to be persuaded, convinced

увеличение *n. neuter* (16) increase, rise

у- + великий great

увеличивать (Reg. A) – увеличить (Reg. B-2) *v. tr.* to increase

-ся to be increased

уверенность *n. fem.* (12) confidence, conviction

у- + вера belief

увидеть *see* видеть

увлажнённый (17) moistened (*perf. pas. past. part. of* увлажнять – увлажнить)

увлажнять (Reg. A) – увлажнить (Reg. B-2) *v. tr.* to moisten

у- + влага moisture

углами *instr. plural of* угол

углевод *n. masc.* (1) carbohydrate

уголь coal; вода water

углеводород *n. masc.* (1) hydrocarbon

уголь coal; водород hydrogen

углекислый *adj.* (17) (pertaining to) carbonic acid or carbon dioxide

уголь carbon; кислый sour, acidic

углекислый газ *fixed expr.* carbonic acid gas, carbon dioxide

углерод *n. masc.* (1) carbon

уголь coal; род birth, tribe, genus

углём *instr. sing. of* угол

углы *nom. and acc. plural of* угол

угля *gen. sing. of* уголь

угол *n. masc.* (1a) angle, corner

уголь *n. masc.* (6a) coal, charcoal (Cf. Note 4, p. 86)

удаваться (Irr. B) – удаться (Irr. I-3) *v. refl.* to succeed

у- + давать – дать to give

удалять (Reg. A) – удалить (Reg. B-2) to remove, to take away

-ся to be removed, taken away

у- + дальний distant

удар *n. masc.* (1) blow, impact

удастся *refl. perf. future third person sing. of* удаться – удаться

удаться *see* удаваться

удельный *adj.* (17) specific

у- + дело thing

удобно *adv. and pred. adj.* conveniently, (it is) convenient

удобный *adj.* (17a) convenient (Cf. § 166, p. 254)

удобрение *n. neuter* (16) (agricultural) fertilizer

у- + добрый good

УДОВЛЕТВОРЯ́ТЬ (Reg. A) - УДОВЛЕТВОРИ́ТЬ (Reg. B-2) *v. tr.*
  -СЯ to be satisfied           *(with dat.)* to satisfy
    у- + ДО- + ВО́ЛЯ will, freedom; ТВОРИ́ТЬ to be creating
УДУША́ТЬ (Reg. A) - УДУШИ́ТЬ (Reg. B-2) *v. tr.* to suffocate
    у- + ДУХ breath, spirit
УЖЕ́ *adv.* already
У́ЖЕ *comp. adj. and adv. (undecl.)* narrower, more narrowly
У́ЗКИЙ *adj.* (21a) narrow
УЗНАВА́ТЬ (Irr. B) - УЗНА́ТЬ (Reg. A) *v. tr.* to recognize,
    у- + ЗНАТЬ to be knowing           to understand
УЗНА́ЕМ *fut. tense first person plu. of* УЗНАВА́ТЬ -
                                      УЗНА́ТЬ

УКАЗА́НИЕ *n. neuter* (16) indication
    у- + КАЗА́ТЬ to be showing
УКА́ЗЫВАТЬ (Reg. A) - УКАЗА́ТЬ (Irr. D-1, З → Ж) *v. tr.*
                            to point out, to indicate
УКОРЕНЯ́ТЬ (Reg. A) - УКОРЕНИ́ТЬ (Reg. B-2) *v. tr.* to plant, to
  -СЯ to take root, to be inculcated      implant, to inculcate
    у- + КО́РЕНЬ root
УКРАША́ТЬ (Reg. A) - УКРА́СИТЬ (Irr. D-2, С → Ш) *v. tr.*
    у- + КРА́СНЫЙ red, beautiful        to adorn, to ornament
УКРЕПЛЁННЫЙ (17) fastened (*perf. pas. past part. of*
                            УКРЕПЛЯ́ТЬ - УКРЕПИ́ТЬ)

УКРЕПЛЯ́ТЬ (Reg. A) - УКРЕПИ́ТЬ (Irr. C-2) *v. tr.* to fasten
    у- + КРЕ́ПКИЙ strong                 to strengthen
У́КСУСНАЯ КИСЛОТА́ *fixed expr.* acetic acid
У́КСУСНЫЙ *adj.* (17) pertaining to vinegar, acetic
    У́КСУС vinegar
УЛА́ВЛИВАТЬ (Reg. A) - УЛОВИ́ТЬ (Irr. C-2) *v. tr.* to catch,
                                to snatch
УЛЕТА́ТЬ (Reg. A) - УЛЕТЕ́ТЬ (Irr. D-2, Т → Ч) *v. tr.* to fly away
    у- + ЛЕТА́ТЬ, ЛЕТЕ́ТЬ to be flying (Cf. § 381, p. 626)
УЛУЧША́ТЬ (Reg. A) - УЛУ́ЧШИТЬ (Reg. B-2) *v. tr.* to improve
  -СЯ to be improved
    у- + ЛУ́ЧШИЙ better, best
УЛУЧШЕ́НИЕ *n. neuter* (16) improvement
УЛУ́ЧШЕННЫЙ (17) improved (*perf. pas. past part. of*
                         УЛУЧША́ТЬ - УЛУ́ЧШИТЬ)

* УЛЬТРАВИОЛЕ́ТОВЫЙ *adj.* (17) ultraviolet
УМЕНЬША́ТЬ (Reg. A) - УМЕ́НЬШИТЬ (Reg. B-2) *v. tr.* to decrease,
УМЕНЬШЕ́НИЕ *n. neuter* (16) decrease, drop     to make smaller
    у- + МЕ́НЬШИЙ less
УМЕНЬШЁННЫЙ (17) decreased (*perf. pas. past part. of*
                   УМЕНЬША́ТЬ - УМЕ́НЬШИТЬ)

умира́ть (Reg. A) – умере́ть (Irr. J-1) *v. tr.* to die, to expire
  у- + мир peace
умножа́ть (Reg. A) – умно́жить (Reg. B-2) *v. tr.* to multiply,
  у- + мно́го many                  to increase
*универса́льный *adj.* (17b) universal
*университе́т *n. masc.* (1) university
уноси́ть (Irr. D-2, C → Ш) – унести́ (Irr. H-2) *v. tr.* to carry
                               away (Cf. § 382, p. 630)
  у- + носи́ть, нести́ to be carrying (Cf. § 381, p. 626)
упа́сть (Irr. H-7) *v. intr. perf.* to fall (Cf. па́дать)
  у- + пасть to fall      (Cf. па́дать)
уплотне́ние *n. neuter* (16) condensation
  у- + пло́тный dense, compact
употребле́ние *n. neuter* (16) application, use
  у- + по- + тре́бовать to be needing
употребля́ть (Reg. A) – употреби́ть (Irr. C-2) *v. tr.* to apply,
  -ся to be applied, used               to use
управля́ть (Reg. A) – упра́вить (Irr. C-2) *v. tr.* to control,
  у- + пра́во right            to direct, to operate
упру́гий *adj.* (21) elastic
  у- + пружи́на spring
уравне́ние *n. neuter* (16) equalization, equation (chemical)
  у- + ра́вный equal
*ура́н *n. masc.* (1) uranium
*Ура́н *n. masc.* (1) Uranus (planet)
у́ровень *n. masc.* (6) level, surface
  у- + ра́вный equal
у́ровнем *instr. sing. of* у́ровень
усили́тельный *adj.* (17) strengthening, amplifying (electronics)
  у- + си́ла strength
ускоре́ние *n. neuter* (16) acceleration
  у- + ско́рый fast
уско́ренный *perf. pas. past part. of* ускоря́ть – уско́рить

ускоря́ть (Reg. A) – уско́рить (Reg. B-2) *v. tr.* to accelerate,
усло́вие *n. neuter* (16) conditions, stipulation      to hasten
успе́х *n. masc.* (3) success
успе́шно *adv.* successfully
устана́вливать (Reg. A) – установи́ть (Irr. C-2) *v. tr.*
                         to set up, to establish
  -ся to be set up, established
  у- + станови́ться to become, to place
устано́вленный (17) established (*perf. pas. past part. of*
                    устана́вливать – установи́ть)
усто́йчивость *n. fem.* (12) stability
  у + стоя́ть – постоя́ть to stand

устойчивый *adj.* (17) stable

устраивать (Reg. A) - устроить (Reg. B-2) *v. tr.* to arrange, to build up
  -ся  to be built up, arranged
  у- + строить  to be building

устремлять (Reg. A) - устремить (Irr. C-2) *v. tr.* to direct, to aim, to steer
  -ся  to be directed, aimed, to approach, to rush
  у- + стремить  to direct

устройство *n. neuter* (13) construction
  у- + строить  to be building

утолщать (Reg. A) - утолстить (Irr. D-2, СТ → Щ) *v. tr.* to make thicker
  у- + толстый  thick

утолщённый (17) thickened (*perf. pas. past part. of* утолщать - утолстить)

утренний *adj.* (19) morning
  утро  morning

участвовать (Irr. A-1) *v. intr. imperf.* to participate ( В, in)
  у- + часть  part

участвует, участвуют *pres. tense third person sing. and plu. of* участвовать)

участие *n. neuter* (16) participation

учение *n. neuter* (16) teaching, doctrine

учёный *adj.* (17) learned (*adj.*) learned person, scientist

ущелье *n. neuter* (15) ravine, chasm

уяснять (Reg. A) - уяснить (Reg. B-2) *v. tr.* to explain
  у- + ясный  clear

Ф

*фабричный *adj.* (17) industrial, plant (*adj.*)

фа́кел *n. masc.* (1) torch

*факт *n. masc.* 91) fact

*фактически *adv.* factually, in fact

*фактор *n. masc.* (1) factor

фарфоровый *adj.* (17) porcelain

*фашизм *n. masc.* (1) Fascism

*февраль *n. masc.* (6) February

*фенол *n. masc.* (1) phenol

*фермент *n. masc.* (1) enzyme, ferment

*ферроалюминий *adj.* (5) ferroaluminum

*фигурировать (Irr. B-2) *v. intr. imperf. and perf.* to figure, to be involved

*физик *n. masc.* (3) physicist

*физика *n. fem.* (9) physics

*физически *adv.* physically

*физический *adj.* (21) physical

*философ *n. masc.* (1) philosopher

\*филосо́фский *adj.* (21) philosophical
\*фильтр *n.masc.* (1) filter
\*фильтра́т *n.masc.* (1) filtrate
\*фильтрова́ть (Irr. A-1) *v.tr.imperf.* (§ 42, p. 61)     to be filtering
\*флот *n.masc.* (1) fleet
\*фо́кус *n.masc.* (1) focus
\*фон *n.masc.* (1) background
\*фоно́граф *n.masc.* (1) phonograph
\*фо́рма *n.fem.* (7) form
\*форма́ция *n.fem.* (11) formation
\*фо́рмула *n.fem.* (7) formula
\*фо́сфор *n.masc.* (1) phosphorus
\*фото́граф *n.masc.* (1) photographer
\*фотографи́ровать - \*сфотографи́ровать (Irr. A-1) *v.tr.*
\*фотографи́ческий *adj.* (21) photographic          to photograph
\*фотогра́фия *n.fem.* (11) photography, photograph
\*фото́н *n.masc.* (1) photon
\*фотоэлектри́ческий *adj.* (21) photoelectric
\*фотоэлеме́нт *n.masc.* (1) photoelement, photoelectric device
\*фотоэффе́кт *n.masc.* (1) photoeffect
\*фра́кция *n.fem.* (11) fraction
\*Фра́нция *n.fem.* (11) France
\*францу́зский *adj.* (21) French
\*фрауенго́феровый *adj.* (17) (pertaining to) Frauenhofer
\*фронт *n.masc.* (1) front
\*фрукт *n.masc.* (1) fruit
 фтори́стый *adj.* (17) (pertaining to or containing) flourine
  фтор flourine
\*фу́нкция *n.fem.* (11) function


# X


\*хара́ктер *n.masc.* (1) character
\*характеризова́ть - \*охарактеризова́ть (Irr. A-1) *v.tr.*
  -ся to be characterized                    to characterize
\*характеризу́емый *pas. pres. part. of* \*характеризова́ть -
                                 \*охарактеризова́ть
\*характеризу́ет, \*характеризу́ют *pres. tense third person,
    sing. and plu. of* \*характеризова́ть - \*охарактеризова́ть
\*характеризу́ющийся (22) being characterized (*refl. act.
    pres. part. of* \*характеризова́ть - \*охарактеризова́ть)
\*характери́стика *n.fem.* (9) characteristic (*n.*)
\*характери́ческий *adj.* (20) characteristic (*adj.*)
\*характе́рный *adj.* (17a) characteristic (*adj.*)
\*хемилюминесце́нция *n.fem.* (11) chemiluminescence
\*хи́мик *n.masc.* (3) chemist

*химически *adv.* chemically
*химический *adj.* (21) chemical
*химия *n.fem.* (11) chemistry
*хинин *n.masc.* (1) quinine
 хлеб *p.masc.* (1) bread
 ХЛОПКА *gen. sing.* of ХЛОПОК
 ХЛОПОК *n.masc.* (3a) clap
 ХЛОПОК *n.masc.* (3a) cotton floc
*хлор *n.masc.* (1) chlorine
*хлорид *n.masc.* (1) chloride
*хлорировать (Irr. A-1) *v.tr. perf. and imperf.* to be chlorin-
                                                      ating, to chlorinate
*хлористый *adj.* (17) (pertaining to or containing) chlorine
*хлористый водород *fixed expr.* hydrogen chloride, HCl
*хлористый *метил *fixed expr.* methyl chloride, $CH_3Cl$
*хлористый *натрий *fixed expr.* sodium chloride
*хлорофилл *n.masc.* (1) chlorophyll
*хлороформ *n.masc.* (1) chloroform
 ХОД *n.masc.* (1) course, movement
 ХОДИТЬ – ПОХОДИТЬ (Irr. D-2, Д ⟶ Ж) *v.intr.* to go,
                         to walk, to move (Cf. § 381-2, pp. 626-630)
 ХОЗЯЙСТВО *n.neuter* (13) business, economy
*Холл *n..masc.* (1) Hall
 ХОЛМИК *n.masc.* (3) heap, (little) hill
   ХОЛМ  hill
 ХОЛОДНЫЙ *adj.* (17a) cold, chill
 ХОРОШИЙ *adj.* (22) good
 ХОРОШО *adv.* well
 ХОТЕТЬ – ЗАХОТЕТЬ (Irr. D-5) *v.tr.* to wish
 ХОТЯ *conj.* although
 ХОТЯ БЫ *conj.* although, even though (Cf. § 316, p. 496)
*ХРОМ *n.masc.* (1) chromium
*ХРОМОСОМ *n.masc.* (1) chromosome


Ц


Ц. *abbr. for* *Цельсий *n.masc.* (5) Celsius (Swedish inventor of
                                              the Centigrade thermometer)
 ЦВЕТ *n.masc.* (26 *gen. plu.* ЦВЕТОВ) color, (1) *plu. only* flower
 ЦВЕТКОВ *gen. plu.* of ЦВЕТОК         (Cf. ВЕС § 359, p. 580)
 ЦВЕТОК *n.masc.* (3a) flower  *(plu. used  in scientific*
*цезий *n.masc.* (5) cesium                    *sense only)*
 ЦЕЛЬ *n.fem.* (12) goal, purpose, target
 ЦЕЛЫЙ *adj.* (17) whole, complete
*цемент *n.masc.* (1) cement

це́нный *adj.* (17a) valuable
  цена́ price
\*Цента́вра *n.fem.* (7) Centaurus
\*це́нтр *n.masc.* (1) center
\*центрифу́га *n.fem.* (9) centrifuge
\*циклотро́н *n.masc.* (1) cyclotron
\*цили́др *n.masc.* (1) cylinder
\*цинк *n.masc.* (3) zinc
  цынга́ *n.fem.* (9) scurvy

Ч

\*Чарль́з *n.masc.* (1) Charles
части́ца *n.fem.* (8) particle
  часть part
α-части́ца *n.fem.* (8) α-particle
части́чка *n.fem.* (9) little particle
части́чно *adv.* partially
ча́стность *n.fem.* (12) particularity, detail
ча́сто *adv.* often, frequently
частота́ *n.fem.* (7) frequency
часть *n.fem.* (12) part
ча́шка *n.fem.* (9 *gen. plu.* ча́шек) cup, pan, small (of balance)
чего́ *see* ЧТО
чего́-то *see* ЧТО́-ТО
челове́к *n.masc.* (3) man, person
челове́чество *n.neuter* (13) humanity
чем *conj.* than (Cf. § 337, p. 530)
чём *see* ЧТО
че́рез *prep.* (*with acc.*) through, after (of time), by
чёрный *adj.* (17a) black
черпа́ть (Reg. A) – черпну́ть (Reg. B-2) *v.tr.* to extract, to draw off
черта́ *n.fem.* (7) feature, trait
черти́ть – начерти́ть (Irr. D-2) *v.tr.* to sketch, to draw
  чёрный black
четвёртый *adj. numeral* (17) fourth
че́тверть *n.fem.* (12) (one) fourth
четы́ре *numeral* (§ 370, p. 600) four
четы́режды *adv.* four times (repetition)
четырёх *see* четы́ре
четырехта́ктый *adj.* (17) four cycle (motor)
  четы́ре four; такт stroke
четыреххлори́стый *adj.* (17) tetrachloro (product)
  четы́ре four; \*хлор chlorine
четыреххлори́стый углеро́д *fixed expr.* carbon tetrachloride

четырьмя *instr. of* четы́ре
чи́сел *gen. plural of* число́
число́ *n.neuter* (13b) number
числово́й *adj.* (18) numerical
чи́сто *adv.* purely, clearly
чистота́ *n.fem.* (7) purity
чи́стый *adj.* (17) pure
чрезвыча́йно *adv.* extremely
че́рез through
ЧТО *pronoun* (§ 152, p. 232) *and conj.* (Cf. § 145, p. 217)
that, which what
что́бы *conj.* in order to (Cf. § 168, p. 256; § 315, p. 495)
что́-то *pronoun* (§ 154, p. 236) something
чувстви́тельность *n.fem.* (12) sensitivity
чу́вствовать to feel
чувстви́тельный *adj.* (17b) sensitive
чугу́н *n.masc.* (1) cast iron
чудеса́ *nom. and acc. plu. of* чу́до
чу́до *n.neuter* (§ 359, p. 578) wonder, miracle
чуть-чу́ть *adv.* little by little
*Чэ́двик *n.masc.* (3) Chadwick

## Ш

шаг *n.masc.* (3) step
шар *n.masc.* (1) globe
ша́рик *n.masc.* (3) little sphere
шату́н *n.masc.* (1) connecting rod
ша́хта *n.fem.* (7) (mining) shaft
*Швейца́рия *n.fem.* (11) Switzerland
шёл *imperf. past tense masc. sing. of* ИТТИ́-ПОЙТИ́ (Cf.
шерсть *n.fem.* (12) wool    § 224, p. 352)
шесто́й *adj.* (18) sixth
шесть *numeral* (§ 370, p. 602) six
ширина́ *n.fem.* (7) breadth
широ́кий *adj.* (21) wide, broad
широко́ *adv.* widely, extensively
*Шко́ла *n.fem.* (7) school
ши́хта *n.fem.* (7) charge (of material)
*шпина́т *n.masc.* (1) spinach
*штат *n.masc.* (1) state

## Щ

щелочноземе́льный *adj.* (17) alkaline earth (*adj.*)
щёлочь alkali;    земля́ earth
щелочно́й *adj.* (18) alkaline

щёлочь *n.fem.* (12) alkali

Э

*Эйнштейн *n.masc.* (1) Einstein
*экватор *n.masc.* (1) equator
*экзаменовать – *проэкзаменовать (Irr. A-1) *v.tr.* to examine
*экономический *adj.* (21) economical (student)
*экран *n.masc.* (1) screen
*эксперимент *n.masc.* (1) experiment
*экспериментально *adv.* experimentally
*экспериментальный *adj.* (17b) experimental
*экстракт *n.masc.* (1) extract
*экстракция *n.fem.* (11) extraction
*эластичность *n.fem.* (12) elasticity
*электрический *adj.* (21) electrical, electric
*электричество *n.neuter* (13) electricity
*электрод *n.masc.* (1) electrode
*электродинамика *n.fem.* (9) electrodynamics
*электролиз *n.masc.* (1) electrolysis
*электролизёр *n.masc.* (1) electrolyzer
*электролит *n.masc.* (1) electrolyte
*электролитический *adj.* (20) electrolytic
*электромагнитный *adj.* (17) electromagnetic
*электрометр *n.masc.* (1) electrometer
*электрон *n.masc.* (1) electron
*электронно-лучевой *adj.* (18) electron-beam
  *электрон electron; луч beam
*электронный *adj.* (17) electronic, electron (*adj.*)
электропроводимость *n.fem.* (12) electrical conductivity
*электро- electro-; про- + водить to be leading
электропроводность *n.fem.* (12) electrical conductivity
*электроскоп *n.masc.* (1) electroscope
электросопротивление *n.neuter* (16) electrical resistance
  *электро- electro-; со- + против against
электростанция *n.fem.* (11) electrical (power) plant
*электротермический *adj.* (21) electrothermal
*электроэнергия *n.fem.* (11) electrical energy
*элемент *n.masc.* (1) element
*Элизабет *see* *Куин *Элизабет
*эллиптический *adj.* (21) elliptical
*эмпирический *adj.* (21) empirical
*эмульсия *n.fem.* (11) emulsion
*энергетический *adj.* (21) (relating to) energy
*энергично *adv.* energetically, violently
*энергия *n.fem.* (11) energy

\*энзи́м, n.masc. (1) enzyme

\*энтро́пия n.fem. (11) entropy

\*эпо́ха n.fem. (9) epoch

\*эрг n.masc. (3) erg

\*Э́рстед n.masc. (1) Oersted

\*Эру́ n.masc. ( undecl., § 363, p. 587) Héroult

э́ти, э́тим, э́тих see Э́ТОТ

\*эти́ловый adj. (17) (pertaining to) ethyl, ethyl (adj.)

\*эти́ловый \*спирт fixed expr. ethyl alcohol

э́то that (is) (Cf. § 120, p. 174)

э́то и есть fixed expr. this is in fact

э́того, э́той, э́тому see Э́ТОТ

э́тот pronoun, demonstrative (§ 142, p. 212) this

э́ту see Э́ТОТ

\*эфи́р n.masc. ether, ester (1)

\*эффе́кт n.masc. (1) effect

\*эффекти́вный adj. (17a) effective

\*э́хо n.neuter (undecl. § 363, p. 587) echo


## Ю


\*ювели́рный adj. (17) jewelry (adj.)

\*Юпи́тер n.masc. (1) Jupiter (planet)

\*Ю́та n.neuter (undecl. § 363, p. 587) Utah


## Я


я pronoun (§ 136, p. 204) I

явле́ние n.neuter (16) phenomenon

явля́ть (Reg. A) – яви́ть (Irr. C-2) v.tr. to show

-ся to show self, to appear, to be (Cf. § 94, p. 136; § 123, p. 181)

явля́ющийся (22) showing self, being, (refl. act. pres. part.
                                        of ЯВЛЯ́ТЬ - ЯВИ́ТЬ)

яд n.masc. (1) poison

я́дер gen. plu. of ядро́

я́дерный adj. (17) nuclear

ядро́ n.neuter (13b) nucleus

язы́к, n.masc. (3) language

яйцо́ n.neuter (13 gen. plu. яи́ц) egg

я́мка n.fem. (9a) (little) hole

я́ркий adj. (21a) bright

я́рко adv. brightly

я́рко-жёлтый adj. (17) bright-yellow

я́ркость n.fem. (12) brightness

ярча́йший *adj. superl.* (22) brightest (Cf. § 346, p. 546)
  я́ркий bright
я́сно *pred. adj. and adv.* clearly, (it is) clear (Cf. §§ 166-7,
я́сный *adj.* (17a) clear                              pp. 254-5)

# NOTES ON ENGLISH-RUSSIAN VOCABULARY

This vocabulary lists all English words found in the Translation Exercises. The general arrangement and abbreviations used
are the same as those of the Russian-English vocabulary as
discussed in §§ 401-404, p. 671-674.

It is important to note that a single English word may be
translated differently depending on the sense in which it is used.
Thus, "solution," denoting a composition prepared by dissolving
one substance in another, is translated by pаствóр while
"solution," meaning the answer to a problem, is translated as
решéние.

Many verbs in English may be used either transitively or
intransitively. Many Russian verbs, as discussed in § 52, p. 71,
are used in their reflexive forms to translate the corresponding
English verb when used intransitively. This relationship is
specifically noted in listing verbs.

# ENGLISH-RUSSIAN
# VOCABULARY

## A

ability n. спосо́бность n. fem. (12)
able adj. спосо́бный adj. (17a)
   to be able мочь – смочь (Irr. G-4) v. intr. (with inf.)
about prep. о́коло prep. (with gen.)
above prep. над prep. (with instr.)
    above mentioned вышеупомянутый adj. (17)
    above stated вышеска́занный adj. (also used as noun
absolute adj. *абсолю́тный adj. (17a)     Cf. § 286, p. 452)
to absorb v. tr. поглоща́ть (Reg. A) –поглоти́ть (Irr. D-2,
   to be absorbed –ся            т → щ) v. tr.
absorber n. *абсо́рбер n. masc. (1)
absorption n. *абсо́рбция n. fem. (11)
academy n. *акаде́мия n. fem. (11)
accelerate v. tr. and intr. ускоря́ть (Reg. A) – уско́рить
   to be accelerated, to accelerate intr. –ся   (Reg. B-2) v. tr.
accelerated past part. уско́ренный (perf. pas. past part.
                        of ускоря́ть – уско́рить)
accomplish v. tr. *реализова́ть (Irr. B-1) v. tr. perf. and
imperf. осуществля́ть (Reg. A) – осуществи́ть (Irr. C-1) v. tr.
according to prep. expr. по prep. (with dat.)
accumulation n. скопле́ние n. neuter (16)
acetate n. *ацета́т n. masc. (1)
acetic acid fixed expr. у́ксусная кислота́ fixed expr.
achieve, attain v. tr. достига́ть (Reg. A) – дости́гнуть
   to be achieved, attained –ся     (Irr. J-3) v. tr. with gen.
   having achieved дости́гший act. past part. of
                достига́ть – дости́гнуть
acid, acidic adj. кисло́тный adj. (17)
acid n. кислота́ n. fem. (7)
acidified past part. подки́сленный perf. pas. past part.
             of подкисля́ть – подки́слить
acquaint v. tr. знако́мить – познако́мить (Irr. C-2)
   to be made or become acquainted –ся
act (on) v. intr. де́йствовать – поде́йствовать (на)
action n. де́йствие n. neuter (16)     (Irr. A-1) v. intr.
activate v. tr. *активи́ровать (Irr. A-1) v. tr. perf. and
activity n. *акти́вность n. fem. (12)        imperf.

actuality n. действительность n.fem. (12)

adult adj. взрослый adj. (17)

aerobic adj. *аэробный adj. (17а)

after (following) после prep. (with gen.) по prep. (with prep l.)

after (according to), по prep. (with dat.)

against prep. против prep. (with gen.)

ago adv. тому назад adv l. expr.

agriculture, n. сельское хозяйство fixed expr.

aid n. помощь n.fem. (12)
    with the aid (of) с помощью, при помощи (with gen.)
    by means of See review of instr. case § 91, p. 131

air n. воздух n.masc. (3)

alcohol n. *спирт n.masc., *алкоголь n.masc. (6)

aliphatic adj. *алифатический adj. (12)

alkaline adj. щелочной adj. (18)

alkaline earth adj. щелочноземельный adj. (17)

all adj. and pronoun every, whole adj. весь adj. and pronoun
                            (decl. § 150, p. 22 idioms § 389, p. 647)

alloy n. сплав n.masc. (1)

alloy v.tr. сплавлять (Reg. A) - сплавить (Irr. C-2) v.tr.
    to be alloyed -ся

almost adv. почти adv.

alpha-rays n. *альфа-луч n.masc. (2)

already adv., уже adv.

also adv. также adv.

alumina n. глинозём n.masc. (1)

aluminum n. *алюминий n.masc. (5)

aluminum adj. *алюминиевый adj. (17)

aluminum chloride, *хлористый*алюминий, *хлорид
                                *алюминия

amalgam n. *амальгама n.fem. (7)

to amalgamate v.tr. and intr. *амальгамировать
                  (Irr. A-1) v.tr. perf. and imperf.

always adv. всегда adv.,

American adj. *американский adj. (21)

among (between) prep. между prep. (with instr.)

among (near, at) prep. у prep. (with gen.) (Cf. § 388, p. 646)

amorphous adj. *аморфный adj. (17а)

amount n. количество n.neuter (13)

amplitude n. *амплитуда n.fem. (7)

anaerobic adj. *анаэробный adj. (17а)

analysis n. *анализ n.masc. (1)

ancient adj. древний adj. (19)

and conj. и, а conj. (Cf. § 61, p. 84)

aniline n. *анилин n.masc. (1)

animal adj. животный adj. (17)

animal *n.* ЖИВО́ТНЫЙ (17 *neuter forms only* Cf. Note 8,
§ 62, p. 86 and § 392, p. 652)

annually *adv.* ежего́дно *adv.*

another *adj. and pronoun* ДРУГО́Й *adj. and pronoun* (20)

    one from another друг от дру́га (Cf. § 156, p. 241)

antenna *n.* \*анте́нна *n.fem.* (7)

any (any at all) *adj.* КАКО́Й-НИБУДЬ, КАКО́Й-ЛИ́БО *adj.*

any (all) *adj.* ВСЯ́КИЙ *adj.* (21)         (§ 154, p. 236)

any (each) *adj.* КА́ЖДЫЙ *adj.* (17)

apparatus *n.* \*аппара́т *n.masc.* (1)

appearance *n.* появле́ние *n.neuter* (16)

application, utilization *n.* примене́ние, испо́льзование,
употребле́ние *n.neuter* (16)

apply, use *v.tr.* ПРИМЕНЯ́ТЬ (Reg. A) - ПРИМЕНИ́ТЬ (Reg. B-2)
    to be applied, used -СЯ          *v.tr.*

aqueous *adj.* ВО́ДНЫЙ *adj.* (17)

argon *n.* \*арго́н *n.masc.* (1)

are *pres. tense form of* to be *v.intr.* есть, суть *emphasizing affirmation or making enumeration* (Cf. § 122, p. 180)

arise, appear *v.intr.* ВОЗНИКА́ТЬ (Reg. A) - ВОЗНИ́КНУТЬ

aromatic *adj.* \*ароматический *adj.* (21)   (Irr. J-3) *v.intr.*

around *prep.* ВОКРУ́Г *prep. (with gen.)*

artificial *adj.* ИСКУ́СТВЕННЫЙ *adj.* (17 *pred.masc. sing.*
ИСКУ́СТВЕН § 356, p. 570)

artificially *adv.* ИСКУ́ССТВЕННО *adv.*

artillery *adj.* \*артиллери́йский *adj.* (21)

as *adv., conj.* как
    as (in the quality of) в ка́честве *(with gen.)*
    as it were как бы (Cf. § 316, p. 496)
    as (for purpose of, in fashion of) *Often expressed by the inst. case.* (Cf. Lessons 12 and 13)
    as to (with regard to) *prepl. expr.* ПО *prep. (with dat.)*

asbestos *n.* \*асбе́ст *n.masc.* (1)       Cf. § 110, p. 160)

asbestos *adj.* \*асбе́стовый *adj.* (17)

ashe, ashes *n.* зола́ *n.fem.* (7 *sing. only*)

asphalt *n.* \*асфа́льт *n.masc.* (1)

at (during, while, near, on) *prep.* ПРИ *prep.,* НА *prep.* В (ВО)
*prep. (with prepl.)* К (КО) *prep. (with dat.)* У *prep. (with gen.)*

at (onto, into, toward) *prep.* НА *prep.,* В (ВО) *prep. with acc.*
К (КО) *prep. with dat.*

atmosphere *n.* \*атмосфе́ра *n.fem.* (7)

atom *n.* \*а́том *n.masc.* (1)

atomic *adj.* \*а́томный *adj.* (17)

attain *v.tr.* ДОСТИГА́ТЬ (Reg. A) - ДОСТИ́ГНУТЬ (Irr. J-3)
*v.tr. (with gen.)* ПРИОБРЕТА́ТЬ (Reg. A) - ПРИОБРЕСТИ́ (Irr. H-3)
*v.tr. (with acc.)*

author *n.* *áвтор *n.masc.* (1)
automobile *n.* *автомобúль *n.masc.* (6)
autumn *n.* óсень *n.fem.* (12)
avail self of *verbal expr.* ПÓЛЬЗОВАТЬСЯ – ВОСПÓЛЬЗОВАТЬСЯ
         (Irr. A-1) *v.refl.* (*with instr.*)
 (while) availing self ПÓЛЬЗУЯСЬ
aviation *n.* *авиáция *n.fem.* (11)
axis *n.* ОСЬ *n.fem.* (12)

# B

background *n.* *фон *n.masc.*
bacteria *n.* *бактéрия *n.fem.* (11)
bacteriophage *n.* *бактериофáг *n.masc.* (3)
base, establish *v.tr.* ОСНÓВЫВАТЬ (Reg. A) – ОСНОВÁТЬ
  to be based, established –СЯ    (Irr. A-1) *v.tr.*
basic (fundamental) *adj.* ОСНОВНÓЙ *adj.* (18)
basic (alkaline) *adj.* ОСНÓВНЫЙ *adj.* (17)
beam (ray) *n.* ЛУЧ *n.masc.* (2)
beautiful *adj.* прекрáсный *adj.* (17a)
begin *v.tr. and intr.* НАЧИНÁТЬ (Reg. A) – НАЧÁТЬ (Irr. C-3,
           H added) *v.tr.*
beginning *n.* НАЧÁЛО *n.neuter* (13)
be *v.intr.* БЫТЬ *v.intr. imperf.* (Irr. I-2) (*Present tense
virtually obsolete.* Cf. § 120, p. 174, §§ 121-123, pp. 178-181)
 (*Past tense* § 213, p. 336) (*Future tense* § 230, p. 360)
belong (to), pertain (to) *v.intr.* ОТНОСÚТЬСЯ (Irr. D-2)
    – ОТНЕСТÚСЬ (Irr. H-2) *v.refl.* (К *with dat.*)
beri-beri *n.* *бéри-бéри *n.neuter* (*undecl.* § 363, p. 587)
beryllium *n.* *берúлий *n.masc.* (5)
best *supl. adj.* наилýчший *supl. adj.* (22)
beta-ray *n.* *бéта-луч *n.masc.* (2)
between *prep.* мéжду *prep.* (*with instr.*)
beyond *prep.* зá *prep.* (*with instr.*)
big *adj.* большóй *adj.* (20)
biological *adj.* *биологúческий *adj.* (21)
bismuth *n.* *вúсмут *n.masc.* (1)
blade (knife) *n.* лéзвие *n.neuter* (16)
blade (turbine) *n.* лопáтка *n.fem.* (9a)
body *n.* тéло *n.neuter* (13)
boil (liquid) *v.tr. and intr.* КИПÉТЬ (Irr. C-2) *v.intr. imperf.*
boiler *n.* КОТЁЛ *n.masc.* (1a е *deleted*)
bombardment *n.* *бомбардирóвка *n.fem.* (9)
boring (holes) *pres. part.* *буровóй *adj.* (18)
both *adj. and pronoun* óба *numeral* (§ 370, p. 601)
both --- and --- И --- И ---

bran *n.* óтрубú *n.plu. only* (Cf. ШИ § 356, p. 579)

branch *n.* ВЕТВЬ *n.fem.* (12)

Brazilian *adj.* \*бразúльский *adj.* (21)

bright (shining) *adj.* СВЕТОВÓй *adj.* (18)

bright (intense light) *adj.* ярКИй *adj.* (21a)

brightness *n.* яркостЬ, *n.fem.* (12)

bring about *verbal expr.* ПРОИЗВОДúТЬ (Irr. D-2) – произвестú (Irr. H-5) *v.tr.*

brother *n.* брат *n.masc.* (§ 359, p. 577)

British *adj.* \*брИтáнский *adj.* (21)

bulb *n.* КОЛбá *n.fem.* (7)

Bunsen *n.* \*БýНзен *n.masc.*, (1)

burn *v.tr. and intr.* ГОРÉТЬ – сгорéтЬ(Reg. B-2)*v.intr.*
жечь – сжечь (Irr. G-2) *v.tr.*

burner *n.* горéлКА *n.fem.* (9a)

bush *n.* КУСТ *n.masc.* (1)

but *conj.* а, НО *conj.* (Cf. § 61, p. 84)

by *prep.* (*For use of instrumental case to express means or agency see* § 91, p. 131)

by (near) *prep.* У *prep.* (*with gen.*) прИ *prep.* (*with prepl.*)

by (through, across) *prep.* чéрез *prep.* (*with acc.*)


## C


calcium *n.* \*кáльцИй *n.masc.* (5)

calcium *adj.* \*кáльцИевый, *adj.* (17)

calibrate *v.tr.* \*калИбровáТЬ – \*прокалИбровáТЬ (Irr. A-1)*v.tr.*

call, name *v.tr.* называ́ТЬ (Reg. A)– назвáТЬ (Irr. E-1 О *insert*)
to be called, named –СЯ (*with instr.*) *v.tr.*

call forth, cause *v.tr.* вызывáТЬ (Reg. A) – вýзватЬ (Irr. E-2) *v.tr.*

camphor *n.* \*кáмфорá *n.fem.* (7)

can, be able *v.intr.* (*with inf.*) МОЧЬ – СМОЧЬ (Irr. G-4) *v.intr.* (*with inf.*)

cannot, must not, it is forbidden *negated verbal expr.* нельзя́ *adv.* (*with inf.*)(Cf. § 178, p. 280)

capillary *n.* \*кáпИлляр *n.masc.*

capillary *adj.* \*кáпИллярный *adj.* (17a)

carbide *n.* \*карбúд *n.masc.* (1)

carbohydrates *n.,* углевóд *n.masc.* (1)

carbon *n.* углерóд *n.masc.* (1)

carbon dioxide *fixed expr.* углекúслый газ *fixed expr.*

carbonate *n.* \*карбонáт *n.masc.* (1)

carbonic acid *adj.* углекúслый *adj.* (17)

carry, bear *v.tr.* носúТЬ – поносúТЬ (Irr. D-2, С → Ш) *v.tr.*
нестú – понестú (Irr. H-5) *v.tr.* (Cf. §§ 381-2, pp. 626-630)

carry out, accomplish  v.tr.  производить (Irr, D-2, Д → Ж)
　　　　　　　　　　　　　　　- произвести (Irr. H-5)v.tr.
　　to be carried out, accomplished，-ся
carry out, complete  v.tr.  совершать (Reg. A) - совершить
　　to be accomplished, completed -ся　　(Reg. B-2) v.tr.
case  n. случай  n.masc. (4)
cast (metal)  v.tr.  отливать (Reg. A) - отлить (Irr. E-3) v.tr.
catalyst  n.  *катализатор  n.masc. (1)
catalytic  adj.  *каталитический adj.(21)
cathode  n. *катод  n.masc. (1)
cathode  adj.  *катодный adj. (17)
cation  n.  *катион  n.masc. (1)
cause  n.  причина  n.fem. (7)
cause, call forth  v.tr.  вызывать(Reg. A)- вызвать (Irr. E-2)
caustic soda  fixed expr.  едкий натр  fixed expr.　　　　v.tr.
cement  n.  *цемент  n.masc. (1)
center  n.  *центр  n.masc.(1) середина  n.fem. (7)
centrifuge  n.  *центрифуга  n.fem. (9)
century  n.  век  n.masc. (3)
cereals  n.  злак  n.masc.  (3) sing. forms  grass, plu. forms
　　　　　　　　　　　　　　　　　　　　　　cereals
certain (several, particular) adj.  некоторый adj. (17)
cesium  n.  *цезий  n.masc. (5)
change (alteration)  n.  изменение,  n.neuter (16)
change (conversion)  n.  превращение n.neuter(16)
change  v.tr. and intr.  изменять(Reg. A) - изменить
　　to be changed, undergo change -ся　　(Reg. B-2) v.tr.
character  n.  *характер  n.masc.(1)
characteristic adj.  *характерический adj. (21)
characterize  v.tr.  *характеризовать - *охарактеризовать
　　to be characterized -ся　　　　　(Irr. A-1) v.tr.
charge (electrical or explosive)  n.  заряд  n.masc. (1)
charged (electrical or explosive) past part.  заряжённый perf.
　　　　　　　　　　pas. past part. of заряжать - зарядить
　　doubly-charged двухзаряжённый (17)
Charles  n.  *Чарльз  n.masc.(1)
chemical  adj.  *химический adj. (21)
chemically adv.  *химически adv.
chemist  n.  *химик  n.masc. (3)
chemistry  n.  *химия  n.fem. (11)
chloride  n.  *хлорид  n.masc. (1)
chlorinate v.tr. and intr.  *хлорировать(Irr. A-1)v.tr. perf. and
chlorine  n.  *хлор  n.masc. (1)　　　　　　　　imperf.
chloroform  n.  *хлороформ  n.masc. (1)
chlorophyll n.  *хлорофилл  n.masc.(1)
chromium  n.  *хром  n.masc. (1)
chromosome  n.  *хромосом  n.masc. (1)

clear, lucid *adj.* ЯСНЫЙ *adj.* (17a)
  (it is) clear ЯСНО (Cf. §§ 166-7, pp. 254-5)
close, near *adj.* БЛИЗКИЙ *adj.* (21a)
closer *comp. adj. and adv.* БЛИЖЕ *comp. pred. adj. and adv.*
clothing *n.* ОДЕЖДА *n.fem.* (7)
coal *n.* КАМЕННЫЙ УГОЛЬ *fixed expr.* (Cf. Note 4, p. 86)
coefficient *n.* \*КОЭФФИЦИЕНТ *n.masc.* (1)
coefficient (hydrogen ion) *n.* ПОКАЗАТЕЛЬ *n.masc.* (6)
coincide *v.intr.* (with) СОВМЕЩАТЬСЯ (Reg. A) – СОВМЕСТИТЬСЯ
        (Irr. D-2, СТ → Щ) *v.refl.* (С *with instr.*)
  to unite, to bring into agreement СОВМЕЩАТЬ – СОВМЕСТИТЬ
cold *adj.* ХОЛОДНЫЙ *adj.* (17a)
college *n.* \*КОЛЛЕДЖ *n.masc.* (3 *instr. sing.* КОЛЛЕДЖЕМ,
collision *n.* СТОЛКНОВЕНИЕ, *n.neuter* (16) *gen. plu.* КОЛЛЕДЖЕЙ)
colloidal *adj.* \*КОЛЛОИДАЛЬНЫЙ *adj.* (17b)
color *n.* ЦВЕТ *n.masc.* (1)
colorimeter *n.* \*КОЛОРИМЕТР *n.masc.* (1)
combine with, annex, unite *v.tr.* ПРИСОЕДИНЯТЬ (Reg. A)
                ПРИСОЕДИТЬ (Reg. B-2) *v.tr.*
  to become combined, undergo combination -СЯ
combustible *adj.* ГОРЯЧИЙ *adj.* (22)
combustion *n.* ГОРЕНИЕ, СГОРАНИЕ *n.neuter* (16)
come, approach *v.intr.* НАСТУПАТЬ (Reg. A) – НАСТУПИТЬ
comet *n.* \*КОМЕТА *n.fem.* (7)        (Irr. C-2) *v.intr.*
common (general) *adj.* ОБЩИЙ *adj.* (22)
common salt *fixed expr.* ПОВАРЕННАЯ \*СОЛЬ *fixed expr.*
commutator *n.* \*КОММУТАТОР *n.masc.* (1)
complete *adj.* ЦЕЛЫЙ *adj.* (17) ПОЛНЫЙ (17 *masc. pred.*
               *sing.* ПОЛОН Cf. § 356, p. 570)
completely *adv.* ПОЛНОСТЬЮ *instr. sing. used as adv.*
completeness *n.* ПОЛНОСТЬ *n.fem.* (12)
complex *adj.* СЛОЖНЫЙ *adj.* (17a)
complicated *adj* СЛОЖНЫЙ *adj.* (17a)
composition *n.* СОСТАВ *n.masc.* (1)
compound *n.* СОЕДИНЕНИЕ *n.neuter* (16)
concentrate (solution) *v.tr.* \*КОНЦЕНТРИРОВАВАТЬ –
             \*СКОНЦЕНТРИРОВАТЬ (Irr. A-1) *v.tr.*
concentrated *past part.* \*КОНЦЕНТРИРОВАННЫЙ *imperf., pas.*
   *past part of* \*КОНЦЕНТРИРОВАТЬ – \*СКОНЦЕНТРИРОВАТЬ
concentration (solution) *n.* \*КОНЦЕНТРАЦИЯ *n.fem.* (11)
conclusion (logical) *n.* ВЫВОД *n.masc.* (1)
conclusion (termination) *n.* КОНЕЦ *n.masc.* (1a)
condensation *n.* УПЛОТНЕНИЕ, СГУЩЕНИЕ *n.neuter* (16)
condense (vapor) *v.tr.* thicken *v.tr. and intr.* СГУЩАТЬ
      (Reg. A) – СГУСТИТЬ (Irr. D-2, СТ → Щ) *v.tr.*
  to undergo condensation, to thicken *intr.* -СЯ
condition *n.* УСЛОВИЕ *n.neuter* (16)

conduct *v.tr.* ПРОВОДИ́ТЬ (Irr. D-2, Д → Ж) провести́
     to be conducted -СЯ          (Irr. H-5) *v.tr.*
conductivity *n.* ПРОВОДИ́МОСТЬ *n.fem.* (12)
     electrical conductivity *n.* электропроводи́мость *n.fem.* (12)
conductor    *n.* ПРО́ВОД *n.masc.* (1)
configuration    *n.* *КОНФИГУРА́ЦИЯ *n.fem.* (11)
confirm    *v.tr.* ПОДТВЕРЖДА́ТЬ (Reg. A) - ПОДТВЕРДИ́ТЬ
                 (Irr. D-2, Д → Ж ) *v.tr.*
confirmed *past part.* ПОДТВЕРЖДЁННЫЙ (17 *perf. pas. past*
              *part.* of ПОДТВЕРЖДА́ТЬ - ПОДТВЕРДИ́ТЬ)
confront *v.tr.* ПРЕДСТОЯ́ТЬ (Reg. A) *v.tr. imperf. (with dat.)*
connected, bound to *past part.* ОБЯ́ЗАННЫЙ *perf. pas. past*
              *part.* of ОБЯ́ЗЫВАТЬ - ОБЯЗА́ТЬ
connecting rod *fixed expr.* ШАТУ́Н *n.masc.* (1)
consequently *adv.* СЛЕ́ДОВАТЕЛЬНО *adv.*
consider (regard as) *v.tr.* СЧИТА́ТЬ (Reg. A) - СЧЕСТЬ (Irr.
     to be considered, regarded -СЯ    СОЧТУ́, -ёшь,-ёт, etc.)*v.tr.*
considerable *adj.* ЗНАЧИ́ТЕЛЬНЫЙ *adj.* (17b)
consist (of) *v.intr.* СОСТОЯ́ТЬ (Reg. B-2) (ИЗ) *v.intr.imperf.*
СОСТАВЛЯ́ТЬСЯ (Reg. A) - СОСТА́ВИТЬСЯ (Irr. C-2) (ИЗ) *v.refl.*
     to constitute, to compose, to form СОСТАВЛЯ́ТЬ - СОСТА́ВИТЬ
constant *n.* *КОНСТА́НТА *n.fem.* (7); ПОСТОЯ́ННЫЙ (17 *Fem. forms*
           *only* Cf. Note 8, § 62, p. 86 and § 392, p. 652)
constant *adj.* ПОСТОЯ́ННЫЙ *adj.* (17a)
construct *v.tr.* СТРО́ИТЬ - ПОСТРО́ИТЬ (Reg. B-2) *v.tr.*
construction *n.* УСТРО́ЙСТВО *n.neuter* (13)
consume (dissipate) *v.tr.* ЗАТРА́ЧИВАТЬ (Reg. A) - ЗАТРА́ТИТЬ
                 (Irr. D-2, Т → Ч) *v.tr.*
contact, be in contact (with) СОПРИКАСА́ТЬСЯ (Reg. A)
       - СОПРИКОСНУ́ТЬСЯ (Reg. B-1) *v.refl. (C with instr.)*
contain    *v.tr.* СОДЕРЖА́ТЬ (Reg. B-2) *v.tr. imperf.*
contemporary *adj.* СОВРЕМЕ́ННЫЙ *adj.* (17a)
continue, prolong *v.tr.* ПРОДОЛЖА́ТЬ (Reg. A) - ПРОДО́ЛЖИТЬ
     to be continued, prolonged -СЯ        (Reg. B-2) *v.tr.*
convenient *adj.* УДО́БНЫЙ *adj.* (17a)
conversion *n.* превраще́ние, преобразова́ние *n.neuter* (16)
convert (change) *v.tr. and intr.* превраща́ть (Reg. A)
     - преврати́ть (Irr. D-2, Т → Щ) *v.tr,* преобразо́вывать
               преобразова́ть (Irr. B-1) *v.tr.*
     to undergo conversion, to be changed -СЯ
convert (transfer) *v.tr.* ПЕРЕВОДИ́ТЬ (Irr. D-2, Д → Ж) -
               перевести́ (Irr. H-5) *v.tr.*
cooling (process) *n.* охлажде́ние *n.neuter* (16)
coordinate    *n.* *КООРДИНА́ТА *n.fem.* (7)
copper    *n.* МЕДЬ *n.fem.* (12)
correspond (to) *v.intr.* СООТВЕ́ТСТВОВАТЬ (Irr. A-1) *v.intr.imperf.*
correspondingly *adv.* СООТВЕ́ТСТВЕННО *adv.*      *(with dat.)*

cosmic *adj.* МИРОВОЙ *adj.* (18)
could (was able) *See past tense of* МОЧЬ – СМОЧЬ (§ 223, p. 348)
could (might have) *See subjunctive of* МОЧЬ – СМОЧЬ (§ 312, p. 491;
course (of instruction) *n.* КУРС *n.masc.* (1) § 223, p.348)
    in the course (of), В течение (*with gen.*)
cover *v.tr.* покрывать (Reg. A) – покрыть (Irr. E-4) *v.tr.*
Cowles *n.* *Каулес *n.masc.* (1)
crank shaft *fixed expr.* кривошип *n.masc.* (1)
create *v.tr.* создавать (Irr. B) – создать (Irr. I-3) *v.tr.*
creation *n.* создание *n.neuter* (16)
critical *adj.* *критический *adj.* (21)
criticize *v.tr.* *критиковать – *раскритиковать (Irr. A-1)
crystal *n.* *кристалл *n.masc.* (1) *v.tr.*
crystalline *adj.* *кристаллический *adj.* (21)
crystallize *v.tr. and intr.* *кристаллизовать (Irr. A-1)
                              *v.tr. imperf.*
    to undergo crystallization, become crystallized –СЯ
cube *n.* *куб *n.masc.* (1)
cubic *adj.* *кубический *adj.* (21)
cure (heal) *v.tr.* излечивать (Reg. A) – излечить (Reg. B-2)
current *n.* ток *n.masc.* (3) *v.tr.*
cyclotron *n.* *циклотрон *n.masc.* (1)
cylinder *n.* *цилидр *n.masc.* (1)

## D

daily *adv.* ежедневно *adv.*
Dalton *n.* *Дальтон *n.masc.* (1)
dangerous *adj.* опасный *adj.* (17a)
dark *adj.* тёмный *adj.* (17a)
day *n.* день *n.masc.*(6a)
Davy *n.* *Дэви *n.masc.* (*undecl.* § 363, p. 587)
decompose *v.tr. and intr.* разлагать (Reg. A) – разложить
(Reg. B-2) *v.tr.* расщеплять (Reg. A) – расщепить (Irr. C-2)
    to undergo decomposition –СЯ *v.tr.*
decrease *v.tr. and intr.* уменьшать (Reg. A) – уменьшить
                          (Reg. B-2) *v.tr.*
    to undergo decrease, become smaller –СЯ
decrease (fall e.g. temperature) *v.intr.* падать (Reg. A) –
                        пасть (Irr. H-7)*v.intr.*
definite *adj.* определённый (17 *pas. past part. of*
                  определять – определить)
deflect *v.tr.* отклонять (Reg. A) отклонить (Reg. B-2) *v.tr.*
    to be deflected –СЯ
depend (on) *v.intr.* зависеть *v.intr. imperf.* (ОТ *with gen.*)
dependence *n.* зависимость *n.fem.* (12)

dephlegmator *n.* *дефлегматор *n.masc.* (1)

describe *v.tr.* описывать (Reg. A) – описать (Irr. D-1) *v.tr.*

designate *v.tr.* обозначать (Reg. A) – обозначить
(Reg. B-2) *v.tr.*

destroy *v.tr.* разрушать (Reg. A) – разрушить (Reg. B-2) *v.tr.*

detail *n.* *деталь *n.fem.* (12)

detect *v.tr.* обнаруживать (Reg. A) – обнаружить (Reg. B-2)
*v.tr.*

detected *past. part.* обнаруженный *perf. pas. past part.*
*of* обнаруживать – обнаружить

determine *v.tr.* определять (Reg. A) определить (Reg. B-2)
*v.tr.*
to be determined -ся

detonation *n.* *детонация *n.fem.* (11)

develop *v.tr.* развивать (Reg. A) – развить (Irr. E-3) *v.tr.*
to undergo development, be developed -ся

device *n.* прибор, *аппарат *n.masc.* (1)

diameter *n.* *диаметр *n.masc.* (1)

diet *n.* *диэта *n.fem.* (7)

differ (from) *v.intr.* отличаться (Reg. A) – отличиться
(Reg. B-2) *v.refl.* (ОТ *with gen.*)
to distinguish (from) отличать – отличить (ОТ)

difference *n.* разность *n.fem.* (12)

different (distinct) *adj.* отличный *adj.* (17a) (*from,* ОТ)

different (various) *adj.* различный *adj.* (17a)

difficult *adj.* трудный *adj.* (17a)
(it is) difficult трудно
(it is) not difficult нетрудно (Cf. §§ 166-7, pp. 254-5)

difficulty *n.* трудность *n.fem.* (12)

dimension *n.* размер *n.masc.* (1)

direction *n.* направление *n.neuter* (16)

direction (side) *n.* сторона *n.fem.* (7)

discover *v.tr.* открывать (Reg. A) – открыть (Irr. E-4) *v.tr.*

discovered *past part.* открытый (17) *perf. pas. past part.*
*of* открывать – открыть

dish (small) *n.* чашка *n.fem.* (9 *gen. plu.* чашек)

disk *n.* *диск *n.masc.* (3)

dissipate *v.tr.* растрачивать (Reg. A) – растратить (Irr. D-2,
Т → Ч) *v.tr.*
to be dissipated -ся

dissociation *n.* диссоциация *n.fem.* (11)

distant *adj.* дальний *adj.* (19)
more distant дальше (*undecl. pred. form* § 334, p. 527)

distribute *v.tr.* распространять (Reg. A) – распространить
(Reg. B-2) *v.tr.*
to undergo or be distributed -ся

divalent *adj.* двухвалентный *adj.* (17a)

dominate *v.intr.* преобладать (Reg. A) *v.intr. imperf.*

double *adj.* двойной *adj.* (18)

doublet *n.* *дублёт *n.masc.* (1)

doubly *adv. Often indicated by prefix* ДВУ- *or* ДВУХ-

doubt *n.* сомнёние *n.neuter* (16)

dove *n.* гóлубь *n.fem.* (12)

downward *adv.* ВНИЗ *adv.*

draw (sketch) *v.tr. and intr.* чертúть – начертúть
(Irr.D-2, т → ч) *v.tr.*

draw (conclusion) *v.tr.* дéлать – сдéлать (Reg. A) *v.tr.*

drive (chase) *v.tr.* гнать – погнáть (Irr. E-2) *v.tr.* (Cf.
§§ 381-2, pp. 626-630)

drop (fall) *v.intr.* пáдать (Reg. A) – пасть (Irr. H-7) *v.intr.*

dry (dry out) *tr. and intr.* высыхáть (Reg. A) – вы́сохнуть
(Irr. J-3) *v.tr. and intr.*

during (along with) *prep.* ПРИ *prep.* (*with prepl.*)

during (within a time interval) *prep.* В (ВО) *prep.* (*with acc.*)

Dutch *adj.* *голлáндский *adj.* (21)

dye *n.* красúтель *n.masc.* (6)

E

each *adj.* кáждый *adj.* (17)

earth *n.* земля́ *n.fem.* (10)

easy *adj.* лёгкий *adj.* (21a)

(it is easy) легкó (Cf. §§ 166-7, pp. 254-5)

eat (to be eating) *v.tr. and intr.* есть (Irr. I-1)  *v.tr. and intr.*
*imperf.*

echo *n.* *эхо *n.neuter* (*undecl.* § 363, p. 587)

economical *adj.* *экономúческий *adj.* (21)

edge *n.* край *n.masc.* (4)

editor *n.* *редáктор *n.masc,* (1)

effect *n.* *эффéкт *n.masc.* (1)

eject *v.tr.* вышибáть (Reg. A) – вы́шибить (Irr. J-3) *v.tr.*
выбрáсывать (Reg. A) – вы́бросить (Irr. D-2, с → ш) *v.tr.*
to be ejected   -ся

ejected *past part.* вы́брошенный (17 *pas.. past part. of*

ejection *n.* выбивáние *n.neuter* (16) выбрáсывать – вы́бросить)

elastic *adj.* *эластúческий *adj.* (21)

elasticity *n.* *эластúчность *n.fem.* (12)

electrical, electrical *adj.* *электрúческий *adj.* (21)

electric power station *fixed expr.* электростáнция *n.fem.* (11)

electrical resistance *fixed expr.* электросопротивлéние
*n.neuter* (16)

electricity *n.* *электрúчество *n.neuter* (13)

electrification *n.* *электризáция *n.fem.* (11)

electrode *n.* *электрóд *n.masc.* (1)

electrolysis *n.* *электролúз *n.masc.* (1)

electrolyte *n.* *электролúт *n.masc.* (1)

electron *n.* *электрóн *n.masc.* (1)

electron-beam *adj.* *электронно-лучевой *adj.* (18)

electronic, electron *adj.* *электронный *adj.* (17)

electrothermal *adj.* *электротермический *adj.* (21)

element *n.* *элемент *n.masc.* (1)

elliptical *adj.* *эллиптический *adj.* (21)

elucidation *n.* выяснение *n.neuter* (16)

emission *n.* вылет *n.masc.* (1)

emit *v.tr.* испускать (Reg. A) - испустить (Irr. D-2,

    to be emitted, radiated -ся       ст → щ) *v.tr.*

emulsion *n.* *эмульсия *n.fem.* (11)

enable *v.tr.* позволять (Reg. A) - позволить (Reg. B-2)

                                    *v.tr.* (*with dat.*)

encounter *v.tr.* встречать (Reg. A) - встретить (Irr. D-2) *v.tr.*

    to be encountered, found, to occur (e.g., minerals) -ся

end *n.* конец *n.masc.* (1a)

energy *n.* *энергия *n.fem.* (11)

engine, machine *n.* *машина *n.fem.* (7)

    steam engine паровая *машина

English *adj.* *английский *adj.* (21)

enormous *adj.* громадный *adj.* (17a)

enormously *adv.* гораздо *adv.*

envelop, enclose *v.tr.* обволакивать (Reg. A) - обволочь

envelope *n.* оболочка *n.fem.* (9a)         (Irr. G-3) *v.tr.*

enzyme *n.* *энзим, *фермент *n.masc.* (1)

epoch *n.* *эпоха *n.fem.* (9)

equal *adj.* равный *adj.* (17a)

equation *n.* уравнение *n.neuter* (16)

equilibrium *n.* равновесие *n.neuter* (16)

essence *n.* сущность *n.fem.* (12)

essential *adj.* необходимый *adj.* (17)

establish *v.tr.* устанавливать (Reg. A) - установить (Irr. C-2)

    to be established, set up -ся              *v.tr.*

ether *n.* *эфир *n.masc.* (1)

ethyl (group) *n.* *этил *n.masc.* (1)

ethyl *adj.* *этиловый *adj.* (17)

ethyl alcohol *fixed expr.* *этиловый *алкоголь

ethyl acetate *fixed expr.* *этиловый *ацетат *fixed expr.*

evaporate (off) *v.tr.* выпаривать (Reg. A) - выпарить

                      (Reg. B-2) *v.tr.*

evaporate (out) *v.tr. and intr.* испарять (Reg. A) - испарить

    to be evaporated, to undergo evaporation -ся (Reg. B-2) *v.tr.*

evaporation *n.* испарение, выпаривание *n.neuter* (16)

even (level) *adj.* равный *adj.* (17a)

    even (even as, also) и

    even though хотя бы (Cf. § 316, p. 496)

every (each) *adj.* каждый *adj.* (17)

every (all) *adj.* всякий *adj.* (21)

everywhere *adv.* ПОВСЮ́ДУ *adv.*.

evolve (emit) *v.tr.* ВЫДЕЛЯ́ТЬ (Reg. A) - ВЫ́ДЕЛИТЬ (Reg. B-2)
to be evolved, emitted -СЯ             *v.tr.*

evolve (develop) *v.tr. and intr.* развива́ть (Reg. A) - разви́ть
to be evolved, developed -СЯ       (Irr. E-3) *v.tr.*

evolution (e.g., of heat or gas) ВЫДЕЛЕ́НИЕ *n.neuter* (16)

example *n.* приме́р *n.masc.* (1)
for example наприме́р

excitation *n.* возбужде́ние *n.neuter* (16)

exert pressure (on) *verbal expr.* дави́ть (на) (Irr. C-1)
                 *v.intr. imperf.*

exhale *v.tr. and intr.* ВЫДЫХА́ТЬ (Reg. A) - ВЫ́ДОХНУТЬ
                 (Reg. B-1) *v.tr.*

exist *v.intr.* существова́ть - просуществова́ть (Irr. A-1)
                 *v.intr.*

expand *v.tr. and intr.* расширя́ть (Reg. A) - расши́рить
to be expanded, to expand *intr.* -СЯ     (Reg. B-2) *v.tr.*

expense *n.* СЧЁТЪ *n.masc.* (1)
at expense (of) за счёт (*with gen.*)

experiment *n.* *экспериме́нт, о́пыт *n.masc.* (1)

experimental *adj.* *эксперимента́льный *adj.* (17b)

explain, clarify *v.tr.* УЯСНЯ́ТЬ (Reg. A) - УЯСНИ́ТЬ (Reg. B-2)

explosive *n.* взры́вчатое вещество́ *fixed expr.*     *v.tr.*

express *v.tr. and intr.* выража́ть (Reg. A) - вы́разить.
to be expressed -СЯ     (Irr. D-2, З → Ж) *v.tr.*

expression *n.* выраже́ние *n.neuter* (16)

extinguish *v.tr.* ГАСИ́ТЬ - ПОГАСИ́ТЬ (Irr. D-2) *v.tr.*

extremely *adv.* черезвыча́йно *adv.*

eye *n.* ГЛАЗ *n.masc.* (§ 359, p. 576)


## F

fact *n.* *факт *n.masc.* (1)

factor *n.* *фа́ктор *n.masc.* (1)

factor (of number) *n.* мно́житель *n.masc.* (16)
prime factor просто́й мно́житель

failure *n.* неча́да *n.fem.* (9 *instr. sing.* неуда́чей)

fall *v.intr.* па́дать (Reg. A) - пасть (Irr. H-7) *v.intr.*

farther *adv.* да́льше *adv.*

fascism *n.* *фаши́зм *n.masc.* (1)

fashion, style, vogue *n.* *мо́да *n.fem.* (7)
in this fashion таки́м о́бразом

fasten, secure *v.tr.* прикрепля́ть (Reg. A) - прикрепи́ть
                 (Irr. C-2) *v.tr.*

fat *n.* жир *n.masc.* (1)

favorable *adj.* ВЫ́ГОДНЫЙ *adj.* (17a)

February n. *февра́ль n.masc. (6)

ferment v.tr. and intr. броди́ть - поброди́ть (Irr. D-2,

fermentation n. брожéние n.neuter (16)     д → ж) v.intr.

field (land) n. по́ле n.neuter (15)

field (region, branch of science, etc.) n. о́бласть n.fem. (12)

filings n.plu. опи́лки n.plu. only (9a Cf. § 359, p. 579)

filter v.tr. and intr.*фильтровáть (Irr. A-1) v.tr.

filter out verbal expr.*отфильтро́вывать (Reg. A)-*отфильтровáть

filtrate n. *фильтра́т n.masc. (1)          (Irr. A-1) v.tr.

final adj. конéчный adj. (17)

find v.tr. находи́ть (Irr. D-2, д → ж) - найти́ (Irr. H-10)
                                                           v.tr.

  to be found, located, to be  -ся (Particularly imperf. forms)

find (encounter) v.tr. встречáть (Reg. A) - встрéтить (Irr. D-2,
                                                  т → ч) v.tr.

  to be encountered, found, to occur (e.g., minerals) -ся

firefly n. светля́к n.masc. (3)

first adj. пéрвый adj. (17)

  at first снача́ла

flame n. пла́мя n.neuter (§ 358, p. 575)

flask  n. ко́лба n.fem. (7)

flax  n. лён n.masc. (1c)

flee v.tr. and intr. бéгать - побéгать (Reg. A) v.intr.

flight  n. лёт, полёт n.masc. (1)

flow v.intr. течь (Irr. G-3) v.intr. imperf.

fly out (of, from) verbal expr. вылетáть (Reg. A) - вы́лететь
                    (Irr. D-2, т → ч ) (из) v.intr.

fly through verbal expr. пролетáть (Reg. A) - пролетéть
                    (Irr. D-2, т → ч) v.tr.

follow (logically, of necessity) v.intr. слéдовать - послéдовать

food n. пи́ща n.fem. (8)                (Irr. A-1) v.intr.

foodstuff n. пищево́е вещество́ fixed expr.

for prep. для prep. (with gen.)

force n. си́ла n.fem. (7)

fork n. ви́лка n.fem. (9a)

form, shape  n. вид, о́браз n.masc. (1)

form, produce v.tr. образо́вывать (Reg. A) - образовáть

  to be formed, produced -ся          (Irr. A-1) v.tr.

formation  n. образовáние n.neuter (16)

formula  n. *фо́рмула n.fem. (7)

found past part. нáйденный (17 perf. past part. of
                            находи́ть - найти́)

four numeral четы́ре numeral (§ 370, p. 600)

four-stroke adj. четырехта́ктый adj. (17)

fourth adj. четвёртый adj. (17)

fractions  n. *фра́кция n.fem. (11)

France n. *Фрáнция n.fem. (11)

Frauenhofer  *n.* *Фрауенгóфер *n.masc.* (1)
Frauenhofer *adj.* *Фрауенгóферовый *adj.* (17)
free *adj.* СВОБÓДНЫЙ *adj.* (17a)
frequency *n.* частотá *n.fem.* (7)
from *prep.* ИЗ, ОТ *prep.* (*with gen.*)
fruit *n.* *фрукт *n.masc.* (1)
fuel *n.* тóпливо *n.neuter* (16)
function *n.* *фýнкция *n.fem.* (11)
function, work *v.intr.* рабóтать – порабóтать (Reg, A) *v.intr.*
furnish (supply) *v.tr.* доставлять (Reg. A)   – достáвить
                                                    (Irr. C-2) *v.tr.*
fused, melted  *past part.* расплáвленный (17 *perf.* *past*
                          *part.* of расплавлять – расплáвить)
fusion *n.* плавлéние *n.neuter* (16)
    fusion together, melting together сплавлéние *n.neuter* (16)
future *n. and adj.* бýдущий *adj.* (17)   (*Used also as noun –*
                                        Cf. Note 9, p. 500)

# G

gamma-ray (1)  *гáмма-лýч *n.masc.* (2)
gas *n.* *газ *n.masc.* (1)
gaseous *adj.* *гáзовый *adj.* (17)
gaseous *adi.* газообрáзный *adj.* (17a)
gear *n.* зубчáтое колесó *fixed expr.*
general (common) *adj.* óбщий *adj.* (22)
    in general вообще
geological *adj.* *геологúческий *adj.* (21)
geometry *n.* *геомéтрия *n.fem.* (11)
glass *n.* стеклó *n.neuter* (13a)
glowing (light emission) *n.* свечéние *n.neuter* (16)
glycerine *n.* глицерúн *n.masc.* (1)
go, walk *v.intr.* ХОДИТЬ – ПОХОДИТЬ (Irr. D-2, Д → Ж)
            ИТТИ – ПОЙТИ (Irr. H-10) (Cf. §§ 381-2, pp. 626-630)
go over, go beyond *verbal expr.* переходить (Irr. D-2, Д → Ж)
                    – перейти (Irr. H-10) *v.intr.*
go up (to) *verbal expr.* ДОХОДИТЬ (Irr. D-2) – ДОЙТИ (Irr. H-10)
gold *n.* зóлото *n.neuter* (13)                    *v.intr.* ( ДО)
good *adj.* хорóший *adj.* (22)
gradually *adv.* постепéнно *adv.*
grain *n.* зернó *n.neuter* (13b)
granite *n.* гранúт *n.masc.* (1)
great *adj.* большóй *adj.* (20)
Greece *n.* *Грéция *n.fem.* (11)
ground, earth *n.* пóчва *n.fem.* (7)
group *n.* *грýппа *n.fem.* (7)

grow *v.intr.* расти́ – вы́расти　(Irr.　расту́, -ёшь, -ёт,
gun powder *fixed expr.* по́рох *n.masc.*　　　　etc.)　*v.intr.*

# H

Hall *n.*　*Холл *n.masc.*(1)
happen (occur) *v.intr.*　случа́ться (Reg. A) – случи́ться
　　　　　　　　　　　　　　　　(Reg. B-2)　*v.refl.*
happy *adj.*　рад *adj.* (*pred. forms only* § 357, p. 571)
hardness *n.*　тве́рдость *n.fem.* (12)
have　*v.tr.*　име́ть (Reg. A) *v.tr. imperf.*
he *pronoun* он *pronoun* (§ 136, p. 204)
heat *n.*　тепло́ *n.neuter* (13)　теплота́ *n.fem.* (7)
heat *adj.*　теплово́й *adj.* (18)
heat *v.tr. and intr.*　нака́ливать (Reg. A) – накали́ть
　　　　　　　　　　　　　　　　(Reg. B-2) *v.tr.*
heating up (process) *n.*　нагрева́ние *n.neuter* (16)
heating up, warming up (process) *n.*　разогрева́ние *n.neuter* (16)
heavenly *adj.*　небе́сный *adj.* (17)
helium *n.*　*ге́лий *n.masc.* (5)
her *pronoun and poss.* её　(Cf.　он § 136, p. 204 also § 138,
Heroult *n.*　*Эру́ *n.masc.*　(*undecl.* § 363, p. 587)　　　　p. 207)

hexagonal *adj.*　*гексагона́льный *adj.* (17b)
high (lofty)　*adj.*　высо́кий *adj.* (21)
high (big)　*adj.*　большо́й *adj.* (18)
highly *adv.*　высоко́ *adv.*
　　highly developed　высокоразви́тый *adj.* (17) (Cf. § 286,
　　　　　　　　　　　　　　　　　　　　　p. 452)
his　*poss.*　его́ *pronoun and poss.* (Cf. он § 136, p. 204, also
　　　　　　　　　　　　　　　§ 138, p. 207)
　　his (*referring to subject of sentence*) свой *poss.*
　　　　　　　　　　　　　　(18) (Cf. § 148, p. 225)
history *n.*　*исто́рия *n.fem.* (11)
honey *n.*　мёд *n.masc.* (1)
horizontal *adj.*　*горизонта́льный　*adj.* (17b)
hormone *n.*　*гормо́н *n.masc.* (1)
how (so, in what fashion)　*adv.*　как *adv.*
hydrated oxide *fixed expr.* гидроо́кись *n.fem.* (12)
hydrocarbon *n.*　углеводоро́д *n.masc.* (1)
hydrochloric acid　*fixed expr.* соляна́я кислота́ *fixed expr.*
hydrodynamics *n.*　*гидродина́мика *n.fem.* (9)
hydrogen *n.*　водоро́д *n.masc.* (1)
hydrogen *adj.*　водоро́дный *adj.* (17)
hydrogen ion　*fixed expr.* водоро́дный *ио́н

hydrogen ion coefficient *fixed expr.* водоро́дный показа́тель

hydrolysis *n.* \*гидро́лиз *n.masc.* (1)

hygroscopic *adj.* \*гигроскопи́ческий *adj.* (21)

hypothesis *n.* \*гипоте́за *n.fem.* (7)

## I

I *pronoun* Я *pronoun* (§ 136, p. 204)

ice *n.* лёд *n.masc.* (1c)

identify *v.tr.* \*идентифици́ровать (Irr. A-1)*v.tr. perf. and*

if *conj.* е́сли *conj.*                      *imperf.*

ignite, become ignited *v.intr.* загора́ться (Reg. A) – загоре́ться

                                     (Reg. B-2) *v.refl.*

      to scorch, to burn загора́ть – загоре́ть

illumination *n.* освеще́ние *n.neuter* (16)

immobile *adj.* неподви́жный *adj.* (17a)

immunity *n.* \*иммуните́т *n.masc.* (1)

impact *n.* уда́р *n.masc.* (1)

impart (to)*v.tr.* придава́ть(Irr. B) – прида́ть (Irr. I-3) *v.tr.*

imparted *past part.* при́данный *perf. pas. past part. of*

                           придава́ть – прида́ть

impedence *n.* \*импеда́нц *n.masc.*

importance *n.* ва́жность *n.fem.* (12)

important *adj.* ва́жный *adj.* (17a)

important (big) *adj.* большо́й *adj.* (20)

improve *v.tr. and intr.* улучша́ть (Reg. A) – улу́чшить

                             (Reg. B-2) *v.tr.*

      to be improved, to improve *intr.* –ся

impulse *n.* \*и́мпульс *n.masc.* (1)

in (inside, within) *prep.* В (ВО) *prep.* (*with prepl.*)

in (into *implying motion*) *prep.* В (ВО) *prep.* (*with acc.*)

in (while, during) *prep.* В (ВО) *prep.* (*with acc.*)

in (on surface of, at) *prep* на *prep.* (*with prepl.*)

in order to *conj. expr.* что́бы *conj.* (Cf. § 168, p. 256; § 315,

incandescence *n.* нака́ливание *n.neuter* (16)       p. 495)

increase (in size, etc.) *n.* увеличе́ние *n.neuter* (16)

increase (rise) *n.* повыше́ние *n.neuter* (16)

increase (grow larger) *v.intr.* возраста́ть (Reg. A) –

      возрасти́ (Irr. возрасту́, -ёшь, -ёт, etc.) *v.intr.*

increase (make larger) *v.tr.* увели́чивать (Reg. A) –

      to be increased, made larger –ся увели́чить(Reg. B-2)*v.tr.*

increased (made larger) *past part.* увели́ченный *perf. pas.*

             *past part. of* увели́чивать – увели́чить

increased (made higher) *past part.* повы́шенный *perf. pas.*

             *past part. of* повыша́ть – повы́сить

independently *adv.* незави́симо *adv.* (of) (ОТ *with gen.*)

indivisible *adj.* недели́мый *adj.* (17)

industrial *adj.* промы́шленный *adj.* (17)

industry *n.* промы́шленность *n.fem.* (12)

inelastic *adj.* *неэласти́ческий *adj.* (21)

infection *n.* *инфе́кция *n.fem.* (11)

influence *n.* влия́ние *n.neuter* (16)

    exert influence (on) ВЛИЯ́ТЬ-ПОВЛИЯ́ТЬ (Reg. A) *v.intr.*
                                 (НА *with acc.*)

initial *adj.* нача́льный *adj.* (17b)

inner *adj.* вну́тренний *adj.* (19)

inorganic *adj.* *неоргани́ческий *adj.* (21)

install *v.tr.* *монти́ровать -*смонти́ровать (Irr. A-1) *v.tr.*

installation *n.* *монта́ж *n.masc.*

instrument *n.* прибо́р *n.masc.* (1)

insulator *n.* *изоля́тор *n.masc.* (1)

interest *v.tr.* *интересова́ть -*заинтересова́ть (Irr. A-1)
                                        *v.tr.*

    to become interested (in), to take interest (in) ‑СЯ (*with*
interesting *adj.* *интере́сный *adj.* (17a)  *instr. or* В *with prepl.*)

internal *adj.* вну́тренний *adj.* (19)

interplanetary *adj.* *межплане́тный *adj.* (17)

interruption *n.* переры́в *n.masc.* (1)

into (implying motion) *prep.* В (ВО) *prep.* (*with acc.*)

intra-atomic *adj.* *внутриато́мный *adj.* (17a)

introduction (preliminary statement) *n.* введе́ние *n.neuter* (16)

introduction (process of bringing in) *n.* внесе́ние *n.neuter* (16)

invent *v.tr.* изобрета́ть (Reg. A) - изобрести́ (Irr. Н-3) *v.tr.*

invention *n.* изобрете́ние *n.neuter* (16)

investigate *v.tr.* иссле́довывать (Reg. A) - иссле́довать
                                 (Irr. A-1) *v.tr.*

investigated *past. part.* иссле́дованный *perf. pas. past*
                              *part.* (Cf. *preceding entry*)

investigated (studied) *past part.* изу́ченный *pas. past part.*
                                изуча́ть-изучи́ть

investigation *n.* иссле́дование *n.neuter* (16)

invisible *adj.* невиди́мый *adj.* (17)

ion *n.* *ио́н *n.masc.* (11)

ionization *n.* *иониза́ция *n.fem.* (11)

iron *n.* желе́зо *n.neuter* (13)

iron *adj.* желе́зный *adj.* (17)

    ferric желе́зный *adj.* (17)

    ferrous желе́зистый *adj.* (17)

iron-aluminum *adj.* железно-*алюми́ниевый *adj.* (17)

irrational *adj.* *иррациона́льный *adj.* (17b)

irreplaceable *adj.* незамени́мый *adj.* (17)

is *pres. tense form of* to be ЕСТЬ (*implying emphasis,*
Cf. § 122, p. 180) (*For various circumlocutions replacing
obsolete present tense of* БЫТЬ "to be" *see* § 123, p. 181)
isolate *v.tr.* *ИЗОЛИРОВАТЬ (Irr. A-1) *v.tr. perf. and
isoprene *n.* *ИЗОПРЕН *n.masc.* (1)                    *imperf.*
isotope *n.* *ИЗОТОП *n.masc.* (1)
it *pronoun* ОНО (ОН, ОНА *when referring to masc. or fem. nouns*
Italian *adj.* *ИТАЛЬЯНСКИЙ *adj.* (21)          Cf. § 136, p. 204)
its *poss.* ЕГО *undecl. poss.* (Cf. § 136, p. 204 and § 138, p. 207);
СВОЙ § 148, p. 225) (*When referring to subject of sentence*
СВОЙ § 148, p. 225)

## J

Japanese *adj.* *ЯПОНСКИЙ *adj.* (21)
juice *n.* СОК *n.masc.* (3)
Jupiter *n.* *ЮПИТЕР *n.masc.* (1)

## K

Kensington *n.* *КЕНСИНГТОН *n.masc.* (1)
kerosene *n.* *КЕРОСИН *n.masc.* (1)
ketone *n.* *КЕТОН *n.masc.* (1)
kilometer *n.* *КИЛОМЕТР *n.masc.* (1)
kind (any kind) *see* any
kinetic *adj.* *КИНЕТИЧЕСКИЙ *adj.* (21)
known *adj.* ИЗВЕСТНЫЙ *adj.* (17a)

## L

laboratory *n.* *ЛАБОРАТОРИЯ *n.fem.* (11)
laboratory *adj.* *ЛАБОРАТОРНЫЙ *adj.* (17)
lamp *n.* *ЛАМПА *n.fem.* (7)
large, big *adj.* БОЛЬШОЙ *adj.* (20)
larger, bigger *comp. adj.* БОЛЬШИЙ *adj.* (22) (Cf. § 332, p. 525)
latex *n.* *ЛАТЕКС *n.masc.* (1)
latter *adj.* ПОСЛЕДНИЙ *adj.* (19)
Laval *n.* *ЛАВАЛЬ *n.masc.* (6)
law *n.* ЗАКОН *n.masc.* (1)
layer *n.* СЛОЙ *n.masc.* (4)
lead (the metal) *n.* СВИНЕЦ *n.masc.* (3a)
leading *pres. part.* ВЕДУЩИЙ (22) *act. pres. part. of*
ВЕСТИ - ПОВЕСТИ

least *superl. adj.* НАИМЕ́НЬШИЙ (22) *superl. adj.*(Cf.

length *n.* ДЛИНА́ *n.fem.* (7)

less *comp. adj. and adv.* МЕ́НЬШЕ *pred. comp. adj. and adv. (undecl.*§ 334, p. 528)

let (permit, allow) *v.tr.* ПУСТЬ *verbal auxiliary*(Cf. § 306, p. 484)

liberate *v.tr.* ОСВОБОЖДА́ТЬ (Reg. A) – ОСВОБОДИ́ТЬ(Irr. D-2,

    to be liberated, set free   –СЯ      Д → Ж) *v.tr.*

life *n.* ЖИЗНЬ *n.fem.*(12)

life *adj.* ЖИ́ЗНЕННЫЙ *adj.* (17 *pred. masc. sing.* ЖИ́ЗНЕН)

light *n.* СВЕТ *n.masc.* (1)

    light-giving *adj.* СВЕТООТДА́ЮЩИЙ (22) (Cf. § 286, p. 452)

light (pertaining to light, illumination) *adj.* СВЕТОВО́Й *adj.*(18)

light (not heavy, easy) *adj.* ЛЁГКИЙ *adj.* (21)

light source *n.* СВЕТОИСТО́ЧНИК *n.masc.*(3)

(like (similar to) *prep.* ПОДО́БНО *prep. (with dat.)*

    and the like И ПРО́ЧЕЕ (*Sometimes abbreviated as* И пр.)

limited, restricted *past part.* ОГРАНИ́ЧЕННЫЙ (17) *perf. pas. past part. of* ОГРАНИ́ЧИВАТЬ – ОГРАНИ́ЧИТЬ

line *n.* *ЛИ́НИЯ *n.fem.* (11)

linear *adj.* *ЛИНЕ́ЙНЫЙ *adj.*(17)

linear-reciprocating *adj.* ПРЯМОЛИНЕ́ЙНО-ВОЗВРА́ТНЫЙ *adj.* (17)

linseed (pertaining to flax) *adj.* ЛЬНЯНО́Й *adj.*(18)

liquid *n.* ЖИ́ДКОСТЬ *n.fem.* (12)

liquid *adj.* ЖИ́ДКИЙ *adj.* (21a)

litharge *n.* МАССИКО́Т *n.masc.*(1)

little, small, slight *adj.* МА́ЛЫЙ *adj.* (17) ; МА́ЛЕНЬКИЙ *adj.* (21)

little by little *advl. expr.* МА́ЛО-ПО-МА́ЛУ *advl.expr.*

living, alive *adj.* ЖИВО́Й *adj.* (18)

logarithm *n.* *ЛОГАРИ́ФМ *n.masc.* (1)

    to take the logarithm*ЛОГАРИФМИ́РОВАТЬ –*ПРОЛОГАРИФМИ́РОВАТЬ

                                    (Irr. A-1) *v.tr.*

low *adj.* НИ́ЗКИЙ *adj.* (21a)

lowering (process) *n.* ПОНИЖЕ́НИЕ *n.neuter* (16)

# M

machine *n.* *МАШИ́НА *n.fem.* (7)

magnetic *adj.* *МАГНИ́ТНЫЙ *adj.* (17)

maintenance *n.* ПОДДЕРЖА́НИЕ *n.neuter* (16)

majority *n.* БОЛЬШИНСТВО́ *n.neuter* (13)

make, do *v.tr.* ДЕ́ЛАТЬ – СДЕ́ЛАТЬ (Reg.A) *v.tr.*

manganese *n.* МА́РГАНЕЦ *n.masc.* (3a *instr. sing.*                                                        МА́РГАНЦЕМ)

many *pronoun* МНО́ГО *pronoun*

many *adj.* МНО́ГИЕ *adj.* (21 *plu. only*)

manner (form, shape)    n.  о́браз n.masc. (1)

   in this manner, in this way  таки́м о́бразом

   in the following manner or way  сле́дующим о́бразом

manufacture n.  вы́работка n.fem.(7)

map n.  *ка́рта n.fem. (7)

March n.  *март n.masc. (1)

mass n.  *ма́сса n.fem. (7)

material n.  *материа́л n.masc. (1)

mathematical adj.  *математи́ческий adj. (21)

mathematician n.  *матема́тик n.masc. (3)

mathematics n. *матема́тика n.fem. (9)

matter (substance) n. *мате́рия n.fem. (11)

matter, affair n.  де́ло n.neuter (13)

may, can be, be able v.intr.  мочь – смочь (Irr. G-4) v.intr.

   may be, might be, can be  мочь – смочь (with быть)

   (he, she, it) might be, can be  мо́жет быть

   (they) might be, can be  мо́гут быть

means, agency n.  сре́дство n.neuter (13)

   by means of prepl. expr.  посре́дством (with gen.)

   by means of (Often expressed by instr. case -- Cf. § 91, p. 131)

   by means of see also with the aid (of) under  aid

measure v.tr.  измеря́ть (Reg. A) – изме́рить (Reg. B-2) v.tr.

mechanical adj.  *механи́ческий adj. (21)

mechanics n.  *меха́ника n.fem. (9)

medicine n.  *медици́на n.fem. (7)

medium (milieu) n.  среда́ n.fem. (7)

melt v.tr. and intr.  пла́вить – распла́вить (Irr. C-2) v.tr.

   to be melted, to melt intr.  -ся

meniscus n.  *мени́ск n.masc.(3)

mention v.tr.  отмеча́ть (Reg. A) – отме́тить (Irr.D-2, Т → Ч)

                                      v.tr.

mercury (the metal) n.  ртуть n.fem. (12)

Mercury (the planet) n.  *Мерку́рий n.masc. (5)

metal n.  *мета́лл  n.masc. (1)

metallic adj.  *металли́ческий adj. (21)

metallurgy n.  *металлу́ргия n.fem. (11)

methane n.  *мета́н n.masc. (1)

method n. *ме́тод, спо́соб n.masc. (1)

methyl (the $CH_3$- radical) n.  *мети́л n.masc. (1)

methyl adj.  *мети́ловый adj. (17)

   methyl chloride  *мети́ловый *хлори́д

methylate v.tr. and intr.  *метили́ровать (Irr. A-1) v.tr.

                        perf. and imperf.

micrometer n.*микроме́тр n.masc.(1)

microorganism n.  *микроорганизм n.masc.  (1)

milk n. *молоко́ n.neuter (13)

mineral (substance) n.  го́рная поро́да fixed expr.

minimum *adj.* \*МИНИМА́ЛЬНЫЙ *adj.* (17b)
mining (industry) *n.* ГО́РНОЕ ДЕ́ЛО *fixed expr.*
mining (operation) *n.* ДОБЫВА́НИЕ *n.neuter* (16)
mining (production) *n.* ДОБЫ́ЧА *n.fem.* (9 *instr. sing.* ДОБЫ́ЧЕЙ)
minute *n.* \*МИНУ́ТА *n.fem.* (7)
mix *v.tr. and intr.* СМЕ́ШИВАТЬ – СМЕША́ТЬ (Reg. A) *v.tr.*
    to be mixed, undergo mixing  –СЯ
mixture *n.* СМЕСЬ *n.fem.* (12)
modern, contemporary *adj.* СОВРЕМЕ́ННЫЙ *adj.*
modification *n.* \*МОДИФИКА́ЦИЯ *n.fem.* (11)
moisten *v.tr.* СМА́ЧИВАТЬ (Reg. A) СМОЧИ́ТЬ (Reg. B-2) *v.tr.*
                      УВЛАЖНЯ́ТЬ (Reg. A)– УВЛАЖНИ́ТЬ (Reg. B-2)
moistened *past part.* УВЛАЖНЁННЫЙ *perf. pas. past part.*
                         *of* УВЛАЖНЯ́ТЬ – УВЛАЖНИ́ТЬ
molecular *adj.* \*МОЛЕКУЛЯ́РНЫЙ *adj.* (17a)
    high molecular *adj.* ВЫСОКОМОЛЕКУЛЯ́РНЫЙ *adj.* (17a)
molecule *n.* \*МОЛЕ́КУЛА *n.fem.* (7)
monoclinic *adj.* \*МОНОКЛИНИ́ЧЕСКИЙ *adj.* (21)
moon *n.* \*ЛУНА́ *n.fem.* (7)
more (*in comp. of adjs.*) *adv.* БО́ЛЕЕ *adv.* (Cf. § 331, p. 523)
*See Lesson* 36 *for summary of comp. forms of adjs. and*
                                 *advs.*
most (*in superl. of adjs.*) *adv.* НАИБО́ЛЕЕ *adv.;* СА́МЫЙ
                                      *adj.*
*See Lesson* 37 *for summary of superl. forms of adjs. and*
mother *adj.* \*МАТЕРИ́НСКИЙ *adj.* (21)            *advs.*
motion *n.* ДВИЖЕ́НИЕ *n.neuter* (16)
motor *n.* \*МОТО́Р *n.masc.* (1)
move *v.tr. and intr.* ДВИ́ГАТЬ (Irr. D-1, Г → Ж) – ДВИ́НУТЬ
    to be moved, to move *intr.* –СЯ         (Reg. B-1) *v.tr.*
moving *act. part. intr.* ДВИ́ЖУЩИЙСЯ *act. pres. part.*
                      *refl. of* ДВИ́ГАТЬ – ДВИ́НУТЬ
movement *n.* ДВИЖЕ́НИЕ *n.neuter* (16)
mover *n.* ДВИ́ГАТЕЛЬ *n.masc.* (6)
much, many *pronoun* МНО́ГО *pronoun*
much *adv.* О́ЧЕНЬ, ГОРА́ЗДО *adv.*
multiple *adj.* КРА́ТНЫЙ *adj.* (17a)
multiplicity *n.* МНО́ЖЕСТВО *n.neuter* (13)
music *n.* \*МУ́ЗЫКА *n.fem.* (9)
must be *see* necessary
    (it) must not, (it) is forbidden *see* not
mutually *adv.* ВЗАИ́МНО *adv.*

# N

narrow *adj.* У́ЗКИЙ *adj.* (21a)
natural *adj.* ПРИРО́ДНЫЙ *adj.* (17) \*НАТУРА́ЛЬНЫЙ *adj.* (17b)

nature *n.* приро́да *n.fem.* (7)
navigation *n.* \*навига́ция *n.fem.* (11)
near *adj.* бли́зкий *adj.*(21a)
near *adv.* бли́зко *adv.*
near *prep.* близ, вблизи́ *prep.* (with gen.)
nearer *comp. adj. and adv.* бли́же *comp. prep. adj. undecl. and comp adv.*
necessary *adj.* необходи́мый *adj.* (17)
  (it is) necessary необходи́мо, на́до (Cf. §§ 166-7, pp. 254-5)
    to be necessary, to follow сле́довать - после́довать
negative *adj,* отрица́тельный *adj.* (17)   (Irr.A-1) *v.tr. and irtr.*
neither -- nor -- НИ --- НИ ---
neoprene *n.* \*неопре́н *n.masc.* (1)
Neptune *n.* \*Непту́н *n.masc.* (1)
neutral *adj.* \*нейтра́льный *adj.* (17b)
neutron *n.* \*нейтро́н *n.masc.* (1)
new *adj.* \*но́вый *adj.* (17)
New (in English names) *adj.* \*Нью *adj.* (undecl.)
New York *n.* \*Нью-Йо́рк *n.masc.* (3)
Newton *n.* \*Ньюто́н *n.masc.* (1)
nickel *n.* ни́ккель *n.masc.* (6)
nitric acid *fixed expr.* азо́тная кислота́ *fixed expr.*
nitrogen *n.* азо́т *n.masc.* (1)
  nitrogen-containing азотосодержа́щий (22) (Cf. § 286, p. 452)
no *see* not
noble *adj.* благоро́дный *adj.* (17a)
nonaqueous *adj.* нево́дный *adj.* (17)
non-luminous *adj.* несветя́щийся (22) (Cf. § 286, p. 452)
nonetheless *adv.* тем не ме́нее *adv l. expr.*
normal *adj.* \*норма́льный *adj.* (17b)
not *adv.* не, нет *adv.*
  (it) must not, (it) is forbidden *verbal expr.* (with inf.)
    нельзя́ *adv.* (with inf.)
not only --- but also --- не то́лько --- но та́кже ---
nozzle *n.* сопло́ *n.neuter* (13b)
nuclear *adj.* я́дерный *adj.* (17)
nucleus *n.* ядро́ *n.neuter* (13b)
number *n.* число́ *n.neuter*
numerical *adj.* числово́й *adj.* (18)

## O

observe *v.tr.* наблюда́ть (Reg. A) - наблюсти́ (Irr. H-5)
  to be observed -ся *v.tr.*
  being observed наблюда́ющийся (22) *act. pres. part.*
    *refl. of* наблюда́ть - наблюсти́

observe (detect) *v. tr.* обнаруживать (Reg. A) – обнаружить
                                       (Reg. B-2)

     observed, detected обнаруженный *pas. past part. of*
                         обнаруживать – обнаружить

obtain *v. tr. and intr.* получать (Reg. A) – получить

     to be obtained, produced, prepared -ся    (Reg. B-2) *v. tr.*

obtaining (acquisition) *n.* получение *n. neuter* (16)

obvious *adj.* очевидный *adj.* (17a)

     (it is) obvious очевидно (Cf. §§ 166-167, pp. 254-256)

occur *see* happen *and* encounter

ocean *n.* \*океан *n. masc.* (1)

Oersted *n.* \*Эрстед *n. masc.* (1)

of *prep.* от, из *prep. (with gen.)*

     *Possession and similar relationship are usually*
     *expressed by using the gen. case. Cf.* § 83, p. 120

often *adv.* часто *adv.*

oil *n.* масло *n. neuter* (13b)

on (while, during, along with) *prep.* при *(prep. with prepl.)*

on (on surface of) *prep.* на *prep. (with prepl.)*

on (onto *implying motion) prep.* на *prep. (with acc.)*

once more *adv l. expr.* вновь *adv.*

one *adj. numeral* один *adj. numeral* (Cf. § 370, p. 600)

one and the same *fixed expr.* один и тот же *fixed expr.*

one from another *fixed expr.* друг от друга *fixed expr.*

oneself *see* self

only *adv.* лишь *adv.*

orbit *n.* \*орбита *n. fem.* (7)

order (arrangement) *n.* порядок *n. masc.* (3a)

     in order to для того чтобы

ordinary *adj.* обычный, обыкновенный *adj.* (17a)

ordinarily *adv.* обыкновенно *adv.*

ore *n.* руда *n. fem.* (7)

organic *adj.* \*органический *adj.* (21)

organism *n.* \*организм *n. masc.* (1)

origin *n.* происхождение *n. neuter* (16)

original *adj.* первоначальный *adj.* (17)

other (another) *adj.* другой *adj.* (20)

other (different) *adj.* иной *adj.* (18)

Otto *n.* \*Отто *n. masc. (undecl.* § 363, p. 587)

our *poss.* наш *poss.* (§ 136, p. 208)

outside *prep.* вне *prep. (with gen.)*

over (above, in space above) *prep.* над (надо) *prep. (with*
                                             *instr.)*

over (on surface of) *prep.* на *prep. (with prepl.)*

oxidation *n.* окисление *n. neuter* (16)

oxide *n.* óкисел *n.masc.* (12)
   (higher) oxide óкись *n.fem.*(12)
   (lower) oxide зáкись *n.fem.* (12)
oxygen *n.* кислорóд *n.masc.* (1)


Р


paper *n.* бумáга *n.fem.* (9)
paraffin *n.* *парафин *n.masc.* (1)
paragraph *n.* *парáграф *n.masc.* (1)
parallelogram *n.* *параллелогрáм *n.masc.* (1)
part *n.* часть *n.fem.* (12)
partially *adv.* частѝчно *adv.*
participate (in) *v.intr.* учáствовать (Irr. A-1) *v.intr.*
                    *imperf.* (B *with prepl.*)
participation *n.* учáствие *n.neuter* (16)
particle *n.* частѝца *n.fem.* (8)
particle *n.* частѝца *n.fem.* (8)
pass (proceed, go) *v.intr.* иттѝ-пойтѝ (Irr. H-10) *v.intr.*
pass (through) *v.intr.* проходѝть (Irr. D-2, Д → Ж) -
                  пройтѝ (Irr. H-10) *v.intr.*
pass (through) *v.tr.* пропускáть (Reg. A) - пропустѝть
             (Irr. D-2, СТ → Щ) *v.tr.*
passage (through) *n.* пропускáние *n.neuter* (16)
passed (having passed through) *act. past part. intr.*
прошéдший (22) *act. past part. intr. of* проходѝть - пройтѝ
passenger *adj.* *пассажѝрский *adj.* (21)
passing (through) *act. pres. part. intr.* проходя́щий (22)
     *act. pres. part. intr. of* проходѝть - пройтѝ
patent *n.* *патéнт *n.masc.* (1)
peaceful *adj.* мировóй *adj.* (18)
peculiarity *n.* осóбенность *n.fem.*(12)
pentane *n.* *пентáн *n.masc.* (1)
period *n.* *перѝод *n.masc.* (1)
periodic *adj.* *периодѝческий *adj.* (21)
perpendicular *adj.* *перпендикуля́рный *adj.*(17a)
person *n.* человéк *n.masc.*
to pertain *v.intr.* относѝться (Irr. D-2, С → Ш) -
               отнестѝсь (Irr. H-2) *v.refl.*
petroleum *n.* нефть *n.fem.* (12)
petroleum *adj.* нефтянóй *adj.*(18)
pharmacy *n.* *фармáция *n.fem.* (11)
phenomenon *n.* явлéние *n.neuter* (16)
philosopher *n.* *филóсоф *n.masc.* (1)
phosphorus *n.* *фóсфор *n.masc.* (1)
photoelectric *adj.* *фотоэлектрѝческий *adj.* (21)

photograph, photography *n.* *фотогра́фия *n.fem.* (11)
photographer *n.* *фото́граф *n.masc.* (1)
photographic *adj.* *фотографи́ческий *adj.* (21)
photon *n.* *фото́н *n.masc.* (1)
physical *adj.* *физи́ческий *adj.* (21)
physically *adv.* *физи́чески *adv.*
physicist *n.* *фи́зик *n.masc.* (3)
physics *n.* *фи́зика *n.fem.* (9)
piston *n.* по́ршень *n.masc.*
place *n.* ме́сто *n.neuter* (13)
place *v.tr.* полага́ть (Reg. A)- положи́ть (Reg. B-2) *v.tr.*
Planck *n.* *Планк *n.masc.* (3)
plane (geometric figure) *n.* пло́скость *n.fem.* (12)
planet *n.* *плане́та *n.fem.* (7)
plant (botanical organism) *n.* расте́ние *n.neuter* (16)
plant (pertaining to a botanical organism) *adj.* расти́тельный *adj.* (17)
plant (factory) *n.* заво́д *n.masc.* (1)
plant (installation of equipment) *n.* ста́нция *n.fem.* (11)
plastic *adj.* *пласти́чный
plasticity *n.* *пласти́чность *n.fem.* (12)
plate (photographic, etc.) *n.* пласти́нка *n.fem.* (9a)
platinum *n.* *пла́тина *n.fem.* (7)
platinum *adj.* *пла́тиновый *adj.* (17)
play *v.tr. and intr.* игра́ть - сыгра́ть (Reg. A) *v.tr. and intr.*
Pluto *n.* *Плуто́н *n.masc.* (1)
plutonium *n.* *плуто́ний *n.masc.* (5)
porcelain *n.* фарфо́р *n.masc.* (1)
porcelain *adj.* фарфо́ровый *adj.* (1)
position *n.* положе́ние *n.neuter* (16)
positive *adj.* положи́тельный *adj.* (17b)
positively *adv.* положи́тельно *adv.*
possess *v.tr.* облада́ть (Reg. A) *v.tr.* (*with instr.*)
possible *adj.* возмо́жный *adj.* (17b)
   (it is) possible возмо́жно, мо́жно (Cf. §§ 166-7, pp. 254-5)
potassium *n.* *ка́лий *n.masc.* (5)
potential *n.* *потенциа́л *n.masc.* (1)
potential *adj.* *потенциа́льный *adj.* (17b)
pour, to be pouring *v.tr.* лить (Irr. E-3) *v.tr. imperf.*
powder *n.* порошо́к *n.masc.* (3a)
   gun powder по́рох *n.masc.* (3)
power *n.* си́ла *n.fem.* (6) мо́щность *n.fem.* (12)
power *adj.* силово́й *adj.* (18)
powerful *adj.* мо́щный *adj.* (17a)
practical *adj.* *практи́ческий *adj.* (21)
practically *adv.* *практи́чески *adv.*

preceding, foregoing *adj.* предыдущий *adj.* (22) (*Also used as noun*)

precious *adj.* драгоце́нный *adj.* (17 *pred. masc. sing.* драгоце́нен)

predict *v.tr.* предска́зывать (Reg. A) -предсказа́ть (Irr. D-1, з → ж) *v.tr.*

preparation (substance) *n.* *препара́т *n.masc.* (1)

preparation (production, acquisition) *n.* получе́ние *n.neuter* (16)

presence *n.* прису́тствие *n.neuter* (16)

present (offer, exhibit, represent) *v.tr.* представля́ть (Reg. A) - предста́вить (Irr. C-2) *v.tr.*
to present self, to appear as, to be *with* собо́й *and acc. case.* (Cf. § 99 p. 144)

present (on hand, contemporary, real) *adj.* настоя́щий *adj.* (22)

pressure *n.* давле́ние *n.neuter* (16)
to exert pressure (on) дави́ть (Irr. C-1) *v.intr. imperf.* на

previously *adv.* пре́жде *adv.* (*with acc.*)

prime (simple) *adj.* просто́й *adj.* (18)
prime factor просто́й мно́житель *fixed expr.*
prime mover дви́гатель *n.masc.* (16)

principally *adv.* гла́вным о́бразом *advl. expr.* (Cf. § 98, p. 141)

principle *n.* *при́нцип *n.masc.* (1)

problem *n.* *пробле́ма *n.fem.* (7)

proceed (from) *v.intr.* исходи́ть (Irr. D-2, д → ж) - изойти́ (Irr. H-10) *v.intr.* (из *with gen.*)

proceed (transpire, occur) *v.intr.* происходи́ть (Irr. D-2, д → ж) - произойти́ (Irr. H.10) *v.intr.*

proceed (flow along) *v.intr.* протека́ть (Reg. A) - проте́чь (Irr. G-3) *v.intr.*

process *n.* *проце́сс, спо́соб *n.masc.* (1)

processing *n.* обрабо́тка *n.fem.* (9)

produce (make, effect, cause) *v.tr.* производи́ть (Reg. A) - произвести́ (Reg. B-2) *v.tr.*
to be caused, effected, produced -ся

produce (obtain, acquire) *v.tr.* получа́ть (Reg. A) - получи́ть (Reg. B-2) *v.tr.*

product (article, substance, work) *n.* *проду́кт *n.masc.* (1); произведе́ние *n.neuter* (16)

product (of multiplication) *n.* произведе́ние *n.neuter* (16)

production (preparation, manufacture) *n.* произво́дство *n.neuter* (13) получе́ние, добыва́ние *n.neuter* (16)

production (yield, output of factory or mine) *n.* *проду́кция *n.fem.* (11) добы́ча *n.fem.* (9 *instr. sing.* добы́чей) (particularly mining production)

professor *n.* *профе́ссор *n.masc.* (1, Footnote 1, p. 5)

prominent *adj.* ви́дный *adj.* (17b)

property (inherent attribute) n. СВОЙСТВО n.neuter (13)
proportion n. ОТНОШЕНИЕ n.neuter (16)
proportional adj. *пропорциональный adj. (with dat.)
                                        (Cf. § 112, p. 164) (17b)
protect (forestall harm) v.tr. предохранять (Reg. A) -
                               предохранить (Reg. B-2) v.tr.
protect (keep safe) v.tr. охранять (Reg. A) - охранить
protein n. белок n.masc. (3a)                    (Reg. B-2) v.tr.
proton n. *протон n.neuter (1)
pulse n. *импульс n.masc. (1)
pure adj. чистый adj. (17)
purpose, goal n. цель n.fem. (12)

## Q

quality n. качество n.neuter (13)
quantity (amount) n. количество n.neuter (13)
quantity (magnitude) n. величина n.fem. (7)
quantum n. *кванта n.fem. (6), *квант n.masc. (1)
quantum adj. *квантовый adj. (17)
quartz n. *кварц n.masc. (1 instr. sing. *кварцем)
quartz adj. *кварцовый adj. (1)
Queen Elizabeth name *Куин *Элизабет name (undecl. Note 15,
question n. вопрос n.masc. (1)                          p. 290)
quick adj. быстрый adj. (17)
quickly adv. быстро adv.
quiet adj. спокойный adj. (17 pred. masc. sing.
quietly adv. спокойно adv.
quinine n. *хинин n.masc. (1)

## R

radar n. *радиолокация n.fem. (11) *радар n.masc. (1)
radar adj. *радиолокационный adj. (17)
radiate (light, etc.) v.tr. излучать (Reg. A) - излучить
                                 (Reg. B-2) v.tr.
radiate (emit, eject) v.tr. испускать (Reg. A) - испустить
                            (Irr. D-2, ст → щ) v.tr.
radiation n. *радиация n.fem. (11), излучение n.neuter (16)
                     (particularly process of radiation)
radio n. *радио n.neuter (undecl. § 363, p. 589)
radio wave fixed expr. радиоволна n.fem. (7)
radioactive n. *радиоактивный adj.
radioactivity n. *радиоактивность n.fem. (12)
radium n. *радий n.masc. (5)

rail *n.* *рельс *n.masc.* (1) (Cf. Note 1, p. 21)

railroad *n.* железная дорога *fixed expr.*

railroad *adj.* железнодорожный *adj.* (17)

range (extent, internal) *n.* *интервал *n.masc.* (1)

rapid, fast *adj.*, быстрый, скорый *adj.* (1)

rapidly *adv.* быстро, скоро

    more rapidly быстрее, скорее *adv.* (Cf. § 336, p. 529)

rare (seldom) *adj.* редкий *adj.* (21)

rarely *adv.* редко *adv.*

rate (speed, velocity) *n.* скорость *n.fem.* (12)

rather (comparitively) *adv.* сравнительно *adv.*

ratio *n.* соотношение *n.neuter* (16)

raw material(s) *n.neuter* сырьё *n.neuter.* (16)

ray (light, etc.) *n.* луч *n.masc.*, (2)

react *v.tr. and intr.* *реагировать – *прореагировать
                              (Irr. A-1) *v.intr.*

  reacting *pres. part.* *реагирующий (22) *act. pres. part. of*
                          *реагировать – *прореагировать

reaction *n.* *реакция *n.fem.* (11)

reactivity *n.* *реактивность *n.fem.* (12)

reagent *n.* *реагент, *реактив *n.masc.* (1)

realize (accomplish), *v.tr.* *реализовать (Irr. A-1) *v.tr.*
    осуществлять (Reg. A) – осуществить (Irr. C-2) *v.tr.*

realize (understand, learn) *v.tr.* узнавать (Irr. узнаю,
                   -ешь, -ет, etc.) – узнать (Reg. A) *v.tr.*

receiver *n.* приёмник *n.masc.*, (3)

recent (latter, last) *adj.* последний *adj.* (19)

reception *n.* приём *n.masc.* (1)

reduce (make smaller) *v.tr.* уменьшать (Reg. A) – уменьшить
    to be reduced, made smaller -ся     (Reg. B-2) *v.tr.*

reduce (chemically) *v.tr.* восстановлять (Reg. A) –
                    восстановить (Irr. C-2) *v.tr.*

reduction (decrease in size, etc.) *n.* уменьшение *n.neuter* (16)

reduction (chemical) *n.* восстановление *n.neuter* (16)

regulate, control, correct *v.tr.* исправлять (Reg. A) –
                  исправить (Irr. C-2) *v.tr.*

relatively *adv.* сравнительно *adv.*

remaining *pres. part.* остальной *adj.* (18)

remember *v.tr.* помнить – вспомнить (Reg. B-2) *v.tr.*

remove *v.tr.* удалять (Reg. A) – удалить (Reg. B-2) *v.tr.*
    to be removed, taken away -ся

repulse, thrust aside *v.tr.* отталкивать (Reg. A) –
                  оттолкнуть (Reg. B-1) *v.tr.*

require, need *v.tr.* требовать (Irr. A-1) *v.tr. imperf.* (*with*
    to be required, needed -ся             *gen.*)

required *past part.*, потребный *adj.* (17a)

requirement *n.* требование *n.neuter* (16)

resist *v.tr.* противостоя́ть(Reg. B-2)- противоста́ть
               (Irr. C-5) *v.tr.* (*with dat.*)

resistance (opposition) *n.* сопротивле́ние *n.neuter* (16)
    electrical resistance электросопротивле́ние *n.neuter* (16)

resistance (stability) *n.* сто́йкость *n.fem.* (12)

respect (relation, regard) *n.* отноше́ние *n.neuter* (16)

result *n.* *результа́т *n.masc.* (1)
    as a result of вследствие *prep.* (*with gen.*)

retort *n.* *рето́рта *n.fem.* (7)

reversible *adj.* обрати́мый *adj.* (17)

revolution (rotation) *n.* враще́ние *n.neuter* (16)

revolution (political) *n.* *револю́ция *n.fem.* (11) переворо́т
                               *n.masc.*(1)

revolve *v.tr. and intr.* обраща́ть (Reg. A) - обрати́ть (Irr. D-2)
    to be revolved, to revolve *intr.* -ся       *v.tr.*

rhombic *adj.* *ромби́ческий *adj.* (21)

rice *n.* *рис *n.masc.* (1)

rice *adj.* *ри́совый *adj.* (17)

ring *n.* кольцо́ *n.neuter* (13d)

rise, increase *n.* повыше́ние *n.neuter* (16)

road *n.* доро́га *n.fem.* (9)

rocket *n.* *раке́та *n.fem.* (7)

rock *n.* ка́мень *n.masc.* (6a)
    rock salt ка́менная соль

role *n.* *роль *n.fem.* (12)

room *n.* ко́мната *n.fem.* (6)

room *adj.*, ко́мнатный *adj.* (17)

root *n.* ко́рень *n.masc.* (6a)

rotary (rotating or involving rotating) *adj.* враща́тельный *adj.* (17)

rotate *v.tr. and intr.* враща́ть (Reg. A) *v.tr. imperf.*
    to be rotated, to rotate *intr.* -ся

rotation *n.* враще́ние *n.neuter* (16) поворо́т *n.masc.*(1)

rubber *n.* каучу́к *n.masc.* (3) (unvulcanize) рези́на *n.fem.*
                              (7) (vulcanized)

rubber *adj.*, *рези́новый *adj.* (17)

rust *n.* ржа́вчина *n.fem.* (7)

rust *v.intr.* ржаве́ть - заржаве́ть (Reg. A) *v.intr.*

rusting (process) *n.* ржавле́ние *n.neuter* (16)

Rutherford *n.* *Резерфо́рд *n.masc.* (1)

rye *n.* рожь *n.fem.* (Cf. § 357, p. 574)

S

sailor *n.* *моря́к *n.masc.* (3)

Saint Clair Deville *n.* *Сен-Клер-Деви́лль *n.masc.* (6)

salt　*n.*　\*СОЛЬ *n.fem.* (12)

same　*pronoun and adj.* САМ *pronoun* (§ 148, p. 223) са́мый
*adj.* (18) (§ 148, p. 223)
　　one and the same ОДИ́Н И ТОТ же (Cf. § 144, p. 215)

sample　*n.* про́ба *n.fem.* (7)

sandstone　*n.* песча́ник *n.masc.* (3)

satellite　*n.* спу́тник *n.masc.* (3)

satisfy　*v.tr.* УДОВЛЕТВОРЯ́ТЬ (Reg. A)　- УДОВЛЕТВОРИ́ТЬ
　　to be satisfied ⁻СЯ　　　(Reg. B-2) *v.tr.* (*with dat.*)

say, speak　*v.tr. and intr.* ГОВОРИ́ТЬ (Reg. B-2)- сказа́ть
　　　　　　(Irr. D-1, З → Ж) *v.tr. and intr.*

scalar　*adj.* \*скаля́рный *adj.* (17)

scatter　*v.tr.* рассеива́ть - рассе́ять (Reg. A) *v.tr.*
　　to be scattered ⁻СЯ

scattered　*past part.* рассе́янный *perf. pas. past part. of*
　　　　　　　　　　　　　　рассеива́ть - рассе́ять

scheme　*n.* \*схе́ма *n.fem.* (6)

science　*n.* нау́ка *n.fem.* (8)

scientific　*adj.* нау́чный *adj.* (17a)

scientist　*n.* учёный *adj.* (*used as noun*) (17)

screen　*n.* \*экра́н *n.masc.* (1)

scurvy　*n.* скорбу́т *n.masc.* (1)

sea　*n.* \*мо́ре, *n.neuter* (15)

sea　*adj.* \*морско́й *adj.* (21)

second (time unit)　*n.* \*секу́нда *n.fem.* (7)

second (ordinal number)　*adj.* второ́й *adj.* (18)

see *v.tr. and intr.* ВИ́ДЕТЬ - УВИ́ДЕТЬ(Irr. D-2, Д → Ж) *v.tr. and intr.*

seed　*n.* се́мя *n.neuter* (Footnote 1, p. 574)

seeming (apparent)　*adj.* ка́жущийся *act. pres. part. refl.*
　　　　　*of* каза́ться - показа́ться (Cf. Footnote 1, p. 425)

self　*refl. pronoun* себя́ (Cf. § 148, p. 223)

self　*emphatic pronoun* са́мый (17), сам (Cf. § 148, p. 223)

separate (detach, divide, isolate)　*v.tr.* ОТДЕЛЯ́ТЬ (Reg. A) -
　　　　　　　　　　ОТДЕЛИ́ТЬ (Reg. B-2) *v.tr.*

series　*n.* (*plu. only*) РЯД *n.masc.* (1　*s.ing, and plu.*)

several　*pronoun and adj.* не́который *pronoun and adj.* (17)
　　　　　не́сколько *pronoun, adv.* (Cf. § 184, p. 236)

shaft (in machine)　*n.* вал *n.masc.* (1)

shaft (mining)　*n.* ша́хта *n.fem.* (16)

sharp *adj.* ре́зкий *adj.* (21a)

sharply　*adv.* ре́зко *adv.* (Cf. § 136, p. 204)

she　*pronoun* она́ *pronoun* (§ 136, p. 204)

shell (artillery shell)　*n.* снаря́д *n.masc.* (1)

shining, glittering　*act. pres. part.* блестя́щий (22) *act.*
　　　　　*pres. part. of* блесте́ть - заблесте́ть

ship　*n.* кора́бль *n.masc.* (6)

show (display, exhibit) *v.tr.* ЯВЛЯ́ТЬ (Reg. A) - ЯВИ́ТЬ
(Irr. C-2) *v.tr.*
to show self, to appear, to be ⁻СЯ (Cf. § 94, p. 136; § 123, p. 181)
show (manifest, render, exert) *v.tr.* ОКА́ЗЫВАТЬ (Reg. A) -
ОКАЗА́ТЬ (Irr. D-1, З → Ж) *v.tr.*
to become manifested, to turn out, to be -СЯ
show (prove) *v.tr.* ДОКА́ЗЫВАТЬ (Reg. A) - ДОКАЗА́ТЬ (Irr. D-1,
З → Ж) *v.tr.*

sick *adj.* БОЛЬНО́Й *adj.* (18 *pred. masc. sing.* БО́ЛЕН
Cf. § 356, p. 569)
sickness *n.* ЗАБОЛЕВА́НИЕ *n.neuter* (16)
significant *adj.* ЗНАЧИ́ТЕЛЬНЫЙ *adj.* (17b)
silver *n.* СЕРЕБРО́ *n.neuter* (13)
similar *adj.* ПОХО́ЖИЙ *adj.* (22)
simple *adj.* ПРОСТО́Й *adj.* (18)
simultaneous *adj.* ОДНОВРЕМЕ́ННЫЙ *adj.* (17)
simultaneously *adv.* ОДНОВРЕМЕ́ННО *adv.*
since *prep.* С (СО) *prep.* (*with gen.*)
since those times С ТЕХ ПОР (Cf. § 390, p. 650)
six *numeral* ШЕСТЬ *numeral* (§ 370 p. 602)
sixth *adj.* ШЕСТО́Й *adj.* (18)
sketch (draw) *v.tr.* ЧЕРТИ́ТЬ - НАЧЕРТИ́ТЬ (Irr. D-2,
Т →Ч) *v.tr.*
sky *n.* НЕ́БО *n.neuter* (Cf. ЧУ́ДО § 359, p. 578)
slight *adj.* МА́ЛЫЙ *adj.* (17) НЕБОЛЬШО́Й *adj.* (20)
slightly (lightly, superficially, gently) *adv.* СЛЕГКА́ *adv.*
slightly (not much, some) *adv.* НЕМНО́ГО *adv. and pronoun*
(§ 150, p. 228)
slow *adj.* МЕ́ДЛЕННЫЙ *adj.* (17)
slow (not big) *adj.* НЕБОЛЬШО́Й *adj.* (20)
slowly *adv.* МЕ́ДЛЕННО *adv.*
small (not big) *adj.* НЕБОЛЬШО́Й *adj.* (20)
small (little, finely divided) *adj.* МЕ́ЛКИЙ *adj.* (21a)
very small, very fine МЕЛЬЧА́ЙШИЙ *superl. adj.* (22)
(Cf. § 346 p. 546)
small (slight) *adj.* МА́ЛЫЙ *adj.* (17)
small (tiny) *adj.* МА́ЛЕНЬКИЙ *adj.* (21)
smaller, lesser *comp. adj.* МЕ́НЬШИЙ *comp. adj.* (22) (Cf. § 332,
p. 525) МЕ́НЬШЕ *comp. adv. and pred. adv.* (*undecl.*) (Cf. § 334, p. 527)
so-called *adj.* ТАК НАЗЫВА́ЕМЫЙ *fixed expr.* (Cf. Note 10, p. 170)
soap *n.* МЫ́ЛО *n.neuter* (13)
soda *n.* *СО́ДА *n.fem.* (7)
sodium *n.* *НА́ТРИЙ *n.masc.* (5)
sodium *adj.* *НА́ТРИЕВЫЙ *adj.* (17)
sodium chloride *ХЛО́РИСТЫЙ *НА́ТРИЙ (17)
soft *adj.* МЯ́ГКИЙ *adj.* (21 a)

soften *v.tr. and intr.* размягчать (Reg. A) – размягчить (Reg. B-2) *v.tr.*

to be softened, to soften *intr.* –ся

solar *adj.* солнечный *adj.* (17a)

soluble *adj.* растворимый *adj.* (17)

solubility растворимость *n.fem.* (12)

solution *n.* раствор *n.masc.* (1)

solvent *n.* растворитель *n.masc.* (1)

some (any) *adj.* какой-нибудь *adj.* (§ 154, p. 236)

sound *n.* звук *n.masc.* (3)

source *n.* источник *n.masc.* (3)

space *n.* пространство *n.neuter* (13)

spark *n.* искра *n.fem.* (7)

special *adj.* *специальный *adj.* (17b)

spectrograph *n.* *спектрограф *n.masc.* (1)

spectroscope *n.* *спектроскоп *n.masc.* (1)

spectrum *n.* *спектр *n.masc.* (1)

spectrum *adj.* *спектральный *adj.* (17)

speed *n.* скорость *n.fem.* (12)

sphere *n.* *сфера *n.fem.* (7)

sphere *n.* шар *n.masc.* (1)

spherical *adj.* *сферический *adj.* (21)

spontaneous *adj.* самопроизвольный *adj.* (17b)

spontaneously *adv.* самопроизвольно *adv.*

stable *adj.* *стабильный *adj.* (17b) устойчивый *adj.* (17)

stalk *n.* стебель *n.masc.* (6a)

stand *v.intr.* стоять – постоять (Reg. B-2) *v.intr.*

star *n.* звезда *n.fem.* (7)

start *n.* начало *n.neuter* (13)

start (from), issue (from) *v.intr.* исходить (Irr. D-2, д → ж) – изойти (Irr. H-10) *v.intr.* (из *with gen.*)

starting, initial *adj.* исходный *adj.* (17)

state (condition) *n.* состояние *n.neuter* (16)

state (of U.S.A.) *n.* *штат *n.masc.* (1)

state (governmental authority) *n.* государство *n.neuter* (13)

state (stage, status) *n.* *стадия *n.fem.* (11)

station (installation) *n.* станция *n.fem.* (11)

statistical *adj.* *статистический *adj.* (21)

steam *n.* (водяной) пар *n.masc.* (1)

steam *adj.* паровой *adj.* (18)

steam engine паровая *машина

steel *n.* *сталь *n.fem.* (12)

steel *adj.* *стальной *adj.* (18)

stimulate *v.tr.* *стимулировать (Irr. A-1) *v.tr.perf. and imperf.*

stormily *adv.* бурно *adv.*

stormy *adj.* бурный *adj.* (17a)

strength n. си́ла n.fem. (7)

strike (against), hit (on) v.intr. попада́ть (Reg. A) – попа́сть (Irr. H-7) v.intr. (В or На with acc.)

stroke (of piston) n. такт n.masc. (1) (time of music)

strong adj. си́льный adj.

strongly adv. си́льно adv.

structure n. *структу́ра n.fem. (7), строе́ние n.neuter (16)

student n. *студе́нт n.masc. (1)

studied past part. изу́ченный perf. pas. past part. of изуча́ть – изучи́ть

study n. изуче́ние n.neuter (16)

study v.tr. изуча́ть (Reg. A) – изучи́ть (Irr. J-3) v.tr.

submit (to), to yield (to) v.tr. and intr. подверга́ть (Reg. A) – подве́ргнуть (Irr. J-3) v.tr. (with dat.)
      to be submitted to, to yield to -ся (with dat.)

substance n. вещество́ n.neuter (13)

succeed v.intr. удава́ться (Irr. B) – уда́ться (Irr. I-3) v.refl. (with dat.) Cf. § 386, p. 642)

success n. успе́х n.masc. (3)

such adj. тако́й adj. (20)
      to be sucked заса́сываться

sufficient adj. доста́точный adj. (17a)

sugar n. *са́хар n.masc. (1)

sulfate n. *сульфа́т n.masc.,

sulfuric acid fixed expr. се́рная кислота́ fixed expr.

sun n. со́лнце n.neuter (1 instr. sing. со́лнцем, nom. and acc. plu. со́лнца)

sunk past part. погружённый perf. pas. past part. of погружа́ть – погрузи́ть

superconductivity n. сверхпроводи́мость n.fem. (12)

supply, supplies n. запа́с n.masc. (1)

surface n. пове́рхность n.fem. (12)

surpass exceed v.tr. превосходи́ть (Irr. D-2, Д → Ж) – превозойти́ (Irr. H-10) v.tr.

Swiss adj. *швейца́рский adj. (21)

switching off (process, action) n. выключе́ние n.neuter (16)

switching on (process action) n. включе́ние n.neuter (16)

symbol n. *си́мвол n.masc. (1)

symbolic adj. *символи́ческий adj. (21)

symmetrical adj. *симметри́чный adj. (17)

symmetry n. *симме́трия n. (11)

synthesis n. *синте́з n.masc. (1)

synthesize v.tr. *синтези́ровать (Irr. A-1) v.tr. perf. and imperf.

synthetic adj. *синтети́ческий adj. (17)

systems n. *систе́ма n.fem. (7)

T

take on, acquire  *v.tr.* ПРИНИМА́ТЬ (Reg. A) – ПРИНЯ́ТЬ (Irr. ПРИМУ́, -ешь, -ет etc.)  *v.tr.*
    to take place  ИМЕ́ТЬ МЕ́СТО
target  *n.* ЦЕЛЬ *n.fem.* (12)
technical  *adj.* *ТЕХНИ́ЧЕСКИЙ *adj.* (21)
technology  *n.*  *ТЕ́ХНИКА
temperature  *n.*  *ТЕМПЕРАТУ́РА *n.fem.* (7)
terrestrial *adj.* ЗЕМНО́Й *adj.* (18)
tetragonal *adj.* *ТЕТРАГОНА́ЛЬНЫЙ *adj.* (17b)
than  *conj.* (*used with comp.*) ЧЕМ *conj.* (*used with comp.*)
                                (Cf. § 337, p. 530)
    *For replacement by gen. case see* § 338, p. 532
thanks to  *prepl. expr.* БЛАГОДАРЯ́ *prep.* (*with dat.*)
that  *conj.* ЧТО *conj.* (Cf. § 145, p. 217)
that  *rel. pronoun* КОТО́РЫЙ *rel. pronoun* (17)(Cf. § 140, p. 210)
that *pronoun, demonstrative* ТОТ *pronoun, demonstrative*
                                (§ 142, p. 213)
    that same ТОТ ЖЕ (Cf. § 144, p. 215)
    that is (in fact) ЭТО (И ЕСТЬ) (Cf. § 120, p. 174)
their *poss.* ИХ *poss.* (*undecl.* § 138, p. 207)
    *Referring to subject of sentence.* СВОЙ *refl. poss.*
                                (§ 148, p. 225)
then (at that time) *adv.* ТОГДА́ *adv.*
then *conj.* (*following conditional clause*) ТО *conj.*
                (Cf. § 169, p. 258, §§ 313-4, pp. 492-5)
theorem  *n.*  *ТЕОРЕ́МА *n.fem.* (7)
theoretical *adj.*  *ТЕОРЕТИ́ЧЕСКИЙ *adj.* (21)
theory  *n.*  *ТЕО́РИЯ *n.fem.* (11)
there (yonder) *adv.* ТАМ *adv.*
    there is *see* is
thereby  *adv.* ПРИ ЭТОМ *advl. expr.*
these *pronoun, demonstrative* ЭТИ *pronoun, demonstrative*
they *pronoun* ОНИ́ *pronoun*
                                (§ 142, p. 213)
thick *adj.* ТО́ЛСТЫЙ *adj.* (17)
thicken *v.intr.* ГУСТЕ́ТЬ – ЗАГУСТЕ́ТЬ (Reg. A) *v.intr.*
think *v.intr.* ДУ́МАТЬ – ПОДУ́МАТЬ (Reg. A) *v.intr.*
third *adj.* ТРЕ́ТИЙ *adj.* (§ 360, p. 581)
this *pronoun, demonstrative* ЭТОТ *pronoun, demonstrative*
                                (§ 142, p. 212)
thread, filament *n.* НИТЬ *n.fem.* (12)
three *numeral* ТРИ *numeral* (§ 370, p. 600)
through (across, by way of) *prep.* ЧЕ́РЕЗ *prep.* (*with acc.*)

through (through the middle of) *prep.* СКВОЗЬ *prep.* (*with acc.*)

thus *adv.* ТАК *adv.*

    thus (in this fashion, in this way) таки́м о́бразом

    thus, for example так наприме́р

time *n.* вре́мя *n. neuter* (§ 358, p. 575)

tin *n.* о́лово *n. neuter* (13)

tissue, fabric *n.* ткань *n. fem.* (12)

titanium *n.* \*тита́н *n. masc.* (1)

to (at, on) *prep.* на, в (во) *prep.* (*with prep.*)

to (onto, implying motion) *prep.* на *prep.* (*with acc.*)

to (into, implying motion) *prep.* в (во) *prep.* (*with acc.*)

to (directed toward, particularly figuratively) к (ко) (*with dat.*)

to (as far as, up to) *prep.* до *prep.* (*with gen.*)

to be growing, fermenting, etc. *see imperf. inf. entered under* grow, ferment, etc.

total (general, common) *adj.* о́бщий *adj.* (22)

train (railroad) *n.* по́езд *n. masc.* (1)

transfer *v. tr.* переноси́ть (Irr. D-2) – перенести́ (Irr. H-2) *v. tr.*

transform, convert *v. tr.* преобразо́вывать (Reg. A) – преобразова́ть (Irr. A-1) *v. tr.*

    to be transformed, converted, to undergo transformation -ся

transition (leap, jump) *n.* переско́к *n. masc.* (3)

transmitted *past part.* по́сланный (17) *perf. past part.* of слать – посла́ть

transmitter *n.* переда́тчик *n. masc.* (3)

transport *n.* \*тра́нспорт *n. masc.* (1)

travel *v. intr.* е́хать – пое́хать (Irr. е́ду, е́дешь, etc.) *v. intr.*

triclinic *adj.* \*триклини́ческий *adj.* (21)

tropical *adj.* \*тропи́ческий *adj.* (21)

tube *n.* тру́бка *n. fem.* (9a)

turbine *n.* \*турби́на *n. fem.* (7)

twentieth *adj.* двадца́тый *adj.* (17)

two *numeral* два *numeral* (§ 370, p. 600)

type (variety, kind) *n.* \*тип *n. masc.* (1)

## U

unaided (simple) *adj.* просто́й *adj.* (18)

undergo change *verbal expr.* изменя́тся (Reg. A) – измени́ться (Reg. B-2) *v. refl.*

    to change *v. tr.* изменя́ть – измени́ть

understand *v. tr. and intr.* понима́ть (Reg. A) – поня́ть (Irr. F-5) *v. tr. and intr.*

undissociated *adj.* \*недиссоции́рованный *adj.* (17) (Cf. § 286, p. 452)

unit *n.* едини́ца *n. fem.* (8)

united *past part.* СОЕДИНЁННЫЙ *perf. pas. past part. of* СОЕДИНЯ́ТЬ

universal, cosmic *adj.* МИРОВО́Й *adj.* (18)      – СОЕДИНИ́ТЬ

unsaturated (solution, chemical compound) *adj.* НЕНАСЫ́ЩЕННЫЙ
                                 *adj.* (17) (Cf. § 286, p. 452)

unsaturated (chemical compound only) *adj.* НЕПРЕДЕ́ЛЬНЫЙ *adj.* (17)

unsolved, undecided *adj.* НЕРЕШЁННЫЙ *adj.* (17) (Cf. § 286, p. 452)

unsuitable *adj.* НЕВЫ́ГОДНЫЙ *adj.* (17a)

until, up to, as far as, *prep.* ДО *prep.* (*with gen.*)

     up to this time (these times) ДО СИХ ПОР (Cf. § 390, p. 650)

uranium (the chemical element) *n.* \*УРА́Н *n. masc.* (1)

     uranium bearing УРАНОНО́СНЫЙ *adj.* (17)

Uranus (planet) *n.* \*УРА́Н *n. masc.* (1)

us *see decl. of* МЫ "we" *in* § 136, p. 204)

U.S.A. *abbrev.* США *abbrev. for* Соединённые \*Шта́ты \*Аме́рики

use (apply) *v. tr.* ПРИМЕНЯ́ТЬ (Reg. A) – ПРИМЕНИ́ТЬ (Reg. B-2)

     to be used, applied –СЯ                       *v. tr.*

use, application *n.* ПРИМЕНЕ́НИЕ *n. neuter* (16)

use (avail self of, utilize) *v. tr.* ПО́ЛЬЗОВАТЬСЯ – ВОСПО́ЛЬЗОВАТЬСЯ
                           (Irr. A-1) *v. refl.* (*with instr.*)

     utilization *n.* ИСПО́ЛЬЗОВАНИЕ *n. neuter* (16)


# V


valence, valency *n.* \*ВАЛЕ́НТНОСТЬ *n. fem.* (12)

valence *adj.* \*ВАЛЕ́НТНЫЙ *adj.* (17a)

valuable *adj.* ЦЕ́ННЫЙ *adj.* (17a)

value (magnitude) *n.* ВЕЛИЧИНА́ *n. fem.* (7)

vanishingly *adv.* ИСЧЕЗА́ЮЩЕ *adv.* (Cf. § 287, p. 455)

various *adj.* РАЗЛИ́ЧНЫЙ *adj.* (17a)

velocity *n.* СКО́РОСТЬ *n. fem.* (12)

Venus *n.* \*ВЕНЕ́РА *n. fem.* (7)

very *adv.* О́ЧЕНЬ *adv.* (Cf. § 351, p. 553)

very (the very, the most) *adv.* СА́МЫЙ *adj.* (18) (Cf. § 148, p. 223;

view, form, type, kind *n.* ВИД *n. masc.* (1)         § 354, p. 544)

viewing (pertaining to or used for viewing) *adj.* ЗРИ́ТЕЛЬНЫЙ *adj.*

virus *n.* \*ВИ́РУС *n. masc.* (1)                         (17)

visible, prominent *adj.* ВИ́ДНЫЙ *adj.* (17a)

vitamin *n.* \*ВИТАМИ́Н *n. masc.* (1)

vodka *n.* ВО́ДКА *n. fem.* (9a)

volatile *adj.* ЛЕТУ́ЧИЙ *adj.* (22)

volcano *n.* \*ВУЛКА́Н *n. masc.* (1)

volt *n.* \*ВОЛЬТ *n. masc.* (1)

voltmeter *n.* \*ВОЛЬТМЕ́ТР *n. masc.* (1)

volume *n.* ОБЪЁМ *n. masc.* (1)

vulcanization *n.* \*ВУЛКАНИЗА́ЦИЯ *n. fem.* (11)

# W

was *past tense form of* to be   *See past tense of* БЫТЬ

water *n.* ВОДА *n.fem.* (7)

wave   *n.* ВОЛНА *n.fem.* (7)

way (road, path, thoroughfare) *n.* ПУТЬ *n.masc.* (§ 359, p. 577)

    by way of ПУТЁМ *with gen.*

    in this way, in this fashion ТАКИМ ОБРАЗОМ

    by means of *See review of instr. case in* Lesson

we *pronoun* МЫ, *pronoun* (§ 136, p. 204)    *particularly*

weak *adj.* СЛАБЫЙ *adj.* (17)

weight *n.* ВЕС *n.masc.* (§ 359, p. 580)

weight *adj.* ВЕСОВОЙ *adj.* (18)

went *past tense form of* "to go." *See past tense of*

                         ИТТИ, *in* § 224, p. 352

went over, went across *See past tense of* ПЕРЕЙТИ *in* § 224, p. 352

what (interrogative) *pronoun* ЧТО *pronoun* (§ 152, p. 232)

wheat *n.* ПШЕНИЦА *n.fem.* (8)

when *adv.* КОГДА *adv.*

whether *adv.* ЛИ *particle used to indicate interrogation*

                             (Cf. § 387, p. 644)

which *pronoun* КОТОРЫЙ *pronoun* (17) (Cf.

while *conj.* БУДУЧИ

    during the course (of) В ТЕЧЕНИЕ (*with gen.*)

whole, all, every *adj.* ВЕСЬ *adj. pronoun* (§ 150, p. 229)

whole (complete) *adj.* ЦЕЛЫЙ *adj.* (17)

why *interr. adv.* ПОЧЕМУ *interr. adv.*

will *Auxiliary for forming future tense. See*

          *in particular*

wish *v.tr.* ХОТЕТЬ – ЗАХОТЕТЬ (Irr. D-5) *v.tr.*

with (during, while, at same time) *prep.* ПРИ *prep.* (*with prepl.*)

with (together) *prep.* С (СО) *prep.* (*with instr.*)

without *prep.* БЕЗ *prep.* (*with gen.*)

Wöhler *n.* ВЁЛЕР *n.masc.* (1)

wonder *n.* ЧУДО *n.neuter* (§ 359, p. 578)

wood *n.* ДЕРЕВО *n.neuter* (§ 359, p. 578)

wooden *adj.* ДЕРЕВЯННЫЙ *adj.* (17)

word *n.* СЛОВО *n.neuter* (13)

work, working *n.* РАБОТА *n.fem.* (6)

work *v.tr. and intr.* РАБОТАТЬ – ПОРАБОТАТЬ (Reg. A)

                                *v.intr.*

    work out, develop *v.tr.* РАЗРАБАТЫВАТЬ – РАЗРАБОТАТЬ

                             (Reg. A) *v.tr.*

write *v.tr. and intr.* ПИСАТЬ – НАПИСАТЬ (Irr. D-1) *v.tr.*

                             *and intr.*

# Y

year  *n.*  ГОД *n.masc.* (1) ЛЕ́ТО *n.neuter* (13) (summer)
yellow *adj.* ЖЁЛТЫЙ *adj.* (17)
you  *pronoun* ВЫ *pronoun* (*Formal*) ТЫ *pronoun* (*Informal*)
young  *adj.* МОЛОДО́Й *adj.* (18)                    (Cf. § 136, p. 204)

# Z

zero  *n.* *НУЛЬ *n.masc.* (6)
zinc  *n.* *ЦИНК *n.masc.* (3)

INDEX

*Numbers refer to pages.*

*Numbers refer to pages.*

*Numbers refer to pages.*

Articles, definite and indefinite
    absence from Russian language, 35
Attributive modifiers. See Adjectives

Cardinal numerals. See Numerals
Cases, use of. See Prepositions, Verbs, Numerals, Negative
    Sentences, Participles, Gerunds
Circumlocation of БЫТЬ "to be." See Verbs
Clauses
    as subject of sentence, 639-640
    introduced by relative pronouns, 210-212, 232-236
    introduced by conjunction ЧТО and ЧТОбЫ, 217, 495-496
    consisting of adjective or noun standing alone, 255-256
    negative dependent clauses, care needed in interpreting, 274-
    275
Cognates. See Adjectives, Adverbs, Nouns, Verbs and Word
    formation
Collective numerals. See Numerals, collective
Collectives
    declension of, 228-230
    use in various idioms, 647-649
Comparative degree. See also Adjectives. Adverbs and individual
    participles
    closely related expressions, 553-555
Conditional sentences
    involving future tense, 364-365
    involving infinitives, 258-259
    involving subjunctive mood, 492-493
Conjugation, of verbs. See also Gerunds, Imperative mood, Sub-
    junctive mood, individual tenses and individual
    participles
    irregular
        importance of present and perfective future tense forms,
        292
        involving irregular endings for present and perfective
        future tenses, 323-326
        relative importance of irregular conjugation, 516, 518
    regular
        general review, 503-519
        introduction, 279-280
        summary of endings used, 510-512
        tabulations of typical conjugation, 516-518
Complex sentences. See Clauses, Conditional sentences, Gerunds,
    Negative sentences, Pronouns, relative and individual
    participles

*Numbers refer to pages.*

*Numbers refer to pages.*

*Numbers refer to pages.*

*Numbers refer to pages.*

*Numbers refer to pages.*

*Numbers refer to pages.*

*Numbers refer to pages.*

*Numbers refer to pages.*

*Numbers refer to pages.*

*Numbers refer to pages.*

Past tense (contd.)
   sentences illustrating use, 338-340
Perfective aspect, relationship to imperfective aspects, 55, 63, 504-509
Possessive adjectives -- special declension, 582
Possessive adjectives and related names
   declension of, 586
Possessives
   declension of, 207-208
   use in sentences, 208-209
Possessives, reflexive
   declension, 225
   use in sentences, 226-228
Possession
   denoted by genitive case, 117-118
   denoted by idiom involving preposition у, 646-647
   denoted by idioms involving the dative case
Predicative forms
   masculine singular of adjectives, irregular formation, 565-572
   neuter singular of passive past participles in impersonal sentences, 388-389
   of adjectives, 171-173
     use in sentences, 176-177
   of passive past participles, sentences involving, 377-378
   of passive present participles, sentences involving, 456-457
Prefixes
   effect on meaning of verbs, 57-63, 504-506
   having numerical significance, 612-616
   summary list, 673-674
Prepositional case
   adjective endings, 108-109
   noun endings, 105-107
   sentences illustrating use, 109-110
   special forms with certain nouns after в and на, 111
   summary of uses, 105
Prepositions
   governing accusative case, 95-100
   governing dative case, 162-164
   governing genitive case, 121-123
   governing instrumental case, 146-148
   idiomatic use of preposition x, 646-647
   idiomatic use with numerals, 610-612
   review of cases governed, 185-187
   sentences illustrating при, 73

*Numbers refer to pages.*

*Numbers refer to pages.*

*Numbers refer to pages.*

*Numbers refer to pages.*